Crime and Criminal Justice

The International Library of Essays in Law and Society
General Editor: Austin Sarat

Titles in the Series

Law and Religion
Gad Barzilai

Police and Policing Law
Jeannine Bell

Law and Society Approaches to Cyberspace
Paul Schiff Berman

Law and Families
Susan B. Boyd and Helen Rhoades

Rhetoric of Law
Marianne Constable and Felipe Gutterriez

Law in Social Theory
Roger Cotterrell

Ethnography and Law
Eve Darian-Smith

International Law and Society
Laura Dickinson

Legal Lives of Private Organizations
Lauren Edelman and Mark C. Suchman

Courts and Judges
Lee Epstein

Consciousness and Ideology
Patricia Ewick

Prosecutors and Prosecution
Lisa Frohmann

Intellectual Property
William T. Gallagher

Human Rights, Law and Society
Lisa Hajjar

Race, Law and Society
Ian Haney Lopez

The Jury System
Valerie Hans

Regulation and Regulatory Processes
Robert Kagan and Cary Coglianese

Crime and Criminal Justice
William T. Lyons, Jr.

Law and Social Movements
Michael McCann

Colonial and Post-Colonial Law
Sally Merry

Social Science in Law
Elizabeth Mertz

Sexuality and Identity
Leslie J. Moran

Law and Poverty
Frank Munger

Rights
Laura Beth Nielsen

Governing Risks
Pat O'Malley

Lawyers and the Legal Profession, Volumes I and II
Tanina Rostain

Capital Punishment, Volumes I and II
Austin Sarat

Legality and Democracy
Stuart A. Scheingold

The Law and Society Canon
Carroll Seron

Popular Culture and Law
Richard K. Sherwin

Law and Science
Susan Silbey

Immigration
Susan Sterett

Gender and Feminist Theory in Law and Society
Madhavi Sunder

Procedural Justice, Volumes I and II
Tom R. Tyler

Trials
Martha Merrill Umphrey

Crime and Criminal Justice

Edited by

William T. Lyons, Jr

University of Akron, USA

ASHGATE

Published by
Ashgate Publishing Limited
Gower House
Croft Road
Aldershot
Hants GU11 3HR
England

Ashgate Publishing Company
Suite 420
101 Cherry Street
Burlington, VT 05401-4405
USA

Ashgate website: http://www.ashgate.com

British Library Cataloguing in Publication Data
Crime and criminal justice. – (The international library of
    essays in law and society)
    1. Criminal justice, Administration of – Political aspects –
    United States 2. Police – United States 3. Punishment in
    crime deterrence – United States 4. Community policing –
    United States 5. Crime and race – United States 6. Crime –
    Sociological aspects – United States
    I. Lyons, William. 1960-
    364.9'73

Library of Congress Cataloging-in-Publication Data
Crime and criminal justice / edited by William T. Lyons, Jr.
        p. cm. — (International library of essays in law and society)
    Includes bibliographical references.
    ISBN 0-7546-2510-9 (alk. paper)
        1. Law enforcement—United States. 2. Racial profiling in law enforcement—United
States. 3. Imprisonment—United States. 4. Criminal justice, Administration of—United
States. I. Lyons, William, 1960- II. Series.

HV8139.C75 2005
365—dc22

                                                        2005048254

ISBN 0 7546 2510 9

Printed in Great Britain by The Cromwell Press, Trowbridge, Wiltshire

Contents

PART III   THE INCARCERATION EXPLOSION

PART IV   POLITICAL CHALLENGES

Acknowledgements

The editor and publishers wish to thank the following for permission to use copyright material.

American Sociological Association for the essay: Bruce Western (2002), 'The Impact of Incarceration on Wage Mobility and Inequality', *American Sociological Review*, **67**, pp. 526–46.

Blackwell Publishing for the essays: Jason Sunshine and Tom R. Tyler (2003), 'The Role of Procedural Justice and Legitimacy in Shaping Public Support for Policing', *Law and Society Review*, **37**, pp. 513–47; Robert J. Sampson and Dawn Jeglum Bartusch (1998), 'Legal Cynicism and (Subcultural?) Tolerance of Deviance: The Neighborhood Context of Racial Differences', *Law and Society Review*, **32**, pp. 777–804; Benjamin Fleury-Steiner (2002), 'Narratives of the Death Sentence: Toward a Theory of Legal Narrativity', *Law and Society Review*, **36**, pp. 549–76.

Cambridge University Press for the essay: Richard C. Fording (2001), 'The Political Response to Black Insurgency: A Critical Test of Competing Theories of the State', *American Political Science Review*, **95**, pp. 115–30. Copyright © The American Political Science Association. Published by Cambridge University Press and reprinted with permission.

Fordham Urban Law Journal for the essay: Jeffrey Fagan and Garth Davies (2000), 'Street Stops and Broken Windows: *Terry*, Race, and Disorder in New York City', *Fordham Urban Law Journal*, **28**, pp. 457–504.

Sage Publications for the essays: Peter K. Manning (2001), 'Theorizing Policing: The Drama and Myth of Crime Control in the NYPD', *Theoretical Criminology*, **5**, pp. 315–44. Copyright © 2001 Sage Publications; Loïc Wacquant (2001), 'Deadly Symbiosis: When Ghetto and Prison Meet and Mesh', *Punishment and Society*, **3**, pp. 95–133. Copyright © 2001 Sage Publications; Michael Tonry (1999), 'Why Are U.S. Incarceration Rates So High?', *Crime and Delinquency*, **45**, pp. 419–37. Copyright © 1999 Sage Publications; Vanessa Barker (forthcoming), 'The Politics of Punishing: Building a State Governance Theory of American Imprisonment', *Punishment and Society*, **8**.

Oxford University Press for the essay: Tali Mendelberg (1997), 'Executing Hortons: Racial Crime in the 1988 Presidential Campaign', *Public Opinion Quarterly*, **61**, pp. 134–57.

Taylor & Francis for the essays: Albert J. Meehan and Michael C. Ponder (2002), 'Race and Place: The Ecology of Racial Profiling African American Motorists', *Justice Quarterly*, **19**, pp. 399–430. Copyright © 2002 Academy of Criminal Justice Sciences http://www.tandf.co.uk/journals; Todd R. Clear, Dina R. Rose, Elin Waring and Kristen Scully (2003), 'Coercive Mobility

Series Preface

The International Library of Essays in Law and Society is designed to provide a broad overview of this important field of interdisciplinary inquiry. Titles in the series will provide access to the best existing scholarship on a wide variety of subjects integral to the understanding of how legal institutions work in and through social arrangements. They collect and synthesize research published in the leading journals of the law and society field. Taken together, these volumes show the richness and complexity of inquiry into law's social life.

Each volume is edited by a recognized expert who has selected a range of scholarship designed to illustrate the most important questions, theoretical approaches, and methods in her/his area of expertise. Each has written an introductory essay which both outlines those questions, approaches, and methods and provides a distinctive analysis of the scholarship presented in the book. Each was asked to identify approximately 20 pieces of work for inclusion in their volume. This has necessitated hard choices since law and society inquiry is vibrant and flourishing.

The International Library of Essays in Law and Society brings together scholars representing different disciplinary traditions and working in different cultural contexts. Since law and society is itself an international field of inquiry it is appropriate that the editors of the volumes in this series come from many different nations and academic contexts. The work of the editors both charts a tradition and opens up new questions. It is my hope that this work will provide a valuable resource for longtime practitioners of law and society scholarship and newcomers to the field.

AUSTIN SARAT
William Nelson Cromwell Professor of Jurisprudence and Political Science
Amherst College

Introduction

When I was conducting my research for *The Politics of Community Policing* (Lyons, 1999), the first thing a leading citizen activist handed to me was a copy of the 'Broken Windows' essay (Wilson and Kelling, 1982). With nearly no empirical evidence at the time to support the notion, popularized in this essay, that the more aggressive policing of minor disorders would reduce serious crime, I was struck then by the fact that this simple metaphor, circulating in the form of a familiar sounding parable, was able to mobilize such enormous persuasive power. Today, as our conversations about crime, punishment, and politics tend to focus, in part, on competing explanations for crime rate fluctuations in New York City, it is still remarkable that what is now frequently upgraded to the 'broken windows theory' remains at the centre of policy and political debates. This volume will begin with a section on policing, and include sections on racial profiling, the incarceration explosion, and the political challenges we face in an attempt to make some sense out of the unusually long life of this simple metaphor, familiar fable and popularized justification for the NYPD's zero-tolerance approach to community policing. This approach has become a model for policing reform across the United States, institutionalizing in the deployment of local police powers the racially disparate and excessively punitive forms of social control seen in our incarceration explosions at the state and national levels.

In 'Broken Windows' Wilson and Kelling begin their analysis with data showing that an experimental return to foot patrols in Newark did not reduce crime rates and conclude that because the residents of the target neighbourhood 'seemed to feel more secure' and 'had a more favorable opinion of the police' it was justified to conclude that police foot patrols did make neighbourhoods safer (1982, p. 29). Their logic was simple: residents were afraid of 'being bothered by disorderly people' and foot patrols elevated the level of public order by keeping 'an eye on strangers' and making 'certain that the disreputable regulars observed some informal but widely understood rules' (1982, p. 32).

> Drunks and addicts could sit on the stoops, but could not lie down. People could drink on side streets, but not on the main intersection. Bottles had to be in paper bags. Talking to, bothering, or begging from people waiting at the bus stop was forbidden. If a dispute erupted between a businessman and a customer, the businessman was assumed to be right, especially if the customer was a stranger . . . Persons who broke the informal rules, especially those who bothered people waiting at bus stops, were arrested for vagrancy. Noisy teenagers were told to keep quiet. (Wilson and Kelling, 1982, p. 30)

Wilson and Kelling assert that these informal rules were enforced through a police–community collaboration, although they provide no evidence either that these unstated rules were ever agreed upon by anyone or of any citizen role in enforcement, other than calling the police and 'ridiculing the violator' (1982, p. 31). Given their own account it should come as no surprise that a zero-tolerance approach to community policing that deploys traditional – that is, neither innovative, community-driven nor reintegrative (see Lyons, 1999; Braithwaite, 1989) – law enforcement tools and citizen participation is structurally limited to providing the police with information (Lyons, 2000). The moral that Wilson and Kelling draw from their largely fictional account of collaboration – where no effort whatsoever is made to actually ask residents what their concerns and priorities might be for their neighbourhood – is the central theme of the essay: 'disorder and crime are usually inextricably linked in a kind of developmental sequence. Social psychologists and police officers tend to agree that if a window in a building is broken and left unrepaired, all the rest of the windows will soon be broken . . . one unrepaired broken window is a signal that no one cares' (1982, p. 31). At this point, even though it is based on imaging collaboration, the central claim that social disorganization matters has both common-sense appeal and social scientific support.

However, Wilson and Kelling are not interested in the social disorganizing messages sent by levels of untended public or private property. Instead, they ignore what Skogan (1990) calls the physical disorder of our most victimized communities, what Sampson and Bartusch (Chapter 5, this volume) analyse as the social disorders rooted in systematic public and private disinvestment, and the political–economic disorders highlighted by Clear and Western, in favour of narrowing the scope of the conflict to the unarticulated discomfort of residents about sharing public space with rowdy teenagers. Indeed, Wilson and Kelling reduce their observations regarding ongoing, often minor but festering physical, social, political and economic disorders, captured in the image of untended broken windows, to a metaphor that suggests that the most thoughtful response to the situation is for the police to more aggressively target strangers who do not know their place for more extreme punishment according to a set of informal rules that more probably reflect the fears driving the authors themselves than represent any serious effort to find out what the actual residents in the neighbourhood cared about. In this way, the target preferred by Wilson and Kelling, the 'unchecked panhandler' is transformed into 'the first broken window' (1982, p. 34) in a classic bait-and-switch.

According to Clear (Chapter 14 of this volume):

> Until recently, theorists of social disorganization have not regarded the effects of public policies as important considerations for their models of public safety. Public policies were generally thought of as responses to crime, not antecedents of it, so these theorists tended to concentrate on informal social control, rather than formal social control. (Wilson and Kelling, 1982, p. 35)

This is an oversight encouraged by framing actual broken windows as a metaphor to justify the more aggressive policing of the homeless. However, research that takes the observation of broken windows seriously is increasingly providing us with an alternative, sober and policy-relevant literature on the relationship between formal approaches to social control (public policy, institutions, bureaucratic routines, campaign strategies and the messages sent by the broken windows that public and private leaders tend to leave untended) and less formal approaches (informal social controls, social capital or collective efficacy). The data presented in this volume powerfully illustrates that literature, showing that social disorganization weakens both formal and informal mechanisms of social control and that the excessively punitive formal mechanisms currently popularized by scholars such as Wilson and Kelling have measurable criminogenic impacts on the informal social controls assumed to exist within communities that are increasingly being sought after to work in partnership with police, prison administrators or prosecutors.

Several essays in this volume treat the initial observation of untended broken windows as evidence that disadvantage concentrates at the neighbourhood level. That it can be traced directly to formal elite (state and corporate) actions as well as to the indirect impact of these actions on less formal cultural practices and social norms. And that seeing broken windows as simply a justification for punishing panhandlers diminishes our capacity to prevent – or even to understand – crime. When Wilson and Kelling reduce broken windows to a metaphor that justifies the more aggressive policing of the most disadvantaged, it turns their argument into a fable that asserts what must be achieved – the social bonding or social capital or collective efficacy or reciprocal relational networks that might become the foundation for the kind of police–community collaboration that they imagine already exists. This unfortunate choice underlies the resilience of 'broken windows' as a powerful soundbite, implicitly mobilizing a nostalgic image of neighbourhood standards that is both historically inaccurate (Walker, 1984) and continues to misdirect policing reform, with particularly negative impacts on how we think about deterrence (Harcourt, 1998) and on the possibility of a sober analysis of crime, punishment, and politics.

Police Powers

The essays in Part I of this volume provide an opportunity to examine the relevant empirical evidence from the NYPD and beyond. In Chapter 1 Jeffrey Fagan and Garth Davies argue that there is a political conflict within policing, made salient by the rediscovery of police–community collaboration, between the policing of place and the policing of persons:

> [P]olice were reluctant to adhere to a new set of markers for performance and competence based on social interactions with law-abiding citizens. By emphasizing the aggressive pursuit of social disorder, or disorderly persons, police returned to the more comfortable performance indicators of stops and arrests, while restoring to the workplace their traditional cultural dichotomy of 'disorderly people and law abiders'. (Fagan and Davies, this volume, p. 14; see also Thatcher, 2001, p. 779)

Fagan and Davies find that 'the NYPD version of disorder policing rejected the emphasis on alternatives to arrest' (p. 17), favouring instead a 'strategy focused on policing poor people' (p. 29), replacing place-based policing with person-focused tactics such that race replaced place. Stop rates were ten times higher for blacks on violence and weapons, and the ratio of arrests to stops was 18.7 per cent higher for blacks on weapons stops, producing a 'style of racial policing' (pp. 33–42). Further, 'community standards were no longer identified through structured and systematic interactions between police and community leaders. Instead, the NYPD turned to its sophisticated data-driven management accountability system – Compstat – to identify community needs' (p. 18), blocking the decentralization necessary for effective police–community partnerships that might identify actual broken windows.[1]

Finally, while Fagan and Davies find that 'the relationship between public disorder and crime is spurious' (p. 21) in a context where a popularized misunderstanding of this relationship justifies more aggressive and less accountable forms of traditional police work, the 'punitive component of the D.P.s [declined prosecutions] and dismissed arrests – being taken into custody, handcuffed, transported, booked, often strip-searched, and jailed overnight – impregnates these events with its own social meaning quite different from the origins of Broken Windows theory' (p. 22). As Thatcher (2001, p. 779) noted, the 'broken windows metaphor synthesizes police and community values in the minds of individual officers', as managers use it to reassure officers that community policing is not soft on crime.

In Chapter 2, Peter Manning provides a detailed discursive and historical analysis of the symbolic communication strategies deployed by the NYPD and city leaders to make salient their 'good-policing of broken windows' explanation of crime rate declines. He argues that '[t]he police, like other occupations, manage uncertainties by manipulating symbols' because 'imagery is crucial to retaining market share, public trust, and funding' (pp. 53–54), and that this often leads top managers to dramatize events. This means that the meaning of observed broken windows is reframed as the police struggle to control their image in the news. 'While the rhetoric of police–community partnerships and reduced social distance is publicized widely, punitive crime control tactics are more widely adopted' (p. 55),[2] confusing residents interested in better managing the conflicts that cause the greatest harm in their lives by making salient other, bureaucratically- and politically-driven conflicts that 'dissipate public energies', as Schattschneider (1975, p. 137) warned against, by focusing them on fears that distract attention from leadership and on to the dangerous classes (Glassner, 1999; Davis and Silver, 2004; Lyons and Drew, 2006).

Manning describes the evolution of policing in New York under Mayor Guiliani and Police Commissioner Bratton as a combination of zero-tolerance crime-fighting justified with increasing reference to militaristic metaphors and a 'words that succeed for policies that fail' (Edelman, 1977), and a rhetorical representation of this as community policing made possible because, '[w]hile the "broken windows" perspective made arrest a last solution, absent changes in social disorder, arrest was elevated in the NYPD to its central weapon in the war against "street crime"' (p. 57). Taken together, this combination made the police more aggressive, less accountable and more insulated from critical public scrutiny. '"Zero tolerance" crime-control tactics, encouraged and supported by Bratton, were fused with a rhetorical strategy called "taking back the streets," a war-tinged metaphor following the "broken windows" theory' (p. 57).

Not only has a narrowing of the scope of 'broken windows' to the more aggressive policing of disorderly strangers prevented the development of what is genuinely promising about reforms like community policing, it has also mobilized formal and informal approaches to public safety that further concentrate disadvantage within America's already most victimized communities in ways that fail to deter deviance because they fail to encourage the kind of public support for state deployment of police powers that makes democratic policing possible and cost-effective.

In their 2003 *Law & Society Review* essay, Jason Sunshine and Tom Tyler (Chapter 3) build on Tyler's other work (Tyler 2000, 2001; Tyler and Wakslak, 2004) in examining the relationship between police legitimacy and public support for the police department. Their findings:

> . . . reinforce the argument that over time, the police can best regulate public behavior by focusing on engaging the social values, such as legitimacy, that lead to self-regulation on the part of most of the public, most of the time. If the public generally view the police as legitimate, much of their everyday behavior will conform to the law, freeing the police up to deal with problematic people and situations. Further, the efforts of the police to manage such problematic people and situations will be aided by cooperation from the public. Finally, when the police need discretionary authority, their use of such authority will be supported by the public. Hence, a procedural justice-based approach to regulation creates social order by engaging public cooperation with law and legal authority. Such cooperation is engaged when people in the communities being policed experience the police as exercising their authority fairly. (Sunshine and Tyler, this volume, p. 103)

The process-based, relational regulation model provided by Sunshine and Tyler 'seeks to manage the relationship between legal authorities and the communities they police through self-regulation that flows from the activation of people's own feelings of responsibility and obligation' (p. 83), thus linking formal and informal social control through attentiveness to political struggle, legitimacy and the processes through which we achieve the shared values constitutive of resilient communities. It turns out that policing with respect is not only something that police have more control over than crime rates (p. 103), it also has a significant impact on their ability to reduce crime (see Mastrofski and Reisig, 2002; Seron, Pereira and Kovath, 2004; Heyman, 2002; for similar data on courts see Tyler 2001 and Tiersma and Salon, 2002). The strong connections between the structure and routine practices of state institutions, citizen identities, collective solidarities, social bonding and disorder highlighted in these policing studies also suggest that the most effective approach to deploying police powers is one that understands these relationships as embedded within particular relational networks, including schools.

Payne, Gottfredson and Gottfredson (2003) expanded our examination of police powers to the school context and found that communally organized schools had less disorder because the relationships enabled by these particular formal structures and routine practices increased student commitment to the school and encouraged the internalization of norms. Like collective efficacy at the neighbourhood level, achieving shared expectations and valuing cross-cutting forms of supportive engagement increase the resilience and deterrent power of informal social controls, reducing deviance and the cost of crime control, while also improving teacher efficacy and morale, reducing dropout rates and improving academic achievement. Further, students or citizens in these contexts became more empathetic, socially well-adjusted, altruistic and better able to prevent, resolve or reduce the harms associated with the routine conflicts in their everyday lives. In short, tending to actual broken windows can reduce crime in ways that also revitalize communities, enabling them to effectively partner with more formal agents in the production of public safety (see also Colvin, Cullen and Vander Ven, 2002).

The final essay in Part I suggests a way of utilizing all this information to reframe the original observations about untended broken windows. In Chapter 5 Robert Sampson and Dawn Bartusch illustrate the power of taking actual broken windows seriously in order to frame our analysis of police powers and deterrence. This particular version of Sampson's extensive research agenda focuses on dispelling the myth that there is a violent black subculture, a them dramatically unlike us and therefore appropriately targeted for more extreme punishment. This essay was chosen because it provides useful connections between the emerging literature on collective efficacy, social capital – the work of Tom Tyler (above), Lawrence Sherman (1993) Michael Tonry (1995), Meares and Kahan (1998) and others – that focuses on encouraging 'policymakers to attend to the unintended consequences of get-tough policies and heavy-handed enforcement practices on a community's ability to contribute to crime-reduction efforts' (Sampson and Bartusch, p. 171). This essay helps us understand the multiple layers of conflict that concentrate in power-poor communities and prevent self-governance at the local level in ways that invite state-privileging solutions to collective action problems, further encouraging the atrophy of alternatives to state agency (see Sennett, 1970; also Rosenfeld, Messner and Baumer (2001) on social capital and homicide).

Since areas of concentrated disadvantage have a higher tolerance for deviance, other than violent deviance (p. 165), this is additional evidence that proximity to crime turns out to produce less punitive, rather than more punitive and vengeful citizens. At the same time, 'blacks appear more cynical because they are disproportionately likely to live in residential environments of concentrated disadvantage' (p. 167). Moreover, whites rush to judge this experience-based cynicism as evidence in support of negative stereotypes about blacks as violent and lazy, which are themselves important attitudinal and cultural sources for white support of more punitive approaches to conflict (Peffley and Hurwitz, 2002). But the ideological and cultural foundations for legal cynicism, a willingness to voluntarily comply with the law, or a readiness to collaborate with the police, reflect neighbourhood experiences, not race (Sampson and Bartusch, p. 168), and the authors 'suggest that inner-city contexts of racial segregation and concentrated disadvantage, where inability to influence the structures of power that constrain lives is greatest . . . breed cynicism and perceptions of legal injustice' (p. 153). These political, economic, and physical disorders, made visible in untended broken windows, provide a neighbourhood context for policing that demands a serious examination of race, the blackening of the US prison system and fear-driven politics before we can begin to understand the dimensions of the various, overlapping and competing conflicts we face.

Racial Profiling

One way of thinking about the disadvantages concentrated within those communities most victimized by crime is to observe their actual broken windows and conclude that these are one powerful sign of the multiple forms of disorder concentrating in power-poor, blackening, inner-city communities. These untended broken windows are concrete manifestations of physical disorders linked to the unequal distribution of resources and employment opportunities; economic disorders linked to absentee landlords, redlining, or neighbourhood disinvestment; and political disorders linked to representation, citizenship, fearmongering, and race-baiting – an area examined in Part II of this volume.

Part II begins with Loïc Wacquant's powerful argument that the explosion of imprisonment and the blackening nature of our prison population are best explained as two aspects of a larger evolution in our 'peculiar institutions', from slavery to Jim Crow to the ghetto to the hyperghetto. As Wacquant argues, '[t]he recent upsurge in black incarceration results from the crisis of the ghetto as device for caste control and the correlative need for a substitute apparatus for the containment of lower-class African Americans'. In this essay the author provides a broad historical framework for making sense of current and ongoing developments in both inner-city neighbourhoods and the criminal justice system. In fact, he argues that these developments cannot be intelligently examined in isolation from each other, because they are two central and integrated mechanisms for the distribution of the physical, political, economic and social disorders that are increasingly concentrating in those inner-city neighbourhoods whose residents cycle and recycle from prisons that look more like ghettos to the communities that look more like prisons and back.

One of the more important micro-mechanisms for the creation and maintenance of this blackening carceral system is the court-sanctioned and police-deployed tactic of racial profiling. In Chapter 7 Albert Meehan and Michael Ponder (2002) analyse racial profiling and argue that 'society expects police officers to preserve the boundaries of place' (p. 424), and like Fagan and Davies above, when tending broken windows is reframed as punishing rowdy teenagers, place becomes more easily confused with race (Black, 1971). In this study, comparing roadway data to the data collected automatically by police cruiser Mobile Data Terminals they found that the most significant factor for explaining variations in which drivers were profiled was race:

African-American drivers are twice as likely as are white drivers to be queried . . . As African-American drivers move from these border sectors to the farthest sectors of the white community, their chances of being the subject of a query increase dramatically . . . [with] query rates that are 325% and 383% greater than their number in the driver population. (pp. 223 and 235)

Similarly, Kane, in a study also done in NYC, found that 'communities characterized by structural disadvantages and increases in Latino populations may have experienced processes that both attenuated informal social control mechanism while providing a source of conflict necessary to encourage police misconduct' (Kane, 2002, p. 884).

Terrill and Mastrofski also find, in their study of the situational determinants of police use of force, that 'male, nonwhite, poor, and younger suspect were all treated more forcefully, irrespective of their behavior' (2002, p. 215). If policing without being attentive to respect and fairness undermines support for the police, that effect is multiplied many times over when we consider the legacy established by persistently disrespectful social control practices like racial profiling on the streets or students on the prison track in American state schools (see Ferguson, 2000) or the even more insidious ways that unexamined, and inaccurate, folk knowledge about race, crime and punishment can have 'a substantial influence on juror decisionmaking during sentencing deliberations . . . So pervasive is the folk knowledge about early release that some jurors regard any contrary belief as frivolous' (Steiner, Bowers, and Sarat, 1999, pp. 485 and 481).

Benjamin Fleury-Steiner (Chapter 8) provides a powerful analysis of juror reasoning over death penalty cases that investigates the various ways in which race is mobilized as a hegemonic narrative and offers three related critical findings. First, '[f]indings among white jurors reveal a hegemonic tale of racial inferiority' (p. 249). Second, stories about racial inferiority are articulated by white jurors in one of four frames, reflecting the profound impact of extra-legal factors, such as their personal experiences, on constructing the meaning of the law and legal institutions. Third, black jurors, similarly influenced by their own experiences, employ two distinct frames in response to the racism of their white counterparts.

As Fleury-Steiner puts it, these 'stories . . . frame and impart meanings' to the law, legal institutions, race and the '[r]acial discourses [that] constitute taken-for-granted understandings and practices' (p. 249), operating as an implicit and often unexamined, or only partially examined, background consensus upon which those making life and death decisions decide when, how and upon whom to deploy law's violence (see Sarat and Kearns, 1995). 'They serve as "mechanisms of social control" because they assert and instantiate a differentiation but do not reveal the basis for those distinctions – do not bring them to the surface for examination and resistance – and thus "conceal the social organization of their production and plausibility"' (pp. 249–50). Like the metaphoric reformulation of broken windows as a call for punishing disorderly people, these frames narrow the scope of sentencing conflicts to often contradictory personal anecdotes that reflect an inattentiveness to power cultivated by the messages from public and private officials delivered by formal mechanisms of social control such as zero-tolerance policing, racial profiling and police disrespect.

This essay provides a powerful empirical explanation for why ordinary citizens, mobilizing a prevailing punitive approach to conflict management, can appear to be taking structure into account in their analysis, even as they dismiss it in favour of volitional explanations in constructing their preferred response. Scheingold (1991, pp. 8–10) pointed out that both liberals and conservatives tend to mix structural and volitional explanations, even as 'dichotomous interpretations [and] symbolic shortcuts [like "structural" or "volitional"] dominate political discourse' to screen out 'criminological complexity'. We see that, in each of the four story frames highlighted by Fleury-Steiner, the white juror begins with some sort of structural analysis only to conclude with a strictly volitional and punitive response. Stories about individual responsibility begin as anecdotes about growing up in, or knowing about, poor communities. Stories about the racial concentration of disadvantage begin with recognition of the tragedy, angry stories expressing indignation that this kid got lost in the system, but conclude that, once he has become a street thug, he no longer knows right from wrong like the rest of us and only understands severe punishment. And, finally, frightening stories mobilizing fears about serious harms move easily from more generalized anxiety to its unexamined volitional source in white fear of young black men (Fleury-Steiner, pp. 260–62; see also Rosenfeld, Messner and Baumer, 2003).

And this fear does not come out of nowhere. In *Public Opinion Quarterly*, Tali Mendelberg (Chapter 9) analysed the now infamous Willie Horton ads to argue persuasively that 'racial campaigns affect far more than voters' behavior at the ballot box' (p. 277). In a controlled experiment, Mendelberg found that 'exposure to Horton coverage increases the effect of prejudice' (p. 288), activates prejudice where it was nearly dormant, 'inclines prejudiced whites to reject the legitimacy of welfare programs and to endorse the idea that African Americans can do without them' (p. 290). Further:

> . . . without Horton exposure, prejudiced individuals are 25 percentage points more likely than unprejudiced people to oppose racially egalitarian policies; with exposure to Horton, prejudiced individuals are 40 percentage points more likely to do so than unprejudiced people. (p. 288)

Testing the alternative hypothesis, that Horton activated people's concerns about crime, the author found that 'Horton did not bring out the power of crime salience . . . [and] did not move perceptions of the importance of crime as a problem' (p. 293).

Horton was about race, the mobilization of which increased resistance to policy that focused on redressing racial inequalities and 'heightened perceptions of racial conflict' (p. 294). Horton also represents, homologous to Wacquant, an evolution in the ways in which Americans deploy race, from a more explicit to a more plausibly deniable, implicit form of the race card: race-coded appeals to law and order. In Chapter 10 Ted Chiricos, Kelly Welch and Marc Gertz conclude that the 'racial typification of crime is a significant predictor of punitive attitudes toward crime, even with controls for various demographic factors, crime salience variables and attitudinal dimensions. In addition, we found that this relationship exists only for white respondents, and more particularly, whites who are less concerned about crime . . .' (p. 320). According to Chiricos, Welch and Gertz:

> The relationship demonstrated here between the racial typification of crime and punitiveness is consistent with the mechanism of 'essentialism' that Young (1999) has shown to be an instrumental moment in the politics of 'exclusion.' The belief that 'others' are essentially different from oneself or one's own group 'allows people to believe in their own superiority while being able to demonize the other, as essentially wicked, stupid or criminal' (Young, 1999: 109). Indeed, the racial typification of crime essentializes race in terms of crime and crime in terms of race, thereby 'demonizing' blacks as the locus of threat. In other historical contexts, such demonizing has been a precursor to the most extraordinary atrocities (Cohen, 1995). Today, it energizes the mechanisms of social exclusion that include, but are surely not limited to, what Young has called 'the great penal gulag' (1999: 190) that has been created in this country during the past twenty years. (p. 321)

Expanding our discussion of more implicit, deadly and symbiotic forms of modern racism, the authors conclude that:

> In some ways 'modern racism' may be more pernicious than the 'traditional' overt expressions of racial antipathy, because of its oblique character. Consider James Q. Wilson's assertion that 'it is not racism that makes whites uneasy about blacks moving into their neighborhoods . . . it is fear. Fear of crime, of drugs, of gangs, of violence' (1992: A-16). Such an assertion, in one short sentence, simultaneously disavows white racism while equating blacks with a list of negative attributes. There may be no more apposite expression of what has been called 'modern racism' than the simple equation of violence, gangs, drugs and crime with blacks. (p. 322)

And this simple equation – articulated most often in the approach to broken windows that narrows the conflicts to how to more aggressively punish power-poor minorities – will be further unpacked in Part III of this volume, which focuses directly on the political utility and social costs associated with our incarceration explosion.

The Incarceration Explosion

Angela Behrens, Christopher Uggen and Jeff Manza argue, in Chapter 11, that:

> the racial composition of state prisons is firmly associated with the adoption of state felon disenfranchisement laws. States with greater nonwhite prison populations have been more likely to ban convicted felons from voting . . . In many Southern states, the percentage of nonwhite prison inmates nearly doubled between 1850 and 1870. Whereas 2% of the Alabama prison population was nonwhite in 1850, 74% was nonwhite in 1870, though the total nonwhite population increased by only 3%. (pp. 372 and 374)

The explanation of this mid-nineteenth-century 'astounding over-representation of blacks behind bars' (Wacquant, this volume, p. 177) draws our attention again to policy decisions taken by public officials that articulate with market decisions by private leaders – in this case, the decision to distribute disintegrative forms of retribution (Braithwaite, 1989) in policies to disenfranchise particular citizens, grouped by a discourse about crime coded to punish on the basis of race.

As Behrens, Uggen and Manza put it, the political utility for leaders willing to create a 'shadowy form of citizenship . . . as punishment for criminal behavior' (p. 375) is that '. . . felon disenfranchisement laws persist [because of] their compatibility with modern racial ideologies. The laws are race neutral on their face . . . [And] a strong anticrime consensus allows contemporary political actors to disenfranchise racial minorities without making explicit the implications for minority suffrage' (p. 374). And, while this particular essay focuses on ballot manipulation as a form of racial subordination that reaches beyond the electoral arena, we also know from Uggen and Manza that, in a narrower focus, these decisions have been far from electorally benign:

> Analysis shows that felon disenfranchisement played a decisive role in US Senate elections in recent years. Moreover, at least one Republican presidential victory would have been reversed if former felons had been allowed to vote, and at least one Democratic presidential victory would have been jeopardized had contemporary rates of disenfranchisement prevailed during that time. (Uggen and Manza, 2002, p. 777)

Incarcerating more of those already most victimized by crime, and then disempowering them within a shadowy form of citizenship upon release, mobilizes blackness to win elections and concentrate additional disadvantages within the families and communities least able to subject public and private forms of unaccountable power to critical scrutiny. In Chapter 12 Bruce Western, continuing to document the unequal distributions of costs associated with a 'penal expansion [that] has deepened racial inequality' (p. 399) and is unlikely to deter criminal behaviour, argues persuasively that '[t]here is strong evidence that incarceration reduces the wages of ex-inmates by 10 to 20 percent . . . [and] incarceration was also found to reduce the rate of wage growth by about 30 percent' (p. 398). Western finds that the negative, lifelong and community-level effect of incarceration on African Americans is twice that on white Americans and that it is the 'low wages earned by ex-inmates' that is 'associated with further crime after release from prison' (p. 399).

In Chapter 13 Devah Pager provides a powerful experimental analysis that directly measures the impact of a criminal record on employment to identify a mechanism of 'carceral channeling' (to use Wacquant's term). These findings further confirm that incarceration has an enormous impact on employment, and that this impact is larger on blacks than whites:

> The effect of race on these findings is strikingly large. Among blacks without criminal records, only 14% received callbacks, relative to 34% of white noncriminals (P<.01). In fact, even whites *with* criminal records received more favorable treatment (17%) than blacks *without* criminal records (14%) . . . The effect of a criminal record is thus 40% larger for blacks than for whites. (pp. 425–6, 427)

Pager concludes that:

> In our frenzy of locking people up, our 'crime control' policies may in fact exacerbate the very conditions that lead to crime in the first place. Research consistently shows that finding quality employment is one of the strongest predictors of desistance from crime. The fact that a criminal record severely limits employment opportunities – particularly among blacks – suggests that these individuals are left with few viable alternatives . . . No longer a peripheral institution, the criminal justice system has become a dominant presence in the lives of young disadvantaged men, playing a key role in the sorting and stratifying of labor market opportunities. (pp. 429–30)

Framing our crime control efforts this way clearly links up with Wacquant, Sampson and Bartusch, Clear *et al.*, Western and others in this volume as they seek to explain the puzzle of the American incarceration explosion in terms of the consequences and costs of massive – and massively racialized – incarceration. According to Pager, the recent period is one in which 'incarceration has changed from a punishment reserved primarily for the most heinous offenders to one extended to a much greater range of crimes and a much larger segment of the population' (p. 406). She argues that '[w]hile stratification researchers typically focus on schools, labor markets, and the family as primary institutions affecting inequality, a new institution has emerged as central to the sorting and stratifying of young and disadvantaged men: the criminal justice system' (p. 405).

Todd Clear, Dina Rose, Elin Waring and Kristen Scully (Chapter 14) continue this line of inquiry by examining the impact of growing incarceration rates at the neighbourhood level. In short, the unequally distributed incarceration explosion weakens community, because 'high concentrations of incarceration' (like poverty, heterogeneity, residential mobility, single-parent families, structural density and urbanization) operate as an additional 'disorganizing factor' to undermine the family, occupational and political resources that enable informal social control (p. 446). Studying incarceration as a form of 'coercive mobility' that has various negative impacts on community stability, this essay explicitly highlights the role of elite decision-making – on the part of both public and private leadership – in our ongoing failure to deter criminal behaviour.

The US prison population has risen every year since 1972 without regard to crime rates, unemployment or other factors which we would expect incarceration to be responsive to, and this massive removal is inescapably linked to the ongoing re-entry of these shadowy citizens into the communities they were forcibly removed from, at a rate of over 600 000 per year (Clear *et al.*, p. 449). The prevailing explanations focus on incapacitation and deterrence – that is, they highlight an expectation that the removal of these 'broken windows' sends a message that will deter future crime by changing the decision-making calculus of those incarcerated and others in their communities. However, a sober analysis of the communities in question reveals that the removal creates a job-opening for another drug dealer; it fails to remove crime. Furthermore, the harsh treatment and diminished life opportunities associated with the punishment of offenders encourages more, not less criminal behaviour upon their release.

Prevailing explanations miss how community safety is maintained – that is, by crafting formal approaches to crime control that support and invest in the neighbourhood-level informal social controls that make cost-effective crime control in a democratic society possible. This means investing in the human capital (quality education, conflict management and other skills, lifetime earning capacity, mobility) of those who live and work in those communities most victimized by crime to build the reciprocal relational networks that generate social capital (achieving, in practice, the shared values that produce resilient communities and collective efficacy). In this study of 80 Tallahassee neighborhoods, Clear *et al.* (p. 462) find that prison releases and high levels of prison admissions are a strong predictor of increases in crime – incarceration is a form of neighbourhood disinvestment. When increases in imprisonment exceed a 'tipping point' (p. 448) and the re-entry of individuals from prison into these communities reduces the level of human capital and disables the social networks that contribute to public safety, it contributes to the creation and exacerbation of places of concentrated disadvantage, constituting an attack on the stability of poor neighbourhoods – an attack on family values – with foreseeably disparate racial impacts (Tonry, 1995).

> The result of an emergent underclass is a kind of permanent system of urbanized social disorganization for the most destitute areas of inner-city life. In today's world of entrenched poverty, the processes of heterogeneity and mobility may no longer work as they once did . . . The inner-city areas that are dominated by the underclass have the greatest levels of crime, as well as little racial heterogeneity and little outward mobility. They also have the greatest concentrations of cycling into and out of prison, and our data suggest that these processes of coercive mobility compound problems of informal social control for the neighborhoods that start out with depleted collective efficacy. (Clear *et al.*, p. 470)

In opposition to the popularly supported idea that increasing formal and punitive attention to minor incivilities is a way of revitalizing informal social controls, this study 'shows that growing formal social control has a negative impact on the capacity for informal social control, especially when that growth is concentrated among certain groups' (p. 471). Colvin, Cullen and Vander Ven (2002, p. 27) similarly argue that coercive approaches cause crime because coercion, like coercive mobility, invests in criminal capital that intimidates the already weak into becoming even more desperately driven by fear and anxiety, while supportive approaches invest in social capital, '*creating* the context' in which the strong social bonds that provide resources useful in preventing or resolving conflicts can emerge.

Given the data presented here, what is driving our rush to punish? According to Kevin Smith in the *Journal of Politics*, growth in imprisonment rates is neither related to crime rates nor to public opinion: 'Instead, it is the most basic elements of the political environment (partisanship and elections) and the continuing legacy of racial social cleavages that explain why incarceration rates have increased' (Smith, 2004, p. 925; see also Beckett and Sasson, 2000; Tonry, 1995). In the final essay in Part III, Michael Tonry provides a detailed examination of precisely this question, and his findings lead us to consider more seriously the politics of crime and punishment in Part IV.

Tonry organizes his investigation as an assessment, from a more internationalist perspective, of several increasingly complex explanations for the American incarceration explosion. First, the claim that this explosion has been in response to a high crime rate 'has virtually no validity' (p. 479). The evidence in support of the related claim that it has been in response to rising crime is more mixed, but still weak, because the most drastically punitive responses were put in place as many as 15 years after crime rates had already peaked and settled into a steady decline (p. 480; see also Savelsberg, 1994).

Second, the claim that the public demanded it is misleading because public opinion is more ambivalent and as often follows, rather than precedes, elite political initiatives (Beckett, 1997). As Tonry puts it, '[t]his leads to the third explanation for American exceptionalism – politicians for partisan advantage have persistently banked the fires of public fear of crime, and then offered harsh policies to dampen those fires. Assessing that explanation requires a look back at how and why crime control became a focal issue in American politics' (p. 483).

While Tonry's argument that, before Barry Goldwater ran for president in 1964, crime control 'debates were seldom partisan or ideological' (p. 483) begs an explanation for the American vigilante tradition (Brown, 1969), the Salem witch trials and McCarthyism and the Red Scare that does not involve partisan and ideological struggles over the political and criminological 'forces that determine how, why and with what consequences societies choose to deal with crime and criminals' (Scheingold, 1998, p. 4), his claim that recent decades are marked by the increased salience of more politicized ways of framing crime control remains persuasive. 'Crime's role as a wedge issue has important consequences' (p. 485), including the oversimplification of complex issues to make them fit into familiar soundbites that will allow a candidate to better control his or her image in the news. 'Matters judges and prosecutors agonize over in individual cases are addressed in slogans and symbols, which often leads to the adoption of ham-fisted and poorly considered policies' (p. 485) that polarize and divide the public in ways that make them less able to understand the nature of crime and more dependent on formal state intervention as a consequence.

Concluding with a focus on larger political trends fragmenting the public into single-issue groups as one way of exploring why crime serves so well as a wedge issue, Tonry draws heavily on Caplow and Simon (1999) to argue that the nationalization of governance and crime control has led to dramatically reduced confidence in government for not only failing in its excessively formal and punitive approaches to these new tasks, but also failing in ways that hasten the atrophy of alternatives, namely less formal approaches that depend on resilient communities rich in social capital.

In this context, marked by 'political balkanization' as the elite-led roots of our culture of fear (Glassner, 1999), 'harsh policies on crime and welfare can be debated in moral terms, respond to broad-based anxieties and empathies, and affront no powerful constituency' (p. 488). And this leads to the final component of Tonry's explanation: our historically contingent political and cultural struggles over how tolerant our collective responses to crime and deviance ought to be. Following the work of David Musto (1987), Tyler and Boeckmann (1997) and Stuart Scheingold (1984, 1991), Tonry argues that, in our current contexts, 'people do not really care about the effectiveness of crime and drug-abuse policies but, instead, support harsh policies for expressive reasons' (p. 491). This is an explanation that highlights both the cultural resonance of punitive approaches to crime control and the ability of public and private elites to prime public sentiments to amplify the salience of punitive responses to crime. All of this brings us to our Part IV which discusses the political challenges of crime control in a free society.

Political Challenges

Stuart Scheingold argues that there is an emerging field of inquiry examining many of the questions posed in this volume: political criminology. 'It is criminology in that it is rooted in conceptions of, and concerns about, the ramifications of street crime; It is political in that its focus is on the way in which crime control strategies both reflect and influence the distribution of power within the polity' (Scheingold, 1998, p. 1). While all the essays so far have offered valuable contributions to the 'study of forces that determine how, why and with what consequences societies choose to deal with crime and criminals' (Scheingold, 1998, p. 4), the final five essays focus much more explicitly on the politics of crime and punishment.

David Jacobs and Jason Carmichael (Chapter 16), in their analysis of the political determinants of punishment, find that 'expansions in the strength of the Republican party and stronger conservative values produce subsequent increases in the prison population' (p. 518), that (after controlling for violent crime) incarceration rates were higher in states with larger black populations and that this relationship was stronger in states where leaders put 'increased political emphasis on black street crime' (p. 518). Their findings contradict previous analyses suggesting that Republican party strength can be read as a democratic response to pre-existing conservative views by demonstrating that 'the strength of the Republican party continues to explain the imprisonment rates after citizen ideology and membership in fundamentalist Protestant churches have been held constant' (p. 520). Finally, over the time-series, the strength of the primary predictor, Republican strength, increased, and the authors conclude that their findings support the position that 'incarceration is one method the modern state uses to manage latent political conflicts created by racial and ethnic divisions' (p. 521), that this method involves 'conservative shifts in political climates' (p. 522) that are measured at the state level here as local political entrepreneurial activities taking electoral advantage of the larger symbolic and policy-making environment associated with national shifts.

Jacobs and Helms demonstrate further 'that punishment is intrinsically political' and partisan, since 'correctional expenditures grow after expansions in the political strength of the Republican Party' (1999, p. 11). Both studies suggest a politics of dependency and the continued analytical force contained in Ira Katznelson's observation that:

> . . . most of the 'social problems' of contemporary cities are the result of the uneven development of American capitalism . . . All have to be dealt with by city governments, yet all are quite obviously generated by causes *external* to the cities in which their impact is felt . . . Their dependency places urban political elites in a situation analogous to the role indigenous rulers performed in classic colonial situations of indirect rule. The 'arbiter governments' they lead must *manage the consequences of their inability to solve urban problems.* (Katznelson, 1976, pp. 218–20, emphasis in original)

In a detailed historical analysis of state-level politics, Vanessa Barker combines quantitative and qualitative data to argue that political structures and political cultural practices channel collective action in ways that account for state policy outcomes such as the subnational variations in imprisonment examined. In a period of transition from one governing coalition to another, in this case from the New Deal coalition and culture and into an emerging zero-tolerance coalition and culture (Lyons and Drew, forthcoming), fear and uncertainty strain existing political arrangements as culture wars and moral panics are made more salient features of the political landscape (Franks, 2004). Barker argues that it has been in these moments of 'political turmoil' that American states have transformed the nature of governance in ways that demonstrate an additional aspect of the politics of crime and punishment.

While changes in state imprisonment policy were central indicators of state political transformation, these changes varied according to the structure and routine bureaucratic practices characteristic of different state political-cultures. One centrally relevant characteristic institutionalized in each state political culture – an animating characteristic of each state's political structures, bureaucratic routines, and how these determined the state's unique approach to incarceration – was how each state had responded differently to the civil rights movement and black demands for political participation. Those states that worked harder to include blacks, supporting civil rights and black political participation rhetorically, institutionally and in policy and bureaucratic practice created formal mechanisms that enabled, enriched and invested in informal mechanisms – in a political culture – that reduced racial conflict, racial hostility, and provided 'a crucial buffer against the use of incarceration as a blunt instrument of social control' (p. 549). Those states that did not include, or actively sought to continue and expand the exclusion of blacks, remaining hostile to civil rights and blocking black political participation, created a formal state apparatus that enabled and encouraged a rancid populism resurgent 'anti-statism, and intensified reliance on confinement in order to bring about a new social order based on exclusion' (p. 20).

Thomas Stucky similarly offers:

> . . . more evidence for the notion that certain local political arrangements enhance or inhibit the accessibility of local officials in ways that affect crime. In addition, the effects of structural indicators of deprivation, such as poverty and family disruption, on violent crime were lower in cities with mayor-council forms of government and as the number of traditional local governmental structures increased. Thus, there appears to be something about certain local government structures that weakens the relationship between deprivation and crime . . . [and] cities with African-American mayors had lower violent crime rates. (Stucky, 2003, pp. 1122–23)

While Barker's analysis builds on work throughout this volume, this selection adds another dimension to our understanding. 'Race and economic marginality may indeed influence the extent to which states rely on confinement . . . but these social factors matter differently in different political contexts with varying effects on imprisonment' (p. 530). This essay is about the unexpected but foreseeable long-term consequences of routine practices and policy structures. When actual broken windows are tended, citizens support effective, non-punitive approaches to conflict management. When leaders 'diffuse and fracture political authority' to amplify expressive fears about broken windows as a metaphor providing only superficial coherence to a collection of moral panics designed to realign the electorate (rather than prevent crime), then citizens learn to direct their frustration at government itself and demand a government limited to punishment.

According to Barker, this approach to leadership 'amplifies anti-statist political cultural practices . . . [that] tend to atomize and frustrate political participants . . . heighten conflict, decrease compromise, and increase animosity', encouraging 'ideological battles rather than pragmatic politics of compromise and coalition' (pp. 536–37). The structures and routine practices in states whose leadership chose to rely on 'high levels of state repression' (incarceration) atomized and frustrated citizens, *constructing* compromise as unthinkable, as irresolute, as weak and permissive, and encouraging citizens to instead feel 'sincerely threatened by opposing views, values, and ideas' (p. 539). Conversely, when state leaders institutionalize inclusion, 'routines of debate, discussion, open exchange of ideas and opinions – in other words, the habits of communicative action', the political culture in these states tends to develop in ways that 'strengthen reciprocal and trusting networks . . . [and] encourage compromise and collaboration between the state and civil society' (p. 541), weakening both the crime control and the political forces that might otherwise demand more punitive approaches to crime.

Richard Fording (Chapter 18) provides further evidence of the importance of leadership in tending to actual broken windows, including attending to the critical relationship between formal and informal mechanisms of social control – political, economic, cultural – when he argues that 'in the absence of electoral power, insurgency is likely to receive only a coercive response from the state' (p. 564). In a pooled cross-sectional time-series analysis of the relationship between welfare recipient rates, incarceration rates and black political unrest, Fording finds that unrest correlated with both increased welfare and increased incarceration, though only for the immediate period and only when blacks had electoral access. When blacks did not have electoral access, insurgency resulted in only a coercive response: incarceration rates rose without a concomitant rise in welfare recipient rates.

Fording claims that:

> States are the most important actors in the American federal system, at least with respect to these two policy areas. States are generally responsible for about half the welfare expenditures in the country. In the case of criminal justice, most arrests are made by local law enforcement agencies, but criminal courts are under state control, and nearly all convicted offenders are sent to state prisons. (p. 588)

He further argues that, at the state level, there is a 'welfare-incarceration tradeoff' (p. 565) – that is, 'a decline in welfare generosity by states is related to an increase in incarceration levels' (p. 568) and that, in the ongoing debate about the motivations of New Deal reformers, 'extrainstitutional politics' was found to be important, but so were 'conventional electoral channels' in conditioning the response to insurgency (p. 567):

> It appears that many states were unsuccessful in reducing AFDC in the years immediately after unrest subsided. If the social control model is correct, however, labor market imperatives, coupled with the mobilization of the business community, eventually would motivate policymakers to reduce welfare

generosity . . . If this dynamic at least partly explains recent contraction of the welfare rolls, then this research may explain a second important policy trend in recent years. If a welfare-incarceration tradeoff exists, then efforts to reduce welfare throughout the 1980s and 1990s should have been matched by some increase in incarceration. (Fording, p. 568)

Aggregate national trend data, and Fording's state-level analysis, support the claim that declining welfare generosity is related to rising use of incarceration, and the combination illustrates both continuities and new trends in the complex relationship between governance and crime control in America. In Chapter 19 Jonathan Simon analyses the role of criminal law in governance traced from our revolutionary roots to Megan's Law, arguing that '[c]riminal law . . . [has] served as the definitive grammar of American democratic governance' (p. 575). He argues that:

Deterrence is both a penal and political theory. It is here that penal strategy and liberal government rationality most perfectly correlate. It is here that the penal machinery seems to operate directly on the cumulative rationality of the democratic body politic. Deterrence has been the original and most enduring way of governing people through their freedom (i.e., through their capacity to make choices).
      Perhaps for this reason, deterrence has been so frequently reinvented and rediscovered as a penal rationale. (pp. 576–77)

When deterrence was married to rehabilitation it continued to operate as both penal and political theory, seeking to 'transform those too unsettled by the Revolution and its aftermath to fully take up its invitation to self-government . . . Deterrence operated like a communicative system "broadcasting" its message of norm compliance across society as a whole, while disciplinary normalization was rooted in particular locations . . .' (p. 578). Wilson and Kelling's (1982) bait-and-switch suggestion that we ought to tend to metaphorical broken windows in order to justify ignoring actual broken windows is a particularly odd mixture of broadcasting one script to mobilize citizen support for a national and symbolic commitment to deterrence and narrowcasting another script to simultaneously mobilize professional support for a localized and expressive punishing of the disadvantaged. As Simon puts it:

Like deterrence, the rehabilitative project has failed many times without disappearing . . . [because] politicians have incentives to make crime a central focus in campaigning. Promises of sweeping economic reforms could yield immediate problems on the markets. Promising to strike hard against crime is likely to offend no important interests . . . Governing through crime in this sense is attractive to people because it permits popular fears and experiences to be valorized in the strongest and most public terms. (pp. 578 and 579)

And it is made all the more attractive when metaphorical broken windows underwrite scripts that mobilize more aggressively punitive approaches to both expanding social control and diminishing social welfare efforts. Simon points out that '[t]he historical deposit of power in the scripts and metaphors of crime control has several consequences' (p. 580). They enable:

. . . political actors to express commitment to the security of the people while avoiding debate on the difficult questions of how to manage the major forms of modern public security (pensions, insurance, public education). [This] also makes it possible to criticize more elaborate measures of government social policy (whether funding for the arts or fighting poverty) as undervaluing and even undercutting the strength of government's primary commitment to physical security. (p. 581)

This has particularly disastrous consequences for the power-poor, African Americans, and the survival of traditional mechanisms of collective risk-sharing (state schools, insurance, government loans and policy preference, pensions). Today, as economic uncertainty accompanied by 'a widespread rollback in the institutions of collective risk sharing' recode racial divisions as the benign struggle between law-breakers and the law-abiding, we are further constructed as even less able to understand the relationship between crime, punishment, race and politics.

'Seen from the governance perspective, this hybrid of race and crime poses a serious threat to democracy in its tendency to intensify the disaggregation of those collective opportunity and risk structures of modern government that American democracy has always relied on to resolve group conflicts in civil society' (p. 586), dividing publics in ways that dissipate their democratic energies in the 'extreme terms of moral outrage that make resolution through negotiation less likely' (p. 590).

> Identities based on victimization . . . [ironically in more inclusive form when based on being a potential victim of crime] produce subjects that are increasingly less capable of defining their interests in terms that can be effectively resolved within the boundaries of democratic politics. The astounding political success of recent punitive legislation like 3-strikes and Megan's Law shows that crime is not necessarily a wedge issue. Almost all demographic segments of the population, and both political parties, supported these measures. On the other hand, one may fear that they produce a kind of false unity around narratives whose compelling facts provide potent political mobilizaztion but little mandate to govern . . . (p. 593)

> Megan's Law describes a kind of political community that may incorporate nearly everybody but in an inert and passive form that is anything but self-governing. (p. 597).

And it transforms political interactions into much more of a zero-sum game, weakening the political, cultural and economic foundations upon which we might deliberate about risk-sharing, constructing resilient communities where individual liberty strengthens families and catalyses the best minds – white or black, male or female – to innovatively address the complex challenges America faces as a nation. Instead, a zero-sum calculus focuses our fears on our neighbours as threatening strangers, rather than as potential partners, diverting our resources from innovation to imprisonment and 'insulating government from failure'. Those without the private resources to live in affluent areas are constructed as targets for punishment and 'their plight can now only look more like a kind of irresponsibility on their part' (p. 602), while even those who do escape to suburban fortress communities are increasingly punishing their children in schools that look more like prisons, producing passive and dependent consumers rather than active democratic citizens empowered with the skills necessary to innovate, lead and prosper.

In the final essay, William Lyons and Stuart Scheingold (Chapter 20), bring together many of the political themes highlighted in this volume. The authors argue that crime control policy, like all law-making, emerges from a complex, ongoing, overlapping, sometimes data-conscious but always electorally driven, political process. Their essay explores the ways in which good data can be marginalized by this political process, particularly the ways in which, in the current political climate, they are marginalized to encourage excessively punitive and less-than-effective approaches to crime control that inescapably impose additional costs upon family and community life – particularly within those communities already most victimized by crime.

After reviewing the politically contested debates over the relationship between our incarceration explosion and deterrence, Lyons and Scheingold focus on three costs of our current political fascination with increasingly severe, disproportionately punitive and racially discriminatory approaches to crime control. This approach represents a retreat from our commitment to the rule of law; it is weakening inner-city families and communities; and it is undermining the possibility of rational public deliberations about crime and punishment. Given the costs associated with ineffective approaches to crime control, how can we explain the creation and maintenance of these policies in a democratic society? Lyons and Scheingold respond as follows:

> A substantial, and in our view convincing, body of data indicates that the politics of crime and punishment are a classic instance of what Murray Edelman (1977) refers to as 'words that succeed and policies that fail.' Winning and holding public office, not crime control, are driving the policy making process . . . Our reading of the data indicates that punitive policies are driven from above as well as from below. The *top-down* explanations are much closer to the mark and, at the very least, provide insightful correctives to the *bottom-up* mainstream narratives. Political leaders are not, however, free agents in this process. And although there is a punitive impulse from below, it is neither as insistent nor as decisive as the conventional wisdom suggests. Finally, the available data fail to establish a reliable association between crime, fear of crime, or criminal victimization and either punitive initiatives from above or punitive impulses from below. Instead, the politics of punishment draw sustenance from other more fundamental problems – many of which might reasonably be seen as root causes of crime. (p. 624)

The remainder of the essay examines in detail the complex and contingent, cross-cutting and indeterminate political struggles that centre around crime and punishment, play out within and without those communities most victimized by crime, and continue to derail the effective deployment of police powers to prevent, resolve or reduce the harms associated with crime and criminal violence.

Summary

In this volume you will find 20 of the best essays published in 14 different leading scholarly journals over the past five years and deploying a wide variety of approaches to the study of crime, punishment and politics. The essays included here provide readers with a detailed examination of the political struggles surrounding crime and punishment today, focused for analytical purposes around a critical deconstruction of Wilson and Kelling's broken windows metaphor. This Introduction represents my own personal assessment of the insights contained in these essays and the ways in which they cohere into stories about crime, punishment and politics. While I hope that you have found it a thoughtful assessment, the selections are also so rich and varied – both substantively and methodologically – that you should also be able to draw your own insights and conclusions. I enjoyed putting the volume together and appreciated being offered the opportunity to do so; it is now up to you to take it from here.

Notes

1   See Weisburg *et al.* (2003), for a detailed analysis of Compstat that similarly concludes that it is driven more by bureaucratic control imperatives than by responsive place-based policing; see also Fagan (1994), for a critical analysis of the deterrence effects of policing strategies in New York City; and Nagin, 2003.

2   See Skogan and Hartnett (1997, pp. 126–28) on the tendency to continue using the same techniques in community policing programs and for perhaps the most thoughtful empirical analysis of community policing to date.

References

Beckett, Katherine (1997), *Making Crime Pay: Law and Order in Contemporary American Politics*, New York: Oxford University Press.

Beckett, Katherine and Sasson, Theodore (2000), *The Politics of Injustice*, Thousand Oaks, CA: Pine Forge Press.

Black, Donald (1971), 'The Social Organization of Arrest: Citizen Discretion', *Stanford Law Review*, **23**, June, pp. 1087–111.

Blumstein, Alfred (1993), 'Making Rationality Relevant: The American Society of Criminology 1992 Presidential Address', *Criminology*, January, pp. 1–16.

Braithwaite, John (1989), *Crime, Shame and Reintegration*, New York: Cambridge University Press.

Brown, Richard Maxwell (1969), 'Historical Patterns in Violence in America', in *The History of Violence in America*, New York: Bantam, pp. 154–226.

Caplow, Theodore and Simon, Jonathan (1999), 'Understanding Prison Policy and Population Trends', in M. Tonry and J. Petersilia (eds), *Prisons*, Crime and Justice: A Review of Research series, ed. M. Tonry, Chicago: University of Chicago Press.

Colvin, Mark, Cullen, Francis and Vander Ven, Thomas (2002), 'Coercion, Social Support, and Crime: An Emerging Theoretical Consensus', *Criminology*, **40**(1), pp. 19–43.

Davis, Darren and Silver, Brian (2004), 'Civil Liberties vs. Security: Public Opinion in the Context of the Terrorist Attacks on America', *American Journal of Political Science*, **48**(1), pp. 28–46.

Edelman, Murray (1977), *Political Language: Words that Succeed and Policies that Fail*, New York: Academic Press.

Fagan, Jeffrey (1994), 'Do Criminal Sanctions Deter Crimes?', in Doris Layton MacKenzie and Craig Uchida (eds), *Drugs and Crime: Evaluating Public Policy Initiatives*, Thousand Oaks, CA: Sage Publications, pp. 188–215.

Ferguson, Ann (2000), *Bad Boys: Public Schools in the Making of Black Masculinity*, Ann Arbor, MI: University of Michigan Press.

Franks, Thomas (2004), *What's the Matter with Kansas? How Conservatives Won the Heart of America*, New York: Metropolitan Books.

Glassner, Barry (1999), *The Culture of Fear: Why Americans are Afraid of the Wrong Things*, New York: Basic Books.

Harcourt, Bernard (1998), 'Reflecting on the Subject: A Critique of the Social Influence Conception of Deterrence, the Broken Windows Theory, and Order-Maintenance Policing New York Style', *Michigan Law Review*, **97**(2), pp. 291–389.

Heyman, Josiah (2002), 'US Immigration Officers of Mexican Ancestry as Mexican Americans, Citizens, and Immigration Police', *Current Anthropology*, **43**(3), June, pp. 479–507.

Jacobs, David and Helms, Ronald (1999), 'Collective Outbursts, Politics, and Punitive Resources: Toward a Political Sociology of Spending on Social Control', *Social Forces*, **77**(4), June, pp. 1–24.

Kane, Robert (2002), 'The Social Ecology of Police Misconduct', *Criminology*, **40**(4), November, pp. 867–97.

Katznelson, Ira (1976), 'The Crisis of the Capitalist City: Urban Politics and Social Control', in Willis Hawley and Michael Lipsky (eds), *Theoretical Perspectives on Urban Politics*, Englewood Cliffs, NJ: Prentice Hall.

Lyons, William (1999), *The Politics of Community Policing: Rearranging the Power to Punish*, Ann Arbor, MI: University of Michigan Press.

Lyons, William (2000), Review of *Community Policing, Chicago Style*, by Wesley Skogan and Susan Hartnett, for *The Law and Politics Book Review*, February, pp. 133–36.

Lyons, William and Drew, Julie (2006), *Punishing Schools: Fear and Citizenship in American Public Education*, Ann Arbor, MI: University of Michigan Press.

Mastrofski, Stephen and Reisig, Michael (2002), 'Police Disrespect Toward the Public: An Encounter-Based Analysis', *Criminology*, **40**(3), August, pp. 519–52.

Meares, Tracey and Kahan, Dan (1998), 'Law and (Norms of) Order in the Inner City', *Law and Society Review*, **32**(4), pp. 804–38.

Mendelberg, Tali (2001), *The Race Card: Campaign Strategy, Implicit Messages, and the Norm of Equality*, Princeton, NJ: Princeton University Press.

Musto, David (1987), *The American Disease: Origins of Narcotic Control* (rev. edn), New Haven, CT: Yale University Press.

Nagin, Daniel (2003), 'An Experimental Investigation of Deterrence: Cheating, Self-Serving Bias, and Impulsivity', *Criminology*, **41**(1), pp. 167–94.

Peffley, Mark and Hurwitz, Jon (2002), 'The Racial Components of "Race-Neutral" Crime Policy Attitudes', *Political Psychology*, **23**(1), pp. 59–75.

Rosenfeld, Richard, Messner, Steven and Baumer, Eric (2001), 'Social Capital and Homicide', *Social Forces*, **80**(1), pp. 283–309.

Sarat, Austin (1993), 'Speaking of Death: Narratives of Violence in Capital Trials', *Law & Society Review*, **27**, pp. 19–58.

Sarat, Austin and Kearns, Thomas (eds) (1995), *Law's Violence*, Ann Arbor, MI: University of Michigan Press.

Savelsberg, Joachim (1994), 'Knowledge, Domination, and Criminal Punishment', *American Journal of Sociology*, **99**, pp. 911–43.

Savelsberg, Joachim, King, Ryan and Cleveland, Lara (2002), 'Politicized Scholarship? Science on Crime and the State', *Social Problems*, **49**(3), pp. 327–48.

Schattschneider, E.E. (1975), *The Semisovereign People: A Realist's View of Democracy in America*, New York: Harcourt Brace.

Scheingold, Stuart (1984), *The Politics of Law and Order: Street Crime and Public Policy*, New York: Longman.

Scheingold, Stuart (1991), *The Politics of Street Crime: Criminal Process and Cultural Obsession*, Philadelphia: Temple University Press.

Scheingold, Stuart (1998), 'Constructing the New Political Criminology: Power, Authority, and the Post-liberal State', *Law and Social Inquiry*, **23**(4), Fall, pp. 857–95.

Sennett, Richard (1970), *The Uses of Disorder: Personal Identity and City Life*, New York: Knopf.

Seron, Carroll, Pereira, Joseph and Kovath, Jean (2004), 'Judging Police Misconduct: "Street-Level" versus Professional Policing', *Law & Society Review*, **38**(4), pp. 665–710.

Sherman, Lawrence (1993), 'Defiance, Deterrence, and Irrelevance: A Theory of the Criminal Sanction', *Journal of Research in Crime and Delinquency*, **30**(4), November, pp. 445–73.

Skogan, Wesley (1990), *Disorder and Decline: Crime and the Spiral of Decay in American Neighborhoods*, New York: The Free Press.

Skogan, Wesley and Hartnett, Susan (1997), *Community Policing, Chicago Style*, New York: Oxford University Press.

Smith, Kevin (2004), 'The Politics of Punishment: Evaluating Political Explanations of Incarceration Rates', *The Journal of Politics*, **66**(3), August, pp. 925–38.

Steiner, Benjamin, Bowers, William and Sarat, Austin (1999), 'Folk Knowledge as Legal Action: Death Penalty Judgments and the Tenet of Early Release in a Culture of Mistrust and Punitiveness', *Law & Society Review*, **33**(2), pp. 461–505.

Stucky, Thomas (2003), 'Local Politics and Violent Crime in US Cities', *Criminology*, **41**(4), pp. 1101–36.

Terrill, William and Mastrofski, Stephen (2002), 'Situational and Officer-Based Determinants of Police Coercion', *Justice Quarterly*, **19**(2), June, pp. 215–48.

Thatcher, David (2001), 'Conflicting Values in Community Policing', *Law & Society Review*, **35**(4), pp. 765–99.

Tiersma, Peter and Salon, Lawrence (2004), 'Cops and Robbers: Selective Literalism in American Criminal Law', *Law & Society Review*, **38**(2), pp. 229–67.

Tonry, Michael (1995), *Malign Neglect: Race, Crime, and Punishment in America*, New York: Oxford University Press.

Tyler, Tom (2000), 'Multiculturalism and the Willingness of Citizens to Defer to Law and to Legal Authorities', *Law & Social Inquiry*, **25**(4), Fall, pp. 983–1020.

Tyler, Tom (2001), 'Public Trust and Confidence in Legal Authorities: What Do Majority and Minority Group Members Want from the Law and Legal Institutions?', *Behavioral Sciences and the Law*, **19**, pp. 215–35.

Tyler, Tom and Boeckmann, Robert (1997), 'Three Strikes and You are Out, But Why? The Psychology of Public Support for Punishing Rule Breakers', *Law & Society Review*, **31**(2), pp. 200–14.

Tyler, Tom and Cheryl Wakslak (2004), 'Profiling and Police Legitimacy: Procedural Justice, Attributions of Motive, and Acceptance of Police Authority', *Criminology*, **42**(2), May, pp. 253–82.

Uggen, Christopher and Manza, Jeff (2002), 'Democratic Contradiction? Political Consequences of Felon Disenfranchisement in the United States', *American Sociological Review*, **67**, December, pp. 777–803.

Unseem, Bert and Goldstone, Jack (2002), 'Forging Social Order and Its Breakdown: Riot and Reform in US Prisons', *American Sociological Review*, **67**, August, pp. 499–525.

Walker, Samuel (1984), '"Broken Windows" and Fractured History: The Use and Misuse of History in Recent Police Patrol Analysis', *Justice Quarterly*, **1**, pp. 75–90.

Weisburg, David, Mastrofski, Stephen, McNally, Ann Marie, Greenspan, Rosann and Willis, James (2003), 'Reforming to Preserve: COMPSTAT and Strategic Problem Solving in American Policing', *Criminology and Public Policy*, **2**(3), July, pp. 421–55.

West, Cornell (1993), *Race Matters*, Boston, MA: Beacon Press.

Wilson, James Q. and Kelling, George (1982), 'Broken Windows', *Atlantic Monthly*, March, pp. 29–38.

Yngvesson, Barbara (1993), *Virtuous Citizens, Disruptive Subjects: Order and Complaint in a New England Court*, New York: Routledge.

Part I
Police Powers

[1]

STREET STOPS AND BROKEN WINDOWS: *TERRY*, RACE, AND DISORDER IN NEW YORK CITY

*Jeffrey Fagan and Garth Davies**

Patterns of "stop and frisk" activity by police across New York City neighborhoods reflect competing theories of aggressive policing. "Broken Windows" theory[1] suggest that neighborhoods with greater concentration of physical and social disorder should evidence higher stop and frisk activity, especially for "quality of life" crimes.[2] However, although disorder theory informs quality of life policing strategies, patterns of stop and frisk activity suggest that neighborhood characteristics such as racial composition, poverty levels, and extent of social disorganization are stronger predictors of race- and crime-specific stops. Accordingly, neighborhood "street stop" activity reflects competing assumptions and meanings of policing strategy. Furthermore, looking at the rate at which street stops meet Terry *standards of reasonable suspicion[3] in various neighborhoods provides additional perspective on the social and strategic meanings of policing. Our empirical evidence suggests that policing is not about disorderly places, nor about improving the quality of life, but about policing poor people in poor places. This strategy contradicts the policy rationale derived from Broken Windows theory, and deviates from the original emphasis on communities by focusing on people. Racially disparate policing reinforces perceptions by citizens in minority neighborhoods that they are under non-particularized suspicion and are therefore targeted for aggressive stop and frisk policing. Such broad targeting raises concerns about the legitimacy of law, threatens to weaken citizen participation in the co-production of*

---

* Jeffrey Fagan is a professor at the Mailman School of Public Health, Columbia University, and a visiting professor at Columbia Law School. Garth Davies is a doctoral candidate, School of Criminal Justice, Rutgers University. All opinions are those of the authors. Peter K. Manning provided helpful comments on this article. Brandon Garrett provided timely and thorough research assistance.

1. James Q. Wilson & George L. Kelling, *The Police and Neighborhood Safety: Broken Windows*, ATLANTIC MONTHLY, Mar. 1982, at 29-38 (using the analogy of a broken window to describe the relationship between disorder and crime).

2. *Id.*

3. Terry v. Ohio, 392 U.S. 1 (1968) (establishing *reasonable suspicion*, as opposed to the higher quantum of proof of *probable cause*, as the constitutional standard to govern stop and frisks).

security, and undercuts the broader social norms goals of contemporary policing.

When it comes to debating theories of crime and law, some people pretend that race does not matter at all, while others accord it undue, if not determinative, significance.[4] Unfortunately, recent events in policing seem to tip the balance of reality toward the latter view. There is now strong empirical evidence that individuals of color are more likely than white Americans to be stopped, questioned, searched, and arrested by police.[5] This occurs in part because of their race, in part because of heightened law enforcement intensity in minority communities, in part because of the temptation among law enforcement officers to simply "play the base rates" by stopping minority suspects because minorities commit

    4. *See generally* RANDALL KENNEDY, RACE, CRIME, AND THE LAW (1997) (exploring the impact of race relations on criminal law and criminal justice); *see also* Kim Taylor-Thompson, *The Politics of Common Ground*, 111 HARV. L. REV. 1306 (1998) (emphasizing the role of race in criminal justice issues through a critical review of RACE, CRIME, AND THE LAW).

    5. United States v. New Jersey, No. 99-5970 (MLC) (D. N.J. Dec. 30, 1999) (consent decree) (establishing the state of New Jersey's consent to comply with various procedures and policies to remedy racial profiling by the state police), http://www.usdoj.gov/crt/split/documents/jerseysa.htm; U.S. GEN. ACCOUNTING OFFICE, RACIAL PROFILING LIMITED DATA AVAILABLE ON MOTORIST STOPS, GAO-GGD-00-41, 7-13 (2000), *available at* http://www.gao.gov/AIndexFY00/title/tocR.htm; CIVIL RIGHTS BUREAU, OFFICE OF THE ATTORNEY GEN. OF THE STATE OF N.Y., THE NEW YORK CITY POLICE DEPARTMENT'S "STOP & FRISK" PRACTICES 89 (1999) [hereinafter OAG REPORT]; DAVID COLE, NO EQUAL JUSTICE: RACE AND CLASS IN THE AMERICAN CRIMINAL JUSTICE SYSTEM, 34-41 (1999) (describing the explicit use of race in criminal profiles by police departments in Maryland, Colorado, Louisiana, and New Jersey); Sean Hecker, *Race and Pretextual Traffic Stops: An Expanded Role for Civilian Review Boards*, 28 COLUM. HUM. RTS. L. REV. 551, 551 (1997); Kris Antonelli, *State Police Deny Searches are Race-Based; ACLU Again Challenges I-95 Stops*, BALT. SUN, Nov. 16, 1996, at 18B; David Kocieniewski & Robert Hanley, *Racial Profiling Was The Routine, New Jersey Finds*, N.Y. TIMES, Nov. 28, 2000, at A1; Barbara Whitaker, *San Diego Police Found to Stop Black and Latino Drivers Most*, N.Y. TIMES, Oct. 1, 2000, at A31; Jim Yardley, *Studies Find Race Disparities in Texas Traffic Stops*, N.Y. TIMES, Oct. 7, 2000, at A12. Similar patterns of stops, searches, and arrests of citizens have been observed in London. *See generally* DAVID SMITH ET AL., POLICE AND PEOPLE IN LONDON: VOLUME I: A SURVEY OF LONDONERS 89-119, tbl.IV.3 (1983) (showing racial disparity in police contacts with black citizens in London). The London survey was conducted in 1981-82, with a stratified random sample of 2420 Londoners ages fifteen and older. Minorities were over-sampled to ensure adequate representation in the study. Overall, 16% of Londoners were stopped in the twelve months preceding the survey. West Indians were slightly more likely to be stopped than whites (18% as compared with 14%), and Asians were least likely to be stopped (5%). The average number of stops was twice as high for West Indians (0.56) compared with whites (0.21) or Asians (0.8). The average number of arrests per person stopped was also far greater for West Indians (3.19) than for whites (1.46) or Asians (1.59). *Id.*

more crimes, and in part because of the tacit approval of these practices given by their superiors.[6]

Whether the legal system should consider race in its every day decision-making is a hotly contested and much-litigated issue.[7] Yet the modern practice of racial policing should surprise no one. Racial profiling is often defended as a useful means to detect criminal behavior.[8] The legal system has long used race as a signal of increased risk of criminality. Examples include: immigration exclusion and other discrimination against Chinese immigrants in the 19th century;[9] the racialization of the debate on the passage of the Harrison Narcotics Act;[10] the internment of the Japanese during World War II;[11] border interdictions to halt illegal immigration;[12]

---

6. *See generally* STATE POLICE REVIEW TEAM, OFFICE OF THE ATTORNEY GEN. OF THE STATE OF N.J., INTERIM REPORT OF THE STATE POLICE REVIEW TEAM REGARDING ALLEGATIONS OF RACIAL PROFILING (1999) (admitting that New Jersey State Police officers engaged in racial profiling, but also that profiling is part of the culture of the State Police), *available at* http://www.state.nj.us/lps/intm_419.pdf (Apr. 20, 1999); *see generally* Jeffrey Goldberg, *The Color of Suspicion*, N.Y. TIMES MAG., June 20, 1999, at 51 (examining various perspectives on racial profiling).

7. Brandon Garrett, *Standing while Black: Distinguishing* Lyons *in Racial Profiling Cases*, 100 COLUM. L. REV. 1815, 1816 n.5 (2000) (reviewing recent lawsuits and investigations of racial profiling). Consent decrees stemming from racial profiling have been signed in many cases. *E.g.*, United States v. New Jersey, No. 99-5970 (MLC) (D. N.J. Dec. 30, 1999) (consent decree entered); Memorandum of Agreement, Between the United States Department of Justice, Montgomery County, Maryland, the Montgomery County Department of Police, and the Fraternal Order of Police, Montgomery County Lodge 35, Inc., Jan. 14, 2000, http//www.usdoj.gov/crt/cor/Pubs/mcagrmt.htm; United States v. City of Pittsburgh, No. 97-0354 (W.D. Pa. Apr. 16, 1997) (consent decree entered); United States v. City of Steubenville, C2-97-966 (S.D. Ohio Sept. 3, 1997) (consent decree entered), http://usdoj.gov/cit/split/documents/steubensa.htm; United States v. City of Los Angeles, No. 00-11769 (C.D. Cal.) (consent decree entered). For reviews of consent decrees involving police departments generally, see Debra Livingston, *Police Reform and the Department of Justice: An Essay on Accountability*, 2 BUFF. CRIM. L. REV. 815 (1999); Myriam E. Gilles, *Reinventing Structural Reform Litigation: Deputizing Private Citizens in the Enforcement of Civil Right*, 100 COLUM. L. REV. 1384 (2000).

8. KENNEDY, *supra* note 4, at 145-46 (discussing race as a predictor of criminality). For a review of the historical uses of ethnic and racial exclusion in the United States based on attributions of greater danger to ethnic minorities, see generally SAMUEL WALKER ET AL., THE COLOR OF JUSTICE: RACE, ETHNICITY AND CRIME IN AMERICA (2d ed. 2000).

9. Yick Wo v. Hopkins, 118 U.S. 356 (1886) (inferring intentional discrimination against Chinese citizens from disparate enforcement of an ordinance banning laundries).

10. Harrison Narcotics Act, ch. 1, 38 Stat. 785 (1914); *see also* DAVID F. MUSTO, THE AMERICAN DISEASE 65 (1973) ("Cocaine raised the specter of the Wild Negro, opium the devious Chinese . . . .").

11. Korematsu v. United States, 323 U.S. 214 (1944) (finding forced internment troubling but ultimately upholding its constitutionality).

460   *FORDHAM URBAN LAW JOURNAL* [Vol. XXVIII

racial components of drug courier profiling;[13] and the so-called
Carol Stuart stops in Boston.[14]

Generally, courts have refused to disallow the use of race as an
indicia of criminality.[15] Most courts have accepted this practice, so
long as (1) race alone is not the rationale for the interdiction, and
(2) it is not done for purposes of racial harassment.[16] This practice
has been reflected in case law as the sound exercise of "professional judgment" by police officers.[17]

---

12. United States v. Martinez-Fuerte, 428 U.S. 543, 556-57 (1976) (affirming the
U.S. Border Patrol's right to conduct checkpoint stops of vehicles near the Mexican
border with or without reasonable suspicion).

13. United States v. Harvey, 16 F.3d 109, 115 (6th Cir. 1994) (Keith, J., dissenting)
("African-Americans are more likely to be arrested because drug courier profiles reflect the erroneous assumption that one's race has a direct correlation to drug
activity.").

14. MASS. ATTORNEY GEN.'S OFFICE, REPORT OF THE ATTORNEY GENERAL'S
CIVIL RIGHTS DIVISION ON BOSTON POLICE DEPARTMENT PRACTICES (Dec. 18, 1990)
(reporting results of an investigation into allegations that, in violation of constitutional mandates, the Boston Police Department "rounded up" African American men
in the wake of the murder of Carol Stuart, a white woman).

Shortly before this article went to press, a sharply-divided United States Court of
Appeals for the Second Circuit declined to reconsider its ruling upholding its dismissal of *Brown v. City of Oneonta*, 221 F.3d 329 (2000). The plaintiffs in *Brown* alleged
that police unconstitutionally swept the 10,000-resident town and stopped and in-
spected the hands of black men after an elderly woman alleged she had been attacked
in her home by a young black male who cut his hand during a struggle.

> The panel reaches a grave conclusion by holding that the police act constitu-
> tionally under the Fourteenth Amendment when, based on a witness's
> predominantly racial description, they stop every young African American
> male in town to determine whether he can exclude himself from a vague
> class of potential suspects that has been defined in overwhelmingly racial
> terms.

Brown v. City of Oneonta, — F.3d — (2d Cir. 2000), *available in* 2000 WL 1855047.

15. *See* Whren v. United States, 517 U.S. 806 (1996). In *Whren*, the U.S. Supreme
Court ruled that as long as an officer observes a traffic violation, a traffic stop is
constitutional, even if the officer has no intention to enforce the law the driver violated. Even if purely pretextual, a racially-motivated stop is constitutional under the
Fourth Amendment if also motivated by a second, non-racial factor. The Court did
state, however, that a stop motivated by race alone would violate Fourteenth Amendment protections. *Id.* at 813. COLE, *supra* note 5, at 39-40 (citing the extraordinarily
high concentration of minority complainants in unsuccessful federal appellate cases
involving pretextual traffic stops). *See also Harvey*, 16 F.3d at 115 (Keith, J., dissenting); KENNEDY, *supra* note 4, at 14 ("Racist perceptions of blacks have given energy
to policies and practices (such as racial exclusion in housing, impoverished schooling,
and stingy social welfare programs) that have facilitated the growth of egregious
crime-spawning conditions that millions of Americans face in urban slums and rural
backwaters across the nation.") (citation omitted).

16. *See Whren*, 517 U.S. at 813.

17. Although courts may be reluctant explicitly to identify and endorse the use of
race as a proxy for criminal behavior, the factual underpinnings of many cases reveal
tacit judicial approval of racial profiling. *E.g.*, Papachristou v. City of Jacksonville, 405

Contemporary criminal justice theory and practice accord with this view, but substitute sociological language for the more formal legal endorsement of race-based practices. In New York City, law enforcement strategies emphasize the aggressive patrol of areas containing manifestations of physical and social disorder. Thus, police aggressively enforce laws on public drinking and loitering. They also actively patrol neighborhoods with empty lots, abandoned cars, and dilapidated buildings. Collectively, these strategies are based on the "Broken Windows" theory, named after the influential essay on the contagious effects of unchecked signs of disorder.[18]

Beginning in 1994, officials altered the police strategies in New York City to address low-level disorder problems that might invite more serious crime problems.[19] These signs of disorder often are more prevalent in urban neighborhoods with elevated rates of pov-

---

U.S. 156 (1972) (reviewing the enforcement of a vague vagrancy ordinance against two black men accompanied by two white females); Florida v. J.L., 529 U.S. 266 (2000) (reviewing the adequacy of a stop and frisk based on an anonymous informant's description of a "young black male" wearing a plaid shirt and carrying a gun).

The "professional judgment" of Detective McFadden provided the basis for his stop and search of the defendant in *Terry v. Ohio*, 392 U.S. 1, 28 (1968). What has been lost in the *Terry* discourse in the ensuing years is the explicit racial component of the events. Terry was African American, McFadden was white. McFadden's "professional judgment" concerning Terry was based on the racial incongruity of Terry being observed outside a storefront in a commercial district far from the areas of Cleveland where most African Americans lived. Anthony C. Thompson, *Stopping the Usual Suspects: Race and the Fourth Amendment*, 74 N.Y.U. L. Rev. 956, 966 (1999). *But see Terry*, 392 U.S. at 5-7 (detailing the suspicious activity the *Terry* defendants engaged in after Detective McFadden, a thirty-nine year veteran of the police department, first observed them and felt "they didn't look right to [him] at the time").

In *Illinois v. Wardlow*, 528 U.S. 119, 124 (2000), the Court noted that although an individual's presence in a "high crime area" does not meet the standard for a particularized suspicion of criminal activity, a location's characteristics are relevant in determining whether an individual's behavior is sufficiently suspicious to warrant further investigation. Since "high crime areas" often are areas with concentrations of minority citizens, this logic places minority neighborhoods at risk for elevating the suspiciousness of its residents. *See e.g.*, DOUGLAS S. MASSEY & NANCY A. DENTON, AMERICAN APARTHEID: SEGREGATION AND THE MAKING OF THE UNDERCLASS (1993).

18. Wilson & Kelling, *supra* note 1, at 31. *See generally* GEORGE L. KELLING & CATHERINE M. COLES, FIXING BROKEN WINDOWS: RESTORING ORDER AND REDUCING CRIME IN OUR COMMUNITIES (1996).

19. Bernard E. Harcourt, *Reflecting on the Subject: A Critique of the Social Influence Conception of Deterrence, the Broken Windows Theory, and Order-Maintenance Policing New York Style*, 97 MICH. L. REV. 291, 292 (1998); Debra Livingston, *Police Discretion and the Quality of Life in Public Places: Courts, Communities, and the New Policing*, 97 Colum. L. Rev. 551, 556 n.14 (1997); Sarah E. Waldeck, *Cops, Community Policing, and the Social Norms Approach to Crime Control: Should One Make Us More Comfortable with the Others?*, 34 GA. L. REV. 1273, 1273 (2000).

erty and social fragmentation.[20] Accordingly, the implementation of Broken Windows policies was disproportionately concentrated in minority neighborhoods and conflated with poverty and other signs of socio-economic disadvantage. Thus, what was constructed as "order-maintenance policing" ("OMP") was widely perceived among minority citizens as racial policing, or racial profiling.[21] The fact that its principle tactic was an aggressive form of stop and frisk policing involving intrusive *Terry* searches,[22] and that at least two deaths of unarmed citizens of African descent were linked to OMP,[23] further intensified perceptions of racial animus.[24]

---

20. WESLEY G. SKOGAN, DISORDER AND DECLINE: CRIME AND THE SPIRAL OF DECAY IN AMERICAN NEIGHBORHOODS 59 (1990); Robert J. Sampson & Stephen W. Raudenbush, *Systematic Social Observation of Public Spaces: A New Look at Disorder in Urban Neighborhoods*, 105 AM. J. SOCIOLOGY 603, 622-30 (1999); Stephen W. Raudenbush & Robert J. Sampson, *Ecometrics: Toward a Science of Assessing Ecological Settings, with Application to the Systematic Social Observation of Neighborhoods*, 29 SOCIOLOGICAL METHODOLOGY 1 (1999).

21. OAG REPORT, *supra* note 5, at 74; David Kocieniewski, *Success of Elite Police Unit Exacts a Toll on the Streets*, N.Y. TIMES, Feb. 15, 1999, at A1 (discussing reactions of citizens to aggressive policing in New York City); Kit R. Roane, *Minority Private-School Students Claim Police Harassment*, N.Y. TIMES, Mar. 26, 1999, at B5 (citing complaints by minority students of indiscriminate and frequent police harassment).

22. There is an irony here about the use of such citizen detentions and searches as a crime fighting tool. The *Terry* decision itself located the frisk less as an investigative aid than as a protection for the patrolling officer: "The frisk . . . was essential to the proper performance of the officer's investigatory duties, for without it the answer to the police officer may be a bullet." Terry v. Ohio, 392 U.S. 1, 8 (1968) (citation omitted). That the stop and frisk engenders animosity was made explicit in the original *Terry* decision. The Supreme Court in *Terry* noted that a frisk "is a serious intrusion upon the sanctity of the person, which may inflict great indignity and arouse strong resentment, and is not to be undertaken lightly." *Id.* at 17. The Court also noted that *Terry* stops had the potential to inflict psychological harm: "Even a limited search . . . constitutes a severe, though brief, intrusion upon cherished personal security, and it must surely be an annoying, frightening, and perhaps humiliating experience." *Id.* at 24-25.

23. David Jackson, *Winning War on Crime Has a Price Giuliani Alienates Many in New York City's Black and Hispanic Communities*, DENVER POST, Apr. 20, 2000, at A23 (discussing the shootings by the New York City Police Department ("NYPD") of Amadou Diallo and Patrick Dorismond); Symposium, *Is Our Drug Policy Effective? Are There Alternatives?*, 28 FORDHAM URB. L.J. 3, 95 (2000) ("[A] team of undercover police approached a man [Patrick Dorismond] . . . even though they had no reason to believe that he was involved in any criminal activity.").

24. Citizens who are stopped and frisked based on a profiling or racial policing strategy understand that they have been singled out because of their race. These encounters have been termed "race-making situations." David R. James, *The Racial Ghetto as a Race-Making Situation: The Effects of Residential Segregation on Racial Inequalities and Racial Identity*, 19 LAW & SOC. INQUIRY 407, 420-29 (1994). The outrage of many minority citizens over the NYPD's policing of aggressive stop and frisks reflects not only the emotional harm from being targeted because of one's race, but also the fear that such situations can escalate into dangerously violent encounters. *See generally* David A. Harris, *The Stories, the Statistics, and the Law: Why "Driving*

Moreover, by explicitly linking disorder to violence, OMP (as informed by Broken Windows theory) further focused police resources and efforts on the neighborhoods with the highest crime and violence rates.[25] That these were predominantly minority neighborhoods further reinforced the disproportionate exposure of New York City's minority citizens to policing. Thus, this construction of disorder broadened the concept to include places where violent and other serious crimes were most likely to occur. Those places tended to be ones with the highest concentrations of socially-disadvantaged minority populations.

In this paper, we assess empirical evidence designed to sort out these competing claims about the underlying theoretical basis for New York City's aggressive policing policy. We analyze patterns of stop and frisk activity to assess whether practice reflected the place-based strategies embodied in Broken Windows theory, or if instead, practice was focused on the social markers of race and disadvantage. We ask whether, after controlling for disorder, the city's stop and frisk policy is, in fact, a form of policing that disproportionately targets racial minorities. We begin by reviewing the history and evolution of these policies, showing the links between race, Broken Windows theory, and aggressive policing. In Part II, we review evidence of the racial skew in policing as reported in recent studies. In Part III, we offer the results of empirical tests of data conducted on trends and patterns of policing to resolve these competing claims about the motivating theories for the observed patterns. We find little evidence to support claims that policing targeted places and signs of physical disorder, and show instead that stops of citizens were more often concentrated in minority

---

While Black" Matters, 84 MINN. L. REV. 265, 273 (1999). The shared danger of profiling encounters reflects the concept of "linked fate" among residents of minority neighborhoods. "Linked fate" refers to the empathy that people have with family and friends. It can also exist among strangers. In the African American community, linked fate has its foundation in the fact that the life chances of African Americans historically have been shaped by race. MICHAEL C. DAWSON, BEHIND THE MULE: RACE AND CLASS IN AFRICAN-AMERICAN POLITICS 77 (1994). Linked fate suggests that when race over-determines an individual's life chances, it is much more efficient for that individual to use the relative and absolute status of the group as a proxy for individual utility. The long history of race-based constraints on life chances among blacks generates a certain efficiency in evaluating policies that affect minority individuals. *Id.*

25. OAG REPORT, *supra* note 5, at 53 (citing N.Y. CITY POLICE DEP'T, POLICE STRATEGY NO. 1: GETTING GUNS OFF THE STREETS OF NEW YORK (1994) (explicitly linking disorder to violence and rationalizing the concentration of order-maintenance policing ("OMP") strategies in the city's neighborhoods with the highest crime rates) [hereinafter POLICE STRATEGY NO.1].

neighborhoods characterized by poverty and social disadvantage. In Part IV, we conclude by returning to the theoretical arguments supporting current police policies. In this last section, we address claims about the positive link between aggressive policing and the prospects for creating social norms changes to restore social regulation of behavior. The counterfactual of crises in legitimacy provides the context for concluding remarks on race and policing in New York.

I. DISORDER AND AGGRESSIVE POLICING IN NEW YORK CITY

A. From Theory to Practice: Broken Windows and Order-Maintenance Policing

As stated, the policy of aggressive stop and frisk practices reflects theoretical and strategic innovations derived from what has become popularly known as Broken Windows theory.[26] The originators of the Broken Windows theory, James Q. Wilson and George L. Kelling, argued that police should address minor disorders to strengthen police-citizen interactions, and consequently, informal social control.[27] For Wilson and Kelling, signs of physical and social disorder invite criminal activity.[28] Disorder indicates to law-abiding citizens that their neighborhoods are dangerous places, leading to their withdrawal from informal social control and regulation.[29] The theory suggests that there is a tipping point at which disorder trumps order by defeating the willingness of citizens to interact with the police and with each other to co-produce security. Accordingly, disorder invites more disorder in a contagious process that progressively breaks down community standards and also sug-

---

26. Wilson & Kelling, *supra* note 1, at 31. For excellent reviews, see Livingston, *supra* note 19, at 578 (discussing the relationship between Broken Windows theory and current policing practices); Harcourt, *supra* note 19, at 301-08 (critiquing Broken Windows theory and empirical research claiming to support the link between disorder and crime); Tracey L. Meares & Dan M. Kahan, *Law and (Norms of) Order in the Inner City*, 32 LAW & SOC'Y REV. 805 (1998) (discussing the link between social norms theory and law enforcement policies).

27. Wilson & Kelling, *supra* note 1, at 31; Livingston, *supra* note 19, at 576; Waldeck, *supra* note 19, at 1255.

28. Wilson & Kelling, *supra* note 1, at 32. They define "minor" disorder to include such problems and crimes as littering, loitering, public drinking, panhandling, teenage fighting on street corners, and prostitution. They also mention signs of physical disorder, including abandoned cars—with broken windows, naturally—and dilapidated buildings, also with broken windows.

29. *Id.* at 33 ("In response to fear, people avoid one another, weakening controls.").

gests to would-be criminals that crime will not be reported. Disorder ultimately invites criminal invasion.

Broken Windows theory comports well with social norms theories. In this framework, individuals form social norms through interactions with others in social spaces, creating norms of either legal or illegal behavior in their communities.[30] Wilson and Kelling argue that when police focus on repairing or removing these disorder problems, they combat crime by promoting the types of social interactions among law-abiding citizens that strengthen the dynamics of social regulation and produce security and social control.[31] To restate this in terms of Broken Windows theory, disorder conveys a social message that there is no effective social regulation of behavior in a neighborhood with such visible and prevalent signs of disorder.[32] In turn, disorder communicates the absence of restraints to others who may interpret this as either tolerance of, or an invitation to, criminal behavior. Thus, as both disorder and criminal behavior spread, they communicate a mutually reinforcing social norm regarding crime and social disorder, all the while communicating danger to those who would attempt to reinforce social norms that oppose crime and disorder.

Empirical support for Broken Windows and disorder theories of crime is reported by Wesley Skogan in an analysis of survey data collected in 1977 and 1983 in six cities.[33] Additional empirical support is reported by George L. Kelling and Catherine M. Coles.[34] Bernard Harcourt, however, reanalyzed Skogan's data and failed to replicate the results, citing numerous inconsistencies and errors in measurement.[35] Dan Kahan attributes New York City's crime decline in the 1990s to the adoption by its police department of a tactical strategy based on Broken Windows theory, although em-

---

30. Meares & Kahan, *supra* note 26, at 805. For an illustration based on ethnographic research, see ELIJAH ANDERSON, CODE OF THE STREET (1999).

31. Wilson & Kelling, *supra* note 1, at 35; ANDERSON, *supra* note 30, at 32; *see also* Harcourt, *supra* note 19, at 302-3. *See generally* Robert C. Ellickson, *Controlling Chronic Misconduct in City Spaces: Of Panhandlers, Skid Rows, and Public-Space Zoning*, 105 YALE L.J. 1165 (1996).

32. *See generally* Lawrence Lessig, *The Regulation of Social Meaning*, 62 U. CHI. L. REV. 943 (1995) (discussing the construction of social meaning); Ellickson, *supra* note 31.

33. SKOGAN, *supra* note 20. Surveys were conducted in Atlanta, Chicago, Houston, Newark, Philadelphia, and San Francisco. His basic model was a regression analysis predicting robbery rates from measures of social and physical disorder, controlling for characteristics of the cities derived from social disorganization theory: poverty, residential stability, and racial heterogeneity.

34. *See generally* KELLING & COLES, *supra* note 18.

35. Harcourt, *supra* note 19, at 312-39.

pirical and conceptual assessments of the crime decline contest that view.[36] Empirical work by Robert Sampson and Jacqueline Cohen provide indirect support for a Broken Windows model of policing by focusing on factors that influence perceptions of the tolerance of disorder, especially higher arrest ratios (relative to the crime rate).[37] Despite the implicit developmental and deontological underpinnings of Broken Windows theory (and corresponding social norms theories), none of the supportive studies included prospective tests of the effects of disorder on changes in crime rates in subsequent periods. In fact, all these studies rely on cross-sectional research that is unable to determine whether the observed relationships are temporally-ordered and therefore causally related, or if they are simply correlations whose causal order is unknown.[38]

The most comprehensive empirical test of the underlying premise of Broken Windows theory—that disorder gives rise to higher crime rates—was a study of disorder in Chicago neighborhoods by Robert Sampson and Stephen Raudenbush.[39] Rather than rely on either official records or self-reports, the researchers constructed highly reliable measures of social disorder from a randomized schedule of videotaping of locations. They combined these disorder measures with reports of social control mechanisms from a random sample of 3864 residents in 343 neighborhoods, and both self-reported and official records of crime. Sampson and Raudenbush re-

---

36. Dan M. Kahan, *Between Economics and Sociology: The New Path of Deterrence*, 95 MICH. L. REV. 2477, 2488 n.63, n.65 (1997). Kahan states that the decline in crime must be attributable to the new policing strategy: order-maintenance policing. *Id. But see* Jeffrey Fagan et al., *Declining Homicide in New York City: A Tale of Two Trends*, 88 J. CRIM. L. & CRIMINOLOGY 1277, 1285-86, 1289-91(1998) (claiming that changes in crime rates are actually predictable cyclical changes in violence rates, and that only gun crime rates have changed); ANDREW KARMEN, NEW YORK MURDER MYSTERY 13-24 (2000) (discussing competing causal claims for the decline in New York City's homicide rate from 1991-98, but finding insufficient evidence to support any single explanation).

37. Robert J. Sampson & Jacqueline Cohen, *Deterrent Effects of the Police on Crime: A Replication and Theoretical Extension*, 22 LAW & SOC. REV. 163, 175-79 (1988) (reporting that more aggressive stop and frisk enforcement produces higher arrest ratios that, in turn, communicate a high punishment likelihood to would-be law violators).

38. For a general discussion of this type of validity threat in cross-sectional, non-experimental research designs, see generally THOMAS D. COOK & DONALD T. CAMPBELL, QUASI-EXPERIMENTATION DESIGN AND ANALYSIS ISSUES FOR FIELD SETTINGS (1979); KENNETH ROTHMAN, MODERN EPIDEMIOLOGY (1986); LEON ROBERTSON, INJURY EPIDEMIOLOGY (1992).

39. Sampson & Raudenbush, *supra* note 20 (reporting results of an observational survey of physical and social disorder in Chicago neighborhoods and its weak association with crime rates).

ported that social interactions and social controls among neighbors are more closely related to crime than is disorder, while these social processes—which they term "collective efficacy"—are unrelated to disorder. Similar to Harcourt's re-analysis of the Skogan data, Sampson and Raudenbush also discredit the relationship between crime and disorder.[40]

These empirical doubts about the efficacy of Broken Windows theory have not stopped its influence on American policing. The development of police strategies that operationalize Broken Windows theory proceeded apace in the past two decades.[41] It was widely translated into a police strategy known as "order-maintenance policing," or OMP.[42] At the same time, Broken Windows theory stimulated a body of academic writing on the subject of order maintenance.[43]

Under OMP, police aggressively enforce laws against social disorder with "zero tolerance" that requires arrest for any law infraction.[44] Widely viewed as an adaptation of an earlier movement

---

40. *Id.* at 603.

41. For example, Commissioner William Bratton had earlier implemented an OMP strategy while head of the New York City Transit Police, called the Clean Car Program ("CCP"). The strategy focused on ridding New York City's subway cars of graffiti. Maryalice Sloan-Hewitt & George L. Kelling, *Subway Graffiti in New York City: "Gettin' up" vs. "Meanin' it and Cleanin' it*," in SITUATIONAL CRIME PREVENTION: SUCCESSFUL CASE STUDIES 242, 244-45 (Ronald V. Clarke, ed., 2d. ed. 1997).

42. Livingston, *supra* note 19, at 632.

43. *E.g.*, George L. Kelling, *Order Maintenance, the Quality of Urban Life, and Police: A Line of Argument*, in POLICE LEADERSHIP IN AMERICA 296 (William A. Geller ed., 1985); Carl B. Klockars, *Order Maintenance, the Quality of Urban Life, and Police: A Different Line of Argument*, in POLICE LEADERSHIP, *supra*, at 309; Carl B. Klockars, *Street Justice: Some Micro-Moral Reservations: Comment on Sykes*, 3 JUST. Q. 513 (1986); Gary W. Sykes, *Street Justice: A Moral Defense of Order Maintenance Policing*, 3 JUST. Q. 497 (1986) [hereinafter *Street Justice*]; Gary W. Sykes, *The Functional Nature of Police Reform: The "Myth" of Controlling the Police*, 2 JUST. Q. 51 (1985). *But see generally* Jack R. Greene & Ralph B. Taylor, *Community-Based Policing and Foot Patrol: Issues of Theory and Evaluation*, in COMMUNITY POLICING: RHETORIC OR REALITY, 195, 201-03 (Jack R. Greene & Stephen D. Mastrofski eds., 1988) [hereinafter COMMUNITY POLICING].

44. Definitions of the crimes that constitute disorder vary, but generally include: unlicensed peddling and vending, public drunkenness and open drinking, vandalism (including graffiti), public urination, loitering, littering, panhandling, prostitution, and menacing misbehavior. The latter often is symbolized by "squeegee" men who solicit money in return for unsolicited cleaning of motorists' windshields at stop lights. Cracking down on squeegee men represents the type of OMP enforcement that most closely expressed popular conceptions of the policy. KELLING & COLES, *supra* note 18, at 14-15; Livingston, *supra* note 19, at 553-54; Harcourt, *supra* note 19, at 297; Wilson & Kelling, *supra* note 1; WILLIAM BRATTON & PETER KNOBLER, TURNAROUND: HOW AMERICA'S TOP COP REVERSED THE CRIME EPIDEMIC 214 (1998) (discussing the NYPD's policy to rid the city of the squeegee people); William J. Brat-

toward "community policing,"[45] OMP advocates active engagement with and arrest of law violators. In more traditional community policing, police pursued ameliorative measures that also were consistent with Broken Windows theory, but avoided coercive encounters with citizens on the street.[46] These ameliorative measures were consistent with Broken Windows tenets that police should focus equally on protecting communities as well as protecting individuals.[47] Although community policing and OMP both derive from a social norms basis, the implementation of OMP in New York moved in a very different direction, exchanging amelioration of physical disorder for interdiction of social disorder.

Sarah Waldeck claims that this exchange resolved a conflict that arose in the occupational subculture of policing with the advent of community policing.[48] In addressing non-crime problems, police were reluctant to adhere to a new set of markers for performance and competence based on social interactions with law-abiding citizens.[49] By emphasizing the aggressive pursuit of social disorder, or disorderly persons, police returned to the more comfortable performance indicators of stops and arrests, while restoring to the workplace their traditional cultural dichotomy of "disorderly people and law abiders."[50] Thus, for example, while New York City police identified only seventy-five "squeegee" people,[51] the expanding definition of disorder meant that more and more people were disorderly and subject to aggressive police attention.

---

ton, *The New York City Police Department's Civil Enforcement of Quality-of-Life Crimes*, 3 J.L. & Pol'y 447, 447-48 (1995); N.Y. City Police Dep't, Police Strategy No. 5: Reclaiming the Public Spaces of New York 10-12 (1994) [hereinafter Police Strategy No. 5].

45. Livingston, *supra* note 19, at 562-91. While OMP emphasizes arrest, other forms of community policing eschew arrest in favor of building community contacts. *E.g.*, Wesley G. Skogan & Susan M. Hartnett, Community Policing, Chicago Style 8, 55-56 (1997).

46. These include, for example, cleaning up trash-strewn lots, painting over graffiti, and assisting housing inspectors to address code violations. *E.g.*, Livingston, *supra* note 19, at 584 (citation omitted); Herman Goldstein, Problem-Oriented Policing 134 (1990); George L. Kelling & Mark H. Moore, *From Political to Reform to Community: The Evolving Strategy of Police*, in Community Policing, *supra* note 43, at 3 (Jack R. Greene & Stephen D. Mastrofski eds., 1988); Stephen D. Mastrofski, *Community Policing as Reform: A Cautionary Tale*, in Community Policing, *supra* note 43, at 47, 67.

47. *See* Livingston, *supra* note 19, at 583 n.162.

48. Waldeck, *supra* note 19, at 1267-69.

49. *See id.* at 1267.

50. *Id.* at 1268, 1278.

51. Bratton & Knobler, *supra* note 44, at 214.

It is important to remember that Wilson and Kelling's original social science construction of Broken Windows theory had little to do with social disorder, especially with the aggressive interdiction of disorderly persons. Thus, as we shall see next, the evolution of OMP in New York resulted in a policy and style of policing that violated the subtle connection that Wilson and Kelling drew between crime and disorder, and that deviated in many important ways from its underlying social norms paradigm. As we show below, the exchange of physical disorder for social disorder signified nothing less than a theoretical paradigm shift from the original construction of Broken Windows theory to the more traditional and problematic policing of social disorganization.

B. Violence, Disorder, and Order-Maintenance Policing in New York City

Many observers have noted that OMP in New York City has eschewed (what is for police) the more esoteric dimensions of community policing targeted at physical disorder, for an aggressive policy of arrest and other traditional law enforcement tactics aimed squarely at social disorder. While remaining true to the origins of Broken Windows theory, there were strategic and tactical reasons to reconstruct the Broken Windows theory in this way.

Whereas community policing implies a partnership between police and community, the interpretation of community needs is one of the wild cards of the theory.[52] The partnership required that the parties respond both to a neighborhood's priorities regarding crime and to the more traditional police functions of detecting and deterring criminal behavior.[53] Community policing, then, often appeared to be a Solomonesque split between traditional police goals focusing on major crimes (e.g., murder and armed robbery) and the goals of community residents concerned with chronic low-level crimes and disorder problems.[54]

However, in shifting from community policing to OMP, police strategy in New York City redirected its strategic focus from remedying physical disorder to policing social disorder. The rationale for this shift from physical to social disorder was the theory that low-level crime—social disorder—nurtures and facilitates more serious crime.[55] George L. Kelling and Catherine M. Cole conceptu-

---

52. *See* Skogan & Hartnett, *supra* note 45, at 8.
53. BRATTON & KNOBLER, *supra* note 44, at 94-95.
54. *See generally* Goldstein, *supra* note 46.
55. Wilson & Kelling, *supra* note 1, at 34.

alized OMP as a cooperative variant on community policing: the enforcement of standards of conduct jointly defined by citizens and police.[56] Even so, this strategic shift did not necessarily imply a tactical change toward aggressive policing. Moreover, this tactical shift departed sharply from the Wilson and Kelling and the Kelling and Coles models of Broken Windows, as well as most contemporary models of community policing.[57] As conceptualized by Kelling and Coles, OMP involved the enforcement of these standards "through non-arrest approaches—education, persuasion, counseling, and ordering—so that arrest would only be resorted to when other approaches failed."[58]

The origins of the tactical shift are revealed in strategy documents issued by the New York City Police Department ("NYPD") in 1994.[59] According to the analysis by the Office of the Attorney General of the State of New York ("OAG Report"), these policies remain in effect today.[60] First, *Police Strategy No. 5, Reclaiming the Public Spaces of New York,*[61] articulates a reconstructed version of Broken Windows theory as the driving force in the development of policing policy. It states that the NYPD would apply its enforcement efforts to "reclaim the streets" by systematically and aggressively enforcing laws against low-level *social* disorder: graffiti, aggressive panhandling, fare beating, public drunkenness, unlicensed vending, public drinking, public urination, and other low-level misdemeanor offenses.[62]

Second, *Police Strategy No. 1, Getting Guns Off the Streets of New York,*[63] formalized the strategic focus on the eradication of gun violence through the tactical measure of intensifying efforts to seize illegal firearms. Homicide trends in New York City since 1985 provided strong empirical support for emphasizing gun violence in enforcement policy.[64] Nearly all the increases in homi-

---

56. KELLING & COLES, *supra* note 18, at 22-23.

57. *See* SKOGAN, *supra* note 20; Goldstein, *supra* note 46.

58. KELLING & COLES, *supra* note 18 at 23.

59. OAG REPORT, *supra* note 5.

60. *Id.* at 56-59.

61. POLICE STRATEGY NO. 5, *supra* note 44.

62. This aggressive approach to low-level disorder was "the linchpin of efforts now being undertaken by the New York City Police Department to reduce crime and fear in the city." *Id.*

63. POLICE STRATEGY NO. 1, *supra* note 25.

64. *See* ROBERT C. DAVIS & PEDRO MATEU-GELABERT, VERA INST. OF JUSTICE, RESPECTFUL AND EFFECTIVE POLICING: TWO EXAMPLES IN THE SOUTH BRONX 2, 3 fig.1a (1999) (charting "Homicides (Murder & Non-Negligent Manslaughter), 1978-1997") [hereinafter VERA REPORT].

cides, robberies, and assaults during this period were attributable to gun violence.[65] The political fallout of the homicide crisis lasted for several years more. The homicide crisis was a critical theme in the mayoral election campaign of 1993, and focused the attention of the incoming Giuliani administration's crime-control policy on gun violence.[66]

These two policies, articulated within a relatively brief period in the first few months of the new administration, explicitly cemented the marriage of OMP and "gun-oriented policing"[67] within policy. The logic of this approach was articulated in a series of documents and statements. "By working systematically and assertively to reduce the level of disorder in the city, the NYPD will act to undercut the ground on which more serious crimes seem possible and even permissible."[68] These tactical shifts were intended to raise the stakes for criminals who carried guns: "Stopping people on minor infractions also made it riskier for criminals to carry guns in public."[69] The policy assumed, quite explicitly, that would-be offenders would be deterred from carrying guns since they would be more likely to be stopped for minor crimes or infractions.

The net effect of this marriage was that Broken Windows theory was implemented out of context. Not only was Broken Windows theory recast from physical to social disorder, but community policing and disorder policing both were separated from the theory, reinvented, and implemented with very different tactics.[70]

First, the NYPD version of disorder policing rejected the emphasis on alternatives to arrest and prosecution—essential tenets of the original Broken Windows theory.[71] Although correcting disorder was the focus of policing, the tactic to achieve it was arrest, the most traditional of law enforcement tools. People who committed disorder offenses were questioned and checked for outstanding

---

65. Fagan et al., *supra* note 36, at 1289, 1298, 1304.

66. *See* ELI SILVERMAN, NYPD BATTLES CRIME: INNOVATIVE STRATEGIES IN POLICING 95 (1999); BRATTON & KNOBLER, *supra* note 44, at 219-20. *See generally* KARMEN, *supra* note 36.

67. Fagan et al., *supra* note 36, at 1322.

68. POLICE STRATEGY NO. 5, *supra* note 44.

69. VERA REPORT, *supra* note 64, at 1.

70. Waldeck, *supra* note 19, at 1274-75 n.89; *see also* Bratton, *supra* note 44, at 463-64. This version of community policing eschewed social work functions antithetical to the traditional definition of policing. These tactics robbed rank-and-file police of the activities—searches and arrests—that not only were the staple of police productivity, but also the stepladder to status on the force and advancement within the department. Among police administrators, the emerging paradigm of community policing took away their primary method of keeping order.

71. Waldeck, *supra* note 19, at 1274.

warrants. Those without identification were taken to a precinct, and many were held until fingerprint checks were completed.[72] In other words, disorder policing was used not to disrupt the developmental sequence of disorder and crime, but instead disorder offenses became opportunities to remove weapons and wanted criminals from the streets.

Second, community policing also was reinvented in this marriage. Community standards were no longer identified through structured and systematic interactions between police and community leaders. Instead, the NYPD turned to its sophisticated data-driven management accountability system—Compstat—to identify community needs. The result was that the locus of the standard-setting process shifted from police-community partnerships to precinct commanders.[73] Presumably, precinct commanders were still involved in their communities, developing plans and setting priorities for enforcement.[74] However, the precinct commanders, who continued to meet with community groups, were now accountable to the NYPD's operational hierarchy for both their successes and their failures to produce declining crime rates.[75] As a result, precinct commanders set the crime-fighting priorities for that precinct and developed overall plans of action, based on meeting NYPD priorities, rather than the standards set in cooperation with communities.[76]

C. Disorganization and Disorder: Competing Theories of Place and Crime

For decades before Broken Windows, criminological theories emphasized the notion of "place."[77] In the 1920s, Clifford Shaw

---

72. *Id.* at 1279. These tactics were developed and widely implemented in the transit police under Bratton's leadership in the early 1990s. BRATTON & KNOBLER, *supra* note 44, at 152.

73. BRATTON & KNOBLER, *supra* note 44, at 233.

74. *See id.*

75. *Id.*

76. OAG REPORT, *supra* note 5, at 54-56. According to the Report, accountability was implemented through Compstat meetings. Compstat ("comparison statistics") is a system of electronic computer mapping of weekly crime statistics within precincts and larger police commands. Monthly Compstat sessions focus on analysis of specific crime issues of any of the eight patrol boroughs. Each patrol bureau spans eight to ten precincts. Commanders are asked to explain, often on the spot and in front of an audience of the commissioner and other high ranking department personnel, changes in crime trends in their areas. *Id.*

77. "Place" in the criminological literature is an enduring concept that alternately refers to neighborhoods, larger sections of cities, or other aggregates of areas. *See generally* CLIFFORD R. SHAW & HENRY D. MCKAY, JUVENILE DELINQUENCY AND

and Henry McKay showed that high rates of juvenile crime were persistent in specific neighborhoods over time, despite changes in the racial and ethnic composition of the persons who lived there. Shaw and McKay concluded that place, not the characteristics of the persons who live there, is implicated in crime. Factors such as poverty rates, a downward skewed age distribution, racial and ethnic heterogeneity, and population turnover (residential mobility) explain variations in crime rates across neighborhoods. Shaw and McKay defined the conditions that produced persistently elevated juvenile crime rates as social disorganization.[78]

Recent revisions to this theory emphasize the social organization—the actions of residents within neighborhoods to produce social control and realize their shared values—as protective against high crime rates. Robert Sampson, Stephen Raudenbush, and Felton Earls reported in a study of residents in 343 Chicago neighborhoods that social cohesion among neighbors is linked to lower levels of violence, net of poverty rates, demography, or other socioeconomic factors.[79] This dynamic conceptualization of neighborhood emphasizes social interactions among neighborhood residents, including:

> (1) the strength and interdependence of social networks; (2) the efficacy of collective supervision that residents exercise; (3) the personal responsibility they assume in addressing neighborhood problems; and (4) the level of resident participation in formal and informal organization such as churches, block clubs, and

---

URBAN AREAS: A STUDY OF RATES OF DELINQUENCY IN RELATION TO DIFFERENTIAL CHARACTERISTICS OF LOCAL COMMUNITIES IN AMERICAN CITIES (rev. ed. 1969) (presenting data on the stability of delinquency rates in Chicago neighborhoods across generations of residents of changing composition); ROBERT J. BURSIK JR. & HAROLD G. GRASMICK, NEIGHBORHOODS AND CRIME: THE DIMENSIONS OF EFFECTIVE COMMUNITY CONTROL (1993) (articulating a systemic theory of delinquency that includes elements of the physical attributes of neighborhoods, their social composition and demography, and the institutions that are influential for the people who live there); *Robert J. Sampson & Janet Lauritsen, Violent victimization and offending: Individual-, Situational-, and Community-Level Risk Factors, in* UNDERSTANDING AND PREVENTING VIOLENCE 1 (Albert J. Reiss Jr. & Jeffrey A. Roth, eds. 1994) (reviewing empirical studies that show a relationship between individuals and communities or neighborhoods and delinquency rates).

78. SHAW & McKAY, *supra* note 77, at 383-87. Recent studies show that these factors are stable explanations over time of variations in crime and violence rates across cities and larger ecological aggregates. Kenneth Land et al., *Structural Covariates of Homicide Rates: Are There any Invariances Across Time and Space?*, 95 AM. J. SOC. 922 (1990).

79. Robert J. Sampson et al., *Neighborhoods and Violent Crime: A Multilevel Study of Collective Efficacy*, SCIENCE, Aug. 15, 1997, at 918 (examining neighborhoods in a way that ensured diversity by race, ethnicity, and class).

PTAs. The idea is that community-level social processes such as the level of supervision of teenage peer groups, the prevalence of friendship networks, and the level of residential participation in formal organizations, mediate the link often noted between individual-level factors, such as race and socioeconomic status, and crime.[80]

As Tracey Meares and others point out, the conditions that characterize poor, minority, inner-city communities generally conform to a place-based social organization model of crime. In urban areas, many poor people of color live in conditions of residential segregation, concentrated poverty, and unemployment that predict the breakdown of community social processes,[81] which in turn predict elevated crime rates.[82] For example, many poor African Americans live in the overwhelmingly poor communities marked by unemployment, family dislocation, and high residential turnover.[83] The challenges to social control in socially disorganized neighborhoods are greater for blacks and Hispanics than for whites.[84]

Social disorganization also predicts social and physical disorder. Both theoretically and empirically, disorder and disorganization are confounded. In the study of Chicago neighborhoods by Sampson and colleagues, they included in regression models measures traditionally associated with social disorganization theory to predict disorder in census tracts.[85] Neighborhood characteristics including concentrated disadvantage[86] and weak social ties (collective efficacy) were significant predictors of the rates of disorder. Disorder, however, did not predict rates of homicide, and only

---

80. Tracey Meares, *Place and Crime*, 73 CHI.-KENT L. REV. 669, 673 (1998); *see also* Robert J. Sampson & William Julius Wilson, *Toward a Theory of Race, Crime, and Urban Inequality*, *in* CRIME AND INEQUALITY 37, 45-48 (John Hagan & Ruth D. Peterson eds., 1995); Sampson et al., *supra* note 79.

81. MASSEY & DENTON, *supra* note 17, at 130-31.

82. Sampson & Wilson, *supra* note 80; *see also* Robert J. Sampson, *Urban Black Violence: The Effect of Male Joblessness and Family Disruption*, 93 AM. J. SOCIOLOGY 348 (1987) (discussing the effect of family disruption on crime independent of joblessness and welfare receipt).

83. MASSEY & DENTON, *supra* note 17, at 166-67; WILLIAM JULIUS WILSON, THE TRULY DISADVANTAGED: THE INNER CITY, THE UNDERCLASS, AND PUBLIC POLICY 20-62 (1987); JAMES SHORT, POVERTY, ETHNICITY AND VIOLENT CRIME (1997).

84. Meares, *supra* note 80, at 673-74; Sampson & Wilson, *supra* note 80, at 42 ("[R]acial differences in poverty and family disruption are so strong that the 'worst' urban contexts in which whites reside are considerably better than the average context of black communities."). *See generally* Sampson et al., *supra* note 79.

85. Sampson & Raudenbush, *supra* note 20, at 633-36, and tbl.6.

86. *Id.* This measure included tract-level rates of poverty and unemployment, single parent households, and receipt of public assistance. Racial concentration of blacks was a moderate contributor to the empirical derivation of this construct.

weakly predicted rates of robbery. After controlling for these neighborhood characteristics, the relationship between disorder and crime disappeared for four of their five empirical tests.[87]

Accordingly, social disorganization predicts crime and disorder, but disorder does not predict crime after controlling statistically for the effects of social disorganization. Sampson and colleagues conclude that: "Contrary to the Broken Windows theory . . . the relationship between public disorder and crime is spurious" for most crimes, and is weakly associated only with the crime of robbery.[88] Disorder is only a moderate predictor of robbery, and it co-varies with other neighborhood characteristics such as concentrated disadvantage. Disorder may have a cascading effect on antecedents of crime—encouraging business migration, for example—but it has very weak indirect effects on crime itself. Sampson and colleagues concluded that disorder takes a back seat to other factors, including structural disadvantage and social ties, in explaining crime rates. Controlling crime through disorder policing is, in their words, "simplistic and largely misplaced."[89] Disorder policing, or OMP, leaves the causes of crime untouched.

II. AGGRESSIVE POLICING: OMP, STREET STOPS, AND RACE

Under the tactical shift to order-maintenance policing in New York City, patrol was reinvented to include pro-active interdiction of persons suspected of violating both minor and serious crimes.[90] The importance of stop and frisk interventions to crime fighting was never formally acknowledged in official documents, but has been discussed in detail by the policy's architects and theorists. Kelling and Coles claim that for OMP to be successful, patrol officers should intervene in observed or suspected low-level disorder.[91]

Critics claim that OMP tactics increased the opportunity for pretextual stops leading to searches and arrests.[92] Stops for minor

---

87. *Id.* at 637.

88. *Id.* at 603, 636-37.

89. *Id.* at 638.

90. OAG REPORT, *supra* note 5, at 56-57.

91. KELLING & COLES, *supra* note 18, at 243-48; OAG REPORT, *supra* note 5, at 57; Waldeck, *supra* note 19, at 1282-83; *accord* James Q. Wilson, *Just Take Their Guns Away*, N.Y. TIMES MAG., Mar. 20, 1994, at 47 (stating that police should make street stop and frisks in order to find persons carrying illegal weapons, without stating a legal or practical rationale for these stops).

92. Waldeck, *supra* note 19, at 1282 ("Nor is there any doubt that the police use quality-of-life offenses as excuses to fish for drugs, guns, or evidence of a more serious crime.").

crimes or infractions were easier to justify under a lower constitutional standard (i.e., "reasonable suspicion") than stops for more serious offenses. Accordingly, OMP stops provided opportunities for police to check for warrants, and, again under reasonable suspicion standards, search suspects for contraband or weapons, and make arrests. Many such offenses—such as public drinking or loitering—take place in public, making their observation easier and an encounter with the putatively offending citizen more likely.

The result was a vast increase in misdemeanor arrests, but also a sharp decline in their quality and sustainability in court. OMP has been activated through vast increases in misdemeanor arrests of adults, increasing from 129,404 in 1993 (the year prior to OMP implementation) to 181,736 in 1996, and 215,158 in 1998.[93] But the evidentiary quality of arrests suffered as their number rose. As arrests increased under OMP, the rate at which prosecutors declined to pursue these cases rose dramatically. In 1998, prosecutors dismissed 18,000 of the 345,000 misdemeanor and felony arrests, approximately twice the number dismissed in 1993.[94] Overall, more than 140,000 cases completed in 1998 ended in dismissals, an increase of 60% compared with 1993.[95] Prosecutors say that refusals to prosecute as well as the high dismissal rate can indicate a decline in the quality of arrest.[96] Many of the declined cases, known as "declined prosecutions" or "D.P.s" in the court, came from predominantly minority neighborhoods, the focus of OMP efforts.[97] The punitive component of the D.P.s and dismissed arrests—being taken into custody, handcuffed, transported, booked, often strip-searched, and jailed overnight—impregnates these events with its own social meaning quite different from the origins of Broken Windows theory.

---

93. DIV. OF CRIMINAL JUSTICE SERVS., STATE OF N.Y., CRIMINAL JUSTICE INDICATORS: NEW YORK CITY, 1995-1999, *at* http://criminaljustice.state.ny.us/crimnet/cjsa/areastat/areastat.htm (using search parameters: "Region: New York City," years 1995-1999) [hereinafter CJI: NEW YORK CITY].

94. Ford Fessenden & David Rohde, *Dismissed Before Reaching Court: Flawed Arrests Rise in New York*, N.Y. TIMES, Aug. 23, 1999, at A1 (citing the sharp rise in the number of arrests that prosecutors declined to prosecute in 1998). The number of cases rejected by prosecutors rose by 41% in the Bronx and 23% in Manhattan, even as the crime rate declined sharply in the same year. Approximately fifty persons each day were arrested and booked, but then released—many spending a night in jail before their cases were dismissed. *Id.*

95. *Id.*

96. *Id.*

97. *Id.*

Analyses of 1998 police stop and frisk reports—UF-250s—showed that OMP policing had drifted from street stops in quality of life crimes to widespread stops of citizens in search of guns.[98] Stop and frisk actions became the primary method for removing illegal handguns from the street. The OAG Report showed that from January 1998 through March 1999, weapons possession was suspected in more than one-third of documented stop and frisk encounters.[99]

The OAG Report also showed that the reconstructed OMP policy was implemented in a manner that was not race-neutral. The OAG Report showed that stops were disproportionately concentrated in the city's poorest neighborhoods, neighborhoods with high concentrations of racial minorities. Table 1 below shows the percentage of stops, according to the distribution of minority populations in the precincts. In precincts with the highest concentrations of minorities, stops of black and Hispanic suspects were highest (by percentage), as might be expected. However, in the thirteen precincts with the lowest minority populations,[100] stops of blacks and Hispanics were well above what their population percentage would predict. In those precincts, 30% of the persons "stopped" were black, more than ten times greater than their percentage of the overall population of those precincts.[101] Hispanics comprised 23.4% of the persons "stopped," more than three times their population share. Whites make up 80% of the population of those precincts, but only 41.5% of the persons "stopped." Even in precincts where neighborhoods had the lowest minority concentration, whites were stopped less. The pattern invokes an enduring empirical fact in criminological research: police officers are more likely to treat as suspicious persons who seem out of place from their surroundings.[102] To police officers, race serves as a marker of

98. OAG REPORT, *supra* note 5, at tbl.I.B.3.

99. *Id.* The Street Crime Unit was disproportionately responsible for the use of stop and frisk actions to search for guns. During the fifteen month study period in the OAG Report, the Street Crime Unit ("SCU") had a "particular emphasis on recovering illegal firearms." Its 435 officers (out of nearly 40,000 in the NYPD) effected more than 10% of all documented stop and frisk encounters citywide. *Id.* at 58-59.

100. *Id.* at tbl.I.A.2.

101. *Id.* The OAG Report established the population of each precinct, using census data for day and night populations. *Id.* at 96.

102. JONATHAN RUBINSTEIN, CITY POLICE 225 (1973); John van Maanen, *Working the Street: A Developmental View of Police Behavior, in* THE POTENTIAL FOR REFORM OF CRIMINAL JUSTICE 83, 118 (Herbert Jacobs, ed. 1974).

where people "belong," and racial incongruity as a marker of suspicion.[103]

TABLE 1. DISTRIBUTION OF STOPS BY RACE OF SUSPECT AND RACIAL COMPOSITION OF PRECINCT (MANDATED REPORT STOPS ONLY)[104]

% Hispanic Population in Precinct	% Black Population in the Precinct		
	Over 40%	10% to 40%	Under 10%
Over 40%	57.0	38.0	17.1
	38.8	55.1	67.0
	3.3	4.9	10.1
	(4)	(11)	(3)
20% to 40%	74.6	31.6	29.5
	19.2	52.0	40.8
	2.9	12.7	22.3
	(2)	(6)	(6)
10% to 20%	84.8	56.9	22.9
	11.0	22.2	40.1
	2.9	18.2	26.3
	(8)	(9)	(5)
Less than 10%	91.6	74.7	30.0
	4.6	8.0	23.4
	2.0	15.4	41.5
	(6)	(2)	(13)
	Legend		% Black Suspects
			% Hispanic Suspects
			% White Suspects
			(Number of Precincts)

Racial incongruity is one of several patterns observed in the OAG Report that depict the racial component of OMP in New York. The ratio of 9.5 stops of black citizens for each arrest made was 20% higher than the 7.9 ratio for whites.[105] Such higher stop-arrest ratios suggest either that stops for blacks were pretextual and largely unfounded, or that police were less discriminating or skillful in assessing "suspicion" for minority citizens.

Stops, alone or in proportion to the population, tell only part of the story. The NYPD points out, for example, that the higher stop

103. Stephen Mastrofski et al., *Race and Every-Day Policing: A Research Perspective*, Presented at the 12th International Congress on Criminology, Seoul, Aug. 24-29, 1998. Anthony C. Thompson reminds us that racial incongruity was one of the markers that aroused the suspicion of Officer McFadden in the original *Terry* case. *See generally* Thompson, *supra* note 17, at 962-73 (discussing the racial dimensions of the original *Terry* case and the centrality of race to Fourth Amendment jurisprudence).

104. OAG REPORT, *supra* note 5, at tbl.I.A.2.

105. *Id.* at tbl.I.B.2.

rate for minorities reflects higher participation of blacks and Hispanics in crimes, especially in the city's highest crime neighborhoods. Using crime data on race- and crime-specific arrest rates within precincts, the OAG Report estimated the extent to which race- and crime-specific stops were predicted by crime, or whether actual stop rates exceeded the predicted stop rates. The results show that crime rates only partially explain stop rates overall, and fail to explain the rates at which minority citizens are "stopped" by the NYPD. After controlling for race- and crime-specific crime rates and the population composition of the precinct, the results showed that black and Hispanic citizens were significantly more likely to be stopped than were white citizens.[106] The overall differences between races were statistically significant, and were significant specifically for stops where the suspected crime was either violence or weapons possession.[107]

Table 2 illustrates the exponentiated coefficients—or comparative odds—from these models, showing the magnitude of the differences for each race- and crime-specific stop rate. This table only includes stops where reports were mandated by NYPD policy. The results are divided into three sections, according to the precinct's black population. This display illustrates the importance of concentration effects. Each coefficient shows the stop-rate adjusted for the crime rate, disaggregated by race of suspect and suspected crime. In other words, each table shows the rate at which blacks, Hispanics, and whites were "stopped" in proportion to the rate at which they were arrested for each crime type. Comparing the coefficient by race illustrates the magnitude of the differences between races.

---

106. *Id.* at tbl.I.C.1.
107. *Id.*

TABLE 2. LOG ODDS OF RACE- AND CRIME-SPECIFIC STOP
RATES, CONTROLLING FOR 1997 RACE- AND CRIME-SPECIFIC
ARREST RATES, BY BLACK POPULATION IN PRECINCT
(MANDATED REPORT STOPS ONLY)[108]

Race of Suspect	Black Population in Precinct: Less Than 10% Suspected Crime			
	Violent	Weapon	Property	Drug
Black	0.37	2.17	0.26	0.10
Hispanic	0.32	1.87	0.39	0.11
White	0.11	0.97	0.33	0.10

Race of Suspect	Black Population in Precinct: From 10% to 40% Suspected Crime			
	Violent	Weapon	Property	Drug
Black	0.36	2.12	0.25	0.09
Hispanic	0.31	1.83	0.38	0.10
White	0.17	0.95	0.32	0.10

Race of Suspect	Black Population in Precinct: Greater Than 40% Suspected Crime			
	Violent	Weapon	Property	Drug
Black	0.30	1.76	0.21	0.08
Hispanic	0.26	1.52	0.31	0.09
White	0.14	0.79	0.27	0.08

For example, Table 2 shows that in precincts where the black population was less than 10%, blacks were 2.17 times more likely to be stopped for weapons offenses compared to the arrest rate for blacks for that crime. Whites were 0.97 times more likely to be stopped compared to the arrest rate for whites for that crime. Comparing the coefficients, blacks were more than twice as likely (2.17/0.97) to be stopped as whites for weapons offenses, relative to their race-specific arrest rates for that crime.

The comparisons throughout this table show the elevated rates at which blacks and Hispanics were stopped for suspected violence and weapons offenses as compared to stop rates for whites. In precincts with more than 40% black population, the black-white ratios were still more than twice as high for violent crimes (0.3/0.14) and nearly three times higher (1.76/0.79) for weapons offenses. The Hispanic-white ratios in these precincts were comparably disproportionate for stops for violent crimes (0.26/0.14) and for weapons offenses (1.52/0.79). The disparities were confined to these two crime types. The coefficients were either comparable or lower for

108. *See id.* at Appendix tbl.1.C.1.

whites where stops related to alleged drug or property crimes, regardless of precinct demography.

The higher-than-predicted stop rates of minorities suggest that the police had cast suspicion more often—than would be predicted by their crime participation—on the city's minority population.[109] Although race may not be determinative in the decision to stop a suspect, race certainly appeared to be a motivating factor in the patterns of stop.and frisk interventions. The prominence of race in the decision to stop citizens may not rise to the threshold of racial profiling, but it does seem to create a racial classification of "suspicion."

To assess whether that suspicion met *Terry* standards of "reasonable suspicion," the OAG Report examined the stop rationales articulated by police officers on the UF-250 stop report form. The researchers examined the reasons that police officers provided for "stopping" civilians, and estimated the rate at which the reasons, as stated, met Fourth Amendment standards of "reasonable suspicion." The narrative rationales for "stops" came from a citywide sample of 10,000 coded and analyzed UF-250 forms from eight precincts plus a supplemental sample of cases across all precincts.[110] The narratives were coded into sixty-seven categories, and the OAG staff then determined whether the stated rationale in each category met *Terry* standards of "reasonable suspicion."[111] These codes were then collapsed into seven categories, or rationales, which were determined as either meeting or failing to meet *Terry* standards.[112]

Table 3, adopted from the OAG Report, shows that in nearly two-thirds of the stops, the articulated "reasonable suspicion" for the stop met *Terry* standards, and that racial disparities were small. However, stops of black suspects more often failed to meet *Terry*

---

109. *Id.* at 126-27.
110. *Id.* at 135-36. The researchers coded rationales for a citywide sample plus a supplemental sample of specifically chosen precincts. For the individual precinct sample, a purposive sample of eight precincts was selected—the 79th, 42nd, 30th, 43rd, 33rd, 107th, 72nd, and the 19th—based on variation in stop rates and population parameters. For each precinct, approximately half of the UF-250 forms were randomly sampled. In all, 4383 UF-250 forms were randomly sampled for the citywide analysis, including 3282 stops where reports were "mandated." *Id.* at 158-60.
111. *Id.* at 145, tbl.II.A.1.
112. *Id.* at 135-60, tbl.II.A.2. Categories where rationales were sufficient to meet *Terry* standards were: (1) crime observed, (2) suspect fit description, (3) weapon observed, (4) suspicious activity plus other criterion behavior. Categories where rationales failed to meet *Terry* standards included: (1) suspicious activity and (2) suspect in wrong place. *Id.* at tbl.II.A.2.

standards (15.4%) than did stops of whites (11.3%). In contrast, there were only minimal differences between stops involving Hispanic and whites suspects.

TABLE 3. ASSESSMENT OF *TERRY* RATIONALES FOR STOPS BY RACE OF SUSPECT, CITYWIDE SAMPLE (MANDATED REPORT STOPS ONLY)[113]

Assessment of Reasonable Suspicion Standard	Race of Person Stopped				
	Black	Hispanic	White	Other	Total
Facts, as stated, articulate	1,172	690	192	60	2,114
reasonable suspicion	64.3%	65.4%	60.4%	69.8%	64.4%
Facts, as stated, do not articulate	281	133	36	9	459
reasonable suspicion	15.4%	12.6%	11.3%	10.5%	14.0%
Insufficient information	370	232	90	17	709
	20.3%	32.7%	28.3%	19.8%	21.6%
Total	1,823	1,055	318	86	3,282

The pattern of evidence in the OAG Report suggests that race evidently became a factor in "everyday policing" in New York City under OMP. Working within a legally permissible but lower standard of "reasonable" racial discrimination, where a second motivating factor (such as "reasonable suspicion") may be present, police over-stopped black and Hispanic citizens relative to their crime participation, well in excess of their white neighbors, and more often without constitutional justification. Black citizens in particular tend to generalize these experiences, with potentially toxic consequences for their perception of the legitimacy of the law.[114] Disproportionate stops of black citizens is an important "race-making" factor,[115] generalized through the sense of linked fate that many blacks share.[116] It conveys social stigma and under-

---

113. *See id.* at tbl.II.B.4.

114. Tracey Maclin, *Race and the Fourth Amendment*, 51 VAND. L. REV. 333, 386 (1998) ("Blacks correctly see pretextual traffic stops as another sign that police officers view blacks, particularly black males, as criminals who deserve singular scrutiny and treatment as second class citizens."). *See generally* David A. Harris, *"Driving While Black" and All Other Traffic Offenses: The Supreme Court and Pretextual Traffic Stops*, 87 J. CRIM. L. & CRIMINOLOGY 544, 571 (1997).

115. This term is borrowed from Professor David James, who has written of the ghetto as a "race-making situation." James, *supra* note 24, at 420-28.

116. DAWSON, *supra* note 24, at 77 (using the "linked fate" concept to explain the way that African Americans perceive what is in their individual self interest). Experiences such as "stop and frisk" encounters could easily undermine the social meaning of the OMP strategy. *Id.* at 80-84; *see also* JEFFREY FAGAN & TRACEY L. MEARES, PUNISHMENT, DETERRENCE AND SOCIAL CONTROL: THE PARADOX OF PUNISHMENT IN MINORITY COMMUNITIES (2000) (discussing how the perceived illegitimacy of the criminal justice system in the African American and Hispanic communities has kept

mines the perceived and attributed legitimacy of law and legal institutions necessary to promote compliance with the law. The harm to individuals stopped but not arrested cannot be discounted in a social framework where events and experiences are linked in this manner.[117]

III. RESOLVING COMPETING THEORETICAL CLAIMS ABOUT STOP AND FRISK ACTIVITY: EMPIRICAL RESULTS

Returning to OMP in New York City, then, we can ask whether the emphasis on disorder was, in fact, a strategy focused on policing poor people rather than disordered places. Of course, at the neighborhood level, race interacts with other neighborhood factors, ones that also correlate with social and physical disorder.[118] In the reconstructed Broken Windows theory that informed OMP in New York City, social disorder, or person-focused tactics, replaced physical disorder, or place-based tactics. Empirical evidence shows that the epidemiology of stop and frisk actions in turn was concentrated among minority persons in poor neighborhoods.[119] Accordingly, it appears that place was switched for race in the reality of OMP. Thus, what began as policing informed by a nuanced Broken Windows theory, in fact reflects criminological theories focused on social disorganization.

This raises two questions for understanding the racial patterns of policing. First, what are the net effects of race on patterns of policing after we control for disorder? If OMP was in fact targeted at disorder, race differences at the neighborhood level should disappear after we introduce measures of disorder. Unlike, for example, race-explicit drug-courier profiles, OMP should be racially and facially neutral once we control for the level of disorder in the neighborhood.

crime rates steady despite harsher sentencing), http://papers2.ssrn.com/paper.taf?abstract-id=223148.

117. William J. Stuntz, Terry's Impossibility, 72 ST. JOHN'S L. REV. 1213, 1218 (1998) (summarizing harms from encounters of innocent citizens with police, including violations of privacy, public shame at being singled out and treated like a criminal suspect, the emotional damage of discrimination, and the potential for police violence and physical injury).

118. Sampson & Raudenbush, supra note 20. See generally ROBERT J. BURSIK, JR. & HAROLD GRASMICK, NEIGHBORHOODS AND CRIME: THE DIMENSIONS OF EFFECTIVE COMMUNITY CONTROL (1993).

119. OAG REPORT, supra note 5, at 92-94 (citing New York City Police Commissioner Howard Safir's statement that minorities are more likely to be "stopped" because they live in high crime neighborhoods with an increased police presence).

Second, if disorder itself is predicted by neighborhood or ecological characteristics, factors that also are correlated with race, are these other factors significant predictors of stop and frisk patterns after we control for disorder? While some neighborhood characteristics are correlated with disorder, these factors also are part of competing theoretical explanations, explanations that are based on characteristics of persons, rather than places. Accordingly, we question whether OMP produces the dramatic racial disparities reported in the OAG Report because of the characteristics of people who live in the neighborhood, or whether these disparities reflect policing targeted in fact at disorder. Analytically, we can compare these two explanations to estimate the ecological locus of racial policing. The results of this competition follow, where we present findings of empirical tests designed to assess these competing claims about the theoretical meaning of OMP in New York City.

A. Social and Physical Disorder

Data on the social organization and physical characteristics of neighborhoods were obtained from the 1999 New York City Housing and Vacancy Survey ("HVS").[120] The HVS is sponsored by the New York City Department of Housing Preservation and Development ("HPD")[121] to comply with New York State and New York City's rent regulation laws. It is conducted every three years with respondents in a stratified random sample of New York City housing units. The sample is based on housing units recorded in the decennial census, and updated every three years as part of the enumeration process preceding the HVS. The HVS emulates the population dimensions of the decennial census and generates measures of household and person characteristics for the city.[122]

---

120. U.S. CENSUS BUREAU, DEP'T OF COMMERCE, 1999 NEW YORK CITY HOUSING AND VACANCY SURVEY (1999), *at* http://www.census.gov/hhes/www/nychvs.html [hereinafter NYC HOUSING SURVEY].

121. THE GREEN BOOK: OFFICIAL DIRECTORY OF THE CITY OF NEW YORK (2000) (providing names and contact information for HPD). The Department of Housing Preservation and Development is responsible for setting and administering housing policy in the city, including development of urban renewal programs, enforcement of civil codes for housing, management of city-owned properties, rehabilitation of abandoned buildings, and construction of low-income housing.

122. NYC HOUSING SURVEY, *supra* note 120, at Overview, http://www.census.gov/ hhes/www/housing/nychvs/overview.html. Differences between the 1999 HVS and the 1990 census include interviewing procedures, staff experience and training, processing procedures, sample design, the sampling variability associated with the HVS and the sample data from the census, and the non-sampling errors associated with the HVS and the census.

The sample includes "vacant available for rent" units as well as occupied units. Both public and privately owned housing units, as well as in rem units,[123] are included. The public-use data set is made available by the U.S. Census Bureau, and includes weights to generate estimates of households and persons for the city. The response rate in the 1999 survey sample of 18,180 was 94%. Interviews were conducted between January and May, 1999 by "field representatives" hired by HPD.[124]

Measures of physical disorder and social structure were aggregated from individual-level responses in the HVS to sub-boroughs. The residential location of each respondent is coded to the borough (county) and the *community district* ("CD"), or sub-borough. CD's are administrative units of each borough; there are fifty-five in the city. Members of the councils of each CD meet periodically to assist city agencies in zoning and other regulatory planning functions. Sub-boroughs include one or two police precincts.

Measures of physical disorder in the sub-borough were computed from responses to items regarding the physical condition of the dwelling and the neighborhood. Respondents were asked to report whether there was damage or disrepair in the exterior walls and windows, stairwells and stairways, and floors. Respondents also were asked to report generally on the condition of other dwellings in their neighborhood: the presence of broken or boarded up windows, and whether the building was "deteriorated" or "dilapidated."[125] Responses were aggregated to the sub-borough level to measure the percentage of housing units with these characteristics.

To avoid redundancy among the disorder variables, a principle components factor analysis with varimax rotation[126] was completed to reduce the variables to a single dimension. The model yielded

---

123. In rem housing units are housing units that are acquired and owned by the City of New York following tax forfeitures or failure to pay other charges such as correcting violations of the housing codes. NYC HOUSING SURVEY, *supra* note 120, at H-2, Definitions of Rent Regulation Status, http://www.census.gov/hhes/www/housing/nychvs/defin99.html.

124. NYC HOUSING SURVEY, *supra* note 120, at Overview. Interviews were conducted to elicit information about the demographic characteristics of each household member, and the housing characteristics of the dwelling.

125. NYC HOUSING SURVEY, *supra* note 120, at Glossary, http://www.census.gov/hhes/www/housing/nychvs/gloss99.html. For vacant units, responses were recorded by the HPD field representatives.

126. "Varimax rotation" is a statistical procedure that permits the extraction of distinct factors or dimensions from a set of highly correlated variables, and assumes that the factors do not overlap statistically or conceptually. GERHARD ARMINGER ET AL., HANDBOOK OF STATISTICAL MODELING FOR THE SOCIAL AND BEHAVIORAL SCIENCES 205-6 (1995).

one factor explaining 85.9% of the variance. Factor coefficients ranged from 0.865 to 0.959, indicating uniform loading and high multicollinearity. Because of its conceptual clarity and importance to the construction of "physical disorder," we used the "broken windows" variable as the measure of disorder.[127]

Measures of social disorganization were computed using similar procedures. Both household and person characteristics were constructed by aggregating individual responses to sub-boroughs. Means and variances for the measures are shown in Appendix A, *infra*. A principle components factor analysis with varimax rotation was again completed and yielded three factors that explained 74.0% of the variance. The first factor describes neighborhoods characterized by concentrations of persons with low education, persons under- or unemployed, households receiving public assistance, households with Hispanic residents, and female-headed households. These neighborhoods also were characterized by low white population. The second factor describes neighborhoods with high racial fragmentation (racial heterogeneity)[128] and high concentrations of male population. These neighborhoods also were characterized by low black population. The third factor describes neighborhoods characterized by high concentrations of immigrants and residential mobility.[129]

These three factors reflect the classic dimensions of social disorganization.[130] The variables within factors were highly correlated, again permitting selection of specific variables to represent each factor. For conceptual clarity and theoretical specificity, we chose specific variables as measures of social disorganization: the percent of households with one or more persons receiving public assistance, racial fragmentation, and residential mobility.[131] Because of the importance of immigration to the social composition of New York City,[132] we included as a predictor the percentage of house-

---

127. Analyses available from authors.
128. *See* CHARLES LEWIS TAYLOR & MICHAEL C. HUDSON, WORLD HANDBOOK OF POLITICAL AND SOCIAL INDICATORS 216 (2d ed. 1972). Racial fragmentation is a measure of the racial heterogeneity within an area, and is computed as:
$1 - ((P)^2)$
Where P = proportion of each race within the spatial unit.
129. *Id.*
130. SHAW & MCKAY, *supra* note 77, at 183-89; SHORT, *supra* note 83, at 55; *see* Sampson & Lauritsen, *supra* note 77, at 1, 51-75; Meares, *supra* note 80, at 673.
131. SHAW & MCKAY, *supra* note 77, at 32, 37, 205.
132. I. M. Miyares & K. S. Gowen, Recreating Boundaries: The Geography of Latin American Immigrants to New York City, CLAG YEARBOOK 2431 (1998); *see* Arun Peter Lobo et al., *Immigration to the New York Metropolitan Region in the*

hold heads who were born outside the U.S. We also included two additional measures that are predictors of crime rates at the community level: the housing vacancy rate[133] and the percentage of housing units in the area that are public housing.[134]

Finally, we included a global measure of crime in the sub-borough: the count of 1997 arrests within each precinct, aggregated to the sub-borough. Arrest counts, published in the OAG Report,[135] were obtained by the OAG from the New York State Division of Criminal Justice Services. State crime counts include "finger-printable" crimes, or crimes that are punishable by jail or prison sentences.

B. Stops and Arrests

Counts and rates of stops and arrests within precincts were compiled from data published by the OAG.[136] In addition to stop counts, the ratio of stops to arrests was computed for each precinct and each type of crime. Cases involving stops that occurred from January 1998 - March 1999 were included. The data tables were compiled by the OAG from files created by the NYPD from UF-250 forms.[137] UF-250 forms are completed by officers following

---

1990's, in MIGRATION WORLD, Volume XXVII, No. 5. (1999); ARUN PETER LOBO ET AL., THE NEWEST NEW YORKERS 1990-1994: AN ANALYSIS OF IMMIGRATION TO NYC IN THE EARLY 1990s (1996); I. M. Miyares, *Little Odessa: Brighton Beach, Brooklyn: An Examination of the Former Soviet Refugee Economy in New York City*, 19 URB. GEOGRAPHY 518 (1998).

133. *See* Ralph B. Taylor, *The Impact of Crime on Communities*, 539 THE ANNALS OF THE AMER. ACAD. POL. & SOC. SCIENCE 28 (1995).

134. *E.g.*, TAMARA DUMANOVSKY ET AL., THE NEIGHBORHOOD CONTEXT OF CRIME IN NYC'S PUBLIC HOUSING PROJECTS (1999) (manuscript on file with author); TERENCE DUNWORTH & AARON SAIGER, NAT'L INST. OF JUSTICE, SUMMARY: DRUGS AND CRIME IN PUBLIC HOUSING: A THREE-CITY ANALYSIS, at viii (1994); Harold Holzman, *Criminological Research on Public Housing: Toward a Better Understanding of People, Places and Spaces*, 42 CRIME & DELINQUENCY 361 (1996).

135. OAG REPORT, *supra* note 5, at tbl.I.C.3; *see also id.* at 120 n. 25 (explaining that arrest counts for 1997 were used—instead of 1998 arrest data—to avoid autocorrelation between stops and arrests that both occurred in 1998). Arrest counts are preferable to crime complaint data, since many types of crime (such as drug crimes or minor property crimes) are not reported in citizen complaints to the police. *Id.* at 121. In addition, complaints often include crimes with no suspect information, while arrests include information on the demographic characteristics of the suspect. *See id.*

136. *Id.* at tbl.I.C.3. Race-specific rates for the total number of stops were computed from the percentages included in the table. The race-specific ratios of stops to arrests were computed from data in tbl.I.B.1 and I.B.2, and Appendix tbl.I.B.1 and I.B.2. tbl.I.B.2 also included data on weapons stops by race.

137. *Id.* at 88.

each stop event.[138] Both global stops and arrests were analyzed, as well as stops where the suspect was alleged to have a weapon. Weapons stops were analyzed separately because of the heavy emphasis on the control of gun violence in the formulation and implementation of NYPD policy.[139]

The analyses included only stops where a UF-250 form was mandated. NYPD policy mandates that officers complete a UF-250 under four specific circumstances: when (1) force is used in the course of the stop; (2) the suspect is frisked (i.e., pat down) and/or searched during the course of the stop;[140] (3) the suspect is arrested; or (4) the suspect refuses to identify him or herself.[141] Nonmandated reports also were submitted during this time, but compliance with reporting requirements when reports were not mandated was uneven, raising reliability problems in assessing the consistency of these reports across precincts.[142]

---

138. *Id.* at 63 (describing the UF-250 form and the NYPD policies regulating the filing of these reports). Although initially designed as a tool for investigation, completion of the UF-250 form has been required by the NYPD Patrol Guide since 1986. *Id.* at 65. In 1997, the police commissioner assigned a high priority to filing UF-250s. N.Y. CITY POLICE DEP'T, PATROL GUIDE: PROCEDURE No. 116-33 (effective Nov. 14, 1986) (detailing policy police officers, in certain circumstances, to document stop and frisk street encounters on the UF-250 form) [hereinafter PATROL GUIDE].

139. For a discussion of the policy, see POLICE STRATEGY No. 1, *supra* note 25, and OAG REPORT, *supra* note 5, at 53. The memo described the NYPD's plan to reduce gun violence by intensified efforts to find and seize illegal firearms. Guns and violent crime also were a primary focus of the NYPD's Street Crime Unit ("SCU"), an elite unit of plain-clothes officers tasked to "hot spots" of concentrated criminal activity. The SCU's "mission" is to "effect the arrests of violent street criminals, with a particular emphasis on recovering illegal firearms." OAG REPORT, *supra* note 5, at 53 n.32 (citing Police Commissioner Howard Safir, Statement Before the New York City Council Public Safety Committee (Apr. 19, 1999)) [hereinafter Safir Statement].

140. That is, searches inside his or her clothing.

141. PATROL GUIDE, *supra* note 138; OAG REPORT, *supra* note 5, at 63-64.

142. Analyses in the OAG Report show that whites were over-represented in cases involving non-mandated reports. OAG REPORT, *supra* note 5, at 95 n.9. Although whites comprised 12.9% of all cases and 10.4% of cases where reports were required, whites comprised 19.3% of cases where a form was not mandated. However, completion of non-mandated reports varied from precinct to precinct, when compared as a ratio to the number of stops with mandated reports. *See id.* at tbl.I.A.1. The OAG Report constructed two scenarios to explain the racial disparity in non-mandated reports. In one scenario, "the police completed non-mandated UF-250's for 'stops' of minorities and non-minorities at the same rate, but [found] that 'stops' of whites were less likely to rise to the more intrusive level of force, a frisk or an arrest." *Id.* at 95 n.9. In the second scenario, "the police were more likely to . . . complet[e] a UF-250 form . . . in a non-mandated situation when the person 'stopped' was white." *Id.* In either scenario, analyzing only mandated report cases—which by definition are more intrusive—would show greater racial disparity than would an analysis of all cases. *Id.*

C. Results

Two dimensions of police stops of citizens were computed to test the hypothesis that crime rates alone do not explain differences in stop rates by race or type of crime. First, comparisons of stop rates by race and type of crime are shown in Table 4.[143] Stop rates by race and type of crime are shown, and the overall race-specific crime rate is shown as a basis of comparison. We used the 1997 race-specific crime counts to compute a per capita stop rate over the fifteen month interval. The results show large disparities by race. Stop rates were nearly five times higher for blacks compared to non-Hispanic whites, and four times higher for Hispanics.[144] The citywide stop rate is heavily weighted by the concentration of stops among blacks and Hispanics. The disparities by race are consistent across crime types, and the heaviest disparities between stops of black and white citizens. For violence and weapons, stops of blacks occur at a rate ten times higher than the rate for whites, and more than twice as high as the rate for Hispanics. Disparities remain for other crime types, but are narrower. Comparisons of race-specific stop rates per 1000 population to arrest rates per 1000 population show that blacks and Hispanics were stopped at rates higher than their arrest rates.

143. *Id.* at 120 n.25 (describing types of crimes). Crimes were reported using four generic crime categories. *Violent crimes* included robbery, assault, homicide, kidnapping and sex crimes. *Weapons crimes* included arrests for both gun and other illegal weapons. *Property crimes* included larceny and burglary. *Drug crimes* included both possession and sale offenses. *Id.*

144. The OAG analysis constructed four categories of race from the eight recorded on the NYPD documentation in the UF-250 data: white, black, Hispanic white, Asian, American Indian, other, unknown. OAG REPORT, *supra* note 5. We use four: black, white, Hispanic, and other. The UF-250 form has no category for black Hispanics, so we were unable to determine whether officers classified black Hispanics as black or Hispanic, or whether officers were consistent in their classification decisions. *Id.* The NYPD classification is based on officers' observations, the Census Bureau classification is based on self-report. In constructing race-specific population rates from the HVS for the sub-boroughs, we classified both white and black Hispanics as black, consistent with classifications in the U.S. Census. The construction of the Hispanic classification from census data involves a two-stage process regarding both race and ethnicity. Once race is determined, a secondary question asks whether the individual identifies himself or herself as a person of "Hispanic origin."

TABLE 4. RACE-SPECIFIC AND CRIME-SPECIFIC STOP RATES PER 1,000 PERSONS, CRIME RATES PER 1,000 PERSONS, AND RACE-SPECIFIC POPULATION CITYWIDE[145]

Type of Crime	Stop Rate: Citywide	Stop Rate: Black	Stop Rate: Hispanic	Stop Rate: White	Stop Rate: Other
Violent	3.2	7.5	3.5	0.7	1.0
Property	2.0	3.1	2.6	1.1	0.9
Drug	1.4	2.7	1.8	0.6	0.3
Weapon	7.6	18.0	8.7	1.3	1.8
Quality of life offenses	1.3	1.8	1.5	0.1	0.5
All offenses	17.1	22.6	20.0	4.8	5.2
Total arrests	104,847	53,472	31,454	16,776	3,145
Arrest rate per 1,000 persons	14.1	29.0	15.1	6.0	4.4
1999 population	7,428,162	1,845,306	2,089,149	2,775,637	718,070

These differences are consistent with significant differences reported in the OAG Report.[146] Controlling for race- and crime-specific crime rates and population, that report showed that stop rates for blacks and Hispanics were significantly higher than the stop rates for whites.[147] These effects were most acute for stops for weapons and violent crimes.[148]

The second measure of police stop activity is the ratio of stops to arrests by race and type of crime. Once police officers decide to stop a citizen, the outcomes of those stops—including whether a frisk or search is conducted, and whether an arrest is made—should not differ by race. Presumably, the "reasonable suspicion" articulated in *Terry v. Ohio* and incorporated into both the formal training and professional judgment of police officers,[149] should lead to stops with race-neutral outcome probabilities. In other words, there is no rationale for police to exercise discretion differently by race that would lead to a higher rate of "false positives" for any racial group. Accordingly, stop rates should reflect a similar efficiency and strategic allocation of police efforts across races.

---

145. OAG REPORT, *supra* note 5, at tbl.I.A.1, tbl.I.A.5; DEP'T OF CITY PLANNING, CITY OF N.Y., 1990-99 POPULATION CHANGE ESTIMATES, *available at* http://www.ci.nyc.ny.us/html/dcp/pdf/9099pop.pdf.

146. OAG REPORT, *supra* note 5, at 94-95. Citywide, blacks constituted 50% of the total "stops" and 51% of the arrests for the covered period. Hispanics constituted 33% of all "stops" and 30% of all arrests. Whites constituted 13% of all "stops" and 16% of all arrests. However, this evidence of proportionality masks differences by neighborhood. *Id.* at 95 n.9, 123.

147. *Id.* at tbl.I.C.1 and I.C.2.

148. *Id.* at tbl.I.C.1 and I.C.2.

149. *See* Thompson, *supra* note 17, at 971.

Table 5 shows the ratio of stops to arrests by race of suspect and suspected charge. A higher rate indicates less efficiency in stops, or an excessive rate of stops needed to affect an arrest. A high stop rate may also indicate more indiscriminate stop practices, or simply broadened suspicion of individuals based on race alone.[150] Overall, the total stop-to-arrest ratio of blacks (7.3 stops per arrest) is 58.7% higher than the ratio for non-Hispanic whites (4.6); the ratio for Hispanics (6.4) is 39% higher than the rate for non-Hispanic whites. For weapons stops, the stop-to-arrest ratio for blacks is 18.7% higher than the ratio for whites, but the ratio for Hispanics is less than 23.0% higher.

TABLE 5. RACE- AND CRIME-SPECIFIC STOP-ARREST
RATIOS CITYWIDE[151]

Type of Crime	Citywide	Black	Hispanic	White	Other
Weapon	16.5	16.5	17.1	13.9	17.3
All Stops	6.5	7.3	6.4	4.6	5.5

To test whether stops were proportionate to crime rates, and to assess factors that might explain stop rates higher than would be predicted by crime rates, multivariate analyses were completed incorporating three potential explanations: the crime rate within the sub-borough (or strategic theory), disorder (or place-based theory), or social disorganization (or person-based theory). Trends in both Tables 4 and 5 confirm the emphasis on weapons stops articulated in NYPD strategy memoranda. Accordingly, separate analyses were completed on the overall stop counts, and then on stops where weapons were the suspected charge or rationale for the stop.

Table 6 shows the bivariate correlations—the correlation between two variables—among these predictors and the outcome variables.[152] Correlations were statistically significant and in the predicted directions for stops overall and stops involving non-white

---

150. One could also argue that a higher stop rate for one group may indicate "under-stops" of other groups, or a reluctance to stop more often persons of one race or another. That is an unlikely explanation, however, since the OAG Report shows that the racial distribution of stops were consistent across precincts and stable over the fifteen months. *See* OAG REPORT, *supra* note 5, at 92-110. It is unlikely that the pattern of under-documentation or depressed stop rates for whites would remain so consistent across the NYPD's many precincts and neighborhoods.

151. OAG REPORT, *supra* note 5, at tbl.I.C.1.

152. For example, stop rates for whites were negatively correlated with vacancy rates, concentrations of public assistance recipients, and housing units with broken windows.

TABLE 6. CORRELATION MATRIX (PEARSON R, P)

	Total Arrests	% in Public Housing	Vacancy Rate	% Units with Broken Windows	% Receiving Public Assistance	Racial Fragmentation	Mobility	% Immigrants
ALL STOPS								
Stops - All	.707**	.474**	.397**	.461**	.573***	.082	-.039	.418**
Stops - Blacks	.582***	.361**	.477**	.423**	.474***	-.120	-.154	.259
Stops - Hispanics	.481**	.388**	.147	.337*	.502***	.236	.142	.418**
Stops - Whites	-.107	-.155	-.337*	-.344*	-.435***	.207	.025	-.033
Stops - Other	.098	.024	-.201	-.136	-.219	.371**	.009	-.126
WEAPONS								
Stops - All	.645**	.449**	.460**	.514***	.664***	-.017	-.124	.336*
Stops - Blacks	.509***	.321*	.462**	.425***	.495***	-.157	-.201	.169
Stops - Hispanics	.518**	.447***	.255	.429***	.641***	.185	.069	.451**
Stops - Whites	.052	-.094	-.244	-.204	-.230	.200	-.015	.015
Stops - Other	.223	-.008	-.110	-.065	-.076	.316*	.080	-.092

* $p < .05$
** $p < .01$
*** $p < .001$

suspects. Stops involving whites either were not correlated with the disorder or disorganization variables, or were correlated negatively with disorganization variables.[153]

Results of multivariate tests of the relative contributions of crime, disorder, and disorganization to stop counts are shown in Table 7. A fixed effects Poisson regression analysis was used, with predictors from each of these three domains.[154] The model estimates the expected value of the number of events in relation to the causal factors and other explanatory variables of interest. The question in this analysis is whether the count of events (stops) in an area (sub-borough) is predicted by factors that might influence these events (arrest rates, social disorganization variables, and physical disorder variables). The baseline model tests the hypothesis that the race-specific stop count is proportional to the number of arrests in the area. The full model assesses whether factors beyond the arrest count predict the stop count in the area.

---

153. Overall, whites in New York City live in neighborhoods that are marked by the absence of social isolation or economic deprivation, as well as neighborhoods with lower crime rates. *See, e.g.*, JOHN MOLLENKOPF & MANUAL CASTELLS, DUAL CITY: RESTRUCTURING NEW YORK 29-31, 304-05 (1991). However, the correlation of stops of whites and crime rates in the neighborhood were not statistically significant. This may reflect the fact that whites often were stopped when they were observed in non-white neighborhoods, usually on suspicion of drugs. *Id.* This illustrates the "racial incongruity" source of disparity, where a stop is triggered by a racial "mismatch" of a person of one color moving through a neighborhood with population dominated by persons of another color. In the case of whites in non-white neighborhoods, it is often on suspicion of drug buying or possession. When black or Hispanic suspects are stopped in predominantly minority neighborhoods, it often is on suspicion of violence or weapons crimes. OAG REPORT, *supra* note 5, at 126-28, and tbl.I.C.1.

154. P. McCULLAGH & J. NELDER, GENERALIZED LINEAR MODELS 193-08 (1989); WILLIAM H. GREENE, ECONOMETRIC ANALYSIS (2d ed. 1993); PETER KENNEDY, A GUIDE TO ECONOMETRICS (3d ed. 1994). Poisson regression is an ideal method to analyze factors that predict counts of events, and determining the relationship of these counts to a set of explanatory or predictive variables. The loglinear Poisson model is the one utilized for these analyses. Standard errors are corrected for overdispersion.

TABLE 7. POISSON REGRESSION OF RACE-SPECIFIC STOPS FOR ALL STOPS AND WEAPONS STOPS ONLY [T, P(T)]

	All Stops				Weapons Stops			
	All Suspects	Black Suspects	Hispanic Suspects	White Suspects	All Suspects	Black Suspects	Hispanic Suspects	White Suspects
Intercept	12.71***	7.74***	3.47**	6.36***	8.86***	6.51***	2.18*	4.86***
1997 Arrests	4.61***	3.24**	3.16**	.81	4.20***	3.17**	3.79***	1.41
% in Public Housing	.30	.01	.28	.95	-.80	-.43	-.68	.16
Vacancy Rate	-1.21	.88	-3.73***	-.94	-.80	.80	-3.92***	-1.08
% Broken Windows	.90	-.71	2.09*	-.49	.45	-.83	2.20*	-.26
% Public Assistance	2.54*	1.55	3.50**	-2.09*	3.97***	2.24*	5.67***	-.79
Racial Fragmentation	1.72	-.11	2.92**	1.01	1.14	-.35	3.77***	1.12
Residential Mobility	-.61	-1.44	1.66	-.23	-1.38	-1.80	.96	-.61
% Immigrant	.05	-.56	1.26	.42	-.46	-.99	1.30	.31
-2 Log Likelihood	117.1	172.5	163.3	166.7	147.4	190.7	165.6	166.1
Model Chi-Square	16431.4	27870.4	12198.4	5281.7	12888.2	18624.2	4698.5	1542.9

*   p < .05
**   p < .01
*** p < .001

The results confirm the claim that the arrest rate predicts both total stops and weapons stops in the sub-boroughs. Arrests are a significant predictor of the total number of stops, the total number of weapons stops, and both total and weapons stops for black and Hispanic suspects. However, arrests fail to predict stops for whites. In part, this may reflect the low rate of stops of whites, or the heterogeneity of the locations of white stops. That is, stops of whites may include both "racial mismatch" stops of whites in non-white areas where crime rates may be elevated, but other types of stops occur as well, most in neighborhoods of varying crime rates. Some may simply be based on descriptions from complainants, and others based on the reasonable suspicion grounds articulated in *Terry*.

Crime rates *should* predict stop rates, and should take into account any differences by race in the likelihood that a citizen should be stopped relative to his or her propensity for crime commission. However, when factors other than crime rates affect stops, we attribute these additional factors to policy, or to other tacit assumptions about race, neighborhoods, and criminality. Table 7 shows that for stops overall, factors other than crime in the neighborhood predict the stop counts. For all suspects, after controlling for crime, stops within the sub-boroughs were predicted by their poverty rates. Accordingly, policing in the city's neighborhoods appears to reflect the economic status of people rather than the physical condition of its buildings.

When race-specific stop counts are considered, both disorder and disorganization variables predict stop counts for Hispanics, but not for blacks. The concentration of dwellings with broken windows, low vacancy rates, high concentration of persons in public housing, and racial heterogeneity all predict the stop count for Hispanics. The diversity of this pattern of predictors for Hispanics reflects the heterogeneity of residential patterns and socio-economic factors for Hispanics. For whites, stops are not predicted by crime, but instead are predicted by the absence of poverty. Again, this reflects the tendency for whites to live in areas that although not necessarily affluent, are less likely to be poor.

Finally, Table 7 shows a different picture for weapons stops. For weapons stops of all suspects generally and specifically of black suspects, poverty rates predicted stop counts, after controlling for crime. As above, policing weapons is concentrated in poor neighborhoods. Stop and frisk activity targeted at weapons seems focused on the economic status of people in neighborhoods, not the physical condition of their buildings. For stops of Hispanic suspects, weapons stops were predicted by both disorder and disorganization variables.

These patterns suggest that stop and frisk strategies have departed from their original Broken Windows underpinnings, and more closely resemble policing of poor people in poor places. How the policy in action evolved so far from its complex and nuanced theoretical origins is a potentially important tale. It is important to understand whether and how race became a marker of increased risk of criminality in this hothouse policy context, the ways in which race interacted with the social organization of policing to produce greater intensity of enforcement and over-enforcement against minority citizens, and the cultural and political dynamics that allow the conflation of race, poverty, and disorder in policing policy. These lessons await a different research paradigm, focused on the hot cognitions of police-citizen interactions, and the social contexts in which these events unfold.

IV. SOCIAL NORMS AND AGGRESSIVE POLICING

In New York, the application of Broken Windows theories through OMP strategies and stop and frisk tactics produced a style of racial policing with stigmatizing effects on minority communities. In fact, the implemented strategy departed sharply from the original design of Broken Windows theory, focusing more on the consequences of broken windows than their causes. The strategy as implemented was intensified surveillance and proactive engagement with citizens under a broad standard of "reasonable suspicion." The emphasis on persons rather than place, and the racial demography of places where OMP was most intense and active, suggest that the cues to which police responded were primarily tied to race as well as places that are defined by race. Not only is this a long way from Broken Windows theory, but it invites constitutional problems that can further distance police from minority citizens.[155] The drift from engagement with community in the co-production of security reflects two different dimensions of social norms, dimensions of both community and organization.

---

155. *See generally* OAG REPORT, *supra* note 5, at 15-44 (discussing Fourth and Fourteenth Amendment issues related to stop and frisk activity and racial profiling, respectively); Garrett, *supra* note 7, at 1829-34 (discussing equal protection issues in racial profiling cases).

A. Social Norms and Aggressive Policing Revisited

Although stop and frisk tactics likely contributed to the crime decline in New York, the precise contribution of these tactics is contested.[156] But there also is little doubt that there were social costs from the crackdown on crime that may compromise the original intent to redirect and rebuild social norms.[157] If the mechanism of decline is search, surveillance, and aggressive misdemeanor arrests, there is no causal path to declining crime that runs through order and social norms. As Harcourt observed, these efforts "have little to do with fixing broken windows and much more to do with arresting window breakers—or persons who look like they might break windows, or . . . strangers . . . or outsiders."[158]

The social norms approach underlying Broken Windows theory required that the cues of crime be removed and replaced with alternative cues that signaled order and social regulation. In the causal dynamic hypothesized by the theory, citizens engaged with police to enforce norms of orderliness, conveying a social meaning that influenced behavior of citizens in the orderly milieu.[159]

This construction of social control comports well with the dynamics of collective efficacy discussed by Sampson, Raudenbush, and Earls.[160] Citizen participation in the dynamics of informal social control, such as collective supervision of teenagers and citizen interventions in low-level crimes, are manifestations of the neigh-

---

156. Fagan et al., *supra* note 36, at 1322 (crediting the decline in gun violence in part to "gun-oriented policing" but acknowledging multiple causation by other social factors); Waldeck, *supra* note 19, at 1283-84 (citation omitted) (suggesting that the stop and frisk tactics produced a crackdown that deterred many from carrying weapons or drugs); Harcourt, *supra* note 19, at 339-40 (claiming that the huge increase in misdemeanor arrests under OMP produced a surveillance effect that depressed crime rates). *But see generally* KARMEN, *supra* note 36 (citing interactions among multiple causes for the crime decline that complicated attribution of effects to any single cause).

157. *See generally* Tom R. Tyler, *Public trust and confidence in legal authorities: What do people want from the law and legal institutions?, in* BEHAVIORAL SCIENCE AND THE LAW (forthcoming) (arguing that public views are primarily shaped by evaluating the fairness of police and court procedures). Neighborhood residents in high crime neighborhood often express satisfaction with the lowered crime rate, but greater distrust of police when aggressive stop, search, and arrest tactics are used. OAG REPORT, *supra* note 5, at 74-87.

158. Harcourt, *supra* note 19, at 342.

159. Kahan, *supra* note 36, at 2488; Meares & Kahan, *supra* note 26, at 823.

160. Sampson & Raudenbush, *supra* note 20, at 611-612 (discussing the link between disorder and "collective efficacy"); *see also* Robert J. Sampson et al., *supra* note 79, at 919-21 (showing evidence that crime rates fluctuate according to the neighborhood's collective efficacy, independent of poverty, racial composition, and other socio-demographic factors).

borhood's "collective efficacy" that reduces crime and disorder.[161] Collective behavior of this type may involve citizen-police interactions, but often these are citizen-initiated efforts, such as "phone trees" among residents to call police and report either physical or social disorder, citizen demands to enforce housing codes to rid neighborhoods of crack houses, advocacy in court proceedings for substantive punishment for chronic disorder offenders, and collective political activity on zoning and licensing.[162] However, neither collective efficacy nor social capital is likely to be increased by policing tactics that rely almost exclusively on stopping, searching, and arresting people. Wilson and Kelling, in the original *Broken Windows* essay, did not imagine a scenario where aggressive policing—in the absence of interaction with community groups or social agencies—would create enduring forms of social interaction by citizens to prevent and control crime.[163]

The incentives for people to engage with legal actors in social regulation and the co-production of security may lie in their evaluations of their treatment by the police. Fairness and crackdowns may be inconsistent, but at least citizens know they are tradeoffs. Recent work by Tom Tyler and colleagues in a survey of residents in three Oakland, California neighborhoods suggests that citizens' evaluations of legal actors are not linked to the outcomes of their court cases or interactions with police, or on the crime rate in their neighborhood.[164] They focus instead on the fairness of their treatment from those authorities.[165] Ronald Weitzer reaches the same conclusion in a survey of residents of three neighborhoods in Washington, D.C.[166] He reports contrasting evaluations of police services in two predominantly black neighborhoods. Proactive po-

---

161. Sampson & Raudenbush, *supra* note 20, at 612.

162. *Id.*

163. The original Broken Windows theory recognized that a disorder-focused policing strategy would "only be effective if applied in conjunction with a wide variety of other police tactics" and "pursued in partnership with . . . other social agencies." Waldeck, *supra* note 19, at 1270 (citation omitted). Waldeck shows that the social norms and tactics suggested by the original Broken Windows theory diverged sharply from the traditional social norms of policing as "crime-fighters" where the officer's "basic business" is arresting offenders. *Id.*; *see* George L. Kelling, *Toward New Images of Policing: Herman Goldstein's Problem-oriented Policing*, 17 LAW & SOC. INQUIRY 539, 540 (1992).

164. TYLER, *supra* note 157. Tyler also notes that some judgments are made on vicarious experiences of neighbors and friends, an illustration of the importance of linked fate. *Id.*

165. *Id.*

166. Ronald Weitzer, *Racialized Policing: Residents' Perceptions in Three Neighborhoods*, 34 LAW & SOC'Y REV. 129, 150-52 (2000).

licing of residents of a poor, high crime neighborhood elicited less favorable reactions to police than did the more reactive and respectful treatment of citizens in an "orderly" middle-class neighborhood.[167]

Such empirical findings suggest the viability and importance of an approach to social regulation based on procedural fairness. Procedural fairness—or better treatment—promotes greater trust and confidence in the law, and higher rates of compliance.[168]

These perceptions of law and legal actors have important implications about popular attributions of legitimacy to law. People who view the law as illegitimate are less likely to obey it, and people who view police officers and judges as lacking in legitimacy are less likely to follow their directives.[169] Although the law is based on the implicit or explicit threat of sanctioning for wrongdoing, the legal system depends heavily on voluntary compliance from most citizens to set and enforce norms, and to engage with the police in social control. Hence, lower levels of legitimacy make social regulation more costly and difficult, both materially and politically. The police depend heavily on the voluntary cooperation of citizens to fight crime. Citizens report crime and criminals, informally help to police their neighborhoods, and aid the courts as jurors and witnesses. Without these cooperative acts from the public, the police risk being seen as an intrusive force imposing order. And without these acts, the meaning of order becomes detached from its social basis and loses its moral weight to influence others in the community.

A social norms approach would invite policing of public order laws in the context of corresponding and contemporaneous extra-legal social initiatives aimed at the same or parallel problems. These efforts reflect a more complex view of the interaction of crime and disorder, one that recognizes their spurious relationship to broader underlying social and physical conditions within neighborhoods. The legitimacy of the law benefits from the simultane-

---

167. *Id.* at 151. Weitzer's findings stand Broken Windows theory on its head by suggesting that the police may be reacting to the visible cues of crime and disorder, not just would-be criminals who might journey to a disorderly neighborhood to take advantage of crime opportunities. Weitzer's findings suggest that in neighborhoods with visible signs of disorder, police react with indiscriminate and widespread patterns of aggressive stops and interdiction of citizens.

168. Tom R. Tyler, Why People Obey the Law 172-73 (1990).

169. *Id.* at 172; Robert J. Sampson & Dawn Jeglum Bartusch, *Legal Cynicism and (Subcultural?) Tolerance of Deviance: The Neighborhood Context of Racial Differences*, 32 Law & Soc'y Rev. 777, 793-800 (1998); Tom R. Tyler et al., Social Justice in a Diverse Society 86 (1997).

ous and aligned actions of citizens and legal actors to promote social norms. While OMP approaches might promote a temporary reduction of crime through suppression, a legitimacy-focused approach promotes construction of social networks that integrate community-level social processes with the regulation of crime and disorder.

B. Organizational Norms

Explanations of the importance of race in police decision making—up and down the hierarchy within police organizations—focus on both the occupational culture and social norms of policing.[170] Although the empirical literature on police "subculture" offers inconsistent evidence of generalizable attitudes and beliefs, several studies show that the dynamics and structure of the police workplace may work to reinforce social (behavioral) norms, perceptions, and beliefs.[171] The separation of the policing and non-policing worlds is widely acknowledged, even in the era of reform and innovation.[172] The insularity of the police workplace leads to a closed system of ideas, a reluctance to question the statements or actions of fellow officers, and "matter of fact prejudices" that are reinforced through customs, rituals, and a shared language.[173] If the workplace is where citizens "acquire 'social capital' . . . and develop ties of empathy and solidarity with their fellow citizens,"[174] then the workplace may be the appropriate locus for efforts to change social norms supporting racial policing.

---

170. *See e.g.*, STATE POLICE REVIEW TEAM, *supra* note 6, at 33-34 (1999). *See generally* Jeffrey Goldberg, *supra* note 6; OAG REPORT, *supra* note 5, at Ch. III, Part III (discussing "Police Attitudes Toward Stop and Frisk"). "A recent survey of 650 Los Angeles Police Department officers found that 25% felt that racial bias (prejudice) on the part of officers toward minority citizens currently exists and contributes to a negative interaction between police and the community." REPORT OF THE INDEPENDENT COMMISSION ON THE LOS ANGELES POLICE DEPARTMENT 69 (1991). *But see* Steve Herbert, *Police Subculture Reconsidered*, 36 CRIMINOLOGY 343, 344 (1998) (claiming that norms within police departments are influenced by bureaucratic structures).

171. *See generally* BITTNER, *supra* note 102; ANTHONY V. BOUZA, THE POLICE MYSTIQUE: AN INSIDER'S LOOK AT COPS, CRIME AND THE CRIMINAL JUSTICE SYSTEM 6-7 (1990).

172. BITTNER, *supra* note 102, at 11; *see also* JEROME H. SKOLNICK & JAMES J. FYFE, ABOVE THE LAW: POLICE AND THE EXCESSIVE USE OF FORCE 242 (1993) (citation omitted).

173. POLICING: A VIEW FROM THE STREET 267-70 (Peter K. Manning & John Van Maanen, eds., 1978).

174. Cynthia L. Estlund, *Working Together: The Workplace, Civil Society, and the Law*, 89 GEORGETOWN L. REV. 1, 4 (2000) (describing the workplace as performing crucial functions of the civil society including fostering communication, connectedness, and empathy among diverse individuals).

The skewed version of Broken Windows theory implemented by the NYPD reinforced the crime-fighting image of policing rather than the alternative norms about alternative solutions to crime problems developed carefully in other community-policing models.[175] The "crime fighting" image included stereotypes of citizens and criminals, stereotypes pregnant with racial meaning.[176] After all, the emphasis on social manifestations of disorder, with its demographic and neighborhood correlates, confounded race and disorder, giving rise to broad suspicion of criminal activity and intensified enforcement in minority neighborhoods. Despite recognizing that some citizens were law-abiding and welcomed police presence, the broad reach of stop and frisk policing risked placing many law-abiders under suspicion.

Efforts to reform the police workplace to modify social norms that emphasize race as a risk factor for crime will require complicated and sustained efforts to "admi[t] the workplace into the realm of civil society . . . ."[177] Policing as a workplace is at once both regulated by the state but also subject to hierarchy, rules, coercion, formal sanctions, and restraint. Is social norms theory applicable to changing the everyday logic and rules of policing? The shift in police function to OMP did not significantly modify core police functions, and in turn it was unlikely to modify the occupational "frame of reference" about crime and race.[178] Accordingly, the older social norms that were reinforced by those police functions and rewards that remained intact. How then, to change those norms?[179]

Many efforts to curtail racial profiling have increasingly focused the role of statistics on police stops. Legislators in seven states have passed laws requiring police to keep statistics, and similar legislation is being considered in twenty-one additional states.[180] Rep-

---

175. Waldeck, *supra* note 19, at 1269-70.

176. Thompson, *supra* note 17 at 987-89 (discussing the processes of racial and other stereotyping that may unconsciously influence stop and arrest decision making).

177. Estlund, *supra* note 174, at 5.

178. POLICING: A VIEW FROM THE STREET, *supra* note 173, at 269.

179. Professor Waldeck suggests that changes in police functions, specifically a return to the original intent of community policing and its emphasis on alternatives, will promote changes in social norms based on a different functional definition of policing. Waldeck, *supra* note 19, at 1300-01. But we propose changes that do not necessarily involve substantive modifications in police functions that are disruptive of the structural relationships within police hierarchies and workplaces.

180. An Act Concerning Traffic Stops Statistics, 1999 Conn. Acts 99-198 (Reg. Sess.); An act concerning criminal procedure; relating to the collection of information on traffic stops, 1999 Kan. Sess. Laws 2683; N.C. GEN. STAT. § 114-10 (1999); 2000 Mo. Legis. Serv. 1053 (West); An Act Relating to Motor and Other Vehicles, 1999

502   *FORDHAM URBAN LAW JOURNAL* [Vol. XXVIII

resentative John Conyers, Jr. (D-MI) proposed similar legislation, the National Traffic Stops Statistics Study Act of 1998, which passed unanimously in the U.S. House of Representatives but was rejected in committee by the U.S. Senate.[181] One rationale for the emphasis on data collection is that statistics can lead to transparency in policing,[182] making decisions visible and publicly accountable. Statistics may enable police departments to evaluate their strategies, or assess whether there are disparity costs that come with successes of particular strategies. Data also make officers' actions transparent, making them more accountable for their decisions. As decisions and everyday actions become more democratic, social norms from community stakeholders will be infused into police norms.

But the dynamics of organizational change following the introduction of data raises several challenges. The organizational and democratic structures within which data are introduced, how data-driven facts are evaluated, and how their meaning is interpreted require experimentation to develop open forums for both internal organizational reflection and open policy debates.[183] How information is shared with community stakeholders, whether the agenda for analysis is shared with these groups, and how the findings of data analyses are translated into concrete measures for organizational change are part of a process of community participation that can "civilize" the police workplace through transparency, leading to democratic interactions focused on data-driven facts.[184] The ex-

---

R.I. Pub. Laws 7164; An Act Relating to reporting information on routine traffic enforcement, 1999 Wash. Legis. Serv. S.S.S.B. No. 6683 (SN); *see also* UNIV. OF MINN. LAW SCH., INSTITUTE OF RACE AND POVERTY's RACIAL PROFILING DATA COLLECTION STATUS REPORT (indicating that bills have been introduced in Alabama, Arkansas, Florida, Iowa, Illinois, Indiana, Kansas, Kentucky, Maryland, Massachusetts, New Jersey, New York, Ohio, Oklahoma, Pennsylvania, Rhode Island, South Carolina, Tennessee, Utah, Wisconsin, and Virginia), http://www1.umn.edu/irp/ARB%20.html; Laura Gunderson, *Bill Aims to Track Racial Profiling*, PORTLAND OREGONIAN, Sept. 12, 2000 at B1 (describing proposed bill in Oregon, which following introduction, was hailed by state police and several major local police departments expressing interest in collecting data on stops).

181. *See* H.R. Rep. No. 105-435 (1998). The legislation passed unanimously in the House, but was voted down in the Senate Judiciary Committee due to opposition from police organizations. *E.g.*, Robert Cohen, *Racial profiling Allegations Spur Lawmakers to call for U.S. Study*, THE STAR-LEDGER, Apr. 14, 1999 at 7.

182. For illustrations of the uses of data to assess strategies, see Eric Luna, *Transparent Policing*, 85 IOWA L. REV. 1108, 1167-94 (2000).

183. Susan Sturm & Brandon Garrett. *Moving Beyond Racial Profiling in New Jersey*, PHILA. INQUIRER, Dec. 4, 2000, at A15.

184. Constructing these types of relationships is likely to be contested, even when consent decrees set forth a framework for data collection on stops and monitoring of

tent to which opportunities for community interaction with police
are routinized and institutionalized can break down the insularity
of police social norms at the top and bottom of its hierarchy.

---

statistical trends. National Public Radio ("NPR") reported that civil rights groups including the American Civil Liberties Union of Southern California, and plaintiffs in
prior racial profiling litigation against the Los Angeles Police Department ("LAPD")
have filed motions to be included as monitors in the consent decree involving the
LAPD. *Morning Edition* (Nat'l Pub. Radio broadcast, Dec. 18, 2000) (discussing the
LAPD consent decree described *supra* note 7), *audio clip of report available at* http://
search.npr.org/cf/cmn/cmnps05fm.cfm?SegID=115661. In the wake of statements by
President-elect Bush in the second presidential debate questioning the federal role in
the reform of police departments, these groups are concerned that a court-appointed
federal monitor will not effectively enforce the city's agreement. The NPR report
quotes Mark Rosenbaum, legal director the Southern California ACLU, as stating
that "[t]he decree fences out those individuals who have the greatest interest in the
most conscientious enforcement . . . . " The NPR report quotes attorneys for the City
of Los Angeles, who counter that "involving more people will lead to too much legal
fighting and not improving policing. A federal judge will do the job on enforcing the
court order, so no outside parties are needed." *Id.*

APPENDIX A. DESCRIPTIVE STATISTICS FOR NEIGHBORHOOD VARIABLES

Social Disorganization	Mean	Standard Deviation
% Non-Hispanic White	36.71	28.77
% Hispanic	27.34	20.50
% Black	26.77	27.00
Racial fragmentation	0.51	0.14
% Living in neighborhood < 6 months	25.57	9.32
% Living in residence < 4 years	39.81	4.60
% Immigrants	82.97	10.58
% Households with public assistance	18.88	13.81
% Not in labor force	40.76	8.19
% Worked less than 26 weeks past year	11.54	2.91
% Unemployed since 1997	38.22	8.65
% Education < less than HS graduate	27.69	12.72
Sex ratio: males: females	0.87	0.10
% Female headed households	21.71	10.97
% Population < 15 years old	22.42	6.63
Disorder		
% Dwellings with damaged exterior walls	3.24	17.71
% Dwellings with damaged exterior windows	2.80	19.11
% Dwelling with damaged stairways	5.69	23.17
% Dwellings with broken heat	13.58	34.26
% Dwellings with damaged floors	5.56	22.92
% Reporting any broken windows in neighborhood	8.89	28.46
% Reporting dilapidated buildings in neighborhood	7.78	26.79

[2]

Theorizing policing:
The drama and myth of crime control in the NYPD

PETER K. MANNING
Northeastern University, USA

Abstract

The article uses articles from elite publications to shape a dramaturgically informed case study exploring the decline in the official crime rate in New York City in 1996, the roles of Commissioner Bratton, the media, and the selected experts commenting upon the causes of the decline. The focal period is 1994–6, and includes news of events, such as trials and convictions, related to the events taking place earlier. Victor Turner's (1976) natural history approach organizes the narrative, which sees an established order punctuated by breach, crisis, response and redress, and conciliation or new schism. This analysis requires a brief overview of dramaturgy, the drama of policing, and the centrality of imagery and rhetoric in sustaining police legitimacy and compliance internally. It is argued in conclusion that such analysis may assist in theorizing policing, seeing the dramatic virtues of crime, and the role of media in policing and politics.

Key Words

crime control • crime figures/UCR • dramaturgy • experts • media • spectacles • zero tolerance

Introduction

While police studies is an enduring, well-funded research field in criminology, it is largely descriptive and atheoretical, replete with narrowly defined empirical studies of arrest policies, attitudes toward community policing, and rather anodyne treatments of one segment (white, male, urban, patrol officers) of the occupational culture. Few studies derive propositions from theory, or use systematic criminology to explore police strategies and tactics. The most frequently cited monographs are Trojanowicz and Bucqueroux (1990) and Skogan (1991), and the works of Skolnick, Wilson, and Rubinstein, which were published some 30 years ago. The most frequently cited policing article, arguably Wilson and Kelling's 'Broken Windows' (1982), is a provocative essay published in a non-refereed popular magazine, seasoned with a pinch of research references, and draws loosely and analogically on experimental social psychology. It purports to be a 'theory' but is merely a programmatic statement that has been used to buttress a range of activities by police, from sweeping the homeless away, to arresting people for drinking beer on their front steps. Much police research focuses on citizen–patrol interactions and crime control features of policing, to the exclusion of political and organizational concepts such as compliance, leadership, legitimization, and the socio-political rhetoric and imagery police employ. The political system in which such interactions are cast is left unexplicated. Theorizing police, although considerable organizational research is available (Bordua and Reiss, 1966; Reiss and Bordua, 1966, 1967; Wilson, 1968; Reiss, 1971, 1974, 1992; Brown, 1988; Langworthy and Crank, 1992; Crank, 1994; Fielding, 1995), remains an unfinished task.

Here, I use dramaturgy, a perspective that emphasizes the use of symbols to convey impressions to an audience, and also a natural history method. I use materials drawn largely from the elite media and academic sources to examine the contradictions generated by the myth of command and control in policing.[1] The case study focuses on the crime decline in New York City which media attributed to William Bratton, Commissioner of the NYPD (1994–6), and key events reported in the media, especially those involving police and other political leadership, in New York City from late 1994 until September 1997 (with a few observations prior to 1991 and others through late 2000). Study of the media and experts' analyses, mainly in the *New York Times*, reveals that the reported crime decline in New York City was attributed to the police and Commissioner Bratton, while experts validated a connection between command leadership, strategies, and tactics in the 'war on crime,' and applauded the 'victory,' i.e. reduced crime known to the police. The media and experts elevated the Commissioner to a celebrity only to later reduce his status. Experts and the media functioned to maintain the appearance of police-based crime control, solidify the police mandate, and increase public confidence. The drama's progress falls somewhat naturally into four stages, although these are not tightly chronological (Turner, 1976): (1) Order and its breach; (2) Crisis; (3) Response and redress; and (4) Conciliation (or new schism). I discuss first dramaturgy and the drama of policing before turning to the case study.

Dramaturgy

Dramaturgy examines how symbols (both material and non-material) are selectively presented in order to impress an audience. This implies a temporal dimension and requires an analysis of the relationships between audience and performers. By emphasizing the role of symbols in representation and management of appearances, it links social structure and associated symbols with interactional and collective dynamics (Goffman, 1983; Schwartz and Wagner-Pacifici, 1991).

Dramaturgy best explains social action when analyzing behavior arising under conditions of uncertainty. Uncertainty obtains when the knowledge necessary to decide is either unknowable, unknown, or only partially known. Uncertainty, when present in situations, opens the text of interaction to a range of symbolic representations (signs) whose reference and meaning vary. At times, signs, such as those used in advertising, sport, and political rhetoric, 'float' away, striking only allegorical or emotive responses, and have no syntactical, empirical, or referential properties. Dramaturgy tries to unearth responses to the uncertain, especially in engagements without long history, and to identify means by which uncertainty is reduced or managed. Even secularized societies, when facing threats of sin, crime, death, and disaster, seek myth and ritual to stabilize organizational relations, maintain an organizational hierarchy, and legitimate authority. Expressions of myth and reassertion of normative standards are especially likely to arise during periods of rapid change or discontinuity.

The drama of policing

Organizational analysis of policing suggests inherent tensions exist in managing an inspectorial bureaucracy combining high discretion at the bottom with command distance from events. Research, ethnographic, organizational, and survey-based, reveals the complex character of policing and how shadowy and distorted are perceptions of command when seen from the ground and vice versa (Manning, 1997 [1977]). Most policy directives are inconsistent and often irrelevant in the day-to-day work. On the other hand, directives consistent with the job control and crime-focus of patrol officers are well received since they are redundant messages. The tension between command and deciding on the ground is reflected in the contradictions between the 'paramilitary' imagery (McNamara, 1967), wide latitude to make unreviewed decisions (Reiss, 1974), high ecological dispersion single units (Jermeir and Berkes, 1977), and evidence of the rather creative, subtle management by officers of police–police and police–public interactions (Van Maanen, 1988; Mastrofski et al., 1995).

Because the police are required to act, and often to act quickly, yet cannot fully foresee their actions' consequences, tensions—or unresolved contradictions between actions and the formal public mandate—remain. The tensions reflect fundamental uncertainties in the mandate that require dramaturgical reconciliation. The police, like other occupations, manage uncertainties by manipulating symbols and rhetoric representing their actions as coherent, rational, and co-ordinated. They partake of myth (counterfactual beliefs with an unexamined status), rely on ritual (repeated sequences of action that refer to themselves), and attempt to manage the appearance of consistent control while sustaining internal compliance and loyalty. Sustaining loyalty and legitimacy is a symbolic function, and a fundamental leadership obligation in policing.

Ironically, the police sustain their mandate in part because the un-explained, the accidental and the unexpected arise regularly, not pre-dictably, and they claim responsibility for coping with such risky business. For this reason, they retain slack resources, are somewhat inefficient, and sustain a posture of surveillance and observation over defined territories. These bureaucratic strategies maximize the opportunity to encounter rela-tively rare events, and to respond at the appropriate level with the required resources.

Certainly, it must be accepted that police are perhaps 'naturally' dra-matic in the sense that their actions connote violence, and sacred ideas such as retribution, justice, punishment, and revenge. Visible street policing, the stops, shootings, confrontations, searches, arrests, and chases are exciting, engaging, dangerous, and morally problematic. Police work is fraught with uncertainties, and the police can only partially control events and must be seen as responsive to risk-producing circumstances. Increasingly, the police are known via the media, and are thus subject to 'mediated representa-tions.' The media vacillate in their treatment of the police to suit their notions of 'news,' and thus ripsaw policing with both outrage and un-critical praise, shifting their focus, claims and 'story line' to suit the current ostensive audience interest in 'the news.'

In an organization, imagery is crucial to retaining a market share, public trust, and funding. This is increasingly true in the public sector. The administrative role, like policing itself (Loader, 1997; Manning, 1997 [1977]), is often intended to dramatize rather than to control, and has multifaceted symbolic dimensions (Mastrofski, forthcoming). While the direct influence of Chiefs is limited to a few areas, their capacity to command media attention is considerable. The aim of the police top command is to maintain an organizational image that is sufficiently vague and polyphonic to win public trust, while sustaining multiple definitions of the police role and function. Increasingly, police appoint media officers, issue press releases and hold press conferences, and seek symbiotic relations with the media (Ericson et al., 1989; Mawby, 1996). Yet, as a result of increasing media mobility, speed and intrusiveness, as well as technologies that can be turned against them (e.g. video cameras in patrol cars and jails), the police are more vulnerable than ever to public scrutiny and media scorn.

The myth of policing includes a subtext about command and control, leadership and loyalty, mobilized when untoward events are revealed. Unfortunately, there are few studies of command and control.[2] Police are by design and tradition two-faced. They are bureaucratic organizations, rule-bound, procedure-oriented, and legalistic. They are also highly discretionary, patrimonial bureaux with loyalty to a Chief as a virtue, situationally expedient, and deeply moralistic in practice. The notion that like generals in war, the top command leads, guides, commands, and strategizes while motivating the 'troops,' remains. The command and control myth in policing states implicitly that officers are led, directed, commanded, and evaluated with respect to their capacity to achieve the organization's mission. The mission of police departments is rarely written and is generally unstated. In the last 30 plus years, the primary vehicle through and by which this discipline is achieved is the police communications system (Bordua and Reiss, 1967; Reiss and Bordua, 1967). The notional connection between command and action is revealed in the breach; when punishment is swiftly dealt for known mistakes, errors, and malfeasance.

Media systematically elevate the organizational status of police and police leadership. Chiefs, as with all celebrities, can be glorified and elevated if only then to be seen as scapegoats. Chiefs who succeed do so briefly (the average tenure of a Chief is said to be 2.5 years). In the USA, when a public failure such as a vicious beating or shooting, riot, or death in custody appears, the Chief is the natural target of criticism. He or she embodies and represents the myth and is protected by it. Nevertheless, tragedy, risk, and potential downfall always threaten mythical heroes. The question is, even in a drama, whether the motives are pure and proper, or merely self-serving, and the flaws grand rather than trivial.

The chief, in some respects, must be a politician of considerable skill in the community, as well as in the organization. But since this requires negotiation and bargaining rather than advocacy if success is to be grasped, externally validated political 'success' often produces rancor and distrust within the department.

Tensions remain especially when periodic crises emerge—an unarmed citizen is beaten or shot, evidence of corruption or violent incidents emerges, disorder is publicized, or a large-scale riot is mishandled. Responses to these tensions create new tensions with a new and unpredictable course. While the rhetoric of police–community partnerships and reduced social distance is publicized widely, punitive crime control tactics are more widely adopted (Kraska and Kappeler, 1997). In New York City, as I will proceed to argue, public rhetoric, media co-operation, and crime reduction produced an epiphany. This high point was briefly realized and then eroded by subsequent events.

The NYPD battles crime

The NYPD has long been characterized as a bureaucratic dinosaur, a red-tape morass, clogged with paperwork, top heavy with ambitious police-politicians, and barely able to stem unending, uncontrollable crime waves (Daley, 1971; Murphy and Plate, 1977). Its crime statistics were dubious, dated and slow to be produced, and done laboriously by hand (*New York Times*, 12 December 1997). The 'thin blue line' was not only seen as corrupt and violent, it was intractable, unionized, traditionally focused on job control. It outspokenly defended working officers and attacked and demonstrated against Mayors and Chiefs. Since the early 1970s, it has seen periodic scandals involving bribery, corruption, and excessive force (Kappeler et al., 1997) and been subject to no less than three major investigations (Knapp, 1972; Zuccotti, 1984; Mollen Commission, 1994).

Although gradual change had been underway in the NYPD since perhaps the 1970s under Commissioner Murphy (Silverman, 1999: 21–65), the negative imagery was transformed, largely by media attention to Bratton, his 'spin skills,' and use of the media. He understood their preoccupation with rare, exceptional, and thus 'newsworthy,' events. Other factors were present: the support of the Mayor, increased resources, and a national decline in crime. To summarize briefly the narrative, a tensely moving four-act drama, it has an opening, a breach, response, and then (renewed) schism or conciliation. Discussion of the four acts or stages organizes the following narrative. They are analytic divisions, rather than simply chronological.

Order and its breach

An order is established   The opening events occurred in 1990. Lee Brown, formerly Chief in Atlanta and Houston, was named NYPD Commissioner by Mayor David Dinkins. He began in New York City a program of 'community policing,' based on his well-publicized efforts in Houston that had received academic praise. His plan included hiring 5000 more officers (Kelling and Coles, 1997: 138). In April 1990 William Bratton, later to become Commissioner of the Boston Police in 1993, was hired to head the New York Transit Police. He undertook a reform of the Transit Police, emphasizing officer morale, equipment, including issuing 9mm guns and urging 'control of the subways.'

A riot in the Crown Heights section of New York in August 1992 was sparked after a car in a motorcade of Lubovitcher Jews ran down and killed a black child. Rioting by blacks ensued and a young Hasidic scholar was stabbed fatally. Race and religion were intertwined and led to charges that the Mayor had not provided adequate police protection (Silverman, 1999: 76–9). The police failure to control the riot, when combined with their reticence and tactical mistakes, was widely criticized by an investigative Commission. Mayor Dinkins, and the newly named Police Commissioner Raymond Kelley (Dinkins had replaced Lee Brown as Commissioner in 1992), admitted mistakes and apologized. The riot, subsequent acquittal of the accused murderer, and a civil suit by the Lubivitcher community claiming their civil liberties had been violated, as well as police and public demonstrations (by black and Jewish groups), sustained the issue for more than a year and shaped the fall Mayoral campaign. Dinkins' handling of the riot played a role in his subsequent defeat by Guiliani, a former federal prosecutor (Jackall, 1997: 254–84) who campaigned on crime control.

Shortly after winning the election, Guiliani hired William Bratton as Police Commissioner. Bratton, in turn, promised the Mayor a decrease in crime (Bratton with Knobler, 1998: 12). This marked a shift from Commissioner Brown's stated policy of community policing to a crime control model. Bratton's crime-fighting tactics, combined with a rhetorical commitment to 'community policing' (Kelling and Coles, 1997: 145), had attained recognition when he headed the New York City Transit Police. Bratton, with consultants from the Police Foundation and Harvard's Kennedy School, now focused the Department on crime reduction (Bratton with Knobler, 1998: 249–55).

Policing now was defined as 'crime fighting,' in the name of quality of life, and was viewed by top command in the NYPD as a war, and the strategy, itself a military term, was described by militaristic metaphors, those which make social complexity a matter of winning or losing, and eradication of the 'loser' the aim rather than compromise and non-exclusive outcomes. While the 'broken windows' perspective made arrest a last solution, absent changes in social disorder, arrest was elevated in the NYPD to its central weapon in the war against 'street crime' (Fagan and Davies, 2001). Zero tolerance, a vague undefined label for controlling visible street activities, assumes making arrests for misdemeanors reduces more serious crime. It uses law tactically. (It has been repeatedly challenged by civil libertarians and defended by Kelling and Coles, 1997: 229–34.) 'Zero tolerance' crime-control tactics, encouraged and supported by Bratton (Kelling and Coles, 1997: 146; Bratton with Knobler, 1998), were fused with a rhetorical strategy called 'taking back the streets,' a war-tinged metaphor following the 'broken windows' theory (Kelling and Coles, 1997: 14–16). The code word, 'zero tolerance' was combined with another slang term, 'in your face policing,' which meant the intrusive questioning of people on the street for such serious crimes as having an open beer on a summer night (Bratton with Knobler, 1998: 229). Bratton did not use this term, and with former Deputy Commissioner Maple (1999a), has consistently urged civility and police accountability without mentioning specifics of how this might be accomplished.

Several important administrative changes were made in the NYPD. According to Kelling and Coles, Bratton '. . . implemented many of the techniques conceived by aggressive CEOs . . . to strategically reposition their organizations' (1997: 144). Bratton's 'reengineering' (Hammer and Champy, 1993), including reassigning or forcing to resign most of the top command staff (Silverman, 1999: 94–5); using focus groups to develop written strategy papers (Bratton with Knobler, 1998: 224–39; Silverman, 1999: 205); marketing the strategies to the Department and the media (Bratton with Knobler, 1998: 280). The media and trade publications emphasized the personal, effective direction of Bratton with the sub-text of

'. . . greater accountability to the community and involvement in solving local problems' (Kelling and Coles, 1997: 145). This accountability theme, echoed in 'op ed' pieces in the *New York Times* (23 February 2000a, 15 June 2000b) directed to his successors, included, unfortunately, no content, detail, or explicit mechanisms.

Field stops and arrests were to include questioning concerning guns and crime-information. Information was to be shared between patrol officers and investigators. Crime mapping and weekly morning 'Compstat' meetings were used to motivate precinct captains to respond to recent trends in official crime figures, disorder, and current problems. These meetings, and related PIM units (pattern identification modules or crime packages), were orchestrated by Jack Maple, former transit officer, now Deputy Commissioner. Maple used crime maps to ensure that the stated principles of the Department, crime intelligence, rapid deployment of officers, effective tactics, and 'relentless' follow-through and assessment, were operative.

It is interesting to note in this context that these emphases, strategies, and buzz-word positioning, suggest that basic police work was not being done at this time—questioning suspects about guns, crimes, and their colleagues' activities, checking for outstanding warrants, entering stops into databases, and being 'arrest'-oriented.

The force was increased by 12,000 officers to over 38,000, including the Transit and Housing Police now merged into the NYPD, an additional 6000 civilians, and now enjoyed an operating budget of some $2.3 billion. It now stands at 41,000 plus (December 2000). The increase in officers in the Street Crimes Unit began at this time: from 138 in 1996 to the present 400 officers, yielding an increase in stops from more than 18,000 to more than 27,000 with no increase in arrests and only 2 per cent of gun stops yielding guns (Toobin, 2000). As a result of these additions to the force, Bratton and top command could assign officers to identified (mapped) clusters of incidents or 'hot spots.' It also appears that officers were urged to make misdemeanor arrests as a way of intelligence gathering, broadening their concerns beyond the immediate encounter.

A short epiphany   After about two years in office, Bratton declared crime reductions for 1995 in all categories on average of 40 per cent plus (homicides were down 56 per cent). The evidence of crime's decline was official data gathered and summarized by precinct sergeants, and entered into computers by headquarters staff from discs delivered weekly from the precincts. Bratton, in a working paper for an NIJ conference (1995), argued that criminologists who claimed crime could not be controlled were wrong (Gottfredson and Hirschi, 1990).[3] This claim was later echoed by others (Kelling and Coles, 1997; Silverman, 1998).[4] Bratton claimed that policing produced or caused these crime reductions, dismissing changes in demography, youth crime, and changes in crack use and its effect on crime rates (especially homicide), and emphasizing instead police efforts in gun control, serving warrants, and making arrests. He explained his commonsense theorizing, the posited link between misdemeanor arrests and crime:

> ... for the year-to-date ending November 12 [1995], the total number of arrests for all criminal offenses in New York City—felonies and mis- demeanors—increased 26.73 per cent over 1993 levels for the comparable period. Arrests for the combined index crimes—all felonies—increased 4.27 per cent. The disparity in these data demonstrate the department's shift from a limiting emphasis on the traditionally 'serious' index offenses committed by adults and toward the strategic enforcement of appropriate and applica- ble laws, and they provide evidence of the efficacy of the 'broken windows' theory. By increasing enforcement (as measured through arrests) for misde- meanor quality-of-life offenses among adults and young people, we were able to achieve enormous reductions in felonies, particularly index crimes.
>
> (Bratton, 1995)

At this point, in the first stage of the drama, the hero, the Commissioner and his loyal and passionate followers, has confronted the rather awesome and mysterious foe, crime, and battles it ferociously to exhaustion. The salience of the hero, the absence of alternative explanations, and the audiences' desire for a 'victory,' suppresses debate about supernumerary heroes, less challenging villains, or more mundane causes of crime's defeat. It also obscures unjust distribution of stops and frisks, the resultant human error, pathos, and misery and alternative consequences of police 'crack- downs' (see Fagan and Davies, 2001 on stops and arrests). This modern hero, unlike a medieval knight, has rational theory rather than God on his side.

A *liminal* period of positive media response with reservations followed the brief epiphany. Following this announcement of the success of the 'war on crime' (based on 1995 figures), the early winter of 1996 was a quiet and happy transitional period. Official figures continued to show crime de- creases through 1998. News featuring crime control in New York City filled major newspapers, such as the *New York Times* and *Washington Post,* and, in due time, journals of opinion such as the (London) *Times Literary Supplement* (Siegel, 1997); the *New York Review of Books* (Lardner, 1997b), and the *New Yorker* magazine (Gladwell, 1996).[5] Brat- ton was pictured on the cover of both *Time* and *Newsweek* in early January 1996. Articles in the national and New York City press documented what journalists viewed as the amazing downward spiral of crime. One article called it a 'miracle' (Lardner, 1997b) without attributing a cause directly, but speculating that Bratton's leadership and tactics were fundamental. The crime decline was generally seen by the media and the social scientists quoted as real and a direct effect of Bratton's policies. The media blitz continued from 1996 through 1998 and even late 1999 when crime figures were again released. Lardner later (1998) wrote a sycophantic review of Bratton's book for the *New York Times.*

Foreshadowing   In April 1996, Bratton resigned amid rumors that he had challenged Guiliani's authority and media hegemony, and was now a political threat. Bratton's biography describes disagreement with the Mayor, especially over his failed 'Juggernaut campaign,' maneuvers designed to sweep the streets clean, take back the neighborhoods, and arrest drug sellers (Bratton with Knobler, 1998: 272–3). One journalist, on the basis of interviews with both of the two contestants, concluded that they had struggled over the control of the police (Klein, 1997). Howard Safir, former Fire Commissioner, was appointed Commissioner over Bratton's choice, John Timoney (Timoney was appointed Police Commissioner of Philadelphia in February 1998). In September 2000 Safir was succeeded by Bernard Kerik.

The continuing crisis

The mood of the media is labile   Anticipating a change in the mood and attention of the media is risky because their aim to entertain and inform has few principled limits. At one moment, a writer was reviewing ecstatically the Kelling-Coles book and a few days later the Louima incident burst across the front pages of the *New York Times*. James Lardner wrote:

> . . . what has been surprising is the relatively benign state of police–community relations . . . New York has been through nothing to compare with, say, the Rodney King incident . . . citizen complaints against the police . . . were down 21 percent through the first five months of 1997, while violent crime continued to fall.
>
> (1997b: 56)

A crisis in the crime control epic arose from several sources. It was in part stimulated by Bratton's resignation, inability to ensure succession to leadership of his clique, and in part by public events that suggested problems with aggressive and violent police street tactics. Much of the crime suppression effort involved massive personnel, heavy questioning, and use of a network of civil regulations and criminal law to harass targeted areas and groups (Bratton with Knobler, 1998: 223–39). Aggressive street tactics focused and do focus police attention on visible minorities in high crime areas (New York State Attorney General's Report, 1998) who are believed to be the source of crime. Arrests for misdemeanors and stops rose during the 1994–6 period (Toobin, 2000), and these were disproportionately of minorities.

The media raise questions   In part, the crisis arose because the media raised questions in their constant search for idols, producing celebrities and elevating them only to seek their destruction. Clearly, the media distort other realities based on research (such as fear and risk, crime events, and the meaning of crime), and create, sustain, and make the news rather than 'report it' (Surette, 1992; Mitroff and Bennis, 1993; Fallows, 1996). Larry

Reibstein reports in *Newsweek* (2 June 1997) a 50 per cent rise in complaints to the Citizen Review Board since 1995, and in September of the same year (7 September) reported a 62 per cent rise in complaints in the same time period. The media signaled a querulous mood in August 1997 when they featured a story about an Irish priest who was assaulted in the subway. Guiliani appeared with him on television, gave him a Yankees cap, and was shown on TV hearing the Father's homily: he forgave those who had slashed his face and robbed him.

Claims paid by the City, *Time* (25 August 1997) revealed, increased from 1992 to 1996 from $13.5 to $32 million. Since 1994, the Civilian Review Board had received over 20,000 complaints, 90 per cent of them from minorities. While these claims and complaints were a product of police actions, prior to and including Bratton's term, they tarnished in retrospect the Commissioner's crime control imagery.

More media response   In late August 1997, the first major event punctuating a crisis appeared. This was the arrest, beating, and torturing of Abner Louima, a black Haitian immigrant, in a precinct after he was arrested outside a Brooklyn nightclub. The *New York Times* reported (16 August 1997) as front page news that Louima had been sodomized by two police officers using the wooden handle of a toilet plunger. He was hospitalized with a damaged colon, lost front teeth, and other injuries.

The media treated this event in the context of the crime control metaphor, suggesting that the beating was represented as an exchange—'the darker side of the zero tolerance doctrine' (*Newsweek*, 1 September 1997). Justin Volpe, an officer convicted with two others of the crime, reportedly said as he raped the prisoner: 'This is Guiliani time, not Dinkins time.'

Treating the crime decline and in events following, journalists orchestrated and played up the story line of police crime control via heroic individual actions (Lardner, 1997a, 1997b), arrests made via good police work, and dramatized police command and control leadership (Anderson, 1997). No one stepped forward, academic or other, to claim the drop in crime was too complex to explain, too subtle and multifaceted to understand, or even produced by forces beyond police control. No one suggested that such tactics had a cost to the city's residents.

Response and redress

The beating of Abner Louima, the publication of the rise in complaints and in settlements, and the Mayor's continued emphasis on 'zero tolerance' and 'quality of life issues,' combined to stimulate a new series of events. These responses were designed to encourage redress and reintegration. Demonstrations and marches to City Hall occurred on 30 March 1997 and in April 1999, and later in December 1999 (protesting Guiliani's policy of arresting the homeless if they refuse to move on. The Mayor named a commission to study police violence (*New York Times*, 21 August 1999) and the Federal Government investigated the Louima case as a possible

violation of civil rights (*New York Times*, 6 March 1999). The results of
these investigations have not been made public (as of December 2000).

While the issue of crime control quieted and the City enjoyed good
publicity, rising tourism, and property values, three officers were tried and
convicted of assaulting Louima (March 1999) and were sentenced in May
1999.

Public opinion outside New York remained favourable. 'Compstat'
meetings, conferences that emphasized accountability for crime, became
known worldwide and diffused to other US cities such as Boston and New
Orleans (the NYPD saw 250 visitors from 25 countries during 1996–7
according to Eli Silverman, 1997b). Adapted by Jack Maple while consult-
ing to the New Orleans department, Compstat-like deployment was used to
'Go get the scumbags' (*Newsweek*, 20 October 1997). The Federal COPS
Agency in 1999 funded a study of the diffusion and impact of Compstat.
NIJ now features a Crime Mapping Center.

Conciliation or schism

After the crisis and response, new rallying points arose, efforts to restore
the status of the police or, on the other hand, to examine the costs of crime
control efforts. Some two years after the Louima beating, other media-
amplified events added to the schism. The NYPD police shot an unarmed
black man, Patrick Descombe, in 1998. This shooting was followed by
another with even greater consequence. An unarmed African immigrant
street peddler, Adalo Diallo, was shot by officers on 4 February 1999. An
international media-driven event exploded. Diallo was shot by four officers
who fired 41 bullets, hitting him with 19. Several penetrated his shoes as he
lay, dead. A garish cartoon cover of the *New Yorker* (8 March 1999)
showed a smiling police officer with a gun standing before a shooting
gallery with the sign '41 shots for 5 cents.' The *New York Times* (28
February 1999) featured a story about immigrants' rising fear of the
NYPD. The Descombe shooting, the beating of Louima, and shooting of
Diallo, like the savaging of Rodney King, became key media events
representing an emerging organizational and political schism now appearing between 'the people' and 'the police.'[6] All four officers charged in the
Diallo case were found innocent of all counts in a jury trial (*New York
Times*, 26 February 2000), with criminologist and former NYPD officer,
James Fyfe, defending the officers' decision as being within standard
procedures.

In this stage, the imagery of crime control orchestrated by a hero was
juxtaposed to the imagery of violence and distress, relying on the media's
massive interests in the bizarre, the rare, and the bloody. Some signs
indicate continuing amelioration of urban stress. Official crime figures were
down in all UCR categories in most big cities and throughout the USA in
the 1990s, and continued to decline through 1999 (*New York Times*, 5
November 1999). The apparent police efficacy in crime control, as with

intractable social problems, is soon swallowed by other news and new fears. The underlying tensions in the city between the white working class and immigrant poor and people of color remained and were symbolized by the public violence during the dramatic series of events.

Spectacle politics

In many respects, the drama of crime control is an example of spectacle politics, as most people in New York City, and certainly those outside of it, only experienced crime via television or news reports. A spectacle is a scene to be viewed, felt, and appreciated, rather than to be understood or explained (Edelman, 1988). This particular drama of crime control was created in part by the media, stimulated by public rhetoric concerning controlling 'disorder,' 'homelessness,' 'squeegee men,' and the mentally ill (Kelling and Coles, 1997: Introduction), and managed by creative use of these ideas by Guiliani and Bratton. These standard police street tactics were, and are, supported by improved intelligence information and deployment. They served, among other things to suppress the powerless and reduce visible deviance, increase complaints and misdemeanor arrests, and play on middle-class citizens' fears of crime and disorder in central urban areas. This aesthetic politics creates a morality play, a play orchestrated later by Mayor Guiliani, in which good and evil are bifurcated, evil is opposed, confronted and hunted, and the 'good' is victorious. Inevitably, the power and appeal of such dramas are, that like fairy tales, they resonate with basic concerns—fear, security, change, 'the other,' and with structural features of life that recycle, reappear, change form and transmorgify, only to remerge. A cycle of challenge and response, rise and fall, salvation and redemption, control and chaos is repeated. But unlike citizens in previous centuries who were entertained by tales and distant echoes of exciting events, we are now confronted within minutes of worldwide news, ritualized and distant, the basis for yet another spectacle.

The media role

The media had no small part in sustaining the reality of, and then shifting perspective to, examining the downside costs of crime reduction. In the winter of 1996, they assumed that the reductions were real, not artifactual, and an undiminished good for the city. In 1997, they contrasted it with rising complaints and the beating of Louima, suggesting that the good, the reported drop in crimes known to the police, and the evil, violence and excess, were a 'trade-off' (*Newsweek*, 1 September 1997). Although the Louima incident was not filmed and shown worldwide as was the Rodney King beating, it has image-making power precisely because of the myth of command and control and the metaphor of crime control had been previously accepted and amplified by the media, and used to create a positive image of the NYPD. In the eyes of the media, the driving force in the drama was 'crime' defined by the police, and visible public or street crime targeted by quick shifts of police personnel, and homicide. The costs to social integration of massive militaristic campaigns, the complexity of and differences between types of crime, even 'violent' crime, were not discussed by the media or experts questioned and quoted. It may have reduced fear of crime and moral panic.[7]

This cyclical drama was not merely the product of a sophisticated, media-wise organization and public acceptance. Experts contributed heavily and repeatedly to the drama at every point: as teachers (at the Kennedy School) of several of the NYPD administrators; as consultants (to the NYPD); as reassuring pundits eager to assume the facts of a 'decline in crime' and offer explanations; and as media-quoted celebrities.

Experts as celebrities

An essential part of modern politics is the manipulation of imagery and the appearance of competence. Celebrities substitute for those with substance and enduring knowledge. Experts' analyses of the causes of the drop in crime were various. Some intellectuals said they were wary of conclusions—James Q. Wilson (Butterfield, 19 August 1997) was the only expert willing from the distance of Los Angeles to say that crime varies. He noted homicides dropped 37 per cent in Los Angeles in a time of organizational stress and reorganization. A sociologist, Richard Moran (quoted in Lardner, 1997a), called Bratton 'lucky,' and the beneficiary of drops in the UCR nationally. All other experts quoted (others may have been asked) accepted the rhetoric of police impact as primary, although they added slight nuances (Dilulio, quoted in the *New York Times*, 19 January 1997). Gladwell (1996—see note 5), for example, quoting criminologists Jeff Fagan (see Fagan et al., 1998) and Alfred Blumstein, suggests that changes in drug markets and perhaps reduced crack cocaine use, demographic shifts (fewer young between 18 and 25), high rates of mortality (including many violent deaths) among urban male cohorts (those most likely to be arrested for crimes), produced a 'tipping point' where high rates began to fall 'naturally.' Two writers (Anderson, 1997; Lardner, 1997a) cited incapacitation as a factor. New York State leads the nation in per capita population in prison, 70 per cent of these (70,000) come from New York City. The incarceration rate nationally quadrupled between 1970 and 1995 (Lardner, 1997). One social scientist (Jackall, 1997: 256–7), after almost three years of fieldwork with the police in Washington Heights, felt that the combination of private security patrols in parks, and sweeping the streets of homeless and 'panhandlers,' may have had a civilizing influence in the subways and parks. Silverman (1999: 6–19) argues that the police were the primary cause of reduced crime, and he dismisses other hypotheses as to cause. In due course, more balanced academic assessments were published (Blumstein and Jacobs, 2000; Fagan and Davies, 2001).

The audiences

Consider now the audiences for these political performances. The hopeful belief in the possibility of crime control, a police theme since J. Edgar Hoover's day, and a constant, variable but enduring, public concern, gives cultural support to 'crime-fighting' achievements. This hope was sustained by the media and emphasized by Bratton while in office. He renewed commitment to crime control (down-played under Commissioner Brown). Kelling and Coles (1997), citing no evidence, claimed that the public was disenchanted with the criminal justice system (p. 254); 911 policing had failed (pp. 89–102); the public demanded that disorder be controlled (p. 36); and people wanted intervention. While the authors caution against supporting a 'siege mentality of the police' (p. 97), and advocate inter-personal skills, this is muted harmony to the 'take back the streets' martial melody. While their views may differ from the published versions, the ideas have been used to rationalize and justify the zero tolerance policies, and they have published no retractions, regrets, or rethinking of their ad-vocacy.

Bratton's performances played to external audiences but also were designed to support officers in the NYPD. He eschewed personal claim for success, pointing to 'team work' (Bratton with Knobler, 1998: 307–9). He did not personally claim responsibility, rather emphasizing his role as leader and motivator (Bratton, 1995). The crime focus played well with the internal audience, the 'troops,' because for several reasons he focused on crime control: making arrests, seizing guns; valuing stops and question-ing; rewarding officers with 9mm guns, uniforms, and cars (as he had done in the Transit Police); and mounting periodic wars on drug dealing areas. Patrol officers, it can be assumed, were enthusiastic about the tactics and focus because they were consistent with their subcultural ideology about how police work should be done. Bratton's overall themes were consistent with traditional policing. A former Chief of San Jose California, a Harvard Ph.D. and former NYPD officer, said: 'They are told they are soldiers in a war . . . in a war, you get atrocities, and that's what this case [Louima] appears to be' (*Time*, 25 August 1997: 38). The pre-emptive and premonitory tactics used in the subways and on the streets against the homeless, the mentally ill, and disorderly (often meaning drunk), the practice associated with the 'broken windows' policy advanced by Kelling and Coles (1997: Chs 4 and 6), and exemplary of NYPD tactics under Bratton, are consistent with police ideology. They have complained that they are 'handcuffed,' by the Miranda warning and the exclusionary rule and that, if 'released,' they can and will con-trol crime. The external audience on the other hand, reached through the media, especially the *New York Times*, also received special atten-tion (Bratton with Knobler, 1998: Ch. 1). His polished approach to the media contrasted with Guiliani's rather abrasive style, and made him a high-profile player in both high (City governance) and low politics (NYPD governance and the internal politics therein).

Tensions and dynamics

There are additional alternative readings of the drama of crime control in the NYPD. These reveal additional tensions and uncertainties, which the crime suppression drama has obscured. These are the counterpoints, or backstage events, that stand in dialectical relationship to events occupying front stage. They await their moment to change places, transform the leading events, and relegate the once key figures in the drama to secondary or supporting status.

Theorizing the decline

Doubtless, the crime control claims by the NYPD (and Kelling and Coles, 1997: 51–56), with media validation, pointed to some valuable changes in the NYPD. Bratton did reorganize and decentralize command to captains at the precinct level. He urged and sanctioned drug arrests by precinct officers (previously restricted to central drug officers). This meant a record number of drug arrests: over 900,000 in the last 10 years (Egan, 19 September 1999). On the other hand, training was unchanged for new recruits and not added for serving officers. No fundamental attention was given to crime prevention, crime causation, or community consultation in training. Given that Commissioner Bratton held office for less than two years, it is difficult to imagine how he reinvented and fundamentally changed the social organization, occupational patrol culture of the NYPD, and/or the habits and practices of offenders and victims in one of the world's largest cities. His policies mirrored the crime-control rhetoric of patrol officers in the city.

These events evidence an orchestrated performance, a drama, a media-amplified spectacle. It was argued that the decline in crime rested on police crime-suppression tactics. Perhaps correctly the police might claim that they do not require an explanation if 'it works.' It matters little to most police that a drop in crime figures, a rise in clearances, or changes disorder result, as long as they can attribute it to their tactics and have media coverage supporting their efforts. Crime-attack and zero tolerance require no theory, fit the conventional street officers' ideology, produce visible scenes and intrusive encounters in public places, and target the weakest and least politically powerful groups for attention.

Although saturation patrol, rapid deployment to street incidents and clusters might temporarily reduce street crimes, the ways in which these assorted patrol tactics alter rates (or absolute numbers) of homicides, rapes, or assault is mysterious. These crimes are insensitive to active police intervention. Street policing has little or no effect on the great bulk of crime, auto thefts and burglaries of cars and dwellings. Tactics have displacement effects, as well as creating shifts in the crime committed by miscreants. Nevertheless, inexplicable fluctuations of specific crimes within the overall rate remain (Young, 1991; Coleman and Moynihan, 1996; Manning, 1997 [1977]: Ch. 7). One hypothesis is that many petty offenders are also felons, have outstanding warrants for their arrest, and that misdemeanor arrests have an incapacitation effect. This could be tested.

The role of police actions in reducing recorded crime remains a cipher because, traditionally, increases in personnel, especially in the short term, tend to increase crimes known to the police (the official UCR definition). Crime suppression feeds into stereotypic notions that the major problem and source of crime is in the streets, committed by people of color and, less importantly, accomplished in corporate board rooms, banks, among politicians and fiduciary agents. Intervention—street sweeps, interrogation, stop and frisk, and saturation patrol, all of which were (and are) used by the NYPD—generally also increases arrests, complaints, and false or mistaken arrests. However, if police actions were aimed at visible social control, reducing scenes and areas worrying to the middle class, then arrests would be avoided, offenses downgraded, felonious drug cases reduced to misdemeanors, and guns seized. Besides criminal sanctions, other forms of control are used: those deemed unworthy being moved along or arrested on violations of civil codes, contempt, or other means; public police cooperating with private police in controlling areas; police working with other city agencies, housing, parks, and welfare, to bring pressure on marginal groups.

Evidentiary questions

What independent evidence supports the crime suppression claim? Recall that the empirical support for the crime control thesis rests on police-created and police-processed data. This question is dealt with minimally by Bratton, Kelling and Coles, and Silverman, and internal research reports (Albrecht, 1998). The urge to sustain and nurture the notion that police can and do control crime was irresistible, in spite of uneven evidence, lack of a theory, and the obvious primacy of other factors (the economy, changes in the law, drug use, composition of social areas (Sampson, Morenoff, and Earls, 1999). What is clear is the increase in stops, arrests, disproportionately of the poor and people of color in poor areas (Fagan and Davies, 2001).

The issue of 'cooking the books,' or shaping crime statistics to suit the police, was mentioned by experts but not explored. Silverman notes in passing, that he does not believe that officials have distorted the crime figures any more recently than in the past (Silverman, 1998: 7). This begs the question of how much lying with statistics went on previously. In general, experts validated the high drama of a rare and significant event, and accepted and augmented the reality of a general decline in crime, something which had not occurred since the 1960s. This gave crime an enduring, aesthetically shaped and palpable reality, and the media had a new 'trend' which in due course they returned to, claiming by late 2000 that all the success, the control of crime, public admiration, and the hard work of the now 41,000 officers was unappreciated, the police underpaid, and suffering low morale (*New York Times,* articles by Kevin Flynn, 25 November 2000b and 26 December 2000c).

Strangely, in connection with this crime blitz and self-promoted success, there has been no discussion of the unreliable nature of police figures.[8] These limitations have been well known by police, academics and journalists for at least 30 years. Consider these. First, the dark figure, which suggests that any changes in reported crime are perhaps doubled by unreported crime revealed in victim surveys, and that reporting figures vary by crime, race, class, and gender. An unreported dark figure of crime remains (Coleman and Moynihan, 1996). All the evidence for some 30 years in this country and in the UK, largely though victim surveys, is that only a small fraction of crime is reported (well under 50 per cent according to that which can be discovered by household surveys). Second, police processing itself, both of calls for service and detective work, shapes and refines citizens' classifications (Ericson, 1982; Nesbary, 1998). Third, once recorded, crime is processed differentially within the criminal justice system. A decreasing fraction is cleared in some fashion, and well under 25 per cent reaches the judicial process (Coleman and Moynihan, 1996). Fourth, it is known that the police–citizen encounter reflects police assessments strongly in non-felony crimes (Black, 1980). In general, there is a long history of police manipulation of statistics (McCleary et al., 1982; Meehan, 1992, 1993); untrustworthy and invalid official crime statistics (Seidman and Couzens, 1974; Chamlin and Kennedy, 1991); and varying accuracy or reporting and recording by category of crime and fluctuations produced by changes in categories or definitions.

Recent developments, including sanctioning a former member of the Transit Police for falsification, and FBI rejection of Philadelphia's crime statistics, do raise reasons to doubt the New York figures (*New York Times*, 3 August 1998). The police have developed traditional means of manipulating crime data officially by changing recording procedures, tightening definitions, reviewing arrests for quality, changing personnel and/or supervision practices in record-keeping and dispatching. They work unofficially through informal and unwritten tacit conventions about receiving information about crime, describing events, evidence and witnesses, identifying and labeling 'suspects,' 'evidence,' 'witnesses' and 'victims,' recording, transcribing, and editing crime reports. This effort is not directed toward increasing the official crime rate, but to reducing its level and seriousness. Evidence in the last three years from Philadelphia, the NYPD, and the Transit Police, as well as Boca Raton, Florida, suggests it is present and operational within policing (Kocieniewski, 28 February 1998, 3 August 1998). The NYPD Commissioner fired a high-ranking officer for manipulating crime data in 1998. Sellin's (1938) rule still holds: the validity of the measure increases as it moves closer to the behavior described. When relying on police data, one relies on second-hand, processed, formatted, stylized material.

No evidence rules out police manipulation of the statistics, a common and well-studied practice. There is no agreed adequate method to compare the variations in official data among large cities. Internal traditions and tacit conventions in recording create subtle time-sensitive variations in crime records (*New York Times*, 3 August 1998). There is no independent validation of crime reports, no internal auditing, and periodic scandals suggest caution in comparing figures across years, across cities, and certainly for cross-national figures.

Let us assume that police data are one estimate of the true or real rate of crime. No independent evidence, from ethnographic studies, victim surveys, self-report studies, records checks or the like, has appeared that speaks to the process. No other measures of 'crime' such as arrests (defined administratively in local departments across the USA), clearances (a ratio of reported to those administratively closed by various means), indictments, convictions, or incidents reported or not to the police according to household or victim surveys are included in any analysis of the crime decline in New York City. To establish firmly the claim of crime reduction, even in official statistics, one would want checks on the validity and reliability of the data-gathering at very least and, ideally, independent sources of data.

Conclusion

There is no systematic theory of the role of police in politics: it is implicit and derivative at best. Police studies focus still on 'street-level' issues. Dramaturgy's value as a perspective is that it reads off public performances as they bear on the politics of mass society, in part shaped by the media through which modern imagery of politics is shaped. Dramaturgical analysis is obligated to interweave events and forms, drama and audience, and explore the ongoing process of meaning-creation as well as micro-interactions or outcomes.

Dramaturgy illuminates the dilemmas of modern command and control. Dependent on the media, yet fearful of their sting, police cautiously adopted visual means of monitoring and defending their own conduct.

The drama of crime control in New York City was socially created and amplified by the media in co-operation with police. Alternative versions and readings are possible which sustain the tension and possibility of new, transformative dramas. This framework can illuminate the actions of police organizations in media-amplified spectacles. The present analysis does suggest the importance of crime as uncertainty. The rise and fall of crime as an issue informs us about the drama of policing because it connotes

uncertainty, a situation in which reassuring dramaturgical presentations are
wanted and needed.

Cast as a drama, the story began around 1991, and is precipitating
events still unfolding. As of late 2000, the cycle of bemoaning the police
and their inefficacy, low morale and, ironically, their putative success, has
begun yet again. A new transformative narrative is taking shape. The
media-driven rise of the NYPD's reputation between 1994 and 1997, with
emphasis on quality of life issues and zero tolerance of disorder and crime
in the City, was significant during Guiliani's terms. This was a counterpoint
to the Mollen Commission's (1994) criticisms and publicity about corruption in 1994. The crime decline had in fact begun some 10 years earlier for
all major crimes in New York City, and the ensuing celebration occurred
with little questioning of its causes. Bratton's leadership, his celebrity status
and magazine-cover presence, were amplified not only by the media, but by
selected quoted experts. Then came a response and a fall from grace.
Questions then arose about police violence against citizens, complaints,
suits and settlements arising, especially as a result of the August 1997–9
controversy over the torture of Louima, and the shooting of Diallo (Berry,
27 February 2000).

Combining the case with a natural history perspective illuminates the
stages and cycles of the crime drama, a fact that is perhaps obvious in a
long-term, elastic, easily manipulated statistic like crimes known to the
police. Some 50 years of criminological research, which has cast severe
doubt on the validity of official police-gathered crime statistics and the
abiding dark figure, occupied no place in the public rhetoric about the
recent well-celebrated demise of crime in New York City. This case study
demonstrates the power of police strategies and tactics augmented by
complicitous experts, used by the media and the police to create and
maintain the appearance of police control of crime, solidify their mandate,
increase public confidence, and claim credit for changes in the quality of life
and tourism in the City.

Many contradictions result from subscribing to the command and
control myth, and its corollary, that police control crime. The police
capacity to eradicate or even shape crime over time and the complementary
notion that top command control and direct officers on the ground to
control the vast range of processes, acts, thoughts, and feelings that are
called 'crime,' is a hopeful administrative fiction. Clearly, when one limits
the denotations of the word 'crime' to that which is observed, reported,
processed, validated, publicized, and made socially real by the police, the
scope of the claim is radically reduced. All forms of crime attack (police
tactics) have short-term effects, are very disruptive of neighborhoods (Rose
and Clear, 1998), and produce unanticipated consequences as well as
frequently displacing crime to other areas. They have sparked protests and
demonstrations in the City. Once adopting a media-orientation, seeking
short-term control of crime, recognizing media amplification of 'news' and
changing audience tastes, police departments are vulnerable to crises

arising from the application of violence to disorder. They are also subject to the fluctuations in crime, especially homicide, that are outside direct police prevention or control.[8]

A drama requires a key theme or focal point; certainly, the object of dramaturgical concern here, a key theme in criminology, is 'crime.' The public and private faces of crime differ. Any discussion of crimes known is a discussion of marginalia in people's lives, but it plays well with the media and fires the public imagination. Crime is a context-based idea, not a thing; it is a representation, a word, a symbol, standing for many things, including vague fears, symbolic villains, threats and assailants, the unknown, generalized anxieties and hopes. It is associated in most people's minds with disorder, incivilities, and urban squalor. It can easily be used to arouse fearful images inconsistent with the banality and property-based nature of crime (auto theft and burglary constituting the vast majority of crimes).

Statistics are shaped, used, manipulated, and presented for social purposes. Theodore Porter suggests that social differentiation and conflict lead to 'trust in numbers' (1992, 1996), and their appearance and use reflect degrees of uncertainty in social relations. Crime statistics were used in this process to reassure and build trust rather than fear. The crime being dramatized in New York City is street crime—the visible delicts of the powerless. Crime is always selectively revealed: dramatized, represented, and articulated in public discourse. Taking back the streets, neighborhood by neighborhood, waging a war on the poor, sad and mad, in known public 'hot spots,' seizing guns and removing the homeless and beggars from the subways, are symbolic representations of one sort of disorder. They were effectively used to illustrate the virtues of middle-class public life style, and remnants of rigid working-class morality.

These illusions of controlling disorder deflect attention from the massive gains in wealth of the top 2 per cent in the USA, and the increasing marginality of the poor. It feeds into stereotypic notions that the major problem and source of crime is in the streets, committed by people of color and, less importantly, accomplished in corporate board rooms, banks, among politicians and fiduciary agents. It further elevates and sanctifies the law in the hands of a vigilant police under courageous leadership, a myth, as the primary resource in creating social order.

Notes

Earlier versions of this article were presented to the Sociology Department at New York University (October 1997) and the Police Foundation (November 1997). I am very grateful to Tracy McGinley who worked diligently to correct my errors, complete the article, and transfer files back and forth from MSU to Northeastern in the early winter of 2001. I also wish to thank Amanda

Robinson for her detailed critique of an earlier draft, the reviewers of this journal for guidance, and Piers Beirne for very helpful editorial suggestions.

1. My evidence consists of files drawn from newspapers, magazines, journal articles, especially from the *New York Times*; Silverman's fieldwork-based book (1999); and NYPD publications on Compstat (Safir, n.d., 1998). I do not claim this is a sample of articles. They are from elite New York and London publications employed as a crude index of media imagery, themes, and use of experts to sustain a 'story line,' or construction of an event or process (Sparks, 1992; Schlesinger and Tumber, 1994).
    A set of papers raising some questions about the decline in crime, focused primarily on the 'zero tolerance' concept rather than the precise workings of it, has been published (Greene, 1999; Innes, 1999; Waldeck, 2000). The most powerful and persuasive work on the impacts of the policing style adapted by the NYPD in the Bratton years through perhaps late 2000, is Jeff Fagan's (Fagan et al., 1998; Fagan and Davies, 2001). The most powerful and consistent empirical evidence that contradicts the ideological spin and misleading claims of 'broken windows' is in the Chicago project headed by Robert Sampson. Based on empirical research in Chicago, it is imaginative, detailed, well analyzed and presented; it is masterful (Sampson, Morenoff and Raudenbusch, 1999, Sampson, Earls and Raudenbusch, 1997 and Sampson, Morenoff and Earls, 1999).
2. This case study illuminates the role of media and politics in policing while recognizing that New York City, like London and Washington, DC, is an exceptional city. It is a high-profile, politically focal, well-resourced city with the USA's largest police force. This should perhaps be treated as an opening and exploratory study, like Wagner-Pacifici's (1994), and its inferences subject to further testing, specification, and elaboration.
3. There is little research on the high politics and leadership decisions of police Chiefs (Hunt and Magneau, 1994; Chatterton and Whitehead, 1997, Mastrofski, forthcoming). Few departments' decision making in connection with community policing have been reported (Sheingold, 1984, 1991; Rosenbaum, 1996; Skogan and Harnett, 1996; Lyons, 1998).
4. Bratton was wrong: some criminologists, namely Lawrence Sherman, on the basis of experimental work in Milwaukee and Minneapolis (1984, 1990, 1991), and James Q. Wilson (1978) in theory, claimed that crime could be controlled. Research by Sherman, Weisburd and associates demonstrates the crime-specific efficacy of the crime-attack model for brief periods (Braga et al., 1999).
5. Reprints of Gladwell's article in the *New Yorker* praising Bratton were circulated by the National Institute of Justice, then headed by Jeremy Travis, a former Deputy Commissioner in the NYPD.
6. The moral drama in the NYPD modifies previous research on moral panics. In the NYPD case, a moral entrepreneur uses reduced crime statistics to emphasize quality of life and fear of crime, to increase public legitimacy, and gain acceptance of the police. It also speaks to the inadequacy of the

labeling–deviancy amplification argument (Young, 1971), because control efforts have not produced more fear, even given media amplification.

7. Dramaturgically, the actual rate of crime is much less important in politics than the belief that crime is down, declining, and under control. This has been interpreted to mean that the city is reaching for a new and vibrant future, has a 'new skyline' (Silverman, 1999), was less crime-ridden, and more attractive to developers, tourists, and investors. Bratton, his media people, Kelling and Coles, the Kennedy School consultants to the NYPD, Silverman, and New York City-based journalists (Butterfield, Gladwell, Lardner, Alter, and *Time* and *Newsweek* editorialists) sustained the myth of command and control, and belief in crime control by direct police intervention.

8. The number of homicides has risen in New York City (Butterfield, *New York Times*, 18 June 2000), by 6 per cent in 1999 and 8.5 per cent by June 2000. The same experts offered plausible ad hoc explanations for why crime had now risen. In an earlier article in the *New York Times*, Blumstein was quoted as saying that homicide is the best indicator of police 'efficiency' because 'It is hard to hide bodies' (3 August 1998). It should be noted that homicide is a rare crime, pursued as diligently as any by police and cleared at a markedly higher rate than other crimes, but is not the crime that creates the greatest workload, leading to pressures for efficiency, (burglary and auto theft are far greater workload factors), is defined differently across the country in practice, is not correlated with crime clearances generally, and is not based in any case on the presence or absence of a 'dead body.' Furthermore such commentary begs the question of what policing is about, what it should produce, and why. These continue to be moot points.

References

ABC News (1997) 'Dateline', 21 August.

Albrecht, James (1997) 'A -45% Reduction in Index Crime: Explaining the Secret to the NYPD's Success', ASC presentation, Washington, DC.

Anderson, D. (1997) 'Why Crime is Down', *New York Times Magazine*, 10 February.

Bai, Matthew and Gregory Beals (1997) 'A Mayor under Siege', *Newsweek*, 5 April.

Barry, Dan (2000) 'Diallo Legacy: Myriad of Questions about the Tactics of Policing the Streets', *New York Times*, 27 February.

Beals, Gregory and Evan Thomas (1996) 'A Crimebuster Falls', *Newsweek*, 6 April.

Beals, Gregory and Matt Bai (1997) 'The Thin Blue Line', *Newsweek*, 1 September.

Becker, H.S. (1963) *Outsiders*. Glencoe: Free Press.

Berger and Luckman (1966) *The Social Construction of Reality*. New York: Doubleday.

Bittner, Egon (1991) *Aspects of Police Work*. Boston, MA: Northeastern.

Black, Donald (1982) *Manners and Customs of the Police*. New York: Academic Press.

Blumstein, Alfred and J. Walthall (eds) (2000) *The Crime Drop in America*. New York: CUP.

Bordua, David and Albert J. Reiss, Jr (1966) 'Command, Control and Charisma: Reflections on Police Bureaucracy', *AJS* 72: 68–76.

Bordua, David and Albert J. Reiss, Jr (1967) 'Law Enforcement', in P. Lazarsfeld, W.J. Sewell and H. Wilensky (eds) *The Uses of Sociology*, pp. 275–303. New York: Basic Books.

Bottoms, Anthony and Paul Wiles (1997) 'Environmental Criminology', in M. Maguire, R. Morgan and R. Reiner (eds) *The Oxford Handbook of Criminology*, pp. 305–59. Oxford: Oxford University Press.

Braga, A. et al. (1999) 'Problem-oriented Policing in Violent Crime Places: A Randomized Controlled Experiment', *Criminology* 37: 541–80.

Bratton, William (1995) 'Great Expectations: How Higher Expectations for Police Departments can Lead to a Decrease in Crime', paper given at NIJ Conference 'Measuring What Matters', Washington, DC, November.

Bratton, William (1998) 'Crime is Down in New York City: Blame the Police', in *Zero Tolerance: Policing a Free Society*, 2nd edn. London: Institute for Economic Affairs.

Bratton, William (2000) 'Why Lowering Crime Did Not Raise Trust', op ed, *New York Times*, 23 February.

Bratton, William (2000) 'The Vigilance that Can't Let Up', op ed, *New York Times*, 15 June.

Bratton, William with Peter Knobler (1998) *Turnaround*. New York: Random House.

Brown, M. (1988) *Working the Street*. New York: Russell Sage.

Butterfield, Fox (1997) 'Crime Fighter's About-Face', *New York Times*, 19 August.

Butterfield, Fox (1998) 'As Crime Falls, Pressure Rises to Alter Data', *New York Times*, 3 August.

Butterfield, Fox (2000) 'Rising Homicide Rate Raises Official Concerns', *New York Times*, 18 June.

Chamlin, M. and M.B. Kennedy (1991) 'The Impact of the Wilson Administration on Economic Crime Rates', *Journal of Quantitative Criminology* 7.

Chan, Janet (1997) *Changing Police Culture*. Melbourne: CUP Australia.

Chatterton, M. and P. Whitehead (1997) 'Strategic Management', unpublished report to British Home Office.

Cohen, Stan (1973) *Folk Devils and Moral Panics*. London.

Coleman, Clive and J. Moynihan (1996) *Understanding Crime Data*. Milton Keynes: Open University Press.

Crank, John (1994) 'Watchman and Community: Myth and Institutionalization in Policing', *Law and Society Review* 28: 325–51.

Crank, John P. and R. Langworthy (1992) 'An Institutional Perspective on Policing', *Journal of Criminal Law and Criminology* 83: 338–63.

Czarniwaska, B. (1997) *The Narrative Approach to Organization*. Chicago, IL: University of Chicago Press.

Daley, Robert (1971) *Target Blue*. New York: Dell.

Edelman, Murray (1966) *The Symbolic Uses of Politics*. Urbana, IL: University of Illinois Press.

Edelman, Murray (1988) *Constructing the Political Spectacle*. Chicago, IL: University of Chicago Press.

Egan, Timothy (1999) 'A Drug Ran its Course and then Hid with its Users', *New York Times*, 19 September.

Ericson, Richard (1982) *Making Crime*. Toronto: Butterworths.

Ericson, Richard and Kevin Haggerty (1997) *Policing the Risk Society*. Toronto: University of Toronto Press.

Ericson, Richard, J. Chan and P. Baranek (1989) *Negotiating Control*. Toronto: University of Toronto Press.

Fagan, Jeffrey, F. Zimring and J. Kim (1998) 'Declining Homicide in New York City', *Journal of Criminal Law and Criminology*.

Fagan, Jeffrey and Garth Davies (2001) 'Street Stops and Broken Windows: Terry, Race and Disorder in New York City', *Fordham Urban Law Review* 28(4): 457–504.

Fallows, James (1996) *Breaking the News*. New York: Pantheon.

Farley, Christopher John (1997) 'A Beating in Brooklyn', *Newsweek*, 25 August.

Fielding, Nigel (1995) *Community Policing*. Oxford: Clarendon.

Flynn, Kevin (1999a) 'Civilian Complaints Said to be Slighted by NY Police', *New York Times*, 9 October.

Flynn, Kevin (1999b) 'Rebound in Murder Rate Puzzling New York Officials', *New York Times*, 5 November.

Flynn, Kevin (1999c) 'State Cites Racial Inequality in New York Police Searches' (summary of the Attorney General of New York's Report), *New York Times*, 1 December.

Flynn, Kevin (1999d) 'Officers' Credibility to be on Trial in Case over Shooting of Immigrant', *New York Times*, 10 December.

Flynn, Kevin (2000a) '9 Police Officers Face Disciplinary Action after Inquiry in Central Park Attacks', *New York Times*, 4 July.

Flynn, Kevin (2000b) 'Behind the Success Story, a Vulnerable Police Force', *New York Times*, 25 November.

Flynn, Kevin (2000c) 'Feeling Scorn on the Beat and Pressure from Above', *New York Times*, 25 December.

Forst, Brian and P.K. Manning (1999) *The Privatization of Policing: Two Views*. Washington, DC: Georgetown University Press.

Gitlin, T. (1980) *The Whole World is Watching*. Berkeley, CA: University of California Press.

Gladwell, M. (1996) 'The Tipping Point', *New Yorker*, 3 June, pp. 32–8.

Goffman, Erving (1960) *Asylums*. Chicago, IL: Aldine.

Goffman, Erving (1974) *Frame Analysis*. New York: Basic Books.

340   *Theoretical Criminology 5(3)*

Goffman, Erving (1983) 'The Interaction Order', *ASR* 48: 1–17.

Greene, Judith (1999) 'Zero Tolerance: A Case Study of Police Policies and Practices in New York City', *Crime and Delinquency* 45: 171–87.

Gusfield, Joseph (1966) *Symbolic Crusade*. Urbana, IL: University of Illinois Press.

Gusfield, Joseph (ed.) (1989) *On Symbols and Society*. Chicago, IL: University of Chicago Press.

Hall, Stuart et al. (1977) *Policing the Crisis*. London: Macmillan.

Hallett, Michael and D. Powell (1995) 'Backstage with the Cops: Dramatic Reification of Police Subculture in American Crime Infotainment', *American Journal of Police* XIV: 101–29.

Hammer, M. and J. Champy (1993) *Reengineering the Corporation*. New York: Harper/Collins.

Herbert, S. (1998) *Policing Los Angeles*. Minneapolis, MN: University of Minnesota Press.

Holdaway, Simon (1983) *Inside the British Police*. Oxford: Blackwells.

Holmes, Steven A. (1999) 'New York Faces Study of Police Acts', *New York Times*, 6 March.

Hughes, E.C. (1958) *Men and their Work*. Glencoe: Free Press.

Hunt, Raymond and John Magneau (1994) *Power and the Police Chief*. Thousand Oaks: Sage.

Innes, Martin (1999) '"An Iron Fist in an Iron glove?" The Zero Tolerance Policing Debate', *Howard Journal* 38: 397–410.

Jackall, Robert (1997) *Wild Cowboys*. Cambridge: Harvard University Press.

Jenner, Eric (2000) 'Computer-based Crime Fighting from the Ground Up', *New York Times*, 12 December.

Jermeir, J. and L. Berkes (1979) 'Leader Behavior in a Police Command Bureaucracy', *ASQ* 23: 1–23.

Kappeler, V., R. Sluder and G. Alpert (1997) *Forces of Deviance Prospect Heights*, 2nd edn. Illinois: Waveland Press.

Kelling, George and Catherine Coles (1997) *Fixing Broken Windows*. New York: Free Press.

Klein, Joe (1997) 'Guiliani Unbound', *New Yorker*, 6 September, pp. 50–61.

Knapp, Whitman (1972) *Report on Corruption in New York City*. New York: George Braziller.

Kocieniewski, David (1998) 'Police Officials' Ouster Swift in Case of Doctored Stats', *New York Times*, 28 February.

Kraska, Peter and V. Kappeler (1997) 'Militarizing the American Police: The Rise and Normalization of Paramilitary Units', *Social Problems* 44: 1–18.

Krauss, Clifford (1996) 'For New York's Finest, it's Slow Going on the Internet', *New York Times*, 3 September.

Lardner, James (1997a) 'The New Blue Line', *NYT Magazine*, 9 February, pp. 50–62.

Lardner, James (1997b) 'Can You Believe the New York Miracle?' New York Review of Books 14 Aug. 54–58.

Lardner, James (1998) 'The Commish' (Review of Bratton and Knoble, 1998), *New York Times*, 1 Feburary.

Loader, Ian (1997) 'Policing and the Social: Questions of Symbolic Power', *British Journal of Sociology* 48: 1–18.

Lyons, William (1998) *The Politics of Community Policing: Rearranging the Power to Punish*. Ann Arbor, MI: University of Michigan Press.

MacCannell, Dean (1989) *The Tourist*, 2nd edn. New York: Schocken Books.

McCleary, Richard, R. Nienstedt and J.M. Erven (1982) 'Uniform Crime Reports as Organizational Outcomes', *Social Problems* 29: 361–72.

McNamara, John (1967) 'Uncertainties in Police Work', in D. Bordua (ed.) *The Police*. New York: Wiley.

Manning, Peter K. (1997 [1977]) *Police Work*. Prospect Heights: Waveland.

Manning, Peter K. (1979) *The Narcs' Game*. Cambridge: MIT Press.

Manning, Peter K. (1988) *Symbolic Communication*. Cambridge: MIT Press.

Manning, Peter K. (1996) 'Dramaturgy, Politics and the Axial Media Event', *The Sociological Quarterly* 37: 261–78.

Manning, Peter K. (forthcoming) *Picturing Policing*.

Maple, Jack *Crime Fighter*. New York: XXX Press.

Maple, Jack (1999) 'Police Must be Held Accountable', *Newsweek*, 21 June.

Mastrofski, Stephen (forthcoming) 'Police Chiefs as Symbolic Leaders', in Elin Waring and David Weisburd (eds) *Fetschrift for Albert J. Reiss, Jr.*

Mastrofski, S., Worden and Snipes (1995) *Systematic Observation of the Police*. Washington, DC: NIJ.

Mawby, Rob (1996) 'Making Sense of Media Representations of British Policing. . .', paper given at International Perspectives on Crime, Justice and Public Order conference, Dublin.

Meares, T. (1998) 'Place and Crime', *Chicago-Kent Law Review* 73: 669.

Meehan, Albert J. (1992) 'I Don't Prevent Crimes, I Prevent Calls', *Symbolic Interaction* 15: 455–80.

Meehan, Albert J. (1993) 'Internal Police Records and the Control of Juveniles', *British Journal of Criminology* 33: 504–24.

Miller, Jerome (1996) *Search and Destroy*. Cambridge: Cambridge University Press.

Mitroff, I. and W. Bennis (1993) *The Unreality Industry*. New York: OUP.

Mollen Commission (1994) *Report*. New York: City of New York.

Moore, Mark (1991) *Creating Public Value*. Cambridge: Harvard University Press.

Murphy, Patrick and T. Pate (1977) *Commissioner*. New York: Simon & Schuster.

Nesbary, Dale (1998) 'Handling Emergency Calls for Service: Organizational Production of Crime Statistics', *Policing* 21: 576–99.

New York Times (1999) 'Dispatch Plans Abandoned', 15 September.

New Yorker (1999) (Cover features a police officer at a shooting gallery), 8 March.

Pedersen, Donald (1997) 'Go Get the Scumbags', *Newsweek*, 20 October.

Rappaport, Roy (1998) *Ritual and Religion in the Making of Humanity.* Cambridge: Cambridge University Press.

Reibstein, Larry (1997) 'NYPD: Black and Blue', *Newsweek*, 2 June.

Reiss, Albert J., Jr (1971) *The Police and the Public.* New Haven, CT: Yale University Press.

Reiss, Albert J., Jr (1974) 'Discretionary Justice', in D. Glaser (ed.) *Handbook of Criminology*, pp. 79–99. Chicago, IL: Rand McNally.

Reiss, Albert J., Jr (1992) 'Policing in the Twentieth Century', in M. Tonry and Norval Morris *Crime and Justice.* Chicago, IL: University of Chicago Press.

Reiss, Albert J., Jr and D. Bordua (1967) 'Environment and Organization', in D. Bordua (ed.) *The Police.* New York: John Wiley.

Reppetto, Thomas (1979) *The Blue Parade.* New York: Macmillan.

Rose D.R. and T. Clear (1998) 'Incarceration, Social Capital, and Crime: Implications for Disorganization Theory', *Criminology* 36(3): 441–80.

Rosenbaum, Dennis (ed.) (1996) *Community Policing.* Thousand Oaks, CA: Sage.

Rubinstein, Jonathan (1972) *City Police.* New York: Farrar, Straus & Giroux.

Safir, Howard (n.d.) 'Compstat: Leadership in Action', unpublished zerox, NYPD.

Safir, Howard (1998) *The Compstat Process.* New York: Office of Management Analysis and Planning, NYPD.

Sampson, Robert and S. Raudenbusch (1999) 'Systematic Social Observation of Public Spaces', *AJS* 105: 603-

Sampson, Robert, J. Morenoff and F. Earls (1999) 'Beyond Social Capital', *ASR* 64: 633–60.

Sampson, Robert, S. Raudenbusch and F. Earls (1997) 'Neighborhoods and Violent Crime', *Science* 227: 918–24.

Schlesinger, Philip and H. Tumber (1994) *Reporting Crime.* Oxford: Clarendon Press.

Schwartz, B. and Robin Wagner-Pacifici (1991) 'The Vietnam Veterans Memorial: Commemorating a Difficult Past', *AJS* 97: 376–420.

Seidman, D. and X. Couzens (1974) 'Getting the Crime Rate Down: Political Pressure and Crime Reporting', *Law and Society Review* 8: 457–93.

Sellin, T. (1938) *Crime and Conflict.* SSRC New York.

Shaw, Clifford and H.D. McKay (1942) *Juvenile Delinquency in Urban Areas.* Chicago, IL: University of Chicago Press.

Sheingold, Stuart (1984) *The Politics of Law and Order.* New York: Longmans.

Sheingold, Stuart (1991) *The Politics of Street Crime.* Philadelphia, PA: Temple University Press.

Sherman, Lawrence W. (1990) 'Police Crackdowns . . .', in Albert J. Reiss, Jr (ed.) *Crime and Justice*, Vol. 12. Chicago, IL: University of Chicago Press.

Sherman, Lawrence W. (1991) 'Crime Attack . . .', in M. Tonry and Norval

Morris *Crime and Justice*, Vol. 15. Chicago, IL: University of Chicago Press.

Sherman, Lawrence W. (1992) *Policing Domestic Violence*. New York: Free Press.

Sherman, Lawrence W. et al. (1984) 'The Specific Deterrent Effects of Arrest', *ASR* 49: 261–72.

Siegel, Fred (1997) 'Keeping the Peace or Holding Back the Tide?', *Times Literary Supplement*, 10 January, pp. 9–10.

Silverman, Eli (1996) 'Mapping a Course for Change: How the NYPD Reengineered Itself to Drive Crime Down', *Law Enforcement News* XXII (15 December).

Silverman, Eli (1997a) 'Crime in New York: A Success Story', *The Public Perspective* June/July: 3–5.

Silverman, Eli (1997b) personal communication, November.

Silverman, Eli (1999) *The NYPD Battles Crime*. Boston, MA: Northeastern University Press.

Silverman, Eli and Paul E. O'Connell (1997) 'Revolutionizing the Police: Fighting Crime in New York City', *Security Journal* X: 1–5.

Skogan, Wesley (1991) *Disorder and Decline*. Berkeley, CA: University of California Press.

Skolnick, Jerome (1967) *Justice without Trial*. New York: Wiley.

Sparks, Richard (1992) *Television and the Drama of Crime*. Milton Keynes: Open University Press.

Strong, Philip (1983) *The Ceremonial Order of the Clinic*. London: RKP.

Surette, R. (1992) *Crime and the Media*. Belmont, CA: Wadsworth.

Toobin, J. (2000) 'The Unasked Question', *New Yorker*, 6 March.

Time (1997) 'A Beating in Brooklyn', 25 August.

Trojanowicz, Robert and Bonnie Bucqueroux (1990) *Community Policing*. Cincinnati, OH: Anderson.

Turner, Victor (1974) *Dramas, Fields and Metaphors*. Ithaca, NY: Cornell.

Turner, Victor (1976) *The Ritual Process*. Chicago, IL: Aldine.

Van Maanen, J. (1988) *Tales of the Field*. Chicago, IL: University of Chicago Press.

Wagner-Pacifici, Robin (1984) *The Moro Morality Play*. Chicago, IL: University of Chicago Press.

Wagner-Pacifici, Robin (1994) *Discourse and Destruction*. Chicago, IL: University of Chicago Press.

Waldeck, Sarah (2000) 'Cops, Community Policing and the Social Norms Approach to Crime Control', *Georgia Law Review* 34 (Spring): 1253–310.

Wilson, James Q. (1968) *Varieties of Police Behavior*. Cambridge: Harvard University Press.

Wilson, James Q. (1978) *Thinking about Crime*. New York: Basic Books.

Wilson, James Q. and George Kelling (1982) 'Broken Windows: Police and Neighborhood Safety', *Atlantic Magazine* 249: 29–38.

Young, J. (1971) *The Drug Takers*. London: Palladian.

Young, M. (1991) *An Inside Job*. Oxford: Clarendon Press.

344   *Theoretical Criminology 5(3)*

Zuccotti, John (1984) *Report On New York City Police Management.* New
    York: City of New York.

PETER MANNING holds the Brooks Chair in Policing and Criminal Justice at
Northeastern University, USA.

[3]

The Role of Procedural Justice and Legitimacy in Shaping Public Support for Policing

Jason Sunshine   Tom R. Tyler

This study explores two issues about police legitimacy. The first issue is the relative importance of police legitimacy in shaping public support of the police and policing activities, compared to the importance of instrumental judgments about (1) the risk that people will be caught and sanctioned for wrongdoing, (2) the performance of the police in fighting crime, and/or (3) the fairness of the distribution of police services. Three aspects of public support for the police are examined: public compliance with the law, public cooperation with the police, and public willingness to support policies that empower the police. The second issue is which judgments about police activity determine people's views about the legitimacy of the police. This study compares the influence of people's judgments about the procedural justice of the manner in which the police exercise their authority to the influence of three instrumental judgments: risk, performance, and distributive fairness. Findings of two surveys of New Yorkers show that, first, legitimacy has a strong influence on the public's reactions to the police, and second, the key antecedent of legitimacy is the fairness of the procedures used by the police. This model applies to both white and minority group residents.

Introduction

Mechanisms for social control are a universal feature of all human societies, and it is difficult to imagine a culture that lacks the means of ensuring that its people follow its norms, rules, or laws. Bringing the behavior of members of the public into line with norms, rules, and laws is a core function of legal authorities. As a consequence, understanding how people respond to different potential mechanisms of social control is important to policy makers, legal scholars, and social scientists (Tyler 1990; Tyler & Huo 2002). Our concern here is with public responses to one institution of social control—the police, and to one mechanism of social control—police legitimacy. We examine such responses among two samples of the residents of New York City using questionnaire-based responses to "voice of the community" surveys.

This study has two goals. The first is to test the argument that police legitimacy has an important influence on public support for the police. In this study, we examine the influence of police legitimacy on three aspects of public support: behavioral compliance with the law, behavioral cooperation with the police, and public willingness to support policies that empower the police to use their discretion in enforcing the law. We compare the influence of legitimacy to the influence of three types of instrumental judgments: risk, performance, and distributive fairness.

Legitimacy is a property of an authority or institution that leads people to feel that that authority or institution is entitled to be deferred to and obeyed. It represents an "acceptance by people of the need to bring their behavior into line with the dictates of an external authority" (Tyler 1990:25). This feeling of obligation is not simply linked to the authority's possession of instruments of reward or coercion, but also to properties of the authority that lead people to feel it is entitled to be obeyed (Beetham 1991). Since the classic writing of Weber (1968), social scientists have recognized that legitimacy is a property that is not simply instrumental but reflects a social value orientation toward authority and institutions—i.e., a normative, moral, or ethical feeling of responsibility to defer (Beetham 1991; Kelman & Hamilton 1989; Sparks, Bottoms, & Hay 1996; Tyler 1990). This analysis will explore the importance of legitimacy, beyond the influence of instrumental factors shaping reactions to the police.

Instrumental models suggest that people's willingness to accept and cooperate with legal authorities is linked to evaluations of police performance, to risk, and to judgments about distributive justice. This model, the *instrumental perspective*, suggests that the police gain acceptance when they are viewed by the public as (1) creating credible sanctioning threats for those who break rules (risk), (2) effectively controlling crime and criminal behavior (performance), and (3) fairly distributing police services across people and communities (distributive fairness).

The second goal of this study is to examine the determinants of legitimacy. The procedural justice perspective argues that the legitimacy of the police is linked to public judgments about the fairness of the processes through which the police make decisions and exercise authority. If the public judges that the police exercise their authority using fair procedures, this model suggests that the public will view the police as legitimate and will cooperate with policing efforts. However, unfairness in the exercise of authority will lead to alienation, defiance, and noncooperation.

This procedural justice-based perspective on the antecedents of legitimacy is again contrasted with an instrumental model that links police legitimacy to instrumental judgments about the police. The instrumental model suggests that the police develop and maintain legitimacy through their effectiveness in fighting crime and disorder in the community. This instrumentally based model of legitimacy is often found in studies of political leaders, in which public support is viewed as based upon leader performance in dealing with economic and social problems (Citrin & Muste 1999).

Conceived of more broadly, the two-stage model outlined reflects *process-based regulation* (Tyler & Huo 2002). Process-based regulation seeks to manage the relationship between legal authorities and the communities they police through self-regulation that flows from the activation of people's own feelings of responsibility and obligation to the community and to community authorities. These social values—i.e., legitimacy—are, in turn, linked to public assessments of the fairness of the manner in which authorities exercise their discretionary authority when implementing the law and/or making decisions about whether and how to provide assistance to those in need. This process-based approach to regulation builds upon the recognition by social theorists that legal authorities depend upon their ability to activate feelings of obligation and responsibility for their effectiveness (Weber 1968; Beetham 1991), and that those feelings, in turn, are linked to justice-based judgments about legal authorities (Tyler 1990).

Police and Policing

Since the establishment of the first formal full-time police force in the United States circa 1837, the police have endured numerous challenges to their legitimacy as an institution of social control. Throughout their history, the relationship between the police and the public has been tumultuous. Instances of police misconduct, with recent examples being the police beating of Rodney King in Los Angeles, the shooting of Amadou Diallo in New York, and the sexual assault on Abner Louima in New York, have long sparked reactions ranging from full-scale riots to public indictments of police practices and public mistrust of the police (Skolnick & Fyfe 1993).

The public is clearly divided over their feelings for the police. And, of particular concern, studies of public views about the police typically reveal large racial and ethnic group differences, with minority group members expressing much more negative attitudes about the police and having lower trust and confidence in institutions of social control. A polarized public is problematic on numerous levels. It inhibits the police from fulfilling their regulatory role in society and produces polarization and discontent through the recognition that certain groups feel disproportionately mistreated by the police. Thus, understanding what it is about police behavior that the public finds problematic is important to

516   **The Role of Procedural Justice and Legitimacy**

accurately address the needs of citizens as well as to enable the police to function effectively.

The Influence of Legitimacy on Public Support

The legitimacy of the police in the eyes of the public is important because it is the fulcrum of the relationship between the police and the public. We hypothesize, first, that if the public views the police as legitimate, then they are more likely to obey the law. To test this argument, we examine the relationship between people's evaluations of the legitimacy of the New York City Police Department (NYPD) and their *behavioral compliance* with the law. We compare the extent to which judgments of legitimacy guide people's behavior with the degree of influence of instrumental factors also thought to shape people's behavior. In particular, we consider the influence of people's estimates of the likelihood that they will be caught and punished for wrongdoing (risk).

Traditional law enforcement strategies are hinged on the belief that people will be deterred from engaging in criminal activity if they fear getting caught and being punished. Strategies based on this belief are grouped under the term *deterrence*. Though policing in the United States has undergone numerous changes in the past decades, the belief in deterrence-based strategies as an effective method of crime control has largely been left intact. It is believed that the best way to regulate the public's behavior is by making undesirable behaviors extremely risky (Harcourt 2001; Kelling & Coles 1996; McArdle & Erzen 2001). This is achieved by increasing the number of officers on the street, increasing arrests, and/or increasing the threat or use of force by the police (Silverman 1999).

Second, we examine the relationship between people's judgments about police legitimacy and their *willingness to cooperate with police activities*. This concern with cooperation develops from the recognition that effective crime control and disorder management depends on public cooperation with the police (Sampson, Raudenbush, & Earls 1997). We test the argument that if the public views the police as legitimate, they will be more likely to assist the police with crime prevention (i.e., reporting crime or calling for help). We compare this argument to the view that cooperation develops from instrumental judgments about the effectiveness of police performance in fighting crime. This instrumental perspective suggests that people will help the police when they think that the police are being effective in managing crime and urban disorder.

If the police are viewed as effective, citizens may view the help the police have to offer as more important because it would have a greater likelihood of leading to concrete results. As with the deterrence perspective, this view of public support is instrumental. It suggests that people make instrumental evaluations of authority, working with the police when they think that the police are effectively dealing with community issues and problems (Skogan 1990; Skogan & Hartnett 1997).

Third, we examine the relationship between people's judgments about police legitimacy and their *willingness to empower the police*. We test the argument that, if the police are viewed as legitimate, they are given a wider range of discretion to perform their duties. When they are not viewed as legitimate, their actions are subject to challenge, their decisions are not accepted, and their directives are ignored. We contrast this view with the distributive justice perspective, which suggests that people support and empower officials when they think that those authorities distribute police services fairly across groups (Sarat 1977).

The distributive justice argument is that people will be more willing to give power to legal authorities when they feel that those authorities deliver outcomes fairly to people and groups. Sarat (1977) argues that the demand for equal treatment is a core theme running through public evaluations of the police and courts. He suggests that the

> perception of unequal treatment is the single most important source of popular dissatisfaction with the American legal system. According to available survey evidence, Americans believe that the ideal of equal protection, which epitomizes what they find most valuable in their legal system, is betrayed by police, lawyers, judges, and other legal officials. (1977:434)

This argument roots evaluations of the police and police services in judgments of resource distribution across people and across groups (Tyler et al. 1997).

Legitimacy as a Social Value-Based Motivation

Political scientists, psychologists, and sociologists have long considered legitimacy to be an essential quality for leaders and regimes to have. When people view an authority as legitimate, it is believed that they will voluntarily comply with that individual or institution's edicts. Tyler (1990) has demonstrated that when people believe the police or the courts are legitimate, they are more likely to comply with their directives. The key point is that this motivation is distinct from the belief that one is likely to be caught and punished for breaking the law.

This study tests a broader model of the consequences of legitimacy. In addition to exploring the influence of legitimacy on compliance, as did Tyler (1990), this study also examines the importance of legitimacy in shaping cooperation with the police. It has been recognized that the police want more from people than just their willingness to defer to law by limiting their engagement in illegal behavior. The police also want members of the community to engage in proactive behaviors that help the police fight crime. In fact, recent studies make clear that the police cannot effectively control crime and disorder without the cooperation of community residents (Sampson, Raudenbush, & Earls 1997).

Further, legal authorities want the public to accept the legitimacy of granting discretionary authority to the police to allow them to fight crime in the community. Recent research makes clear that the boundary of police authority is a contested one, with community residents sensitive to being stopped and questioned, arrested, and jailed by the police as part of police crime-fighting authority. The issue of whether and in what way the police have the authority to intrude into people's lives by stopping them on the street or in cars, by questioning them, and by arrests and detentions, is central to current controversies about racial profiling, all of which address the question of when the police have discretion to decide whom to stop, question, and ticket. Clearly, the police must have some discretion about how to do their jobs. And in some areas, such as whom to shoot, the police have traditionally been given wide discretion, since the threshold for retrospectively judging a shooting to be inappropriate is quite high. The question addressed here is what factors shape the boundaries of discretion in the eyes of the public.

The Determinants of Legitimacy

This study also explores the aspects of police behavior that influence people's assessment of the legitimacy of the police. As before, we compare two models, one linked to instrumental judgments about the police and the other to procedural justice. Again, the outcome model is built upon three types of evaluations of the police: (1) their ability to catch rule-breakers, (2) their performance in fighting crime, and (3) the fairness of their distribution of outcomes.

We contrast this outcome perspective with a procedural justice model. The procedural justice model focuses on how the police treat people as antecedents of people's views on police legitimacy, rather than seeing legitimacy as linked to how effective they are or whether they provide people with fair outcomes.

A wide body of research makes clear that people's reactions to their personal experiences with the police are shaped by their evaluations of the fairness of the procedures the police use to exercise their authority (Tyler & Lind 1988; Tyler 1990; Tyler et al. 1997; Tyler & Huo 2002). Further, studies demonstrate that procedural justice is central in other hierarchical situations in which people are dealing with authorities, such as in mediation (Pruitt et al. 1993), work organizations (Tyler & Blader 2000), courts (Casper, Tyler, & Fisher 1988; Tyler & Lind 1988), and prisons (Sparks, Bottoms, & Hay 1996). Hence, considerable evidence suggests that procedural justice will be central to the relationship between people and legal authorities in the arena of policing.

Our hypothesis is that procedural fairness will also be a primary influence on judgments of legitimacy when people are evaluating the police in general, in addition to when they are reacting to personal encounters with particular authorities. This assumption underlies a procedural justice approach of policing. It is supported by prior studies of personal experience (Tyler 1990), by secondary analyses of several public opinion polls of public evaluations of the police and courts (Tyler 2001b), and by the findings of studies of rule-following behavior in work settings (Tyler & Blader 2000). While suggestive, these prior efforts lack a direct comparison of the role of procedural and instrumental factors in shaping legitimacy in legal settings. This study provides such a direct comparison.

In considering the procedural justice-based model of legitimacy, it is important to recognize that we are working with cross-sectional data in the studies outlined. It is always possible that compliance leads to legitimacy and perceptions of procedural justice. While the data examined here cannot address this issue, other longitudinal data (Tyler 1990) suggest that the model articulated here is reasonable. Ultimately, experiments are needed to test the causal sequence outlined.

A procedural justice-based approach to policing has numerous advantages over an instrumental approach—i.e., an approach that links cooperation to risk, performance, and/or distributive fairness. One advantage stems from the intrinsic motivations engaged by legitimacy, which leads to a self-regulatory stance by community residents. In other words, when people view the police as legitimate, they are more likely to voluntarily defer to police action and less likely to challenge it. Further, intrusive police tactics are more widely tolerated by the public when the public trusts the motives that drive those tactics (Tyler & Huo 2002). Greater discretionary authority will enable the police to perform their regulatory role more effectively and efficiently.

Second, research suggests that a procedural approach to citizen interaction may enhance the safety of both law enforcement officers and community residents (Tyler & Huo 2002). As mentioned above, instrumental approaches encourage competitive interaction. The powerful party—the police officer—initiates interaction by establishing dominance over the weaker party. It is thought that in the face of overwhelming power the weaker party will submit out of fear of the consequences of noncompliance. However, current social science evidence does not support this conclusion. Pruitt and Rubin (1986) argue that when power-based tactics are used by one party, they are imitated by the opposing party. Corroborating that finding, Lawler, Ford, and Blegen (1988) argue that anger and resentment stemming from the imposition of power elicits behavior from the weaker party meant to resist and harm the aggressor. Generally, conflicts based on domination tend to become irrational and quickly escalate as hostility increases (Pruitt 1981).

By contrast, interaction based on fairness and cooperation can defuse a fight over dominance. In fact, Axelrod (1984) argues that the most effective negotiation strategy for both sides is usually (although not always) to begin with cooperation but to respond with competition if an opponent reciprocates with competition. Similarly, a procedural justice-based policing strategy doesn't mean the police should not resort to the use of force when faced with a hostile individual. It simply means that to the extent that the police can elicit compliance without the use of force, the police officers, the institution of policing, and society in general will benefit greatly.

A procedural justice-based approach to policing allows the police to focus on controlling crime without alienating the public. As previously argued, deterrence and other performance-based strategies have not faired well for the police in regard to creating and maintaining a favorable climate of public opinion. Research indicates that evaluations of the police are based more on how the police treat people than how well they perform their job (Tyler 1990; Tyler & Huo 2002; Tyler 2001a). For example, Tyler and Huo (2002) found in a study of Oakland residents living in high crime areas that how the police treated people explained more of the variance in police evaluations than did variations in the quality of police performance. Thus, when police change the way they interact with citizens, moving from a command-and-control orientation to a fair and respectful disposition, public evaluations will eventually become more favorable. Effectively controlling crime and maintaining positive public evaluations is not a tradeoff that the police have to make. In fact, on the contrary, the police can engage in effective crime control and increase public support when they exercise their authority fairly.

Our goal in this analysis is not to test the effectiveness of a particular policing strategy. Rather, we are testing the validity of the underlying psychological model upon which such a strategy is based. Unless that psychological model is a correct description of people's psychological dynamics in dealings with the police, the policing strategy outlined is unlikely to be effective.

Policing Strategies

The recognition of the importance of the relationship between the public and the police toward building police legitimacy has already spawned a trend toward community-oriented policing (Kelling & Moore 1988; Friedman 1992; Skogan et al. 1999; Skolnick & Fyfe 1993). The police have learned that they cannot function effectively without public support, and they are building policing strategies designed to build such support.

Traditionally, police strategies for crime fighting were reactive. Officers would patrol neighborhoods in relative isolation from the surrounding community. Contact with citizens would only be made when officers were called to respond to a specific call. Crime prevention and control were thought to be achieved through the threat of arrest and punishment. This belief manifested itself in a policy of "saturation patrols," traffic stops, and field interrogations.

Over the past few decades, it has become clear that this approach to policing alienated citizens and the police from one another (Reiss 1992; Moore 1992). Police could not rely on the public's support for their efforts, and the public lost faith in the ability of the police to provide safety. Community policing quickly became a policy buzzword for numerous strategies aimed at mending the relationship between the police and the public while at the same time improving crime control. Fighting crime and police/community relations were now viewed as intimately related (Friedman 1992).

Many police departments, in response to their problematic relationship with the public, altered the way they policed neighborhoods. Officers were taken out of the squad car and shifted to foot patrols, new posts were constructed to enlist the cooperation of community leaders, and many other initiatives were taken to engage with the community and ultimately rebuild the relationship between citizens and police. This new police/community outreach is a distinct departure from traditional policing methods. However, the premise that increased police interaction with citizens (i.e., more foot patrols, police/community meetings) will lead to improved public opinion has not been thoroughly tested (see Skogan & Hartnett 1997).

What these efforts show is that many police departments are already acting based upon many elements of the psychological model being tested in this study. However, they are doing so without the benefit of a clearly articulated and empirically tested model of the psychological dynamics of the public's reactions to policing activities. Without such a model, efforts to control crime tend to vary depending on the political climate and personal philosophies of community leaders (Blumstein & Wallman 2000; Brodeur 1998; Gest 2000; Wilson & Petersilia 2002).

Policing After September 11, 2001

We have presented the various models of public evaluation as if they were context-free. However, it is clear that public views about law enforcement have changed in the era of counterterrorism that has followed the attack on the World Trade Center towers. How might that influence views about policing? Research suggests that during times of strife and difficulty, people become more focused on the effectiveness of police performance and less concerned about issues of process and rights (Deutsch 1990; Nagata 1993; Sullivan, Piereson, & Marcus 1982). This study tests the role of context by considering public views before and following this important public event.

The Public and the Police: Majority and Minority Perspectives

It is also important to consider whether the models being evaluated apply equally well to everyone in a community. In particular, do the members of majority and minority groups consider the same issues when evaluating the police? The nature of the relationship between the police and the public has a serious impact on the effectiveness of crime control strategies, the welfare of community residents, and the institution of policing, suggesting the importance of maintaining favorable policy/community relations among all the communities dealing with the police.

Numerous surveys explore public views toward the police and confidence in their abilities to fight crime and maintain public safety (Huang & Vaughn 1996). These studies suggest that there is considerable variation between different ethnic groups. For example, Huang and Vaughn (1996) found that 67% of African Americans felt the police were fair (the lowest of all groups surveyed), compared to 87% of whites. When questioning people about the police use of force, they found that 67% of African

Americans thought of police use of force as a problem, compared to 40% of whites.

Other studies, conducted in a variety of American cities (Cole 1999; Worden 1995; Sullivan, Dunham, & Alpert 1987), found that minority citizens were especially likely to report being mistreated by police. This is not surprising because it is minority citizens who are more likely to be subject to police regulatory actions. For example, in New York City between 1998 and 2000,[1] 84% of those stopped and frisked were African American or Hispanic. In addition, minority group members are more likely to need police help—73% of victims of violent crime were African American or Hispanic.

A second type of study does not look at objective differences in the experiences of the members of different ethnic groups but at ethnic group differences in attitudes toward the police. Studies of this type typically consider the three primary ethnic groups in New York: whites, African Americans, and Hispanics. Considerable evidence suggests that minority group members have less trust and confidence in the police, the courts, and the legal system. However, it is not clear whether minority group members base their evaluations of the police on different criteria than do whites. Tyler and associates (Tyler et al. 1997; Tyler & Huo 2002) argue that the members of all ethnic groups evaluate legal authorities in similar ways. We test that argument here by comparing the criteria used by both white and minority community residents to evaluate the legitimacy of the police.

Testing Procedural Justice-Based Strategies of Policing

Procedural justice-based policing rests on four key assumptions. First, people's judgments of police legitimacy are as important or more important than people's calculations of the risk of being caught and punished in predicting compliance with law. In order for policing linked to procedural justice to be a viable alternative to policing based on instrumental judgments, authorities have to be able to rely on people's internal motivations for obeying the law. As described earlier, legitimacy represents this internal motivation. Procedural justice-based policing is based on the expectation that, when people view legal authority as legitimate, they voluntarily follow the law.

Second, legitimacy is also more important than instrumental judgments about issues such as performance for predicting

---

[1] Taken from New York City Police Department Citywide Stop and Frisk Data 1998, 1999, and 2000 (NYPD 2001).

whether the police will experience cooperative behavior, such as helping the police to solve crimes, on the part of community residents. The literature reviewed earlier suggests that deterrence was not an effective strategy for gaining long-term compliance with the law or for eliciting cooperative behavior from community residents. In fact, research on conflict situations suggests that deterrence strategies were likely to be met with resistance. By contrast, legitimacy is connected with people's internal sense of obligation to authority and therefore promotes voluntary, co-operative behavior. When people view the police as legitimate, they are more likely to call them to report crimes or volunteer their time to work with them in their communities.

Third, legitimacy is more important than instrumental judgments in shaping public deference to police activities. In other words, when the public views the police as legitimate, they are more likely to empower the police to perform their policing duties and less likely to try to circumscribe police activity or limit police discretion. Thus, public evaluations of legitimacy influence the degree to which the police have discretionary authority that they can use to function more effectively because the public is likely to give them more leeway to use their expertise.

Finally, evaluations of legitimacy are based on procedural fairness more so than on judgments about distributive fairness or other instrumental indicators. Policymakers and police officials often assume that the police are judged by how effective they are in controlling crime. It is believed that the legitimacy of the police is based on how well they perform, whether they effectively sanction rule-breakers, and/or whether police services are distributed fairly across society. By contrast, policing based on the process judgment of procedural justice rests on the assumption that people form assessments of legitimacy based more on how the police exercise their authority than on their effectiveness or on how equally police provide assistance to the various communities where they work.

This latter aspect of the procedural justice-based model, i.e., the role of procedural justice in shaping legitimacy, is crucial because more often than not, the police cannot provide people with what they want, nor can they control the crime rate. Though they are charged with the responsibility of controlling crime, they only partially control the factors that lead people to become criminals, and the resources may or may not exist for the police to engage in what they think will be effective strategies of crime control. Thus, the police cannot rely on effectiveness defined in terms of performance. They do, however, have some degree of control over how they exercise their authority when dealing with members of the public. According to the procedural justice-based model of regulation, it is through procedurally just interactions with the public that the police can impact their own legitimacy (Tyler & Huo 2002).

Method

The First New York City Sample—Pre-September 11, 2001

To test the assumptions of the process-based model of policing, a self-report survey was mailed to a random sample of registered voters in New York City. The questions used to operationalize each of the variables in the study are shown in Appendix A. The study was conducted during spring and summer 2001 during a period of poor police/community relations but before the September 2001 World Trade Center terrorist attack.

Of the questionnaires sent, a sample of 586 was returned. This reflects a response rate of 22%. Respondent age ranged from 19 to 88 (mean of 48). Gender was 62% female, 75.2% had at least some college education, and income averaged between $40,000 and $60,000 per year. The ethnic breakdown was 56.8% white and 43.5% nonwhite (14.8% Hispanic or Latino; 22.4% African American; 6.3% other ethnicities).

The response rate in this study was typical of mailed questionnaires. However, it was low and raises concerns about potential sample bias. In considering these findings, we need to be aware that there are potential biases in the results that are linked to who chose to respond to the questionnaire. To correct for such biases, we weighted the respondents' answers to adjust for their ethnicity, income, and education. This adjustment first involved removing "other" ethnicities (6.3%) and focusing on those whites, African Americans, and Hispanics who provided complete income and education information. We then weighted this remaining sample of 483 from a total of 576 returned interviews to represent the population of New York City, as measured in the 1990 U.S. Census. This weighting resulted in an adjusted sample of 483 (55% white, 19% African American, 26% Hispanic). For this analysis, we collapsed ethnicity further into a white/minority dichotomous variable.

Results

The Consequences of Legitimacy

The first question is whether legitimacy influences public support for the police. We performed regression analysis using the indexes of legitimacy, risk, distributive justice, instrumental

526   **The Role of Procedural Justice and Legitimacy**

evaluations, and demographic variables to predict compliance with the law, cooperation with police, and the empowerment of law enforcement. Demographic variables included in the analysis were ethnicity, education, age, sex, and education. The purpose of the regression analysis was twofold. First, the results would enable us to determine the relative impact each independent variable has on each dependent variable. Second, regression allowed us to conclude that the impact of any significant variable in the equation was independent of the impact of any other variable in the equation.

The results indicated that both legitimacy (beta = 0.22, $p < 0.001$) and risk estimates (beta = 0.18, $p < 0.001$) influenced compliance (overall $R^2 = 9\%$, $p < 0.001$). No effect was found for distributive justice or other instrumental judgments. Compliance was also found to be influenced by ethnicity, income, and gender, with whites, the more well off, and female respondents more likely to comply with the law. In addition, because the compliance scale was skewed, a Tobit analysis was performed. The results of that analysis supported those already noted. In that analysis, legitimacy (beta = 0.14, $p < 0.001$) and risk (beta = 0.07, $p < 0.05$) influenced compliance. In addition, whites and women were more likely to obey the law.

Perceptions of police legitimacy (beta = 0.30, $p < 0.001$) and evaluations of police performance (beta = 0.11, $p < 0.05$) predicted citizen cooperation with the police (overall $R^2 = 14\%$, $p < 0.001$). Estimates of risk and distributive justice had no impact on cooperation. Ethnicity also impacted cooperation, with minority respondents more likely to cooperate with the police.

Finally, empowerment was predicted by perceptions of legitimacy (beta = 0.40, $p < 0.001$) and distributive justice (beta = 0.21, $p < 0.001$) (overall $R^2 = 40\%$, $p < 0.001$). Those with higher incomes were less likely to support the empowerment of the police.

What Determines Legitimacy?

The second question is which judgments about the police determine legitimacy. We performed a regression analysis using indexes of procedural justice, distributive justice, performance evaluations, risk estimates, and demographic variables to predict legitimacy. The resulting model accounted for 73% of the variance in legitimacy. The results indicated that legitimacy was based predominantly on procedural justice (beta = 0.62, $p < 0.001$), and to a lesser extent on performance evaluations (beta = 0.20, $p < 0.001$) and distributive justice judgments (beta = 0.11, $p < 0.001$), but not on estimates of risk. Significant effects were also found regarding education. More highly educated respondents were likely to indicate lower levels of legitimacy.

Procedural Justice-Based Policing: A Statistical Model

We constructed a latent structural equation incorporating all the variables measured in this study into a single model. This procedure has numerous advantages over standard regression analysis. First, all assumptions of the process-based model of policing could be tested simultaneously, accounting for all variance at once. Second, latent structures correct for measurement inaccuracy, providing a more accurate picture of underlying relationships. Third, intermediate effects can be observed directly (see Joreskog and Sorbom [1986] for review of latent structured equation models).

Figure 1 represents the final model produced using this latent structure approach. The model fit the data well (CFI = 0.90, IFI = 0.90, RMSEA = 0.060, chi-square = 1222.6, df = 411).[2] Thus, this model represents a stringent test of the assumptions upon which a process-based model of regulation rests. In estimating the model shown, all possible paths were allowed. Figure 1 shows only the paths that emerged as significant.

As in the regression equation performed earlier, procedural fairness was the primary driver of perceptions of legitimacy (beta = 0.74). Distributive fairness and estimates of risk had no effect on legitimacy, while performance evaluations had a relatively larger effect than that revealed by the previous regression analysis (beta = 0.15). Finally, confirming the earlier regression equations, legitimacy had a substantial impact on empowerment (beta = 0.47), cooperation (beta = 0.28), and compliance (beta = 0.25). Cooperation was also influenced by performance (beta = 0.16), and compliance by risk (beta = 0.23).

Unlike the earlier regression equations, we found no direct effects on cooperation for procedural justice when legitimacy was in the equation. In other words, the influence of this variable flows through legitimacy. Procedural justice was represented by a "latent" variable reflecting indexes of the quality of treatment, quality of decisionmaking, and a general procedural fairness index.[3]

---

[2] Large numbers of items increase the parameters to be estimated, which increases the chi-square, thereby making it more difficult to fit a model. This model fit well despite the number of items used.

[3] We included items measuring what Tyler and Huo (2002) describe as "trust" in the motives of the authorities in the two studies reported here as aspects of quality of interpersonal treatment.

Figure 1. Study One. Structural Equation Model: Testing the Assumptions of Procedural Justice-Based Regulation.

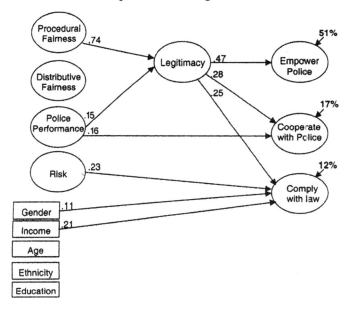

Of course, we need to keep in mind that the model tested was linked to people's judgments about police fairness, rather than to actual police behavior itself. We have no way of knowing what the police are actually doing as they patrol the streets of New York and respond to calls. In other words, the beginning point of our analysis is the self-reports of community residents—policing as they experience it. People's judgments about police fairness may or may not reflect objective police behavior and may or may not be linked to the actual congruity between police behavior and the law.

Method

The Second New York City Sample: Post-September 11, 2001

The second study used to test the assumptions of the process-based policing model was based on telephone interviews with a stratified sample of the residents of the City of New York.[4] In the study, 1,653 interviews were conducted during summer 2002 in both English and Spanish. Appendix B shows the questions used to operationalize each of the variables in the study.

[4] The collection of these data was supported by a grant from the National Institute of Justice (No. 2001IJCX0029).

The response rate of for the survey was 64%, a response rate typical of telephone questionnaires. However, to correct for possible biases, we weighted the respondents' answers. This weighting took account of the sampling procedure and corrected for variations away from random sampling. It also corrected for differences in the proportion of minority group members in the sample vis-à-vis the proportion in each borough in the city (according to U.S. Census figures).

In this analysis, respondents of "other" ethnicities ($n = 210$) were excluded, and the study focused on whites, African Americans, and Hispanics (weighted $n = 1,422$). In this weighted sample, 41% of respondents were ages 18–34, 55% were female; 63% had at least some college education, and 43% had an income of $40,000 per year or less. The ethnic breakdown was 44% white ($n = 628$), 28% Hispanic or Latino ($n = 394$), and 28% African American ($n = 400$).

Results

The Consequences of Legitimacy

The first question is again whether legitimacy influences public support for the police. We performed regression analysis using the indexes of legitimacy, risk, distributive justice, performance evaluations, and demographic variables to predict compliance with the law, cooperation with police, and empowerment of law enforcement authorities. Demographic variables included in the analysis were ethnicity, education, age, sex, and education. The purpose of the regression analysis was twofold. First, the results examined the relative impact each independent variable had on each dependent variable. Second, regression examined the independent impact of any significant variable in the equation.

Results indicated that both legitimacy (beta = 0.14, $p < 0.001$) and risk estimates (beta = 0.06, $p < 0.01$) influenced compliance (overall $R^2 = 8\%$, $p < 0.001$). No effect was found for distributive justice or performance evaluations. We also found that compliance was influenced by age, education, and gender, with older, better-educated, and female respondents more likely to comply with the law. In addition, because the compliance scale was again skewed, we performed a Tobit analysis again. The results of that analysis again supported those already noted, with legitimacy shaping compliance.

Perceptions of police legitimacy (beta = 0.26, $p < 0.001$) and evaluations of risk (beta = 0.16, $p < 0.001$) predicted citizen cooperation with the police (overall $R^2 = 16\%$, $p < 0.001$). Estimates of performance and distributive justice had no impact on

530   **The Role of Procedural Justice and Legitimacy**

cooperation. Age, education, and income also impacted cooperation, with older, higher-education, and higher-income respondents
more likely to cooperate with the police.

Finally, empowerment was predicted by perceptions of
legitimacy (beta = 0.35, $p<0.001$), distributive justice (beta = 0.09,
$p<0.001$), risk (beta = 0.07, $p<0.01$), and neighborhood conditions (beta = 0.06, $p<0.05$) (overall $R^2 = 22\%$, $p<0.001$). Those
higher in education and income were also less likely to support the
empowerment of the police, as were African Americans and older
respondents.

What Determines Legitimacy?

The second question is what determines legitimacy. We
performed a regression analysis using the indexes of procedural
justice, distributive justice, performance evaluations, risk estimates,
and demographic variables to predict legitimacy.

The resulting model accounted for 33% of the variance in
legitimacy. The results indicated that legitimacy is based predominantly on procedural justice (beta = 0.35, $p<0.001$), and to a lesser
extent on distributive justice (beta = 0.21, $p<0.001$) and police
performance, as indexed by assessments of neighborhood conditions (beta = $-.07$, $p<0.01$), but not on estimates of risk.
Significant effects were also found regarding education. African
Americans, older respondents, higher-income respondents, and
women were likely to indicate lower levels of legitimacy.

Procedural Justice-Based Policing: A Statistical Model

We again constructed a latent structural equation incorporating
all the variables measured into a single model. It was similar to that
used with the first study data. The model treated police
performance, neighborhood conditions, and fear of crime as three
indicators of overall police performance (using a latent variable
approach).

Figure 2 represents the final model produced using this latent
structure approach. The model fit the data well (CFI = 0.98,
IFI = 0.98, RMSEA = 0.09, chi-square = 830, df = 80).[5] Thus, this
model represents a stringent test of the assumptions upon which
the process-based model of regulation rests. In the model shown,
all paths were allowed to occur, while Figure 2 shows only the paths
that emerged as significant ($p<0.001$).

---

[5] Large numbers of items increase the parameters to be estimated, which increases
the chi-square, thereby making it more difficult to fit a model. This model fit well despite
the number of items used.

Figure 2. Study Two. Structural Equation Model: Testing the Assumptions of Procedural Justice-Based Regulation.

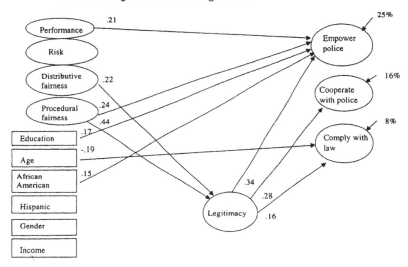

Procedural fairness, a "latent variable" reflecting quality of decisionmaking, quality of treatment, and overall assessments of procedural justice, was the primary driver of perceptions of legitimacy (beta = 0.44). Distributive fairness also had an effect on legitimacy (beta = 0.22). Finally, confirming the earlier regression equations, legitimacy had a substantial impact on empowerment (beta = 0.34), cooperation (beta = 0.28), and compliance (beta = 0.16). Only one direct effect was found for procedural justice when legitimacy was in the equation, and that was on empowerment (beta = 0.24). In other words, the influence of procedural justice generally flowed through legitimacy.

Of course, we need to keep in mind that the model tested was again linked to people's judgments about police fairness, rather than to actual police behavior itself. We have no way of knowing what the police are actually doing as they patrol the streets of New York and respond to calls. In other words, our analysis is about policing as community residents experience it.

Ethnic Group Differences: Study Two

To examine the differences among ethnic groups, we divided respondents into three groups: whites, African Americans, and Hispanics. We then examined the antecedents of compliance,

532   **The Role of Procedural Justice and Legitimacy**

cooperation, and empowerment within each group. Since a more detailed analysis within each of these three dependent variables suggested similar ethnic group effects for each variable, we combined the three measures of cooperation into a single dependent variable. Table 1 shows a separate analysis within each ethnic group for that combined dependent variable. The results shown in Table 1 suggest that legitimacy is the key to cooperation among all ethnic groups. Within each group, legitimacy was the primary factor shaping cooperation with the police.

The second question is whether procedural justice is an antecedent of legitimacy. Again, separate regression analyses within each ethnic group, shown in Table 2, suggested that procedural justice is always a key antecedent of legitimacy. This is true regardless of each respondent's ethnic group background. In addition, whites and African Americans were significantly influenced by their distributive justice judgments, while Hispanics were not. Again, the three ethnic groups were generally similar in the basis upon which they determined how legitimate they viewed police authorities as being.

Finally, we can separate procedural justice into three components: overall evaluations of procedural fairness, evaluations of the quality of decisionmaking, and evaluations of the quality of interpersonal treatment. We can then look at the influence of judgments about decisionmaking and interpersonal treatment on overall procedural justice judgments. Table 3 shows this analysis. In addition, Table 4 shows a similar analysis for legitimacy.

Table 1. Cooperation With the Police (compliance, cooperation, empowerment): Study Two

Beta Weights	All Respondents	Whites	African Americans	Hispanics
Legitimacy	.40***	.41***	.45***	.48***
Performance	−.01	.02	.01	−.03
Crime Problem	.01	.02	.06	−.02
Risk	.17***	.09*	.19***	.23***
Distributive Fairness	.06*	.09*	.06	−.06
Sex	−.01	−.01	.03	.00
Age	−.19***	−.17***	−.21***	−.14**
Income	−.01	−.04	−.02	.03
Education	−.02	.08	−.01	−.04
Af. Am./White	.11***	—	—	—
Hisp./White	−.03	—	—	—
Adj. R^2	29%	26%	31%	28%

NOTE: The three aspects of cooperation were combined into a single dependent variable after separate analysis suggested that this overall combined analysis did not obscure distinct ethnic group effects within the three dependent variables.

*$p < .05$; **$p < .01$; ***$p < .001$.

Table 2. The Antecedents of Legitimacy: Study Two

Beta Weights	All Respondents	Whites	African Americans	Hispanics
Procedural Justice	.35***	.30***	.37***	.46***
Distributive Fairness	.20***	.26***	.23***	.10
Performance	.03	.05	.03	.00
Crime Problem	−.06*	−.09*	−.09*	.02
Risk	−.01	.04	−.05	−.05
Sex	−.06	−.05	−.05	−.12*
Age	−.09**	−.08*	−.12*	−.11*
Income	−.06*	−.09*	−.01	−.06
Education	−.03	−.03	−.05	−.01
Af. Am./White	.16***	—	—	—
Hisp./White	.09**	—	—	—
Adj. R²	34%	30%	28%	24%

$*p < .05; **p < .01; ***p < .001.$

Table 3. The Antecedents of Procedural Justice: Study Two

Beta Weights	All Respondents	Whites	African Americans	Hispanics
Quality of Decisionmaking	.20***	.20***	.29***	.16***
Quality of Treatment	.36***	.37***	.23***	.43***
Distributive Fairness	.05*	.05	.06	−.02
Performance	.15***	.20***	.03	.06
Crime Problem	.10***	.06	.10*	.10*
Risk	.04	.03	.04	.05
Sex	−.02	−.04	−.02	−.03
Age	.03	.03	.05	.06
Income	−.04	.04	−.06	−.08
Education	−.07*	−.11*	−.02	−.07
Af. Am./White	.04	—	—	—
Hisp./White	.00	—	—	—
Adj. R²	41%	46%	36%	34%

$*p < .05; **p < .01; ***p < .001.$

The results of this analysis of the meaning of procedural fairness suggest that whites are especially sensitive to issues of interpersonal treatment. Those issues dominated their procedural justice judgments and were the only factor influencing their legitimacy judgments. In contrast, minority group members were more balanced and considered both issues—quality of decisionmaking and quality of interpersonal treatment— more equally. However, like whites, Hispanics gave considerable weight to interpersonal treatment when evaluating procedural justice. In this respect, Hispanics seem intermediate, falling between whites and African Americans. However, white and African American assessments of legitimacy were influenced by distributive justice, while Hispanic assessments were not. Overall, these findings reinforce those already outlined in pointing to the importance of process-based judgments in shaping reactions to the police and to policing activities.

Table 4. The Antecedents of Legitimacy: Study Two

Beta Weights	All Respondents	Whites	African Americans	Hispanics
Quality of Decisionmaking	.14***	.06	.19**	.24***
Quality of Treatment	.24***	.28***	.23**	.27***
Distributive Fairness	.21***	.26***	.22***	.09
Performance	.04	.05	.02	−.01
Crime Problem	−.06*	−.08*	−.08	.04
Risk	−.01	.05	−.05	−.05
Sex	−.06*	−.05	−.05	−.12*
Age	−.09**	−.07*	−.11*	−.10
Income	−.07**	−.08*	−.02	−.07
Education	−.04	−.04	−.05	−.02
Af. Am./White	.11***	—	—	—
Hisp./White	.04	—	—	—
Adj. R^2	33%	31%	29%	25%

$*p < .05; **p < .01; ***p < .001.$

Discussion

The results of this analysis provide support for the underlying assumptions about psychology upon which procedural justice-based policing rests. The first assumption is that public evaluations of police legitimacy impact people's compliance with law, their willingness to cooperate with and assist the police, and whether the public will empower the police. In both studies, no other independent variable measured had such a sweeping influence on police/community relations. This broad impact of legitimacy explains why, in the final models, it was by far the dominant predictor of orientation toward the police. The other independent variables only influenced particular aspects of community residents' orientation toward police, while legitimacy was important for each component.

These findings support the argument that legitimacy is a social value that is distinct from performance evaluations. They show that such values have an important and distinct influence on people's support for the police, suggesting that there is a strong normative basis of public support for the police that is distinct from police performance. More generally, it is clear that ethical judgments about obligation and responsibility are an important element of public support for the police.

People are *not* primarily instrumental in their reactions to the police—in other words, judging the police in instrumental terms. Instead, their reactions to the police are linked to their basic social values. This finding supports the arguments of Weber (1968) about the normative basis of public reactions to authority. It extends prior research findings (Tyler 1990) by showing that cooperation and empowerment, in addition to compliance, are influenced by legitimacy. These findings oppose the notion that if they are effectively fighting crime the police will inevitably alienate the public. By focusing on the psychology underlying views about their legitimacy among members of the public, the police can enhance their image in the eyes of the public, be objectively more effective in enforcing the law, and gain greater discretion in performing their regulatory duties. This suggests the value of focusing on an understanding of the determinants of legitimacy.

Further, these findings reinforce the argument that over time, the police can best regulate public behavior by focusing on engaging the social values, such as legitimacy, that lead to self-regulation on the part of most of the public, most of the time. If the public generally view the police as legitimate, much of their everyday behavior will conform to the law, freeing the police up to deal with problematic people and situations. Further, the efforts of the police to manage such problematic people and situations will be aided by cooperation from the public. Finally, when the police need discretionary authority, their use of such authority will be supported by the public. Hence, a procedural justice-based approach to regulation creates social order by engaging public cooperation with law and legal authority. Such cooperation is engaged when people in the communities being policed experience the police as exercising their authority fairly.

Of course, it is important to recognize that not all possible instrumental judgments, or even all possible indexes of police performance, are considered in these studies. An important task for future research is to develop and examine a broader range of instrumental issues that might potentially be important to people in their evaluations of the police. Further, we might consider a broader set of philosophical issues, such as people's conceptions of social contracts, their views of democratic theory, and/or their responsibility to the state and state authorities when thinking of alternatives to procedural justice as an antecedent of legitimacy. Legitimacy may also derive from philosophical or political perspectives and is not simply a reflection of police behavior. All of these issues point to directions for future research.

The key assumption upon which procedural justice-based policing is based is that evaluations of legitimacy are primarily based on procedural fairness. That assumption is supported by the findings of these surveys, which identify procedural justice as the primary antecedent of legitimacy among the samples of New Yorkers interviewed. In fact, the strength of the dominance of procedural justice judgments is striking and is clearly the primary factor shaping legitimacy.

This finding is very important from the perspective of policing, since the police have more control over how they treat people than they do over the crime rate. The incidence of crime will fluctuate due to factors beyond police control. Procedural fairness, or treating people with respect and in an unbiased fashion, does not depend on crime rate fluctuations. Rather, it depends on the behavior of the police themselves. Thus, by becoming procedurally sensitive, the police develop a way they are viewed by the public that is to some degree insulated from societal forces, such as demographics or economic conditions, which shape crime rates but are beyond police control. Tyler and Huo (2002) refer to governance based on procedural justice as process-based regulation and argue that it offers many advantages to the police.

The message that authorities need to acknowledge the basic dignity and rights of citizens, to account for decisions that affect them, and to make their decisions in a neutral and objective way is consistent with the work of Sherman on defiance theory (1993) and with the reintegrative shaming model of Braithwaite (1989). Defiance theory argues that without such an acknowledgment of their dignity and rights, people are likely to feel angry and be resistant to the police, while models of reintegrative shaming emphasize the potential for increasing future deference to authority by the respectful treatment of offenders. Here too, the message is that people are more accepting of and cooperative with authorities when they are treated with fairness and respect.

Terrorism and Policing

The two studies reported differ in many ways, including their method of sampling and some of the questions asked. Study Two was improved based upon the problems encountered in Study One. As a result, we need to use caution in comparing the findings of these two studies. However, they do represent a naturally occurring quasi-experiment, in that the first survey was conducted before the World Trade Center attack and the second survey was conducted after that attack. Comparison of the two results, therefore, allows us to address the question of whether procedural concerns are less important when concerns about national security are higher.

A comparison of Figures 1 and 2 suggests that legitimacy plays a similarly important role in judgments about the police and police empowerment both before and following the World Trade Center attack. In both cases, empowerment flows primarily from legitimacy. However, instrumental issues do matter in the second study, where performance directly shaped empowerment. This may be because people feel more threatened, or because performance was better measured in the second study. In the first study, performance mattered because it shaped legitimacy, but performance did not directly shape empowerment. Further, in both studies procedural justice was the key antecedent of legitimacy.

While these findings suggest that the atmosphere of terror and threat following the World Trade Center attack does not strongly alter people's reactions to policing activities, it is important to emphasize that this study is focused on neighborhood policing activities. We might find greater shifts if we focused directly on national-level issues of civil liberties.

Ethnic Group Differences

Tyler and Huo (2002) argue that while the members of different ethnic groups differ in their views about the legitimacy of the law, the courts, and the police, the psychological basis of legitimacy is similar within each group. The findings of Study Two provide strong support for this argument. Regardless of ethnicity, people cooperate with the police when they view the police as legitimate. Further, legitimacy is linked to fairness in the exercise of authority. This is not to say that the views of the various ethnic groups are identical. They are not. But the similarities are striking, and the differences are small.

This finding, based upon general evaluations of the police, is consistent with Tyler and Huo's finding in their study of personal experiences with the police and courts (Tyler & Huo 2002). That study found that the members of different ethnic groups evaluated their personal experiences with the police and the courts using a common psychological model that emphasized fairness of treatment. Hence, on both the personal and the general levels, the evidence suggests that a general psychological model explains the reactions of the members of the three major ethnic groups considered—whites, African Americans, and Hispanics. That model is the procedural justice-based model of policing.

References

Axelrod, Robert (1984) *The Evolution of Cooperation*. New York: Basic.

Beetham, David (1991) *The Legitimation of Power*. Atlantic Highlands, NJ: Humanites Press International, Inc.

Blumstein, Albert, & Joel Wallman, eds. (2000) *The Crime Drop in America*. Cambridge: Cambridge Univ. Press.

Braithwaite, John (1989) *Crime, Shame, and Reintegration*. Cambridge: Cambridge Univ. Press.

Brodeur, Jean-Paul (1998) *How to Recognize Good Policing*. Thousand Oaks, CA: Sage.

Casper, Jonathan D., Tom R. Tyler, & Bonnie Fisher (1988) "Procedural Justice in Felony Cases," 22 *Law & Society Rev.* 483–507.

Citrin, Jack, & Christopher Muste (1999) "Trust in Government," in J. P. Robinson, P. R. Shaver, & L. S. Wrightsman, eds., *Measures of Political Attitudes*. New York: Academic Press.

538   **The Role of Procedural Justice and Legitimacy**

Cole, David (1999) *No Equal Justice: Race and Class in the American Criminal Justice System.* New York: W. W. Norton.

Deutsch, Morton (1990) "Psychological Roots of Moral Exclusion," 46 *J. of Social Issues* 21–6.

Friedman, Robert R. (1992) *Community Policing: Comparative Perspectives and Prospects.* New York: St. Martin's Press.

Gest, Ted (2000) *Crime and Politics: Big Government's Erratic Campaign for Law and Order.* Oxford: Oxford Univ. Press.

Harcourt, Bernard E. (2001) *The Illusion of Order: The False Promise of Broken Windows Policing.* Cambridge: Harvard Univ. Press.

Huang, Wilson S., & Michael S. Vaughn (1996) "Support and Confidence: Public Attitudes Toward the Police," in T. Flanagan & D. Longmire, eds., *Americans View Crime and Justice: A National Public Opinion Survey.* Thousand Oaks, CA: Sage Publications.

Joreskog, Karl G., & Dag Sorbom (1986) *LISREL: Analysis of Linear Structural Relationships by the Method of Maximum Likelihood.* Uppsala, Sweden: University of Uppsala, Department of Statistics.

Kelling, George L., & Catherine M. Coles (1996) *Fixing Broken Windows.* New York: Touchstone.

Kelling, George L., & Mark K. Moore (1988) "The Evolving Strategy of Policing. Perspectives on Policing," No. 4, 1–15. Washington, DC: National Institute of Justice.

Kelman, Herbert C., & V. Lee Hamilton (1989) *Crimes of Obedience.* New Haven: Yale Univ. Press.

Lawler, Edward J., Rebecca Ford, & Mary Blegen (1988) "Coercive Capability in Conflict: A Test of Bilateral Versus Conflict Spiral Theory," 51 *Social Psychology Q.* 93–107.

McArdle, Andrea, & Tanya T. Erzen (2001) *Zero Tolerance: Quality of Life and the New Police Brutality in New York City.* New York: New York Univ. Press.

Moore, Mark H. (1992) "Problem-Solving and Community Policing," in M. Tonry & N. Morris, eds., *Modern Policing: Crime and Justice, A Review of Research,* Vol. 15. Chicago: Univ. of Chicago Press.

Nagata, Donna K. (1993) *Legacy of Injustice.* New York: Plenum.

New York City Police Department (2001) "New York City Police Department Citywide Stop and Frisk Data, 1998, 1999, and 2000." http://www.nyc.gov/html/nypd/pdf/pap/stopandfrisk_0501.pdf.

Pruitt, Dean (1981) *Negotiation Behavior.* New York: Academic Press.

Pruitt, Dean, & Jeff Z. Rubin (1986) *Social Conflict: Escalation, Stalemate, and Settlement.* New York: McGraw-Hill.

Pruitt, Dean, Robert S. Peirce, Neil B. McGillicuddy, Gary L. Welton, & Lynn M. Castrianno (1993) "Long-Term Success in Mediation," 17 *Law and Human Behavior* 313–30.

Reiss, Albert J. Jr. (1992) "Police Organization in the Twentieth Century," in M. Tonry & N. Morris, eds., *Modern Policing: Crime and Justice, A Review of Research,* Vol. 15. Chicago: Univ. of Chicago Press.

Sampson, Robert J., Stephen W. Raudenbush, & Felton Earls (1997) "Neighborhoods and Violent Crime," 277 *Science* 918–24.

Sarat, Austin (1977) "Studying American Legal Culture," 11 *Law & Society Rev.* 427–88.

Sherman, Lawrence W. (1993) "Defiance, Deterrence, and Irrelevance: A Theory of the Criminal Sanction," 30 *J. of Research in Crime and Delinquency* 445–73.

Silverman, Eli B. (1999) *NYPD Battles Crime: Innovative Strategies in Policing.* Evanston, IL: Northwestern Univ. Press.

Skogan, Wesley G. (1990) *Disorder and Decline.* New York: Free Press.

Skogan, Wesley G., & Susan M. Hartnett (1997) *Community Policing, Chicago Style.* New York: Oxford Univ. Press.

Skogan, Wesley G., Susan M. Hartnett, Jill DuBois, Jennifer T. Comey, Marianne Kaiser, & Justine H. Lovig (1999) *On the Beat: Police and Community Problem Solving.* Boulder, CO: Westview Press.

Skolnick, Jerome, & James Fyfe (1993) *Above the Law: Police and the Excessive Use of Force.* New York: Free Press.

Sparks, J. Richard, Anthony Bottoms, & Will Hay (1996) *Prisons and the Problem of Order.* Cambridge: Cambridge Univ. Press.

Sullivan, John L., James E. Piereson, & Gregory E. Marcus (1982) *Political Tolerance and American Democracy.* Chicago: Univ. of Chicago Press.

Sullivan, Peggy S., Roger G. Dunham, & Geoffrey P. Alpert (1987) "Attitude Structures of Different Ethnic and Age Groups Concerning Police," 78 *J. of Criminal Law and Criminology* 177–96.

Tyler, Tom R. (1990) *Why People Obey the Law.* New Haven: Yale Univ. Press.

——— (2001a) "Trust and Law Abidingness: A Proactive Model of Social Regulation," 81 *Boston University Law Rev.* 361–406.

——— (2001b) "Public Trust and Confidence in Legal Authorities: What Do Majority and Minority Group Members Want from the Law and Legal Institutions?," 19 *Behavioral Sciences and the Law* 215–35.

Tyler, Tom R., & Steven L. Blader (2000) *Cooperation in Groups.* Philadelphia: Psychology Press.

Tyler, Tom R., & Yuen J. Huo (2002) *Trust in the Law: Encouraging Public Cooperation With the Police and Courts.* New York: Russell-Sage.

Tyler, Tom R., & E. Allan Lind (1992) "A Relational Model of Authority in groups," 25 *Advances in Experimental Social Psychology* 115–91.

Tyler, Tom R., Robert J. Boeckmann, Heather J. Smith, & Yuen J. Huo (1997) *Social Justice in a Diverse Society.* Boulder, CO: Westview Press.

Weber, Max (1968) *Economy and Society: An Outline of Interpretive Sociology,* G. Roth & C. Wittich, eds. New York: Bedminster Press.

Wilson, James Q., & Joan Petersilia (2002) *Crime: Public Policies for Crime Control.* Oakland, CA: Institute for Contemporary Studies.

Worden, Robert E. (1995) "The 'Causes' of Police Brutality: Theory and Evidence on Police Use of Force," in W. A. Geller, & H. Toch, eds., *And Justice for All: Understanding and Controlling Police Abuse of Force.* Washington, DC: Police Executive Research Forum.

Appendix A: Measures, Study One

Legitimacy

Legitimacy is operationalized as the perceived obligation to obey the directives of a legal authority, trust in the institution of policing and in individual police officers in one's neighborhood, and affective feelings toward the police. We asked respondents to indicate the extent of their agreement to nineteen items on six-point Likert scales ranging from "agree strongly" to "disagree strongly." The overall scale had a mean of 3.9 (3.5 was neutral, with low scores indicating high legitimacy, s.d. = 0.97, alpha = 0.94).

For obligation, we asked respondents to agree/disagree that: (1) "You should accept the decisions made by police, even if you think they are wrong," (2) "Communities work best when people follow the directives of the police," (3) "Disobeying the police is seldom justified," and (4) "It would be difficult for you to break the law and keep your self-respect."

For trust in the institution of policing, we asked people to agree/disagree that (5) "The police can be trusted to make decisions that are right for the people in your neighborhood," (6) "People's basic rights are well protected by the police in your neighborhood," (7) "The police in your neighborhood are generally honest," (8) "New York City has one of the best police forces in the United States," (9) "I am proud of the work of the NYPD," (10) "I am happy to defend the work of the NYPD when talking to my friends," (11) "I agree with many of the values that define what the NYPD stands for," (12) "I cannot think of another police force that I respect more than the NYPD," and (13) "The work of the NYPD encourages me to feel good about our city."

Finally, to measure the emotional component of legitimacy, we asked respondents to rate the extent of their feelings about the NYPD on six six-point scales. The feelings included (14) respect, (15) trust, (16) appreciation, (17) fear, (18) contempt, and (19) anger.

Instrumental Judgments

Risk
We defined risk as the perceived likelihood of being caught and punished for breaking the law. We created an index using three questions based on a six-point Likert scale. We presented respondents with six common types of law-breaking behavior (noted under "compliance") and asked them how likely it was that [they] would be caught and punished if they broke these laws, how much the police would care, and how severely [they] would be punished. We combined these items into a scale of risk (alpha = 0.78, mean = 3.5, s.d. = 1.3).

Performance in Fighting Crime
We measured performance evaluations by nine questions on a six-point Likert scale. Items included questions asking (1–5) "How effective have the police been at controlling violent crime, gang violence, drugs, gun violence, and burglary?" Other items included (6) "How quickly do the police respond when they are called for help?," (7) "How quickly do the police respond when people in your neighborhood call the police for help?," (8) "Are the police effective at providing help?," and (9) "Do the police try to be of assistance?" We combined these items into a performance index (alpha = 0.91; mean = 4.1, s.d. = 0.99).

Distributive Fairness
We measured distributive fairness by five questions on the same six-point scale used for procedural justice. Items included

(1) "How often do people receive the outcomes they deserve under the law when they deal with the police?," (2) "Are the outcomes that people receive from the police better than they deserve, worse than they deserve, or about what they deserve under the law?," (3) "How often do the police give people in your neighborhood less help than they give others due to their race?," (4) "The police do not provide the same quality of service to people living in all areas of the city," and (5) "Minority residents of the city receive a lower quality of service from the NYPD than do whites." We combined these items into a scale of distributive fairness (alpha = 0.76; mean = 3.4, s.d. = 1.04).

Consequences of Legitimacy

Compliance

We assessed compliance by asking respondents to indicate on six-point Likert scales how often they followed rules about seven types of behavior: (1) where to park a car legally, (2) how to legally dispose of trash and litter, (3) not making noise at night, (4) not speeding or breaking traffic laws, (5) not buying possible stolen items on the street, (6) not taking inexpensive items from stores or restaurants without paying, and (7) not using drugs such as marijuana. We initially combined these items into a compliance index (alpha = 0.88). Respondents indicated very high levels of compliance (mean = 5.3, s.d. = 0.94), yielding a highly skewed distribution (skew = − 2.2, s.e. = 0.12). In order to remove this skewness, we collapsed the compliance index into a three-point scale by trichotomizing the original items (alpha = 0.85 for the new scale, mean = 2.5, s.d. = 0.56).

Cooperation

We assessed cooperation by ten questions, on six-point scales similar to previous questions, which asked respondents how likely they would be to (1) "Call the police to report a crime occurring in your neighborhood," (2) "Call the police to report an accident," (3) "Help the police to find someone suspected of committing a crime," (4) "Call and give the police information to help the police solve a crime," (5) "Report dangerous or suspicious activities in your neighborhood to the police," (6) "Voluntarily work as a police-community liaison worker at night or during weekends," (7) "Spend some of your time helping new police officers by showing them around your neighborhood," (8) "Volunteer to attend a community meeting to discuss crime in your neighborhood," (9) "Work with others in your neighborhood on neighborhood watch activities designed to lower crime," and (10) "Be willing to serve on a neighborhood committee to discuss problems in your neighborhood with the police." We combined these items into a single index (alpha = 0.87, mean = 4.38, s.d. = 0.93).

Empowerment

We assessed empowerment by five questions on a six-point Likert type scale. Questions asked the extent to which the subject agreed or disagreed that (1) "The police should have the right to stop and question people on the street," (2) "The police should have the power to decide which areas of the city should receive the most police protection," (3) "Because of their training and experience, the police are best able to decide how to deal with crime in your neighborhood," (4) "The police should have the power to do whatever they think is needed to fight crime," and (5) "If we give enough power to the police, they will be able to effectively control crime." We combined these items into an overall index (alpha = 0.83, mean = 3.26, s.d. = 1.23).

Antecedents of Legitimacy

Procedural Fairness

We measured procedural fairness using questions reflecting three aspects of procedural justice. We combined all the items to create a summary index of procedural fairness (alpha = 0.98; mean = 3.61; s.d. = 1.18).

In the items, we asked respondents to indicate the frequency with which the police engaged in behavior consistent with procedural justice in their neighborhood. Measured on a six-point Likert-type scale, a range was given from "almost always" to "almost never."

The items included two overall assessments of procedural justice: (1) "Make decisions about how to handle problems in fair ways" and (2) "Treat people fairly." The alpha for this subscale was 0.92.

Respondents also evaluated the fairness of police decisionmaking. The items asked if the police (3) "Treat everyone in your neighborhood with dignity and respect," (4) "Treat everyone in your community equally," (5) "Accurately understand and apply the law," and (6) "Make their decisions based upon facts, not their personal biases or opinions." In addition, the index had four items asking about how fairly the police make decisions. These items included how fairly the police decide (7) "Who to stop and question on the street," (8) "Who to stop for traffic violations," (9) "Who to arrest and take to jail," and (10) "How much they will help people with problems." The alpha for this subscale was 0.96.

They also evaluated the quality of treatment people received. The items asked whether the police (11) "Clearly explain the reasons for their actions," (12) "Give honest explanations for their actions," (13) "Give people a chance to express their views before making decisions," (14) "Consider people's opinions when deciding what to do," (15) "Take account of people's needs and concerns," (16) "Treat people with dignity and respect," (17) "Respect people's rights," (18) "Sincerely try to help people with their problems," (19) "Try to find the best solutions for people's problems," and (20) "The NYPD treats citizens with courtesy and respect." The alpha for this subscale was 0.93.

Appendix B: Measures, Study Two

Legitimacy

Legitimacy is operationalized as the perceived obligation to obey the directives of a legal authority and trust in the institution of policing and in individual police officers in one's neighborhood. We asked respondents to indicate the extent of their agreement to 19 items on Likert scales. In the overall scale, low scores indicated high legitimacy (alpha = 0.84, mean = 2.36, s.d. = 0.53).

For obligation, we asked respondents to agree/disagree that (1) "You should accept the decisions made by police, even if you think they are wrong," (2) "You should do what the police tell you to do even when you do not understand the reasons for their decisions," (3) "You should do what the police tell you to do, even when you disagree with their decisions," (4) "You should do what the police tell you to do even when you do not like the way they treat you," (5) "There are times when it is ok for you to ignore what the police tell you (reversed)," (6) "Sometimes you have to bend the law for things to come out right (reversed)," (7) "The law represents the values of the people in power, rather than the values of people like you (reversed)," (8) "People in power use the law to try to control people like you (reversed)," and (9) "The law does not protect your interests (reversed)."

For trust in the institution of policing, we asked people to agree/disagree that (10) "Overall, the NYPD is a legitimate authority and people should obey the decisions that NYPD officers make," (11) "I have confidence that the NYPD can do its job well," (12) "I trust the leaders of the NYPD to make decisions that are good for everyone in the city," (13) "People's basic rights are well protected by the police," (14) "The police care about the well-being of everyone they deal with," (15) "I am proud of the work of the NYPD," (16) "I agree with many of the values that define what the NYPD stands for," (17) "The police are often dishonest (reversed)," (18) "Some of the things the police do embarrass our city (reversed)," and (19) "There are many things about the NYPD and its policies that need to be changed (reversed)."

Instrumental Judgments

Risk

We defined risk as the perceived likelihood of being caught and punished for breaking the law. We presented respondents with seven common types of law-breaking behavior (noted under "compliance") and asked how likely it was that [they] would be caught and punished if [they] broke these laws. The seven behaviors were "parking your car illegally," "disposing of trash illegally," "making too much noise at night," "breaking traffic laws or speeding," "buying stolen items on the street," "taking inexpensive items from stores without paying," and "using drugs such as marijuana in public places." We combined these items into a scale of risk (low scores meant high perceived risk; alpha = 0.87, mean = 2.36, s.d. = 0.95).

Performance in Fighting Crime

We measured performance evaluations in three ways: by asking how effective the police were, by reports about neighborhood conditions, and by reports of fear of victimization.

To assess police effectiveness, we asked respondents: (1) "How effective are the police in fighting crime in your neighborhood?," (2) "When people call the police for help, how quickly do they respond?," and (3) "How effective are the police at helping people who ask for help?" We combined these items into an overall scale, with low scores indicating high effectiveness (alpha = 0.63; mean = 2.01; s.d. = 0.93).

We assessed neighborhood conditions by asking respondents eight questions, including (1) "How often do you see garbage in the streets," (2) "How often do you see empty beer bottles on the streets," (3) "How often do you see graffiti on the walls," (4) "How often do you see gangs hanging out on the streets," (5) "How often do you see people buying beer, wine, or liquor on the street," (6) "How often do you see people buying or selling drugs on the street," (7) "How high is the crime rate in your neighborhood?," and (8) "In the past year, has the crime rate been increasing?" We formed an overall scale, with low scores indicating poor neighborhood conditions (alpha = 0.81; mean = 2.89, s.d. = 0.70).

We assessed fear of victimization using a four-item scale. Items included: (1) "How much do you worry about your home being burglarized?," (2) "How much do you worry about being robbed, assaulted, or mugged on the street?," (3) "How safe is your neighborhood during the day?," and (4) "How safe is your neighborhood in the evening?" We created a single indicator of fear (alpha = 0.75; mean = 3.13, s.d. = 0.72).

Distributive Fairness

We measured distributive fairness by eleven questions. We first asked respondents whether eight groups received the quality of service they deserved from the police: people like the respondent, people in their neighborhood, minorities in their neighborhood, whites, African Americans, Hispanics, poor people, and wealthy people. Respondents could indicate that each group received what they deserved, too much, or too little. Responses for each group were coded as either fair or unfair (too much or too little). Respondents were also asked whether (1) "The police treat everyone equally regardless of their race," (2) "The police provide better services to the wealthy (reversed)," and (3) "They sometimes give minorities less help due to their race (reversed)." We combined these items to form a single scale, with low scores indicating unfairness (alpha = 0.67; mean = 2.37; s.d. = 0.66).

Consequences of Legitimacy

Compliance

We assessed compliance by asking respondents to indicate on six-point Likert scales how often they followed rules about seven types of behavior: (1) where you can legally park your car, (2) how to dispose of trash and litter, (3) against making too much noise at night, (4) against speeding or breaking other traffic laws, (5) against buying possibly stolen items on the street, (6) against taking inexpensive items from stores without paying, and (7) against using drugs such as marijuana in public places. These items formed a compliance scale (alpha = 0.80). Respondents indicated very high levels of compliance, yielding a highly skewed distribution (skew = 2.07, s.e. = 0.07). In order to remove this skewness, we performed a square root transformation, leading to a less skewed scale (skew = 1.55, s.e. = 0.07, with an alpha of 0.80, mean = 1.21, s.d. = 0.25).

Cooperation

We assessed cooperation by three questions, on scales that asked respondents how likely they would be to (1) "Call the police to report a crime occurring in your neighborhood," (2) "Help the police to find someone suspected of committing a crime by providing them with information," and (3) "Report dangerous or suspicious activities in your neighborhood to the police." We combined these items into a single index, with low scores indicating being helpful to the police (alpha = 0.68, mean = 1.43, s.d. = 0.60).

546   **The Role of Procedural Justice and Legitimacy**

Empowerment

We assessed empowerment by six questions on a six-point Likert-type scale. Questions asked the extent to which the subject agreed or disagreed that (1) "The police should have the right to stop and question people on the street," (2) "The police should have the power to decide how much police protection each area of the city receives," (3) "The police should have the power to decide which laws are the most important for them to enforce," (4) "The police should be able to search people's homes without having to get permission from a judge if they think stolen property or drugs are inside," (5) "Community residents need to be equal partners with the police in making decisions about how to fight crime (reversed)," and (6) "There need to be clear limits on what the police are allowed to do in fighting crime (reversed)." We combined these items into an overall index in which low scores indicated empowering the police (alpha = 0.56, mean = 3.10, s.d. = 0.57).

Antecedents of Legitimacy

Procedural Fairness

We measured procedural fairness using questions reflecting three aspects of procedural justice. We combined all the items to create a summary index of procedural fairness (alpha = 0.98; mean = 3.61; s.d. = 1.18).

In the items, we asked respondents to indicate the frequency with which the police engaged in behavior consistent with procedural justice in their neighborhood. Three subscales were used: overall fairness, fairness of decisionmaking, and fairness of treatment. The total scale had 11 items, and low scores indicated fairness (alpha = 0.91, mean = 2.17, s.d. = 0.92).

The items for overall assessments of procedural justice were (1) "Do the police make decisions about how to handle problems in fair ways?" and (2) "Do the police treat people fairly?" Low scores indicated fairness, and the alpha for this subscale was 0.73 (mean = 1.98, s.d. = 1.24).

Respondents also evaluated the fairness of police decisionmaking. The items asked if the police (3) "Usually accurately understand and apply the law," (4) "Make their decisions based upon facts, not their personal biases or opinions," (5) "Try to get the facts in a situation before deciding how to act," (6) "Give honest explanations for their actions to the people they deal with," and (7) "Apply the rules consistently to different people." The alpha for this subscale was 0.84 (mean = 2.27, s.d. = 1.02).

They also evaluated the quality of treatment people received. The items asked whether the police (8) "Consider the views of the people involved when deciding what to do," (9) "Take account of the needs and concerns of the people they deal with," (10) "Treat people with dignity and respect," and (11) "Respect people's rights." The alpha for this subscale was 0.82 (mean = 2.14, s.d. = 0.97).

[4]

SCHOOLS AS COMMUNITIES: THE RELATIONSHIPS AMONG COMMUNAL SCHOOL ORGANIZATION, STUDENT BONDING, AND SCHOOL DISORDER*

ALLISON ANN PAYNE
  The College of New Jersey
DENISE C. GOTTFREDSON
  The University of Maryland
GARY D. GOTTFREDSON
  Gottfredson Associates, Inc.

Research has indicated that school factors such as communal school organization and student bonding are predictive of school disorder, with greater communal organization and greater student bonding leading to less delinquency and victimization. Data from a nationally representative sample of 254 public, nonalternative, secondary schools were used to examine structural equation models representing hypothesized relationships among communal school organization, student bonding, and school disorder. The hypothesis that communally organized schools would have less disorder held true for teacher victimization and student delinquency, but not for student victimization. In addition, the hypothesis that the relationship between communal school organization and school disorder would be mediated by student bonding was supported for student delinquency, but not for teacher victimization.

KEYWORDS: School disorder, school climate, student bonding, school community, school, survey, delinquency, violence

* This research was supported in part by Grant 96-MU-MU-0008 from the National Institute of Justice, U.S. Department of Justice. Additional support was provided by Grant 98-JN-FX-0004 from Office of Juvenile Justice and Delinquency Prevention, U.S. Department of Justice, and by the U.S. Department of Education. The opinions expressed do not necessarily reflect the positions or policy of any sponsor. We thank Suzanne Busby, David Cantor, Scott Crosse, Ellen R. Czeh, Rebecca Gold, Irene Hantman, Elizabeth M. Jones, Jacob Lawrence, Kirsten Mackler, Felicia Morings, Nicole Piquero, April Rose, Lana Ryaboy, Gary Shapiro, Rebecca Silverman, Adriana Wade, and Shannon Womer for assistance with this research. We also thank John H. Laub, Sylvia Rosenfield, Doug Smith, Gary Lafree, Robert Bursik, and three anonymous reviewers for their helpful comments and suggestions For more information, contact Allison Ann Payne, Department of Criminology and Justice Studies, The College of New Jersey, P.O. Box 7718, Ewing, N.J. 08628-0718 (609-771-3366); payne@tcnj.edu.

750   PAYNE ET AL.

Although school-related deaths, violent victimizations in school, and
overall school crime have declined over the past decade (Kaufman et al.,
2001), serious forms of delinquency and victimization in schools are still a
problem. In a 1998 national survey, 37.3% of secondary school students
reported having hit or threatened to hit other students in the past year
(Gottfredson et al., 2000). In the same study, 19% of students reported
having been threatened, 14% reported having been attacked, and 5%
reported having been threatened with a knife or a gun. Similarly, 20% of
teachers reported being threatened, although only 3% reported actually
being attacked (Gottfredson et al., 2000).

Even more common are incidents of less serious delinquency and victimization. In the study mentioned above, 28% of teachers reported damage to property worth less than $10, 24% reported theft of property worth
less than $10, 14% reported damage to property worth more than $10, and
13% reported theft of property worth more than $10 (Gottfredson et al.,
2000). Similarly, 16% of secondary school students reported damaging or
destroying school property and 9% reported engaging in theft.

Aside from the obvious costs of school crime on property damage and
loss and personal injury, school disorder is costly because it reduces the
ability of schools to carry out their educational mission. Surveys of American teachers (e.g., Harris et al., 1993) document some of school disorder's
collateral effects on the learning environment. These surveys show that the
threat of school violence results in lower teacher and student attendance
at school. Teachers in disorderly schools also spend a large proportion of
their time coping with behavior problems rather than in academic instruc-
tion, which results in lower levels of academic engagement, academic performance, and eventually graduation rates. Fear of victimization in
schools has also been shown to influence students' ability to concentrate
and learn (Lawrence, 1998; McDermott, 1980). Finally, disorder is likely
to influence the schooling experience more generally by affecting staffing
quality. A recent analysis of data collected by the National Center for
Education Statistics (Ingersoll, 2001) showed higher teacher turnover in
schools with greater discipline problems, and teachers cited discipline
problems as a major reason for leaving. These problems are especially
severe in urban areas.

Research has identified several characteristics of schools and communities related to school disorder that might be manipulated in efforts to
reduce these problems. This study focuses on two of these predictors of
disorder: the social organization and the level of student bonding in a
school. Research has illustrated the importance of school social organization in general and, more specifically, the importance of communal school
organization (Bryk and Driscoll, 1988; Gottfredson, 2001; Gottfredson et
al., 2003; Welsh, 2000). Communal school organization refers to the

organization of a school as a community, as indicated by supportive relationships between and among teachers, administrators, and students, a common set of goals and norms, and a sense of collaboration and involvement. Schools that are communally organized have more positive student attitudes, better teacher morale, and less student problem behavior (Battistich and Hom, 1997; Battistich et al., 1995; Bryk and Driscoll, 1988). The supportive relationships, common norms and goals, and greater involvement and participation increase the likelihood that students will become more bonded to school. The importance of student bonding in improving student achievement and reducing problem behavior is also supported by previous research (Cernkovich and Giordano, 1992; Gottfredson et al., 2002; Jenkins, 1997; Krohn and Massey, 1980; Liska and Reed, 1985; Welsh et al., 1999).

This study examines the school-level relationships among communal school organization, student bonding, and school disorder. It is hypothesized that more communally organized schools will have students who are more bonded to school and, therefore, have lower levels of student delinquency and student and teacher victimization against students and teachers. Structural equation modeling is used to examine these relationships (Bentler, 1995).

PRIOR RESEARCH IN COMMUNAL SCHOOL ORGANIZATION AND STUDENT BONDING

COMMUNAL SCHOOL ORGANIZATION

As defined by Solomon et al., (1997), a school that has a high sense of community, is one in which ". . .members know, care about, and support one another, have common goals and sense of shared purpose, and to which they actively contribute and feel personally committed" (Solomon et al., 1997:236). A communally organized school emphasizes informal social relations, common norms and experiences, and collaboration and participation; by contrast, more bureaucratic schools emphasize formal organization, technical knowledge, and regulation and standardization (Lee et al.; Rowan, 1990).

The idea of the communal school organization is similar to Sampson's concept of neighborhood collective efficacy (Sampson et al., 1997; Sampson et al., 1999; Morenoff et al., 2001). Collective efficacy "highlights shared expectations and mutual engagement by residents in local social control" (Morenoff et al., 2001:520). Sampson et al. propose that neighborhoods with higher collective efficacy will have higher levels of informal social control, defined as the capacity of a community to regulate the behavior of its members. These higher levels of social control, in turn, lead to lower levels of crime and delinquency (Sampson et al., 1997; Sampson et al., 1999; Morenoff et al., 2001).

Previous research has demonstrated beneficial outcomes of communal school organization. Bryk and Driscoll (1988) found that levels of teacher efficacy, work enjoyment, and morale were higher and teacher absenteeism was lower in schools that were communally organized. These schools also had lower levels of student misbehavior and dropouts, and higher levels of academic interest and math achievement. Similarly, Battistich et al. found that student sense of community was significantly correlated with the students' liking for school, empathy, prosocial motivation, academic motivation, self-esteem, conflict resolution, and altruistic behavior (Battistich et al., 1995; Solomon et al., 1992). Finally, Battistich and Solomon (1997) found that sense of community was highly correlated with teacher efficacy, teacher work enjoyment, teacher satisfaction, teacher perceptions of principal effectiveness, parental supportiveness, and positive relations between teachers and students. Only one study specifically examined the relationship between student sense of community and deviant behavior: Battistich and Hom (1997) found that higher levels of student sense of school community were associated with lower levels of drug use and delinquency.

Previous research, however, has not examined the process leading from communal school organization to these beneficial outcomes. That is, these studies do not examine why students in communally organized schools exhibit higher levels of academic achievement or lower levels of problem behavior. Although some researchers propose that communal school organization leads to greater student sense of belonging, which, in turn, leads to less delinquency, no studies have specifically tested this hypothesized mediating mechanism. Another weakness of some past studies is the small number of schools included in the study. For instance, the findings of Battistich and his colleagues (Battistich et al., 1995; Battistich and Hom, 1997) are based on data from only 24 schools, which, for research on a school-level concept such as communal school organization, constitutes a very small sample. In addition, many of the previous studies do not control for the possibility of a spurious relationship between communal school organization and the outcomes. This study attempts to address these weaknesses by examining the extent to which student bonding mediates the effect of communal school organization on school disorder, by using a large nationally representative sample of secondary schools, and by including exogenous variables such as community poverty and school size.

STUDENT BONDING

Students with a high sense of school community appear to be more bonded to the school. They have greater attachment to the teachers, more commitment to the school, and have internalized the norms of the school to a greater degree. They feel as though they belong to the school, as though they are valued and accepted.

These ideas, suggested by the literature reviewed above, provide a link between communal school organization and delinquency via Hirschi's social control theory (Hirschi, 1969). As discussed by Hirschi (1969), one domain in which an individual's social bond is formed is the school. Attachment to school is shown by the extent to which students care about the school, the teachers, and the teachers' opinions. Commitment to education is shown by the time and energy students invest in school as they pursue the goal of academic achievement. Involvement is simply the time spent on conventional school activities. Finally, belief is the extent to which students give legitimacy to the norms and rules of the school. In general, students who are well integrated in school are less likely to be deviant. Those who have more positive attachments, who have invested greater effort into school, who are involved in more school activities, and who believe in the rules of the school are less likely to engage in deviant activities (Welsh et al., 1999).

Hirschi (1969) provided support for his theory as exhibited in the school domain. Students who cared little about what the teachers think and who did not like school were much more likely to report delinquent acts. Additionally, those with low belief and low commitment were more likely to be delinquent (Hirschi, 1969). Other researchers have also supported the negative relationship between school bonding and delinquency (Cernkovich and Giordano, 1992; Gottfredson et al., 2002; Jenkins, 1997; Krohn and Massey, 1980; Liska and Reed, 1985; Welsh et al., 1999;). Although little research has examined the relationship between student bonding levels and levels of victimization in schools, Gottfredson and Gottfredson (1985) did find that schools with higher levels of student attachment to school and student belief in conventional rules experienced lower levels of teacher and student victimization.

It is clear that student bonding is an important concept when discussing student achievement and delinquency. Research has demonstrated that students who are more attached to teachers, more committed to school, and have stronger belief in the school's norms will display higher academic achievement and less deviant behavior.

The present study contributes to the research regarding social bonding to schools in several ways. It uses a national sample of 307 schools, larger than other recent tests of the theory (Jenkins, 1997; Welsh et al., 1999). It also examines the relationship between communal school organization and student bonding, and the outcome variables of both delinquency and victimization, while controlling for exogenous variables.

754   PAYNE ET AL.

THE LINKS

Discussions about communal school organization naturally lead to discussions about student bonding. Research has demonstrated that students in communally organized schools have a greater sense of belonging, greater commitment to school, and greater internalization of school norms (Battistich et al., 1995; Solomon et al., 1992). As the adults in the school create a school community, the climate of the school becomes warmer and more inclusive and participatory. The students' feelings of belonging or attachment then increase, as do their levels of commitment to school and their levels of belief in or acceptance of school norms and values. These findings directly relate to Hirschi's social control theory. Thus, the link between communal school organization and student bonding is clear: Students in schools that are communally organized will be more bonded to the school.

It is important to note the difference between communal school organization and student bonding, as they could be seen as the same concept on the surface. The major difference is where each theoretical concept lies in relation to the individual. Communal school organization refers to the existence of a specific social organization that is external to the individual; that is, the existence of supportive relations, of collaboration and participation, and of a set of shared norms and goals. Student bonding, however, refers to the internal processes that result from the existence of this communal organization in the school: the personal attachment to the school, the commitment to education, and the belief in school rules. Therefore, communal school organization is external to the individual, whereas student bonding is internal.

HYPOTHESES

Based on the research reviewed above, the hypotheses of this study are as follows:

Hypothesis One: Schools with higher levels of communal school organization will have lower levels of school disorder.

Hypothesis Two: The effect of communal school organization on school disorder will be mediated by student bonding.

METHODS

SAMPLE

The National Study of Delinquency Prevention in Schools (Gottfredson and Gottfredson, 2002; Gottfredson and Gottfredson, 2001; Gottfredson,

SCHOOLS AS COMMUNITIES   755

et al., 2000) was intended to classify and describe existing school-based prevention programs and practices and to examine factors related to successful implementation of these programs and practices. It also provided national estimates of the amount of crime and violence occurring in and around schools. The study was designed to describe schools in the United States as well as characterize schools by level and location. Accordingly a sample of public, private, and Catholic schools, stratified by location (urban, suburban, and rural) and level (elementary, middle, and high) was drawn from the most comprehensive list of schools available—a mailing list maintained by Market Data Retrieval, a commercial mailing list vendor. A probability sample of 1287 schools (143 for each cell in the sample design) was selected with the expectation that if a response rate of 70% could be achieved, there would be 300 schools responding at each level and 300 schools responding from each location (about 100 per cell, or 900 schools overall). The student and teacher surveys were administered in the spring of 1998.

RESPONSE RATES

From the sample of 1287 schools, seven were found to be closed and one was found not to be a school, leaving 1279 schools in the sample. Teacher and student surveys, on which most of the measures in this study are based, were administered only in secondary schools, so this study excludes elementary schools. Of 847 secondary schools asked to participate, 310 (37%) participated in the student survey and 403 (48%) participated in the teacher survey. When the correlations between school and community characteristics and survey participation were examined, it was found that schools located in small towns or rural areas were significantly more likely to have participated. Schools were less likely to have participated if they were located in communities with more female-headed households with children, a greater proportion of urban population, and more households that received public assistance. The factors associated with participation are reported in greater detail in Gottfredson et al. (2000). The implications of the low response rates and the nonrandom attrition from the study are discussed in the Discussion section.

Generally, all teachers in participating schools were sampled, and a sufficient number of students were sampled to produce an estimated 50 respondents per school. When a student roster containing student gender was available, students were systematically sampled within gender. Otherwise, students were stratified by grade level and sampled. In participating schools, the mean student response rate was 76% and the mean teacher response rate was 78%.

SCHOOLS USED IN THIS ANALYSIS

Certain categories of schools are excluded from this analysis. Elementary schools are excluded because student and teacher surveys were administered only in secondary schools. The overall sample also contained alternative schools for disruptive youth, which included a large number of extreme outliers on several of the variables of interest in this study. These too were excluded, reducing the number of secondary schools in the sample from 847 to 778. Further, preliminary analyses indicated that problems of disorder are very different for private and religious schools than for public schools and would require separate analyses. Therefore, because relatively few non-public non-alternative secondary schools are included in the sample, the present study was limited to public schools. Schools were retained in the study sample only if they had participated in both the student survey and the teacher survey. This resulted in a sample of 255 schools. Finally, one school was excluded in which student enrollment was an extreme outlier. The final sample for this study is 254 public, secondary, nonalternative schools that participated in both the teacher and the student surveys. Consequently, the results of this study are most applicable to the nation's public, secondary, nonalternative schools. In this final sample, the within-school response rate for the student survey ranged from 16% to 100%, with a mean of 75%, and the within-school response rate for the teacher survey ranged from 12% to 100%, also with a mean of 75%.

MEASURES

Items and scales composed from teacher and student questionnaires are described below. Reliability coefficients and intra-class correlations are taken from Gottfredson et al., 2000. More detailed descriptions of each of the measures are also provided in that document.[1]

SCHOOL DISORDER

Teacher Victimization is based on an eight-item scale from the teacher questionnaire (adapted from the Effective School Battery (ESB), Gottfredson, 1999) measuring the number of different crimes or acts of incivility experienced by the teacher at school during the current school year. A

---

1. Nonresponse adjustments and the inverse of sampling probabilities were used to compute weights applied to make the sample as representative as possible of the nation's schools. In previously reported national estimates from this data of school crime, school prevention programming, and so on, the estimates were weighted. Gottfredson et al. (2000), however, showed that weighted and unweighted results from *correlational* analyses displayed similar patterns. Therefore, because the present study reports only school-level correlations, unweighted data are used.

school's score is the mean across teachers of the proportion of items endorsed. The individual-level alpha is .61, and the intra-class correlation (the proportion of variance in this scale that lies between schools) is .14.

Student Victimization is based on a seven-item scale from the student questionnaire (adapted from What About You (WAY) Form DC, Gottfredson and Gottfredson, 1999) measuring the number of different crimes, ranging from thefts to physical attacks, experienced by the student at school during the current school year. A school's score is the mean across students of the proportion of items endorsed. The individual-level alpha is .61, and the intra-class correlation is .04.

Student Delinquency is based on 4 of the 13 available delinquency items from the student questionnaire (adapted from WAY, Gottfredson and Gottfredson, 1999) measuring the number of different crimes committed by the student during the current school year. The four items used in this study measure delinquent activities *in school.* These four items are as follows: "In the last 12 months, have you purposely damaged or destroyed property belonging to school?" ". . .hit or threatened to hit a teacher or other adult in school?" ". . .hit or threatened to hit other students?" ". . .stolen or tried to steal something at school, such as someone's coat from a classroom, locker, or cafeteria, or a book from the library?" A school's score is the mean across students of the proportion of items endorsed. The individual-level alpha for this scale is .58, and the intra-class correlation is .05.[2]

COMMUNAL SCHOOL ORGANIZATION

Supportive and Collaborative Relations is based on the Morale scale from the teacher questionnaire (adapted from the ESB, Gottfredson, 1999). It is a five-item scale that highlights the level of collaboration between and among the faculty and administration, the level of support felt by teachers, and the teachers' views of the relations between teachers and administration, teachers and students, and among the faculty. Examples of items include "The administration is supportive of teachers" and

---

2. Note that the individual-level alpha reliability coefficients for several of the measures are low by conventional standards employed in individual-level research. In school-level research, however, the reliability of the *school mean* is more relevant than the reliability of the individual-level measures. The scales used in this study generally contain few items because they were not designed to produce reliable individual-level measurement, but rather stable schools means. Scales of modest reliability at the individual-level, when averaged across multiple respondents in the school, can produce reliable school means (Feldt and Brennan, 1989; Stanley, 1971). Estimates of school-level reliability for the measures used in the National Study of Delinquency Prevention in Schools ranged from .68 to .90 for student measures and from .69 to .85 for teacher measures (Gottfredson et al., 2000).

"Administrators and teachers collaborate." A school's score is the mean across teachers of the proportion of items endorsed. The individual-level alpha for the original Morale scale is .81 and the intra-class correlation is .28.

Common Goals and Norms is based on the Organizational Focus scale from the teacher questionnaire (adapted from the Organizational Focus Questionnaire, Gottfredson, 2000). It is a ten-item scale highlighting the commonality of direction and expected behavior in the school. Examples of items include "The goals of this school are clear" and "Everyone understands what behavior will be rewarded." A school's score is the mean across teachers of individuals' mean responses to the Likert-type items. The individual-level alpha for the original Organizational Focus scale is .94, and the intra-class correlation is .26.

STUDENT BONDING

Attachment is a 13-item scale from the student questionnaire (adapted from What About You (WAY), Form DC, Gottfredson and Gottfredson, 1999) measuring students' emotional bonds to teachers and the school in general, as well as students' feelings of belonging. Examples of items include "I care what teachers think about me" and "I am usually happy when I am in school." A school's score is the mean across students of the students' average item responses. The individual-level alpha is .82 and the intra-class correlation is .05.

Belief is a 23-item scale from the student questionnaire (adapted from WAY, Form DC, Gottfredson and. Gottfredson, 1999) dealing with students' feelings about breaking rules and the legitimacy of norms. Examples of items include "I want to be a person of good character" and "You have to break some rules if you want to be popular." A school's score is the mean across students of the students' average item responses. The individual-level alpha is .86 and the intra-class correlation is .07.

Commitment is a 14-item scale from the student questionnaire (adapted from WAY, Form DC, Gottfredson and Gottfredson, 1999) measuring the effort and value students place on their schoolwork, grades, and homework. Examples of items include "I am proud of my school work" and "I usually quit when my school work is too hard." A school's score is the mean across students of the students' average item responses. The individual-level alpha is .83 and the intra-class correlation is .04.

EXOGENOUS VARIABLES

Percentage students African-American is based on data from the Common Core of Data from the National Center for Education Statistics.

SCHOOLS AS COMMUNITIES 759

Percentage teachers African-American is based on data from the teacher questionnaire.

Poverty and Disorganization is a factor score based on measures obtained from the 1990 Census for the zip code areas in which the school is located. The following census variables are markers for the factor: welfare (the average household public assistance income), female-headed household (the rate of single females with children under 18 to married couples with children under 18), median income (the proportion of households with income below $27,499), poverty (rate of persons below the 1.24 poverty level to persons above), divorce rate (the rate of persons older than 15 years who are married to those who are separated, divorced, or have a spouse absent), and male and female unemployment (proportion of unemployed males/females in the labor force). A few schools' scores that were extreme outliers were trimmed to three standard deviations above the mean.

Residential Crowding is a factor score from the 1990 Census. Marker variables for the factor are the ratio of households with five or more people to other households and the proportion households not English speaking.

Student enrollment is based on principal reports of the number of students enrolled in the school from the first principal questionnaire. These principal reports were compared with data from the Common Core of Data and Market Data Retrieval. Clarification from the schools was sought when substantial discrepancies occurred. The natural log of the enrollment was taken to reduce skew.

Number of different students taught is calculated from a question in the teacher questionnaire. Teachers were asked to report how many different students they taught within an average week; responses were "Fewer than 35," "35 to 70," "71 to 100," and "More than 100." Responses were then coded as follows: "Fewer than 35" was coded as 17.5, "35 to 70" was coded as 52.5, "71 to 100" was coded as 85.5, and "More than 100" was coded as 120.

Urbanicity is a factor score based on 1990 Census data for the school's zip code area. The following variables are markers for the factor: population size (total population), urban level (city level type), and urbanicity (the proportion of people living within an urban area). A few extreme outliers were trimmed to three standard deviations above the mean.

Percentage students male is based on the self-reported gender of students who completed the student questionnaire.

Grade level is a binary variable indicating whether the school is a middle/junior high school (0) or a vocational/senior high school (1).

760   PAYNE ET AL.

Table 1 shows the means, standard deviations, actual range, and *N*s for all of the variables described above.

Table 1.   Mean, Standard Deviation, Range, and *N* for All Variables

Variable	Mean	Standard Deviation	Range	*N*
School Disorder				
Student Delinquency	.175	.059	.060–.410	254
Student Victimization	.219	.047	.100–.340	254
Teacher Victimization	.162	.069	.000–.520	254
Communal School Disorder				
Supportive and Collaborative Relations	.758	.158	.297–1.000	254
Common Norms and Goals	.743	.146	.300–.986	254
Student Bonding				
Attachment	.618	.065	.416–.790	254
Belief	.660	.062	.399–.813	254
Commitment	.736	.057	.499–.871	254
Exogenous Factors				
Percentage Students African-American	14.609	23.249	.000–99.690	235
Percentage Teachers African-American	7.657	16.011	.000–90.630	254
Poverty and Disorganization	−.109	.698	−1.200–3.000	242
Residential Crowding	−.010	.786	−1.500–3.000	242
Student enrollment	790.31	478.401	97.000–2912.000	254
Student enrollment (natural log)	6.489	.636	4.570–7.980	254
Number of different students taught	90.070	15.100	24.230–120.000	254
Urbanicity	−.198	.953	−2.325–2.390	242
Percentage students male	48.643	6.666	25.000–68.900	253
Grade level	.343	.475	.000–1.000	254

ANALYSIS STRATEGY

The distributional characteristics of the measures to be included in the study were examined first. Some variables were transformed and others were trimmed to deal with outliers and skew. Exploratory factor analyses were conducted separately for the exogenous variables, the communal school organization measures, and the student bonding measures to guide decisions about the measurement model. Highly related items and scales were treated as multiple indicators of an underlying construct. The EQS Structural Equations Program (version 5.7B for Windows; Bentler, 1995) was then used to estimate a structural equations model (SEM) of the direct and indirect effects of the exogenous factors and communal school organization and the direct effects of student bonding on school disorder, based on the variance-covariance matrix for the transformed and rescaled

SCHOOLS AS COMMUNITIES 761

variables. A critical value of $p < .05$ was used to determine if structural paths were significant.

Estimation of these models proceeded in several steps. First, variables were rescaled so that their variances would be approximately equal and the small amount of missing data was imputed for some of the exogenous variables for between 1 and 19 schools, depending on the variable. With one exception, the regression method was used for imputation, using variables from the census that are not included in the model to predict scores for the missing variables. For one variable, percent students male, mean substitution was used because no census variable predicted it.

Next, measurement models were estimated separately for the exogenous variables, the communal school organization latent construct, and the student bonding latent construct, using the exploratory factor analysis results as a guide, but adding paths as suggested by the Lagrange multiplier test to improve the fit of the model to the data.

To test the first hypothesis, an initial SEM was estimated, allowing all nonrecursive paths from the exogenous factors to the communal school organization construct and to each of the disorder measures and all nonrecursive paths from the communal school organization construct to the disorder measures to be unconstrained. In this model, the previously estimated measurement models were fixed and the error terms for the three school disorder measures were allowed to covary. This model was improved by deleting paths that, according to the Wald test, could be eliminated without degrading the fit of the model and by adding a few paths or covariances that the Lagrange multiplier test suggested should be added to improve the fit.

To test the second hypothesis, the student bonding construct was included in the model, with all paths from the exogenous factors and the communal school organization construct to the student bonding construct and all paths from the student bonding construct to each of the school disorder measures unconstrained. This second model was also improved by deleting paths that could be eliminated without degrading the fit of the model and by adding a few paths or covariances that would improve the fit.

Several indices of fit are reported for each of these steps: the ratio of the X^2/df (best if 3 or less), the nonnormed fit index, and the comparative fit index (both best if greater than .9).

762   PAYNE ET AL.

RESULTS

Table 2 shows the rotated factor loadings from an exploratory factor analysis of the exogenous variables. This analysis was conducted using the 224 schools with complete data for the exogenous variables. Several factor solutions were examined, and a five-factor solution that accounted for 82% of the variance in the observed measures was selected. In this solution, the first factor represents the racial composition of the school and the level of poverty and disorganization in the community surrounding the school. It is named Concentrated Poverty/African-American and explains 26% of the variance in the observed variables. The second factor measures the size of the school and the urbanicity of the community surrounding the school; it is named Size and Urbanicity and accounts for 20% of the variance in the observed variables. For the remaining factors, a single measure loads high on and describes the factor: Residential Crowding of the surrounding community, explaining 12% of the variance; Grade Level, explaining 12%; and Percentage Students Male, explaining 11%.

Table 2.   Varimax Rotated Factor Loadings for Exogenous Factors

Variable	Concentrated Poverty/ African-American	Size and Urbanicity	Residential Crowding	Grade Level	Percentage Students Male
Percentage students African-American	*.930*	.027	−.050	.008	−.129
Percentage teachers African-American	*.901*	−.023	.028	−.035	−.098
Poverty and Disorganization	*.802*	−.104	.166	.066	.121
Student enrollment	.084	*.857*	.145	.201	.100
Urbanicity	−.033	*.797*	.089	−.176	−.111
Number of different students taught	−.163	*.654*	−.295	−.117	.021
Residential crowding	.070	.029	*.962*	.006	−.037
Grade level	−.013	−.066	.013	*.982*	−.024
Percentage students male	−.075	−.006	−.038	−.022	*.982*
Percentage variance explained	26.283%	20.166%	11.940%	11.722%	11.431%

N = 224

The two indicators of Communal School Organization (Supportive and Collaborative Relations and Common Norms and Goals) have factor loading values of .95, indicating one underlying factor that explains 90% of the variance. Finally, the three indicators of Student Bonding (Attachment, Belief, and Commitment) load highly on one factor, with loading values ranging from .85 to .91; this underlying factor explains 78% of the variance of the observed measures.

Table 3 shows the correlations among the three school disorder measures and between each disorder measure and the exogenous factors, Communal School Organization, and Student Bonding. As expected, the three measures of disorder are positively correlated—especially the two measures taken from the student survey. Each of the exogenous factors is significantly related to at least one measure of disorder. Concentrated Poverty/African-American and Residential Crowding are more highly related to Teacher Victimization than to either Student Victimization or Student Delinquency. The correlations of Size and Urbanicity are smaller than anticipated, and this factor's correlation with Student Delinquency is in the opposite direction anticipated. When the correlations between Student Delinquency and the individual indicators of the Size and Urbanicity factor were examined, it was found that school enrollment has a significant negative correlation with Student Delinquency ($-.164$**), whereas Urbanicity and number of different students taught are not significantly correlated with Student Delinquency. Thus, the negative correlation between Student Delinquency and the overall Size and Urbanicity factor is being driven by the single indicator school enrollment, which displays a negative correlation with Student Delinquency that was unanticipated.[3]

Table 3.   Correlations among Study Variables[a]

	Student Delinquency	Student Victimization	Teacher Victimization
School Disorder			
Student Delinquency	—	—	—
Student Victimization	.500**(254)	—	—
Teacher Victimization	.275**(254)	.189**(254)	—
Communal School Organization	−.054 (254)	.087 (254)	−.440**(254)
Student Bonding	−.697**(254)	−.229**(254)	−.156**(254)
Exogenous Factors			
Concentrated Poverty/African-American	.171* (224)	.059 (224)	.391**(224)
Residential Crowding	−.016 (242)	.021 (242)	.226**(242)
Size and Urbanicity	−.219**(224)	−.083 (224)	.022 (224)
Percentage Students Male	.087 (253)	.128* (253)	−.036 (253)
Grade Level	−.101 (254)	−.461**(254)	−.112 (254)

[a] Ns are in parentheses
** $p < .01$, * $p < .05$

3.   Additional analyses were conducted to explore the possibility of a tipping point in the relationship between student enrollment and Student Delinquency, however no clear point was found. One possible explanation for this unanticipated negative correlation is the link among school size, truancy, and delinquency. It is very likely that larger schools have higher rates of truancy. In addition, previous research has shown

764   PAYNE ET AL.

Schools with a higher percentage of males experience significantly higher levels of student victimization, and high schools experience significantly lower levels of student victimization, but these exogenous factors are not significantly related to the other disorder measures. Communal School Organization is significantly correlated with Teacher Victimization in the expected direction, but is not significantly correlated with either student-reported measure of disorder.[4] Finally, Student Bonding is significantly related to all three disorder measures in the expected direction.

Figure 1 shows the standardized measurement models estimated with EQS. They accord with the Factor Analysis results, except that three correlations are added: Schools located in areas of concentrated poverty and with higher percentages of African-American students and teachers have lower percentages of males, probably because of higher dropout rates for males in these areas. Grade level is correlated with Size and Urbanicity, such that high schools score lower on this factor, but the error term for one of the indicators for this factor—student enrollment—is strongly and positively correlated with grade level. This pattern suggests that high schools are larger than middle schools (not surprising), and that high schools are less likely to be found in urban areas. This latter association is

Table 4.   Summary of Model Fit Indices[a]

Model	df	NNFI	CFI	χ^2/df
CFA, Exogenous Factors	27	.93	.95	2.09
STR, Hypothesis One	64	.85	.90	2.95
STR, Hypothesis Two	112	.88	.90	2.62

[a]CFI = comparative fit index; NNFI = nonnormed fit index; CFA = confirmatory factor analysis; STR = structural or path model

that truant students are more likely to engage in delinquency (Hirschi, 1969; McCarthy and Hagan, 1992). Therefore, the negative correlation between student enrollment and Student Delinquency might actually be an artifact of the absentee rate of the more delinquent students in larger schools. We would like to thank Robert Bursik for suggesting this possible explanation.

4.   Recall that the school disorder measures included in the summary scales for the outcome variables include a relatively wide range of behavior. Additional exploratory analyses were conducted to determine whether more serious forms of victimization and delinquency had different patterns of correlations with Communal School Organization measures than less serious forms. Scales were rescored to include (a) only violent victimization and delinquency items and (b) only nonviolent and less serious items. The scales containing less serious/nonviolent items generally had slightly higher correlations with Communal School Organization measures than the scales containing only violent items; this is probably because there is more variability with less serious behaviors. However, the direction and significance levels of the correlations of the Communal School Organization measures with violent victimization and delinquency were generally the same as with nonviolent\less serious victimization and delinquency.

most likely due to the lower response rate obtained for urban high schools. Table 4 shows that all of the fit indices suggest a good fit to the data for this measurement model. The measurement model for Communal School Organization is exactly as anticipated by the Factor Analysis results, as is the measurement model for Student Bonding. All of the coefficients in the measurement models are statistically significant.

Figure 2 shows the standardized SEM results for the model estimated to test hypothesis one. This figure shows only the structural paths because the measurement paths were fixed. All coefficients in the model are significantly different from zero, and the fit indicators exceed or are close to the conventional levels recommended.

The model shows that the exogenous factors are related to school disorder as expected. Schools with higher percentages of male students experience higher levels of student delinquency and victimization. Schools in areas of concentrated poverty and with high percentages of African-American students and teachers experience higher levels of teacher victimization and student delinquency; these schools are also less communally organized. As found with the zero-order correlations, the Size and Urbanicity factor is related to lower levels of student victimization and delinquency but is not related to teacher victimization. Schools in areas with higher levels of residential crowding experience more teacher victimization. Finally, high schools experience lower levels of delinquency and victimization, and are less communally organized.

As hypothesized, Communal School Organization influences school disorder net of the effects of the exogenous factors. Schools that are more communally organized experience significantly lower levels of teacher victimization and student delinquency. Communal School Organization does display the anticipated negative effect on Student Victimization, but the path is not statistically significant. Note also that the magnitude of the effect on Teacher Victimization (–.41) is much larger than on either of the student-reported disorder measures (–.11 and –.06).

Figure 3 shows the standardized SEM results for the model estimated to test hypothesis two. As in Figure 2, only the structural paths are shown because the measurement paths were fixed. The measurement path is shown for the Attachment indicator of Student Bonding, however, because a direct path to Attachment was added from constructs other than the Student Bonding construct on which it loaded in the measurement model.[5] As suggested by the Lagrange multiplier tests, the addition of

5. As can be seen in Figure 3, Grade level has a negative effect on the latent construct Student Bonding but a positive effect on the single indicator Attachment. To explore this finding, the zero-order correlations among Grade level, the latent construct Student Bonding, and the individual indicators of Student Bonding were examined. It

766   PAYNE ET AL.

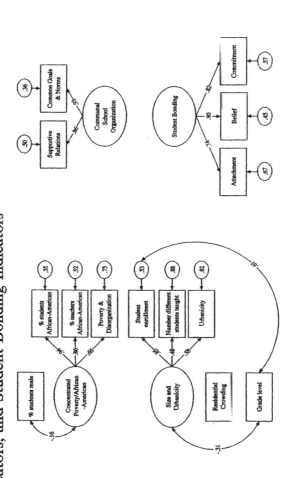

Figure 1   Measurement Models for Exogenous Factors, Communal School Organization Indicators, and Student Bonding Indicators

SCHOOLS AS COMMUNITIES

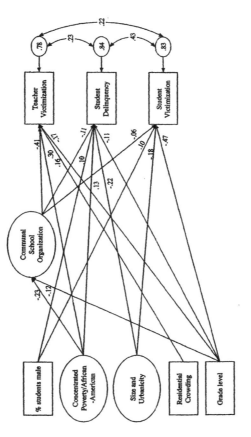

Figure 2   Standardized Structural Equation Model Results for Hypothesis One

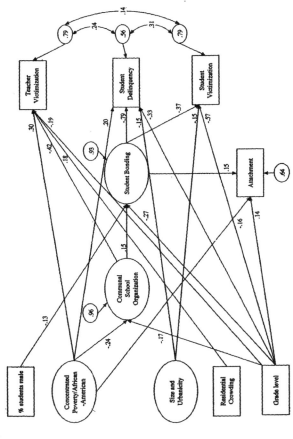

Figure 3   Standardized Structural Equation Model Results for Hypothesis Two

SCHOOLS AS COMMUNITIES 769

these paths improved the model fit of the initial SEM. All coefficients in the model are significantly different from zero, and the fit indicators exceed or are close to the conventional levels recommended.

The relationships between the exogenous factors and the school disorder measures are similar to those in Figure 2, although some differences are seen. The paths from percentage students male to the two student-reported disorder measures are no longer significant. Instead, schools with higher percentages of male students have lower levels of student bonding, which then affects the levels of disorder in the school. Thus, the effect of percentage male students on school disorder is mediated by student bonding. As in Figure 2, schools in areas of concentrated poverty and with high percentages of African-American students and teachers experience higher levels of teacher victimization and student delinquency; these schools are also less communally organized and have lower levels of student bonding. Also as before, the Size and Urbanicity factor is related to lower levels of student victimization and delinquency but is not related to teacher victimization. Schools in areas with higher levels of residential crowding experience more teacher victimization. Finally, high schools experience lower levels of delinquency and victimization, are less communally organized, and have lower levels of student bonding than middle schools.

Communal School Organization and Student Bonding display effects on the school disorder measures net of the exogenous variables. Communal School Organization also influences Student Bonding net of these variables. Schools that are more communally organized have higher levels of student bonding and lower levels of teacher victimization. The significant path from Communal School Organization to Student Delinquency seen in Figure 2 is no longer significant in this model, which suggests that the negative effect of communal school organization on student delinquency is mediated by student bonding, as hypothesized. Finally, schools with higher levels of student bonding experience less student delinquency and student victimization.

---

was found that Grade level has strong negative correlations with the majority of the Student Bonding indicators, with the exception of Attachment, which has a positive but nonsignificant correlation with Grade level. Thus, the negative correlations between the majority of the indicators and Grade level resulted in a negative relationship between the overall Student Bonding construct and Grade Level in the EQS model. However, the nonsignificant zero-order correlation between the single indicator Attachment and Grade level becomes a separate significant positive effect in the EQS model. This suggests that high school students may have stronger feelings of belonging and may be more emotionally attached to their teachers, but are less committed to school and have lower levels of belief in conventional rules, which then result in lower levels of overall student bonding.

770   PAYNE ET AL.

DISCUSSION

This study examined the process by which the communal organization of a school influences the level of disorder in that school. Specifically, it tested the hypotheses that (1) schools that are more communally organized will have lower levels of school disorder and (2) the relationship between communal school organization and school disorder will be mediated by student bonding. Both hypotheses were supported, but this support did not hold for all three measures of disorder. Schools that were more communally organized did experience less disorder, but the effects were small for the student-reported measures of disorder and statistically significant only for the measure of student delinquency. In addition, levels of student bonding did mediate the relationship between communal school organization and student delinquency, but not the relationship between communal school organization and teacher victimization.

LIMITATIONS AND FUTURE RESEARCH

The most important limitation is the cross-sectional nature of the data. Because all data were collected at the same time, it is impossible to truly determine the causal direction of the associations found in this study. For instance, the negative association between communal school organization and teacher victimization could indicate that a strong sense of community in the school leads to less teacher victimization, as predicted by the hypotheses. However, it could also indicate that lower teacher victimization rates lead to a strong sense of community or that the relationship between the two constructs is reciprocal. To assess proper temporal ordering, future studies should be longitudinal in nature, collecting data on communal school organization, student bonding, and school disorder at several points in time.

Another important limitation is the low school response rate overall and the relationship between survey participation and community characteristics. Schools in urban areas, with more female-headed households with children, a greater proportion of urban population, and more households that received public assistance were significantly less likely to have participated in the study. Therefore, the study results may not generalize well to schools located in such communities. It is unlikely, however, that the basic results of the study would change had these schools been included. Exploratory analyses of potential biases introduced by the low response rates suggested that participating schools located in similar communities as the majority of nonparticipating schools were more likely to have lower levels of communal school organization and higher rates of disorder. It therefore seems likely that the inclusion of the nonparticipating schools would have resulted in actually intensifying the relationships reported in this study. Of course, it is possible that the relationships of interest are not linear in the region of the distribution in which the nonparticipating schools fall, or that some characteristic unmeasured by the study and related to participation, communal school organization, and school disorder might alter the relationships. However, the linear relationship between the community characteristics related to nonparticipation and levels of communal school organization and school disorder seem to indicate that, if anything, the results presented here provide conservative estimates of the effect of communal school organization on school disorder. Nevertheless, future research should replicate this study with samples that are more representative of schools in urban, disadvantaged communities.

Another limitation is the absence of data to measure certain key constructs. For instance, no data on parental involvement in the school or on student academic achievement are available. These data would be helpful in adding additional dimensions and outcomes of communal school organization. Student reports of sense of community are also lacking; such reports would be valuable to further investigate the relationships among communal school organization, student bonding, and school disorder. This lack of student data on communal school organization is the most likely explanation for the fact that, in this study, communal school organization has a stronger effect on teacher-reported measures of school disorder than on student-reported measures. This study also lacks information on the content of the shared goals and norms in a communally organized school, which would be helpful in exploring the effect of different systems of goals and norms. Also missing from the data are measures of school governance. While this study relies on the elements of communal school organization discussed by Bryk and Driscoll (1988) (system of shared values, common agenda of activities, and ethos of caring), others discuss the importance of participatory governance as an additional element of communal school organization (Battistich et al., 1997; Welsh et al., 1999). In communally organized schools, the planning and decision making are more likely to be influenced by all members of the school community, which is likely to lead to a greater sense of belonging and greater internalization of the common norms and goals. Future research should include measures of these various constructs.

In addition, further exploration of the relationships *among* the elements of communal school organization is necessary. Do these elements occur simultaneously or is there an order in which each element develops? One could envision a process whereby the supportive and collaborative relations found in more communally organized schools leads to a more participatory style of governance, which then affects the creation of common goals and norms. Conversely, it could be that the participatory governance leads to the more supportive relations. Are all elements equally important in affecting school disorder? And are all elements necessary in order to achieve high levels of student bonding? Must supportive relations exist or are common norms and goals sufficient, and vice versa? These questions are similar to the discussion by Sampson et al. on the community-level relationships among social cohesion, collective efficacy, and social control (Sampson, 2002; Morenoff et al., 2001), and lead to the possibility of a misspecification in the definition of communal school organization. *If* each element of communal school organization develops at a different point in time, with one element possibly leading to another, or *if* every element is not necessary to achieve high levels of student bonding and low levels of school disorder, then perhaps these elements are truly independent concepts and should not be linked under one underlying construct. Future research should certainly explore these possibilities.

Finally, future research should include a multilevel analysis of the concepts examined in this study. Although communal school organization is clearly a school-level concept, the other constructs in this study, such as student bonding, delinquency, and victimization, should be examined at both the individual and school level.

CONCLUSION

The results found in this study are valuable, despite the limitations. The findings confirm that the social organization of a particular school influences the level of disorder in that school: As predicted by hypothesis one, schools that were more communally organized had lower levels of teacher victimization and student delinquency. In addition, the effect of communal school organization on student victimization was in the expected direction, although nonsignificant. These negative relationships accord with previous research. They suggest that schools in which teachers agree that the relationships among school members are supportive and collaborative and that there are common organizational goals and norms will experience less disorder.

The second hypothesis explored this relationship further. It was predicted that the negative relationship between communal school organization and school disorder would be mediated by student bonding. That is, schools that are more communally organized would have students who are more bonded to the school, which would then lead to less disorder. The first part of this hypothesis was confirmed: Schools that were more communally organized did indeed have students who were more bonded to the school. The second part of the hypothesis was confirmed for student delinquency: The effect of communal school organization on student delinquency became non-significant once student bonding was included in the model. This implies that the supportive and collaborative relationships and common norms and goals reported by the teachers were internalized by the students, resulting in higher levels of student bonding. These higher bonding levels, in turn, lead to less delinquency.

This indirect effect of communal school organization through student bonding was not seen for teacher victimization, however. That is, the effect of communal school organization on teacher victimization did not change when student bonding was included in the model. This is curious because, presumably, the delinquent acts being committed by the students result at least partially in victimization of teachers; one would, therefore, expect the two disorder measures to act similarly. However, the stronger relationship between the social organization measures and teacher victimization is consistent with previous results reporting similar findings with regards to school climate (Gottfredson and Gottfredson, 1985; Gottfredson et al., 2003). This may indicate that teachers are being victimized by nonstudents and students. Another possible explanation is that the unmediated relationship between communal school organization and teacher victimization is a methodological artifact due to the lack of student measures of communal school organization previously discussed. Future research should explore this pattern further.

The findings of this study regarding the positive effects of communal school organization have great potential for school-based delinquency prevention. Interventions that can strengthen the communal organization of the school and, in turn, increase student bonding could lead to reductions in the amount of delinquency and victimization in the school. Examples of such interventions include the School Development Program and the Child Development Project, both of which have demonstrated positive results on teacher and student outcomes (Battistch et al., 1996; Cook et al., 1998; Haynes and Comer, 1996). By improving the relationships among school members, the collaboration and participation of these members, and the agreement on common goals and norms, schools could increase students' attachment to school, commitment to education, and belief in school rules and norms. With these improvements in communal school organization and student bonding, schools could experience a reduction in disorder, thereby improving the schools' ability to carry out their educational mission.

REFERENCES

Battistich, Victor, Daniel Solomon, Dong-il Kim, Marilyn Watson, and Eric Schaps
    1995   Schools as communities, poverty levels of student populations, and students' attitudes, motives, and performance: A multilevel analysis. American Educational Research Journal 32: 627–658.

774 PAYNE ET AL.

Battistich, Victor, Eric Schaps, Marilyn Watson, and Daniel Solomon
1996   Prevention effects of the child development project: Early findings from an ongoing multi-site demonstration trial. Journal of Adolescent Research 11: 12–35.

Battistich, Victor, and Allen Hom
1997   The relationship between students' sense of their school as a community and their involvement in problem behavior. American Journal of Public Health 87(12):1997–2001.

Battistich, Victor, and Daniel Solomon
1997   Caring school communities. Educational Psychologist 32(3) 137–151.

Bentler, Peter M.
1995   EQS Structural Equations Program Manual. Encino, Calif.: Multivariate Software, Inc.

Bryk, Anthony S. and Mary Driscoll
1988   The school as community: Shaping forces and consequences for students and teachers. Madison: University of Wisconsin, National Center on Effective Secondary Schools.

Cernkovich, Stephen, and Peggy Giordano
1987   Family Relationships and Delinquency. Criminology 25: 295–321.

Cook, Thomas, H. David Hunt, and Robert Murphy
1998   Comer's School Development Program in Chicago: A theory-based evaluation. Working papers. Evanston, Ill.: Northwestern University Institute for Policy Research.

Feldt, Leonard S. and Robert L. Brennan
1989   Reliability. In Linn, R. L. (ed.), Educational Measurement (3^d edition). New York: American Council on Education–McMillan.

Fleury, Kathryn Chandler, Michael Planty, and Michael Rand.
2001   Indicators of School Crime and Safety: 2001. U.S. Department of Education and Justice. NCES 2002-113/NCJ-190075. Washington, D.C.: 2001.

Gottfredson, Denise
2001   Delinquency and schools. New York: Cambridge University Press.

Gottfredson, Denise and Gary Gottfredson
2002   Quality of School-Based Prevention Programs: Results from a National Survey. Journal of Research in Crime and Delinquency 39(1) 3–35

Gottfredson, Denise, David Wilson, and Stacy Najaka
2002   School-Based Crime Prevention. In Sherman, Lawrence, David Farrington, Brandon Welsh, and Doris MacKenzie. Evidence-Based Crime Prevention. London, U.K.: Routledge.

Gottfredson, Gary
1999   User's manual for the Effective School Battery. Ellicot City, MD: Gottfredson Associates. [Originally published in 1984].
2000   Environmental focus in a large national sample of schools. Paper presented at annual meeting of the American Psychological Association. Washington, D.C. (ERIC No. ED 446 314)

Gottfredson, Gary, and Denise Gottfredson
1985   Victimization in schools. New York: Plenum.

1999 Development and applications of theoretical measures for evaluating drug and delinquency prevention programs: Technical manual for research editions of What About You (WAY). Ellicot City, MD: Gottfredson Associates.

2001 What Schools do to Prevent Delinquency and Promote Safe Environments. Journal of Educational and Psychological Consultation, 12(4)313–344.

Gottfredson, Gary, Denise Gottfredson, Ellen Czeh, David Cantor, Scott Crosse, and Irene Hantman
2000 A National Study of Delinquency Prevention in School Final Report. Ellicott City: Gottfredson Associates, Inc.

Gottfredson, Gary, Denise Gottfredson, Allison Ann Payne, and Nisha Gottfredson
2003 School Climate Predictors of School Disorder: Results from the National Study of Delinquency Prevention in Schools. (manuscript under review)

Harris, Louis and Associates
1993 Violence in America's Public Schools: A Survey of the American Teacher. New York: Metropolitan Life Insurance Company.

Haynes, Norris, and James Comer
1996 Integrating schools, families, and communities through successful school reform: The school development program. School Psychology Review, 25(4)501–507.

Hirschi, Travis
1969 Causes of Delinquency. Berkeley, Calif.: University of California Press.

Ingersoll, Richard
2001 Teacher turnover and teacher shortages: An organizational analysis. American Educational Research Journal, 38:499–534.

Jenkins, Patricia
1997 School delinquency and the school social bond. Journal of Research in Crime and Delinquency, 34(3)337–368.

Kaufman, Phillip, Xianglei Chen, Susan Choy, Katharin Peter, Sally Ruddy, Amanda Miller, Jill

Krohn, Marvin, and James Massey
1980 Social control and delinquent behavior: An examination of the elements of the social bond. The Sociological Quarterly 21:529–544.

Lawrence, Richard
1998 School Crime and Juvenile Justice. New York: Oxford University Press, Inc.

Lee, Valerie E., Anthony S. Bryk, and Julia B. Smith
1992 The organization of effective secondary schools. Review of Research in Education 19:171–267.

Liska, Allen, and Mark Reed
1985 Ties to conventional institutions and delinquency: estimating reciprocal effects. American Sociological Review 50:547–560.

McCarthy, Bill and John Hagan
1992 Mean Streets: The theoretical significance of situational delinquency among homeless youths. American Journal of Sociology 98(3): 597–628.

776   PAYNE ET AL.

McDermott, Joan
    1980   High anxiety: Fear of crime in secondary schools. Contemporary Education
            52: 18–23.

Morenoff, Jeffrey D., Robert J. Sampson, and Stephen W. Raudenbush
    2001   Neighborhood inequality, collective efficacy, and the spatial dynamics of
            urban violence. Criminology 39(3)517–560.

Rowan, Brian
    1990   Commitment and control: Alternative strategies for the organizational
            design of schools. Review of Research in Education 16:353–392.

Sampson, Robert
    1999   What "Community" Supplies. In Ronald F. Fergusen and William T. Dick-
            ens (eds.), Urban Problems and Community Development. Washington,
            D.C.: Brookings Institution Press.
    2002   Transcending tradition: New directions in community research, Chicago
            style. Criminology 40:213–230.

Sampson, Robert, Jeffery D. Morenoff, and Felton Earls
    1999   Beyond spatial capital: Spatial dynamics of collective efficacy for children.
            American Sociological Review 64: 633–660.

Sampson, Robert, Stephen W. Raudenbush, and Felton Earls
    1997   Neighborhoods and violent crime: A multilevel study of collective efficacy.
            Science 277(5328) 918–924.

Solomon, Daniel, Victor Battistich, Dong-il Kim, and Marilyn Watson
    1997   Teacher practices associated with students' sense of the classroom as a com-
            munity. Social Psychology of Education 1:235–267.

Solomon, Daniel, Marilyn Watson, Victor Battistich, Eric Schaps, and Kevin Delucchi
    1992   Creating a caring community: Educational practices that promote children's
            prosocial development. In Oser, Fritz, Andreas Dick, and Jean-Luc Patry
            (eds.), Effective and responsible teaching: The new synthesis. San Fran-
            cisco: Jossey-Bass, pp. 383–396.

Stanley, Julian C.
    1971   Reliability. In Robert L. Thorndike (ed.), Educational Measurement (2d
            edition). Washington D.C.: American Council on Education .

Welsh, Wayne, Jack Greene, and Patricia Jenkins
    1999   School disorder: The influence of individual, institutional, and community
            factors. Criminology 37(1)73–115.

Welsh, Wayne.
    2000   The Effects of School Climate on School Disorder. ANNALS of AAPSS,
            567, 88–107.

    Allison Ann Payne is Assistant Professor at The College of New Jersey, Department
of Criminology and Justice Studies. She recently received her Ph.D. from the University of Maryland, Department of Criminology and Criminal Justice. Her research interests include juvenile delinquency, school-based delinquency prevention, and program
evaluation. She has previously worked on an evaluation of Positive Action Through
Holistic Education (PATHE) in Charleston, S.C., and an evaluation of the Strengthening Washington D.C. Families Program.

SCHOOLS AS COMMUNITIES 777

Denise C. Gottfredson is a Professor at the University of Maryland, Department of Criminology and Criminal Justice. She received a Ph.D. in Social Relations from The Johns Hopkins University. Gottfredson's research interests include delinquency and delinquency prevention, and particularly the effects of school environments on youth behavior. She currently directs evaluations of Baltimore City's Drug Treatment Court and the Maryland After School Opportunity Grant Fund Program, and is PI on a grant to work with the prevention community in the State of Maryland to increase the use of research-based prevention practices. She is also Co-PI on an evaluation of the Strengthening Washington D.C. Families Program.

Gary D. Gottfredson, president of Gottfredson Associates, Inc., specializes in psychometrics, evaluation research, career assessment, organization development, preventing problem behavior, and personality assessment. He received a Ph.D. in Psychology from The Johns Hopkins University.

[5]

Legal Cynicism and (Subcultural?) Tolerance of Deviance: The Neighborhood Context of Racial Differences

Robert J. Sampson   Dawn Jeglum Bartusch

We advance here a neighborhood-level perspective on racial differences in legal cynicism, dissatisfaction with police, and the tolerance of various forms of deviance. Our basic premise is that structural characteristics of neighborhoods explain variations in normative orientations about law, criminal justice, and deviance that are often confounded with the demographic characteristics of individuals. Using a multilevel approach that permits the decomposition of variance within and between neighborhoods, we tested hypotheses on a recently completed study of 8,782 residents of 343 neighborhoods in Chicago. Contrary to received wisdom, we find that African Americans and Latinos are *less* tolerant of deviance—including violence—than whites. At the same time, neighborhoods of concentrated disadvantage display elevated levels of legal cynicism, dissatisfaction with police, and tolerance of deviance unaccounted for by sociodemographic composition and crime-rate differences. Concentrated disadvantage also helps explain why African Americans are more cynical about law and dissatisfied with the police. Neighborhood context is thus important for resolving the seeming paradox that estrangement from legal norms and agencies of criminal justice, especially by blacks, is compatible with the personal condemnation of deviance.

Over three decades ago, David Matza (1964) argued that "subculture" was the central concept of the prevailing sociological view of delinquency. Indeed, much classic criminological theory takes as a starting point the concept of social conflict over values, beliefs, and norms that govern behavior (e.g., Sutherland 1947; Cohen 1955; Miller 1958; Cloward & Ohlin 1960). This conflict is thought to allow for the emergence of subcultures composed of individuals who, by not sharing in the beliefs of the dominant ideology, are freed from societal constraints. Subcul-

Originally presented at the 1997 Annual Meeting of the Law and Society Association, St. Louis. The article was prepared while the senior author was a Fellow at the Center for Advanced Study in the Behavioral Sciences, Stanford, CA. Funding support from the American Bar Foundation, Carnegie Corporation of New York (Grant B-6346), and the Project on Human Development in Chicago Neighborhoods is gratefully acknowledged. Thanks are due the anonymous reviewers for helpful comments. Address correspondence to Robert J. Sampson, Department of Sociology, University of Chicago, 1126 E. 59th St., Chicago, IL 60637 (email: rjsam@srcuchicago.edu).

tures are thus alleged to turn tables on society—delinquency is itself normative and law is viewed with cynicism.

Although the concept of subculture has been the subject of many debates in criminology, attempts to verify directly the existence of subcultural values and beliefs are rare and have yielded inconsistent results. Typically subcultures are inferred from behavioral patterns, and in American criminology this procedure has most often produced the notion of a subculture of violence in the inner city (Wolfgang & Ferracuti 1967; Curtis 1975). Blacks and low-income residents of the so-called underclass, in other words, have been posited to evince a cultural tolerance of violence. Moreover, there has been a tendency to conflate individual attitudes favorable to deviance with a system of what Merton called "normlessness" and Durkheim called "anomie." Perhaps most important, extant research focuses primarily on individual and demographic attributes rather than situating the study of norms in a larger structural context. As Claude Fischer (1995:547) observed in a recent assessment of 20 years of research on the matter, subcultural theory is, at core, an ecological theory about places, not a theory of persons.

We capitalize here on a recent multilevel study of 8,782 residents of 343 Chicago neighborhoods in order to highlight sociodemographic and neighborhood sources of variation in tolerance of deviance (including violence) and attitudes about the legitimacy of law. We argue that "anomie" about law—what we call "legal cynicism"—is a concept distinct from subcultural tolerance of deviance. Our basic premise is that orientations toward deviance and its control are not subcultural in origin in the sense envisioned by traditional theory, nor are they solely attributable to the aggregated characteristics of individuals (social composition). We hypothesize that an important source of variation lies in the differential social-ecological structure of neighborhoods— notably, in levels of concentrated disadvantage, residential instability, and immigrant concentration that reflect larger inequalities in American society (Sampson & Wilson 1995). In particular, our results show that racial differences in normative orientations are either contrary to subculture of violence expectations or confounded with neighborhood.

Subcultural Tolerance of Deviance and Violence

Although subculture has been defined in terms of social networks and interaction patterns, we focus here on the more cultural component: norms and attitudes about deviance (Fischer 1976:259). Attempting to assess normative differences in survey ratings of the seriousness of crimes, Rossi et al.'s (1974) influential study found widespread agreement among respondents, irrespective of their social-demographic characteristics (e.g., race, gender, educational attainment). Erlanger (1974:283; Erlanger & Winsborough 1976) reported a similar "absence of major differences by race or class in approval of interpersonal violence" and relationships between fighting and peer respect that were inconsistent with the subculture of violence thesis. Using nationally representative data from the General Social Survey, Cao, Adams, and Jensen (1997) also found no support for a subculture of violence tied to blacks. White males expressed more violent beliefs regarding defensive situations, and whites and blacks did not differ in beliefs about violence in offensive situations. This general pattern was supported by the survey research of Shoemaker and Williams (1987) and Ellison (1991). In addition, a recent study that controlled for random measurement error in attitudinal variables found no differences between whites and nonwhites in attitudes about retribution, courage, and "disputatiousness" (Markowitz & Felson 1998).

Against a backdrop of consensus, however, even Rossi et al. (1974:231) noted a "hint of subcultural differences," evidenced by the fact that black males with less than a high school education ranked crimes against persons somewhat differently than did the rest of the sample. In another major study, Blumenthal (1972) and colleagues (Blumenthal et al. 1972) found that black males were considerably more likely than white males to favor violence for the purpose of social change. Hartnagel (1980) also found that blacks were significantly more likely than whites to approve of the use of serious violence ("knifing" another person), although this pattern did not hold for a less serious form of violence (punching). A more recent body of research, drawn largely from Sutherland's (1947) differential association theory, argues that attitudes toward delinquency and law violation account for the effects of sociodemographic characteristics on delinquent behavior (Matsueda 1982; Matsueda & Heimer 1987; Heimer & Matsueda 1994; Heimer 1996, 1997). Definitions specifically favorable to violence have been shown to vary by class position, with those in the lower socioeconomic class more likely to maintain such definitions than the middle or the upper class (Heimer 1997). For males, attitudes favoring deviance more generally vary by race and age, with blacks and older respondents more likely to hold such attitudes (Heimer 1996).

Examining the use of "techniques of neutralization," Hindelang (1974) provided further evidence that attitudes favorable to delinquency are highly variable across individuals. Testing hypotheses derived from the work of Matza (1964) and Sykes and Matza (1957), Hindelang found that those reporting no involvement in illegal acts were more disapproving of the same acts than those reporting illegal involvement. Casting doubt on the necessity of neutralizing techniques, Hindelang concluded:

> In all groups, for virtually all acts, Matza and Sykes' premise of
> subscription to a common value system, regardless of illegal in-
> volvement, does not find support in these data. . . . The data
> here suggest a more generalized and more enduring release
> from moral constraint, which derives from a value system per-
> mitting involvement in certain illegal behaviors *independent of*
> *extenuating circumstances.* (Hindelang 1974:383–84; emphasis in
> original)

On the other hand, a more recent study by Agnew (1994) found
that techniques of neutralization were substantially associated
with delinquency, especially among those who disapproved of violence and who associated with delinquent peers.

Contextualizing Subculture

As is clear from the preceding review, survey research on subcultures and attitudes toward deviance has focused on individual-
level variations, and with varying results. Remarkably little research in this area takes a contextual perspective. One exception
is a study by Felson et al. (1994) that provides an aggregate-level
analysis of subcultural values and violence between schools,
along with analysis of the effect of school context on individual
variations in violence. Felson et al. found significant associations
of a school-level culture of violence with individual-level measures of interpersonal violence, theft/vandalism, and school delinquency, controlling for individual-level measures of subcultural orientations to violence. Cao et al. (1997:375–76) support
the Felson et al. strategy by calling for more contextualization in
research on subcultures: "It is possible that a subculture of violence may involve belief systems that characterize a particular urban community. . . . Inclusion of this ecological element, thus,
would shift focus from subcultural beliefs in violence, which
could transcend place, to a more complicated interaction between community and value system."

Although ethnographic studies are very different in research
design, the rich tradition of such studies provides support for this
notion. Suttles's (1968) account of the social order of a Chicago
neighborhood characterized by poverty and heterogeneity emphasized age, sex, ethnicity, and territory as markers for the ordered segmentation of slum culture. Suttles found that single-
sex, age-graded primary groups of the same ethnicity and territory emerged in response to threats of conflict and community-
wide disorder and mistrust. Also in Chicago, Anderson's (1978)
ethnography of a South Side ghetto bar suggested that primary
values coexisted alongside residual values associated with deviant
subcultures such as "toughness," "getting big money," and "going
for bad" (pp. 129–30, 152–58). According to Anderson, lower-
class black residents did not value violence as a primary goal, but
it was nonetheless expected as a fact of life in that context. An-

derson's (1990, 1997) recent research elaborates this idea further by suggesting that a "code of violence" is more likely to emerge in the inner city. Because aggression at the hands of others is a central concern of public life in the inner city, he argues that solutions for dealing with such situations have evolved into shared informal understandings—a set of prescriptions of engagement for those who would effectively manage themselves in their everyday relations with others. Much like Suttles (1968) and Horowitz (1987), Anderson suggests that in certain contexts the wider cultural values are simply not relevant—they become "unviable."

Extant research is thus decidedly mixed and paints a complex picture of subcultural orientations that is not reducible to simplistic accounts of either "consensus" or "conflict" (Hagan, Silva, & Simpson 1977). Perhaps Shaw and McKay (1942) had it right when they argued long ago that traditions of delinquency and crime were powerful forces in certain communities, yet remained only a part of the community's system of values. They wrote, "the dominant tradition in every community is conventional, even in those having the highest rate of delinquents" (p. 180). Indeed, the very notion of subculture implies a larger dominant culture. In the social disorganization tradition of Shaw and McKay, Kornhauser (1978:75) argued a similar point; namely, that poverty, ethnic heterogeneity, mobility, and the accompanying structural features of social disorganization (e.g., anonymity, mutual distrust) impede communication and obstruct the quest for what are still common values. From her viewpoint, the attenuation of societal values fostered by structural disorganization leads to a state of cultural disorganization. In such disorganized communities, conventionality clashes with a "street culture" where crime, disorder, and drug use are expected and serve as a symbolic embodiment of the precariousness of everyday life (Anderson 1997). This interpretation may help to explain the inconsistent support shown for subcultural values in surveys. Survey research designs, particularly national samples, are often insensitive to ecological and situational variations (see also Sullivan 1989).

We suggest, then, that both streams of research evidence—ethnographic and survey based—may be reconciled so long as we emphasize the situational and contextual basis of value attenuation, rather than an autonomous culture that positively values violence at all times and places. Although conventional norms are pervasive in any community, it may be that tolerance of deviance, a cultural emphasis on "toughness" and "bravado" in the face of danger, and an overt readiness to use violence varies across structural and situational contexts. In this regard, community contexts may shape "cognitive landscapes" (Sampson 1997) of appropriate standards and expectations of conduct. The purpose of

this article is to measure directly the contextual variations by
neighborhood in such subculture-related orientations.

"Anomie" and Legal Cynicism

The research reviewed to this point concerns subcultural tolerance of violence or deviance more generally. Yet, as we suggested early on, there has been a tendency in the literature to
confuse tolerance of deviance with "normlessness" or "anomie."
Distinguishing these constructs, we suggest that support for what
one personally views as "appropriate" (or normative) forms of
conduct does not necessarily imply support for the regulations of
the larger society or the mechanisms used to enforce such conduct (i.e., laws, policing). In the classic Durkheimian sense, anomie refers to a state of normlessness in which the rules of the
dominant society (and hence the legal system) are no longer
binding in a community or for a population subgroup (Kapsis
1978:1139). Anomie in this sense is conceived as part of a social
system and not merely a property of the individual. Normlessness
and powerlessness tend also to go hand in hand, breeding cynicism about the rules of the society and their application, regardless of individual values. We thus maintain that tolerance of deviance and anomie—especially the component related to what we
call "legal cynicism"—are distinct normative structures that do
not necessarily operate in concert.

There is a long literature on the psychometric measurement
of individual differences in anomie. The Srole (1956) anomie
scale, for example, has generated an entire body of validation
research (see, e.g., Kapsis 1978). By contrast, we are concerned
here with neighborhood differences in perceptions of normlessness and legal cynicism. In one of the major studies looking at
neighborhood-level differences, Wilson (1971) challenged the assertion common in prior research (e.g., Bullough 1967) that residents of black "ghettos" can be characterized by high levels of
anomie. Examining three neighborhoods of varying levels of racial heterogeneity, Wilson found that, for blacks, anomie was lowest in the "ghetto" neighborhood that was most racially homogeneous (96% black) and highest in the most racially diverse
neighborhood. Wilson's explanation conformed to a subcultural
perspective, especially the idea that blacks in ghetto neighborhoods learn to redefine success "in ways in keeping with the
shared symbols of a black, lower-class reference group" (Wilson
1971:86).

As an alternative interpretation, Kapsis (1978) relied on Suttles's (1972) concept of "defended" versus "defeated" communities to offer a more structural or "sociopolitical" perspective that
attributes low levels of anomie to effective linkages between the
neighborhood and the larger society or, more specifically, be-

tween the neighborhood and the political clout of the city. Kapsis studied a neighborhood similar in many respects to Wilson's black "ghetto," but which could be divided into an incorporated portion under the jurisdiction of the city and an unincorporated portion under the jurisdiction of the county and characterized by inadequate services and facilities. Kapsis found support for his hypotheses that anomie or "perceived normlessness" was higher in the "ghetto" neighborhood than in the more racially heterogeneous neighborhood he studied and that anomie was higher in the "defeated" county portion of the ghetto neighborhood than in the "defended" city portion, where links to political structures were stronger. The implication of Kapsis's (1978) work is that members of economically and racially isolated communities, that is, those who were least able to exercise political influence to obtain community services, were more likely than others to report high normlessness.

We would further suggest that inner-city contexts of racial segregation and concentrated disadvantage, where inability to influence the structures of power that constrain lives is greatest, also breed cynicism and perceptions of legal injustice. As Hagan and Albonetti (1982:330) wrote, "conceptions and perceptions of justice are determined in large part by the times, places, and positions in the social structure from which they are derived." They examined perceptions of "criminal injustice" with questions concerning law enforcement and the judicial system: for example, "police who do not treat poor suspects the same as well-to-do suspects," "judges who are biased and unfair," "courts that do not treat blacks and other minorities the same as whites" (p. 340). They found that blacks and members of the lowest social class were more likely to perceive criminal injustice than whites and the upper class, respectively. Hagan and Albonetti also found that while race was significantly related to all measures of criminal injustice, the relationship between race and perceptions of injustice was particularly strong for items involving the police. Blacks, they found, were substantially more likely than whites to report that police treat poor and "well-to-do" suspects differently, and to view the police as unrepresentative of the communities in which they work. Numerous other studies support the finding that blacks are less favorable than whites in their judgments about police (see, e.g., Block 1971; Hahn 1971; Smith & Hawkins 1973). Dunham and Alpert (1988), for example, relying on a sample of five neighborhoods in Miami, found that blacks were more likely to report negative perceptions of police demeanor and to disapprove of police use of discretion than were Cuban American and white respondents in the sample.

Although sparse, extant research thus suggests that members of low-income and minority-group populations are most likely to perceive injustice in the application of legal norms and to ex-

press cynicism about the legitimacy of laws and the ability of police to do their job in an effective and nondiscriminatory manner. From our perspective, moreover, the important point is that
these patterns may be contextual in origin and not reducible to
differences in crime rates. In particular, differential ecological
distributions of social resources by race mean that *at all levels of
socioeconomic status* (SES), observed relationships involving race
are likely to reflect unmeasured advantages in the ecological
niches that whites occupy (see Wilson 1987:58–60; Sampson &
Wilson 1995). Subcultural interpretations often overlook these
racial differences in the structural context of disadvantage and
resource exploitation across neighborhoods.

Research Strategy

Extending Fischer's (1995) insight that subcultural theory is
largely a theory about places, we propose that subcultural norms
and legal cynicism are not necessarily (or only) about individual-
level variations, especially those by race/ethnicity. Rather, we argue for the importance of neighborhood-level variations by correlated dimensions of concentrated disadvantage and social stability. Individual-level variations still matter, of course, a point
Fischer (1995:548–49) carefully acknowledges in a call also for
contextually based research on subcultural orientations among
individuals. We therefore integrate these analytical perspectives
by systematically examining individual-level variations in tolerance of deviance and beliefs about the legitimacy of law *in conjunction with* an analysis of whether structural characteristics explain neighborhood-level variance in subcultural orientations—
above and beyond the sociodemographic characteristics of the
people residing in those neighborhoods. In this way we partition
the variance in tolerance of deviance and legal cynicism into be-
tween-individual and between-neighborhood components; our
main theoretical interest resides in the latter.

We have also proposed a distinction between the tolerance of
deviance and cynicism about the applicability of law. One can be
highly intolerant of crime, but live in a disadvantaged context
bereft of legal sanctions and perceived justice. In fact, we suggest
that this is exactly the sort of context found in many ghetto-pov-
erty areas of our large cities where lower-income minorities are
disproportionately concentrated. Crime there is usually high, but
that does not imply, nor is there consistent evidence, that African
American residents are tolerant of crime (Shoemaker & Williams
1987; Ellison 1991). In terms of rational self-interest, intolerance
of crime makes more sense than a culturally sanctioned endorsement of life-threatening behavior. Yet cynicism about the police
may still be high, along with perceptions of criminal injustice
(Hagan & Albonetti 1982) and a sense that legal norms are not

binding or are too weak to warrant social trust (Kapsis 1978). We attempt to resolve this seeming paradox of criminal intolerance and legal cynicism by considering, simultaneously, individual position in the social structure (especially race) and neighborhood structural differentiation.

Data and Methodology

The data for our article are drawn from a recent study explicitly designed to examine social context—the Project on Human Development in Chicago Neighborhoods (PHDCN). "Neighborhood" is conceptualized as an ecological subsection of a larger community—a collection of both people and institutions occupying a spatially defined area that is conditioned by a set of ecological, sociodemographic, and often political forces (cf. Park 1916:147–54). In addition to its long history of neighborhood differentiation, the extensive social-class, racial, and ethnic diversity of the population was a major reason Chicago was selected for the study. At present, whites, blacks, and Latinos each represent about a third of the population.

To operationalize neighborhood, Chicago's 847 populated census tracts were combined to create 343 "Neighborhood Clusters" (NCs). The overriding consideration in forming NCs was that they should be ecologically meaningful units composed of geographically contiguous census tracts and internally homogeneous with regard to distributions on a variety of census indicators. The study settled on an ecological unit smaller than the established 77 community areas in Chicago (average size = 40,000) but large enough to approximate local neighborhoods—on average, around 8,000 people. Major geographic boundaries (e.g., railroad tracks, parks, freeways), knowledge of Chicago's local neighborhoods, and cluster analyses of census data were used to guide the construction of relatively homogeneous NCs with respect to distributions of racial-ethnic mix, socioeconomic status, housing density, and family organization.

The Community Survey (CS) of the PHDCN is a multidimensional assessment by residents of the structural and cultural properties of their neighborhoods. To gain a complete picture of the city's neighborhoods, 8,782 Chicago residents representing all 343 NCs were personally interviewed in their homes in 1995. The basic design for the CS had three stages: at stage 1, city blocks were sampled within each NC; at stage 2, dwelling units were sampled within blocks, and at stage 3, one adult resident (18 or older) was sampled within each selected dwelling unit. Abt Associates carried out the screening and data collection in cooperation with the research staff of PHDCN, achieving a final response rate of 75%. The sampling plan yielded a representative probability sample of Chicago residents and a large enough within-cluster sample to create reliable between-neighborhood measures. The samples within clusters were designed to be approximately self-weighting, and thus the between-neighborhood analysis is based on unweighted data (see Sampson, Raudenbush, & Earls 1997:924). All descriptive statistics designed to reflect the city population (e.g., means, proportions) are based on weighted data.

Individual Measures

Tolerance of deviance is measured by four questions that asked respondents about "how wrong" they thought various acts were if committed by 13-year-olds and 19-year-olds. Rather than ask about crimes such as robbery or rape that are near universally condemned, the study probed attitudes about "minor" deviance along with a more common manifestation of violence. Respondents were asked, "How wrong is it for teenagers around thirteen years of age to (a) smoke cigarettes, (b) use marijuana, (c) drink alcohol, and (d) get into fist fights." These items were measured on a five-point Likert scale: "not wrong at all" (1), "a little wrong" (2), "wrong" (3), "very wrong" (4), and "extremely wrong" (5). Four corresponding questions asked how wrong the same acts were for "teenagers around nineteen years of age." To assess attitudes specific to violence, we report the replication of analyses with just the fighting item (d).

We drew on and modified Srole's (1956) anomie scale. Under our modification, *legal cynicism* is measured by five items assessing general beliefs about the legitimacy of law and social norms. Respondents reported their level of agreement with five statements: "Laws were made to be broken," "It's okay to do anything you want as long as you don't hurt anyone," "To make money, there are no right and wrong ways anymore, only easy ways and hard ways," "Fighting between friends or within families is nobody else's business," and "Nowadays a person has to live pretty much for today and let tomorrow take care of itself" (1 = strongly disagree, 2 = disagree, 3 = neither agree nor disagree, 4 = agree, and 5 = strongly agree). The common idea is the sense in which laws or rules are not considered binding in the existential, present lives of respondents. Taken as a whole, that is, the items tap variation in respondents' ratification of acting in ways that are "outside" of law and social norms.

Satisfaction with police is measured by five variables concerning the ability of police to respond effectively and fairly to neighborhood crime concerns. On a five-point Likert scale similar to that used for legal cynicism, respondents were asked to report their level of agreement with five statements: "The police in this neighborhood are responsive to local issues," "The police are doing a good job in dealing with problems that really concern people in this neighborhood," "The police are not doing a good job in preventing crime in this neighborhood" (reverse coded), "The police do a good job in responding to people in the neighborhood after they have been victims of crime," and "The police are not able to maintain order on the streets and sidewalks in the neighborhood" (reverse coded).

Measurement Models

Each observed indicator of attitudes toward deviance, legal cynicism, and satisfaction with police was specified as a linear combination of a latent factor plus random measurement error. This strategy enabled us to estimate and control for the biasing effects of random response error, which one might expect to be relatively large for attitudinal variables. We used Jöreskog and Sörbom's (1993b) PRELIS 2 program to generate polychoric correlation and asymptotic covariance matrices, accounting for the ordinal nature of measures. These matrices were then analyzed using the weighted least-squares method of estimation in LISREL 8 (Jöreskog & Sörbom 1993a).

Table 1 shows descriptive statistics of all indicators and parameter estimates of the measurement models. Because the same four items were used to assess attitudes toward deviance at both ages, we included four measurement-error correlations among like items across age (e.g., cigarette smoking at age 13 and age 19). We also included two measurement-error correlations within each age between smoking cigarettes and drinking alcohol. The fit of this model to the data was acceptable: $\chi^2 = 224.29$, df = 13 (goodness of fit index = .997, adjusted goodness of fit index = .991). The correlation between the two latent factors in this model was .72. More important, validity coefficients (standardized loadings) for the empirical indicators of both factors were relatively high, ranging from .73 to .96 at age 13 and from .76 to .93 at age 19.

We estimated single-factor measurement models for both legal cynicism and police satisfaction. We included three measurement-error correlations in the legal cynicism model, which fit the data well: $\chi^2 = 9.68$, df = 2 (goodness of fit index = 1.00, adjusted goodness of fit index = 0.997). Validity coefficients ranged from .44 to .69. We also included three measurement-error correlations in the police satisfaction model, which fit the data extremely well: $\chi^2 = 0.10$, df = 2 (goodness of fit index = 1.00, adjusted goodness of fit index = 1.00). Validity coefficients ranged from .44 to .95.

Taking into account these patterns of measurement error, we obtained factor scores representing OLS coefficients of the regression of latent variables on all observed indicators (Bollen 1989:305). We used these factor scores to estimate tolerance of

788   **Legal Cynicism and (Subcultural?) Tolerance of Deviance**

Table 1. Descriptive Statistics and Parameter Estimates of the Individual-Level Measurement Models, PHDCN Survey, 1995

	Observed Mean	Observed Variance	Error Variance	Metric Slope	Validity Coefficient
Tolerance of deviance, age 13[a]					
Smoke cigarettes	4.46	0.65	0.23	1.00[b]	0.88
Use marijuana	4.66	0.46	0.07	1.10	0.96
Drink alcohol	4.63	0.48	0.09	1.09	0.96
Fist fights	4.25	0.97	0.46	0.83	0.73
Tolerance of deviance, age 19[a]					
Smoke cigarettes	3.35	1.94	0.42	1.00[b]	0.76
Use marijuana	4.11	1.27	0.14	1.21	0.93
Drink alcohol	3.79	1.60	0.22	1.16	0.89
Fist fights	3.92	1.29	0.43	0.99	0.76
Legal cynicism[c]					
Laws to be broken	2.03	0.89	0.57	1.00[b]	0.65
Okay to do anything you want	2.42	1.17	0.53	1.05	0.68
No right/wrong ways to make money	2.20	1.06	0.53	1.05	0.69
Fighting is nobody else's business	2.67	1.22	0.80	0.68	0.44
Person has to live for today	2.52	1.32	0.72	0.81	0.53
Satisfaction with police[d]					
Responsive to local issues	3.46	0.96	0.35	1.00[b]	0.80
Good job dealing with problems	3.31	1.03	0.10	1.18	0.95
Not doing good job preventing crime[e]	3.21	1.09	0.72	0.66	0.53
Good job responding to victims	3.41	0.88	0.70	0.68	0.55
Not able to maintain order[e]	3.36	1.07	0.81	0.55	0.44

[a] $N = 7,841$; range 1 (not wrong) to 5 (extremely wrong).
[b] Fixed coefficient.
[c] $N = 7,925$; range 1 (strongly disagree) to 5 (strongly agree).
[d] $N = 7,918$; range 1 (strongly disagree) to 5 (strongly agree).
[e] Reverse coded.

deviance at ages 13 and 19, legal cynicism, and satisfaction with police for each respondent. To accomplish this, we weighted the observed indicators by the factor scores and then summed the weighted components for each factor. The ranges for the tolerance of deviance factor are 0.91 to 4.56 (age 13) and 0.79 to 3.93 (age 19); for the legal cynicism scale, 0.80 to 4.01; and for police satisfaction, 0.85 to 4.24. The resulting factor-score estimates are best viewed as summary "indicators" of true latent constructs that account for measurement-error correlations; these factor scores served as the basic input to the multivariate hierarchical linear models. Suggesting the robustness of results, however, our factor-analytic approach produced scales similar to those obtained by calculating an unweighted average of the relevant items for each scale.

Neighborhood Structure

Three indexes of neighborhood structural differentiation are examined based on prior theory (Wilson 1987; Sampson & Wilson 1995) and analysis of census data in Chicago over three decades (Morenoff & Sampson 1997; Sampson et al. 1997). We focus here on 1990 census data because they were measured independently from the PHDCN community survey and were collected five years earlier, permitting temporal sequencing. Ten census variables were selected to reflect structural differences in poverty (percentage below the poverty line and percentage receiving public assistance), race/ethnicity (percentage black, percentage Latino American, percentage foreign born), the labor market (percentage unemployed), age composition (percentage under age 18), family structure (percentage female-headed families with children), housing (percentage home ownership), and residential stability (percentage living in the same house as in 1985). To simplify the dimensionality of the regressor space and account for the extensive multicollinearity among these 10 census variables, we used alpha-scoring factor analysis with an oblique factor rotation to create three summary indexes (see Sampson et al. 1997:920).

Concentrated disadvantage represents an economic disadvantage factor in racially segregated urban neighborhoods that was dominated by high loadings (> .8) for poverty, public assistance, unemployment, female-headed families with children, and percentage under age 18, followed by, to a lesser extent, percentage black. This factor reflects the neighborhood concentration of resource disadvantage, to which African Americans and single-parent families with children are disproportionately exposed (Wilson 1987; Land, McCall, & Cohen 1990). The second factor captures areas of *concentrated immigration*. The variables that define this dimension are percentage Latino (approximately 70% of Latinos are Mexican American in Chicago) and percentage foreign born. The third factor is dominated by just two variables with very high (> .8) loadings—percentage living in the same house as five years earlier and percentage owner-occupied homes. The emergence of a *residential stability* factor is consistent with much past research. Using factor loadings as weights, summary scales were created to reflect the three dimensions.[1]

Hierarchical Linear Models

The nested structure of the PHDCN data is addressed by adapting appropriate hierarchical linear models (HLM) that account for the nonindependence of observations within neighborhood contexts. The HLM procedures of Bryk and Raudenbush (1992) were used to estimate two equations simultaneously: within neighborhood and between neighborhood. The major ad-

---

[1] We also examined several other procedures, including weighted scales based on principal components analysis and unit-weighted scales based on standardized z-scores. An analysis of three decades worth of census data in Chicago, from 1970 to 1990, yielded a similar factor structure (Morenoff & Sampson 1997). Overall the substantive results were not sensitive to these alternative estimation and scoring procedures.

vantage of HLM for present purposes is that it unifies levels of
analysis rather than forcing a choice of one against the other;
that is, both individual-level and neighborhood-level relationships are simultaneously modeled and estimated.[2] As Garner and
Raudenbush (1991:253) argue, such partitioning allows the appropriate interpretation of the explanatory power of hierarchical
models.

Our analysis strategy accounts for a rich array of individual-
level and group-level covariates. Specifically, the within-neighborhood model regresses the three key measures—legal cynicism,
tolerance of deviance, and satisfaction with police—on 11 characteristics: race/ethnicity (composed of indicators for Latino
American and non–Latino African American; non–Latino Cauca-
sian is the reference category), a composite measure of socioeconomic status (first principal component of education, income,
and occupational prestige), sex (1 = female, 0 = male), marital
status (composed of separate indicators for married, separated or
divorced, and single), home ownership, mobility (number of
moves in the past five years), years in the neighborhood, and age.
With tolerance of deviance as the example, the within-neighborhood model can be written as:

$$(\text{Tolerance})_{ij} = \beta_{0j} + \Sigma_{(q=1-11)} \beta_q X_{qij} + e_{ij},$$

where β_{0j} is the intercept; X_{qij} is the value of covariate q associated
with respondent i in neighborhood j; and β_q is the partial effect
of that covariate on tolerance of deviance. The error term, e_{ij}, is
the unique contribution of each individual, which is assumed to
be independently, normally distributed with constant variance σ^2.
Importantly, because the person-level covariates are centered
about the sample means, β_{0j} is the mean tolerance of deviance in
a neighborhood after the effects of the 11 covariates have been
adjusted.

The between-neighborhood model can be written as

$$\beta_{0j} = \theta_{00} + \theta_{01} (\text{con. disad.}) + \theta_{02} (\text{con. immig.}) + \theta_{03} (\text{res. stability}) + U_{0j},$$

where θ_{00} is the average tolerance score, and θ_{01}, θ_{02} and θ_{03} are
the regression coefficients of the effects of concentrated disad-
vantage, immigrant concentration, and residential stability, respectively, on the adjusted neighborhood level of tolerance. U_{0j} is
the neighborhood-level error term, or the unique contribution
of each neighborhood, assumed to be normally distributed with
variance τ. Based on preliminary analysis, we constrain all within-
neighborhood slopes to be constant across neighborhoods.[3] Our
interest is main effects on parameter variance across neighbor-

---

[2] All models were estimated with HLM 4.0, which provides robust standard errors.
For statistical details on the empirical Bayes and maximum-likelihood estimation, see
Bryk & Raudenbush (1992:ch. 3) and Sampson et al. (1997:924).

[3] We explored random slope models but generally found that there were no multilevel interactions in the data for the key variables. In particular, variance in the slope

hoods in tolerance of deviance, legal cynicism, and satisfaction with policing, adjusting for measurement error and individual-level differences in sociodemographic composition.[4]

Sociodemographic Patterns

To aid in identifying descriptive patterns, we began our analysis by dividing the tolerance of deviance, legal cynicism, and satisfaction with police scales into equal thirds. Table 2 presents the crosstabulation, weighted to reflect the Chicago population, of the three scales by race/ethnicity, socioeconomic status, gender, and age. Because of the large sample, significance tests are less informative than percentage differentials.

The measures of tolerance of deviance at ages 13 and 19 reveal similar patterns that contradict common stereotypes regarding the magnitude of tolerance and its connection to sociodemographic differences. Overall, respondents are rather intolerant of deviance among youth (see also Table 1, descriptive statistics), with mean values above 4 ("very wrong") for all items among 13-year-olds. Even for 19-year olds, respondents are highly intolerant except for smoking items. More interesting, African Americans and Latino respondents are much less tolerant of deviance than are white respondents. Whereas 42% of blacks and 47% of Latinos score low on the tolerance of deviance scale at age 13, only 31% of whites do so. The pattern is similar for tolerance of deviance at age 19. These rather substantial differences in magnitude are all highly significant. Perhaps most striking, when we limited the analysis to the fighting item, the race/ethnic differences actually increased: for example, the percentage of whites who responded that fighting among 13-year-olds was extremely wrong was 42% compared with 54% for blacks and 63% for Latinos (table not shown). Even for violence, then, racial and ethnic minorities are apparently less tolerant than European Americans.

Table 2 also shows that respondents of low socioeconomic status are less tolerant of deviance than are those of high SES, again contrary to common perceptions. Some 45% of low-SES respondents score low on the tolerance of deviance at age 13

---

estimate for race/ethnicity across neighborhoods was not reliably predicted by the measured characteristics of concentrated poverty, immigrant concentration, or stability.

[4] There is another adjustment of potential importance that we addressed as well—spatial autocorrelation. As a check on the sensitivity of results to the spatial dependence of dependent variables across neighborhood clusters, we replicated the main results introducing spatial lags (see Morenoff & Sampson 1997:42–43). Essentially, these models controlled for the cumulative effect on each neighborhood of the levels of the dependent variable of *all other* neighborhoods in the city, weighted by geographical proximity to the reference neighborhood. OLS regressions of these "spatial diffusion" models yielded identical substantive patterns for the main explanatory variables, suggesting the robustness of results to potential diffusion processes. In future work, we hope to integrate the simultaneous estimation of HLM and spatial diffusion models.

Table 2. Tolerance of Deviance, Legal Cynicism, and Satisfaction with Police by Key Sociodemographic Characteristics, PHDCN Survey, 1995

	Race/Ethnicity			SES			Sex		Age		
	White	Black	Latino	Low	Medium	High	Male	Female	18-32	33-47	48-100
Tolerance of deviance, age 13											
Low	31%	42%	47%	45%	39%	34%	32%	43%	34%	39%	44%
Medium	32	25	26	23	27	31	27	28	29	29	25
High	37	33	27	33	34	35	40	29	38	32	31
Tolerance of deviance, age 19											
Low	27%	32%	43%	37%	33%	29%	28%	35%	25%	32%	40%
Medium	42	32	34	34	38	38	35	38	38	35	37
High	32	36	23	29	29	34	37	27	37	33	23
Legal cynicism											
Low	46%	38%	35%	29%	37%	49%	36%	43%	33%	42%	46%
Medium	35	32	34	35	34	33	36	33	37	32	32
High	19	29	31	36	29	18	28	25	30	26	22
Satisfaction with police											
Low	14%	38%	36%	40%	31%	18%	28%	28%	33%	27%	23%
Medium	38	36	37	36	39	37	35	39	36	39	37
High	49	26	27	24	30	45	37	34	31	34	41

NOTE: Percentage estimates are weighted to reflect sampling design.

scale, compared with 34% of high SES respondents. A similar pattern exists for tolerance of deviance at age 19. More in line with common belief, Table 2 shows that males are more tolerant of deviance among 13- and 19-year-olds than are females and that younger respondents are more tolerant of deviance at both ages than are older respondents.

For the legal cynicism scale, Table 2 reveals substantial differences in beliefs about the legitimacy of law by race/ethnicity, age, and socioeconomic status. Twenty-nine percent of black respondents and 31% of Latino respondents score in the highest one-third of the legal cynicism scale, compared with only 19% of white respondents. Older respondents score lower on the legal cynicism scale than do those who are younger. The most significant variation in legal cynicism is by socioeconomic status. Respondents of low SES are significantly less likely than those of high SES to view legal norms as legitimate; 36% of low-SES respondents score in the highest one-third of the legal cynicism scale, compared with only 18% of high-SES respondents. To the extent that SES and race are confounded, Table 2 suggests that we need to consider them simultaneously in later models.

The findings for the satisfaction with police scale are similar to those for the legal cynicism scale. Black and Latino respondents report much lower levels of satisfaction with policing in their neighborhoods than do white respondents. Not surprisingly, persons of low SES report less satisfaction with the police than do those of high SES. Sex differences are immaterial, but younger respondents are less satisfied with policing in their neighborhoods than are older respondents.

At the descriptive level, the data suggest that minority respondents are less tolerant of deviance than whites, even as they are more cynical about the police and legal norms. Hence it appears that the data do not support a simplistic black subculture of deviance or violence thesis, but they do support research on perceptions of injustice and alienation from police (e.g., Hagan & Albonetti 1982). We now turn to simultaneous sources of variation in these scales at the person and neighborhood levels.

Multilevel Results

Table 3 presents the HLM decomposition of variance components for attitudes toward deviance.[5] We analyzed both the age 13 and age 19 scales separately, a summary measure that averaged the two, and the individual fighting item. The HLM results were substantively identical for deviance at ages 13 and 19. To

---

[5] All multivariate HLM models are based on listwise deletion of missing data. On average, the models with complete data on all items captured about 85% of the original sample. Further analysis of missing data patterns revealed nothing systematic that would appear to bias the conclusions derived from the substantive results.

simplify, Table 3 displays results for the combined scale, scored so that a higher value indicates greater *in*tolerance of deviance. The reliability of the scale at the neighborhood level is .60, where reliability is defined as $\Sigma \, [\tau_{00}/(\tau_{00} + \sigma^2/nj)] \, / \, J$. Thus the reliability of tolerance of deviance averaged across J (342) neighborhoods[6] increases as the sample size (n) in each of the j neighborhoods increases and the between-group variance (τ_{00}) increases relative to the within-group variance (σ^2). A magnitude of .60 suggests that we are able to tap, with a reasonable degree of precision, neighborhood differences in subcultural orientations to deviance as our research strategy demands (cf. Fischer 1995).

Table 3. Hierarchical Linear Model of Low Tolerance for Deviance (Age 13/ 19 Summary Scale, Neighborhood-Level Reliability = .60): Variance Decomposition and Correlates, PHDCN Survey, 1995

	Coefficient	S.E.	t-Ratio
Intercept	3.655	.009	402.04**
Person level $(N = 7,267)$			
African American	.128	.032	3.97**
Latino American	.175	.025	6.95**
Female	.167	.015	10.86**
SES	−.010	.007	−1.52
Age	.004	.001	6.93**
Married	.085	.022	3.85**
Separated/divorced	.042	.023	1.84
Single	−.055	.025	−2.26*
Own home	.014	.018	0.77
Residential moves	−.027	.006	−4.49**
Years in neighborhood	−.001	.001	−1.82
Neighborhood level $(N = 342)$			
Concentrated disadvantage	−.048	.018	−2.69**
Immigrant concentration	.069	.012	5.59**
Residential stability	.057	.009	5.87**

	Variance Components	Variance Explained
Within neighborhoods	.363	5%
Between neighborhoods	.030	64%

$* \, p < .05$ $** \, p < .01$

The HLM estimate of the intraclass correlation (ICC) reveals that about 8% of the scale's parameter variance lies between neighborhoods, with the remainder apportioned to a combination of random error and individual-level variation. This relatively low level of between-neighborhood variation is similar to what has been found in other studies looking at contexts such as schools and even families. Duncan and Raudenbush (1997:10) advise caution in interpreting small intraclass correlations, as effect sizes commonly viewed as large translate into small propor-

---

6 The neighborhood cluster containing O'Hare International Airport was deleted because there were not enough sample respondents residing there to obtain reliable measures.

tions of variance in individual outcomes explained by neighbor-hood membership. In fact, neighborhood effect sizes as large as .8 of a standard deviation difference give rise to an ICC as low as .14. Therefore, a small correlation among neighbors does not rule out a large effect size associated with a measured difference between neighborhoods (Duncan & Raudenbush 1997:11).

The multivariate HLM results confirm the descriptive finding from Table 2 regarding race/ethnicity that contradicts common assumptions. With SES, eight other person-level predictors, and neighborhood context controlled for, we found that African Americans and Latino Americans report significantly less toler-ance for deviance than whites (t-ratios of 3.97 and 6.95, $p < .01$, respectively).[7] Not only are Latinos especially intolerant of devi-ance, residents of concentrated immigrant areas, which are predominantly Latino in composition, are also higher in intoler-ance (t-ratio = 5.59). This contextual result suggests something emergent about Latino culture, perhaps religious in nature, which yields a consistent pattern of condemnation of deviance.

The neighborhood-level results reveal two other distinct find-ings. Areas of concentrated disadvantage and residential *in*stability appear to have increased levels of tolerance of devi-ance. The HLM model adjusts for compositional differences in the sample survey with respect to race/ethnicity and SES (among other sociodemographic characteristics), pointing to a contex-tual component of subcultural theory. Namely, tolerance of devi-ance does appear to be ecologically patterned—it is higher in neighborhoods of ghetto poverty and instability but lower in con-centrated immigrant neighborhoods. At the same time, however, minority groups are more intolerant of deviance than whites, even when neighborhood context is controlled.

Because of the historical connection of subcultural theory to violence, we replicated the results with the tolerance of fighting item. Perhaps not surprisingly, respondents were less likely to see fighting among 19-year-olds as extremely wrong (40%) com-pared with 13-year-olds (51%). Further analysis of the fighting item by individual covariates also indicated that we were better able to discriminate among differences at age 13 than at age 19, especially by race/ethnicity. Table 4 thus presents the HLM re-sults for intolerance of fighting among 13-year-olds. Although somewhat less reliable at the neighborhood level, the basic pat-terns remain the same. African Americans and Latinos are signif-icantly more likely to condemn fighting than European Ameri-cans (t-ratios = 2.89 and 6.38, respectively). And stable neighborhoods and Latino immigrant neighborhoods are more intolerant of fighting. The only difference that emerges for the

---

[7] In the model without any measured neighborhood characteristics, the coefficients for African Americans and Latinos were similarly positive, indicating greater intolerance of deviance (t-ratios = 2.47 and 7.97, respectively).

Table 4. Hierarchical Linear Model of Low Tolerance for Fighting at Age 13 (Neighborhood-Level Reliability = .56): Variance Decomposition and Correlates, PHDCN Survey, 1995

	Coefficient	S.E.	t-Ratio
Intercept	4.226	.016	265.22**
Person level (N = 7,410)			
African American	.139	.048	2.89**
Latino American	.255	.040	6.38**
Female	.247	.025	10.01**
SES	−.018	.010	−1.82
Age	.004	.001	3.94**
Married	.082	.033	2.48*
Separated/divorced	.044	.038	1.15
Single	−.046	.039	−1.17
Own home	.000	.028	0.01
Residential moves	−.014	.010	−1.31
Years in neighborhood	−.001	.001	−1.33
Neighborhood level (N = 342)			
Concentrated disadvantage	.013	.023	0.57
Immigrant concentration	.066	.021	3.18**
Residential stability	.049	.019	2.66**

	Variance Components	Variance Explained
Within neighborhoods	.919	3%
Between neighborhoods	.063	35%

* $p < .05$ ** $p < .01$

fighting item is that the effect of concentrated poverty is no longer significant. Apparently, the greater tolerance of deviance found in ghetto poverty areas (Table 3) does not extend specifically to violence, yet another finding which undercuts a racially linked subculture of violence argument.[8]

Table 5 examines the HLM model of legal cynicism. The neighborhood-level reliability estimate of .54 is somewhat less than that for the tolerance of deviance scales. In addition, the variance components reveal that only about 6% percent of the variance in the measure lies between neighborhoods. These results are not altogether surprising given the attitudinal nature of the survey questions and the "individualistic" bent of the psychometric history of anomie scales. Our ability to detect neighborhood differences is thus somewhat attenuated, but we are still within the bounds of acceptability (see Duncan & Raudenbush 1997). Model 1 in Table 5 presents just the person-level predictors to reveal differential patterns in the data as we integrate levels of analysis. Note that the coefficient for African

---

[8] Recall the strong connection of neighborhood percentage black with economic disadvantage. As a further test, we examined whether blacks residing in inner-city neighborhoods of concentrated disadvantage approve of fighting more than do blacks in middle-class neighborhoods. They do not. When the disadvantage factor was divided into thirds (low, medium, and high), the percentage of African Americans reporting that fighting among 13-year-olds is extremely wrong was 53, 53, and 55, respectively. Thus, if anything, blacks in high-poverty areas are more intolerant of fighting.

Table 5. Hierarchical Linear Model of Legal Cynicism (Neighborhood-Level Reliability = .54): Variance Decomposition and Correlates, PHDCN Survey, 1995

	Model 1			Model 2		
	Coefficient	S.E.	*t*-Ratio	Coefficient	S.E.	*t*-Ratio
Intercept	1.852	.008	231.25**	1.850	.008	235.23**
Person level (*N* = 7,408)						
African American	.060	.017	3.58**	.022	.021	1.01
Latino American	.039	.021	1.88	.027	.023	1.18
Female	−.068	.013	−5.08**	−.069	.013	−5.15**
SES	−.089	.006	−15.58**	−.083	.006	−13.64**
Age	−.002	.000	−3.96**	−.002	.000	−3.62**
Married	−.079	.021	−3.79**	−.079	.021	−3.76**
Separated/divorced	−.050	.023	−2.20*	−.051	.023	−2.20*
Single	.011	.023	0.50	.012	.023	0.52
Own home	−.018	.016	−1.12	−.016	.016	−0.99
Residential moves	.006	.005	1.13	.008	.005	1.45
Years in neighborhood	−.000	.000	−0.36	−.000	.000	−0.63
Neighborhood level (*N* = 342)						
Concentrated disadvantage				.047	.011	3.99**
Immigrant concentration				.008	.010	0.76
Residential stability				.013	.008	1.65

	Variance Components	Variance Explained	
		Model 1	Model 2
Within neighborhoods	.291	5%	5%
Between neighborhoods	.018	56%	61%

* *p* < .05   ** *p* < .01

Americans is both positive and significant (*p* < .01), meaning that blacks report higher levels of cynicism about legal norms than do whites. The other pattern is that high-SES respondents, females, older respondents, and those either married or separated/divorced report lower levels of estrangement from legal norms.

Model 2 introduces neighborhood context into the picture. Once neighborhood-level differences in concentrated disadvantage are accounted for, the coefficient for blacks is reduced to insignificance. *Note that no other person-level predictors change.* For example, the coefficient for SES remains virtually invariant (-.089 vs. -.083), whereas the coefficient for African Americans is cut by more than 50% (.060 to .022). It seems, then, that minority status is confounded with neighborhood context—blacks appear more cynical because they are disproportionately likely to live in residential environments of concentrated disadvantage. The magnitude of difference in ecological niches of residence by race is in fact striking: 20% of blacks live in neighborhoods with a poverty rate greater than 40%, compared with 3% of Latinos and less than 1% of whites. Even more disturbing, over 50% of blacks in Chicago live in neighborhoods in the upper one-third of the city-wide distribution on the concentrated disadvantage factor, compared with 17% of Latinos and just 2% of whites. Thus African

Americans in particular, relative to *both* whites and Latinos, are much more likely to reside in ecologically distinct environments of concentrated disadvantage. The data in Table 5 suggest that it is precisely this contextual reality of ecologically structured disadvantage—and not race at the person level—that is the driving component of the legal cynicism result. Interestingly, the strong influence of concentrated disadvantage is such that residential instability and immigrant concentration do not matter in predicting legal cynicism.

The concentrated disadvantage result in Table 5 held up when we introduced a multisource measure of the violent crime rate across neighborhoods. It may be, for example, that experience with personal victimization or the perception of rampant crime in the neighborhood breeds hopelessness and cynicism about sociolegal norms of responsibility (Skogan 1990). Because we know that concentrated disadvantage is strongly linked to violent crime (Sampson et al. 1997), we explicitly entertained this rival hypothesis. A measure for violence was created by combining standardized measures of homicide (incidents of police-recorded homicide in the neighborhood, normed by population size),[9] survey-reported personal victimization by violence, and a scale of perceived violent acts committed in the neighborhood. All three constituent measures of violence refer to the year 1995. Although the summary measure of violence was rather highly correlated with concentrated disadvantage ($r = .66$, $p < .01$), the results were invariant to its consideration. The coefficient estimate for concentrated disadvantage remained significant and at the same magnitude (.047, t-ratio = 3.70), but the estimate for violent crime was close to zero (t-ratio = $-.41$). This test reveals that concentrated disadvantage is a robust predictor of legal cynicism that adjusts for not only compositional differences in respondents but also rates of violent crime in the neighborhood.[10]

Table 6 presents the HLM results for the final measure tapping satisfaction with the Chicago police. Again we present separate models that reveal the confounding of race and neighborhood. Unlike the analysis for Table 5, however, we retain the models that control for violent crime rates because they reveal significant relationships. This is not surprising. In evaluating attitudes about the police, one would expect that those living in high-crime areas would express less satisfaction with the police than those living in relatively crime-free environments. The more interesting questions from our perspective are: Does the ecological context of concentrated disadvantage predict satisfaction with

[9] Homicide is generally agreed to reflect smaller biases in police recording than other crimes. Nevertheless, we obtained similar results for total violent crime (per capita incidents known to the police of murder, rape, robbery, and aggravated assault).

[10] The results for tolerance of deviance and fighting (Tables 3 and 4) also held when the violent crime rate was controlled.

Table 6. Hierarchical Linear Model of Satisfaction with the Police
(Neighborhood-Level Reliability = .77): Variance Decomposition
and Correlates, PHDCN Survey, 1995

	Model 1			Model 2		
	Coefficient	S.E.	*t*-Ratio	Coefficient	S.E.	*t*-Ratio
Intercept	2.837	.016	179.06**	2.845	.011	254.67**
Person level (*N* = 7,396)						
African American	−.156	.028	−5.50**	−.016	.029	−0.55
Latino American	−.041	.028	−1.45	−.014	.028	−0.49
Female	−.039	.016	−2.36*	−.037	.016	−2.26*
SES	.047	.008	6.03**	.033	.008	4.20**
Age	.007	.001	9.80**	.007	.001	9.14**
Married	−.043	.026	−1.68	−.050	.025	−1.99*
Separated/divorced	−.028	.029	−0.93	−.026	.029	−0.91
Single	.006	.029	0.21	.007	.029	0.23
Own home	.007	.021	0.35	−.023	.020	−1.14
Residential moves	−.003	.007	−0.41	−.006	.007	−0.87
Years in neighborhood	−.002	.000	−2.78**	−.002	.000	−1.96*
Neighborhood level (*N* = 342)						
Concentrated disadvantage				−.148	.017	−8.90**
Immigrant concentration				−.028	.013	−2.10*
Residential stability				.002	.012	0.15
Violent crime rate				−.061	.007	−8.30**

	Variance Components	Variance Explained	
		Model 1	Model 2
Within neighborhoods	.505	1%	2%
Between neighborhoods	.092	36%	82%

* *p* < .05   ** *p* < .01

the police independent of the crime rate? And does the combination of concentrated disadvantage and violent crime account
for the relationship established in Table 2 whereby African
Americans express more negative attitudes than do whites toward
the police?

The answers given in Table 6 are fairly clear and affirmative
on both counts. First, in the within-neighborhood regression
with no structural characteristics (Model 1), African Americans,
along with low-income respondents, females, younger persons,
and long-term residents, express significantly lower levels of satisfaction with the police. The negative evaluation of criminal justice agents by minority groups conforms to the earlier finding of
Hagan and Albonetti (1982). Second, the measure of police satisfaction is very reliable at the neighborhood level (.77), with more
than 15% of the variance lying between neighborhoods. To explain this variation, we introduce in Model 2 the three neighborhood characteristics in conjunction with the violent crime rate.
As expected, the data show that higher-crime areas emit the least
satisfaction with the police. Yet concentrated immigrant neighborhoods and poverty areas show lower levels of police satisfaction regardless of the violent crime rate. To be sure, when the

violent crime rate is dropped from the model, the size of the concentrated disadvantage coefficient increases substantially to −.23 (*t*-ratio = −13.32). This finding tells us that violent crime *is* a major part of the story of why residents of concentrated poverty areas rate the police so negatively. Still, violent crime is not the whole story nor is individual race/ethnicity—the contextual effect of disadvantage retains its strong predictive power.

Third, and perhaps most intriguing, introducing the combined influence of concentrated neighborhood disadvantage and violent crime completely accounts for the race/ethnic differences observed in Model 1. Model 2 shows that the coefficient estimate for African Americans is reduced by a factor of 10 (−.156 to −.016) and is now insignificant. Again, by contrast, the other sociodemographic correlates of satisfaction barely change when neighborhood context is simultaneously considered. The large change in individual-level coefficients when neighborhood context is simultaneously considered is thus specific to blacks. Apparently, then, it is a neighborhood context more than a race-specific attitude that explains estrangement from the police.

Conclusion

Direct measurement of cultural values and normative orientations is rare in the social sciences, especially in contextual perspective. Addressing this limitation, we developed three scales tapping dimensions of subcultural tolerance, cynicism about legal norms and police effectiveness. Although the proportion of variance that lies between neighborhoods was relatively small, we were able to measure neighborhood-level differences reliably. The HLM models explained a reasonably large amount of this variance in systematic ways. The results suggested that if there is a subcultural system that tolerates deviance and turns a cynical eye toward the law and agents of criminal justice, it is not linked in a simple way to race. Put simply, there is no "black" subculture of violence. If anything, African Americans are *less* tolerant of crime than their European American counterparts.

At the same time, inner-city "ghetto" areas displayed elevated levels of legal cynicism, dissatisfaction with the police, and tolerance of deviance generally defined. This consistent finding cannot be explained away by compositional differences or by levels of violent crime in the neighborhood, even though these factors clearly matter. In support of contextual accounts of subculture (e.g., Anderson 1990, 1997; Sampson 1997), it thus appears that there is an ecological structuring to normative orientations—"cognitive landscapes" where crime and deviance are more or less expected and institutions of criminal justice are mistrusted. These differences are not large, but they are consistent nonetheless. We would thus offer the take-away message that normative orientations toward law and deviance are rooted more in experiential differences associated with neighborhood context than in a racially induced subcultural system. Because race and neighborhood are confounded, the tendency in the literature has been, incorrectly in our view, to attribute to African Americans a distinct culture of violence.[11]

Perhaps we should not be surprised that those most exposed to the numbing reality of pervasive segregation and economic subjugation become cynical about human nature and legal systems of justice—even as they personally condemn acts of deviance and violence that make life more precarious. Meares and Kahan (1997), proponents of the "New Chicago School" (Lessig 1998) of legal reasoning, examine the relationship between law and norms from a different angle but with similar implications. They argue that law has the potential to be most effective when it operates in concert with social norms of order that informally control behavior, and is sensitive to norms against *dis*order that may give rise to crime. Meares and Kahan encourage policymakers to attend to the unintended consequences of get-tough policies and heavy-handed enforcement practices on a community's ability to contribute to crime-reduction efforts. As an alternative, they advocate crime-control strategies in disadvantaged African American communities that bolster neighborhood social organization and involve the community in significant ways to show that crime is not tolerated there. Such norm-sensitive strategies have the potential to alleviate some of the legal cynicism that pervades disadvantaged communities, expressed even by residents with little tolerance for the crime that surrounds them. The implications of our findings for rethinking how the police and other agents of criminal justice should approach social norms in inner-city America are thus potentially far-reaching.

---

[11] Davis (1997) maintains that "race of interviewer effects" may bias responses to both racial and nonracial survey questions, as respondents adjust their answers according to their perceptions of the "racial expectations" of the interviewer. From this view, nonrandom measurement error could mask honest reports on issues such as voting behavior, trust in government, or attitudes about violence. Davis, for example, demonstrated the inhibitory effect that white interviewers had on African Americans' reports of racial consciousness and support for Jesse Jackson as a presidential candidate. An anonymous reviewer pointed out that this type of "race of interviewer effect" could be responsible in part for the lack of support for the subculture hypothesis in previous survey research. In the present study, however, interviewers were quite diverse in race/ethnic background (covering all three major groups) and language. Indeed, many interviews were conducted in Spanish and Polish. Moreover, if the race of interviewer in any way biased blacks' responses to the tolerance of deviance items (assuming for the sake of argument that interviewers were white), we should have seen bias in the same direction for the legal cynicism and satisfaction with policing questions. Specifically, blacks would report low levels of cynicism and high satisfaction with police. That they clearly did not suggests that race of interviewer cannot explain the findings.

References

Agnew, Robert (1994) "The Techniques of Neutralization and Violence," 32 *Criminology* 555–80.

Anderson, Elijah (1978) *A Place on the Corner.* Chicago: Univ. of Chicago Press.

——— (1990) *Streetwise: Race, Class, and Change in an Urban Community.* Chicago: Univ. of Chicago Press.

——— (1997) "Code of the Streets," in McCord, ed. 1997.

Block, Richard (1971) "Fear of Crime and Fear of the Police," 19 *Social Problems* 91–101.

Blumenthal, Monica D. (1972) "Predicting Attitudes toward Violence," 176 *Science* 1296–1303.

Blumenthal, Monica D., Robert L. Kahn, Frank M. Andrews, & Kendra B. Head (1972) *Justifying Violence: Attitudes of American Men.* Ann Arbor: Institute for Social Research, Univ. of Michigan.

Bollen, Kenneth A. (1989) *Structural Equations with Latent Variables.* New York: John Wiley & Sons.

Bryk, Anthony, & Stephen Raudenbush (1992) *Hierarchical Linear Models.* Newbury Park, CA: Sage Publications.

Bullough, Bonnie (1967) "Alienation in the Ghetto," 72 *American J. of Sociology* 469–78.

Cao, Liqun, Anthony Adams, & Vickie J. Jensen (1997) "A Test of the Black Subculture of Violence Thesis: A Research Note," 35 *Criminology* 367–79.

Cloward, Richard A. & Lloyd E. Ohlin (1960) *Delinquency and Opportunity: A Theory of Delinquent Gangs.* Glencoe, IL: Free Press.

Cohen, Albert K. (1955) *Delinquent Boys.* Glencoe, IL: Free Press.

Curtis, Lynn A. (1975) *Violence, Race, and Culture.* Lexington, MA: D. C. Heath.

Davis, Darren W. (1997) "Nonrandom Measurement Error and Race of Interviewer Effects among African Americans," 61 *Public Opinion Q.* 183–207.

Duncan, Greg, & Stephen Raudenbush (1997) "Getting Context Right in Quantitative Studies of Child Development." Presented at conference on Research Ideas and Data Needs for Studying the Well-being of Children and Families, October.

Dunham, Roger G., & Geoffrey P. Alpert (1988) "Neighborhood Differences in Attitudes toward Policing: Evidence for a Mixed-Strategy Model of Policing in a Multi-Ethnic Setting," 79 *J. of Criminal Law & Criminology* 504–23.

Ellison, Christopher G. (1991) "An Eye for an Eye? A Note on the Southern Subculture of Violence Thesis," 69 *Social Forces* 1223–39.

Erlanger, Howard S. (1974) "The Empirical Status of the Subculture of Violence Thesis," 22 *Social Problems* 280–92.

Erlanger, Howard S., & Halliman H. Winsborough (1976) "The Subculture of Violence Thesis: An Example of a Simultaneous Equation Model in Sociology," 5 *Sociological Methods & Research* 231–46.

Felson, Richard B., Allen E. Liska, Scott J. South, & Thomas L. McNulty (1994) "The Subculture of Violence and Delinquency: Individual vs. School Context Effects," 73 *Social Forces* 155–73.

Fischer, Claude S. (1976) *The Urban Experience.* 1st ed. San Diego: Harcourt Brace Jovanovich.

——— (1995) "The Subcultural Theory of Urbanism: A Twentieth-Year Assessment," 101 *American J. of Sociology* 543–77.

Garner, Catherine, & Stephen W. Raudenbush (1991) "Neighborhood Effects on Educational Attainment: A Multilevel Analysis," 64 *Sociology of Education* 251–62.

Hagan, John, & Celesta Albonetti (1982) "Race, Class, and the Perception of Criminal Injustice in America," 88 *American J. of Sociology* 329–55.

Hagan, John, Edward T. Silva, & John H. Simpson (1977) "Conflict and Consensus in the Designation of Deviance," 56 *Social Forces* 320–40.

Hahn, Harlan (1971) "Ghetto Assessments of Police Protection and Authority," 6 *Law & Society Rev.* 183–94.

Hartnagel, Timothy F. (1980) "Subculture of Violence: Further Evidence," 23 *Pacific Sociological Rev.* 217–42.

Heimer, Karen (1996) "Gender, Interaction, and Delinquency: Testing a Theory of Differential Social Control," 59 *Social Psychology Q.* 39–61.

——— (1997) "Socioeconomic Status, Subcultural Definitions, and Violent Delinquency," 75 *Social Forces* 799–834.

Heimer, Karen, & Ross L. Matsueda (1994) "Role-Taking, Role Commitment, and Delinquency: A Theory of Differential Social Control," 59 *American Sociological Rev.* 365–90.

Hindelang, Michael J. (1974) "Moral Evaluations of Illegal Behaviors," 21 *Social Problems* 370–85.

Horowitz, Ruth (1987) "Community Tolerance of Gang Violence," 34 *Social Problems* 437–50.

Jöreskog, Karl G., & Dag Sörbom (1993a) *LISREL 8: A Guide to the Program and Applications.* Chicago: Scientific Software International.

——— (1993b) *PRELIS 2: A Program for Multivariate Data Screening and Data Summarization.* A Preprocessor for LISREL. Chicago: Scientific Software International.

Kapsis, Robert E. (1978) "Black Ghetto Diversity and Anomie: A Sociopolitical View," 83 *American J. of Sociology* 1132–53.

Kornhauser, Ruth Rosner (1978) *Social Sources of Delinquency: An Appraisal of Analytic Models.* Chicago: Univ. of Chicago Press.

Land, Kenneth, Patricia McCall, & Lawrence Cohen (1990) "Structural Covariates of Homicide Rates: Are There Any Invariances across Time and Space?" 95 *American J. of Sociology* 922–63.

Lessig, Lawrence (1998) "The New Chicago School," __ *J. of Legal Studies* (in press).

Markowitz, Fred E., & Richard B. Felson (1998) "Social-Demographic Attitudes and Violence," 36 *Criminology* 117–38.

Matsueda, Ross L. (1982) "Testing Control Theory and Differential Association: A Causal Modeling Approach," 47 *American Sociological Rev.* 489–504.

Matsueda, Ross L., & Karen Heimer (1987) "Race, Family Structure, and Delinquency: A Test of Differential Association and Social Control Theories," 52 *American Sociological Rev.* 826–40.

Matza, David (1964) *Delinquency and Drift.* New York: John Wiley & Sons.

McCord, Joan, ed. (1997) *Violence and Childhood in the Inner City.* New York: Cambridge Univ. Press.

Meares, Tracey, & Dan Kahan (1997) "Law and (Norms of) Order in the Inner City." Presented at Law & Society Association annual meeting, St. Louis, MO, June.

Miller, Walter B. (1958) "Lower-Class Culture as a Generating Milieu of Gang Delinquency," 14 *J. of Social Issues* 5–9.

Morenoff, Jeffrey, & Robert J. Sampson (1997) "Violent Crime and the Spatial Dynamics of Neighborhood Transition: Chicago, 1970–1990," 76 *Social Forces* 31–64.

Park, Robert E. (1916) "The City: Suggestions for the Investigations of Human Behavior in the Urban Environment," 20 *American J. of Sociology* 577–612.

Rossi, Peter H., Emily Waite, Christine E. Bose, & Richard E. Berk (1974) "The Seriousness of Crimes: Normative Structure and Individual Differences," 39 *American Sociological Rev.* 224–37.

Sampson, Robert J. (1997) "The Embeddedness of Child and Adolescent Development: A Community-level Perspective on Urban Violence," in McCord, ed. 1997.

804   **Legal Cynicism and (Subcultural?) Tolerance of Deviance**

Sampson, Robert J., & William Julius Wilson (1995) "Toward a Theory of Race, Crime, and Urban Inequality," in J. Hagan & R. D. Peterson, eds., *Crime and Inequality*. Stanford, CA: Stanford Univ, Press.

Sampson, Robert J., Stephen W. Raudenbush, & Felton Earls (1997) "Neighborhoods and Violent Crime: A Multilevel Study of Collective Efficacy," 277 *Science* 918–24.

Shaw, Clifford R., & Henry D. McKay (1942) *Juvenile Delinquency and Urban Areas*. Chicago: Univ. of Chicago Press.

Shoemaker, Donald J., & J. Sherwood Williams (1987) "The Subculture of Violence and Ethnicity," 15 *J. of Criminal Justice* 461–72.

Skogan, Wesley (1990) *Disorder and Decline: Crime and the Spiral of Decay in American Neighborhoods*. Berkeley: Univ. of California Press.

Smith, Paul E., & Richard O. Hawkins (1973) "Victimization, Types of Citizen-Police Contacts, and Attitudes toward the Police," 8 *Law & Society Rev.* 135–52.

Srole, Leo (1956) "Social Integration and Certain Corollaries: An Exploratory Study," 21 *American Sociological Rev.* 709–16.

Sullivan, Mercer (1989) *"Getting Paid": Youth Crime and Work in the Inner City*. Ithaca, NY: Cornell Univ. Press.

Sutherland, Edwin H. (1947) *Principles of Criminology*. 3d ed. Philadelphia: J. B. Lippincott.

Suttles, Gerald D. (1968) *The Social Order of the Slum: Ethnicity and Territory in the Inner City*. Chicago: Univ. of Chicago Press.

——— (1972) *The Social Construction of Communities*. Chicago: Univ. of Chicago Press.

Sykes, Gresham M., & David Matza (1957) "Techniques of Neutralization: A Theory of Delinquency," 22 *American Sociological Rev.* 664–70.

Wilson, Robert A. (1971) "Anomie in the Ghetto: A Study of Neighborhood Type, Race, and Anomie," 77 *American J. of Sociology* 66–88.

Wilson, William Julius (1987) *The Truly Disadvantaged: The Inner City, the Underclass, and Public Policy*. Chicago: Univ. of Chicago Press.

Wolfgang, Marvin E., & Franco Ferracuti (1967) *The Subculture of Violence: Towards an Integrated Theory in Criminology*. London: Tavistock.

Part II
Racial Profiling

[6]

Deadly symbiosis

When ghetto and prison meet and mesh

LOÏC WACQUANT
University of California, Berkeley
Centre de sociologie européenne du Collège de France

Abstract

To explain the astounding over-representation of blacks behind bars that has driven mass imprisonment in the United States, one must break out of the 'crime-and-punishment' paradigm to reckon the extra-penological function of the criminal justice system as instrument for the management of dispossessed and dishonored groups. This article places the prison in the *historical sequence of 'peculiar institutions'* that have shouldered the task of defining and confining African Americans, alongside slavery, the Jim Crow regime, and the ghetto. The recent upsurge in black incarceration results from the crisis of the ghetto as device for caste control and the correlative need for a substitute apparatus for the containment of lower-class African Americans. In the post-Civil Rights era, the vestiges of the dark ghetto and the expanding prison system have become linked by a triple relationship of functional equivalency, structural homology, and cultural fusion, spawning a carceral continuum that entraps a population of younger black men rejected by the deregulated wage-labor market. This carceral mesh has been solidified by changes that have reshaped the urban 'Black Belt' of mid-century so as to *make the ghetto more like a prison* and undermined the 'inmate society' residing in U.S. penitentiaries in ways that *make the prison more like a ghetto*. The resulting symbiosis between ghetto and prison not only perpetuates the socioeconomic marginality and symbolic taint of the black subproletariat, feeding the runaway growth of the carceral system. It also plays a pivotal role in the remaking of 'race', the redefinition of the citizenry via the production of a racialized public culture of vilification of criminals, and the construction of a post-Keynesian state that replaces the social-welfare treatment of poverty by its penal management.

Key Words

ghetto • prison • inmate society • racial disproportionality • caste control • race making • post-Keynesian state • African Americans • United States

PUNISHMENT AND SOCIETY 3(1)

REFRAMING BLACK HYPER-INCARCERATION

Three brute facts stare the sociologist of racial inequality and imprisonment in America in the face as the new millenium dawns. First, since 1989 and for the first time in national history, African Americans make up a majority of those walking through prison gates every year. Indeed, in four short decades, the ethnic composition of the US inmate population has *reversed*, turning over from 70 percent white at the mid-century point to nearly 70 percent black and Latino today, although ethnic patterns of criminal activity have not been fundamentally altered during that period (LaFree et al., 1992; Sampson and Lauritzen, 1997).

Second, the rate of incarceration for African Americans has soared to astronomical levels unknown in any other society, not even the Soviet Union at the zenith of the Gulag or South Africa during the acme of the violent struggles over apartheid. As of mid-1999, close to 800,000 black men were in custody in federal penitentiaries, state prisons and county jails, a figure corresponding to *one male out of every twenty-one* (4·6 percent) and one out of every nine ages 20 to 34 (11·3 percent). An additional 68,000 black women were locked up, a number higher than the *total* carceral population of any one major western European country (Beck, 2000).[1] Several studies, starting with a series of well-publicized reports by the Sentencing Project, have documented that, on any given day, upwards of one-third of African-American men in their twenties find themselves behind bars, on probation or on parole (Donziger, 1996: 104–5). And, at the core of the formerly industrial cities of the North, this proportion often exceeds two-thirds.

A third trend interpellates the social analyst of race, state, and punishment in the United States: the past two decades have witnessed a swift and steady *deepening of the gap* between the imprisonment rates of blacks and whites (from about one for 5 to one for 8·5), and this rising 'racial disproportionality' can be traced directly to a single federal policy, namely, the War on Drugs launched by Ronald Reagan and expanded by the administrations of George Bush and William Jefferson Clinton. In 10 of the 38 states in which this black-white disparity has grown, African Americans are imprisoned at more than ten times the rate of their compatriots of European origin.[2] The political elite of the country is well placed to take note the phenomenon since the jurisdiction that sports the highest racial gap in the land is none other than the District of Columbia, where blacks were 35 times more likely than whites to be put behind bars in 1994 (Mauer, 1997).

These grim statistics are well-known and agreed among students of crime and justice – though they have been steadfastly ignored or minimized by analysts of urban poverty and policy, who have yet to register the enormously disruptive impact that imprisonment has on low-income black communities, as shown by Miller (1997). What remains in dispute are the causes and mechanisms driving this sudden 'blackening' which has turned the carceral system into one of a few national institutions dominated by African Americans, alongside professional sports and selected sectors of the entertainment industry. Most analysts have focused on trends in crime and endeavored to decompose the source of black over-representation in prison by sorting and sifting through patterns of criminality, bias in arrest, prosecution, and sentencing, and prior criminal records (see Blumstein, 1993, for a model study, and Tonry, 1995: 56–79, for a vigorous and rigorous review). A few have expanded their compass to measure the influence of such non-judicial variables as the size of the black population, the poverty rate, unemployment, inflation, income, value of welfare payments, region, support for religious fundamentalism, and political party in office (e.g., Lessan, 1991; Yates, 1997; Greenberg and West, 1999). But none of these factors, taken separately or jointly, accounts for the sheer magnitude, rapidity, and timing of the recent racialization of US imprisonment, especially as crime rates have been flat and later declining over that period. For this, it is necessary, first, to take a longer historical view and, second, to break out of the narrow 'crime-and-punishment' paradigm to reckon the extra-penological role of the penal system as instrument for the management of dispossessed and dishonored groups.[3]

In this article, I put forth two interconnected theses, the first *historical*, replacing the carceral institution in the full arc of ethnoracial division and domination in the United States, the second *institutional*, explaining the astounding upsurge in black incarceration in the past three decades as a result of the obsolescence of the ghetto as a device for caste control and the correlative need for a substitute apparatus for keeping (unskilled) African Americans 'in their place', i.e. in a subordinate and confined position in physical, social, and symbolic space. I further argue that, in the post-Civil Rights era, the remnants of the dark ghetto and the fast-expanding carceral system of the United States have become tightly linked by a triple relationship of functional equivalency, structural homology, and cultural fusion. This relationship has spawned a *carceral continuum* that ensnares a supernumerary population of younger black men, who either reject or are rejected by the deregulated low-wage labor market, in a never-ending circulus between the two institutions. This carceral mesh has been solidified by two sets of concurrent and interrelated changes: on the one end, sweeping economic and political forces have reshaped the structure and function of the urban 'Black Belt' of mid-century to *make the ghetto more like a prison*. On the other end, the 'inmate society' that inhabited the penitentiary system of the US during the postwar decades has broken down in ways that *make the prison more like a ghetto*. The resulting symbiosis between ghetto and prison not only enforces and perpetuates the socioeconomic marginality and symbolic taint of the urban black subproletariat, feeding the runaway growth of the penal system that has become a major component of the post-Keynesian state. It also plays a pivotal role in the remaking of 'race' and the redefinition of the citizenry via the production of a racialized public culture of vilification of criminals.

A fuller analysis, extending beyond the black ghetto, would reveal that the increasing use of imprisonment to shore up caste division in American society partakes of a broader 'upsizing' of the penal sector of the state which, together with the drastic 'downsizing' of its social welfare sector, aims at imposing desocialized wage labor as a norm of citizenship for the deskilled fractions of the postindustrial working class (Wacquant, 1999a). This emerging *government of poverty* wedding the 'invisible hand' of the deregulated labor market to the 'iron fist' of an intrusive and omnipresent punitive apparatus is anchored, not by a 'prison industrial complex', as political opponents of the policy of mass incarceration maintain (e.g. Davis, 1998), but by a *carceral-assistential complex* which carries out its mission to surveil, train and neutralize the populations recalcitrant or superfluous to the new economic and racial regime according to a gendered division of labor, the men being handled by its penal wing while (their) women and children are managed by a revamped welfare-workfare system designed to buttress casual employment. It is this shift from the social to the penal treatment of poverty and its correlates at the bottom of the class and caste structure, subsequent to the denunciation of the

PUNISHMENT AND SOCIETY 3(1)

Fordist-Keynesian social contract, that has brought the prison back to the societal center, counter to the optimistic forecasts of its impending demise by analysts of the criminal justice scene in the early 1970s.

To recognize that the hypertrophic growth of the penal institution is one component of a more comprehensive restructuring of the American state to suit the requirements of neoliberalism is not to negate or even minimize the special office of race in its advent. If the prison offered itself as a viable vehicle of resolving the 'black question' after the crisis of the ghetto – that is, for reformulating it in a way that both *invisibilizes it and reactives it* under new disguises: crime, 'welfare dependency', and the 'underclass' – it is surely because America is the one society that has pushed the market logic of commodification of social relations and state devolution the furthest (Esping-Andersen, 1987; Handler, 1997). But, conversely, if the US far outstrips all advanced nations in the international trend towards the penalization of social insecurity, it is because, just as the dismantling of welfare programs was accelerated by the conflation of blackness and undeservingness in national culture and politics (Gilens, 1999), the 'great confinement' of the rejects of market society, the poor, the mentally ill, the homeless, the jobless and the useless, can be painted as a welcome 'crackdown' on *them*, those dark-skinned criminals issued from a pariah group still considered alien to the national body. Thus, just as the color line inherited from the era of Southern slavery directly determined the mishappen figure of America's 'semi-welfare state' in the formative period of the New Deal (Lieberman, 1998), the handling of the 'underclass' question by the prison system at the close of the 20th century is key to fashioning the visage of the post-Keynesian state in the 21st.

FOUR PECULIAR INSTITUTIONS

To ascertain the pivotal position that the penal apparatus has come to assume within the system of instruments of (re)production of ethnoracial hierarchy in the post-Civil Rights era, it is indispensable to adopt an historical perspective of the *longue durée* so as to situate the prison in the full lineage of institutions which, at each epoch, have carried out the work of race making by drawing and enforcing the peculiar 'color line' that cleaves American society asunder.[4] Put succinctly, the task of *defining, confining, and controling* African Americans in the United States has been successfully shouldered by four 'peculiar institutions': slavery, the Jim Crow system, the urban ghetto, and the novel

TABLE 1 The four 'peculiar institutions' and their basis

PECULIAR INSTITUTION	FORM OF LABOR	CORE OF ECONOMY	DOMINANT SOCIAL TYPE
Slavery (1619–1865)	unfree fixed labor	plantation	slave
Jim Crow (South, 1865–1965)	free fixed labor	agrarian and extractive	sharecropper
Ghetto (North, 1915–1968)	free mobile labor	segmented industrial manufacturing	menial worker
Hyperghetto + Prison (1968–)	fixed surplus labor	polarized postindustrial services	welfare recipient & criminal

organizational compound formed by the vestiges of the ghetto and the expanding
carceral system, as set out in Table 1.

The first three of these institutions, chattel slavery until the Civil War, the Jim Crow
regime of racial exclusion operative in the agrarian South from Emancipation to the Civil
Rights revolution, and the ghetto in the 20th century Northern industrial city, have,
each in its own manner, served two joined yet discordant purposes: to recruit, organize,
and extract labor out of African Americans, on the one hand; and to demarcate and ultimately seclude them so that they would not 'contaminate' the surrounding white society
that viewed them as as irrevocably inferior and vile because devoid of ethnic honor. These
two goals of *labor extraction and social ostracization* of a stigmatized category are in
tension with one another inasmuch as to utilize the labor power of a group inevitably
entails bringing it into regular intercourse with oneself and thereby invites the blurring
or transgression of the boundary separating 'us' from 'them'. Conversely, to immure a
group in a separate physical and sociosymbolic space can make it more difficult to draw
out and deploy its labor in the most efficient way. When the tension between these two
purposes, exploitation and ostracization, mounts to the point where it threatens to
undermine either of them, its excess is drained, so to speak, and the institution restabi-
lized, by resort to *physical violence*: the customary use of the lash and ferocious suppression of slave insurrections on the plantation, terroristic vigilantism and mob lynchings
in the post-bellum South, and periodic bombings of Negro homes and pogroms against
ghetto residents (such as the six-day riot that shook up Chicago in 1919) ensured that
blacks kept to their appointed place at each epoch.[5]

But the built-in instabilities of unfree labor and the inherent anomaly of caste partition in a formally democratic and highly individualistic society guaranteed that each
'peculiar institution' would in time be undermined by the weight of its internal contradictions as well as by mounting black resistance and external opposition,[6] to be replaced
by its successor regime. At each new stage, however, the apparatus of ethnoracial domination would become less total and less capable of encompassing all segments and all
dimensions of the social life of the pariah group. As African Americans differentiated
along class lines and acceded to full formal citizenship, the institutional complex charged
with keeping them 'separate and unequal' grew more differentiated and diffuse, allowing a burgeoning middle and upper class of professionals and salary earners to *partially*
compensate for the negative symbolic capital of blackness by their high-status cultural
capital and proximity to centers of political power, while lower-class blacks remained
burdened by the triple stigma of 'race', poverty, and putative immorality.[7]

1. Slavery (1619–1865)

From the first years of the colony to the Civil War, slavery was the institution that determined the collective identity and individual life chances of Americans of African parent-
age. Orlando Patterson (1982: 334 and passim) has rightly insisted that slavery is
essentially 'a relation of domination and not a category of legal thought', and, moreover,
a relation unusual for the inordinate amounts of material and symbolic violence it
entails. In the Americas (as opposed to, say, in the Islamic world, where it served no productive purpose), this violence was channeled to fulfil a definite economic end: to
appease the nearly insatiable appetite of the plantation for labor. The forcible importation of Africans and West Indians, and the rearing of their descendants under bondage

PUNISHMENT AND SOCIETY 3(1)

(the US enslaved population tripled to reach 4 million in the half-century after the slave trade was cut off in 1808), supplied the unfree and fixed workforce needed to produce the great staples that were the backbone of North America's preindustrial economy, tobacco, rice, sugar, and cotton.

In the early colonial period indentured servitude was economically more advantageous than slavery but, by the second half of the 17th century, the increase in life expectancy, the growth of the tobacco trade, the need to encourage further voluntary immigration and the relative powerlessness of African captives compared to European migrants and native Americans combined to make slaves the preferred source of labor (Morgan, 1975). After the Revolution, human bondage was abolished along the Eastern seaboard and prohibited north and west of the Ohio River, but it spread and solidified throughout the South, as the economic value of slaves rose in concert with the increase in the demand for cotton and the scarcity of labor in the new territories of the Southwest. Once it generalized, slavery transformed all of society, culture, and politics in its image, fostering the concentration of economic and state power in the hands of a small slaveholder class tied to lower-class whites by patronage relations and to their slaves by a paternalistic code and elaborate rituals of submission that reinforced the latter's lack of cultural autonomy and sense of inferiority (Williamson, 1986: 15–27).

Whereas in the early decades of the colony the status of slave and servant were virtually indistinguished – the terms were even used interchangeably – by the 19th century the dichotomous opposition between bondsmen and freemen had been racialized: the militant defense of slavery generated an elaborate ideology justifying the subhuman condition imposed upon blacks by their inferior biological makeup, exemplified by the animalistic traits, in turn childish and bestial, attributed to the archetypal figure of Sambo. In the decades leading to the Civil War, the specter of insurrection and of the abolition of bondage resulted in increased hostility toward manumission, miscegenation, and 'passing' by Negroes, as well as in the generalization of a rigid twofold racial schema, based on the mythology that God had created blacks to be slaves and that one drop of 'Negro blood' made one a Negro – persons of mixed descent were believed to be against nature and fated to physical extinction (Davis, 1992: 41–2). Slavery as a system of unfree labor thus spawned a suffusive racial culture which, in turn, remade bondage into something it was not at its outset: a color-coded institution of ethnoracial division.[8]

2. Jim Crow (South, 1865–1965)

Emancipation posed a double and deadly threat to Southern society: the overthrow of bondage made slaves formally free laborers, which potentially eliminated the cheap and abundant workforce required to run the plantation economy; black access to civil and political rights promised to erode the color line initially drawn to bulwark slavery but since entrenched in both the South and the North of the country. In a first phase, during Reconstruction, the Dixie ruling class promulgated the Black Codes to resolve the first problem by establishing 'forced labor and police laws to get the freedman back to the fields under control' (Woodward, 1971: 250–1). In a second phase, through the 1880s, the white lower classes, pressed by the dislocations wrought by declining farm prices, demographic pressure and capitalist industrialization, joined with the plantation elite to demand the political disenfranchisement and systematic exclusion of former slaves from all major institutions (Wilson, 1980: 57–61): the Jim Crow regime of racial segregation was born which would hold African Americans in its brutal grip for nearly a century in the Southern states and beyond.[9]

Under this regime, backed by custom and elaborate legal statutes, superexploitative sharecropping arrangements and debt peonage fixed black labor on the land, perpetuating the hegemony of the region's agrarian upper class – and the work discipline of the antebellum plantation: the lash remained in use in Mississipi into the interwar years. The economic opportunities of African Americans were severely restricted not only in the cotton fields but also in the emerging mining and industrial towns of the uplands by limiting their employment to the most dirty and dangerous 'nigger work'. Former slaves and their descendants were prohibited from attending churches and schools with whites (in some states, biracial education was even made unconstitutional). And they were methodically banished from the ballot box thanks to an assortment of residency requirements, poll taxes, literacy tests, 'grandfather clauses' and disqualifying criminal offenses.[10]

Most crucially, the second 'peculiar institution' sharply curtailed social contacts between whites and blacks by relegating the latter to separate residential districts and to the reserved 'colored' section of commercial establishments and public facilities, saloons and movie houses, parks and beaches, trolleys and buses, waiting rooms and bathrooms. Any and all forms of intercourse that might imply social equality between the 'races' and, worse yet, provide an occasion for sexual contact across the color line were rigorously forbidden and zealously surveiled, and any infringement, real or imagined, savagely repressed. The hysterical dread of 'racial degeneracy' believed to ensue from mixing, and justified by the self-evident query 'Would you want your sister to marry a nigger?' (Dollard, 1937: 62), climaxed in periodic explosions of mob violence, beatings, whippings, and rioting against blacks who failed to 'stay in their place' and display proper caste deference. In the last two decades of the 19th century, some 2,060 African Americans were lynched, one third of them after being accused of sexual assault or mere improprieties towards white women (Williamson, 1982: 292). These veritable carnivals of caste rage, during which the bodies of 'bad niggah' were ritually desecrated by burning, mutilation, and public exhibition, were fanned by the press, tacitly supported by the churches, and encouraged by the complicity of the forces of order and immunity from the authorities. African Americans could hardly turn to the courts for protection since the latter openly put the law of caste above the rule of law: lynchings were perpetrated by lower-class 'rednecks' but with the consent and approval of white 'quality ', for, as a Mississippi gentleman put it, 'race is greater than law now and then, and protection of women transcends all law, human and divine' (cited by McMillen, 1990: 240).

3. The ghetto (North, 1914–1968)

The very ferocity of Jim Crow on both the labor and the ostracization fronts sowed the seeds of its eventual ruin, for blacks fled the South by the millions as soon as the opportunity came. Three forces combined to rouse them to desert Dixie and rally to the surging metropolitan centers of the Midwest and Northeast in the half-century following the outbreak of World War I. The first was the economic crisis of cotton agriculture caused by the boll weevil and later by mechanization, as well as arrested urbanization in the South due to the industrial underdevelopment of the region (Fligstein, 1981). The second was the booming demand for unskilled and semiskilled labor in the steel mills,

packinghouses, factories and railroads of the North, as the war cut off immigration from Europe and employers sent their recruiting agents scurrying through the South to entice African Americans to come work for them (Marks, 1989). But economic push and pull factors merely set conditions of possibility: the trigger of the Great Migration that transformed the black community from a landless peasantry to an industrial proletariat, and with it the visage of American society *in toto*, was the irrepressible will to escape the indignities of caste and its attendant material degradation, truncated life horizon, and rampant violence – the outmigration of blacks was heaviest in those counties of the Deep South where lynchings were most frequent (Tolnay and Beck, 1992). These indignities were made all the more intolerable by the ongoing incorporation of 'white ethnics' into national institutions and by the paradoxical role that the US played on the world stage as champion of those very freedoms which it denied Negros at home. The trek up to Chicago, Detroit, New York and Philadelphia was thus undertaken by Southern blacks not only to 'better their condition' but also to board the 'train of freedom' (to recall the title of a well-known poem by Langston Hughes) on a journey filled with biblical imagery and political import (Grossman, 1989: esp. 16–37): it was a race-conscious gesture of collective defiance and self-affirmation.[11]

    Yankee life did offer salutory relief from the harsh grip of Southern caste domination and significantly expand the life chances of the former sharecroppers, but it did not turn out to be the 'promised land' of racial equality, economic security, and full citizenship for which migrants yearned. For, in the Northern metropolis, African Americans came upon yet another device designed to allow white society to exploit their labor power while keeping them confined to a separate *Lebensraum*: the ghetto. As the Negro population rose, so did the animosity of whites towards a group they viewed as 'physically and mentally unfit', 'unsanitary', 'entirely irresponsible', and therefore 'undesirable as neighbors', in the terms reported to the 1920 Chicago Commission on Race Relations (cited in Spear, 1967: 22). Patterns of ethnoracial discrimination and segregation that had hitherto been inconsistent and informal hardened in housing, schools, and public accomodations such as parks, playgrounds and beaches. They were extended to the polity, where the promotion of a small cadre of black politicians handpicked by party leaders served to rein in the community's votes to the benefit of the white-controlled city machine (Katznelson, 1976: 83–5). They were systematized in the economy, where a 'job ceiling' set conjointly by white employers and unions kept African Americans trapped in the lower reaches of the occupational structure, disproportionately concentrated in semi-skilled, manual, and servant work that made them especially vulnerable to business downturns (Drake and Cayton, 1945: 223–35; Wilson, 1980: 71–6). And, when they tried to breach the color bar, for instance by attempting to settle outside of their reserved perimeter in violation of restrictive covenants, blacks were assaulted on the streets by white 'athletic clubs' and their houses bombed by so-called 'neighborhood improvement societies'. They had no choice but to take refuge in the secluded territory of the Black Belt and to try to build in it a self-sustaining nexus of institutions that would both shield them from white rule and procure the needs of the castaway community: a 'Black Metropolis' lodged 'in the womb of the white', yet hermetically sealed from it (Drake and Cayton, 1945: 80).[12]

    This 'black city within the white', as black scholars from DuBois and Frazier to Oliver Cox and Kenneth Clark have consistently characterized the ghetto (Wacquant, 1998a), discharged the same two basic functions that slavery and the Jim Crow system had performed earlier, namely, to harness the labor of African Americans while cloistering their tainted bodies, so as to avert both the specter of 'social equality' and the odium of 'miscegenation' that would inevitably result in loss of ethnic honor for whites. But it differed from the preceding 'peculiar institutions' in that, by granting them a measure of organizational autonomy, the urban Black Belt enabled African Americans to fully develop their own social and symbolic forms and thereby accumulate the group capacities needed to escalate the fight against continued caste subordination.[13] For the ghetto in full-fledged form is, by its very makeup, a *double-edged sociospatial formation*: it operates as an instrument of *exclusion* from the standpoint of the dominant group; yet it also offers the subordinate group partial *protection* and a platform for succor and solidarity in the very movement whereby it sequesters it.

Specifying the workings of the ghetto as mechanism of ethnoracial closure and control makes readily visible its *structural and functional kinship with the prison*: the ghetto is a manner of 'ethnoracial prison' in that it encloses a stigmatized population which evolves within it its distinctive organizations and culture, while the prison functions as a 'judicial ghetto' relegating individuals disgraced by criminal conviction to a secluded space harboring the parallel social relations and cultural norms that make up the 'society of captives'.[14] This kinship explains why, when the ghetto was rendered inoperative in the sixties by economic restructuring that made African-American labor expendable and mass protest that finally won blacks the vote, the carceral institution offered itself as a substitute apparatus for enforcing the shifting color line and containing the segments of the African-American community devoid of economic utility and political pull. The coupling of the transformed core of the urban Black Belt, or hyperghetto, and the fast-expanding carceral system that together compose America's fourth 'peculiar institution' was fortified by two concurrent series of changes that have tended to 'prisonize' the ghetto and to 'ghettoize' the prison. The next two sections examine each of these trends in turn.

FROM COMMUNAL GHETTO TO HYPERGHETTO: HOW THE GHETTO BECAME MORE LIKE A PRISON

The *fin-de-siècle* hyperghetto presents four main characteristics that differentiate it sharply from the communal ghetto of the Fordist-Keynesian era and converge to render its social structure and cultural climate more akin to those of the prison. I consider each in turn by drawing a schematic contrast between the mid-century 'Bronzeville' depicted by St. Clair Drake and Horace Cayton (1945) in *Black Metropolis* and the South Side of Chicago as I observed it some forty years later through fieldwork, official statistics, and survey data.

1. Class segregation overlays racial segregation

The dark ghetto of mid-century held within itself a full complement of classes, for the simple reason that even the black bourgeoisie was barred from escaping its cramped and compact perimeter while a majority of adults were gainfully employed in a gamut of occupations. True, from the 1920s onward, Chicago's South Side featured clearly demarcated subdivisions stratified by class, with the small elite of doctors, lawyers, teachers, and businessmen residing in the stabler and more desirable neighborhoods adjacent to white districts at the southern end, while the families of laborers and domestic workers massed themselves in areas of blight, crime and dissolution towards the northern end (Frazier, 1932). But the social distance between the classes was limited by physical propinquity and extensive family ties; the black bourgeoisie's economic power rested on supplying goods and services to its lower-class brethens; and all 'brown' residents of the city were united in their common rejection of caste subordination and abiding concern to 'advance the race', despite its internecine divisions and the mutual panning of 'big Negroes' and 'riff-raff' (Drake and Cayton, 1945: 716–28). As a result, the postwar ghetto was *integrated both socially and structurally* – even the 'shadies' who earned their living from such illicit trades as the 'numbers game', liquor sale, prostitution and other *risqué* recreation, were entwined with the different classes.

Today's black bourgeoisie still lives under strict segregation and its life chances continue to be curtailed by its geographic and symbolic contiguity with the African-American (sub)proletariat (Patillo-McCoy, 1999). Nonetheless, it has gained considerable physical distance from the heart of the ghetto by establishing satellite black neighborhoods at its periphery inside the city and in the suburbs.[15] Its economic basis has shifted from the direct servicing of the black community to the state, with employment in public bureaucracies accounting for most of the growth of professional, managerial and technical positions held by African Americans over the past thirty years. The genealogical ties of the black bourgeoisie to the black poor have also grown more remote and less dense. What is more, the historic center of the Black Belt has experienced massive depopulation and deproletarianization, such that a large majority of its residents are no longer employed: two-thirds of the adults in Bronzeville did not hold a job in 1980, compared to fewer than half thirty years earlier (cf. Table 2); and three out of every four households were headed by women, while the official poverty rate hovered near the 50 percent mark.

This marked lowering and homogenization of the social composition of the ghetto

TABLE 2 The changing class structure of Chicago's South Side, 1950–1980 *

	1950 TOTAL	%	1980 TOTAL	%
Proprietors, managers, professional & technical	5,270	3.3	2,225	3.2
Clerical, sales	10,271	6.4	5,169	7.5
Operative, laborers, craftsmen	42,372	26.7	6,301	9.3
Private household and service workers	25,182	15.8	5,203	7.5
Total employed adults	83,095	52.2	18,898	27.5
Adults not employed	75,982	47.8	50,148	72.5
Total adult population	159,077	100	69,046	100

* Comprising the three community areas of Grand Boulevard, Oakland, and Washington Park; adults are persons 15 and over for 1950, 18 and over for 1980.

Source: Chicago Fact Book Consortium, *Local Community Fact Book*, Chicago, Center for the Study of Family and Community, 1955, and Chicago Review Press, 1985.

makes it akin to the monotonous class recruitment of the carceral institution, dominated as the latter is by the most precarious fractions of the urban proletariat of the unemployed, the casually employed, and the uneducated. Fully 36 percent of the half-million detainees housed by US jails in 1991 were jobless at the time of their arrest and another 15 percent worked only part-time or irregularly. One-half had not finished high school and two-thirds earned less than a thousand dollars a month that year; in addition, every other inmate had been raised in a home receiving welfare and a paltry 16 percent were married (Harlow, 1998). Residents of the hyperghetto and clients of the carceral institution thus present germane profiles in economic marginality and social dis-integration.

2. Loss of a positive economic function

The transformed class structure of the hyperghetto is a direct product of its evolving position in the new urban political economy ushered by post-Fordism. We have seen that, from the Great Migration of the interwar years to the 1960s, the dark ghetto served a positive economic function as reservoir of cheap and pliable labor for the city's factories. During that period, it was 'directly exploited by outside economic interests, and it provide[d] a dumping ground for the human residuals created by economic change. These economic conditions [we]re stabilized by transfer payments that preserve[d] the ghetto in a poverty that recreate[d] itself from generation to generation', ensuring the ready availability of a low-cost workforce (Fusfeld and Bates, 1982: 236). By the 1970s, this was no longer true as the engine of the metropolitan economy passed from manufacturing to business and knowledge-based services, and factories relocated from the central city to the mushrooming industrial parks of the suburbs and exurbs, as well as to anti-union states in the South and to foreign countries.

Between 1954 and 1982, the number of manufacturing establishments in Chicago plunged from 10,288 to 5,203, while the number of production workers sank from nearly half a million to a mere 172,000. The demand for black labor plummeted accordingly, rocking the entire black class structure (Wacquant, 1989: 510–11), given that half of all employed African Americans in Chicago were blue-collar wage earners at the close of World War II. Just as mechanization had enabled Southern agriculture to dispense with black labor a generation earlier, 'automation and suburban relocation created a crisis of tragic dimension for unskilled black workers' in the North, as 'for the first time in American history, the African American was no longer needed in the economic system' of the metropolis (Rifkin, 1995: 79; also Sugrue, 1995: 125–52). The effects of technological upgrading and postindustrialization were intensified by (1) unflinching residential segregation, (2) the breakdown of public schools, and (3) the renewal of working-class immigration from Latin America and Asia to consign the vast majority of uneducated blacks to economic redundancy. At best, the hyperghetto now serves the *negative economic function of storage of a surplus population* devoid of market utility, in which respect it also increasingly resembles the prison system.

3. State institutions of social control replace communal institutions

The organizations that formed the framework of everyday life and anchored the strategies of reproduction of urban blacks in the 1950s were group-based and group-specific establishments created and run by African Americans. The black press, churches, lodges and fraternal orders, social clubs and political (sub)machine knit together a dense array of resources and sociability that supported their quest for ethnic pride and group uplift. To its 200,000 members, the five hundred religious congregations that dotted the South Side were not only places of worship and entertainment but also a potent vehicle for individual and collective mobility within the specific order of the ghetto that cut across class lines and strengthened ingrown social control, even as black proletarians chaffed in endless 'protest against the alleged cupidity and hypocrisy of church functionaries and devotees' (Drake and Cayton, 1945: 710–11, 650).

In the economic realm also, African Americans could seek or sustain the illusion of autonomy and advancement. Now, Negro entreprise was small scale and commercially weak, the three most numerous types of black-owned firms being beauty parlors, grocery stores and barber shops. But the popular 'doctrine of the 'Double-Duty Dollar', according to which buying from black concerns would 'advance the race' (Drake and Cayton, 1945: 430–1, 438–9), promised a path to economic independence from whites, and the 'numbers game' seemed to prove that one could indeed erect a self-sustaining economy within Black Metropolis. With some 500 stations employing 5,000 and paying yearly wages in excess of a million dollars for three daily drawings, the 'policy racket' was at once big business, a fixture of group fellowship, and a popular cult. Protected by criss-crossing ties and kickbacks to court officials, the police, and politicians, the 'policy kings' were regarded as 'Race Leaders, patrons of charity, and pioneers in the establishment of legitimate business' (Drake and Cayton, 1945: 486; also Light, 1977).

By the 1980s, the organizational ecology of the ghetto had been radically altered by the generalized devolution of public institutions and commercial establishments in the urban core as well as by the cumulative demise of black associations caused by the confluence of market withdrawal and state retrenchment (Wacquant, 1998a). The physical infrastructure and business base of the South Side had been decimated, with thousands of boarded-up stores and abandoned buildings rotting away along deserted boulevards strewn with debris and garbage. Arguably the most potent component of the communal ghetto, the church lost its capacity to energize and organize social life on the South Side. Storefront operations closed in the hundreds and the congregations that have endured either battle for sheer survival or battle local residents: in the early 1990s, on 63rd Street near Stony Island Avenue, the Apostolic Church of God, lavishly financed and patronized by an expatriate black bourgeoisie, was engaged in a trench war with the surrounding poor population which viewed it as an invader, so that the church had to fence itself up and hire a phalanx of security guards to enable its members to come into the neighborhood and attend its three services on Sunday.[16] Similarly, the black press has grown outside of the ghetto but virtually disappeared within it as a vector of public opinion: there were five black weeklies in Bronzeville when World War II broke out; forty years later, the *Chicago Defender* alone remains in existence and then, only as a pale shadow of its former glorious self – it is sparsely distributed even at the heart of the South Side whereas an estimated 100,000 read it and everyone discussed it fervently in the 1940s.[17]

The vacuum created by the crumbling of the ghetto's indigenous organizations has been filled by *state bureaucracies of social control*, themselves largely staffed by the new black middle class whose expansion hinges, not on its capacity to service its community, but on its willingness to assume the vexing role of *custodian* of the black urban sub-proletariat on behalf of white society. By the 1980s, the institutions that set the tone of daily life and determined the fate of most residents on Chicago's South Side were (1) astringent and humiliating welfare programs, bolstered and replaced by 'workfare' after 1996, designed to restrict access to the public aid rolls and push recipients into the low-wage labor market; (2) decrepit public housing that subjected its tenants and the surrounding population to extraordinary levels of criminal insecurity, infrastructural blight and official scorn (its management was so derelict that the Chicago Housing Authority had to put under federal receivership); (3) permanently failing public health and public schools operating with resources, standards, and results worthy of Third World countries; and (4), not least, the police, the courts, and on-the-ground extensions of the penal system such as probation officers, parole agents, and 'snitches', recruited by the thousands by law enforcement agencies, often under threat of criminal prosecution, to extend the mesh of state surveillance and capture deep into the hyperghetto (Miller, 1997: 102–3).[18]

4. Loss of 'buffering function' and the depacification of everyday life

Along with its economic function of labor pool and the extensive organizational nexus it supported, the ghetto lost its capacity to buffer its residents from external forces. It is no longer Janus-faced, offering a sheltered space for collective sustenance and self-affirmation in the face of hostility and exclusion, as in the heyday of the Fordist-Keynesian era. Rather, it has devolved into a one-dimensional machinery for naked relegation, a human warehouse wherein are discarded those segments of urban society deemed disreputable, derelict, and dangerous. And, with the conjoint contraction of the wage-labor market and the welfare state in the context of unflinching segregation, it has become saturated with economic, social, and physical insecurity (Massey and Denton, 1993; Krivo and Peterson, 1996). Pandemic levels of crime – gunfire and assaults have become habitual, with homicide rates topping 100 for 100,000 at the core of the South Side in 1990 – have further depressed the local economy and ruptured the social fabric. The depacification of everyday life, shrinking of networks, and informalization of survival strategies have combined to give social relations in the hyperghetto a distinct carceral cast (Kotlowitz, 1991; Jones and Newman, 1997; Wacquant, 1998b): fear and danger pervade public space; interpersonal relations are riven with suspicion and distrust, feeding mutual avoidance and retraction into one's private defended space; resort to violence is the prevalent means for upholding respect, regulating encounters, and controling territory; and relations with official authorities are suffused with animosity and diffidence – patterns familiar to students of social order in the contemporary US prison (e.g., Carroll, 1974; Jacobs, 1977; Irwin, 1980).

Two examples illustrate well this increasing conformance of the hyperghetto to the carceral model. The first is the *'prisonization'* *of public housing*, as well as retirement homes, single-room occupancy hostels, homeless shelters, and other establishments for collective living, which have come to look and feel just like houses of detention.[19] 'Projects' have been fenced up, their perimeter placed under beefed-up security patrols and authoritarian controls, including identification-card checks, signing in, electronic monitoring, police infiltration, 'random searches, segregation, curfews, and resident counts – all familiar procedures of efficient prison management' (Miller, 1997: 101). Over the past decade, the Chicago Housing Authority has deployed its own police force and even sought to institute its own 'misdemeanor court' to try misbehaving tenants on the premises. Residents of the Robert Taylor Homes, at the epicenter of the South Side, have been subjected to video surveillance and required to bear special ID cards as well as pass through metal detectors, undergo patdown searches, and report all visitors to a housing officer in the lobby (Venkatesh, 2000: 123–30). In 1994, the CHA launched massive paramilitary sweeps under the code name 'Operation Clean Sweep,' involving pred-dawn surprise searches of buildings leading to mass arrests in violation of basic constitutional rights quite similar to the periodic 'shakedowns' intended to rid prison wards of shanks and other contraband. As one elderly resident of a District of Columbia project being put under such quasi-penal supervision observed: 'It's as though the children in here are being prepared for incarceration, so when they put them in a real lock-down situation, they'll be used to being hemmed in' (cited by Miller, 1997: 101).

Public schools in the hyperghetto have similarly deteriorated to the point where they operate in the manner of *institutions of confinement* whose primary mission is not to educate but to ensure 'custody and control' – to borrow the motto of many departments of corrections. Like the prison system, their recruitment is severely skewed along class and ethnoracial lines: 75 percent of the pupils of Chicago's establishments come from families living under the official poverty line and nine of every ten are black or Latino. Like inmates, these children are herded into decaying and overcrowded facilities built like bunkers, where undertrained and underpaid teachers, hampered by a shocking penury of equipment and supplies – many schools have no photocopying machines, library, science laboratory, or even functioning bathrooms, and use textbooks that are thirty-year-old rejects from suburban schools – strive to regulate conduct so as to maintain order and minimize violent incidents. The physical plant of most establishments resembles fortresses, complete with concertina wire on outside fences, bricked up windows, heavy locks on iron doors, metal detectors at the gates and hallways patroled by armed guards who conduct spot checks and body searches between buildings. Over the years, essential educational programs have been cut to divert funds for more weapons scanners, cameras, emergency telephones, sign-in desks, and security personnel, whose duty is to repel unwanted intruders from the outside and hem students inside the school's walls.[20] Indeed, it appears that the main purpose of these school is simply to 'neutralize' youth considered unworthy and unruly by holding them under lock for the day so that, at minimum, they do not engage in street crime. Certainly, it is hard to maintain that educating them is a priority when half of the city's high schools place in the bottom 1 percent of establishments nationwide on the American College Test and two thirds of ghetto students fail to complete their cursus while those who do graduate read on average at the 8th grade level (Chicago Tribune, 1992: 12–3). At any rate, the carceral atmosphere of schools and the constant presence of armed guards in uniform in the lobbies, corridors, cafeteria, and playground of their establishment habituates the children of the hyperghetto to the demeanor, tactics, and interactive style of the correctional officers many of them are bound to encounter shortly after their school days are over.

FROM 'BIG HOUSE' TO WAREHOUSE:
HOW THE PRISON BECAME MORE LIKE A GHETTO

The two decades following the climax of the Civil Rights movement not only witnessed a sea change in the function, structure and texture of the dark ghetto in the postindustrial metropolis. The racial and class backlash that reconfigured the city also ushered a sweeping transformation in the purpose and social organization of the carceral institution. Summarily put, the 'Big House' that embodied the correctional ideal of melioristic treatment and community reintegration of inmates[21] gave way to a race-divided and violence-ridden 'warehouse' geared solely to neutralizing social rejects by sequestering them physically from society – in the way that a classical ghetto wards off the threat of defilement posed by the presence of a dishonored group by encaging it within its walls, but in an ambience resonant with the fragmentation, dread, and despair of the post-Fordist hyperghetto. With the explosive growth of the incarcerated population leading to rampant overcrowding, the rise in the proportion of inmates serving long sentences, the spread of ethnically-based gangs, the flood of drug offenders and especially of young offenders deeply rooted in the informal economy and oppositional culture of the street, the 'inmate society' depicted in the classic prison research of the postwar decades foundered, as John Irwin (1990: vi) observes in his 1990 preface to *The Felon*:

> There is no longer a single, overarching convict culture or social organization, as there tended to be twenty years ago when *The Felon* was written. Most prisoners restrict their association to a few other prisoners and withdraw from prison public life. A minority associates with gangs, gamble, buy and sell contraband commodities, and engage in prison homosexual behavior. If they do so, however, they must act 'tough' and be willing to live by the new code, that is, be ready to meet threats of violence with violence.

It is not easy to characterize the changes which have remade the American prison in the image of the ghetto over the past three decades, not only because of the 'astonishing diversity' of establishments and regimes across levels of the carceral system and the different states (Morris, 1995: 228), but also because we have remarkably little on-the-ground data on social and cultural life inside the contemporary penitentiary. Sociologists have deserted the institution – with a firm push from corrections administrations that have grown increasingly closed and secretive – just as it was ascending to the front line of the instruments for the regulation of poverty and race. With the partial exception of women's facilities, field studies based on direct observation have virtually disappeared, as research on imprisonment shifted from close-up accounts of the internal order of the prison, its hierarchies, values, and mores, to distant analyses of incarceration rates, the dynamics and cost-effectiveness of penal management, sentencing, and fear of crime based primarily on official statistics, administrative reports, litigation findings, and large-scale surveys (DiIulio, 1991; Simon, 2000).[22] Nonetheless, one can provisionally single out five tendencies that fortify the structural and functional meshing of ghetto and prison in the large (post)industrial states that have put the United States on the path to mass imprisonment.

1. The racial division of everything

The relatively stable set of positions and expectations defined primarily in terms of criminal statuses and prison conduct that used to organize the inmate world has been replaced by a chaotic and conflictual setting wherein 'racial division has primacy over all particular identities and influences all aspects of life' (Irwin, 1990: v; also Carroll, 1982; Johnson, 1996; Hassine, 1999: 71–8). The ward, tier, cell and bed-bunk to which one is assigned; access to food, telephone, television, visitation and in-house programs; one's associations and protections, which in turn determine the probability of being the victim or perpetrator of violence: all are set by one's ethnic community of provenance. Elective loyalty to inmates as a generic class, with the possibility of remaining non-aligned, has been superseded by forced and exclusive loyalty to one's 'race' defined in rigid, caste-like manner, with no in-between and no position of neutrality – just as within the urban ghetto. And the central axis of stratification inside the 'pen' has shifted from the vertical cleavage *between prisoners and guards*, marked by the proscription to 'rat on a con', exploit other inmates, and 'talk to a screw', to horizontal cleavages *among prisoners* between blacks, Latinos, and whites (with Asians most often assimilated to whites and Middle Easterners given a choice of voluntary affiliation).

In Sykes's (1958) classic account, the 'argot roles' that compose the social structure and cultural fabric of the prison are all *specific to the carceral cosmos*. 'rats' and 'center men' are defined as such because they betray the core value of solidarity among inmates by violating the ban on communication with custodians; 'merchants' peddle goods in the illicit economy of the establishment while 'gorillas' prey on weak inmates to acquire cigarettes, food, clothing, and deference; similarly, 'wolfs', 'punks' and 'fags' are descriptors of sexual scripts adopted behind bars. Finally 'ball busters' and 'real men' are categories defined by the type of intercourse they maintain with guards: defiant and hopeless, the former give 'screws' a hard time while the latter 'pull their own time' without displaying either subservience or aggression. In John Irwin's (1990) portrait of the social organization of convicts in California prisons in the 1960s, the inmate subculture is not a response to prison deprivation but an import from the street. Yet it is the criminal identities of 'thief', 'convict' and 'square' that nonetheless predominate behind bars. In today's warehouse prison, by contrast, racial affiliation has become the 'master status trait' (Hughes, 1945) that submerges all other markers and governs all relations and spaces, from the cells and the hallways to the dining hall, the commissary and the yard.[23]

To be sure, American prisons, both North and South, have always been strictly segregated along ethnoracial lines. But these lines used to *crosscut and stabilize* penitentiary demarcations as the social worlds of black and white inmates ran parallel to each other in 'separate but equal' fashion, so to speak (Jacobs, 1983: 75–6). In the aftermath of the black mobilization of the 1960s and the rapid 'darkening' of the imprisoned population, racial cleavages have grown to *undercut and supplant* carceral ones. And the perennial pattern of separation and avoidance that characterized race relations in the postwar years has been amplified by open hostility and aggression, particularly through the agency of gangs.

2. The 'code of the street' overwhelms the 'convict code'

Along with racial division, the predatory culture of the street, centered on hypermasculinist notions of honor, toughness, and coolness has entered into and transfigured the social structure and culture of jails and prisons. The 'convict code', rooted in solidarity among inmates and antagonism towards guards (Sykes and Messinger, 1960), has in

effect been swamped by the 'code of the street' (Anderson, 1998), with its ardent imperative of individual 'respect' secured through the militant display and actualization of
readiness to mete out physical violence. Accordingly, 'the old 'hero' of the prison world
– the 'right guy' – has been replaced by outlaws and gang members. These two types
have raised toughness and mercilessness to the top of prisoners' value systems' (Irwin,
1990: vii). Ethnically-based street gangs and 'supergangs', such as the Disciplines, El
Rukn, Vice Lords, and Latin Kings in Illinois, the Mexican Mafia, Black Guerrilla
Family, and Aryan Brotherhood in California, and the Netas in New York City, have
taken over the illicit economy of the prison and destabilized the entire social system of
inmates, forcing the latter to shift from 'doing your own time' to 'doing gang time'. They
have even precipitated a thorough restructuring of the administration of large-scale
prison systems, from Illinois to California to Texas (Jacobs, 1977: 137–74; Irwin, 1980:
186–92; Martin and Ekland-Olson, 1987).

Together with the compositional changes of the prison's clientele, the rising tide of
drugs circulating *sub rosa*, and the consolidation of racially-based gangs, the eclipse of the
old inmate structure of power has resulted in increased levels of interpersonal and group
brutality.[24] So that 'what was once a repressive but comparatively safe 'Big House' is now
often an unstable and violent social jungle' (Johnson, 1996: 133) in which social intercourse is infected with the same disruption, aggression, and unpredictability as in the
hyperghetto. Today's prisoners 'complain about the increased fragmentation and disorganization that they now experience. Life in prison is no longer organized but instead is
viewed as capricious and dangerous' (Hunt et al., 1993: 407). Those who return behind
bars after spending extended periods outside invariably find that they do not recognize
'the joint' and that they can no longer get along with their fellow inmates due to the prevailing anomie.[25] When my best friend and informant from Chicago's South Side,
Ashante, was sent to serve a six-year sentence in a low-security facility in downstate Illinois after having 'stayed clean' on the outside for a decade following a stint of eight years
at Stateville penitentiary, he promptly requested a transfer to a maximum-security prison:
he was dismayed by the arrogance and unruliness of 'young punks' from the streets of
Chicago who ignored the old convict code, disrespected inmates with extensive prison
seniority, and sought confrontation at every turn. Ashante knew well that, by moving to
Stateville or Pontiac, he would endure a much more restrictive regimen in a more dreary
physical setting with access to fewer programs, but he believed that a more predictible
environment ruled by the norms of the 'inmate society' of old made for a less risky
sojourn.[26] The increased entropy and commotion that characterizes prison life today
explains that 'it is not uncommon to find ten percent of the population of large prison
in protective custody' (Morris, 1995: 248). It accounts also for the proliferation of 'supermax' penitentiaries across the country as authorities strive to restore order by relegating
'the worst of the worst', inmates in special facilities where they are kept in near-total lockdown under detention regimes so austere that they are indistinguishable from torture in
the light of international human rights covenants (King, 1999).

3. Purging the undesirables

The 'Big House' of the postwar decades was animated by a consequentialist theory of
punishment that sought to resocialize inmates so as to lower the probability of re-offense

once they returned society, of which they were expected to become law-abiding if not productive members. Following the official repudiation of the philosophy of rehabilitation in the 1970s (Allen, 1981), today's prison has for sole purpose to *neutralize* offenders – and individuals thought to be likely to violate the law, such as parolees – both *materially*, by removing them physically into an institutional enclave, and *symbolically*, by drawing a hard and fast line between criminals and law-abiding citizens. The 'law-and-order' paradigm that has achieved undivided hegemony in crime and justice policy over the past two decades jettisons any notion of prevention and proportionality in favor of direct appeals to popular resentment through measures that dramatize the fear and loathing of crime viewed as the abhorrent conduct of defective individuals.[27] 'Such appeals to resentment', writes Hirsch (1999: 676), 'reflect an ideology of purging "undesirables" from the body politic' in which incarceration is essentially a means for social and moral excommunication. That makes the mission of today's prison identical to that of the classical ghetto, whose *raison d'être* was precisely to quarantine a polluting group from the urban body.

When the prison is used as an implement for social and cultural purging, like the ghetto, it no longer points beyond itself; it turns into a self-contained contraption which fulfils its function, and thus justifies itself, by its mere existence. And its inhabitants learn to live in the here-and-now, bathed in the concentrate of violence and hopelessness brewing within the walls. In his autobiographical description of the changing social structure and culture of a maximum-security facility in Pennsylvania over the past sixteen years, inmate Victor Hassine (1999: 41) captures well the devolution of the Big House, pointing to eventual reentry into society, into a Warehouse leading nowhere but to a wall of despair:

> Through this gradual process of deterioration, Graterford the prison became Graterford the ghetto, a place where men forgot about courts of law or the difference between right and wrong because they were too busy thinking about living, dying, or worse. Reform, rehabilitation, and redemption do not exist in a ghetto. There is only survival of the fittest. Crime, punishment, and accountability are of little significance when men are living in a lawless society where their actions are restrained only by the presence of concrete and steel walls. Where a prison in any real or abstract sense might promote the greater good, once it becomes a ghetto it can do nothing but promise violent upheaval.

4. The proto-racialization of judicial stigma

The contemporary prison can be further likened to the ghetto in that, in the revanchist penal climate of the past two decades, the stigma of penal conviction has been prolonged, diffused, and reframed in ways that assimilate it to an ethnoracial stigma attached *ad aeternitum* to the body of its bearer. In other liberal-democratic societies, the status dishonor and civic disabilities of being a prisoner are temporary and limited: they affect offenders while they are being processed by the criminal justice system and typically wear off upon coming out of prison or shortly thereafter; to ensure this, laws and administrative rules set strict conditions and limits to the use and diffusion of criminal justice information. Not so in the United States, where, on the contrary, (1) convicts are subjected to ever-longer and broader post-detention forms of social control and symbolic branding that durably set them apart from the rest of the population; (2) the criminal

files of individual inmates are readily accessible and actively disseminated by the authorities; (3) a naturalizing discourse suffused with genetic phraseology and animalistic
imagery has swamped public representations of crime in the media, politics, and significant segments of scholarship.

All but two states require *postprison supervision* of offenders and 80 percent of all
persons released from state penitentiaries are freed under conditional or community
release; the average term spent on parole has also increased steadily over the past two
decades to surpass 23 months in 1996 – nearly equal to the average prison term served
of 25 months (Petersilia, 1999). At the same time, parole services have become entirely
focused on the administrative enforcement of safety and security, to the near-total
neglect of job training, housing assistance, and substance abuse treatment, even
though official records indicate that over three- fourths of inmates suffer from psy-
chotropic dependency. With fully 54 percent of offenders failing to complete their
term of parole in 1997 (compared to 27 percent in 1984), and parole violators making
up a third of all persons admitted in state penitentiaries every year (two-thirds in California), parole has become an appendage of the prison which operates mainly to
extend the social and symbolic incapacities of incarceration beyond its walls. With the
advent of the Internet, corrections administrations in many states, among them Illinois, Florida, and Texas, have put their entire inmate data bases on line, further
stretching the perimeter of penal infamy by making it possible for anyone to delve
into the 'rap sheet' of prisoners via the World Wide Web, and for employers and land-
lords to discriminate more broadly against ex-convicts in complete legality (Wacquant,
1999a: 76–7).[28]

This general movement towards longer and more encompassing post-detention
measures of criminal justice supervision finds an extreme instantiation in the management of sex offenders under the regime of 'Megan's Laws' voted in 1996 by federal and
state governments in a mad rush to appease displaced popular ire over child abuse.
These laws mandate that authorities not only keep a registry of all (ex-)sex offenders in
their jurisdiction, for periods extending up to life, but also notify the public of their
whereabouts via mailings, posters, media announcements and CD-Roms containing
the files of ex-offenders coded by geographic area (Martin, 1996), thus making permanent and highly visible the blemish attached to their conviction. In Louisiana, for
instance, the (ex-)sex offender himself must notify in writing his landlord, neighbors,
and the director of the local school and municipal parks of his penal status; he must
also post warnings of his presence in a community newspaper within thirty days of his
arrival. The law further authorizes 'all forms of public notification ', including posters,
handbills, and bumper stickers – a judge can even request that the offender wear 'a distinctive garb' that will readily identify him as a sex offender (Cooper, 1998), in the
manner of the yellow star or hat donned by Jews in the principalities of Medieval
Europe and Hitler's Germany. Upon release of this information, former sex offenders
have been routinely insulted, publicly humiliated, harassed and attacked; many have
lost their jobs and been forced to relocate to escape the open hostility of their neighbors; a few have reacted by committing suicide. Reinforced by the systematic media
(mis)representation of sex offenders as congenital perverts whose behavior cannot be
prevented or corrected, Megan's Laws send the unmistakable message, 'once an
offender, always an offender',[29] turning judicial stigma into negative symbolic capital

that cannot be shed and will therefore weigh on its bearer for life, like the stain of 'race' construed as a dishonoring form of denegated ethnicity.

The resurgence and popularity of genetic pseudo-explanations of crime is another indicator of the bent towards the compulsive *racialization of criminals*, whose counterpart is the elective *ethnicization of crime victims*, who have recently been fabricated into a quasi-ethnic group (Best, 1997), complete with its distinctive idiom, insignia, pageantry, and official organizations that mobilize to demand 'affirmative action' from the state on behalf of their members. One illustration from among a myriad: the compendium on crime edited by James Q. Wilson and Joan Petersilia, in which 'twenty-eight leading experts look at the most pressing problem of our time' (according to the book's front cover blurb), opens with two long chapters that review 'Criminogenic Traits' and 'Biomedical Factors in Crime' (Herrnstein, 1995; Brennan et al., 1995). For Richard Herrnstein (1995: 40, 41, 62, 56–7, 58), a renowned Harvard psychologist and co-author, with ultraright-wing ideologue Charles Murray, of the infamous treatise in scholarly racism, *The Bell Curve*, serious crimes are not culturally or historically defined but *male in se*, 'crimes that are wrong in themselves'. Now, 'it would be an overstatement to say "once a criminal always a criminal", but it would be closer to the truth [sic] than to deny the evidence of a unifying and long-enduring pattern of encounters with the law for most serious offenders'. This pattern cannot be explained by 'accidents, situations, and social forces', as these only 'modulate the criminogenic factors' of low intelligence, antisocial personality and male chromosomes.[30] The genetic roots of crime are further confirmed by the fact that offenders are 'disproportionately nonectomorphic mesomorphs' (chunky and muscular with large bones) and sport 'lower heart rates', 'lower nervous system responsiveness to sudden stimuli', and 'atypical patterns [of] brain waves'. Herrnstein regrets that research has turned up 'only weak association between male hormones and criminal behavior or antisociality' but he promptly consoles himself by asserting that the Y chromosome elevates criminal behavior in 'supermales' and 'increases the risk of criminal incarceration by a factor of about ten' – based on the fact that the proportion of XYY male prisoners is ten times that in the general population.[31] Interestingly enough, Herrnstein does not discuss ethnoracial differences in criminality and, in his conclusion, he even disingenuously disavows – on feigned epistemological grounds – any effort to 'frame questions about behavior in terms of causes' (although he has repeatedly turned correlation into causation in this very chapter). But it requires little effort to infer from his argumentation that, 'just as night follows day', the hyper-incarceration of blacks must be caused in part by their innate criminal propensity, given what he calls 'a scientific consensus that criminal and antisocial behavior can have genetic roots' (Herrnstein, 1995: 62, 58).[32]

5. Bifurcated socioracial patterning of carceral recruitment and authority

Today's prison further resembles the ghetto for the simple reason that an overwhelming majority of its occupants originate from the racialized core of the country's major cities, and returns there upon release, only to be soon caught again in the police dragnet to be sent away for another, longer sojourn behind bars in a self-perpetuating cycle of escalating socioeconomic marginality and legal incapacitation. To take but one example, in the late 1980s, three of every four inmates serving a sentence in the prisons of the entire state of New York came from only *seven* black and Latino neighborhoods of New York

City, which also happen to be the poorest areas of the metropolis, chief among them Harlem, the South Bronx, East New York, and Brownsville (Ellis, 1993). Every year these segregated and dispossessed districts furnished a fresh contingent of 25,000-odd inmates while 23,000 ex-convicts were discharged, most of them on parole, right back in these devastated areas. A conservative estimate, given a statewide felony recidivism rate of 47 percent, is that within a year, some 15,000 of them found their way back 'upstate' and under lock.[33] The fact that 46 percent of the inmates of New York state prisons issue from neighborhoods served by the 16 worst public schools of the city (Davidson, 1997: 38) ensures that their clientele will be duly replenished for years to come.

The contemporary prison system and the ghetto not only display a similarly skewed recruitment and composition in terms of class and caste. The former also duplicates the authority structure characteristic of the latter in that it places a population of poor blacks under the direct supervision of whites – albeit, in this case, lower-class whites. In the communal ghetto of the postwar, black residents chaffed under the rule of white land-lords, white employers, white unions, white social workers and white policemen (Clark, 1965). Likewise, at century's end, the convicts of New York City, Philadelphia, Balti-more, Cleveland, Detroit and Chicago, who are overwhelming African-American, serve their sentence in establishments staffed by officers who are overwhelmingly white (see Figure 1). In Illinois, for instance, two-thirds of the state's 41,000 inmates are blacks who live under the watch of a 8,400 uniformed force that is 84 percent white. With the proliferation of detention facilities in rural areas, perversely, the economic stability and social welfare of lower-class whites from the declining hinterland has come to hinge on the continued socioeconomic marginality and penal restraint of ever-larger numbers of subproletarian blacks from the urban core.

The convergent changes that have 'prisonized' the ghetto and 'ghettoized' the prison in the aftermath of the Civil Rights revolution suggest that the inordinate and mount-ing over-representation of blacks behind bars does not stem simply from the discrimi-natory targeting of specific penal policies such as the War on Drugs, as proposed by Tonry (1995), or from the sheer destabilizing effects of the increased penetration of ghetto neighborhoods by the penal state, as Miller argues (1997). Not that these two factors are not at work, for clearly they are deeply involved in the hyper-incarceration of African Americans. But they fail to capture the precise nature and the full magnitude of the transformations that have interlocked the prison and the (hyper)ghetto via a relation of *functional equivalency* (they serve one and the same purpose, the coercive con-finement of a stigmatized population) and *structural homology* (they comprise and comfort the same type of social relations and authority pattern) to form a *single insti-tutional mesh* suited to fulfil anew the mission historically imparted to America's 'pecu-liar institutions'.

The thesis of the structural-functional coupling of the remnants of the ghetto with the carceral system is supported by *the timing of racial transition*: with a lag of about a dozen years, the 'blackening' of the carceral population has followed closely on the heels of the demise of the Black Belt as a viable instrument of caste containment in the urban-industrial settting, just as, a century earlier, the sudden penal repression of African Americans had helped to shore up 'the walls of white supremacy as the South moved from an era of racial bondage to one of racial caste' (Oshinsky, 1996: 57). It is also ver-ified by the *geographic patterning* of racial disproportionality and its evolution: outside

115

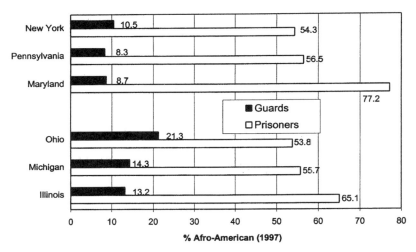

•Figure 1 Black prisoners guarded by white correctional officers
Source: Camp and Camp (1998: pp. 13 and 130)

of the South – which for obvious historical reasons requires a separate analysis – the black-white gap in incarceration is more pronounced and has increased faster in those states of the Midwest and Northeast that are the historic cradle of the Northern ghetto (Mauer, 1997).

The intertwining of the urban Black Belt and the carceral system is further evidenced, and in turn powerfully abetted, by the *fusion of ghetto and prison culture*, as vividly expressed in the lyrics of 'gangsta rap' singers and hip hop artists (Cross, 1993), in graffitti and tattooing (Phillips, 1999: 152–67), and in the dissemination, to the urban core and beyond, of language, dress, and interaction patterns innovated inside of jails and penitentiaries. The advent of hyper-incarceration for lower-class blacks and Latinos has in effect rendered moot the classic dispute, among scholars of imprisonment, between the 'deprivation thesis,' canonized by Gresham Sykes, and the 'importation thesis,' proposed in response by John Irwin and Donald Cressey. This alternative has been transcended by the melting of street and carceral symbolism, with the resulting mix being *re-exported* to the ghetto and diffused throughout society via the commercial circuits catering to the teenage consumer market, professional sports, and even the mainstream media.[34] Witness the widespread adolescent fashion of baggy pants worn with the crotch down to mid-thigh and the resurgent popularity of body art featuring prison themes and icons – more often than not unbeknownst to those who wear them.

HOW PRISON IS REMAKING 'RACE' AND RESHAPING THE CITIZENRY

I indicated earlier that slavery, the Jim Crow system and the ghetto are 'race making' institutions, which is to say that they do not simply *process* an ethnoracial division that would somehow exist outside of and independently from them. Rather, each *produces* (or co-produces) this division (anew) out of inherited demarcations and disparities of group power and inscribes it at every epoch in a distinctive constellation of material and symbolic forms.[35] And all have consistently *racialized* the arbitrary boundary setting African Americans apart from all others in the United States by actively denying its cultural origin in history, ascribing it instead to the fictitious necessity of biology.

The highly particular conception of 'race' that America has invented, virtually unique in the world for its rigidity and consequentiality, is a direct outcome of the momentous collision between slavery and democracy as modes of organization of social life *after* bondage had been established as the major form of labor conscription and control in a underpopulated colony home to a precapitalist system of production (Fields, 1982). The Jim Crow regime reworked the racialized boundary between slave and free into a rigid caste separation between 'whites' and 'Negros' – comprising all persons of known African ancestry, no matter how minimal – that infected every crevice of the postbellum social system in the South (Powdermaker, 1939). The ghetto, in turn, imprinted this dichotomy onto the spatial makeup and institutional schemas of the industrial metropolis. So much so that, in the wake of the 'urban riots' of the 1960s, which in truth were uprisings against intersecting caste and class subordination, 'urban' and black became near-synonymous in policy making as well as everyday parlance. And the 'crisis' of the city came to stand for the enduring contradiction between the individualistic and competitive tenor of American life, on the one hand, and the continued seclusion of African Americans from it, on the other.[36]

As a new century dawns, it is up to the fourth 'peculiar institution' born of the adjoining of the hyperghetto with the carceral system to remould the social meaning and significance of 'race' in accordance with the dictates of the deregulated economy and the post-Keynesian state. Now, the penal apparatus has long served as an accessory to ethnoracial domination by helping to stabilize a regime under attack or bridge the hiatus between successive regimes: thus the 'Black Codes' of Reconstruction served to keep African-American labor in place following the demise of slavery while the criminalization of civil rights protests in the South in the 1950s aimed to retard the agony of Jim Crow. But the role of the carceral institution today is different in that, for the first time in US history, it has been elevated to the rank of main machine for 'race making'.

Among the manifold effects of the wedding of ghetto and prison into an extended carceral mesh, perhaps the most consequential is the practical revivification and *official solidification of the centuries-old association of blackness with criminality* and devious violence. Along with the return of Lombroso-style mythologies about criminal atavism and the wide diffusion of bestial metaphors in the journalistic and political field (where mentions of 'superpredators', 'wolf-packs', 'animals' and the like are commonplace), the massive over-incarceration of blacks has supplied a powerful common-sense warrant for 'using color as a proxy for dangerousness' (Kennedy, 1997: 136). In recent years, the courts have consistently authorized the police to employ race as 'a negative signal of increased risk of criminality' and legal scholars have rushed to endorse it as 'a rational adaptation to the demographics of crime', made salient and verified, as it were, by the blackening of the prison population, even though such practice entails major inconsistencies from the standpoint of constitutional law (Kennedy, 1997: 143, 146). Throughout the urban criminal justice system, the formula 'Young + Black + Male' is now openly equated with 'probable cause' justifying the arrest, questioning, bodily search and detention of millions of African-American males every year (Gaynes, 1993).

In the era of racially targetted 'law-and-order' policies and their socio-logical pendant, racially skewed mass imprisonment, the reigning public image of the criminal is not just that of 'a *monstruum* – a being whose features are inherently different from ours' (Melossi 2000: 311), but that of a *black* monster, as young African-American men from the 'inner city' have come to personify the explosive mix of moral degeneracy and mayhem.[37] The conflation of blackness and crime in collective representation and government policy (the other side of this equation being the conflation of blackness and welfare) thus re-activates 'race' by giving a legitimate outlet to the expression of anti-black animus in the form of the public vituperation of criminals and prisoners. As writer John Edgar Wideman (1995: 504) points out,

> It's respectable to tar and feather criminals, to advocate locking them up and throwing away the key. It's not racist to be against crime, even though the archetypal criminal in the media and the public imagination almost always wears 'Willie' Horton's face. Gradually, 'urban' and 'ghetto' have become code words for terrible places where only blacks reside. Prison is rapidly being re-lexified in the same segregated fashion.

Indeed, when 'to be a man of color of a certain economic class and milieu is equivalent in the public eye to being a criminal', being processed by the penal system is tantamount to being made black, and 'doing time' behind bars is at the same time 'marking race' (Wideman, 1995: 505).[38]

A second major effect of the penalization of the 'race question' via the hypertrophic expansion of the prison system has been to thoroughly *depoliticize* it. For reframing the problems posed by the maintenance of ethnoracial division in the wake of the ghetto's demise as issues of law enforcement automatically delegitimates any attempt at collective resistance and redress. Established organizations of civic voice for African Americans cannot confront head on the crisis of hyperincarceration in their community for fear that this would seem to validate the very conflation of blackness and crime in public perception that fuels this crisis. Thus the courteous silence of the NAACP, the Urban League, the Black Congressional Caucus, and black churches on the topic, even as the penal tutelage of African Americans has escalated to heights experienced by no other group in history, even under the most repressive authoritarian regimes and in Soviet-style societies. This reticence is further reinforced by the fact, noted long ago by W.E.B. DuBois, that the tenuous position of the black bourgeoisie in the socioracial hierarchy rests critically on its ability to distance itself from its unruly lower-class brethen: to offset the symbolic disability of blackness, middle-class African Americans must forcefully communicate to whites that they have 'absolutely no sympathy and no known connections with any black man who has committed a crime' (DuBois cited in Christianson, 1998: 228).

Even riots, the last weapon of protest left to an urban subproletariat spurned by a political system thoroughly dominated by the white suburban electorate and corporations, have been rendered purposeless by mass penal confinement. It is commonly believed that 'race riots' in the United States crested in the 1960s and then vanished, save for anomalous outbursts such as in Miami in 1980 and Los Angeles in 1992. In reality, the ghetto uprisings of 1963–1968 have been succeeded by a rolling *wave of upheavals inside of prisons,* from Attica and Soledad to facilities throughout Michigan, Tennessee, Oklahoma, Illinois, West Virginia, and Pennsylvania, among others (Morris, 1995: 248–9; Useem and Kimball, 1989). But, by moving from the open stage of the streets to the closed perimeter of penitentiaries, these outbursts differed from their predecessors of the 1960s in three important ways. First, ghetto riots were highly visible and, through the media, interpellated the highest authorities in the land. Carceral riots, on the contrary, were never conspicuous to start with (unless they caused major destruction), and they have rapidly grown less and less perceptible to the point of virtually *disappearing* from the public scene.[39] Next, they have received *administrative* responses from within the correctional bureaucracy in lieu of political responses from without, and these responses have only compounded the problem: the approach of the state to inmate belligerence in the 1950s was to 'intensify the therapeutic thrust in prisons' (Rotman, 1995: 189); thirty years later, it is to intensify the drive to 'classify, separate, and isolate' (Irwin, 1980: 228), to toughen discipline, routinize the use of 'lockdown', and to multiply 'special housing units' and 'supermax' facilities. A third difference between the uproarious ghetto riots of decades past and the diffuse, muffled, carceral riots that have replaced them is that they typically pit, not blacks against whites, but *one subordinate ethnic group against another,* such as blacks versus Mexicans, thereby further diminishing the likelihood that they will receive a broad sociopolitical interpretation connecting them to the transformed ethnoracial order on the outside.[40] By entombing poor blacks in the concrete walls of the prison, then, the penal state has effectively smothered and silenced subproletarian revolt.

By assuming a central role in the post-Keynesian government of race and poverty, at the crossroads of the deregulated low-wage labor market, a revamped 'welfare-workfare' apparatus designed to support casual employment, and the vestiges of the ghetto, the overgrown carceral system of the United States has become a major engine of symbolic production in its own right.[41] It is not only the preeminent institution for signifying and enforcing blackness, much as slavery was during the first three centuries of US history. Just as bondage effected the 'social death' of imported African captives and their descendants on American soil (Patterson, 1982), *mass incarceration also induces the civic death* of those it ensnares by extruding them from the social compact. Today's inmates are thus the target of a threefold movement of exclusionary closure:

1. Prisoners are denied access to valued *cultural capital:* just as university credentials are becoming a prerequisite for employment in the (semi-)protected sector of the labor market, inmates have been expelled from higher education by being made ineligible for Pell Grants, starting with drug offenders in 1988, continuing with convicts sentenced to death or lifelong imprisonment without the possibility of parole in 1992, and ending with all remaining state and federal prisoners in 1994. This expulsion was voted by Congress for the sole purpose of accentuating the symbolic divide between criminals and 'law-abiding citizens' in spite of overwhelming evidence that prison educational programs drastically cut recidivism as well as help to maintain carceral order (Page, 2000).

2. Prisoners are systematically excluded from *social redistribution* and public aid in an age when work insecurity makes access to such programs more vital than ever for those dwelling in the lower regions of social space. Laws deny welfare payments, veterans

benefits and food stamps to anyone in detention for more than 60 days. The Work Opportunity and Personal Responsibility Act of 1996 further banishes most ex-convicts from Medicaid, public housing, Section 8 vouchers, and related forms of assistance. In spring of 1998, President Clinton denounced as intolerable 'fraud and abuse' perpetrated against 'working families' who 'play by the rules' the fact that some prisoners (or their households) continued to get public payments due to lax bureaucratic enforcement of these prohibitions. And he proudly launched 'unprecedented federal, state, and local co-operation as well as new, innovative incentive programs' using the latest 'high-tech tools to weed out any inmate' who still received benefits (Clinton, 1998), including the disbursement of bounties to counties who promptly turn in identifying information on their jail detainees to the Social Security administration.

3. Convicts are banned from *political participation* via 'criminal disenfranchisement' practiced on a scale and with a vigor unimagined in any other country. All but four members of the Union deny the vote to mentally competent adults held in detention facilities; 39 states forbid convicts placed on probation from exercising their political rights and 32 states also interdict parolees. In 14 states, ex-felons are barred from voting even when they are no longer under criminal justice supervision – *for life* in ten of these states. The result is that nearly 4 million Americans have temporarily or permanently lost the ability to cast a ballot, including 1.47 million who are not behind bars and another 1.39 million who served their sentence in full (Fellner and Mauer, 1998). A mere quarter of a century after acceding to full voting rights, one black man in seven nationwide is banned from the electoral booth through penal disenfranchisement and seven states permanently deny the vote to more than one fourth of their black male residents.

Through this *triple exclusion*, the prison, and the criminal justice system more broadly, contribute to the ongoing *reconstruction of the 'imagined community' of Americans* around the polar opposition between praiseworthy 'working families'- implicitly white, suburban, and deserving – and the despicable 'underclass' of criminals, loafers, and leeches, a two-headed antisocial hydra personified by the dissolute teenage 'welfare mother' on the female side and the dangerous street 'gang banger' on the male side – by definition darkskinned, urban, and undeserving. The former are exalted as the living incarnation of genuine American values, self-control, deferred gratification, subservience of life to labor;[42] the latter is vituperated as the loathsome embodiment of their abject desecration, the 'dark side' of the 'American dream' of affluence and opportunity for all believed to flow from morality anchored in conjugality and work. And the line that divides them is increasingly being drawn, materially and symbolically, by the prison.

On the other side of that line lies an institutional setting unlike any other. Building on his celebrated analyses of Ancient Greece, classical historian Moses Finley (1968) has introduced a fruitful distinction between 'societies with slaves' and 'genuine slave societies'. In the former, slavery is but one of several modes of labor control and the division between slave and free is neither impermeable nor axial to the entire social order. In the latter, enslaved labor is epicentral to both economic production and class structure, and the slave-master relation provides the pattern after which all other social relations are built or distorted, such that no corner of culture, society and self is left untouched by it. The astronomical overrepresentation of blacks in houses of penal confinement and the increasingly tight meshing of the hyperghetto with the carceral system suggests that, owing to America's adoption of mass incarceration as a queer social policy designed to discipline the poor and contain the dishonored, lower-class African Americans now dwell, not in a society with prisons as their white compatriots do, but in *the first genuine prison society* of history.

Acknowledgements

A shorter version of this paper was presented at the Conference on Mass Imprisonment in the United States: Social Causes and Consequences, New York University Law School, 26 February 2000. It benefited from the comments, criticisms, and queries of fellow participants and audience members; the pointed encouragements of Jack Katz, Michael Tonry, James Jacobs, and Franklin Zimring were particularly stimulative. Special thanks are due to David Garland, first, for inviting a neophyte to participate in this fateful event and, second, for the extraordinary patience and persistence he mustered in awaiting the final text, which benefited from the editorial vigilance of Megan L. Comfort.

Notes

1 Because males compose over 93 percent of the US state and federal prison population and 89 percent of jail inmates, and because the disciplining of women from the lower class and caste continues to operate primarily through the agencies of the social arm of the American state (namely, welfare and workfare), this article focuses solely on men. But a full-fledged analysis of the distinct causes and consequences of the astonishing growth in the imprisonment of black (and Hispanic) women is urgently needed, among other reasons because the penal confinement of women has immensely deleterious effects on their children (Hagan and Dinovitzer, 1999).

2 It must be stressed, moreover, that this increase in 'racial disproportionality' is notably underestimated since the category 'whites' comprises a significant and growing number of Latinos, as the latter's share of the total inmate population increases over time (and the more so in states that have led the march to mass incarceration, such as Texas, California and Florida).

3 In this, I follow the exhortation of Georg Rusche (1933: 11) in a short but pointed article that sums up the intention of his and Kirchheimer's classic *Punishment and Social Structure*: 'The bond, transparent or not, that is supposed to exist between crime and punishment. . . must be broken. Punishment is neither a simple consequence of crime, nor the reverse side of crime, nor a mere means which is determined by the end to be achieved. Punishment must be understood as a social phenomenon freed from both its juristic concept and its social ends', that is, its official mission of crime control, so that it may be replaced in the complete system of strategies, including social policies, aimed at regulating the poor. But I do *not* follow Rusche in (1) postulating a *direct* link between brute economic forces and penal policy; (2) reducing economic forces to the sole state of the *labor market*, and still less the supply of labor; (3) limiting the control function of the prison to lower *classes*, as distinct from other subordinate categories (ethnic or national, for instance); and (4) omitting the ramifying *symbolic* effects that the penal system exercises by

PUNISHMENT AND SOCIETY 3(1)

drawing, dramatizing, and enforcing group boundaries. Indeed, in the case of black Americans, the symbolic function of the carceral system is paramount. For a terse application of this approach to the penal containment of immigrants in the European Union today, see Wacquant (1999b).

4 Two features of America's *racial exceptionalism* must be noted briefly here: the United States is the only nation in the world to define as 'black' all persons with *any* recognized African *ancestry*, creating a rigid black/white division between two mutually exclusive communities; second, within the United States, the 'one-drop rule' and the principle of hypodescent (whereby the offspring of any mixed couple are automatically assigned to the inferior category, here blacks, irrespective of their phenotype, upbringing, and other social properties) are applied solely to African Americans, making them the only U.S. ethnic group that cannot merge into white society through intermarriage. This highly peculiar conception of 'blackness' arose in the American South to protect the institution of slavery and later served to solidify the Jim Crown system of segregation (Davis, 1992).

5 Thus also the central place of violence in the black American collective experience and imagination, from Nat Turner, Frederick Douglass and Martin Delany to Ralph Ellison, Bayard Rustin and Malcolm X (Levine, 1977; Takaki, 1993; Broderick and Meier, 1965).

6 The 'inherent instability of the slave relation' has been demonstrated by Patterson (1982: 336) and that of unfree labor by Kolchin (1987: 359); the congenital incompatibility of caste separation and democracy is the fulcrum of Gunnar Myrdal's (1944) classic analysis of the 'American dilemma' of race (which, *pace* Myrdal, is *not* a value conflict amenable to moral resolution but a structural disjuncture between principles of social vision and vision, maintained or overturned by relations of power).

7 This historical schema should not be read as an ineluctable forward march towards ethnoracial equality. Each new phase of racial domination entailed retrogression as well as progress. And, while it is true that there has been a kind of 'civilizing' of racial domination (in Norbert Elias's sense of the term), it remains that each regime has to be evaluated in light of the institutional possibilities it harbors, not simply by contrast to its predecessor(s).

8 The interaction of slavery and race, and how each transformed the other across the three broad 'generations' of slaves during the 17th and 18th century, the 'charters generations', the 'plantation generations', and the 'revolutionary generations', is well depicted by Ira Berlin (1998).

9 This regime was supported and abetted by the federal government, which acted as a powerful engine for the national legitimation and diffusion of exclusionary racial practices and patterns in the half-century preceding the Civil Rights Act of 1964: every major federal institution, from the US civil service and public employment exchanges to public housing and the armed forces, engaged in the systematic discrimination and ostracization of blacks (King, 1995).

10 In Mississippi, 'the list of disqualifying offenses – which included arson, bigamy, fraud, and petty theft, but not murder, rape, or grand larceny – was tailored, in the opinion of the state supreme court, to bar blacks, a "patient, docile people . . . given rather to furtive offenses than to the robust crimes of the whites" ' (McMillen, 1990: 43).

11 As an uprooted people, African Americans have always migrated in search of improved economic opportunities and a less oppressive racial climate. Before World War I, their peregrinations took them throughout the South as well as to the frontier states of the West, in a quest for land as fount of material security. The Great Migration redirected these population streams towards the urban North and amplified them by linking them to industrial wage employment. With the onset of mass imprisonment, lower-class blacks are being forcibly 'migrated' back to the declining rural areas where most state and federal prisons are located.

12 The New Deal helped this parallel city coalesce by (1) further stimulating outmigration from the South via agricultural programs that excluded black farmers and farm laborers; (2) extending public aid to jobless African Americans living in the Northern metropolis (half of Chicago's Negro families were on relief in 1940); and (3) building up its physical infrastructure through public works and the massing of social housing projects in the segregated urban core, while refusing to guarantee loans to blacks seeking residence in white neighborhoods. After the Second World War, federal housing, lending, and transportation policies conspired to keep blacks firmly hemmed in the ghetto.

13 The urbanization of blacks accelerated the 'melting' of mulattos and Negros into a single overarching African-American identity. It also supplied the impetus for the gestation and growth of the gamut of organizations that took up the struggle for racial equality on the national stage, from the gradualist Urban League and National Association for the Advancement of Colored People to the militant Brotherhood of Sleeping Car Porters to the secessionist Universal Negro Improvement Association of Marcus Garvey.

14 A fuller discussion of the homologies between ghetto and prison as institutions of forced confinement of dishonored categories is in Wacquant (2000: 382–5).

15 It is not so much that the black middle class *moved out* of the 'inner city,' as argued by Wilson (1987); rather, it has *grown* outside of the historic core of the ghetto after its heyday. For the black bourgeoisie was miniscule at the mid-century point, and as early as the 1930s it had already established outposts beyond the perimeter of Bronzeville, as Drake and Cayton (1945: 384) point out.

16 On Christmas night of 1988, I attended mass at a Baptist church near the Robert Taylor Homes, the single largest concentration of public housing in Chicago (and, for that matter, in the United States) with a population of some 15,000. Participation was so sparse (about sixty people) that members of the audience had to join the choir impromptu to allow it to wade through its piteous repertoire. The atmosphere upon leaving the cavernous building was one of disaffection and depression. A few months later, the ramshackle structure was boarded up and, by the following Christmas, it had been razed and its lot left vacant.

17 The *Chicago Defender*'s role a 'race paper' has been partially taken up by *The Call*, the official organ of the Nation of Islam, but the latter's circulation is but a fraction of its predecessor's and its impact incomparably smaller.

18 For detailed accounts of the gross and systematic dysfunctioning of these institutions and their impact on residents of Chicago's hyperghetto, see, respectively, Abraham (1992) on public health, Venkatesh (2000) on public housing, Ayers (1997) on the juvenile court, *Chicago Tribune* (1992) on public schools, and Conroy (2000) and

Amnesty International (1999) on the police (including reports of more than a decade of rampant torture at Area 2 station on the South Side, involving mock executions, 'Palestinian hangings', electric shocks with cattle prods, burnings with radiators and asphyxiation with plastic bags, in addition to the usual pattern of brutality, unjustified shootings and cover-ups, and the detention and interrogation of children in custody).

19 See the account of Gerstel et al. (1996) on homeless shelters and the vivid description of Chicago's 'SRO Death Row' by Klinenberg (1999: 269–72). Parallels between prison culture and the management of the Armory, New York's biggest homeless shelter, are suggested by Dordick (1997: 126-49)

20 In 1992, the Division of School Safety of the New York City Board of Education had a budget of 73 million dollars, a fleet of ninety vehicles, and over 3,200 uniformed security officers, which made it the ninth largest police force in the country, just ahead of that of Miami. In 1968, this division did not exist. John Devine (1996: 80–2) notes that lower-tier principals now have as one of their major concerns the management of this 'paramilitary force [which] has taken on an independent existence with its own organization and procedures, language, rules, equipment, dresssing rooms, uniforms, vans, and lines of authority'.

21 One must be careful not to romantizice the carceral past: even in the heyday of rehabilitation (corresponding to the full maturation of the Fordist economy and Keynesian state), the prison did not much rehabilitate, owing to the abiding 'priority given to institutional order, discipline, and security' (Rotman, 1995: 295). But the ideal of treatment, the intervention of therapeutic professionals, and the deployment of rehabilitative routines did improve conditions of detention and reduce arbitrariness, cruelty, and lawlessness behind bars. What is more, extensive 'programming' helped achieve internal stability and instilled a forward-looking outlook among inmates.

22 Note the parallel with social research on the ghetto: the field studies of the sixties, focusing on ghetto *institutions* seen at ground level from the insider's point of view, disappeared by the 1970s to be replaced a decade later by survey-based research on the 'underclass', i.e., *population aggregates* constructed from afar and from above via the manipulation of quantitative indicators. Note also that the disappearance of the inmate society from social science partakes at a cognitive level of a distinctively US policy of 'invisibilization' of social problems and problem populations (the same technique is now being applied to welfare recipients). By contrast, ethnographic research on the prison is alive and productive in Europe, especially England and France.

23 The caste-like organization of the Warehouse extends to the management of relations with the outside. At the San Quentin prison near San Francisco, whenever a black (or Latino) inmate is assaulted inside the facility, all African-American (Latino) inmates from that housing unit are automatically barred from visitation and the women who are thus refused entry to see them learn to think of themselves in such categorical terms in their dealings with the prison (personal communication from Megan Comfort, based on ongoing field work in 'the Tube', the enclosed area where prison visitors wait for their visit).

24 'The activities of these violent groups who, in the pursuit of loot, sex, and revenge,

will attack any outsider have *completely unraveled any remnants of the old codes of honor* and tip networks that formerly helped to maintain order. In a limited, closed space, such as a prison, threats or attacks like those posed by these groups cannot be ignored. Prisoners must be ready to protect themselves or get out of the way. Those who have chosen to continue to circulate in public, with few exceptions, have formed or joined a clique or gang for their own protection. Consequently, violence-oriented groups dominate many, if not most, large men's prisons' (Irwin, 1980: 192, emphasis added).

25 See, for instance, Hassine (1999: 41–2) first-hand account of the conflict between 'new inmates vs. old heads' in the ghettoized 'prison subcultures' marked by 'their disrespect for authority, drug addition, illiteracy, and welfare mentality', in short, 'all the evils of the decaying American inner city'.

26 The same reasoning applies in big-city jails, which have become so disrupted, violent, and punitive that many detainees hasten to plead guilty in order to be 'sent to state' right away: 'Better do a year in state [prison] than three months in this hell of a jail' is how several detainees at LA's Men's Central Jail put it to me in summer of 1998.

27 'Three Strikes and You're Out', which mandates the lifelong incarceration of offenders at the edge of their criminal career in response to double recidivism, epitomizes this approach to 'vengeance as public policy' (Shichor and Sechrest, 1996) in its disregard for proportionality and penological efficacy, as well as in its unabashed use of a catchy baseball metaphor that likens crime fighting to a kind of sport.

28 Florida is at the vanguard of the trend to diffuse the criminal justice files of prisoners over the Internet 'in the interest of public safety.' The 'Corrections Offender Network' rubric of its prison administration allows one to run searches by name, race, sex, identifiers (Social Security, passport or alien number, driver's licence) and offense category. It provides not only the usual personal data (name and aliases, birth date, hair and eye color, height and weight, 'scars, marks, and tattoos' with their exact description and location) and criminal justice information (current offense date, offense type, sentence date, case number and prison sentence length, plus an abrievated incarceration history), but also a full-size color picture and the date of release as well as the current address for former inmates out on parole. This site received some 300,000 visits during its first year of operation.

29 As indicated by the disappearance of the term '*ex*-sex offender' in legal, political, and even scholarly discourse, which makes sex crimes the act of a particular *species* of individual, rather than a particular type of legally proscribed *conduct*.

30 'Inasmuch as criminal behavior is associated with [inferior] intelligence and [antisocial] personality, and inasmuch as personality and intelligence have genetic influences on them, then *it follows logically, as night follows day, that criminal behavior has genetic ingredients*' (Herrnstein, 1995: 55, emphasis added). The conceptual sleight-of-hand here lies both in the predicates (that intelligence and antisocial personality, inasmuch as they are themselves coherent variables, are genetically determined), in the vagueness of the terms 'influences' and 'ingredients', and in the locution 'inasmuch as' . . .

31 Not a single source is cited for this rather stunning statistic, despite superabundant notes and references throughout the chapter.

32 This is reaffirmed in the companion article by Brennan et al. (1995: 87–8), who sum up their findings thus: 'Criminal behavior in parents increases the likelihood of nonviolent crime in the offspring. This relationship is due, in part, to genetic transmission of criminogenic characteristics. This genetic effect is stronger for females and is especially important for recidivistic crime'. They also report that perinatal factors (delivery complications), frontal lobe dysfunction, and reduced cerebrospinal serotonin fluid levels are associated with violent crime while EEG slow alpha activity correlates with property crimes! For an up-to-date compendium of gene-based theories of crime and their resurgent popularity in mainstream US criminology, read Ellis and Walsh (1997).

33 It is revealing that these data should come from a survey of the geographic provenance of prisoners carried out by inmates themselves: they sensed at ground level what prison activist and scholar Eddie Ellis (1993: 2; also 1998) calls the 'relation of symbiosis' emerging between the ghetto and the carceral system, even as government officials and social scientists were oblivious or indifferent to it.

34 Hardly a week goes by without the *New York Times* featuring one or several articles reporting on some aspect of prison unrelated to crime control attesting to the seeping out and normalization of carceral culture: e.g. 'Accessories for the Big House: Corrections Officers Survey the Options for Keeping Inmates in Line' (in the Sunday magazine); 'In Jailhouse Chic, an Anti-Style Turns into a Style Itself' (Fashion rubric); 'Rooms Available in Gated Community: $20 a Day'(Society's Journal); 'Using Internet Links from Behind Bars' (Society); 'A Hard-Case Study Approach to Executive Training' (seminars on communication techniques for executives held inside of Attica, in the Business Section); 'Confined in Prisons, Literature Breaks Out' (in Arts and Ideas) (14 May, 13 June, 10 July, 1, 23 and 26 August, 2000 respectively).

35 That 'race' as a social principle of vision and division (to invoke Pierre Bourdieu's notion) is *made* and therefore contested, as are all social entities, does not mean that it is *eo ipso* infinitely malleable, endowed with a 'fluency', 'inherent instability' and even 'volatility' that would allow it to be reconfigured anew at every historical turn (as argued by Berlin, 1998: 1–3). The welcome emphasis on contention, resistance and change that has been the hallmark of recent populist, 'bottom up' approaches to the historiography and sociology of ethnoracial domination should not blind us to the fact that the ductility and durability of 'race' is highly variable across epochs and societies, depending, precisely, on the nature and workings of the extant 'peculiar institutions' that produce and reproduce it in each particular setting.

36 Two indicators suffice to spotlight the enduring ostracization of African Americans in US society. They are the only group to be 'hypersegregated', with spatial isolation shifting from the macro-level of state and county to the micro-level of municipality and neighborhood so as to minimize contacts with whites throughout the century (Massey and Denton, 1993; Massey and Hajnal, 1995). They remain barred from exogamy to a degree unknown to any other community, notwithstanding the recent growth of so-called multiracial families, with fewer than 3 percent of black women marrying out compared to a majority of Hispanic and Asian women (DaCosta, 2000).

37 Thus the commercial success, based on prurient fascination, of the autobiographical account of the well-named Los Angeles gang member, Monster Kody (Shakur, 1993).

38 Teresa Gowan (2000) reports that white ex-convicts forced to settle in inner-city St. Louis to be close to parole agencies upon being released from Missouri prisons complain that the criminal justice system 'turning them into blacks'.

39 So much so that they escape even the attention of prison scholars: two days before the conference at which this paper was presented, a race riot pitting some 200 black and Latino inmates broke out at California's high-tech Pelican Bay prison (a maximum-security facility reputed as 'the nation's most-secure' and notorious for being a 'war zone' between African Americans and whites), during which guards killed one prisoner and seriously wounded twelve others. It took 120 correctional officers a full half-hour to quell the frenzied mêlée, despite the use of tear gas, pepper spray, rubber and wooden bullets and two dozen rounds from Ruger Mini-14 rifles. The next day, authorities placed all 33 prisons in the state on security alert ('Guards Kill Prisoner in Brawl at Pelican Bay', *San Francisco Chronicle*, 24 February 2000; 'Inmate Dies and 12 Are Hurt as Riot Erupts in California Prison', *New York Times*, 24 February 2000; 'State Puts all Prisons on Security Alert: Authorities are on Lookout for Signs of Racial Tension after Riot Ended in Shooting Death of an Inmate at Pelican Bay', *Los Angeles Times*, 25 February 2000). None of the participants to the conference mentioned this disturbance, the single most violent in California prisons in two decades, during the two days of discussions.

40 This is not to say, of course, that all prison upheavals are caused by racial conflict. The typical carceral riot involves a range and mix of grievances, from inadequate food and medical care to arbitrary and repressive management to idleness and lack of rehabilitative programs. But racial divisions and tensions are always a propitious backdrop, if not a major causal factor, of violent incidents, real or perceived, inside of U.S. detention houses (in summer of 1998, the word among detainees of the Los Angeles County Jail was that some facilities had to be avoided at all costs because they witnessed 'a race riot every day').

41 The argument that follows is influenced by Garland's (1991: 219) neo-Durkheimian explication of 'penality as a set of signifying practices' that 'help produce subjectivities, forms of authority and social relations' at large.

42 As when Albert Gore, Jr., declared in his prime-time speech at the Democratic Convention on 20 August of 2000: 'In the name of all the working families who are the strength and soul of America, I accept your nomination for President of the United States', indicating that non-working families and detached individuals, being unfit to be included in the act of political delegation, are not and need not be concerned by the election. The Vice-President uttered the locution 'working families' a record nine times in only 52 minutes and every major speaker that night invoked it repeatedly.

References

Abraham, Laurie Kay (1993) *Mama might be better off dead: The failure of health care in urban America*. Chicago: The University of Chicago Press.

Allen, Francis A. (1981) *The decline of the rehabilitative ideal*. New Haven: Yale University Press.

Amnesty International (1999) *Summary of Amnesty International's concerns on police abuse in Chicago*. London: Amnesty International, AMR/51/168/99.

PUNISHMENT AND SOCIETY 3(1)

Anderson, Elijah (1998) *Code of the street: Decency, violence, and the moral life of the inner city.* New York: Knopf.

Ayers, William (1997) *A kind and just parent: The children of juvenile court.* Boston: Beacon Press.

Beck, Allan (2000) *Prison and jail inmates at midyear in 1999.* Washington, D.C.: Bureau of Justice Statistics.

Berlin, Ira (1998) *Many thousands gone : The first two centuries of slavery in North America.* Cambridge MA: Harvard University Press.

Best, Joel (1997) 'Victimization and the victim industry'. *Society* 34(4): 9–17.

Blumstein, Alfred (1993) 'Racial disproportionality of US prison revisited'. *University of Colorado Law Review* 64: 743–60.

Brennan, Patricia, Sarnoff A. Mednick and Jan Volacka (1995) 'Biomedical factors in crime'. In James Q. Wilson and Joan Petersilia (eds.), *Crime.* San Francisco: ICS Press, pp. 65–90.

Broderick, Francis L. and August Meier (1965) *Negro protest thought in the twentieth century.* Indianapolis: Bobbs-Merrill.

Camp, C. and G. M. Camp (eds.) (1998) *The Corrections Yearbook 1998.* Middletown: Criminal Justice Institute.

Carroll, Leo (1974) *Hacks, Blacks, and cons.* Lexington: D.C. Heath & Co.

Carroll, Leo (1982) 'Race, ethnicity, and the social order of the prison.' In Robert Johnson and Hans Toch (eds.), *The pains of imprisonment.* Beverly Hills: Sage, pp. 181–201.

Clark, Kenneth C. (1965) *Dark ghetto: Dilemmas of social power.* Amherst: University of Massachussetts Press.

Clinton, William Jefferson (1998) 'Saturday radio address'. 25 April 1998 (available on the White House web site).

Chicago Tribune (Staff of the). (1992). *The worst schools in America.* Chicago: Contemporary Press.

Christianson, Scott (1998) *With liberty for some: Five hundred years of imprisonment in America.* Boston: Northeastern University Press.

Conroy, John (2000) *Unspeakable acts, ordinary people: The dynamics of torture.* New York: Knopf.

Cooper, Scott A. (1998) 'Community notification and verification practices in three states' in *National Conference on Sex Offender Registries.* pp. 103–6. Washington: Bureau of Justice Statistics.

Cross, Brian (1993) *It's not about a salary: Rap, race, and resistance in Los Angeles.* New York: Verso.

DaCosta, Kim (2000) 'Remaking the color line: Social bases and implications of the multiracial movement'. Ph.D Dissertation Department of Sociology, University of California, Berkeley.

Davidson, Joe (1997) 'Caged cargo: Cashing in on black prisoners'. *Emerge* 23 October: 36–46.

Davis, Angela Y. (1998) 'Globalism and the prison industrial complex: An interview with Angela Davis'. *Race and Class* 40(2/3): 145–57.

Davis, F. James. (1992) *Who is Black? One's nation definition.* University Park: Penn State Press.

Devine, John (1996) *Maximum security: the culture of violence in inner-city schools*
Chicago: The University of Chicago Press.

DiIulio, John J. (1991) 'Understanding prisons: The new old penology'. *Law & Social Inquiry* 16(1): 65–99.

Dollard, John (1937) *Caste and class in a southern town*. New York: Doubleday Anchor, reprint 1957.

Donziger, Steven (1996) *The real war on crime*. New York: Basic Books.

Dordick, Gwendolyn (1997) *Something left to lose: Personal relations and survival among New York's homeless*. Philadelphia: Temple University Press.

Drake, St. Clair and Horace Cayton (1945) *Black metropolis: A study of Negro life in a northern city*. New York: Harper and Row, 1962.

Ellis, Edwin (1993) *The non-traditional approach to criminal justice and social justice*. Harlem: Community Justice Center, mimeographed, 8 pages.

Ellis, Edwin (1998) 'An interview with Eddie Ellis'. *Humanity and Society* 22(1): 98–111.

Ellis, Lee and Anthony Walsh (1997) 'Gene-based evolutionary theories in criminology'. *Criminology* 35(2): 229–76.

Esping-Andersen, Gösta (1987) *Three world of welfare*. Princeton: Princeton University Press.

Fellner, Jamie and Marc Mauer (1998) *Losing the vote: The impact of felony disenfranchisement in the United States*. Washington DC: The Sentencing Project and Human Rights Watch.

Fields, Barbara Jean (1982) 'Race and Ideology in American History'. In J. Morgan Kousser and James M. McPherson (eds.), *Region, race, and reconstruction: Essays in the honor of C. Vann Woodward*. New York: Oxford University Press, pp. 143–77.

Finley, Moses (1968) 'Slavery'. *International encyclopedia of the social sciences*. New York: Free Press.

Fligstein, Neil (1981) *Going north: Migration of blacks and whites from the South, 1900–1950*. New York: Academic Press.

Frazier, E. Franklin (1932) *The negro family in Chicago*. Chicago: The University of Chicago Press.

Fusfeld, Daniel R. and Timothy Bates (1984) *The political economy of the ghetto*. Carbondale: Southern Illinois University Press.

Garland, David (1991) 'Punishment and Culture: The Symbolic Dimension of Criminal Justice'. *Studies in Law, Politics, and Society* 11: 1911–22.

Gerstel, Naomi, Cynthia J. Bogard, Jeff McConnell, and Michael Schwartz (1996) 'The therapeutic incarceration of homeless'. *The Social Service Review* 70(4): 543–72.

Gilens, Martin (1999) *Why Americans Hate Welfare: Race, Media, and the Politics of Anti-Poverty Policy*. Chicago: The University of Chicago Press.

Gowan, Teresa (2000) 'Excavating Globalization from Street Level: Homeless Men Recycle their Pasts'. In Michael Burawoy et al., *Global ethnography*. Berkeley: University of California Press.

Greenberg, David and Valerie West (1999) 'Growth of state prison populations, 1971–1991'. Paper presented at the Annual Meetings of the Law and Society Association, Chicago, May.

PUNISHMENT AND SOCIETY 3(1)

Grossman, James R. (1989) *Land of hope: Chicago, black southerners, and the great migration*. Chicago: The University of Chicago Press.

Hagan, John and Ronit Dinowitzer (1999) 'Collateral consequences of imprisonment for children, communities, and prisoners'. In Michael Tonry and Joan Petersilia (eds.), in *Prisons*. Chicago: The University of Chicago Press, pp 121–62.

Handler, Joel (1997) *Down with bureaucracy*. Princeton: Princeton University Press.

Harlow, Caroline Wolf (1998) *Profile of jail inmates 1996*. Washington: Bureau of Justice Statistics.

Hassine, Victor. (1999) *Life without parole: Living in prison today*. Boston: Roxbury Publications, 2nd ed.

Herrnstein, R.J. (1995) 'Criminogenic traits'. In James Q. Wilson and Joan Petersilia (eds.). *Crime*. San Francisco: ICS Press, pp. 39–64.

Hirsch, Andrew von. (1998) 'Penal theories'. In Michael Tonry (ed.), *The handbook of crime and punishment*. Oxford: Oxford University Press, pp. 659–83.

Hughes, Everett C. (1945 [1984]) 'Dilemmas and Contradictions of Status'. Reprinted in *The sociological eye*. New Brunswick: Transaction, pp. 141–52.

Hunt, Geoffrey, Stephanie Riegel, Tomas Morales, and Dan Waldorf (1993) 'Changes in prison culture: Prison gangs and the case of the "Pepsi Generation"'. *Social Problems* 40(3): 398–409.

Irwin, John (1980) *Prisons in turmoil*. Boston: Little, Brown.

Irwin, John (1970 [1990]). *The felon*. Berkeley: University of California Press, new edition.

Jacobs, James B. (1977) *Stateville: The penitentiary in mass society*. Chicago: The University of Chicago Press.

Jacobs, James B. (1983) 'Race relations and the prisoner subculture'. In *New perspectives on prisons and imprisonment*. Ithaca: Cornell University Press, pp. 61–79.

Johnson, Robert (1996). *Hard Time: Understanding and reforming the prison*. 2nd ed. Belmont: Wadsworth Publishing.

Jones, LeAlan and Lloyd Newman (1997) *Our America: Life and death on the South Side of Chicago*. New York: Washington Square Press.

Katznelson, Ira (1976) *Black men, white cities: Race, politics and migration in the United States, 1900–1930, and Britain, 1948–68*. Chicago: The University of University Press.

Kennedy, Randall (1997) 'Race, law, and suspicion: Using color as a proxy for dangerousness'. In *Race, crime and the law*. New York, Pantheon, pp. 136–67.

King, Desmond (1995) *Separate and unequal: Black Americans and the U.S. Federal Government*. Oxford: Oxford University Press.

King, Roy D. (1999) 'The rise and rise of Supermax: An American solution in search of a problem?'. *Punishment & Society* 1(2): 163–86.

Klinenberg, Eric (1999) 'Denaturalizing disaster: A social autopsy of the 1995 Chicago heat wave'. *Theory and Society* 28(2): 239–95.

Kolchin, Peter (1987) *Unfree labor: American slavery and Russian serfdom*. Cambridge: The Belknap Press of Harvard University Press.

Kotlowitz, Alex (1991) *There are no children here*. New York: Anchor Books.

Krivo, Lauren J. and Ruth D. Peterson (1996) 'Extremely disadvantaged neighborhoods and urban crime'. *Social Forces* 75(2): 619–650.

Lafree, Gary, K. Drass and P. O'Day (1992) 'Race and crime in post-war America: determinants of African American and white rates, 1957–1988'. *Criminology* 30: 157–88.

Lessan, Gloria T. (1991) 'Macro-economic determinants of penal policy: Estimating the unemployment and inflation influences on imprisonment rate changes in the united states, 1948–1985'. *Crime, Law and Social Change* 16(2): 177–98.

Levine, Lawrence (1977) *Black culture and black consciousness.* Oxford: Oxford University Press.

Lieberman, Stanley (1998) *Shifting the color line: Race and the American welfare state.* Cambridge: Harvard University Press.

Light, Ivan (1977) 'Numbers gambling among blacks: A financial institution'. *American Sociological Review*, 42(6): 892–904.

Marks, Carole (1989) *Farewell, we're good and gone: The Great Black Migration.* Bloomington: Indiana University Press.

Martin, Robert J. (1996) 'Pursuing public protection through mandatory community notification of convicted sex offenders: The trials and tribulations of Megan's Law'. *The Boston Public Interest Law Journal* 26: 26–56.

Martin, Steve J. and Sheldon Ekland-Olson (1987) *Texas prisons: The walls came tumbling down.* Austin: Texas Monthly Press.

Massey, Douglas, and Nancy Denton (1993) *American apartheid: Segregation and the making of the underclass.* Cambridge: Harvard University Press.

Massey, Douglas and Zoltan L. Hajnal (1995) 'The changing geographic structure of black-white segregation in the United States'. *Social Science Quarterly* 76(3): 527–42.

Mauer, Marc (1997) 'Racial disparities in prison getting worse in the 1990s'. *Overcrowded Times* 8(1): 8–13.

McMillen, Neil R. (1990) *Dark journey: Black Mississippians in the age of Jim Crow.* Urbana: University of Illinois Press.

Melossi Dario (2000) 'Changing representations of the criminal'. *British Journal of Criminology* 40(2): 296–320.

Miller, Jerome G. (1997) *Search and destroy: African-American males in the criminal justice system.* Cambridge: Cambridge University Press.

Morgan, Edmund S. (1975) *American slavery, American freedom: The ordeal of colonial Virginia.* New York: W.W. Norton.

Morris, Norval (1995) 'The contemporary Prison, 1965–present'. In Norval Morris and David Rothman (eds.), *The Oxford history of the prison.* New York: Oxford University Press, pp. 226–59.

Myrdal, Gunnar (1944 [1962]) *An American dilemma: The Negro problem and modern democracy.* New York: Harper Torchbook.

Oshinsky, David M. (1996) *Worse than slavery: Parchman farm and the ordeal of Jim Crow justice.* New York: Free Press.

Page, Josh (2000). 'Eliminating the enemy: A cultural analysis of the exclusion of prisoners from higher education'. M.A. paper, Department of Sociology, University of California-Berkeley.

Patillo-McCoy, Mary (1999) *Black picket fences: Privilege and peril among the black middle class.* Chicago: The University of Chicago Press.

Patterson, Orlando (1982) *Slavery as social death.* Cambridge: Harvard University Press.

Pens, Dan (1998) 'Federal prisons erupt'. In Daniel Burton-Rose, Dan Pens and Paul

PUNISHMENT AND SOCIETY 3(1)

Wright (eds.), *The celling of America: An inside look at the U.S. prison industry.*
Monroe, Maine: Common Courage Press, pp. 244–9.

Petersilia, Joan (1999) 'Parole and prisoner reentry in the United States'. In Michael
Tonry and Joan Petersilia (eds.), *Prisons.* Chicago: The University of Chicago Press,
pp. 479–529.

Philipps, Susan A. (1999) *Wallbangin': Graffiti and Gangs in L.A.* Chicago: The University of Chicago Press.

Powdermaker, Hortense (1939 [1993]) *After freedom: A cultural study of the Deep South.*
Madison: University of Wisconsin Press, new ed.

Rifkin, Jeff (1995) *The end of work: The decline of the global labor force and the dawn of
the post-market era.* New York: Tarcher and Putnam.

Rotman, Edgardo (1995) 'The failure of reform: United States, 1865–1965'. In Norval
Morris and David J. Rothman (eds.), *The Oxford history of the prison.* New York:
Oxford University Press, pp. 169–97.

Rusche, Georg. (1933 [1980]). 'Labor market and penal sanction: Thoughts on the sociology of punishment'. In T. Platt and P. Takagi (eds.), *Punishment and penal discipline.*
Berkeley: Crime and Justice Associates, pp. 10–17.

Sampson, Robert J. and Janet L. Lauritsen (1997) 'Racial and ethnic disparities in crime
and criminal justice in the United States'. In Michael Tonry (ed.), *Ethnicity, crime,
and immigration: Comparative and cross-national perspectives.* Chicago: The University
of Chicago Press, pp. 311–74.

Shakur, Sanyika (1993) *Monster: The autobiography of an L.A. gang member.* New York:
The Atlantic Monthly Press.

Shichor, David and Dale K. Sechrest (eds.) (1996) *Three strikes and you're out : Vengeance
as public policy.* Thousand Oaks: Sage Publications.

Simon, Jonathan (2000) 'The "Society of Captives" in the era of hyper-incarceration'.
Theoretical Criminology 4(3): 285–308.

Spear, Allan H. (1967) *Black Chicago: The making of a negro ghetto, 1890–1920.*
Chicago: The University of Chicago Press.

Sugrue, Tom (1996) *The origins of the urban crisis: Race and inequality in postwar Detroit.*
Princeton: Princeton University Press.

Sykes, Gresham (1958 [1974]) *The society of captives: A study in a maximum security
prison.* Princeton: Princeton University Press.

Sykes, Gresham and Sheldon Messinger (1960) 'The inmate social system'. In Richard
Cloward et al., *Theoretical studies in the social organization of the prison.* New York:
Social Science Research Council, pp. 6–10.

Takaki, Ronald T. (1993) *Violence in the black imagination.* Oxford: Oxford University
Press (expanded and revised edition).

Tolnay, Stewart E. and E.M. Beck (1992) '*Racial violence and black migration in the
American south, 1910 to 1930'. American Sociological Review* 57(1): 103–116.

Tonry, Michael (1995) *Malign neglect: Race, class, and punishment in America.* New York:
Oxford University Press.

Useem, Bert and Peter Kimball (1989) *States of siege: U.S. prison riots, 1971–1986.* New
York: Oxford University Press.

Venkatesh, Suhdir (2000) *American project: The rise and fall of a modern ghetto.* Cambridge: Harvard University Press.

Wacquant, Loïc (1989) 'The Ghetto, the state, and the new capitalist economy'. *Dissent* (*Fall*): 508–20.

Wacquant, Loïc (1998a) 'Negative social capital: State breakdown and social destitution in America's urban core'. *The Netherlands Journal of the Built Environment* 13-1: 25–40.

Wacquant, Loïc (1998b) 'Inside the zone: The social art of the hustler in the black American ghetto'. *Theory, Culture, and Society* 15(2): 1–36.

Wacquant, Loïc (1998c) ' "A Black City Within the White": Revisiting America's Dark Ghetto'. *Black Renaissance – Renaissance Noire* 2(1): 141–151.

Wacquant, Loïc (1999a) *Les Prisons de la misère*. Paris: Editions Raisons d'agir (English trans. forthcoming as *Prisons of Poverty*, Minneapolis, University of Minnesota Press, 2001).

Wacquant, Loïc (1999b) ' "Suitable enemies": Foreigners and immigrants in the prisons of Europe'. *Punishment & Society* 1-2: 215–23.

Wacquant, Loïc (2000) 'The new "peculiar institution": On the prison as surrogate ghetto'. *Theoretical Criminology* 4(3), Special issue on 'New Social Studies of the Prison': 377–89.

Williamson, Joel (1986) *A rage for order: Black-white relations in the American south since Emancipation*. New York: Oxford University Press.

Wilson, William Julius (1980) *The declining significance of race*. Chicago: The University of Chicago Press, 2nd edition.

Wilson, William Julius (1987) *The truly disadvantaged: The inner city, the underclass and public policy*. Chicago: The University of Chicago Press

Woodward, C. Vann (1971) *American counterpoint: Slavery and racism in the North-South dialogue*. Boston: Little, Brown.

Wideman, John Edgar (1995) 'Doing time, marking race.' *The Nation* 261 (30 October): 503–505.

Yates, Jeff (1997) 'Racial incarceration disparity among states.' *Social Science Quarterly*, 78-4 (December): 1001–10.

LOÏC WACQUANT is Researcher at the Centre de sociologie européenne du Collège de France and an Associate Professor of Sociology and Research Fellow at the Earl Warren Legal Institute, University of California-Berkeley. He is the author of *Les Prisons de la misère, Corps et âme. Carnet ethnographique d'un apprenti-boxeur*, and of the forthcoming *In the Zone: Life in the Dark Ghetto at Century's End*. Aside from racial domination and the role of carceral institutions in the regulation of social misery in neoliberal society, his interests include comparative urban marginality, social theory, violence and the body.

[7]

RACE AND PLACE: THE ECOLOGY OF RACIAL PROFILING AFRICAN AMERICAN MOTORISTS*

ALBERT J. MEEHAN**

MICHAEL C. PONDER***
Oakland University

We propose an ecological dimension to racial profiling by comparing the distribution of drivers on the roadways with officers' proactive surveillance and stop behavior in a predominantly white suburban community bordering a predominantly African American community. African Americans are subject to significant racial profiling, as reflected in disproportionate *surveillance* and *stopping* by the police when driving through whiter areas. Officers' behavior is not explained by African Americans' criminality because the "hit rates" for African American drivers are lower in whiter areas. Profiling is sensitive to race *and* place and manifests itself organizationally, reflecting community patterns of residential segregation.

Minority motorists, particularly African Americans, have long complained that the police, especially in suburban areas, stop them

* The authors acknowledge the generous assistance of the anonymous police department that provided research access. The Roadway Observation Study was supported by the Oakland University Research Committee and Vice-Provost Randy Hanson. The authors thank their research assistants—Kim Cochrane, Melissa Hall, Lisa Kelley, Tracey Meldrum, John Schiable, and Nicky Spry—and colleagues—Jim Dow, David Maines, Terri Orbuch, Gary Shepherd, Dan Smith, and Winson Taam—for their contributions to this research. Anne Warfield Rawls provided invaluable criticism and editorial changes. Direct all correspondence to Albert J. Meehan, Department of Sociology and Anthropology, Oakland University, Rochester, MI 48309.

** Albert J. Meehan is an associate professor of sociology and director of the Criminal Justice Program at Oakland University. He has a long-standing research interest in police record-keeping practices, the interactional organization of police work, and the impact of information technologies on the police. His work has appeared in the *British Journal of Criminology, Psychiatric Quarterly, Qualitative Sociology, Symbolic Interaction, Sociological Quarterly*, and *Urban Life*

*** Michael C. Ponder is a special instructor in sociology and a research associate in the Public Affairs Research Laboratory at Oakland University. He has served as a consultant to community coalitions, school districts, police departments, and nonprofit agencies, assisting with program evaluation, community surveys, need assessments, and organizational development. His current research focuses on the effect of extreme response style on measures of drug use obtained from teenagers in self-report surveys.

for no legitimate reason but solely because they are black: a practice referred to as racial profiling. Furthermore, they have reported that during such stops, they have been subjected to detailed questioning and searches and given no explanation, or only a vague explanation, of why they were stopped. The phenomenon has achieved such notoriety among African Americans that it is called "driving while black" (Harris, 1997). A national survey of police-citizen contacts indicated that African American drivers *are* more likely than white drivers to be stopped, have their vehicles searched, and be ticketed by the police (U.S. Bureau of Justice Statistics 2001, pp. 15-19).[1] Nationally, 4 out of 10 African Americans report having been "profiled" by the police, and even a majority of white Americans believe that the problem is widespread (Gallup Organization, 1999).[2]

Research suggests that police behavior varies by ecological or neighborhood context (Klinger, 1997). That is, disparate treatment by the police may not be the product of race alone—the racial *and* class composition of a neighborhood influences police behavior and citizens' perceptions of that behavior (Alpert & Dunham, 1988; Smith, Graham, & Adams, 1991; Weitzer, 2000). Weitzer (1999) found that the class composition of a neighborhood can have a positive impact on police-citizen relations, for instance, between middle-class African Americans and the police in a middle-class African American neighborhood. Neighborhood racial composition can also have a negative effect when African American middle-class citizens are outside their neighborhood and in a predominantly white area (Weitzer, 2000). Williams and Murphy (1990) noted that modern police patrol had its origins in southern slave patrols, which legally sanctioned the routine monitoring of all blacks, not just slaves.[3] That current police practice may function in the same way is not lost on many African Americans (Feagin, 1991; Walker, 1997; Weitzer & Tuch, 1999), reinforcing the perception in the African

---

[1] However, in this survey, 75% of African Americans who were stopped reported that the police had a legitimate reason for the stops, and 82% reported that the police behaved properly during the stops. By comparison, whites were more likely to report that the police had a legitimate reason to stop them (86%) and behaved properly (91%).

[2] While whites acknowledge the existence of profiling, they do not necessarily oppose the practice. Weitzer (2000) found that white middle-class respondents justified the racially disparate treatment of African Americans as rational discrimination, citing stereotypical beliefs about the criminality, dangerousness, and disproportionate representation of African Americans in the criminal justice system.

[3] Research on discriminatory behavior toward African Americans by the police has a long and somewhat controversial history (Mann, 1993; Weitzer, 1996). Some studies have suggested bias (e.g., Brown, 1981; Chambliss, 1994), while others have argued that the offender's demeanor, criminal history, and/or seriousness of the instant offense accounts for police decision making that produces higher rates of arrests for minorities (Black, 1971; Black & Reiss, 1967; c.f., Smith & Visher, 1981; Smith, Visher, & Davidson, 1984).

American "collective consciousness" (DuBois, 1903/1989; Rawls, 2000) that the police serve an oppressive function.

In this article, we present data that reveal an ecological dimension to racial profiling. African Americans are subject to disproportionate *surveillance* and *stopping* by the police when they drive through white areas of the community under study. Furthermore, profiling significantly increases as African Americans move farther from stereotypically "black" communities and into wealthier, whiter areas: a phenomenon we call the *race-and-place* effect. Being an African American driver in a whiter area has more negative consequences than being an African American driver in a blacker area of the same community.

RACE AND PLACE

Police conceptions of place constitute a vital part of police work—orienting officers toward physical and social surroundings. As Gieryn (2000, pp. 466-467) observed:

> Place is, at once, the building, streets, monuments and open spaces assembled at a certain geographic spot *and* actor's interpretations, representations and identifications. Both domains, the material and the interpretive, the physical and the semiotic, work autonomously and in a mutually dependent way.

Police officers develop and use an intricate knowledge of place: "area knowledge" (Bittner, 1970), "territorial knowledge" (Brown, 1981; Rubenstein, 1973), and knowledge of "hot spots" (Sherman, 1989). Conceptions of place and the people who occupy places are critically linked to the police assessment of moral character (Sacks, 1972). A patrol officer's sector assignment (place) is not simply a geographic designation; it is the territory over which the officer exerts jurisdictional claims about acceptable and unacceptable behavior (Manning, 1997; VanMaanen, 1974).

Police conceptions of place do not exist in a social vacuum. The police orient toward place in ways that are shared by the community, yet framed by their occupational and professional demands and experiences (Alpert & Dunham, 1988; Brown, 1981). That police attitudes reflect the community (Banton, 1964; Brown, 1981; Reiss, 1971) is not merely a truism, but a feature of the occupational character of police work. By its very nature, police work is divisive and reflects the prejudices of the community and individual officers (Bittner, 1970; Matson & Duncombe, 1992). It is those citizens they must satisfy. Writing about the differential treatment of minorities, Bittner (1970, pp. 9-10) observed that in treating a poor African American differently from an affluent white person,

the policeman [is not] merely expressing personal or institutional prejudice by according the two characters differential treatment. Public expectations insidiously instruct
him to reckon with these "factors." . . . Indeed, the differential treatment they accord them reflects only the distribution of esteem, credit and desserts in society at large.

For the police, race is strongly tied to their conception of place.
Officers know which communities are whiter, blacker (or more minority), or some combination of the two and where in their own
community racial, ethnic, and class composition differ (Brown,
1981). Such "commonsense geography" is a resource for constructing the meaning of "place." Officers develop "typifications" of vehicles, persons, and spaces on the basis of their experience (Sacks,
1972; VanMaanen, 1978). These form the background expectancies
against which typifications of race and place are produced in the
lived, embodied experience of patrol work. They include assumptions and expectations about the criminality of African Americans.

Social psychological studies provide evidence that the police,
when compared to nonpolice, apply a "cognitive schema" that views
the ambiguous behaviors of African Americans as suspicious and
potentially criminal (Ruby & Brigham, 1996; Vrij, 1993). Indeed,
officers are acutely—though uncritically—aware that official statistics show that African Americans are disproportionately represented as offenders throughout the criminal justice process. The
police often associate an imagined propensity toward criminality
with blackness, and hence many police officers (Cleary, 2000) and
citizens (Weitzer, 1999) rationalize the profiling of African Americans as "good police work" that is likely to be productive (e.g., produce arrests). The practice of racial profiling is inextricably tied not
only to race, but to officers' conceptions of place, of what *should* typically occur in an area and *who belongs*, as well as *where they
belong*.

The linkage of race and place does not evolve within police departments without tacit or explicit community support. For example, research on social threats has demonstrated that communities
respond to the greater residential presence of minorities by increasing police expenditures (P. Jackson, 1989, 1992; Liska, 1992). Community support is also reflected in gatekeeping practices that have
produced patterns of residential segregation of African Americans
that are deeply entrenched throughout the United States (Alba &
Logan, 1993; Darden & Kamel, 2000; Massey & Denton, 1993). Although patterns of residential segregation have changed over the
past 30 years—statistics show that 1 in 3 African Americans now
live in suburbs—American suburbs are still predominantly white

(Baldassare, 1992; Thernstrom & Thernstrom, 1997). While community members, real estate agents, and lending institutions are important gatekeepers at strategic points in maintaining or changing a community's racial composition (Gotham, 1998; Massey & Denton, 1993; Pearce, 1979), the everyday monitoring of community boundaries is the responsibility of the police. Indeed, citizens expect the police to protect them from minority outsiders (Weitzer, 1999).[4]

Therefore, we consider racial profiling to be a practice embedded within the police organizational context and emphasize its relationship to the larger societal context from which discrimination, whether intentional or unintentional, emanates (Feagin & Eckberg, 1980). Profiling, viewed this way, is a form of *side-effect institutional discrimination* that "involves practices in one institutional or organizational arena that have an adverse impact because they are linked to intentionally discriminatory practices in another" (Feagin & Eckberg, 1980, p. 13). Specifically, profiling African Americans is linked to the larger context of the community under study, which, like many American communities, is residentially segregated and whose citizens fear African Americans and what "they" symbolize (i.e., danger, criminality, property devaluation). In short, we propose that underlying the police practice of racial profiling is the contested preservation of *place*.

RACIAL PROFILING

Racial profiling is typically defined as the police use of race as the *sole* basis for initiating law enforcement activity (e.g., stopping, searching, and detaining a person) (Ramirez, McDevitt, and Farrell, 2000). By this definition, for an action to constitute racial profiling, the officer's motivation or intent to discriminate by race must be demonstrable. It is extremely difficult to prove racial profiling, particularly in cases involving traffic offenses, which the Supreme Court has ruled can be used as a pretext for investigating other offenses (Abramovsky & Edelstein, 2000; Harris, 1997). Ramirez et al. (2000. p. 3) defined racial profiling more broadly as

> any police initiated action that relies on the race, ethnicity
> or national origin *rather than the behavior* of an individual

---

4 Community support for police protecting community boundaries can be quite explicit. A *Detroit Free Press* analysis of ticketing practices in a predominantly white suburb found that African American drivers from Detroit were disproportionately ticketed. At the next city council meeting, "'keep it up' was the phrase enthusiastically announced . . . by residents and council members alike . . . [in] phone calls to city leaders, the police department and the Free Press, about 100 Harper Woods residents have defended the department's ticketing practices, outweighing critics more than 5-1" ("Harper Woods Supports Its Cops," 2000, p. 7).

404   RACE AND PLACE

or information that leads the police to a particular individual who has been identified as being, or having been, engaged in criminal activity." [italics added]

Justification for police action requires the presence of "suspicious"
behavior or law enforcement information that leads the police reasonably to conclude that a specific person is engaged in or is about
to engage in criminal behavior.

Obviously, racial profiling can occur in contexts other than
driving—while walking, bicycling, taking a bus, boarding a plane,
and moving through customs (Ahmed & Rezmovic, 2001; Cole,
1999; Russell, 1998). However, profiling in the context of driving—
the focus of this research—has drawn the most public attention.
The reasons for this focus reflect important structural changes in
American society related to the automobile's impact on daily life,
combined with law enforcement tactics and legal rulings that grew
from the U.S. preoccupation with the war on drugs.

First, the growth of the automobile as the primary mode of
transport, coupled with the decline of rail transport, led to an increase of vehicles on roadways and the broader ecological distribution of persons to places (Felson, 1998; Hawley, 1971; Kay, 1997).
Thus, private vehicles, subject to constitutional protections of private property, have become the primary means of transporting persons and goods (legal and illegal) that are not always visible to the
police.

Second, the shift of the economy—white-collar and light industrial work, shopping, and leisure venues—from urban to suburban
locations (K. T. Jackson, 1985; Kowinski, 1985; Ward, 1994) has
necessarily brought minorities into traditionally white areas, although not, for the most part, to reside there.

Third, in the 1980s, the war on drugs became the primary concern of law enforcement, and with it came important court decisions
limiting constitutional protections against unreasonable search and
seizure (Skolnick, 1994). The "result-oriented" focus of this "war"
created an atmosphere in which stereotypes about African Americans' drug use and drug dealing contributed to disproportionate police enforcement of drug laws against African Americans (Allen-
Bell, 1997; Currie, 1993), despite research that found that drug use
among African Americans is proportionate to their number in the
general population (Miller, 1996; the Sentencing Project, 1999).

The most significant case involving the automobile was the
1996 U.S. Supreme Court decision in *Whren vs. the United States*
(hereafter *Whren*). The focus on racial profiling in traffic stops
emerged in numerous legal analyses of *Whren*, most notably by
Harris (1997). Although *Whren* affirmed that racially motivated

stops are unconstitutional, it nonetheless permitted the police to use the pretext of a traffic violation to stop a vehicle and investigate (i.e., search and seize evidence) for possible criminal behavior without meeting the standard of reasonable suspicion or probable cause for that specific offense. Thus, a traffic violation is a legitimate pretext for the officer's "real" motivation (i.e., trying to find evidence of some crime; conducting a fishing expedition; or, worse, harassing the driver). Harris argued that discretionary enforcement and harassment using traffic offenses had disproportionately fallen upon minorities before *Whren* and that this disparity would increase after this decision. Thus, in 1997, the focus on "driving while black" received considerable national attention among legal and social science scholars, the mass media, and federal and state legislatures.[5]

While most researchers agree that racial profiling is a problem, the extent of profiling is essentially unknown and difficult to measure (Police Executive Research Forum, 2001; U.S. Bureau of Justice Statistics, 2001; U.S. General Accounting Office, GAO, 2000). As lawmakers debate methods of reducing racial profiling, researchers attempt to measure the extent of the practice and understand its complexities. Most research to date has compared proxy measures of roadway usage (e.g., residential racial composition) with the recorded stops of motorists using traffic tickets issued or stop events recorded in written patrol logs. This procedure seems logical because a statistical database can be derived from these police records (e.g., traffic tickets and patrol logs).

However, measuring the extent of stops, let alone *who* the police stop, on the basis of tickets and log entries is problematic because a significant portion of patrol activity—including traffic stops and field interrogations—is never recorded (Cooney, 1997; Meehan, 1986, 2000; U.S. Commission on Civil Rights, 2000; Weiss & Freels, 1996). This creates an important source of measurement error for research that depends on records created by officers.

More important, studies based on written records of stops, interrogations, or searches overlook a crucial step in the decision-making process: The police use their in-car computers to surveil the population of drivers.[6] Such surveillance may or may not result in a

---

[5] Additional support for 1997 as a watershed year is reflected in our Lexus-Nexus database search using the keywords "racial profiling" and "driving while black." Prior to 1994, these topics are not mentioned in law reviews, wire services, newspaper articles, and radio and television broadcasts. Between 1994 and 1996, a total of 15 articles or stories were about these topics. From 1997 to 2000, the total number of articles or stories increased exponentially each year—from 45 in 1997 to 14,804 in 2000. Also, federal legislation requiring mandatory reporting of data on traffic stops was also introduced in 1997.

[6] The police do not need any particular reason or level of suspicion to conduct a query. For example, Illinois courts have upheld the random running of license plates, ruling that a plate is a public record, not a private one. Current proposals

stop—either recorded or not recorded. However, the in-car computer leaves an electronic trail of officers' query behavior that *can* be used to examine this police activity. This heretofore unexamined, technologically based, aspect of profiling behavior provides a record of who the police surveil, when and where they surveil, and what information is requested.

In-car computers (called Mobile Data Terminals, or MDTs) give police officers immediate access to national (the FBI's National Crime Information Computer), state (Department of Motor Vehicles, state police), and local databases from their patrol cars. Depending on the type of query, information on the vehicle and the driver's (or passenger's) criminal and traffic-violation history are available to determine if a car is stolen or the person has outstanding arrest warrants. If a person is on probation or parole, the conditions are also provided (e.g., no driving except to and from work).

Prior to computers in patrol cars, officers were dependent upon radio communication with the dispatcher who conducted a record check for them. Research suggests this practice was also influenced by race, social class, and place considerations (Brown, 1981; Muir, 1977; Skolnick, 1994). However, the MDT enhances an officer's autonomy by eliminating the dispatcher in this record-checking process—making the officer's surveillance activity virtually invisible to coworkers, supervisors, and dispatchers (Meehan, 1998).[7] The use of computer technology in this capacity illustrates what Marx (1988, p. 2) called the *new surveillance*, whereby "the state's power to seek out violations, even without specific grounds for suspicion, has been enhanced." Marx observed that the new surveillance fosters more "proactive, diffuse, and open-ended investigations of individuals, groups, and property" (pp. 9-10). Computer technology figures prominently in this process (see also Gordon, 1990; Lyon,

---

argue that a higher standard, such as probable cause, should be required to prevent unwarranted police access to information on drivers (see Amirante, 1997; Cedres, 1997; Prime, 1996).

[7] The fact that these computer records exist and can be analyzed may appear to contradict the claim that computer usage increases an officer's autonomy and invisibility. While the computer trail of officers' computer *queries* to various databases does exist, to date, it has not been systematically used by the police department under study or other departments routinely to monitor officers' behavior. It is common practice for departments to report that officers' *car-to car* computer communications—not officers' *queries* of databases—are routinely monitored by supervisors, particularly in the aftermath of the Christopher Commission's investigation of the Rodney King beating. Indeed, officers orient to this possible monitoring even though, in the department under study, supervisory review is infrequent and undertaken only when some "problem" has arisen with a specific officer (e.g., a female dispatcher complains that a male officer is "hitting" on her). Query behavior is not monitored, partly because one would need to create a merged database from various records (MDT queries, patrol logs, and dispatcher records) and have an accurate estimate of roadway composition like we undertook to analyze proactive surveillance behavior. Generally, departments have not constructed such databases, nor have they conceived of the need to do so.

1994). Marx also noted that "computers qualitatively alter the nature of surveillance—routinizing, broadening, and deepening it. Organizational memories are extended over time and across space" (p. 208). The new surveillance is virtually invisible, hard to evade, and subject to database error,[8] or worse—manipulation (Marx, 1988).

Another limitation of research on profiling is that the organizational and ecological contexts studied have concentrated on specialized units, such as drug enforcement teams, or traffic units that are responsible for patrolling specific stretches of highway, rather than on patrol officers in suburban communities.[9] African Americans report that when they are driving through suburban communities or areas outside where they live, they are profiled because they are presumed to be "out of place" (Ramirez et al., 2000). This suggests an ecological distribution to the profiling experience *and* to profiling behavior by suburban police—a logical assumption given that police behavior varies by ecological and neighborhood context (Alpert & Dunham, 1988; Klinger, 1997).

To our knowledge, no study of racial profiling has focused on an *entire* suburban police department, which, in addition to traffic duties, engages in delivering a broad range of police services. If racial profiling is a significant and consistent experience of African Americans traveling in suburban areas, it should be broadly reflected in the practices of a whole department. Furthermore, if there is a place effect, it can be demonstrated only by comparing police behavior in different areas of the same community.

DESCRIPTION OF THE DATA

Data were collected from a medium-sized suburban police department with over 100 sworn officers. This department has no minorities and few women. The city has over 75,000 residents, can be characterized as blue collar and predominantly white (98%), and

---

[8] Database error is particularly serious, since evidence suggests that the "benefit of the doubt" in questionable circumstances is usually given to the computer. Gordon (1990, p. 73) reported that fewer than half the 50 states require updating criminal history files to include dismissals and acquittals and that only 13 states require random audits to ensure accuracy. Yet, all the states require the entry of arrests. Given that African Americans are more likely to be released after arrest without prosecution (Petersillia, 1983), database errors specifically disadvantage them. Zonderman (1990, pp. 164-165) also found that about 11% of arrest warrants in the FBI database had either been cleared, were inaccurate, or invalid and that 7,000 reports of stolen cars and license plates were errors.

[9] For example, studies of the New Jersey State Police and the sheriffs' departments in Florida and Maryland have focused on agencies whose primary function is traffic enforcement on major highways or roads that are considered drug-transport corridors (Harris, 1997; Verniero, 1999). Some research has examined precinct-level behavior in cities like Philadelphia (GAO, 2000) and New York City (U.S. Commission on Civil Rights, 2000). But this research cannot address the suburban racial profiling experience of being out of place.

has a mix of industrial and technological industries. It is among the larger cities in the state and shares one border with a city of predominately African American residents (more than 75%), hereafter called "Black City."[10] Thus, these two communities reflect the pattern of racially segregated communities that is found throughout the United States.

There is considerable variation as one travels through the community, and it is reflected in the pattern of patrol assignments. Patrol assignments use eight sector designations that we labeled A–H, which correspond to geographic boundaries that the officers are responsible for patrolling. Sectors are not all equal in size, but are configured according to levels of crime and citizens' calls for police service. Each of the border sectors (A–D), which constitute about one-third of the square mileage in this community, cover smaller areas because they are densely populated, generate the most calls for service, and have the highest rates of reported property and violent crimes.

The two middle sectors (E–F) and the farthest sectors (G–H) from the border are equal in size and cover one-third of the city each. They contain larger property lots with wealthier residents and businesses. These sectors have less population density, fewer calls for police service, and less reported violent and property crimes. Thus, officers in these sectors (E–F, G–H) have more space to patrol and fewer calls for service.

We used both qualitative and quantitative data in our analysis. In fact, our initial interest in the MDT as an investigative and surveillance tool had its origin in field observations and discussions of this practice with officers in this (and one other) department. Field research conducted over four years (1996–99) prior to the collection of the MDT and roadway data reported here, included extensive ride-alongs[11] with patrol officers (240 hours) and 25 interviews at all levels of the command staff (from the chief to sergeants) and specialized units (e.g., detective bureau, internal affairs). Knowledge of police practices in the field and how different records of these practices are constructed by officers and stored electronically informed the design of two different and unique quantitative data sets: an MDT query database and data from our Roadway Observation Study.

---

[10] We selectively altered aspects of the community and the description of the department to preserve anonymity.

[11] During ride-alongs, a semistructured interview about current information technology was used and observations were made of how the officers used information technology (e.g., in-car computers and cameras) during their patrols. Field notes were written upon leaving the setting.

MDT Query Database

When officers conduct an MDT query, the information they request and receive is preserved electronically. Officers can receive information about a vehicle (e.g., year, make, and model; the name and address of the registered owner; and the status of the vehicle—stolen or unregistered) or of an individual (e.g., criminal career history, outstanding warrants, and probation/parole restrictions). In our data set, each officer's query was compared with subsequent queries the officer made to construct a query's event history. For example, when a plate query (the most common type of query) was processed and the name of the vehicle's owner was subsequently queried for a criminal career history, these queries were coded as continuations of the first query event. The MDT also records which officer is making the query, his or her patrol assignment (place), and time of query. Combining this query information with patrol officers' logs and police dispatchers' records, we could determine an outcome for each query. In sum, we could correlate information about the driver with the place of the query, time of day, officer's characteristics (i.e., age, years of experience on the force, and use of the computer) and outcome of the query.

Data on race are not available in the information the police receive from MDT queries.[12] Thus, we used a proxy measure, like the police do when they use knowledge of community composition to link race with place. Given distinct patterns of residential segregation in the metropolitan area we studied, we assigned a racial identity (African American, white, or other) for each driver, by inference, using the residence of the vehicle owner. A driver was coded as white if the vehicle owner lived in a community whose population was 97% or more white. A driver was coded as African American if the vehicle owner lived in a community whose population was 75% or more African American. The remaining drivers who did not meet either 97% white or > 75% African American residence thresholds were not included in the analysis of race.

This approach assumes (1) that the registered vehicle owner is usually driving the car and (2) that when owners lend their vehicles, they usually do so to family members or friends who reside in the same community and/or are most likely to be the same race. According to our definition, the MDT data indicated that 27% of the drivers (owners) were African American and 73% were white: That

---

12 Race is not even included for a query about an operator's license. Only criminal career history (CCH) queries provide information on race, but this information is usually incomplete. In our data, only 154 (4%) of the CCH queries identified the person's race. Furthermore, most persons do not have criminal records.

is, they lived in communities meeting our definitions of primarily white or primarily African American.

Although this approach leaves room for error, it is in the direction of *undercounting* African Americans. We tested this assumption by comparing race as assigned by residence (a variable we call "resrace") to the actual race observed in three related data sets. In the pilot test of the Roadway Observation protocol, we recorded the license plates, race, and gender of 526 randomly selected drivers. Then, using all African American drivers observed ($N = 76$) and a random sample of the 450 white drivers observed ($N = 78$), the police department conducted a computerized search of those plates similar to what officers do with an MDT. We also compared the residence recorded for all tickets ($N = 339$) and arrests ($N = 258$) during the two weeks of our study with the race recorded by the officer on tickets and arrest reports. In these data sets, the race of the driver or the ticketed or arrested person was known (or, at least, observed and recorded by someone), not merely inferred.

Table 1 compares race as observed to race as inferred (resrace) for each data set. It indicates that resrace reliably predicts race, as observed for both whites and African Americans, across each data set. For example, resrace predicts observed African American drivers 100% of the time in the Roadway Observation pilot data, 92% of the time in the ticket data, and 89% of the time in the arrest data. While there is error because some whites may live in a predominantly African American community and be incorrectly coded as African American and some African Americans may live in a predominantly white community and be incorrectly coded as white, the error is in the direction of undercounting African American drivers. The rate of true positives for African Americans is consistently greater than our assumption of 75%. If anything, African Americans are more likely to be incorrectly coded as white using resrace. Thus, the rate of profiling indicated in our analysis may actually be higher, but not lower, than reported. Furthermore, across each data set, race as assigned by residence is positively and highly correlated with race as observed. We interpret this finding as confirmation of the high degree of residential segregation in the study region. In general, we conclude that, for the purpose of measuring racial profiling of African American drivers, residence reliably serves as a proxy for race.

The MDT query database consists of all 5,604 MDT queries made by 111 patrol officers working during seven days (24-hour periods) spanning two weeks in April 2000. In this article, we analyze the 3,716 queries that occurred in *proactive* time windows during which, we argue, officers have more discretion whether to query the

Table 1. Percentage of Drivers Predicted to Be African American and White Using Residence (Resrace) Who Are Actually African American and White Using Roadway Observations,[a] Ticket,[b] and Arrest Data[c]

	RESRACE PREDICTS WHITE		RESRACE PREDICTS AFRICAN AMERICAN	
WHITE	ROADWAY	82 (*N* = 59)	ROADWAY	0 (*N* = 0)
	TICKET	98 (*N* = 275)	TICKET	8 (*N* = 5)
	ARREST	93 (*N* = 173)	ARREST	11 (*N* = 8)
	True Positive: % of Time Resrace Predicts a White as a White Using Residence		False Positive: % of Time Resrace Predicts a White as an African American Using Residence	
AFRICAN AMERICAN	ROADWAY	18 (*N* = 13)	ROADWAY	100 (*N* = 47)
	TICKET	2 (*N* = 5)	TICKET	92 (*N* = 54)
	ARREST	7 (*N* = 14)	ARREST	89 (*N* = 63)
	False Positive: % of Time Resrace Predicts an African American as a White Using Residence		True Positive: % of Time Resrace Predicts an African American as an African American Using Residence	

[a] All African Americans and a random sample of whites observed in the Roadway Pilot Study (*n* = 119). Correlation of resrace and race = .80, *p* < .001 (two-tailed test).
[b] All tickets issued during the study period in which race was identified (*N* = 339). Correlation of resrace and race = .90, *p* < .001 (two-tailed test).
[c] All arrests during the study period in which race was identified (*N* = 258). Correlation of resrace and race = .80, *p* < .001 (two-tailed test).

MDT. That is, we eliminated all reactive events (and queries) in which the officer was either required, or was more likely, to run a plate or a name (e.g., traffic accidents; calls for service, such as "suspicious vehicles"; or when an arrest was made).[13] Hence, the analysis focuses on the queries that officers *chose* to initiate when they were not engaged in reactive work.

Furthermore, to analyze officers' "pure" surveillance activities, we excluded proactive queries associated with recorded police stops from the analysis. We assumed that when officers decided to record a stop, these proactive events were *more likely* to have been based on an observed violation or suspected illegal activity that could be later justified if necessary. From our perspective, the question is to what extent do police act solely on the basis of race? When officers ran plates and did not stop drivers, we assumed that they did not observe violations that *would have* warranted stops. Therefore, if

---

[13] For this seven-day period, officers made 5,604 queries, of which 3,963 were first queries. Of the 3,963 first queries, 2,673 (67%) were proactive. These 2,673 proactive queries resulted in an additional 1,043 follow-up queries that originated from the first proactive queries. Thus, the total number of proactive queries was 3,716. Our analysis focuses on the 2,673 first proactive queries. The data from the 1,043 proactive follow-up queries were included as a part of the record of the first queries.

significantly more queries *not* related to stops involved African Americans than whites, we had some confidence that those queries were influenced by race. If race is a factor in query behavior, we would also conclude that it is a factor in stops. By focusing on queries that did not result in stops, however, we controlled for possible legal justifications for actions.Thus, we examined the proactive surveillance behavior (measured by queries) of officers who, for the record, did not record stops.

Using an MDT query database offers two advantages. First, officers make more queries than stops, and query behavior is far more prevalent than recorded stops. For example, during these seven days, 3,716 proactive queries were made by 111 officers. By contrast, on the same days, only 333 recorded traffic stops were made by 73 of these officers.[14] Only 9% of the 3,716 proactive queries were related to recorded stops. Thus, there was more query behavior than recorded stops to analyze.

Second, focusing on query behavior uses the "informating" capacity of computers, which record police actions automatically, rather than relying on the memories or note-taking/reporting skills of officers, drivers, or other observers. Zuboff (1987, p. 9) noted that unlike earlier machine technologies that substituted for human labor, "the devices that automate by translating information into action also register data about those automated activities, thus generating new streams of information." Thus, the MDT not only automates the processing of queries, it records that processing as an *action of the user*. As such, MDT technology is a more consistent recorder of police surveillance behavior than are recorded stops.

Roadway Observation Data

On the same seven days during this two-week period, we conducted a rolling Roadway Observation Study in this community. Racial profiling can be assessed reliably only if one compares police data with the racial composition of drivers who are actually using the roadways.[15] Our decision to use a rolling method versus observation of intersections was based on several factors. First, officers typically do not remain in one location for an extended time during their shifts; they roam their sectors. Thus, our observation method

---

[14] We used officers' logs and dispatchers' records to identify all *recorded* traffic stops and coded outcomes reported on the logs (i.e., warn, issue ticket, arrest). These data do not reflect the *actual* number of traffic stops because officers do not record all stops in their logs or call them into the dispatcher who records stops in the dispatch database.

[15] In addition to roadway composition, some have argued that comparable rates of violators and the seriousness of violations are necessary to prove profiling (U.S. Bureau of Justice Statistics, 2001, p. 15). However, no satisfactory method of ascertaining this rate has been agreed upon (GAO, 2000, p. 2).

mimics patrol practice. Second, given the size of the city, coverage of the 50 major intersections, or even sampling them, was impractical because of the lack of personnel. Third, a rolling observation car is less obtrusive to both the citizenry and the police.

Vehicles were sampled on the 15 major roads that run north to south and east to west in this community. A two-person team in an observation car was randomly assigned one of eight designated travel routes (called sorties) that they drove for three-hour time windows. Observation time windows spanned 24 hours a day excluding 3 a.m. to 6 a.m. because of the low traffic volume. Each sortie entailed citywide coverage, and the starting points were randomly chosen.

Using a stopwatch and a tape recorder, an observer recorded information on randomly selected passenger vehicles, vans, and trucks within one-to-three car lengths of the observation vehicle at 30-second intervals. Vehicles already recorded, commercial vehicles, and buses were excluded. Each observation recorded the following data: sortie observation number, license plate, the driver's race (African American, not African American) and gender, the observation location (i.e., main street and cross streets), the target position (e.g., front left) and the time of the observation.

The observer and driver had 60 seconds to observe and record this information. Any information not obtained within 60 seconds was noted (e.g., unable to determine race). If no target vehicle was available at the 30-second interval, this observation was recorded as "no target vehicle available," and the time and location were noted.

A total of 35 sorties, spanning 105 hours, yielded 6,269 observations of this community's roadways. A target vehicle was available in 61% ($n = 3,840$) of the observations; thus no target vehicle was available, within one to three car lengths, in 39% ($n = 2,429$) of the observations. The race and gender composition of drivers using these roadways was calculated from these 3,840 observations and mapped according to time and location.

The analysis compared the rates at which African American and white drivers were the objects of officers' proactive MDT query behavior with the racial composition of drivers on the roadway during the same seven-day period. Our goal was to answer two questions: (1) Do police officers proactively surveil African American drivers at a rate that is significantly higher than their proportion of the actual population of drivers on the road? and (2) Does police behavior vary by place?

RACE AND PLACE MATTER

To determine whether African Americans and whites are equally likely to have proactive MDT queries made about their vehicle or person, we compared the racial composition of the roadway to the racial composition of proactive police queries. Tables 2 and 3 show that the race and gender composition of the roadways varies by place and time. African American drivers tend to use roads closer to the border of Black City and are slightly more likely to drive at night (12 a.m.–8 a.m.) and on weekends. The distribution of men (60%) and women (40%) on the roadway remains relatively stable across place and time except that women are less likely to drive after midnight.[16]

Table 2. Race and Gender of Drivers Observed by Place: Patrol Sector and Type of Street (percentages; numbers in parentheses)

	African American			White		
	Male	Female	Total	Male	Female	Total
Grand Mean	7 (269)	6 (238)	13 (507)	53 (1,981)	34 (1,274)	87 (3,261)
Patrol Sector						
Borders Black City						
A	11 (22)	12 (25)	23 (47)	50 (100)	27 (55)	77 (155)
B	15 (31)	8 (18)	23 (49)	54 (114)	23 (50)	77 (164)
C	12 (56)	14 (64)	26 (100)	48 (216)	26 (118)	74 (334)
D	12 (49)	10 (41)	22 (90)	48 (198)	30 (123)	78 (321)
Middle sectors						
E	6 (38)	6 (38)	12 (76)	54 (353)	34 (224)	88 (577)
F	5 (29)	3 (19)	8 (48)	55 (349)	38 (241)	92 (590)
Farthest from						
Black City						
G	4 (27)	2 (15)	7 (42)	57 (346)	36 (221)	93 (567)
H	3 (17)	3 (18)	6 (35)	52 (305)	42 (242)	94 (547)
Type of Street						
Borders Black City	26 (65)	24 (59)	49 (124)	39 (97)	12 (30)	51 (127)
Interior streets	6 (193)	5 (148)	11 (341)	53 (1,623)	35 (1070)	89 (2693)
Farthest border—						
Black City	2 (3)	1 (2)	3 (5)	59 (92)	37 (92)	97 (150)

Source: Data from the Roadway Observation Study: Drivers (N = 3,840) observed during 35 sorties on 7 days over a 14-day period in April 2000.

Overall, African Americans constitute 13% of the drivers on the roadways but only less than 3% of the residential population. Clearly, more African Americans are employed in or pass through

---

[16] Discussions of racial profiling generally gloss over the issue of gender. Studies of racial discrimination typically focus on the overrepresentation of African American men in the system. However, recent studies have suggested that the war on drugs has had a disproportionate impact on African American women (Sentencing Project, 1999). In our data, women made up 40% of the drivers on the road, and their distribution was uniform throughout the city. White women used interior roads and roads farthest from the Black City border, whereas African American women use roads closer to the Black City border. Our analysis indicates that where gender differences occur, it is African American women who are the target of MDT queries.

Table 3.   Race and Gender of Drivers Observed by Time: Police Shift and Type of Day (percentages; numbers in parentheses)

	African American			White		
	Male	Female	Total	Male	Female	Total
Grand Mean	7 (269)	6 (238)	13 (507)	53 (1,981)	34 (1,274)	87 (3,261)
Police Shift						
Midnights						
(12–8 a.m.)	8 (41)	7 (37)	16 (78)	58 (288)	26 (131)	84 (419)
Days						
(8 a.m.–4 p.m.)	6 (91)	7 (111)	13 (202)	52 (799)	34 (525)	87 (1,324)
Afternoons						
(4 p.m.–12 a.m.)	8 (137)	5 (90)	13 (227)	51 (894)	36 (618)	87 (1512)
Type of Day						
Weekdays	7 (184)	6 (167)	13 (351)	53 (1,456)	34 (951)	87 (2407)
Weekends	8 (85)	7 (71)	16 (156)	52 (525)	32 (323)	84 (848)

Source: Data from the Road Observation Study: Drivers (N = 3,840) observed during 35 sorties on 7 days over a 14-day period in April 2000.

this city than reside there. However, the distribution of African American drivers on these roadways is not a uniform 13% throughout the city.

Sectors (A–D), which border Black City, contain the largest percentage of African American drivers (an overall average of 24%). (See Table 4.) As one moves to the middle sectors (E–F) and sectors (G–H) farthest from Black City, there are significantly fewer African Americans driving these roads. Each border sector (A–D) includes the border road between this city and Black City: About half (49%) the drivers on this border road are African American, whereas the distribution of African Americans on other city border roads, which adjoin predominantly white communities, is much lower. As one compares this border road to the interior roads, one sees that the proportion of African American drivers drops precipitously to an average of 11% overall for interior roadways. The border-sector pattern is dramatically magnified when one compares the Black City border road with the road farthest from this border, where African American drivers constitute only 3% of the drivers.

Overall, a comparison of the roadway data to the MDT data indicates that the most significant finding is the race variable: 13% of the drivers were African American, whereas 27% of all proactive police queries were about African American drivers. Whites, who constituted 87% of the drivers, made up only 73% of the proactive police queries. In other words, if one assumes that the percentage of African American and white drivers on the road should be the same as the percentage of African American and white drivers queried, the ratios in Table 4 should be at or near 1:1. However, this is clearly not the case: African American drivers are twice as likely as are white drivers to be queried (2.1 versus 0.8).

Table 4. Racial Composition of Drivers on the Roadways Compared to Proactive Mobile Data Terminal (MDT) Queries by Individual Patrol Sectors (percentages; numbers in parentheses)

	African American			White		
	Drivers	Queries	D-Q Ratio[a]	Drivers	Queries	D-Q Ratio[a]
Grand Mean	13 (507)	27 (572)	1:2.1***	87 (3,261)	73 (1,581)	1:0.8
Borders Black City						
Sector A	23 (47)	32 (115)	1:1.4***	77 (156)	68 (241)	1:0.9
Sector B	23 (49)	35 (57)	1:1.6**	77 (164)	64 (103)	1:0.8
Sector C	26 (120)	26 (99)	1:0.9	74 (335)	76 (311)	1:1.0
Sector D	22 (90)	25 (113)	1:1.1	78 (322)	75 (331)	1:1.0
Middle Sectors						
Sector E	12 (76)	28 (62)	1:2.4***	88 (579)	71 (154)	1:0.8
Sector F	8 (48)	26 (49)	1:3.3***	92 (590)	74 (141)	1:0.8
Farthest from Black City						
Sector G	7 (42)	16 (15)	1:2.0*	93 (568)	86 (95)	1:0.9
Sector H	6 (35)	22 (62)	1:3.8***	94 (547)	77 (205)	1:0.8

Source: Data on drivers based on data from the Roadway Observation Study for one week in April 2000 (N = 3,840). Data on police queries based on 3,716 proactive MDT queries made by the police during this same one-week period.
[a]D-Q ratio equals the percentage of police queries divided by the percentage of drivers and is expressed as a ratio.
*$p < .01$, **$p < .001$, ***$p < .0001$ (two-tailed tests).

This effect is not constant; it changes as African Americans move from one sector of the city to another. In general, African Americans who are traveling in three of the four sectors (A, B, and D) bordering Black City have query rates that are slightly, but significantly, higher than their number in the driver population. Only in Sector C is the ratio slightly less than 1:1. Given that these sectors include the largest percentage of African American drivers on the roadways, this finding requires an explanation.

Border streets between poorer-wealthier or blacker-whiter communities in police departments are often referred to as "demilitarized" or "combat" zones. Because there are more African American drivers in these sectors, one might predict a higher rate of African American queries. But here, the reverse is the case. In all four border sectors, the police operate with a concept of who belongs in this zone. African American drivers are not considered out of place and receive slightly more queries than do whites.

Within border sectors, Sector C stands out for the police. It generates the highest load of calls and official crime rates in the city. Census data show that it contains the greatest concentration of poor whites, with lower income and educational levels compared to other parts of the city. In short, in this sector, police officers deal with the city's *white criminal element*. While the differences are small, the lowest rates of African American queries and the highest rates of white queries are found here. Officers' concern in this area is not the presence of African Americans but, rather, the activity of whites. Thus, a different conception of race and place operates here: Poor whites in this place (Sector C) require more watching.

As African American drivers move from these border sectors to the farthest sectors of this white community, their chances of being the subject of a query increase dramatically. African Americans who travel in Sectors F and H, which are adjacent and contain the largest pockets of wealthier white neighborhoods, have query rates that are 325% and 383% greater than their number in the driver population. To put this finding in perspective, to achieve such high query rates with fewer African American drivers on these road-ways, officers must be "hunting" for, or clearly noticing, African American drivers in these sectors. By comparison, whites have about the same chance of being the subject of a query *throughout* the whole city.

If surveillance behavior varies by ecological context, does stop behavior display a similar pattern? Table 5 compares the recorded stops of African American persons by place. The African American stop rates of officers in the nonborder sectors are three times greater than African American drivers on these roads. African American drivers are not only surveilled because they are out of place (i.e., in whiter areas), but are also more likely to be stopped in these areas. By contrast, border-sector officers stop African Ameri-can drivers at rates equal to their number on those roadways. Thus, a race-and-place effect is also evident in the stop behavior of officers.

RACE, PLACE, AND THE "HIT" RATE

A common defense of racial profiling is the claim that African Americans are more criminal and that when the police profile by race, they engage in "rational discrimination" (Taylor & Whitney, 1999). As evidence of African Americans' criminality, this position typically cites the disproportionate number of African Americans who are arrested and incarcerated and ignores studies of discrimi-natory decision making by criminal justice officials that makes dis-proportionate "outcomes" a self-fulfilling prophecy. Furthermore, research has consistently found that targeting African Americans and other minorities does not support arguments of greater crimi-nality. For example, a review of police success rates in searches con-cluded that although the police tend to search minorities more often than whites, "Blacks and Latinos are no more likely than Whites to be in possession of narcotics or other contraband" (Ramirez et al., 2000, p. 10).

Table 5.   African American Drivers on the Roadways Compared to Recorded Stops of African Americans, by Patrol Sectors (percentages; numbers in parentheses)

	African American Drivers	African American Stops	Driver-Stop Ratio[a]
Grand Mean	13 (507)	25 (62)	1:1.9***
Borders Black City Sectors A–D	24 (306)	26 (41)	1:1.1
Middle Sectors Sectors E–F	10 (124)	32 (12)	1:3.2**
Farthest from Black City Sectors G–H	6 (77)	18 (9)	1:3.0***

Source: Data on drivers based on data from the Roadway Observation Study for one week in April 2000 ($N = 3,840$). Data on recorded stops based on 3,716 proactive MDT queries made by the police during this same one-week period.
[a] The driver-stop ratio equals the percentage of stops of African Americans divided by the percentage of African American drivers and is expressed as a ratio.
* $p<.01$, ** $p<.001$, *** $p<.0001$ (two-tailed tests).

Whether or not it has any empirical basis, many officers *believe* that querying vehicles with African Americans produces more "hits"—that is, the computer returns information indicating legal problems with the vehicles or drivers. The expectation of productivity and its attendant rewards motivate officers' behavior (Mastrofski, Ritti, & Snipes, 1994). Although there is scant empirical research on the MDT as a tool for generating hits, police officers and administrators generally believe that the MDT makes officers more effective crime fighters (c.f., Meehan, 1998; Nunn, 1994). In the police department under study, officers receive no information about their overall hit-to-query ratio to assess or challenge such beliefs.[17] However, because our data links an officer's query to a hit, we could test the claim that querying African Americans is more productive.

We restricted our analysis to the first query an officer made on a license plate. Unlike the earlier analysis, which excluded recorded stops, we *included* recorded stops to represent fairly all possible hits associated with first queries. By examining the *first query* only, we tested the officer's initial hunch or suspicion about a vehicle—it

---

[17] While officers extol the value of the MDT's crime-fighting capacity, the hit-rate question strains their belief system. Officers readily cite examples of the computer identifying a stolen vehicle or person with a warrant leading to an arrest. However, some officers, particularly supervisory personnel, complain that many MDT arrests for minor traffic violations (e.g., driving with a suspended license) pad an officer's productivity statistics, increase overtime opportunities, and that officers waste time going after these "easy" arrests and miss opportunities to catch serious criminals. Many older officers complain that the computer deskills younger officers in this regard (Meehan, 1998). Nonetheless, officers maintain the belief that the computer enhances their detection abilities.

is closest to testing the value of pure surveillance. Furthermore, we included first queries only of *license plates* because the occurrence of a name or operator license as a first query in these data indicates that the officer most likely stopped the person or vehicle, even if no record was made of this stop.[18]

Table 6 indicates a hit rate of 7.2% for first queries of license plates: 144 of the 2,004 plates queried returned a hit; expired plates comprised 78% ($N = 113$) of these hits. The plates of African American drivers are more likely to return a hit than are the plates of

Table 6. Hit Rate for Officers' First Queries of License Plates ($N = 2,004$) by Border and Nonborder Sectors

	Number of Plate Queries	Number of Hits	Hit Rate[a]
All Drivers (total)	2,004	144	7.2
Border sectors A–D	1,280	83	6.4
Nonborder sectors E–H	724	61	8.4
African American Drivers (total)	541	47	8.6
Borders sectors A–D	365	35	9.6
Nonborder sectors E–H	176	12	6.8
White Drivers (total)	1,463	97	6.6
Border sectors A–D	915	48	5.2
Nonborder sectors E–H	548	49	8.9

[a]The hit rate equals the number of hits divided by the number of plate queries.

white drivers (86% versus 66%)—although this difference is not statistically significant.[19]

When we analyzed the hit rate by border and nonborder sectors, however, important differences emerged. Officers in border sectors have a higher hit rate for African Americans than do officers in nonborder sectors (9.6% versus 6.8%). The hit rate for whites in nonborder sectors is 8.9%, higher than the 6.8% hit rate for African

---

[18] This analysis assumes the officer initiated the query at the time as opposed to using information collected at some previous point in time. Nonetheless, it is possible to estimate the number of unrecorded stops. In our data, there were 333 recorded stops. Among the first queries, there were 6 operator-license and 91 name queries. These 97 queries suggest that the number of unrecorded stops was 97— bringing the total number of stops to 430. So, 23% or, about 1 in 4 stops, were not recorded by officers. This is a conservative estimate; it does not include officers who made a stop and did not use the MDT. Also, officers told us that they estimate that between 30% and 50% of all stops are not recorded.

[19] The possible hits an officer can receive from a plate query include (1) the plate is expired because the registration is not updated; (2) there is no title information recorded for the vehicle; (3) the license plate is not valid; (4) the plate is reported stolen; (5) the vehicle assigned to this plate is reported stolen; (6) the registered owner of this vehicle has a warrant for his or her arrest outstanding; (7) there is no record of this plate, indicating that the plate has not been registered for five or more years; and (8) the vehicle attached to this plate has been impounded or abandoned.

Americans. Yet, officers in nonborder sectors query African American plates at levels that are consistently higher than those of officers in border sectors. If the justification for racial profiling were African American criminality, then the lower hit rates for African Americans in nonborder areas should discourage disproportionate surveillance. The African American drivers in these whiter, nonborder sectors, who are subject to the higher levels of query surveillance, are the *least* likely to have legal problems (i.e., hits). Thus, although African American hit rates are somewhat higher overall, an analysis by place shows that *queries are the highest for African Americans where hits are the lowest*. Therefore, considerations of place, not the productivity from hits, drives the African American query rate.

THE ROLE OF MDT TECHNOLOGY IN RACIAL PROFILING

The availability of MDT technology in police cars has the obvious consequence of increasing officers' proactive surveillance via various databases. However, officers' use of MDT varies widely: Some officers use it a lot, whereas others do so only occasionally. We found that the level of MDT use was a significant predictor of higher levels of racial profiling.

We assigned officers to three groups of high, medium, and low MDT users on the basis of their average number of proactive queries. Each group accounted for one-third of all proactive queries. Twelve officers, who averaged 64.5 queries, were categorized as high users and accounted for one-third (774) of all proactive queries. A second group of 23 officers, who averaged 33.3 queries, were labeled medium users. The remaining 76 officers, labeled low users, averaged 10.3 queries and accounted for the remaining 34% of all proactive queries.

Table 7 shows the racial distribution of queries by high, medium, and low MDT users. As MDT use increased, the proportion of African American queries also increased significantly. The 12 high-MDT users accounted for 43% ($n = 219$) of all proactive African American queries. The African American query rate of these 12 high-MDT users was 1.6 times greater than the African American query rate of the 75 low-MDT users and 1.4 times greater than the 23 medium-MDT users.

Table 8 shows the percentage of African American queries of high, medium, and low MDT users by place (border versus nonborder sectors). Once again, the race-and-place effect is demonstrated. Officers patrolling in whiter areas had a higher percentage of African American queries. But the effect is also related to officers'

Table 7. Racial Distribution of Proactive Mobile Data Terminal (MDT) Queries of High-, Medium-, and Low-Level MDT Users (percentages; numbers in parentheses)

Type of MDT User	African American Queries	White Queries
Low user	26 (134)	36 (527)
Medium user	31 (160)	35 (512)
High user	43 (219)	30 (443)
Total	100 (513)	100 (1,482)

Note: $\chi^2 = 30.334$, $df = 2$, $p < .0001$.

Table 8. African American Drivers on the Roadways Compared to Proactive (MDT) Queries of African Americans by High-, Medium-, and Low-Level MDT Users, by Border and Nonborder Sectors (percentages; numbers in parentheses)

		Low-Level MDT Users		Medium-Level MDT Users		High-Level MDT Users	
	African American Drivers	African American Queries	African American D-Q Ratio[a]	African American Queries	African American D-Q Ratio	African American Queries	African American D-Q Ratio[a]
Borders Black City (Sectors A–D)	24 (306)	24 (70)	1:1.0	26 (131)	1:1.0	34 (142)	1:1.4***
Nonborder sectors (Sectors E–H)	8 (201)	18 (62)	1:2.2***	19 (25)	1:2.3*	37 (77)	1:4.6***
Grand mean	13 (507)	21 (132)	1:1.6***	24 (156)	1:1.8***	35 (219)	1:2.7***

Source: Data on drivers based on data from the Roadway Observation Study for one week in April 2000 ($N = 3,840$). Data on police queries based on 3,716 proactive MDT queries made by the police during this same one-week period.
[a] The D-Q ratio equals the percentage of police queries divided by the percentage of drivers and is expressed as a ratio.
* $p < .01$, ** $p < .001$, *** $p < .0001$ (two-tailed tests).

use of MDT. High-MDT users consistently and disproportionately surveilled African Americans in both the border (34%) *and* nonborder (37%) sectors. Their rate in the border sectors was 1.4 times greater than the number of African Americans driving in those sectors, and in the nonborder sectors, it was 4.6 times greater than the number of African Americans driving in those sectors. Thus, we found that this small group of high MDT-using officers had the highest levels of profiling, regardless of where they were located.

By contrast, low- and medium-MDT users queried African Americans in the border sectors at rates in proportion to the number of African Americans who were driving in these sectors. But consistent with the race-and-place effect already observed, in the nonborder sectors, the query rates of low- and medium-MDT users were disproportionate to the number of African Americans in the driving population but not at the same levels as those of the high-MDT users.

Furthermore, the rates of *recorded* stops of African Americans by high MDT users were significantly *higher* than those of the low- and medium-MDT users. Table 9 indicates that high- query officers recorded more stops for African Americans (36%) than did low-query officers (19% of recorded stops). So, this small group of officers were not only surveilling but also stopping more African Americans.

Table 9.   Racial Distribution of Recorded Stops of High-, Medium-, and Low-Level MDT Users (percentages; numbers in parentheses)

Type of MDT User	Recorded Stops		Total
	African American	White	
Low user	19 (23)	81 (100)	100 (123)
Medium user	22 (19)	78 (66)	100 (85)
High user	36 (22)	64 (39)	100 (61)

Note: χ^2 6.925, df = 2, $p < .01$.

DISCUSSION

Our analysis suggests that racial profiling has an important ecological distribution. Profiling, as measured by the proactive surveillance of African American drivers, significantly increases as African Americans travel farther from "black" communities and into whiter neighborhoods. We also found that MDT technology may facilitate profiling. That is, while most officers queried African Americans at a higher rate than they did whites, a small group of high-MDT users, who represented only about 10% of the patrol force during the period under study, accounted for a significant proportion of all proactive queries of African Americans. These officers also had higher levels of recorded stops of African Americans.

Thus, on the one hand, we found a systemic effect of race-and-place profiling reflected in the behavior of most of the police officers and characterized by greater surveillance of African Americans in whiter areas. Conceptions of place reflect stereotypically negative and prejudicial judgments about the presence of African Americans in a community. Such perceptions are not unique to the police profession. They are typical of American society in which citizens, both white and African American, fear African Americans, whom they perceive as out of place or whose mere presence invokes the fear of victimization.

On the other hand, a small group of officers, characterized by greater levels of MDT use, produced higher levels of surveillance and stops of African American drivers. Although we suggest that the officers overall were responding to institutionalized conceptions of place, which mirror patterns of residential segregation, this group of high-MDT users seemed more responsive to the presence of African Americans regardless of place. The technology, in combination with conceptions of race and place, appears to heighten this effect.

Because racial profiling is a product of pervasive and institutionalized patterns of racial segregation in American society, it is not helpful to treat racial profiling as an effect of individual officers, consciously or unconsciously taking advantage of their occupational positions to act on their individual prejudices. That police officers are often socially conservative in attitude and lifestyle and express prejudices against minorities does not, ipso facto, translate into discrimination against minorities (Black & Reiss, 1967). In fact, findings in the police literature on discrimination have reinforced the classic gap between such prejudicial attitudes and behavior (Chen, 1996; Waddington, 1999).

Discussions of racial profiling must move beyond a consideration of the intent or motivation of police officers in individual cases, which dominates legal thinking, to an examination of its embeddedness as a practice within the organizational (institutional) context of the police and their relationship to the larger societal context from which discrimination, whether intentional or unintentional, emanates (Feagin & Eckberg, 1980). If racial profiling reflects society-wide patterns of segregation and a generalized attitude about who belongs where, focusing on police "attitudes" or "cultural sensitivity" will not solve the problem.

Sensitivity training for officers, for example, is designed to increase cultural awareness of the historical and contemporary plight of minorities in the United States, as well as to sensitize officers to their own covert (unintentional), and even overt (intentional) forms of prejudice and discrimination. However, our findings suggest that a focus on individual attitudes and behavior misses the underlying societal and occupational *structural* problems that produce racial profiling. Racial profiling in our study was a department-wide phenomenon—responsive to place. We propose that even the most racially sensitive officers engaged in it. And although a small group of officers engaged in a higher rate of profiling than the others, it is not clear that prejudicial attitudes or intentions motivated their behavior either. It seems that their behavior was closely linked to the available technology.

Set against the reality of a biased society, a police officer's recourse is an appeal to professional ideals. In response to accusations of racism and discrimination, officers often respond by stating that they are trained to be "color blind." This term is meant to convey conformity to the "professional" ideal of universality and the legal principle that the *behavior* of people—not *who* they are or *what* racial, ethnic, age, or social-class group they belong to—affects the officer's decision to stop; question; arrest; or, in our data, to surveil and query. It is important to note that many officers in the department we studied sincerely believed this to be true of their behavior, such that efforts to persuade them otherwise through cultural awareness seminars gnawed at the core of their professional belief system and training.

However, as we noted earlier, the work of the police, by its very nature and consequences, precludes their ability to act in such a color-blind or nonprejudicial manner. Put more strongly, society expects police officers to preserve the boundaries of place. Add to this structural occupational characteristic and the contradiction it engenders, the following irony: Against the backdrop of police professionalism, various court rulings have supported the legal justification of using race as a proxy for criminality and dangerousness by creating legal precedents in which race can be used either as the *sole* consideration or in *combination* with other contextual factors to trigger "suspicion," thus justifying police intervention (Kennedy, 1997). So, color blindness need no longer be invoked as a defense or explanation by officers or be considered a professional ideal. Legal precedent already permits a full color pallet to enter into police decision making.

As court rulings make challenges to racial profiling more difficult, profiling has been added to the list of those police behaviors that occur when too much discretion is afforded the police (Ramirez et al., 2000). This approach aims to reduce discretion by requiring officers to record traffic-stop information in patrol logs (or some electronic equivalent). The documentation of stops, now legally mandated in three states with legislation pending in others, is considered a method of documenting the "profiling" problem and a means of curtailing highly discretionary stops. That is, if the police know they are accountable via record keeping, they will reduce such stops. Critics of this proposal suggest that monitoring police behavior may discourage police aggressiveness and lead to an increase in crime or have a negative impact on police morale (c.f. Cleary, 2000).

However, there is another predictable police response to consider: The police will continue to conduct such stops but not record them—thus constructing their records to reflect no bias. In our data, about 25 percent of the stops were not recorded. This is not to suggest a simple argument that the police will purposely distort reality through their record-keeping practices, although there are certainly occasions when they do. Rather, the argument has more to do with the fundamental nature of discretion and attempts to control it and some essential features of police record-keeping practices.

In his classic exposition on the police, Bittner (1970, p. 2) argued: " While the proposal that discretion should be reviewable is meritorious, the hope that its scope can be curtailed by the formulation of additional norms is misguided. Contrary to the belief of many jurists, new rules do not restrict discretion but merely shift its locus." Bittner called attention to a philosophical argument regarding the fundamental defeasibility of rules. Rules are open ended, and although they offer a "core of clarity," their application is surrounded by uncertainty and contingency. The task of fitting rules to cases *necessarily* entails discretion, that is, judging "the correctness of the fit."

Officers already manage a variety of realities through their patrol logs (Meehan, 1986), and recording requirements for traffic stops are no exception. It is well known that the police do not *call out* all traffic stops over the radio (a rule in most police organizations), let alone *record* all traffic stops they make (another organizational rule). Currently, patrol logs are primarily internal organizational documents whose uses are primarily actuarial (i.e., used to generate statistics on officers' activities, such as the number and type of calls for service answered and the number of traffic stops sans race and gender). Logs are used to generate internal measures of patrol activity, typically for supervisors, and are constructed with this internal organizational career in mind. They do not represent all activity, nor do they necessarily represent "real" activity because officers often construct their logs to conform to bureaucratic expectations (Meehan, 2000). As such, they have a fictive character.

The new traffic stop-reporting requirements will alter the organizational career and uses of patrol log records. Data on traffic stops will be produced with these projected external organizational careers in mind (i.e., courts assessing profiling behavior). Thus, the use of the logs will become primarily contractual, rather than actuarial (Garfinkel & Bittner, 1967; Meehan, 1986). This change, in turn, will affect how the records are constructed.

Arrest reports illustrate contractual uses of records. The organizational career of an arrest report is primarily external (i.e., sent to the court and available to the defense). It is contractual in that it documents police treatment of persons in accordance with specified bureaucratic and legal constraints. Once patrol logs have the projected external career and contractual use proposed by legislation, the police can fashion their logs to make racial differences invisible. That is, they may continue to stop African Americans, but will not record the stops unless formal actions (i.e., tickets or arrests) are taken. The "harassment" will continue, but no record of it will exist.[20]

CONCLUSION

The surveillance and stopping behavior of the police is sensitive to race and place. This effect manifests itself systemically and organizationally and reflects community patterns of residential segregation. Being African American and out of place is noticed. A small group of officers magnify this pattern through their use of MDT technology.

Although this was a case study of one police department's practices in a large, racially segregated suburban community, we think that this community and its police are not unlike many suburban communities bordering urban areas with a substantial population of African Americans. Torn by racial conflict in the 1960s, waves of whites fled the urban cities to the "safety" of the suburbs. Preservation of place shapes the thinking of suburban residents and officers alike. We suggest that our findings are generalizeable to suburban communities in which racial tension between urban and suburban communities exists and the police are responsive to these community concerns.

The current focus on stops and tickets, while important, overlooks an important data source that is less easy for officers to manipulate. We have developed an alternative methodology focusing on the proactive surveillance of patrol officers via MDT technology. These data provide insights into the surveillance and investigative activities of officers, moving the focus to earlier stages in the profiling process.

Finally, proposed remedies for racial profiling must take into account a more complete sociological understanding of the phenomenon. Sensitivity training that is targeted at the attitudes of individual officers and efforts to structure discretion will not have much

---

[20] Such record keeping was part of a consent agreement with the Maryland State Police (Harris, 1997). When the data subsequently reported to the court showed continued patterns of discrimination, litigation was reopened. Clearly, then, such a record-keeping requirement is not effective for preventing profiling. The police may have thought that despite having to log these data, there would be no repercussions (i.e., supervisors would not monitor it, and the court would not revisit the issue). However, once the police *do* orient to the external career of any record, they are more careful in crafting that record. The legal and political implications of traffic-stop reporting are not lost on officers.

impact on a practice that reflects the values of the community to which the police are accountable.

REFERENCES

Abramovsky, A., & Edelstein, J. I. (2000). Pretext stops and racial profiling after Whren v. United States. *Albany Law Review, 63,* 725-748.

Ahmed, W., & Rezmovic, E. (2001). Racial profiling: A policy issue in need of better answers. *Chance, 14,* 40-41.

Alba, R. D., & Logan, J. R. (1993). Minority proximity to whites in suburbs: An individual-level analysis of segregation. *American Journal of Sociology, 98,* 1388-1427.

Allen-Bell, A. (1997). The birth of the crime: Driving while black (DWB). *Southern University Law Review, 25,* 195-225.

Alpert G. P., & Dunham, R.G. (1988). *Policing multi-ethnic neighborhoods*: Westport, CT: Greenwood Press.

Amirante, S. L. (1997). People v. Barnes—George Orwell's *1984* revisited: Unbridled and impermissible police use of computer power in the modern age. *Loyola University Chicago Law Journal, 28,* 667-684.

Baldassare, M. (1992). Suburban communities. *Annual Review of Sociology, 18,* 475-494.

Banton, M. (1964). *The policeman and the community.* New York: Basic Books.

Bittner, E. (1970). *The functions of the police in modern society.* Chevy Chase, MD: National Institute of Mental Health.

Black, D. (1971). The social organization of arrest. *Stanford Law Review, 23,* 63-77.

Black, D., & Reiss, A. J. (1967). Patterns of behavior in police and citizen transactions. In *Studies in crime and law enforcement in major metropolitan areas.* Washington, DC: U.S. Government Printing Office.

Brown, M. K. (1981). *Working the street: Police discretion and the dilemmas of reform.* New York: Russell Sage Foundation.

Cedres, D. (1997). Mobile data terminals and random license plate checks: The need for uniform guidelines and reasonable suspicion requirement. *Rutgers Computer and Technology Law Journal, 23,* 391-417.

Chambliss, W. (1994). Policing the ghetto underclass: The politics of law and law enforcement. *Social Problems, 41,* 177-195.

Chen, J. (1996). Changing police culture. *British Journal of Criminology, 36,* 109-134.

Cleary, J. (2000). *Racial profiling studies in law enforcement: issues and methodology.* St. Paul: Minnesota House of Representatives Research Department.

Cole, D. (1999). *No equal justice.* New York: New York Press.

Cooney, M. (1997). Hunting among police and predators: The enforcement of traffic law. *Studies in Law, Politics and Society, 16,* 165-188.

Currie, E. (1993). *Reckoning: Drugs, the cities and the American future.* New York: Hill & Wang.

Darden, J. T., & Kamel, S. M. (2000). Black residential segregation in the city and suburbs of detroit: Does socioeconomic status matter? *Journal of Urban Affairs, 22,* 1-13.

DuBois, W. E. B. (1989). *The souls of black folk.* New York: Penguin. (Original work published 1903)

Feagin, J. R. (1991). The continuing significance of race: Antiblack discrimination in public places. *American Sociological Review, 56,* 101-116.

Feagin, J. R., & Eckberg, D. (1980). Discrimination: Motivation, action, effects, and context. *Annual Review of Sociology, 6,* 1-20.

Felson, M. (1998). *Crime and everyday life* (2nd ed.). Thousand Oaks, CA: Pine Forge Press.

The Gallup Organization. (1999, December 9). *Racial profiling is seen as widespread, particularly among young black men.* Princeton, NJ: Author.

Garfinkel, H., & Bittner, E. (1967). Some good organizational reasons for bad clinic records. In H. Garfinkel (Ed.), *Studies in ethnomethodology* (pp. 186-207). Englewood Cliffs, NJ: Prentice Hall.

428   RACE AND PLACE

Gieryn, T. F. (2000). A space for place in sociology. *Annual Review of Sociology, 26,* 463-495.

Gordon, D. (1990). *The justice juggernaut: Fighting street crime, controlling citizens.* New Brunswick, NJ: Rutgers University Press.

Gotham, K. F. (1998). Race, mortgage lending and loan rejections in a U.S. city. *Sociological Focus, 31,* 391-405.

Harper Woods supports its cops. (2000, June 6). *Detroit Free Press,* p. 7.

Harris, D. (1997). "Driving while black" and all other traffic offenses: The Supreme Court and pretextual traffic stops. *Journal of Criminal Law and Criminology, 87,* 544-582.

Hawley, A. H. (1971). *Urban society: An ecological approach.* New York: Ronald Press.

Jackson, K. T. (1985). *Crabgrass frontier: The suburbanization of the United States.* New York Oxford University Press.

Jackson, P. (1989). *Minority group threat, crime and policing: Social context and social control.* New York: Praeger.

Jackson, P. (1992). Minority group threat, social context and policing. In A. Liska (Ed.), *Social threat and social control* (pp. 89-101). Albany: State University of New York Press.

Kay, J. H. (1997). *Asphalt nation: How the automobile took over America and how we can take it back.* New York: Crown.

Kennedy, R. (1997). *Race, crime, and the law.* New York: Vintage Books.

Klinger, D. A. (1997). Negotiating order in patrol work: An ecological theory of police response to deviance. *Criminology, 35,* 277-306.

Kowinski, W. S. (1985). *The malling of America.* New York: William Morrow.

Liska, A. (Ed.). (1992). *Social threat and social control.* Albany: State University of New York Press.

Lyon, D. (1994). *The Electronic eye: The rise of surveillance society.* Minneapolis: University of Minnesota Press.

Mann, C. R. (1993). *Unequal justice: A question of color.* Bloomington: Indiana University Press.

Manning, P. K. (1997). *Police work: The social organization of policing* (2nd ed.). Prospect Heights, IL: Waveland Press.

Marx, G. T. (1988). *Undercover: Police surveillance in America.* Berkeley: University of California Press.

Massey, D. S., & Denton, N. A. (1993). *American apartheid: Segregation and the making of the underclass.* Cambridge, MA: Harvard University Press.

Mastrofski, S. D., Ritti, R. R., & Snipes, J. B. (1994). Expectancy theory and police productivity in DUI enforcement. *Law and Society Review, 28,* 113-147.

Matson, A. O., & Duncombe, S. R. (1992). Public space, private place: The contested terrain of Tompkins Square Park. *Berkeley Journal of Sociology, 37,* 129-161.

Meehan, A. J. (1986). Recordkeeping practices in the policing of juveniles. *Urban Life, 15,* 70-102.

Meehan, A. J. (1998). The impact of Mobile Data Terminal (MDT) information technology on communication and recordkeeping in patrol work. *Qualitative Sociology, 21,* 225-254.

Meehan, A. J. (2000). The organizational career of gang statistics: The politics of policing gangs. *Sociological Quarterly, 41,* 337-370.

Miller, J. G. (1996). *Search and destroy: African-American males in the criminal justice system.* New York: Cambridge University Press.

Muir, W. (1977). *The police: Streetcorner politicians.* Chicago: University of Chicago Press.

Nunn, S. (1994). How capital technologies affect municipal service outcomes: The case of police Mobile Digital Terminals and stolen vehicle recoveries. *Journal of Policy Analysis and Management, 13,* 539-559.

Pearce, D. (1979). Gatekeepers and homeseekers: Institutional patterns in racial steering. *Social Problems, 26,* 325-342.

Petersillia, J. (1983). *Racial disparities in the criminal justice system.* Santa Monica CA: RAND.

Police Executive Research Forum. (2001). *Racially biased policing: A principled response.* Washington DC: Author.

Prime, J. S. (1996). A double-barreled assault: How technology and judicial interpretations threaten public access to law enforcement records. *Federal Communications Law Journal, 48,* 341-369.

Ramirez, D., McDevitt, J., & Farrell, A. (2000). *A resource guide on racial profiling data collection: Promising practices and lessons learned.* Washington DC: U.S. Department of Justice.

Rawls, A. W. (2000). "Race" as an interaction order phenomena: W. E. B. DuBois's "Double consciousness" thesis revisited. *Sociological Theory, 18,* 241-274.

Reiss, A. J. (1971). *The Police and the public.* New Haven, CT: Yale University Press.

Rubenstein, J. (1973). *City police.* New York: Random House.

Ruby, C. L., & Brigham, J. C. (1996). A criminal schema: The role of chronicity, race, and socioeconomic status in law enforcement officials' perception of others. *Journal of Applied Social Psychology, 26,* 95-112.

Russell, K. K. (1998). *The color of crime.* New York: New York University Press.

Sacks, H. (1972). Notes on the police assessment of moral character. In David Sudnow (Ed.), *Studies in social interaction* (pp 280-293). New York: Free Press.

The Sentencing Project. (1999). *Drug policy and the criminal justice system.* Washington, DC: Author.

Sherman, L. (1989). Hot spots of predatory crime: routine activities and the criminology of place. *Criminology, 27,* 27-55.

Skolnick, J. (1994). *Justice without trial.* New York: John Wiley & Sons.

Smith, D. A., Graham, N., & Adams, B. (1991). Minorities and the police: Attitudinal and behavioral questions. In M. J. Lynch & E. B. Patterson (Eds.), *Race and criminal justice* (pp. 22-35). New York: Harrow & Heston.

Smith, D. A., & Visher, C. (1981). Street-level justice: Situational determinants of police arrest decisions. *Social Problems, 29,* 167-177.

Smith, D. A., Visher, C., & Davidson, L. A. (1984). Equity and discretionary justice: The influence of race on police arrest decisions. *Journal of Criminal Law and Criminology, 75,* 234-249.

Taylor, J., & Whitney, G. (1999). Crime and racial profiling by U.S. police: Is there an empirical basis? *Journal of Social, Political and Economic Studies, 24,* 485-510.

Thernstrom, S., & Thernstrom, A. (1997). *America in black and white.* New York: Simon & Schuster.

U.S. Bureau of Justice Statistics. (2001). *Contacts between the police and the public: Findings from the 1999 national survey.* Washington, DC: U.S. Department of Justice.

U.S. Commission on Civil Rights. (2000). *Police practices and civil rights in New York City.* Washington DC: Author.

U.S. General Accounting Office. (2000). *Racial profiling: Limited data available on motorist stops.* Washington, DC: Author.

VanMaanen, J. (1974). Working the street: A Developmental view of police behavior. In H. Jacob (Ed.), *The potential for reform of criminal justice* (pp. 83-130). Beverly Hills, CA: Sage.

VanMaanen, J. (1978). The asshole. In P. K. Manning & J. VanMaanen (Eds.), *Policing: A view from the street* (pp. 221-238). Santa Monica, CA: Goodyear.

Verniero, P. (1999). *Interim report of the state police review team regarding allegations of racial profiling.* Trenton: New Jersey Department of Law and Public Safety.

Vrij, A. (1993). An impression formation framework on police prejudice. An overview of experiments on perceptual bias in police-citizen interaction. *Police Studies, 16,* 28-32.

Waddington, P. A. J. (1999). Police (canteen) sub-culture: An appreciation. *British Journal of Criminology, 39,* 287-309.

Walker, S. (1997). Complaints against the police: A focus group study of citizen perceptions, goals, and expectations. *Criminal Justice Review, 22,* 207-226.

Ward, S. K. (1994). Trends in the location of corporate headquarters: 1969-1989. *Urban Affairs Quarterly, 29,* 468-478.

Weiss, A., & Freels, S. (1996). The effects of aggressive policing: The Dayton Traffic Enforcement Experiment. *American Journal of Police, 15,* 45-64.

Weitzer, R. (1996). Racial discrimination in the criminal justice system: Findings and problems in the literature. *Journal of Criminal Justice, 24,* 309-322.

Weitzer, R. (1999). Citizen perceptions of police misconduct: Race and neighborhood context. *Justice Quarterly, 16,* 820-846.

Weitzer, R. (2000). Racialized policing: Residents' perceptions in three neighborhoods. *Law and Society Review, 34,* 129-155.

430   RACE AND PLACE

Weitzer, R., & Tuch, S. A. (1999). Race, class, and perceptions of discrimination by the police. *Crime and Delinquency, 45,* 494-507.

Williams, H., & Murphy, P.V. (1990, January). The evolving strategy of police: A minority view. *Perspectives on Policing,* No. 13. Bethesda, MD: National Institute of Justice

Zonderman, J. (1990). *Beyond the crime lab.* New York: John Wiley & Sons.

Zuboff, S. (1987). *In the age of the smart machine: The future of work and power.* New York: Basic Books.

[8]

Narratives of the Death Sentence:
Toward a Theory of Legal Narrativity

Benjamin Fleury-Steiner

This article investigates how the consciousness of ordinary citizens enlisted as jurors in death penalty trials is racialized. The study draws on post-trial interviews with some 66 white and black jurors who served on 24 capital trials in which either a white or black defendant received the death sentence. Findings among white jurors reveal a hegemonic tale of racial inferiority. However, other characteristics such as social class or relevant biographical experiences help explain how jurors' stories are racialized. More specifically, racial inferiority is articulated in four congruous narratives: "individual responsibility," "the tragedy of the 'black' group," "the bad kid and the caring family," and "the threatening outsider." Furthermore, black jurors' stories are influenced by their background experiences as well. More-educated black jurors employ a sympathetic discourse toward the "culturally distant whites." On the other hand, working-class blacks that have had negative experiences with whites in public are found to employ a narrative of "resisting white racism." Understanding the subtle influences of legal agents' multiple identities in the remaking of racial hegemony has broader implications for a revised constitutive perspective of law—what I call a "theory of legal narrativity."

T he stories of those who take part in the operations of state law, including jurors in death penalty cases, frame and impart meanings of "race." Racial discourses constitute taken-for-granted understandings and practices. They serve as "mechanisms of social control" because they assert and instantiate a dif-

An earlier version of this work was presented at the Law & Society Association meetings in Vancouver, June 2002, and at the American Sociological Association meetings in Chicago, August 2002. I am grateful to Joseph Sanders and Sally Merry for their patience, guidance, and words of wisdom in helping me bring this project to completion. Many thanks for the insightful comments of Margaret Andersen, Michael Antonio, Ronet Bachman, William Bowers, Anne Bowler, Ursula Bentele, Kitty Calavita, Jennifer Culbert, Valerie Hans, Tim Kaufman-Osborne, Mona Lynch, Anna Maria Marshall, Michael Musheno, Trish Oberweiss, Austin Sarat, Margaret Vandiver, and the LSR's anonymous reviewers. I am especially grateful to Laura Beth Nielsen for her painstaking readings of earlier drafts, her words of encouragement, and, most importantly, her friendship. Finally, I thank my life-partner, Dr. Ruth Fleury-Steiner, for all her love and support throughout the completion of this project. Support for this research was provided by a grant from the Law and Social Sciences Program of the National Science Foundation, grant NSF SES-9013252. Address correspondence to Benjamin Fleury-Steiner, Department of Sociology and Criminal Justice, University of Delaware, 305 Smith Hall, Newark, DE 19716 (e-mail: bfs@udel. edu).

ferentiation but do not reveal the basis of those distinctions—do not bring them to the surface for examination and resistance—and thus "conceal the social organization of their production and plausibility" (Ewick & Silbey 1995:213). These discourses have the capacity to "colonize consciousness" (Ewick & Silbey 1995:214) because they are used colloquially without elaboration or explanation.

How racial meaning is elaborated also depends on the identities of the individuals employing such discourses. As Kimberlee Crenshaw (1995) has observed, identities are not all of a piece; they intersect with each other. For example, a black person living in a marginalized community may have a very different position on the death penalty than one who lives in a middle-class neighborhood. Indeed, they may have very different moral orientations, because "morality is bound to a sense of self, helps determine our sense of others, and then becomes the grounds to legitimate who 'I' am, who I think 'you' are and how 'we' should go on" (Oberweis & Musheno 2001:64). Jurors who have different identities might be expected to "see" themselves, and thus the defendants they sit in judgment of, *differently*.

In the sections that follow, I present a theoretical context for investigating race as a hegemonic narrative (section I). Next, I describe the data from which I draw (section II) and the methodology I employed (section III). The findings presented in section IV demonstrate contrasting and complementary theories of racial inferiority in white capital jurors' stories. By contrast, educated black jurors employ a narrative of "culturally distant whites," while more working-class blacks tell a more explicit tale of "resisting white racism." In closing, I discuss the implications of these findings for what I call a "theory of legal narrativity."

I. A Perspective on Hegemony, Identity, and Legal Consciousness

In this article, I call attention to how individuals' racialized discourses of crime and criminals confirm taken-for-granted *understandings* and how these understandings imply broader hegemonic stories (Ewick & Silbey 1995). By *hegemonic*, I refer to the taken-for-granted wisdom of the majority that is both situational and historically specific: stories that "everyone knows" and is familiar with. In this way, hegemonic tales embody general understandings that "go without saying, because, being axiomatic, they come without saying" (Comaroff & Comaroff 1991:23).

Austin Sarat's (1993) study of narratives of violence in attorneys' arguments in capital trials demonstrates the hegemonic character embedded in capital trial narratives. Problematizing the prosecution's argument—*"We have a right," the prosecutor claimed, "to be vindicated and protected"* (emphasis added)—Sarat elucidates how such narrating simultaneously serves to reinforce whiteness as a legally protected, dominant group "interest":

> "We" is both an inclusive and a violent naming, a naming fraught with racial meaning. Who is included in the "we"? While this "we" reaches from this world to the next as a remembrance of and identification with [the white victim], at the same time, it makes the black [defendant] an outsider in a community that needs protection from people like him. It excludes him by claiming law as an entitlement against him. Law's violence is necessary both to vindicate and protect "us" from him. (Sarat 1993:49)

Beyond race as a taken-for-granted story of "us" and "them," the multiple social identities of those who *do* hegemony has implications for understanding how legal consciousness is constituted. Trish Oberweis and Michael Musheno's (2001) study of legal consciousness among street-level bureaucrats persuasively reveals how moral decision-making is inextricably bound up in state actors' "ordinary," historically specific, and institutionally constrained identities. Focusing on the narratives of police officers and social services administrators, their study provides a fascinating window of how multiple identities constitute discretionary judgments. Having respondents sketch stories about how their own perspectives of morality informed their decision-making (see Oberweis & Musheno 2001:109–12), they present a window into the interconnectedness of identity, morality, and the law-in-action. Describing the arrest of a woman identified as pregnant, a prostitute and an alcoholic, a respondent from their study, a white police officer, Clinton Hinkley, stated:

> She blew a .225 [on a breath test for intoxication], which is over twice the legal limit. . . . She was real happy about it and didn't think anything about the fact that she was drinking. She thought that she was doing good because she was cutting down. That right there caused me a lot of problems, especially because I have a seven-month-old baby. That just really bothers me. My wife didn't touch a single sip of alcohol, didn't take any medications or anything, just because she didn't want any possible thing wrong with the baby. And this one's going to grow up with a mother who doesn't even know who the father is of her unborn child and she's out here drinking up. . . . The only way you can do anything about it is if they make abortions illegal. My understanding is that there are a lot of people who get home abortions and have their own ways of aborting their children. Some of which is through alcohol and drugs, so it's just a form of abortion. That way if you have prostitutes or people out there that are doing drugs or alcohol while they're pregnant, then we can force them into custody for the term of the pregnancy to keep them from abusing the baby. . . . The only other way to help prevent this is to give all drug addicted females, or female prostitutes a hysterectomy (Oberweis & Musheno 2001:75).

Officer Hinkley's story of the intoxicated and pregnant prostitute powerfully demonstrates how morality is constructed at the intersections of experiential, institutional, and historically specific identities. As a "good parent" in the latter half of the twentieth century, Officer Hinkley, a white working-class male, mobilizes a pro-life politics of gendered immorality. Drawing on conservative stories of "welfare queens" and immoral single mothers, Hinkley as both officer and "good parent" wants to "force *them* into custody." In other words, the female suspect represents to him a breed of immoral outsiders who have taken full advantage of "liberal" abortion policies (e.g., "The only way you can do anything about it is if they make abortions illegal.") and therefore must be punished harshly. Framing his arrest story in the context of his own privilege vis-à-vis his wife's pregnancy, he, by implication, ignores the female suspect's marginality. Officer Hinkley blames the "dishonest," "morally reprehensible" victim for her impoverished and marginalized identity (e.g., "She thought that she was doing good"). At the same time, he mobilizes his institutional role as "law enforcer" "to enforce his moral view to the extent that he can, with rather significant consequences for the woman involved" (Oberweis & Musheno 2001:75).

Likewise, how identities are constituted in capital jurors' stories of their life or death decisions has implications for understanding legal consciousness in death penalty judgments. Thus, in this article I build on recent research in legal consciousness theory (Ewick & Silbey 1998; Nielsen 2000) by demonstrating how law as hegemonic narratives is mobilized and resisted at the intersection of the identities of both the punisher *and* the punished.

II. The Data

Jurors' stories come from the Capital Jury Project (CJP), a national study of jury discretion in death penalty cases. While the CJP did not strategically sample for jurors with regard to race, approximately 10 percent (9.8%) were African American.[1] This analysis draws on 66 jurors' stories from some 24 cases in which either a black or white defendant was sentenced to death.[2] Table

---

[1] Less than 4 percent (3.6%) of the sample was made up of Hispanic, Asian, or other racial or ethnic minority jurors and thus did not provide adequate numbers of jurors for the foregoing analysis.

[2] To ensure reliability in the comparison of jurors' interviews from black and white defendant death cases, they were closely matched according to two criteria. First, cases were matched according to circumstances surrounding the crime. More specifically, all 24 cases are relatively similar in the levels of aggravation: 23 of 24 (95.8%) are single victim homicides involving either shootings in the course of a robbery (31.0% black defendants v. 26.0% white defendants) or homicides involving strangers (46.3% black defendant v. 48.7% white defendants), 2 cases (1 black defendant and 1 white defendant) involve multiple aggravating circumstances including either kidnapping, robbery, or rape prior to

1 provides a demographic picture of the jurors who served on these cases.[3]

The survey instrument was designed to chronicle the respondents' entire capital jury experience from *voir dire* to their final decisions whether to impose the life or death sentence.[4] By employing both closed-ended and open-ended questions, the interviewers were able to gather information on what legal or extra legal factors might have influenced jurors' decision making across both the guilt and punishment phases of a bifurcated capital trial. Interviewers also encouraged jurors to expound in their own words on various issues, including "their own impressions of the defendant" and "how the jury arrived at its punishment decision." While such questions did not explicitly focus on the influence of race on jurors' sentencing decisions, they did prove crucial to this analysis of white and African American capital jurors' racialized consciousness; that is to say, as ordinary citizens charged with making life or death decisions, capital jurors could and sometimes did speak of the "natural and normal way of doing things . . . their commonsense understanding of the world" (Merry 1990:5), including their commonsense understandings of racial identities as they pertained to their experiences as capital sentencing jurors.

---

the killing. Second, because the vast majority of juries made their decisions in a relatively short period of time (especially in black defendant death cases especially), to ensure comparability, I selected only those cases decided in four hours or less. The distribution of black and white defendant death cases by the amount of time it took the jury to reach its punishment decision is presented below:

Time it took the jury to reach its punishment decision

	≤4 Hours	>4 Hours
White defendant death cases	66.7%	33.3%
No. of jurors	(N = 28)	(N = 14)
Black defendant death cases	88.4%	11.6%
No. of jurors	(N = 38)	(N = 5)

[3] To ensure that differences in jurors' responses are not due to jurors serving on different cases, the present analysis draws only from those cases in which both whites and blacks were interviewed.

[4] Since the CJP began, some 1,155 former capital jurors from 340 capital trials in 14 states have been interviewed. The original sampling plan for each state focused on an equal representation of capital trials ending in life and death sentences. Moreover, investigators in each state used various strategies to stratify and balance the representation of sentencing outcomes in terms of regions within the state or of urban and rural locations. While the CJP was restricted from selecting cases from all regions of every state in the sample—indeed, states such as California, Texas, and Florida were simply too large and thus statewide sampling became impractical—investigators in some states did conduct interviews with more than the required four jurors. The CJP data include 24 trials represented by five jurors, 8 by six jurors, and 1 by eight jurors. Unfortunately, in some instances, jurors refused to be interviewed, despite a $20 incentive. More specifically, 39 trials are represented by a single juror, 41 by two jurors, 68 by three, 148 by four, 29 by five, 1 by seven, and 1 by eight. (For additional details concerning the CJP's methodology, see Bowers 1995).

Table 1. Demographic Characteristics of Jurors in White and Black Defendant Death Cases

	White Defendant Death Cases	Number of Jurors (N)	Black Defendant Death Cases	Number of Jurors (N)
Number of defendants	12	28	12	38
Race				
White	71.4%	20	71.1%	27
Black	28.6%	8	28.9%	11
Total	100.0%	28	100.0%	38
Gender				
Male	71.4%	20	55.3%	21
Female	28.6%	8	44.3%	17
Total	100.0%	28	100.0%	38
Race and gender				
White Males	50.0%	14	42.1%	16
White Females	21.4%	6	28.9%	11
Black Males	21.4%	6	13.2%	5
Black Females	7.1%	2	15.8%	6
Total	100.0%	28	100.0%	38
Socioeconomic status				
Upper	32.1%	9	31.6%	12
Middle	17.9%	5	13.2%	5
Low	28.6%	8	23.7%	9
Missing	21.4%	6	31.6%	12
Total	100.0%	28	100.0%	38
State identification				
Alabama	10.7%	3	5.3%	2
California	7.0%	2	—	—
Florida	40.5%	10	13.2%	5
Georgia	—	—	7.9%	3
Indiana	7.0%	2	—	—
Kentucky	17.9%	5	—	—
Louisiana	10.7%	3	5.3%	2
Missouri	—	—	—	—
North Carolina	—	—	13.2%	5
Pennsylvania	—	—	13.2%	5
South Carolina	17.9%	5	41.9%	16
Tennessee	—	—	—	—
Texas	—	—	—	—
Virginia	—	—	—	—
Total	100.0%	28	100.0%	38

The Death Qualified Sample

The sample consists of a population of individuals with a unique set of attitudes and beliefs. As "death qualified" capital jurors, such individuals have been shown by social psychological studies to demonstrate greater punitive orientations toward crime and the criminal justice system (Fleury-Steiner 2003) and a greater proneness toward conviction (Thompson 1989). Studies of capital jurors find that white male juries are disproportionately far more likely to impose the death sentence when the defendant is black and the victim is white (Bowers et al. 2001). Furthermore, an imposing collection of studies on racialized stereotypes

(Barkan & Cohn 1994; Sweeny & Haney 1992) and racialized fears of crime find increased punitiveness among whites (Sunnafrank & Fontes 1983). More sophisticated studies demonstrate that white respondents presented with vignettes of violent crimes committed by black offenders yield stronger correlations between the factors of race and punitveness than the diffuse indicators of crime and punitiveness:

> [R]acial stereotypes [are] only modestly correlated with attitudes toward generic crime issues (e.g., the death penalty), our punitiveness and civil liberties scales, and so on. . . . The conditional impact of race, however, in no way minimizes its importance. Violent crimes committed by blacks, and the policies designed to punish them, are the very images which drive public fears . . . They are conflated by the media, by individuals like Charles Stewart and Susan Smith (both of whom blamed African American males for crimes they, themselves, committed), and by cynical political messengers who "Willie Hortonize" campaigns (Hurwitz & Peffley 1997:395–396; see also Hurwitz & Peffley 1998).

Thus, we might expect former capital jurors to employ similar racialized discourses in their stories of *actually making* their sentencing decisions. Indeed, these data offer the unique opportunity to study such stereotypical discourses in punishment decision-making among a sample of citizens who are expected to hold these attitudes and beliefs but differ by identities (see Table 1).

III. Methodology

> Narrative analysis takes as its object of investigation the story itself. . . . The purpose is to see how respondents in interviews impose order on the flow of experience to make sense of events and actions in their lives. The methodological approach examines the informant's story and analyzes how it is put together, the linguistic and cultural resources it draws on, and how it persuades a listener of authenticity. Analysis in narrative studies opens up the forms of telling about experience, not simply the content to which language refers. We ask, why was the story told *that* way? (Riessman 1993)

To encourage respondents to tell stories about their experiences, the CJP survey explicitly asked jurors to *tell* about important moments during the trial, deliberations, and their impressions of the defendant. The goal of these questions was to help jurors construct their responses in their own ways. For example, when asked to tell about their sentencing decisions, jurors would often give a chronological accounting of what the jury did to reach its punishment decision (e.g., "First we took a vote to see where everybody stood on punishment"). While jurors may have told stories of their decisions from only this perspective, others

broke from a strict accounting of the jury's decision-making protocol to tell a story about other experiences. Given the leeway to
answer as they saw fit, in many instances jurors' stories emerged
when least expected. For example, in response to their impressions of the defendant, many jurors took the floor and told extended stories.

Each interview lasted approximately two hours and in most
cases was tape recorded. Several teams of undergraduate research assistants and I transcribed jurors' verbatim responses,
then computerized and analyzed them. Subsequently, I went
through the texts of jurors' responses, coding striking features
that I marked for reanalysis. Although I was not overly concerned
with interruptions or pauses that occurred during the interviews,
I noticed that sometimes transcribers had inserted exclamation
marks, or had written notes in parentheses describing jurors' reactions (e.g., "Juror seems annoyed by this question," or "Juror
got very serious when answering"). To better under these comments, whenever possible, I listened to the tapes again.

Following Riessman's (1993:57) methodology, I instructed a
research assistant to transcribe a juror's entire response, even if it
"wasn't in answer to the question." Indeed, many jurors describing their sentencing decisions told stories about America's "broken justice system" more broadly, as this comment from Leslie
Odom, a 34-year-old white homemaker illustrates:

> *I read the papers everyday, and I'd say 60 percent to 70 percent
> of the crime committed in my area is committed by people who've
> been in prison and got out early on several different occasions.
> We have had a quite a few murders, and early release is the cause
> of it.*

From this response it is clear that analytic induction is extremely useful. *What* is the juror saying? *Why*, in response to,
"Tell me how the jury made its punishment decision," does the
juror tell a story about early release from prison in her community? The more I scrutinized jurors' responses in the context of
my prior theoretical expectations regarding hegemony, identity,
and legal consciousness, the more the features of discourse
"jumped out" at me (Riessman 1993:57).

My interests in critical race theory (e.g., Bell 1987; Butler
1997; Carbado 1999; Crenshaw et al. 1996; Haney-Lopez 1996;
Lawrence 1987; Matsuda 1989; Morrison 1997) in the context of
identity as a "pervasive two-role social process (Goffman
1963:138),"[5] played a central function throughout the analysis as
well. Consider the following from Sheila Brooks, a 38-year-old
white, college-educated hairdresser, in response to a question

---

[5] "The normal and the stigmatized are not persons but rather *perspectives* (emphasis
added) (Goffman 1963:138).

concerning her impressions of the defendant (analyzed in detail later):

> *I saw the defendant as a very typical product of the lower, socio-economic, black group who grew up with no values, no ideals, no authority, no morals, no leadership, and this has come down from generation to generation. And that was one of the problems we had, for me, and in the jury. Because some of the jurors were looking at him as your average white kid: he wasn't a white kid. He came from a totally different environment. I'm just saying that he was the one that was the defendant. And I just saw him as a loser from day one, as soon as he was born into that environment, and into that set of people who basically were into drugs, alcohol, illegitimacy, AIDS, the whole nine yards. This kid didn't have a chance. That's how I saw the defendant. And there are 10,000 others like him out there, which is very tragic.*

Brooks's response is obviously more than a simple description of the defendant. She tells a rich, detailed story that draws on themes of racial identity, morality, and tragedy. However, from Goffmanian and critical race perspectives her story raises several fascinating questions: *How* does identifying the defendant's blackness enable her to understand her own "white" identity? *What* is the purpose of telling a story of her fellow jurors' reactions to the defendant? *How* does her use of ambiguous identifiers such as "that," "totally different," "that set of people," and the "whole nine yards" help her make sense of the defendant's identity? *What* does the statement, "There are 10,000 others like him out there, which is very tragic" say about the role of *tragedy* in Sheila Brooks's story?

The development of these theoretically grounded questions, in combination with my analytical refinement of jurors' stories, was a long and painstaking process. Through numerous rounds of retranscribing and revising, I was able to clarify my interpretations of jurors' stories. Ultimately, I was able to make the difficult decision of how to represent respondents' discourses in the texts presented here. "Determining where a narrative begins and ends and the listener/questioner's place in producing it are textual as well as analytic issues" (Riessman 1993:58).

The Present Study

In this project I drew on the insights gained from seeing law as not separate from prevailing social arrangements, including racial inequality.[6] As a basis, I examined research regarding the popular consciousness of law among ordinary citizens (Ewick & Silbey 1998). I looked at studies of citizen's consciousness of free

---

[6] For a recent review, see Feagin 2000.

speech and their experiences with public harassment (Nielsen 2000). I also considered work on the moral production of identities in the experiences of street-level bureaucrats (Oberweis & Musheno 2001).

To study how the consciousness of African American and white jurors racialized, I focused on ordinary citizens enlisted by the state to make the *extraordinary* decision of life or death. This project does not explore capital jurors in cases that ended in life sentences. Nevertheless, it does provide one important window on how the consciousness of African Americans and whites as jurors in death penalty cases is formed.

I conducted close readings of each of these 66 jurors' responses to open-ended questions concerning their decisions on punishment and their impressions of the defendant. In my examination of jurors' interviews in white defendant death cases, I did not find any explicitly racialized discourses.[7] While my failure to mention race alone is not a reason to exclude such cases from the analysis,[8] given my focus on criminal punishment, and because discourses around black criminality are particularly problematic in the United States,[9] I focused only on black defendant death cases in the foregoing analysis of jurors' stories.

My analysis of black defendant death cases revealed several inconsistencies in jurors' racialized discourses. For example, more-educated[10] white jurors were more likely to express an understanding and sympathy toward a black defendant's upbringing and disadvantaged surroundings. In contrast, less-educated whites made more explicit allusions to "us" and "them." Black jurors' stories also varied. More-educated blacks were more likely to sympathize with the difficulties whites had in relating to a black defendant's marginality. Alternatively, less-educated blacks expressed frustration with their more explicitly racist white counterparts. Although I do not mean to suggest there are no other references or allusions in jurors' responses, I do believe that the narratives I present were the most common and often repeated.

---

7 In a larger analysis of these data involving jurors' identity stories in both life and death cases (Fleury-Steiner, forthcoming), I discovered that jurors in white defendant cases do invoke class marginality and other outsider tropes. Furthermore, regardless of the defendant's race, many jurors justify their sentencing decisions by default, because, in their words, "life is not life" (Steiner, Bowers, & Sarat 1999).

8 Indeed, that jurors do not mention race reveals only that "white" is an invisible or default racial category in the United States (e.g., Haney-Lopez 1996) and thus may be represented in jurors' discourse in other important ways.

9 Perhaps the broadest indicator of how crime discourse in America has been racialized "black" is the vastly disproportionate level of incarceration for African Americans as compared to whites (e.g., Mauer 2000).

10 To examine socioeconomic status, jurors were asked questions about their level education and annual income. A combined measure of high, medium, and low jurors' SES appears in Table 1.

IV. The Tale of Racial Inferiority

White jurors were asked to reflect on the defendant they had sentenced to death. Some chose to tell a story that establishes from the outset "what kind of person (in the defendant) they were dealing with." These stories reveal a hegemonic narrative of *racial inferiority* and white superiority or supremacy. While the racial inferiority narrative may be "built on concepts and explanatory schemes . . . that are themselves abstractions (Sommers & Gibson 1994:59)," whites make the tale of African Americans' racial inferiority *real* in a taken-for-granted story of "not living up to the standards of the white majority."

Whites tell stories that represent the defendant as lacking individual characteristics, as a member of an inferior "other." In short, they tell *cultural distance* stories. Such tales involve the emplotting[11] of episodes from personal experience or popular culture that reveal how they have come to see the defendant as racially inferior. I explicate this narrative in the following presentation of jurors' stories

Cultural Distance Stories

Whites' cultural distance stories are replete with "place images" or with "various discrete meanings associated with real places or regions regardless of their character in reality" (Shields 1991:60). They encompass a broader "cultural distance talk" not unlike what Lisa Frohmann (1997), in her study of prosecutorial decision making in sexual assault cases, has termed "discordant locales." In this way, jurors "construct distinct groups with different cultures who live in geographically separate spaces and have different schemes under which they interpret the everyday world" (1997:533).

How do whites *accomplish* cultural distance in their stories? My analysis reveals that jurors' differing personal experiences and educational backgrounds help explain how cultural distance can vary along four axes of narrative interpretation: (1) individual responsibility, (2) the tragedy of the disadvantaged, (3) the bad kid and the caring family, and (4) the threatening outsider. Although these designations are by no means mutually exclusive—indeed they often overlap and serve to reinforce one another—they are always situational. That is, they vary according to the juror's and defendant's identities and the circumstances sur-

---

11 Emplottment is a critical concept for understanding how narratives across time and space continue to "make sense" to storytellers. As Margaret R. Sommers and Gloria D. Gibson (1994:59) cogently observe: "[E]mplottment gives significance to independent instances, not their chronological or categorical order. . . . [I]t is emplottment which translates events into episodes."

rounding the crime or trial. To clarify the utility of each, however, it is important to describe them separately.

The Story of Individual Responsibility

Generally speaking, cultural distance reveals how whites ob-
jectify the black defendant—how they come to see him as representative of an inferior race.[12] More specifically, how jurors see
themselves and their surroundings may influence such discourse
in one of two ways. First, more-educated whites resort to a more
explicitly race-neutral or "color-blind" discourse that reveals a
heightened awareness of both time and place. They *do* contemporary racial hegemony by emplotting stories of their own experiences into the broader narrative of evaluating the defendant's
responsibility for the crime. As a means of understanding who
the defendant "is" and thus "why people like him act this way,"
they may also tell individual responsibility stories of a "weak" or
"faulty" criminal justice system or other government institutions
(e.g., "The welfare system makes these people"). As Bonnie
Mayer, a 53-year-old white homemaker, explains:

> *I lived in a poor community, and I knew of families that were not
> too far from the defendant's family level of poverty. They had
> difficult lives. They didn't have a lot of personal possessions.
> During the trial, the psychologist brought up that Cal didn't
> have shoes or clothes to wear [as a child]. Both the lack of these
> things he had growing up, and the fact that he didn't have a
> mother and father in the house to discipline him and to really
> love him. I believe that really did affect the defendant. But I had
> seen other people in poverty that did not go onto lead a life of
> crime. That's no excuse. I'm sorry, I felt very bad that he had no
> life, but that's no reason to do what he did.*

The Tragedy of the "Black" Group

The tragedy of the black group narrative enables whites to
rationalize away any doubts about what the defendant they are
dealing with represents. The plot of this story, in effect, is "the
defendant's life may be a tragedy but he is still one of *them*." De-
flecting a more explicit commitment to a tale of racial inferiority,
jurors thus "play the tragedy card," which enables them to articulate feelings of "failure or catastrophe as the ultimate end of the
story" (Jacobs 2001:224). As Avery Anderson, a 42-year-old white,
college-educated business executive, observes: "It was a very sad
situation all the way around, he was black, raised in the ghetto,
and so on."

---

[12] Less 2% of the cases in the CJP sample involved female defendants.

The Bad Kid and the Caring Family

Interconnections between race and gender identities are revealed in the story of the "bad kid and the caring family." More specifically, whites present themselves as disappointed or angry "parents" of an African American defendant. Such a paternalistic narrative goes back to slave times (Litwack 1979) and is emplotted here to belittle the nonwhite defendant, thus to *simplify away* the complexities of his life. According to Deidre Lund a 51-year-old white sales representative, "This kid got lost in system. Like a lost sheep, he had a pitiful background. He's basically a street kid. I'm not so sure he knows right from wrong like the rest of us."

Moreover, as paternalistic figures, whites must deal with members whose views deviate from the rest of the group. Focusing on convincing a nonwhite holdout to join the pro-death majority, they tell stories of lending a sympathetic ear to the African American holdout's plight. As I show in a case study to follow, in effect they tell a story of coaxing the holdout back into the caring "graces of the family." Most typically, compliance is reached by easing the holdout into confronting whether she is "with the jury or against it," "for justice or against it."

The Threatening Outsider

Relying on the only cultural capital they may possess, that indeed *makes sense* to them in the decision to take a life, jurors resort to telling stories of a threatening outsider. In this way, doing death is accomplished in explicit stories of racialized or gendered identities. Jurors focus on the defendant's dark, cold, or menacing appearance or hypermasculinity. However, "threatening outsider" stories often defy simple categorizations of the defendant. In other words, these tales are windows into how jurors construct identities as threatening and how they respond to such identities vis-à-vis punishment. As Shirley Loman, a 58-year-old white secretary stated in response to the question "During the punishment phase did any of the defense witnesses backfire?":

> *His mother, really his reaction to his mother's testimony, he was very unemotional through the whole trial and when his mother got on the stand and pleaded for his life he didn't bat an eye, not a tear, no emotion at all, that pretty much put him in the electric chair.*

Sheila Brooks: "He wasn't a white kid . . ."

Sheila Brooks, a white college-educated hairdresser and mother of two, served on a capital jury that sentenced to death Ray Floyd Cornish a 20-year-old black male convicted of shooting a white male convenience store clerk. This was Sheila Brooks's first time serving on a jury.

Sheila Brooks told the interviewer that her decision to impose the death sentence "was a very hard decision." While she believes the jury made the right choice on punishment, she would prefer not to serve on a capital case again. In the course of her three-hour interview, she did not offer many stories. Indeed, most of her answers were short and straight to the point. However, she was far more forthcoming when the interviewer asked, "During the trial, what were your impressions of the defendant?"

> *I saw the defendant as a very typical product of the lower socio-economic, black group who grew up with no values, no ideals, no authority, no morals, no leadership, and this has come down from generation to generation. And that was one of the problems we had, for me, and in the jury. Because some of the jurors were looking at him as your average white kid: he wasn't a white kid. He came from a totally different environment. I'm just saying that he was the one that was the defendant. And I just saw him as a loser from day one, as soon as he was born into that environment, and into that set of people who basically were into drugs, alcohol, illegitimacy, AIDS, the whole nine yards. This kid didn't have a chance. That's how I saw the defendant. And there are 10,000 others like him out there, which is very tragic.*

Sheila Brooks's tragedy of the "black" group tale conveys what might best be called a "white racial dialectic." Labeling the defendant as part of a valueless, "black" group, she simultaneously reinforces her own superior "white" identity. Comparing her own view to that of her counterparts on the jury, Sheila informs them that "he wasn't a *white* kid." Moreover, her use of ambiguous adjectives and phrases such as "that," "totally different," "that set of people," and the "whole nine yards" reveals a broader and more pervasive ideological means for distancing herself from a defendant she sees as lacking in individuality. Indeed, she sees him as part of a subordinate "black" subculture. Nevertheless, she observes, "there are 10,000 others like him out there, which is very tragic." The defendant is thus just another "character" in her story. Indeed, for Sheila Brooks, Cornish's "black life" fits a tragedy that is *all too familiar.*

In this story, Cornish's life is part of a tragic story that blacks "don't have a chance" *at the same time* that they are pitiful losers. Having difficulty relating to a defendant "born into *that* environment," Sheila Brooks marks entire places as breeding grounds for black inferiority, as drug-ridden, AIDS-infested places—places far away (albeit, tragically) from where 'average white kids" live. Next, she responds to the question, "In your mind, how well do the following words describe the defendant: severely abused as a child?":

> *I believe that was what he endured most as a child: Severe neg-*
> *lect. They were from the lower socioeconomic black group. From*
> *what we read about in the paper a lot, he was definitely from that*
> *group.*

The popular media, as Antonio Gramsci classically observed, is a key transmitter of hegemony. For Sheila Brooks, media confirms that "black" is more than just a category for designating the defendant Cornish, but a story of what "these people are." Next, she emplotts an individual responsibility story of her husband's struggles with addiction into her broader cultural distance narrative:

> *I did think about my first husband who was a drug addict and*
> *that's how I know what a drug addict is. And they didn't prove*
> *that to me. And drug addicts don't go out and kill people.*

The final sentence serves as an important hegemonic end in Sheila Brooks's story. By emplotting the story of her husband's addiction as a matrix for understanding the defendant's addiction, she is able to see Cornish as culturally remote; that is, she is able to confirm what she already *knows* about drug addicts. At the same time, the story of her husband allows her to come across as "color-blind" or race neutral. Because "drug addicts don't go out and kill people," she is able to rationalize away the complexities of Cornish's *own* problems with illicit drugs. In contrast to her earlier story of the "lower socioeconomic black group," by comparing the defendant's and her husband's addictions she allows herself to seamlessly make the transition to an evaluation of Cornish's culpability for murder.

Employing episodes from their private lives, white jurors tell stories that are inconsistent and often contradictory explanations for how they came to *know* the defendant. It is precisely such inconsistencies and contradictions that help explain how the racial inferiority narrative is a taken-for-granted part of "doing" death on the racially defined other. Unlike the subordinate racial group, white jurors need not be consistent. They need only to confirm what they already believe—that the defendant is everything or anything that *they* are not (e.g., "black" *and* "addicted").

Melvin Seagal: "I call them lost souls. . ."

Stories of personal experiences lend an air of authority to jurors' stories. Consider Melvin Seagal, a 63-year-old, retired, white social worker who sat in judgment of Frank Sharpe, a 33-year-old African American male convicted of shooting to death his 72-year-old uncle:

> *I lived in New York City for 17 years, and I saw a lot of young-*
> *sters like him in the ghettos up there, who were just lost souls. I*

call them lost souls. They have the propensity to do great harm to others because they have a lot of rage. They have a lot of unresolved anger. So, yes, I've seen young men and women who very much reminded me of him. They're powder kegs, they're just . . . their emotions are just simmering beneath the surface. And that's where I was exposed to a lot of people like him, when I was living in New York City.

Comparing his own experiences of working with "ghetto youngsters" with Sharpe's experiences bolsters the veracity of Melvin Seagal's story. In contrast to Sheila Brooks's explicitly lay, nonexpert tale of a "lower socioeconomic black group," Melvin Seagal employs his identity as an experienced *insider*. Yet Seagal's story conveys essentially the same plot as Brooks's: Blacks such as Frank Sharpe are "lost souls"; "they have the propensity to do great harm"; "they have a lot of rage." Drawing on his own experiences with blacks, he in effect represents himself as an expert *testifying* to the defendant's outsider identity. By emplotting the story of "ghetto lost souls" into his evaluation of the defendant, Seagal *avoids* evaluating the specific complexities of Frank Sharpe's life.

From Racial Tragedy to Racial Contempt

Media and jurors' personal resources give meaning to an underlying clash of cultures in jurors' cultural distance stories. Both popular culture and personal experiences help them confirm what they already know about "blacks" like the defendant. Using such cultural and personal capital enables jurors to see the defendant as "other" and indeed *worthy* of the death sentence.

"Death worthiness" in whites' stories may also be told through the prism of the defendant's crime. In this way, whites combine an emotionally charged tale of "black violence" with their reactions to the murder. Unlike the previous examples, the tragedy of the "black" group tale gives way to a story of contempt for the defendant and *what* he represents. Such stories convey contempt for the black defendant as part of a broader epidemic that needs to be avenged.

Robert Waingrow: "The blacks are killing the blacks. . . . Just like a gorilla . . . like Rodney King"

This high-school-educated 43-year-old white construction worker served on a case involving the defendant Ivan Strayhorn, an African American man who murdered his stepmother. He begins by telling the "tragically familiar" story of "the blacks are killing the blacks." Here, he offers his reactions to the murder of Strayhorn's stepmother:

[I]t's a shame, a woman that lived a good life, you know? And it's just a shame to see the way she went. I'm not going to be racial about it, but you have to state the facts: The blacks are killing the blacks. And you don't punish gently. It's just brutal. You think that he would do that to somebody who put her hand out to help him?

Robert Waingrow's story of the "all too familiar" escalating black-on-black violence is a matrix for understanding Strayhorn's responsibility for the crime. Indeed, it helps Waingrow make sense of the defendant's senselessness. Trying to save face (e.g., "I'm not going to be racial about it"), Waingrow "knows the facts." He is far less subtle, however, in his representation of Strayhorn's altercation with the courtroom deputies during the trial:

During the trial we determined he was a very violent person, because he jumped up and grabbed a deputy and tried to get the pistol out of his holster in the court, in front of everybody. It took six guys to subdue him. One of the detectives went over, and Strayhorn damn near got his gun and probably would have shot him. And the judge is yelling, "get the jury out, get the jury out!" And everybody is going "oh my god, oh my god!" People scattered like you wouldn't believe. This guy was big, you know. And these big deputies are jumping all over him, and he's just dragging them along. Just like a gorilla. Like Rodney King, you know the same situation.

Robert Waingrow's racial inferiority tale speaks for itself. The black body is but a racist caricature in his story. Drawing on the Rodney King spectacle, he presents Strayhorn as an inhuman beast, a chained gorilla. If "black-on-black" violence helped him broadly locate the defendant's murder of his stepmother, then seeing Strayhorn in this courtroom altercation only confirms for Robert Waingrow *what he already knew* about blacks "like" Rodney King. Waingrow knows from the beginning "who" Ivan Strayhorn "is" and "how" he will vote on punishment. Employing a tale of racial inferiority, Waingrow dehumanizes Strayhorn as a "chained gorilla . . . like Rodney King." Like Toni Morrison's eloquent observation of how race and inhumanity were conflated in the O. J. Simpson spectacle, for Robert Waingrow

race is itself primitive. . . . What might be illogical for a white is easily possible for a black who has never been required to make, assumed to make, or described as making "sense." Therefore when race is at play the leap from one judgment (faithful dog) to its complete opposite (treacherous snake) is a trained reflex. From this reductive point of view blacks are seen to live outside "reason" in a world of phenomena in which motive or its absence is sheltered from debate. Or, as a William Faulkner character put it, "a nigger is not a person so much as a form of behavior." (Morrison 1997:xi)

566   **Narratives of the Death Sentence**

Ralph Lewis: "Every time . . . I meet a nigger. . ."

Older, less-educated white jurors' stories convey an even more explicit contempt for blacks. Such jurors weave racial epithets into their stories; they explicitly see blacks as inferior. Marking the defendant with a racial identity rooted in a hopeless and savagely violent black group, they express an utter lack of surprise over the defendant's actions.

Ralph Lewis, a 62-year-old, white, retired farmer was born and raised in Alabama and is *proud* of his Southern background. Indeed, throughout his interview he seemed to take great pride in "how thick my accent is." While there were some audio problems and thus some difficulties transcribing his three-hour interview, Lewis's description of Alfred Watson, a black man convicted of shooting a black victim in an apparently failed drug deal, was captured by the tape recorder:

> *Anybody that was born and raised in the South when I was born and raised in the South and says they're not prejudice is a liar. I try very, very hard to get over it. Every time . . . I meet a nigger, and I don't like white ones anymore than I do black ones. That's the way it is. And what difference [there] [is] between me and anybody else is that I admit it . . . I mean, like when I heard about the killing, I thought, well, they're just wiping each other out again. You know, if they'd been white people, I would've had a different attitude.*

Obviously, Ralph Lewis's overt racism elucidates his underlying contempt toward African Americans such as Alfred Watson. While only one other juror in the sample referred to the defendant as a "nigger," such contempt stories, albeit more explicitly than Robert Waingrow's story, convey a very similar point: that this defendant's violence is indicative of a racially inferior group. However, the statements "they're just wiping each out again" and "if they'd been white people, I would've had a different attitude" are more than racist blather. Viewed through the lens of punishment at the hands of the state, Lewis's story reveals how sentencing the "other" has as much to do with constructing black identities as it has to do with *confirming* whiteness.

When Blacks Hold Out for Life

The story of the caring family is a matrix for how the white majority is able to convince a black holdout to impose the death sentence. Describing the holdout's reluctance to impose the death sentence because of the holdout's identification with the defendant's race, or more generally her mistrust of the criminal justice system, jurors in the majority tell stories of a sympathetic attempt to understand the fellow jurors' "differences" with the group.

White male jurors, rather than resorting to outright intimidation of the minority, tell a story of "the caring father," in an almost cordial approach, to convince the nonwhite holdout. As Mary R. Jackman (1996:74) observes:

> Within these constraints, the dominant group relies more on love or reasoning as instruments of coercion than on hostility and force. These efforts do not fall into a void, but set the moral parameters of the dialogue with the subordinates. If the structure of the relationship is conducive, subordinates may be trapped into generous compliance.

White males tell stories that show their attempt to understand, or at least acknowledge, the subordinate's point of view. What distinguishes such attempts, however, is how paternalism becomes an especially effective discourse, indeed, a means for trapping the holdout by the serenade into "generous compliance."

Fred Dawson: ". . . the fact that it is one of your brothers"

Fred Dawson, a 38-year-old business executive, served on the Cornish case with Sheila Brooks. The jury was made up of eleven whites (six females and five males) and one black woman. At the sentencing phase, all of the jurors except the black woman had made up their minds that Cornish deserved death. Here Dawson tells how the jury was able to persuade her this one juror to join the majority:

> *The only disagreement was with the black lady. She was a bright, a very nice lady. She had problems before. . . . Her son had been picked up, accused of a crime falsely, because he was black. She was a little bit sour on the system, but he got out of it. They found the other two black kids. So we were talking about that, and she looked across the table and she said, "I was the one who voted for life, you know?" I said, "you don't have to tell me that." I said, "but I know you were having trouble, the fact that it is one of your brothers . . . ." And she said, "he really aint no brother of mine, he's a bad dude, bad." So I said, "well, that's up to you." She said, "Why don't we vote again?" And it was 12–0. And then she sat there and cried for 20 minutes. But she was a good lady.*

Dawson's story of "the caring father" immediately draws attention to the "very nice," "bright," "black" lady. Conveying a sense of sympathy, Dawson then quickly shifts to a story of what "made her different from us." Dawson is indeed careful to acknowledge the validity of the African American holdout's mistrust of a criminal justice system that falsely "accused" her son of a crime. In addition, his introduction creates a sense of rising curiosity in the reader; the focus now is almost completely on the "good black lady."

Dawson's story is also a tragic one. Speaking in the black woman's voice, he is able to sound both sympathetic and understanding of her "black" plight. However, it is not until Dawson recounts her response to the challenge of "having to sentence one of your brothers" that the utility of paternalism as a device for achieving compliance is revealed. Dawson simultaneously expresses sympathy for the black juror's predicament *and* turns the tables on her. Employing a "dominance of care," he coaxes her into confronting what he perceives as her own black protectionism. But Dawson is careful to represent himself as a caring and sympathetic father figure (e.g., "Well, that's up to you."). In a word, care and sympathy allow him to avoid the implications of the obviously racial tactics he has used to make the black holdout *see things his way*. Indeed, paternalism, especially in the context of the give-and-take of deliberations, is perhaps the most effective and indeed subtle discourse for creating the illusion of a "color-blind" and sympathetic decision-making process.

While paternalism and sympathy played a roll in the jury's deliberations, Fred Dawson was anything but sympathetic toward the defendant and what he represents. Consider Dawson's responses to the following questions concerning his impressions of the defendant, his family, and the crime:

INTERVIEWER: *Did you have the following thoughts or feelings about the defendant: "You felt anger or rage toward him?"*

DAWSON: *I was angry because hundreds of thousands of people are like this throughout the country who cause all this aggravation and money to be spent on the court system. It's just ridiculous! It's wasting my time.*

INTERVIEWER: *Did you feel contempt or hatred for the defendant's family?*

DAWSON: *I don't hate anyone. It's the same bullshit that never stops. There's too much of it. Our welfare system makes these people. Our dollars we give them. It's terrible and awful.*

INTERVIEWER: *In your mind how well do the following words describe the killing: It made you sick to think about it?*

DAWSON: *No, because that is a personal thing. I don't get upset*
            about people like that. I just want to put him away from
            society. Hang them if they have to be hung, or the death
            penalty, whatever. I am sick and tired of this. It's a fairly
            universal attitude of people today. There is so much
            stupid crime! It's ridiculous, you know? We have so
            many liberal "do wells"—those bleeding heart liberals.
            This is nonsense. The guy knew what he was doing when
            he pumped four shots into the guy.

The nexus of white middle-class male identity and conservative tough-on-crime rhetoric is audible in each of Fred Dawson's
responses. Replete with racially coded phrases such as "these"
people and "the same bullshit that never stops," his angry responses stem not only from the defendant's actions but also from
whom Cornish and his family represent. Thus Dawson's individual responsibility story has little to do with an "individualized"
assessment of the defendant's conduct. Rather, Dawson's identity
is one of a "conservative avenger"—he sees himself as "evening
the score" against the pro-welfare, liberal establishment he
blames for producing "the Ray Floyd Cornishs of America"—a
racialized discourse heavily employed during the Reagan and
Bush presidencies (Omi & Winant 1986).

Fred Dawson focuses his contempt for Cornish's crime on
the liberal "do wells." In effect, he reconciles the contradiction in
his fellow juror Sheila Brooks's assessment of the defendant as
both responsible for his actions and a product of his tragic "black"
environment. Indeed, in Dawson's story anti-liberal rhetoric is a
justification in and of itself; it is taken for granted as the *way
things are* (e.g., "a fairly universal attitude"). And it enables Dawson to make Cornish's crime *personal* (e.g., "Our dollars we give
them") at the same time that it obscures his own racist stereotypes of a dangerous black welfare class.

V. The Stories of Black Capital Crimes' Jurors

The African Americans in this study challenge the racial inferiority tales of their fellow white jurors. In effect, they offer critiques of whites' localized knowledge that they describe as forms
of both white elitism and racial bias against black defendants.
The more-educated blacks draw on specific examples of something their fellow white jurors said or did as a basis for presenting
a broader critique of the entire capital jury system itself. More of
the working-class black jurors tell stories directed at white folks
whom they describe as individual racists.

Ronald Fredrickson: "They wanted to fry those black boys . . ."

Working-class black males, such as Ronald Fredrickson, voice strong resistance toward their fellow white counterparts on the jury. Fredrickson, a 53-year-old auto mechanic who served on the case of Arthur Chester, a black man convicted of murdering a white police officer, gives this response to the question, "In your own words, can you tell me what the jury did to reach its decision about the defendant's punishment?":

> *They wanted to fry those black boys. I'm serious, that's the feeling I got. I felt that they didn't give a shit one way or the other. They wanted to go home to their husbands or to the football game instead of worrying about whether these people were going to die or not. They felt like these two black boys took a white man's life: We're going to burn them. That's the impression I got from a lot of the jurors . . . I really believe they wanted to burn both of those guys because they were black and because the white defendant had a plea bargain and we didn't even hear his testimony. He was there just as much as the other black guy was.*

Fredrickson's story reveals a deep alienation and hostility toward the white majority. He expresses resistance to the pervasive white hegemonic of black inferiority, of which he is acutely aware. The phrase "to their husbands" is perhaps the clearest example of his resistance to a system he views as privileging whites. His use of the generalized descriptive "their" suggests a more global perspective of the struggle for racial justice as well. Moreover, "football games"—as a trope for white indifference—serves both to articulate to the interviewer the lack of concern the white majority had toward Chester's life and also to suggest a critique of the privileged "white" suburban lifestyle. Fredrickson, as a working-class high-school-educated man, employs a racialized discourse of a society deeply polarized by race and class inequality.

While Ronald Fredrickson never joined the pro-death majority—indeed, he was outnumbered in an eventual majority-rule decision for death—his last two sentences highlight his awareness of racial inequity in the criminal justice system (i.e., "he was there just as much"). Yet Fredrickson's story reveals more than a diffuse mistrust of the criminal justice system. That is, such a broad belief in the context of the Chester case can be heard as galvanizing Fredrickson's own internal resistance toward people such as Ralph Lewis—those who believe that blacks are an inferior race.

Harold Brown: "totally different perspective of what happens in the inner-city . . ."

Other African American jurors share familiar experiences with whites. These stories confirm why they resist white racism.

Another black juror, Harold Brown, a 54-year-old high-school-educated carpenter, explained how the jury made its decision to sentence to death Dwayne Whitmore, an African American convicted of killing another African American in an apparent gang-related dispute:

> *People got their opinion before the trial actually started. Like this guy from up North. He had a totally different perspective of what happens in the inner city compared to the guy out in the suburbs who thinks, "If it's a black thing then its automatic guilty." The white woman on the jury says the same thing. The white woman from West city who gets on the elevator with me, she got a problem. If something went down, the first thing that's gonna come out of her mouth, "It was a black guy." It's an automatic thing. And it's a shame to think that way when these white jurors hooked up that they were so disinterested. They were more concerned about what we were gonna have for lunch, and how long was lunch, and when we're [we] gonna get out of there.*

Like Ronald Fredrickson, Harold Brown tells a story that reveals a powerful sense of resistance toward the racially biased white jurors. He emplotts a story from outside the jury room into his broader resisting-white-racism narrative. In this way the hypothetical "elevator episode" serves not only to highlight racial bias among white jurors but also to convey it as taken for granted. In other words, Brown's story can be interpreted as saying, "If whites are racists in elevators, then obviously they will be racist when deciding whether or not to sentence a black defendant to death."

Shirley Sharpe: "I felt like an outsider . . . "

Shirley Sharpe, a college-educated secretary tells a more sympathetic story of *culturally distant whites.* She begins by describing her attempt to "educate" the white jurors who are unfamiliar with poor, blacks' lifestyles:

> *The main problem I had with the jury as a whole was that they were not considering what background this kid came out of. They were looking at it from a white middle-class point of view. Let me give you an example. There was testimony where they said that the defendant stayed out until eleven o'clock at night. But we are looking at a different kid here. This kid came out of a broken home where there was no structure, no authority figures. . . . He just came as he went. Of course he's going to stay out until eleven o'clock at night! He's going to stay up beyond that. And they were arguing, "Well, my kid comes in at such and such."*

Nevertheless, sympathy for her white counterparts gave way to frustration in Sharpe's story:

> *And I was frustrated. I felt there had to be more blacks on the jury. Because I think that was a big frustration for me. Because they were looking at this thing from a white middle-class perspective, and you have to put yourself into that black lifestyle this kid came out of. That particular lifestyle where there was not a good home, no supervision, there were no authority figures for this kid. So why waste time on talking about, my god, what time this kid comes in the house! There were a lot of little instances like that. That's why I felt like an outsider at times, because I felt I should have been more forceful at trying to get these people to understand. We had to look at it like the lifestyle he came out of, the background he came out of. But nobody wanted to listen. They all wanted to talk. I'm not strong-willed. I'm not forceful enough. That's why I felt like an outsider. So, rather, than get into it, I didn't say much. I mean, I deliberated, but I didn't say much about those types of things. So that was a biggie, and it didn't make me happy. And I felt there should have been more blacks on the jury to balance that out.*

Shirley Sharpe employs two distinct racialized discourses. On one hand, she speaks as an educated black juror who is sympathetic to her culturally distant white counterparts. On the other hand, however, she is unable to educate them on the realities of social disorganization and the absence of social control, so she turns to a narrative of *resisting white racism*. In this story the problem with the jury system is all to clear: Whites are too socially estranged from blacks *to make sense* of their murderous actions. Thus Shirley Sharpe feels like an "outsider" who lacked the will to persuade the whites.

Moreover, it is important to note that this shift in her story from racial educator to resister is emplotted against the very specific backdrop of being the only African American character in this tale. Indeed, this reality and her failure to persuade the white majority help explain her profound sense of racial disconnection, which manifest itself in her own personal estrangement and ultimately in her feelings that the system is in desperate need of reform. This narrative shift can be heard as elucidating *both* a local and a global consciousness. Such a "double consciousness" (Du Bois [1896] 1981) as an African American capital juror *and* as a member of the black community helps explain why black jurors may come to resent the white majority jurors they see as utterly estranged from "black" life outside the legal system.

VI. Conclusion

Racialized discourses among the death qualified jurors are not all of a piece. Whites articulate a tale of racial inferiority, but how such a narrative is made and remade hegemonic is more complex. White jurors are found to employ cultural distance stories of individual responsibility, the tragic "black" group, the "bad kid" and "the caring family," and "the threatening outsider." Who a juror *is*, however, has implications for how such stories make sense to them—indeed, for understanding how the tale of racial inferiority remains taken for granted.

In contrast, African American jurors, who represent a very small percentage of the death qualified jurors (Bowers et al. 2001), tell stories of "culturally distant whites" and "resisting white racism." In a word, blacks clearly "see" things differently than whites in death cases involving black defendants. But there are also subtle differences *within* the sample of blacks. More-educated jurors, such as Shirley Sharpe, are more sympathetic to the defendant and tend to tell stories that are closer in tone to those of their educated white counterparts (e.g., Sheila Brooks's "He wasn't a white kid" story). Alternatively, less-educated working-class blacks such as Ronald Fredickson are far less sympathetic; indeed they are openly hostile to the white majority they perceive as utterly indifferent to the lives of African Americans.

Prior research has attempted to present a more nuanced, "situational" perspective of legal consciousness (Nielsen, 2001), one that looks at legal discourses across *categories* of race, class, and gender. As a complement to Nielsen's perspective, this research points to a far more fluid perspective of the "law" as constituted by respondents' *multiple* identities. In the remainder of this paper I highlight some critical directions for what I have called a "theory of legal narrativity."

Toward a Theory of Legal Narrativity

A theory of legal narrativity posits "that it is through narrativity that we come to know, understand, and make sense of the social world, and it is through narratives and narrativity that we constitute our social identities" (Sommers & Gibson 1994:58). From this perspective, legal consciousness is understood by elucidating both the stories that give meaning to actors' identities (e.g., Oberweis & Musheno 2001) *and in turn* how such identities give meaning to "law" (e.g., Phillips & Grattet 2000; Richman 2002) as a site for competing hegemonic and subversive narratives (e.g., Ewick & Silbey 1995). It is only through the explication of identity stories (e.g., narrativity) and the hegemonic force that constitutes such stories (i.e., which makes law's dominance taken for granted) that we can more fully come to understand the subtleties of legal consciousness.

A theory of legal narrativity also presents a complementary methodological focus to the theory of situational legal consciousness (Nielsen 2001). More specifically, in addition to focusing on "variation across group when examining legal consciousness"

(Nielsen 2001:1088), a focus on narrativity moves beyond an analysis of law as a single isolated phenomenon occurring across or among isolated social groups. In this way, events are made episodic. This is accomplished by focusing on "emplottment":

> It is emplottment that gives significance to independent instances, not their chronological or categorical order. . . . As a mode of explanation, causal emplottment is an accounting (however fantastic or implicit) of why a narrative has the story line that it does. (Sommers and Gibson 1994:59)

It is also through the emplottment of identity stories that we learn *how* the law's hegemonic potential is mobilized and resisted.

Thus these data demonstrate the subtle intersections and tensions among race, identity, and hegemony in death cases. Undoubtedly, "race" has been demonstrated to be a pervasive and complex grammar for "doing" death. Racialized discourses are truly far more complex than "obvious" racial stereotypes of "black" criminals. For example, capital jurors' racialized discourses are constituted by both their "ordinary" identities—as, for example, in Sheila Brooks's story as a "wife of an addict" *and* more broadly by their popular wisdom—as in the example of the use of the trope of "the low socioeconomic, black group" more broadly. Nevertheless, it is only through the explication of narrativity in this context that we are able to see such subtle connections. To better understand legal consciousness in other sites, future research should pay greater attention to hegemonic narratives as both constituting and constituted by multiple identities.

References

Barkan, Steven E., & Steven F. Cohn (1994) "Prejudice and Support for the Death Penalty by Whites," 31 *J. of Research in Crime & Delinquency* 202–9.

Bell, Derek (1987) *And We Are Not Saved: The Elusive Quest for Racial Justice.* New York: Basic Books.

Bowers, William J. (1995) "The Capital Jury Project: Rationale, Design, and a Preview of Early Findings," 70 *Indiana Law J.* 1043–1102.

Bowers, William J., Benjamin D. Steiner, & Marla Sandys (2001) "Death Sentencing in Black and White: An Empirical Examination of Juror Race and Jury Racial Composition in Capital Sentencing," 3 *Pennsylvania J. of Constitutional Law* 171–274.

Butler, Paul (1997) "Affirmative Action and the Criminal Law," 68 *Univ. of Colorado Law Rev.* 841–89.

Carbado, Devon W. (1999) *Black Men on Race, Gender, and Sexuality: A Critical Reader.* New York: New York Univ. Press.

Comaroff, Jean, & John Comaroff (1991) *Of Revelation and Revolution.* Chicago: Univ. of Chicago Press.

Crenshaw, Kimberlee (1995) "Mapping the Margins: Intersectionality, Identity Politics, and Violence Against Women," in Dan Danielsen & Karen Engle, eds., *After Identity.* New York: Routledge.

Crenshaw, Kimberlee, Neil Gotanda, Garry Peller & Kendall Thomas (1996) *Critical Race Theory: The Key Writings that Formed the Movement.* New York: New Press.

Du Bois, W.E.B. ([1896] 1981) *The Souls of Black Folk.* New York: W.W. Norton & Co.

Ewick, Patricia, & Susan S. Silbey (1995) "Subversive Stories and Hegemonic Tales: Towards a Sociology of Narrative," 29 *Law & Society Rev.* 197–226.

——— (1998) *The Commonplace of Law: Stories from Everyday Life.* Chicago: Univ. of Chicago Press.

Feagin, Joe R. (2000) *Racist America.* New York: Routledge.

Fleury-Steiner, Benjamin (forthcoming) *Jurors' Stories of Death: How America's Death Penalty Invests in Inequality.* Ann Arbor, MI: University of Michigan Press.

——— (2003) "Before or Against the Law? Citizens' Legal Beliefs and Experiences as Death Penalty Jurors," 27 *Studies in Law, Politics, & Society* 115–37.

Frohmann, Lisa (1997) "Convictability and Discordant Locales: Reproducing Race, Class, and Gender Ideologies in Prosecutorial Decisionmaking," 31 *Law & Society Rev.* 531–56.

Goffman, Erving (1963) *Stigma: Notes on the Management of Spoiled Identity.* New York: Simon & Schuster.

Haney-Lopez, Ian (1996) *White by Law.* New York: New York Univ. Press.

Hurwitz, Jon, & Mark Peffley (1997) "Public Perceptions of Race and Crime: The Role of Racial Stereotypes," 41 *American J. of Political Science* 375–401.

——— (1998) *Perception and Prejudice: Race and Politics in the United States.* New Haven: Yale Univ. Press.

Jackman, Mary R. (1996) *The Velvet Glove: Paternalism and Conflict in Gender, Class, and Race Relations.* Berkeley: Univ. of California Press.

Jacobs, Ronald N. (2001) "The Problem with Tragic Narratives: Lessons from the Los Angeles Uprising," 24 *Qualitative Sociology* 221–43.

Lawrence, Charles (1987). "The Id, the Ego, and Equal Protection: Reckoning with Unconscious Racism," 39 *Stanford Law Rev.* 317–61.

Litwack, Leon F. (1979) *Been in the Storm So Long: The Aftermath of Slavery.* New York: Routledge.

Matsuda, Mary (1989) "Public Response to Racist Speech: Considering the Victim's Story," 87 *Michigan Law Rev.* 2320–72.

Mauer, Marc (2000) *Race to Incarcerate.* New York: New Press.

Merry, Sally Engle (1990) *Getting Justice and Getting Even: Legal Consciousness among Working-Class Americans.* Chicago: Univ. of Chicago Press.

Morrison, Toni (1997) "The Official Story: Dead Man Golfing," in Toni Morrison & Claudia Brodsky Lacour, eds., *Birth of a Nation 'hood: Gaze, Script, and Spectacle in the O. J. Simpson Case.* New York: Pantheon Books.

Nielsen, Laura Beth (2000) "Situating Legal Consciousness: Experiences and Attitudes of Ordinary Citizens about Law and Sexual Harassment," 34 *Law & Society Rev.* 1055–90.

Oberweis, Trish, & Michael Musheno (2001) *Knowing Rights: State Actors' Stories of Power, Identity, and Morality.* Burlington, VT: Ashgate-Dartmouth.

Omi, Michael, & Howard Winant (1986) *Racial Formation in the United States from the 1960s to the 1980s.* New York: Routledge & Kegan Paul.

Phillips, Scott, & Ryken Grattet (2000) "Judicial Rhetoric, Meaning-Making, and the Institutionalization of Hate Crime Law," 34 *Law & Society Rev.* 567–606.

Richman, Kimberly (2002) "Lovers, Legal Strangers, and Parents: Negotiating Parental and Sexual Identity in Family Law," 36 *Law & Society Rev.* 285–319.

Riessman, Catherine Kohler (1993) *Narrative Analysis.* Newbury Park, CA: Sage.

Sarat, Austin (1993) "Speaking of Death: Narratives of Violence in Capital Trials," 27 *Law & Society Rev.* 19–58.

Shields, Rob (1991) *Places on the Margin: Alternative Geographies of Modernity.* London: Routledge.

Sommers, Margaret R., & Gloria D. Gibson (1994) "Reclaiming the Epistemological 'Other': Narrative and the Social Constitution of Identity," in Craig Calhoun, ed., *Social Theory and the Politics of Identity.* Malden, MA: Blackwell.

Steiner, Benjamin D., William J. Bowers, & Austin Sarat (1999) "Folk Knowledge as Legal Action: Death Penalty Judgments and the Tenet of Early Release in a Culture of Mistrust and Punitiveness." 33 *Law & Society Rev.* 461–506.

Sunnafrank, Michael, & Norman E. Fontes (1983) "General and Crime-Related Racial Stereotypes and Influences on Juridic Decisions," 17 *Cornell J. of Social Relations* 1–15.

Sweeny, Laura T., & Craig Haney (1992) "The Influence of Race on Sentencing: A Meta-Analytic Review of Experimental Studies," 10 *Behavioral Sciences & The Law* 179–95.

Thompson, William C. (1989) "Death Qualification after *Wainwright v. Witt* and *Lockhart v. McCree*," 13 *Law & Human Behavior* 185–207.

[9]

EXECUTING HORTONS
RACIAL CRIME IN THE 1988 PRESIDENTIAL CAMPAIGN

TALI MENDELBERG

> George Bush opposes gun control and favors executing Hor-
> tons. I would guess Willy [*sic*] Horton doesn't. (A white focus-
> group participant, Texas, October 1988)[1]

Introduction

Contemporary historians of the South, following in the steps of Du Bois
and Woodward, have recognized that racial campaigns can affect far more
than voters' behavior at the ballot box. Given the right conditions, a racial
campaign can reinforce a variety of racially conservative views and actions (e.g., Lewis 1993). Scholars of public opinion have been slower to
explore the possibility that elections have broad consequences for public
opinion. This article seeks to remedy that neglect. It examines the way
in which racial campaigns prime racial predispositions in whites' views
of government policies designed to ameliorate racial inequality.

The 1988 presidential campaign's Willie Horton episode is my vehicle
of choice. Perhaps no other campaign tactic has come to represent better
the race card in contemporary elections. Yet, to date no evidence exists
that the Willie Horton story was effective. More generally, few direct
quantitative studies exist of the impact of racial campaign communication.[2] Here I use the Horton episode to test the ways and extent to which

TALI MENDELBERG is an assistant professor at Princeton University. She wishes to
thank R. Douglas Arnold, Larry Bartels, Michael Dawson, Martin Gilens, Fred I. Green-
stein, Jennifer Hochschild, Leonie Huddy, Kathleen Hall Jamieson, Donald Kinder,
Kathleen McGraw, Steven Rosenstone, Gary Shiffman, and Jeff Spinner for helpful comments.
1. Quoted in Jamieson (1992, pp. 32, 35).
2. Exceptions are Kern and Just's study of the Helms affirmative action ad (1995); Metz
and Tate's (1995) investigation of the impact of racial campaigns on turnout; and Kinder
et al.'s (1989) survey-based study of the impact of the Horton appeal on whites' vote.
Jamieson (1992) provides examples of voter response to Horton, drawn from focus groups.
West's study focused on the content of the Horton story rather than on its effect on the
public (1993).

elite trafficking in racial symbols shapes whites' thinking about policies designed to assist African Americans. I test two competing hypotheses: (1) by activating whites' racial prejudice, the Horton appeal weakened the already uncertain public will to remedy racial inequality; (2) the Horton appeal did no such thing; instead, it caused whites to give greater weight to concern over crime when considering various crime control measures. The first hypothesis is drawn from a broader view of the campaign as a racialized one, while the second hypothesis is drawn from a view of the campaign as a racially neutral one, or at least one that featured race only incidentally.

THE IMPACT OF CAMPAIGNS

Both hypotheses share in common the assumption that what elites say during presidential campaigns may have important consequences for public opinion. More than any other event, presidential elections are institutionalized, periodic opportunities to set the public agenda, to define collective problems, and to discuss publicly the future course of the nation. More than at any other time in their elective cycle, politicians have strong incentives to be persuasive, to capture public attention, to mobilize voters' sentiments, and to gain and maintain adherents. Elections are a time in which the symbolic power of political ritual is at its height (Edelman [1964] 1985). What politicians say during their campaigns for office may, on average, prompt stronger and more far-reaching public reaction than what they say during any other time of the electoral cycle. Carmines and Stimson put it this way: "Mass political involvement and issue discourse are episodic and discrete. Largely absent most of the time, they occur during political campaigns and particularly during presidential campaigns" (1989, p. 136).

All of this, however, is largely speculative. While the impact of campaigns on vote choice has preoccupied scholars since the pioneering election studies of the 1940s (Kinder and Sears 1985), there has been no systematic attempt to delineate the breadth of campaign effects. We lack knowledge of the distinctive impact of candidate messages, relative to other kinds of elite communication, on opinions about issues. Issues have been studied as explanatory variables in models of vote choice, not as dependent variables susceptible to campaign shifts. At the same time, studies of opinion about issues, including studies of media agenda-setting, have neglected the causal role of campaigns. Neither mass media studies (e.g., Iyengar and Kinder 1987) nor studies of elite opinion leadership on issues (e.g., Carmines and Stimson 1989; Zaller 1992) have specifically examined campaign effects on issue positions, though Carmines and Stimson do draw attention to elite influences on issue constraint.[3]

Furthermore, it is not as if politicians have abandoned the race card. The white public has certainly moved away from biological racism and segregation and toward endorsement of the principle of racial equality (Schuman, Steeh, and Bobo 1985). But debate over implementation of that principle has, if anything, accelerated since the height of the civil rights movement (Schuman, Steeh, and Bobo 1985; Sniderman and Piazza 1993). Candidates for office no longer promise to "fight relentlessly to prevent amalgamation of races," as did J. Lindsay Almond of Virginia along with most southern gubernatorial candidates in the late 1950s and early 1960s (Black 1976). But they find a variety of ways to appeal to whites' concerns about government attempts to ameliorate racial inequality. Metz and Tate (1995), for example, have documented the continuing use of racial appeals in urban campaigns. Others have begun to study ways in which candidates code their racial appeals, making implicit references to race while claiming no racial intent (Himelstein 1983; Jamieson 1992; Kinder et al. 1989; Mendelberg 1994). Nor should we expect race to fade away from electoral politics anytime soon now that it has worked itself into the fabric of the party system (Carmines and Stimson 1989; Edsall and Edsall 1991; Huckfeldt and Kohfeld 1989). Electoral campaigns, it seems, continue to rely on racial appeals for political advantage, and they do so because of the structural imperatives of American politics. In that case, studying the impact of racial appeals on public opinion opens a window on the way in which the status of African Americans has been negotiated since the civil rights movement reintroduced race into party politics.

DO RACIAL APPEALS MOVE WHITE PUBLIC OPINION?

Here I answer three questions about racial appeals: Do they move public opinion? If so, do they move opinion by priming racial antagonism? Or do they move opinion by priming concern about nonracial matters? For the 1988 presidential election, the questions become: Did the Horton appeal move whites' opinion on issues? If so, did it prime racial antagonism in opinion about racial policies (and racially tinged welfare policies)? Or did it prime concern about crime in opinions about crime policies? In other words, does public reaction cast the Horton appeal as a race card or, instead, as a straightforward vehicle for discussing universal, race-neutral concerns like criminal justice?

---

3. McGraw (1991) found variations in the effect of politicians' accounts of their issue votes on public endorsement of those issues, but has not focused on campaigns.

THE 1988 PRESIDENTIAL CAMPAIGN

During the fall of 1988, the criminal record of Willie Horton became a centerpiece of the presidential campaign. The story of Horton as relayed in George Bush's stump speeches, presidential debates, Republican campaign literature, and political advertisements was that of a young black man convicted of a grisly first-degree murder and sentenced to life without parole in a Massachusetts prison. While on a weekend pass he escaped, and kidnapped and brutally assaulted a white couple in their home, raping the woman and stabbing the man (Drew 1989; Jamieson 1992).

While the release of the Horton advertisement by a group technically unaffiliated with the Bush campaign sparked a heated exchange between the campaigns, the debate was brief, came quite late in the campaign, and mostly steered clear of race. Lloyd Bentsen and Jesse Jackson did accuse the Bush campaign of playing racial politics with the Horton case, but much of the debate did not deal with this charge. For one thing, Bush and his aides immediately and vigorously denied it.[4] Lee Atwater, the Republican strategist who much later apologized for the Horton appeal, at the time admitted no link with it: "Our campaign made no TV commercials about Willie Horton" (O'Reilly 1995, p. 387). Even as he later confessed to having approved the Horton appeal, Atwater still claimed it was not about race at all.

Those who denied the charge of racism implied that the Bush campaign's discussion of crime in general, and the furlough issue and Horton's case in particular, were simply about crime and had little to do with race (O'Reilly 1995). The journalist Robert MacNeil, in summarizing the Horton appeal's impact, reported that voters' response was, "I'm going to vote for George Bush because I can't vote for a man who lets murderers out of jail."[5]

The mass media for the most part did not seriously consider the possibility that the Horton appeal was a play of the race card and inadvertently aided in communicating it (Jamieson 1992, p. 28). Some newspapers handled the questions about the appeal's racism as if they were simply a dirty tactic. The closest journalists came to condemning the Horton appeal was to label it a negative partisan tactic, not a negative racial tactic (Jamieson 1992). Only after the campaign was over did the Horton appeal develop a reputation as an obvious play of the race card.

---

4. Kristin Clark Taylor, Bush's assistant press secretary and a black woman, countered that it was not Bush who sent Horton "out galavanting around on a weekend party pass" (O'Reilly 1995, p. 386).
5. In Jamieson (1992, p. 33). See also Barone and Ujifusa's summary (1989). A different version rested on the supposed truth in the notion that black men are especially prone to violence. "The average voter . . . just plain don't [*sic*] feel guilty for being scared of black criminals," explained one commentator. " . . . They [*sic*] didn't understand why it was racist to talk about reality" (O'Reilly 1995, p. 387).

Neither did the Horton appeal have any overt racial content. Not once did the official Bush campaign organization make a direct reference to race—the news media (unwittingly) and unofficial pro-Bush groups (wittingly) jointly provided the menacing mug shot of Horton and made his victims' white race salient. On the surface, the story seemed to be a dramatic, overly individualized, somewhat distorted, but largely legitimate way to discuss crime. While Horton's case was only one of several elements in Bush's discussion of crime, it was, as the most symbolic element, a rich composite of crime-related issues and concerns, especially drugs, victims' rights, and misguided social reform policies.

The Horton case, however, was saturated with racial meaning as well, largely through images of Horton. The configuration of the criminal (a young black man), the victims (an ordinary white middle-class couple), and the crime (physical assault in the victims' home, kidnapping, and—most notable—rape) has a long and sordid history as a stereotypical myth about the sexual aggression of African American males that, unchecked, directs itself particularly at innocent white women (Fredrickson 1971; Jordan 1968). The message may have worked as a symbol of misguided crime policies, but it may also have worked as a symbol of misguided racial-crime policies.

INTERPRETING THE 1988 CAMPAIGN

The Horton story, then, plausibly—but debatably—qualifies as a strategic use of a racial symbol, and its apparent effectiveness in advancing Bush's candidacy makes it a good case for a preliminary test of the power of racial campaign communication. To test the hypothesis that Horton was importantly about race, we need to find out whether the Horton message primed whites' racial prejudice. Several ways are available for thinking about what form contemporary racial beliefs and sentiments might take. One of these is variously known as symbolic or modern racism, and refers to a particular constellation of racial sentiment, moralism, and traditional American values. There is by now ample evidence that racial prejudice, defined in this way, is an important determinant of opinions on racial matters, and leads to resistance to racial equality as principle and policy. In its various incarnations it has been found to be a powerful predictor of vote choice in local and national elections, and of opposition to various race policies such as busing and affirmative action. It is much more prevalent today than biologically oriented racism, which centers on the notion of blacks' inherent biological inferiority to whites, and it may be on the rise (Kinder and Sanders 1996). The modern racism scale used to measure this kind of prejudice makes no explicit reference to racial inferiority; rather, it assesses hostility and moral indignation regarding blacks' current social, political, and economic status (see Sears [1988] for an overview and validation).

The hypothesis that racial symbols work by priming racial prejudice rests on the assumption that racial prejudice is dynamic, that its power waxes and wanes depending on the prevailing racial mood of the country and the moves of its politicians. This premise rests on an important contribution of cognitive social psychology, namely, the notion that racial stereotypes are more or less used in judgments depending on the information environment (Devine 1989). Personal racial isolation and certain racial issue frames can increase the impact of prejudice on various racial policies (Kinder and Mendelberg 1995; Kinder and Sanders 1996; Nelson and Kinder 1996). Perhaps prejudice is also primed by candidates' racial messages, finding greater expression in whites' policy views as a consequence.

However, if the Horton story did not appeal to whites' racial inclinations, but, as its defenders claim, dramatized the problem of crime, we would expect that racial prejudice would not play an enhanced role in shaping whites' political views. On this view, the Horton message was simply a public airing of the problem of crime and what the government might do about it. While many commentators now view the Willie Horton case as a clear racial appeal, in 1988 it was widely perceived as primarily a message about crime and misguided liberalism, not race. Furthermore, some observers and scholars continue to downplay its racial element. A recent journalistic profile of public response to what it called "Willie Horton" crimes ignored race altogether (Anderson 1995). According to Barone and Ujifusa's *Almanac of American Politics,* voters inferred from the Horton episode the obvious and not altogether inaccurate message that Dukakis might carry liberalism to unreasonable extremes. They argue that "such an inference was neither racist nor irrational" (1989, p. xxxvi). Hagen similarly argues against the "fascination in some quarters with the hidden meanings—especially the hidden racial meanings—of campaign rhetoric and political advertisements, to the exclusion of more obvious and pertinent considerations" (1995, p. 80).

On this view, the Horton appeal may have activated predispositions that match the "more obvious" content of the Horton story: concern about crime. The alternative hypothesis I test, then, is that a rating of crime as an important problem played an enhanced role in shaping public preferences about government crime initiatives. The Horton case would lead those who considered crime a problem to endorse measures designed to reduce crime to a greater extent than they might do otherwise.

Method

To test the two hypotheses, I designed an experiment that allowed me first to measure racial and crime predispositions, then to control exposure to the Horton message (or to a control message about Boston Harbor), and finally to gauge the impact on whites' opinion.[6] The experimental method avoids the common pitfalls of most survey-based attempts to study the impact of elites' opinion leadership (see McGraw [1991] for a similar argument). Ordinarily, these attempts lack strong causal inference because they employ correlational designs and bivariate statistical models. An example of this, notable for its originality and sophistication, is Carmines and Stimson's argument that the rearrangement of public opinion around the civil rights issue was driven by partisan shifts at the elite level (1989). Carmines and Stimson make a passing reference to the dramatic actions of Johnson and Goldwater in 1964 as largely responsible for important public shifts on race (pp. 47, 54). But their evidence on this point simply suggests that elite-partisan patterns crystallized in advance of public-partisan shifts. Many other events were underway at the time that public opinion changed on race; and assessments of racial attitudes in the 1940s and 1950s show a distinct movement toward tolerance well ahead of the legislative fiats and electoral maneuvering of 1964 (Schuman, Steeh, and Bobo 1985).

Kinder et al. (1989) undertook an analysis of 1988 National Election Study data aimed, in part, at assessing the effect of exposure to Horton messages over the campaign, using respondent's date of preelection interview to index level of exposure. They found that the longer the exposure, the greater the influence of prejudice on vote choice. But their effort is clouded by uncertainty about which individuals received what level of exposure (if any). And their general measure of campaign exposure is unable to tease out the effects of Horton messages from concurrent campaign messages and events. Neither can it ensure that recipients of the Horton message are different from nonrecipients only in exposure. Finally, there is the vexing problem of estimating the impact of Horton messages on the public while controlling on the impact of the public on elites and controlling on spurious, mood-of-the-times factors (such as a more general shift toward conservatism).

The most elegant solution to these methodological problems is controlled experimentation. By controlling the exact content and circumstances of exposure to political events, the problem of tracking the unique and unbiased effect of a particular elite move disappears. Of course, we should still worry here about the primary weakness of experiments—the problem of external validity. To partly alleviate this problem, I have taken the unusual step of using actual news segments broadcast during the campaign.[7] This step, and survey-based replication (see the Conclusion),

6. I will rely on "exposure to Horton" as a shorthand to "exposure to the Horton message."
7. The usual trade-off between external and internal validity in this case means that there is less precision in locating the source of the effect than there would be if I had artificially

should give us some confidence in the results, though cautious interpretation is in order.

PARTICIPANTS AND MEASUREMENT

Seventy-seven white non-Hispanic students enrolled in introductory psychology at the University of Michigan participated in the experiment for course credit. The median age was 18, and the group was about evenly divided by gender (58 percent female). Participants were administered the modern racism scale (see McConahay, Hardee, and Batts 1981), which assesses the more subtle prejudice described previously and minimizes socially desirable answers. The scale was administered to the entire class as part of a multistudy prescreening questionnaire.[8] Prejudice was then coded as zero for those lowest and one for those highest.

DESIGN AND PROCEDURE

Participants were randomly assigned either to the experimental condition, in which they viewed a Horton news segment, or to the control condition, in which they viewed a news segment about pollution in Boston Harbor. They were scheduled in small groups for a 50-minute session. Written and oral instructions informed them that after watching a few news segments they would be asked to evaluate the amount of horse race versus substantive coverage, and that they would be asked about their political beliefs so that we could hold these constant in the analysis. It was crucial that the full purpose of the experiment not be revealed, to avoid demand characteristics that might bias the results. Debriefing protocols suggest I succeeded in this.

---

limited the content of the stimulus. So, e.g., creating a condition in which the Horton message is conveyed without Horton's image would strengthen the internal validity of the design, but at the cost to external validity (since a manufactured news segment is usually not the same as a real one).

8. The scale was constructed by averaging seven Likert items (Cronbach's alpha = .83). With $N = 844$, the mean is 2.14 (SD = .68; range = 1.00–4.86), which is substantially less than the sample mean of the 1988 National Election Study (3.05, SD = 1.1; derived from results reported in Kinder et al. [1989]). To ensure a sufficiently large prejudiced group, I selected participants from the upper and lower deciles of the modern racism distribution (a random sample yields almost no prejudiced people). Because the student distribution is liberal, sampling its extremes creates one group of highly unprejudiced people and one group of people who are moderately prejudiced. The fact that the prejudiced group in this study is at the same level of prejudice as the large and politically consequential group at the center of the national prejudice distribution is fortuitous, since it means that findings about the prejudiced group in this study are more plausibly generalizable to the average voter in 1988. Another advantage of using a student sample is that it is less likely to have been exposed to 1988 campaign coverage at the time it unfolded (debriefing revealed very few instances of Horton recall). A probability sample of adults not exposed to Horton coverage would be better, but such a sample is logistically quite difficult to assemble for an experimental design that requires much more time and energy than normal survey participation.

Tali Mendelberg

Those in the Horton condition watched three news segments from 1988 network evening news broadcasts, borrowed from the Vanderbilt News Archives. The segment covering Horton's case was placed in the middle.[9] It featured, in part, the Horton ad (on the increasingly blurry line between news and ads, see West [1993]). The control condition replicated the Horton condition in every respect except the middle segment, which consisted of a story about the pollution of Boston Harbor. The two middle segments were similar in tone, length, the emotional and symbolic nature of the criticism of Dukakis and the factual nature of the rebuttal (see Mendelberg 1994 and appendix for details).

Finally, all participants completed a questionnaire on their political views. It included questions on implicitly racial policies like welfare, on government policies addressing racial inequality, and on perceptions of racial conflict. In addition, participants were asked about their ideology and demographic characteristics and for opinions on nonracial and crime-related issues.[10]

Results

We are now in a position to answer two central questions about the Horton appeal: Did it have an impact on public opinion? And if so, was the impact carried by whites' racial prejudice rather than their concern about crime?

EXPLICITLY RACIAL VIEWS

To test the hypothesis that the impact of racial prejudice increased on opposition to race policies with exposure to the Horton appeal, I estimate

9. See (Mendelberg 1994) for justification of this particular segment. The Horton segment was 3 minutes, 1 second, long; the three segments together lasted 10 minutes, 34 seconds. Abbreviating a standard half-hour evening news broadcast in such a drastic way, and including in it a full 3-minute story, may seem to stack the deck in favor of Horton effects, but on the other hand, the single-exposure treatment may underestimate them (Iyengar and Kinder 1987, p. 25).

10. Several elements of the design reduce the study's demand characteristics, a particular concern for the unobtrusive study of racial views. First, the modern racism items were embedded among several dozen others. Second, the experiment itself took place several weeks after the administration of the modern racism items, to avoid residual priming effects and to dissociate that scale from the experiment. Third, care was taken to avoid the presence of people of color during the experiment (by selecting white fellow participants and experimenters). Fourth, the cover story directed attention to an aspect of the news coverage unrelated to any issue or to race, so as not to artificially call attention to the study's purpose. Fifth, the treatment story and its control counterpart were placed in the middle to avoid drawing undue attention to them. Sixth, the postcoverage questionnaire included items that reinforced the cover story, and nonracial items preceded explicitly racial ones. Debriefing revealed only a few participants who guessed the focus on African Americans, though they made no link with the news stories. The study took place in the spring of 1992.

the following model of opinions on race policies and racial conflict, where Horton and prejudice are 0–1 dummy variables:

$$
\begin{aligned}
\text{Race opinion} = a &+ b_1(\text{prejudice}) + b_2(\text{Horton}) \\
&+ b_3(\text{Horton} \times \text{prejudice}) + b_4(\text{crime salience}) \quad (1) \\
&+ b_5(\text{conservatism}) + b_6(\text{gender}) + b_7(\text{class}).
\end{aligned}
$$

If the Horton story activates racial prejudice, then we should see a positive interactive effect of Horton and prejudice (b_3). Such an effect would suggest that exposure to the Horton story enhances the effect of prejudice on racial views above and beyond its baseline impact under conditions of nonracial communication. Even in the control condition, where there is no exposure to the Horton story, the effect of prejudice (b_1) is expected to be large and positive, because prejudice does not require activation to influence policy. But prejudice should have a greater impact on race policy when it is activated by a racial story. No net effect of the Horton message is expected, since I expect the effect of the message to be interactive (so b_2 may well be zero).

These effects should hold even when other determinants of public opinion on race, which are associated with prejudice, are taken into account. The truncated nature of the sample takes care of this concern for some of these variables: age, region, and education. The rest—crime salience (the tendency to view crime as an important problem), class identification, gender, and ideological conservatism—are included as controls in the right-hand side of equation (1).[11]

I examine nine dependent variables, divided into two categories: policies and perceptions. The first is the extent to which the government should intervene in racial problems: make a special effort to aid blacks, increase spending on blacks, bus school children to achieve desegregation, and engage in affirmative action in school and workplace. Four of these five items are averaged into a race-policy index.[12] The second category is perceptions of African Americans' position in society or of racial conflict: whether blacks' position has improved recently, the chances that a white person will lose a job or promotion because of an equally or less qualified black person, and whether civil rights leaders are pushing too fast.

Table 1 presents unstandardized ordinary least squares (OLS) coefficients on the normal, baseline effect of prejudice (b_1) and on the interactive effect of prejudice under exposure to Horton (b_3), with the standard

11. Conservatism has been measured by the usual 7-point self-identification question (from NES), and was included as a conservatism-liberalism continuum. The correlation between prejudice and conservatism is high ($r = .72$), and the estimated coefficients on prejudice and the interaction are smaller when conservatism is included, though the standard errors are not affected.
12. Busing's interitem correlation was at least 40 percent lower than the rest, so it was excluded.

Table I. Baseline and Incremental Effects of Prejudice
on Racial Views

Racial View	Effect of Prejudice in Control Condition (Baseline)	Effect of Prejudice in Horton Condition (Incremental)
Race policy:		
Government aid	.28**	.12
	(.09)	(.10)
Spending on blacks	.17**	.31**
	(.10)	(.11)
Busing	.31**	−.09
	(.14)	(.17)
Affirmative action, jobs	.27**	.07
	(.08)	(.10)
Affirmative action, schools	.28**	.13*
	(.09)	(.10)
Race policy index	.25**	.15**
	(.07)	(.08)
Racial conflict:		
Blacks' position improved	.13	.34**
	(.11)	(.13)
Blacks get white jobs	.19*	.25**
	(.13)	(.15)
Civil rights push too fast	.22**	.09
	(.10)	(.11)

NOTE.—Entries are unstandardized OLS regression coefficients (standard errors in parentheses). Incremental effects must be added to baseline effects for the total effect. Explanatory variables not shown are conservatism, crime salience, gender, and class. $N = 77$. Prejudice and Horton are 0–1 dummy variables. The same equation applies to all dependent variables in a given table. All variables in all tables were recoded on a 0–1 interval, with 1 as the conservative end (so positive coefficients are expected).
* $p \le .10$, two-tailed test.
** $p \le .05$, two-tailed test.

errors in parentheses (the dependent variables are all recoded from their original metrics to the 0–1 interval scale, with 1 as the conservative end, so OLS is appropriate). Each equation is represented by a row. Taking the left-hand column first, the baseline coefficients on prejudice are clearly and consistently large, and with two exceptions they are statistically significant by the standard ($p \le .05$) criterion. While in two of the three racial-conflict equations the effect of prejudice is small or nonexistent, it ranges from .17 to an impressive .31 in the race-policy equations. All this is consistent with previous findings about the effect of prejudice under average political conditions.

Moving to the right-hand column, which displays the interactive, incremental effect of prejudice with exposure to Horton, it is evident that exposure to the Horton coverage increases the effect of prejudice. The interactive, incremental effect of prejudice on the policy index is a statistically significant .15, which, added to the baseline effect of prejudice (.25), yields a substantial total prejudice effect of .40. The political significance is this: without Horton exposure, prejudiced individuals are 25 percentage points more likely than unprejudiced people to oppose racially egalitarian policies; with exposure to Horton, prejudiced individuals are 40 percentage points more likely to do so than unprejudiced people.[13]

This pattern is even more striking for the racial conflict items. Here the average baseline coefficient on prejudice is lower than it is in the race-policy equations. In at least one of the three equations, the baseline prejudice coefficient approaches zero. Comparing the baseline coefficients with the interactive coefficients in the right-hand column shows that exposure to the Horton condition activates prejudice where it was nearly dormant. For example, in the case of the question of whether blacks get white jobs, the coefficients change from a baseline of .19 to an interactive effect of .25, yielding a total effect of .44 (a 132 percent increase in the power of prejudice). This suggests that, when it is activated by a racially implicit symbol like the Horton story, prejudice will lead to perceptions that African Americans' position has improved and to a sense that whites are losing their jobs to African Americans. While prejudice may not always operate noticeably in the absence of racial communication, when such appeals are made, prejudice becomes a formidable influence.

Taken together, this set of results shows that Horton inflated the mostly substantial, sometimes weak impact of prejudice on opinions about racial matters. It suggests that people who are prejudiced become even more resistant to racial equality with exposure to Horton than they would be without it. But perhaps the increase in the effect of prejudice simply means that individuals low on prejudice reacted against Horton and moved in a more liberal direction, that racial tolerance rather than prejudice was activated, while the prejudiced remained as before. In that case, we can conclude that Horton did not lead people with racial resentments to vent them when making public policy choices and that the public reacts to racially implicit appeals by bringing its tendency to reject stereotypes to bear on racial matters. This, however, does not seem to be the case, as b_2 is essentially zero (table A1 in the appendix illustrates this).

---

13. The magnitude of the effect is not an artifact of the policy index. While some of the coefficients in the five race-policy equations are not much larger than their standard errors, they represent an average incremental increase of 54 percent over the baseline effects.

Table 2. Baseline and Incremental Effects of Prejudice on Nonracial Views

Nonracial View	Effect of Prejudice in Control Condition (Baseline)	Effect of Prejudice in Horton Condition (Incremental)
Defense	.07	.01
	(.09)	(.11)
Limit imports	−.07	−.08
	(.15)	(.18)

NOTE.—Entries are unstandardized OLS regression coefficients (standard errors in parentheses). Incremental effects must be added to baseline effects for the total effect. Explanatory variables not shown are conservatism, crime salience, gender, and class. $N = 77$. Prejudice and Horton are dummy variables. The same equation applies to all dependent variables in a given table. All variables in all tables were recoded on a 0–1 interval, with 1 as the conservative end (so positive coefficients are expected).

NONRACIAL VIEWS

But what if the Horton message activated prejudice generally, moving opinions on nonracial issues as well as on clearly racial questions? If it did, the argument that Horton worked as a racial symbol is considerably weakened. Table 2 presents the impact of prejudice on opinions on nonracial policies. Equation (1) has been reestimated, for the entire sample, but this time the dependent variables are foreign-relations policies (all variables are scaled on the 0–1 interval, with one as the most conservative response). The numbers look quite different in table 2 than in table 1. In both equations in table 2 the interactive effect is statistically indistinguishable from zero. The Horton story did not activate prejudice in nonracial areas.

WELFARE VIEWS

The impact of Horton is clear on views about matters that explicitly involve African Americans, and it is just as clearly absent on views about matters that are not racial. But there is a middle ground. Perhaps Horton exposure also moves opinion on implicitly racial matters, specifically, those that mix race and the traditional American values of self-reliance and hard work. Welfare is such an issue. Given that the majority of whites endorse stereotypes about African Americans' dependence on welfare (Bobo and Kluegel 1991; Kinder and Mendelberg 1995), and that endorsement of these views leads to more opposition to welfare (Gilens 1995),

Executing Hortons   **147**

Table 3. Baseline and Incremental Effects of Prejudice on
Welfare Views

Welfare View	Effect of Prejudice in Control Condition (Baseline)	Effect of Prejudice in Horton Condition (Incremental)
Blacks can do without welfare	.17**	.21**
	(.10)	(.12)
Workfare	−.21**	.21**
	(.10)	(.12)
Reduce welfare benefits	.17**	.11
	(.10)	(.12)
Welfare spending	.26**	.06
	(.12)	(.14)
Welfare feeling thermometer	−.12	−.19**
	(.10)	(.12)
Welfare index	.10	.19**
	(.07)	(.08)

NOTE.—Entries are unstandardized OLS regression coefficients (standard errors in parentheses). Incremental effects must be added to baseline effects for the total effect. Explanatory variables not shown are conservatism, crime salience, gender, and class. $N = 77$. Prejudice and Horton are dummy variables. The same equation applies to all dependent variables in a given table. Except for the feeling thermometer, all variables in all tables were recoded on a 0–1 interval, with 1 as the conservative end (so positive coefficients are expected).
** $p \leq .05$, two-tailed test.

it is reasonable to suspect that prejudice plays a heightened role in opposition to welfare under exposure to the Horton story.

    With this proposition in mind, I asked whether most blacks on welfare could do without it if they tried, whether welfare recipients should be required to work, whether welfare benefits should be reduced to make working for a living more attractive, whether spending on welfare should be reduced, and whether feelings toward people on welfare are essentially negative. I constructed an index averaging the responses to all the welfare items (Cronbach's alpha = .46). All variables are scaled on the 0–1 interval, with 1 as the most conservative response except the feeling thermometer.

    The results show that the Horton story inclines prejudiced whites to reject the legitimacy of welfare programs and to endorse the idea that African Americans can do without them. Coefficient estimates derived from equation (1) are displayed in table 3 (with the welfare items as the dependent variables). Table 3 makes clear that prejudice is an important influence on welfare opinions, though not uniformly so. The baseline coefficient on prejudice is large and statistically beyond question in four of the five individual equations, though in the workfare equation it takes the wrong sign (negative coefficient expected in the feeling thermometer equation). And in the case of feelings toward welfare recipients, Horton activates racial prejudice where it lies dormant, moving the coefficient from a nonsignificant $-.12$ baseline to an impressive total effect of $-.31$. The same pattern appears for the index of welfare items. Again, b_2 is zero, suggesting that Horton exposure moved opinion toward greater resistance to welfare among the prejudiced, while leaving the unprejudiced unaffected. Welfare has become a racial and illegitimate government program in the minds of a significant proportion of the white public, and the Horton message increases the tendency of the prejudiced to reject it.

AN ISSUE OF CRIME?

Before we conclude that Horton worked as a racial appeal, however, the alternative hypothesis must be tested. This view's proponents argue that the Horton story was an appeal about crime, that it was only coincidentally about race. Even if the Horton story did activate racial sentiments, that is an unfortunate and peculiar side effect of an essentially nonracial message. To test this possibility, the first order of business is to treat the salience of crime in the same way I treated prejudice. To do this, I evaluate the extent to which exposure to Horton changes the baseline effect of crime salience on matters of crime. With this purpose in mind, I estimate equation (2):

$$
\begin{aligned}
\text{Crime opinion} = a &+ b_1(\text{prejudice}) + b_2(\text{Horton}) \\
&+ b_3(\text{Horton} \times \text{crime salience}) \\
&+ b_4(\text{crime salience}) + b_5(\text{conservatism}) \\
&+ b_6(\text{gender}) + b_7(\text{class}).
\end{aligned}
\tag{2}
$$

This equation is identical to equation (1) but replaces prejudice with crime salience in the interaction term. Of interest in this equation is b_3, the interaction of crime salience and exposure to Horton. I contrast this coefficient with the baseline effect of crime salience (b_4) to see if there is a difference between the effects of crime salience among those who saw the coverage of Horton and those who saw instead the control story. If the Horton case functioned as a means of discussing crime, pure and simple, then Horton exposure should lead people who care about the crime problem to implement this concern in their opinions on crime-related matters to a greater extent than people who are concerned about crime but did not view the Horton coverage.

Table 4. Baseline and Incremental Effects of Crime Salience on Crime Views

Crime View	Effect of Crime Salience in Control Condition (Baseline)	Effect of Crime Salience in Horton Condition (Incremental)
Capital punishment	−.06 (.18)	−.24 (.29)
Law enforcement spending	.27** (.16)	−.05 (.26)
Spending on war on drugs	.63** (.24)	−.29 (.38)
Bush tough on crime	−.02 (.15)	−.12 (.24)
Dukakis weak on crime	.00 (.16)	−.03 (.25)
Which candidate will solve crime problem	.12 (.18)	−.22 (.28)

NOTE.—Entries are unstandardized OLS regression coefficients (standard errors in parentheses). Incremental effects must be added to baseline effects for the total effect. Explanatory variables not shown are conservatism, prejudice, gender, and class. $N = 77$. The same equation applies to all dependent variables in a given table. All variables in all tables were recoded on a 0–1 interval, with 1 as the conservative end (so positive coefficients are expected).
   ** $p \leq .05$, two-tailed test.

The crime alternative, then, predicts that Horton coverage may incline people worried about crime to favor capital punishment for persons convicted of murder and to favor increased spending on law enforcement and on the war on drugs. If Horton coverage worked as an appeal about crime, it might plausibly lead people concerned about crime to think Bush was tough on crime and Dukakis was not, and to think that Bush would do a better job addressing the problem of crime than Dukakis.

Table 4 presents the baseline and interactive effects of crime salience.[14] The baseline effect of crime salience is inconsistent, ranging from a huge .63 in the case of spending on the war on drugs, to the wrong-signed −.06 in the case of capital punishment. This is not a reliable baseline with which to compare the interactive effects under exposure to Horton. Nevertheless,

14. See appendix for measurement of salience of crime as a problem.

it is apparent that Horton did not bring out the power of crime salience. None of the estimates of the interactive effect of crime salience even reach their standard errors, and all have the wrong sign. There is nothing in equation (2) that redeems the crime hypothesis, not even a single significant Horton coefficient (b_2).[15]

Perhaps, however, the Horton appeal affected views of crime in a more direct way. It may be that the priming model I have used for racial prejudice simply does not fit when it comes to views about crime. Instead, the Horton story may have exercised its impact by making people aware of the severity of the problem of crime. By dramatizing and personalizing the often impersonal and anonymous face of crime, the Horton appeal may have made crime a much more salient concern. To test this version of the crime hypothesis I regressed the salience of crime on exposure to Horton. The results show that exposure to Horton did not move perceptions of the importance of crime as a problem (b = $-.01$, SE = .06). Crime, it seems, was not a more salient problem as a consequence of the Horton message.[16]

Of course, it is possible that exposure to Horton did not affect worries over crime across the board, but did heighten concern about crime among more prejudiced whites. Iyengar and Kinder (1987, p. 41), for example, found that white viewers hostile to blacks were most likely to emphasize the importance of unemployment after viewing a white victim of it. To test the possibility that racial prejudice plays a similar mediating role for crime salience, I included a prejudice × Horton interaction term in the equation for crime salience. Doing this, however, yielded an insignificant unstandardized coefficient estimate (b = .08, SE = .12; the baseline prejudice effect = $-.09$, SE = .11).[17]

Given the absence of interaction effects on crime views, the absence of Horton-exposure effects on the sense that crime is an important problem, or any other sign of life from the crime hypothesis, I tentatively conclude that exposure to Horton had no effect apart from its enhancement of the influence of prejudice on political views regarding race. A caveat is in order, however. It is possible that the measure of crime salience misses the power of concern about crime. Perhaps an alternative measure

15. On the hypothesis that Horton moved crime opinions by activating racial prejudice, I included a Horton × prejudice interaction term, but the coefficient on this term was substantively minuscule and statistically insignificant. Including this term did not affect either of the crime coefficients or their standard errors.

16. Crime salience was measured after exposure to Horton. This would have made the entire crime salience analysis suspect, if crime salience had varied with exposure to Horton, but as reported, this was not the case.

17. Adding crime salience × Horton to the race opinion equations does not change any of the prejudice estimates by a meaningful amount (or their standard errors). The interactive effects of crime salience fluctuate wildly from one racial equation to the next, have very large standard errors, and the total effects range from $-.37$ to 0.05.

that relies on a rank order of national problems would yield better results. Also I measured crime salience with only one item, while my dummy-variable measure of prejudice derives from a multiple-item scale. The baseline effect of the crime-salience measure I used was unexpectedly weak. All this suggests that the crime hypothesis deserves additional tests with different measures.

Conclusion

The Horton appeal was, judging by its effects in this study, about race rather than crime; it mobilized whites' racial prejudice, not their worries about crime. The consequences of this mobilization were greater resistance to government efforts to address racial inequality, heightened perceptions of racial conflict, and greater resistance to policies perceived as illegitimately benefitting African Americans. The experiment I conducted has limitations, of course. It is unclear how long the effects lasted, whether the conclusions apply to cases other than the 1988 election, and whether a nonstudent sample would have yielded similar results. However, Kinder et al.'s (1989) analysis of the 1988 National Election Study corroborates my finding that the Horton message was an effective play of the race card. This replication is especially reassuring given its reliance on a national sample of voters and the fact that it documented effects not after a single exposure but over the course of the campaign.

Iyengar and Kinder (1987) argued that stories about a given issue only affect views of that issue, partly as a by-product of the fragmentation of public opinion. When it comes to racial discourse, however, agenda setting and priming effects do not seem to operate normally, failing to reflect, contrary to Iyengar and Kinder's findings, the surface content of the messages that spark them (1987). Without this specificity, television's power in the domain of race may not be as limited as we might like to think. Whether or not violation of the specificity of priming reflects the special, integrative role of race in whites' public opinion deserves further study.

While the focus here has been on the Horton message in particular, given its prototypical profile, the results, though tentative, speak to racial communication more generally and to the institutional side of racial politics. We are now in a position to conclude, albeit preliminarily, that racial messages probably do matter, that they activate racial prejudice, and that they have serious consequences for public preferences regarding racial inequality. By establishing a three-way link between individuals' prejudice, their racial opinions, and racial appeals generated by the macrolevel dynamics of political campaigns, I have attempted to show how prejudice is activated in political contexts, transformed from an individual trait to collective obstacle.

The 1988 presidential campaign had, on its face, little to do with race (the Democratic primaries were another matter, of course, due to Jesse Jackson's candidacy). But closer attention to one of the more significant messages of that campaign reveals that race can operate even where it is absent on the surface: in a contest featuring white candidates, a large majority of white voters, and communication that carries few overt references to race. Attention to campaigns that seem to be devoid of race can reveal one way in which prejudice remains a potent political force among whites. It also demonstrates how racially modulated electoral strategies are implemented, and how they reinforce the gap between the opinions of African Americans and whites.

One of the significant aspects of Goldwater's 1964 candidacy was his success in conveying a racially conservative message without appearing to espouse segregation, and thus, without appearing to be a racist. But though the Horton appeal followed in the footsteps of the original southern strategy, it was nevertheless path breaking. It took place during a presidential election that was largely devoid of racial issues, certainly more so than the 1964 election, which took place in the wake of the Civil Rights Act. The Horton communication was, in 1988, very much a deniable play of the race card. It netted more political capital than any of its predecessors with the possible exception of Nixon's appeals in 1968 (Mendelberg 1994). As a result, Drew was correct in predicting that the negative style of the 1988 presidential campaign—in particular, its racial component— would be emulated by future campaigns. The racial campaign style of 1988 was echoed in such statewide campaigns as the 1990 Helms-Gantt contest in North Carolina, the 1991 gubernatorial election in Mississippi, the 1991 Duke-Edwards gubernatorial contest in Louisiana, the 1992 presidential bid of Patrick Buchanan, and Wilson's and Huffington's 1994 campaigns in California. All these campaigns included racial symbols: discussions of the supposed rising welfare underclass, condemnation of unfair federal quota bills, or a less subtle discussion of the loss of white jobs to undeserving minorities. While the tactic of coded appeals may have emerged from a national-level struggle for the allegiance of racially conservative whites, it has become a routine tool in the arsenals of candidates at all levels and of both parties.

That a racial campaign message may powerfully shape opinion on issues underscores the scope of presidential campaigns. The influence of elections may extend well beyond voters' choice of parties or candidates to encompass citizens' views of significant national problems. Elections are the linchpin connecting elites and masses, one that allows influence to flow not only from masses to elites, but from elites to masses. When presidential candidates use racial appeals, they raise racial stereotypes and resentments to the national agenda, displacing white individuals' more democratically desirable considerations. Should whites rely on nonracial ideological guidance in response to appeals about issues that implicate subordinate groups, the power of racial appeals may not lessen, but at least their democratically troubling consequence would be muted. But as long as racial appeals prime racial prejudice, we have cause to worry about the health of elections as an instrument of liberal democracy, with its requirement that citizens act out of tolerance rather than factional interests. As long as racial appeals continue, electoral campaigns will be lost opportunities for bridging the nation's racial chasm.

Appendix

Horton News Segment

The segment used was an *NBC Evening News* broadcast. The story was the lead story on October 7, 1988, and was introduced by Tom Brokaw as Bush conducting a "well-orchestrated attack on Dukakis' record on law and order." The story opened with the reporter, Lisa Meyers, saying Bush accused Dukakis of having an "ultra-liberal, ultra-lenient approach to crime." Bush is shown in a rally, saying that "when it comes to the plight of the victims and their families, there is an astounding lack of sensitivity and human compassion." Bush is reported to have recounted in gruesome detail the case of Willie Horton, "a first-degree murderer from Massachusetts who raped and tortured a Maryland couple while out of prison on a weekend furlough." Barnes, one of Horton's victims, is introduced next, speaking at a news conference. He is reported to have said that he and his wife would have been murdered if they hadn't escaped and to have accused Dukakis of insensitivity. Barnes is shown saying, "There's never even been an apology for what happened to us. Whenever it's been brought up it's been treated as an aberration, one failure in a successful system, which is a blatant lie." The reporter says Bush claims he is not faulting Dukakis for the Horton case alone, but because Dukakis refused to meet with crime victims trying to end the furlough program, and because even after Horton, he refused to change the program until public pressure became overwhelming. Bush is shown saying, "As far as I know, the governor has never acknowledged that his furlough program was a tragic mistake." The reporter says the Dukakis camp accuses Bush of trying to exploit a tragedy. Senator DeConcini is shown defending Dukakis's record on crime. The reporter outlines Bush's newly released crime package, which includes tougher sentencing, requiring all criminals on parole to remain drug-free or go to jail, rehabilitating first offenders, and the death penalty for "cop killers and drug kingpins." The reporter says the estimated cost is $300 million a year, but Bush has not said how he will pay it. She ends by saying, "Bush aides believe crime is one of their most powerful issues with Reagan Democrats and independent voters. They claim it takes but two words to raise serious questions about Dukakis's judgment: Willie Horton."

154 **Tali Mendelberg**

Question Wording

Unless otherwise noted, responses to all items were recoded on the 0–1 interval, "don't know" responses in the middle, 1 = conservative. The Modern Racism Scale was used to select participants; the prejudice variable in the actual analysis was a 0–1 dummy, 0 = lowest decile, and 1 = highest decile.

MODERN RACISM SCALE (5-POINT LIKERT FORMAT)

1. It is easy to understand the anger of black people in America.
2. Blacks have more influence upon school desegregation plans than they ought to have.
3. Discrimination against blacks is no longer a problem in the United States.
4. Over the past few years the government and news media have shown more respect to blacks than they deserve.
5. Blacks are getting too demanding in their push for equal rights.
6. Over the past few years blacks have gotten more economically than they deserve.
7. Blacks should not push themselves where they are not wanted.

CRIME SALIENCE

How about the crime problem in the U.S.? Do you personally feel that this problem is: Very important (74 percent); Somewhat important (23 percent); Not much of a problem, (or) Don't know (3 percent)?

RACE POLICIES

1. Some people feel that the government in Washington should make every effort to improve the social and economic position of blacks. Others feel that the government should not make any special effort to help blacks because they should help themselves. Where would you place yourself on this scale? (7-point)
2. If you had a say in making up the federal budget this year, for which of the following programs would you like to see spending increased and for which would you like to see spending decreased? Programs that assist blacks: Increased; Same; Decreased; Don't know.
3. In general, do you favor or oppose the busing of black and white school children from one school district to another? (Favor; Oppose; Don't know)
4. Some people say that because of past discrimination, blacks should be given preference in hiring and promotion. Others say such preference in hiring and promotion is wrong because it discriminates against whites. (5-point Likert; Don't know)
5. Because of past discrimination it is sometimes necessary for colleges and

universities to reserve openings for black students. Others oppose quotas because they say quotas give blacks advantages they haven't earned. What about your opinion—do you favor or oppose quotas to admit black students? (5-point Likert; Don't know)

RACIAL CONFLICT

1. Over the past few years we have heard a lot about improving the position of black people in this country. How much improvement do you think there has been in the position of black people in the past few years? (A lot; Some; Not much at all; Don't know)
2. What do you think the chances are these days that a white person won't get a job or a promotion while an equally or less qualified black person gets one instead? (Very likely; Somewhat likely; Not likely; Don't know)
3. Some say that the civil rights people have been trying to push too fast. Others feel they haven't pushed fast enough. What do you think? (Too fast; About right; Too slow; Don't know)

CRIME POLICIES

1. Do you favor or oppose the death penalty for persons convicted of murder? (5-point Likert scale; Don't know)
2. Law enforcement spending (federal budget spending series).
3. Spending on war on drugs (federal budget spending series).
4. Here are some phrases people may use to describe political figures. For each tell me whether the phrase describes the candidate extremely well, quite well, not too well, or not well at all. George Bush: Tough on crime and criminals.
5. Michael Dukakis: Tough on crime and criminals.
6. Which candidate do you think would do a better job solving the crime problem? (Bush; Dukakis; Neither; Both; Don't know)

Table A1. Effect of Horton on Racial Views, by Prejudice Level

Racial View	Effect of Horton among Prejudiced	Effect of Horton among Unprejudiced
Race policy:		
Government aid	.12**	−.02
	(.06)	(.08)
Spending on blacks	.17**	−.14**
	(.08)	(.08)
Busing	−.12	−.04
	(.13)	(.12)
Affirmative action, jobs	.01	−.06
	(.06)	(.08)
Affirmative action, schools	.15**	.02
	(.06)	(.09)
Race policy index	.11**	−.04
	(.05)	(.07)
Racial conflict:		
Blacks' position improved	.19**	−.16**
	(.10)	(.09)
Blacks get white jobs	.27**	.02
	(.11)	(.10)
Civil rights push too fast	.14**	.07
	(.08)	(.08)

NOTE.—Entries are unstandardized OLS regression coefficients (standard errors in parentheses). Explanatory variables not shown are conservatism, crime salience, gender, and class. $N = 77$. Horton is a 0–1 dummy variable. The same equation applies to all dependent variables in a given table. All variables in all tables were recoded on a 0–1 interval, with 1 as the conservative end (so positive coefficients are expected). Estimates are derived from eq. (1), estimated separately for each of the two prejudice groups: Race opinion $= a + b_1(\text{Horton}) + b_2(\text{crime salience}) + b_3(\text{conservatism}) + b_4(\text{gender}) + b_5(\text{class})$.
** $p \leq .05$, two-tailed test.

References

Barone, Michael, and Grant Ujifusa. 1989. *The Almanac of American Politics, 1990.* Washington, DC: National Journal.

Black, Earl. 1976. *Southern Governors and Civil Rights.* Cambridge, MA: Harvard University Press.

Bobo, Lawrence, and James Kluegel. 1991. "Modern American Prejudice: Stereotypes, Social Distance, and Perceptions of Discrimination toward Blacks, Hispanics, and Asians." Paper presented at the annual meeting of the American Sociological Association, Cincinnati.

Carmines, Edward, and James Stimson. 1989. *Issue Evolution.* Princeton, NJ: Princeton University Press.
Devine, Patricia. 1989. "Stereotypes and Prejudice: Their Automatic and Controlled Components." *Journal of Personality and Social Psychology* 56:5–18.
Drew, Elizabeth. 1989. *Election Journal: Political Events of 1987–1988.* New York: Morrow.
Edelman, Murray. (1964) 1985. *The Symbolic Uses of Politics.* Urbana: University of Illinois Press.
Fredrickson, George. 1971. *The Black Image in the White Mind: The Debate on Afro-American Character and Destiny, 1817–1914.* New York: Harper & Row.
Gilens, Martin. 1995. "Racial Attitudes and Opposition to Welfare." *Journal of Politics* 57:994–1014.
Himelstein, Jerry. 1983. "Rhetorical Continuities in the Politics of Race: The Closed Society Revisited." *Southern Speech Communication Journal* 48:153–66.
Huckfeldt, Robert, and Carol Kohfeld. 1989. *Race and the Decline of Class in American Politics.* Urbana: University of Illinois Press.
Iyengar, Shanto, and Donald Kinder. 1987. *News That Matters.* Chicago: University of Chicago Press.
Jamieson, Kathleen Hall. 1992. *Dirty Politics.* Oxford: Oxford University Press.
Jordan, W. 1968. *White over Black: American Attitudes toward the Negro, 1550–1812.* Chapel Hill: University of North Carolina Press.
Kern, Montague, and Marion Just. 1995. "The Focus Group Method, Political Advertising, Campaign News, and the Construction of Candidate Images." *Political Communication* 12:127–45.
Kinder, Donald, and Tali Mendelberg. 1995. "Cracks in Apartheid: The Political Impact of Prejudice among Desegregated Whites." *Journal of Politics* 57:402–24.
Kinder, Donald, Tali Mendelberg, Michael Dawson, Lynn Sanders, Steven Rosenstone, Jocelyn Sargent, and Cathy Cohen. 1989. "Benign Neglect and Racial Codewords in the 1988 Presidential Campaign." Paper presented at the annual meeting of the American Political Science Association, Atlanta.
Kinder, Donald, and Lynn Sanders. 1996. *Divided by Color.* Chicago: University of Chicago Press.
Kinder, Donald, and David Sears. 1985. "Public Opinion and Political Action." In *Handbook of Social Psychology,* vol. 2, ed. Gardner Lindzey and Elliot Aronson. New York: Random House.
Lewis, David Levering. 1993. *W. E. B. Du Bois: Biography of a Race.* New York: Henry Holt.
McConahay, John, B. Hardee, and V. Batts. 1981. "Has Racism Declined? It Depends Upon Who's Asking and What Is Asked." *Journal of Conflict Resolution* 25:563–69.
McGraw, Kathleen. 1991. "Managing Blame: An Experimental Test of the Effects of Political Accounts." *American Political Science Review* 85:1133–58.
Mendelberg, Tali. 1994. "The Politics of Racial Ambiguity: Origin and Consequences of Implicitly Racial Appeals." Ph.D. dissertation, University of Michigan.
Metz, David H., and Katherine Tate. 1995. "The Color of Urban Campaigns." In *Classifying by Race,* ed. Paul Peterson. Princeton, NJ: Princeton University Press.
Nelson, Thomas E., and Donald R. Kinder. 1996. "Issue Frames and Group-Centrism in American Public Opinion." *Journal of Politics* 58:1055–78.
O'Reilly, Kenneth. 1995. *Nixon's Piano.* New York: Free Press.
Schuman, Howard, Charlotte Steeh, and Lawrence Bobo. 1985. *Racial Attitudes in America: Trends and Interpretation.* Cambridge, MA: Harvard University Press.
Sears, David. 1988. "Symbolic Racism." In *Eliminating Racism,* ed. Phyllis Katz and Dalmas Taylor. New York: Plenum.
Sniderman, Paul, and Thomas Piazza. 1993. *The Scar of Race.* Cambridge, MA: Harvard University Press.
West, Darrell. 1993. *Air Wars: Television Advertising in Election Campaigns, 1952–1992.* Washington, DC: Congressional Quarterly.
Zaller, John. 1992. *The Nature and Origins of Mass Opinion.* Cambridge: Cambridge University Press.

[10]

RACIAL TYPIFICATION OF CRIME AND SUPPORT FOR PUNITIVE MEASURES

TED CHIRICOS
  Florida State University
KELLY WELCH
  Villanova University
MARC GERTZ
  Florida State University

KEYWORDS: race, racial threat, social threat, punitiveness

This paper assesses whether support for harsh punitive policies toward crime is related to the racial typification of crime for a national random sample of households (N=885), surveyed in 2002. Results from OLS regression show that the racial typification of crime is a significant predictor of punitiveness, independent of the influence of racial prejudice, conservatism, crime salience, southern residence and other factors. This relationship is shown to be concentrated among whites who are either less prejudiced, not southern, conservative and for whom crime salience is low. The results broaden our understanding of the links between racial threat and social control, beyond those typically associated with racial composition of place. They also resonate important themes in what some have termed modern racism and what others have described as the politics of exclusion.

In 1994, at the height of a period of intensifying punitiveness within the American criminal justice system (Irwin and Austin, 2001; Tonry, 1995), Jerome Miller,[1] the executive director of the National Center for Institutions and Alternatives, offered a racialized hypothesis for the dramatic rise in rates of incarceration. Miller observed that:

> There are certain code words that allow you never to have to say "race," but everybody knows that's what you mean and "crime" is

---

1. Miller previously headed the Illinois Department of Children and Family Services and directed the Juvenile Corrections Systems of both Massachusetts and Pennsylvania.

one of those ... So when we talk about locking up more and more people, what we're really talking about is locking up more and more black men (Szykowny, 1994:11).

Miller goes on to argue that "when we talk about building more prisons, when we talk about longer sentences, when we talk about throwing away the keys ... everyone knows that we're talking about blacks. And so the sky's the limit now" (Szykowny, 1994:12).

In essence, Miller contends that crime is typified in our culture as a black phenomenon and that our inclination to incarcerate at higher rates than ever before is directly tied to this. Similar points have been made by Beckett and Sasson (2000:136) and by Roberts, who argued that much of the support for an increasingly punitive response to crime is grounded in a "belief system that constructs crime in terms of race and race in terms of crime" (1993:1947). Though plausible, this provocative hypothesis is at best supported by anecdotal evidence[2] or by inferences drawn from racial patterns of incarceration. We offer a direct test of the hypothesis. Specifically, we use national survey data to examine the extent to which support for harsh punitive measures toward criminals is linked to associating crime with race.

The possibility is consistent with, and may help expand, our understanding of the "social threat" approach to the sociology of social control (Liska, 1992). That approach, which builds on Blalock's seminal "power threat" concept (1967), hypothesizes that aggregate measures of social control are to some degree mobilized by the presence of minorities, principally blacks. The hypothesis has been examined by linking the racial composition of place to various measures of social control, such as the size and funding of police departments (Chamlin, 1989; Chamlin and Liska, 1992); rates of arrest (Harer and Steffensmeier, 1992; Liska et al., 1985); rates of incarceration (Bridges et al., 1987; Padgett, 2002) and individuals' chances of incarceration (Myers and Talarico, 1987).

But as Chiricos et al. (2001: 323) suggest, at the heart of such structural relationships are a variety of "microprocesses" that operate at the individual level and help to activate and make the structural relationships possible.[3] For example, Liska and Chamlin note that "the threat hypothesis ... suggests that a high percentage of nonwhites produces an emergent property, 'perceived threat of crime,' which increases arrest

---

2. For example, Miller (1996:87) offers such anecdotal evidence based on a conversation with a judge and Bridges, Crutchfield and Simpson (1987:355-356) provide similar evidence gleaned from interviews of prosecutors and judges.

3. These micro processes are presumed to operate at the level of individuals who may perceive the presence of blacks as threatening and be inclined to call the police (Warner, 1992) or otherwise assist in the mobilization of social control.

rates through increasing pressure on police to control crime" (1984:384–5). The perceived threat of crime in most social threat research is an essential but unmeasured element in the mobilization of social control. A fairly substantial body of research has developed to assess the extent to which fear of crime is related to the actual or perceived racial composition of place (Chiricos et al., 2001; Covington and Taylor, 1991; Liska et al., 1982; Moeller, 1989; Taylor and Covington, 1993; Skogan, 1995).

Measuring the relationship between where people live and their fear of crime is one approach to specifying the race-specific crime threat implicit to the social threat hypothesis. But another is to measure directly the extent to which people associate crime with blacks. Regardless of the racial composition of neighborhoods, an explicit link between race and crime may be the basis for support of more punitive controls—more arrests, more funding for police, greater use of incarceration, or other punitive measures. That, in effect, is what we are testing here. If the evidence supports the hypothesis, we may be in a position to broaden our understanding of how race, threat and social control interact.

RACE AND THREAT IN CONTEXT

Much of the research using racial composition of place as an indicator of race-related threat has shown that its relationship, either to social control at the macro level or to fear and other attitudinal measures at the individual level, is often contextual. Blalock was the first to raise the issue when he noted "the possibility that different kinds of persons will not be similarly motivated by the minority percentage variable" (1967:31). Pamela Jackson, who researched the relevance of racial composition of cities for various policing measures, concluded that "social context acts as a prism, altering perceptions of the degree of minority-group threat" (1992:94).

The most common contexts at the macro level have been time and place. For example, studies of police department size (Greenberg et al., 1985; Jacobs, 1979), police department funding (Jackson, 1985, 1986, 1989) and lynching (Tolnay et al., 1992) have found the relevance of percent black to vary over time. Regional variation in the relationship between racial composition and rates of incarceration (Padgett, 2002), lynching (Corzine et al., 1983), segregation (Emerson, 1994), police strength (Greenberg et al., 1985) and police funding (Jackson, 1989) has also been widely documented.

At the micro-level the contingent nature of racial threat has also been demonstrated. For example, Liska et al. (1981) report that the relationship between percent nonwhite and fear varies by time and place. Ward et al. (1986) found that percent black and perceived safety of elderly respondents were related only among those who reported "competency" difficulties. Chiricos et al. (1997) found that the relationship between racial composition and fear of crime depended on the respondent's race and (2001) varied regionally.

The findings of a number of studies on negative racial perceptions are relevant here. Carmine and Layman, for example, found that, in relation to support for government policies to assist blacks, racial "prejudice has its most powerful influence on white Democrats" and none on Republicans (1998:129). They concluded that "Republicans, whatever their level of prejudice, are committed to a limited role for the national government in the social welfare domain" and for them, prejudice has little consequence (1998:129). Borg (1997) found that support for the death penalty among white respondents to the General Social Survey (GSS) was significantly linked to racial prejudice but only for those classified as "nonsoutherners." Taylor (1998) also used GSS data to find that racial composition of the respondent's city was significantly related to "anti-black prejudice" and "policy-related beliefs about blacks," but only outside of the South. She concluded that the issue of race is so long-standing in the South that individual levels of prejudice might well be "less vulnerable" to it (1998:526).

It is reasonable to anticipate that the relationship of racial typification of crime to punitiveness might also be contextual. Much of the contextual evidence concerning racial threat and related attitudes is regional and we will therefore consider that in our analysis. Borg's (1997) findings about prejudice and punitiveness, Taylor's (1998) about racial composition and prejudice and Carmine and Layman's (1998) about prejudice and policy preferences have a common theme. Racial composition and racial prejudice are least consequential where either racial attitudes, punitiveness or policy preferences are more harsh. We might on that account, expect that racial typification will be weakest where punitiveness is already high.

Before describing our methodology and findings, we briefly review the salience of racial typification of crime and related research on punitive attitudes.

RACIAL TYPIFICATION OF CRIME

The presumed link of crime with black men is well established in American culture (Hawkins, 1995; Russell, 1998). It has been argued however, that since the 1960s, in the wake of civil rights activism and higher levels of integration, it has grown substantially more conspicuous (Barlow, 1998). The image of the black male as a criminal threat—which Russell (1998:71) contends often morphs into the perception of "criminalblackman"—received well documented media support from advertisements featuring Willie Horton in the 1988 presidential campaign of George Bush (Jamieson, 1992; Mendelberg, 1997).

Indeed, it is widely assumed that the media, especially television, has played an important role in establishing the identity of race and crime. Beckett and Sasson (2000:136), for example, observe that "television crime news and the new reality crime programs associate blackness and crime and do so in emotionally charged ways that encourage punitiveness among the viewing public." Fishman notes that "the media have ... propagated the erroneous and racist notion that all poor blacks, especially males are addicted to crack cocaine, involved in drug trafficking and/or involved in heinous drug-related crimes" (1998:112). And former Secretary of Health and Human Services Louis Sullivan contends that "as he [the black male] typically appears in the media, he's either a jewelry bedecked drug pusher, a misogynous pimp or a vicious thug" (quoted in Drummond, 1990:28).

The link between race and crime has become so well established that Barak (1994:137) can reasonably assert that "today's prevailing criminal predator has become a euphemism for young black male." So it may not be surprising that hoaxes about black suspects, such as those involving Charles Stuart in Boston and Susan Smith in South Carolina,[4] are so readily found credible (Russell, 1998). The facile assumption of black criminal suspicion is further demonstrated by a recent experiment at UCLA. Subjects viewing newscasts of crime stories were twice as likely to believe that a black suspect had been identified in stories that made no specific reference to a suspect (Mauer, 1999: 174).

The racial typification of crime is so well established that, as Barlow notes, in much discourse about crime, "it is unnecessary to speak directly of race because talking about crime *is* talking about race" (1998:151). Even public figures with politically "liberal" credentials make the race/crime connection. The Reverend Jesse Jackson, while speaking out against black on black crime, admitted to feeling "relief" when approaching strangers on darkened urban streets are not young black men (Cohen, 1993:A2). And former Democratic Senator Bill Bradley observed with chagrin that "the fear of black crime covers the streets like a sheet of ice" (Skogan, 1995:60).

The consequences of the racial typification of crime—besides the hypothesized support for punitive justice measures to be tested here—are many. At the very least they include the difficulty, if not impossibility, of service delivery in predominantly black neighborhoods and the "unavailability" of taxicabs to black travelers, even in racially mixed or

---

4. In these highly publicized incidents, Susan Smith drowned her children and Charles Stuart shot his wife to death and in both instances police attention was focused for some time on alleged black male assailants.

predominantly white areas (West, 1994). They also include the racial profiling of suspects by law enforcement (Kennedy, 1997) and the increased likelihood of witness error in court testimony (Roberts, 1993). It has also been argued that the assumption of black criminality leads to the more likely use of deadly force in encounters between police and suspects in some urban neighborhoods (Chua-Eoan, 2000).

Finally,the racial typification of crime may contribute to what some have called "modern racism" (McConahay, 1986; Sears, 1988). This is characterized by "a general hostility toward blacks" (Entman, 1990:332) as opposed to direct expressions of racial superiority or inferiority. The result is to increase the likelihood that some whites will "lump all or most blacks into categories with negative characteristics" (Entman, 1992:345). The ready association of blacks with crime is one example.[5]

PRIOR RESEARCH:
PUNITIVE ATTITUDES TOWARD CRIMINALS

Survey research into the correlates and predictors of punitive attitudes toward criminals has been extensive but is difficult to synthesize. One reason is the many methodologies used. Perhaps the most important variable has been the measurement of punitive attitudes. Some researchers have asked a single question, concerning, for example, support for the death penalty (Borg, 1997; Britt, 1998) or judgment about the appropriateness of current sentencing practices (Cohn et al., 1991; Secret and Johnson, 1989; Sprott, 1999). The second type of question has been commonly used in both Gallup and GSS surveys for some time. Another method has been to give respondents an opportunity to choose among a variety of options for dealing with crime in general or with particular crimes. Among the alternatives considered are the use of fines and probation in addition to incarceration (Jacoby, 1989) or the use of community-based options, early release or "rehabilitation" programs (Skovron et al., 1988). Another approach has been to describe particularized crime vignettes and ask respondents either to assess the appropriateness of a hypothetical punishment (Miller et al., 1986, 1991) or to assign a punishment from within a specific range of possibilities (Blumstein and Cohen, 1980; Durham et al., 1996; Rossi and Berk, 1997; Thomas et al., 1976).

---

5. For an excellent discussion of the evolution of modern racism and how it differs from traditional racism, see Sniderman, et. al., who observe that while both "centered on dislike of blacks ... before, racists would say blatantly that blacks were lazy. Now they would say instead that if blacks were only willing to work hard, they could be as well off as whites" (1998:21).

RACIAL TYPIFICATION OF CRIME 365

Given the extraordinary diversity of methods for estimating punitiveness, and because no prior research has dealt with racial typification of crime as a potential predictor, we briefly review here what has been learned about the relationship of punitiveness to race, racial attitudes and fear of crime. Because our theoretical focus is, broadly speaking, the threat of crime that is racially specified, the closest we can come to relevant research is that which deals with crime threat generally (fear) and race or racial attitudes specifically. None of this research bears directly on our hypothesized relationship, but because our analyses will be race specific and control for fear of crime and racial prejudice, this work may be relevant. The results we reference are limited to those based on multivariate analyses.

FEAR OF CRIME AND PUNITIVENESS

The evidence concerning fear and punitiveness is quite inconsistent. Sprott's (1999) Canadian study found no relationship between fear and judgments about the harshness or leniency of adult court sentencing. Similarly, Secret and Johnson (1989) found no relationship in a national random sample between fear and judgments about the appropriateness of court sentencing and spending to control crime. The most consistent support for the relevance of fear is reported by Langworthy and Whitehead (1986) in a national survey about the punitive rather than rehabilitative purpose of incarceration and by Applegate et al. (2002) in their Ohio study of support for harsher court penalties. Young and Thompson (1995) also found that fear predicted support for the death penalty, using national GSS data.

The remaining research involving fear has produced qualified results. For example, fear was unrelated to punitive responses to robbery, burglary, molestation, drug sales and drug possession in a Las Vegas study (McCorkle, 1993) but positively to those for rape. Cohn et al. (1991) found in their national sample that for white respondents fear was unrelated to judgments about the harshness of court sentencing, but for black respondents was highly significant. Tyler and Weber's (1982) Illinois study found fear to be unrelated to support for the death penalty in five estimates, but positively related in three. Using national survey data, Schwartz et al. (1992) found that fear of violent victimization predicted support for several punitive measures, but not for others. Using similar data, Schwartz et al. (1993) found that the same fear measure was related to support for juveniles being sentenced as adults for violent, property and drug crimes.

366   CHIRICOS, WELCH AND GERTZ

RACE AND PUNITIVENESS

There has been much more evidence on the relevance of race for punitiveness than for the fear of crime.[6] The results are quite consistent. Most often, race is a nonsignificant predictor in multivariate estimates of punitiveness (Applegate et al., 1996, 2000, 2002; Grasmick et al., 1992; Harris, 1986; Langworthy and Whitehead, 1986; McCorkle, 1993; Sandys and McGarrell, 1995; Schwartz et al., 1993; Skovron et al., 1989; Tyler and Weber, 1982). Where race does make a difference, whites are almost always more punitive.

For example, Rossi and Berk (1997) used elaborately varied crime vignettes to solicit judgments from a national random sample on the choice of punishments for offenders under specified conditions. When respondent demographics were included with region and city size variables, whites were significantly more punitive in four of nine regression estimates. However, when social and political attitudes as well as personal experience with crime and justice were added to the models, race of respondent was no longer a significant predictor. Grasmick et al. (1993) found that race did not matter in Oklahoma City when it came to support for harsher laws and sentencing. They did find, however, that white respondents were significantly more likely to support the death penalty for both adults and juveniles.

Using national GSS data, Cohn et al. (1991) found that whites were more likely to say that courts in this country do not deal harshly enough with criminals. Secret and Johnson (1989) also made use of GSS survey data to assess whether courts are too harsh or not harsh enough with criminals and whether too much or too little money is being spent on "halting the rising crime rate" and "dealing with drug addicts." Race was not significant in four separate estimates for the spending variables. But for one of two estimates, whites were significantly more punitive. Skovron et al. (1988) surveyed respondents in Columbus and Cincinnati, Ohio. In Columbus race was unrelated to a question concerned with shortening sentences to reduce prison overcrowding, but in Cincinnati whites were more likely to oppose it.

Researchers using national GSS data (Borg, 1997; Britt, 1998; Combs and Comer, 1982; Young, 1992; Young and Thompson, 1995) have consistently found that whites supported the death penalty more than others. The only study to report greater punitiveness among blacks involved support among students at a southern university for the death penalty (Bohm, 1992).

---

6. It should be noted that race was most often not the specific focus of these studies, but a variable that was included in multivariate estimates of punitiveness.

RACIAL TYPIFICATION OF CRIME   367

RACE RELATED ATTITUDES AND PUNITIVENESS

To our knowledge, only a handful of studies have examined race-related attitudes and punitiveness and none of them used racial typification of crime. The results are relatively consistent. For example, Borg (1997) used a national random sample of white respondents to assess support for the death penalty. Among her independent variables were "racial antipathy" and "racial stereotyping." The first was measured by questions that asked about living in a neighborhood where "half your neighbors were blacks" and having a close friend or relative "marry a black person." The second combined responses to statements about blacks being lazy, unintelligent, unpatriotic and wanting to live on welfare. For the full sample, and for a subsample of "southern" respondents, neither racial antipathy nor racial stereotyping was related to support for the death penalty. However, both antipathy and stereotyping were significantly related to punitiveness in a subsample of "nonsouthern" respondents.[7]

Similar results using national GSS data have shown support for the death penalty to be related to racial antipathy and negative stereotyping (Barkan and Cohn, 1994) as well as to a seven-item "racism" scale (Aguirre and Baker, 1993). Cohn et al. (1991) used 1987 GSS data to show that racial prejudice as indicated by a three-item scale involving intermarriage, discrimination in home sales and neighborhood exclusion, was related to judgments that courts were not harsh enough in punishing criminals.

Rossi and Berk (1997) also used a national sample of respondents who were given crime vignettes with variable characteristics, including a judgment about whether minority groups had too few or too many "civil rights." In the fullest models, which included demographic, regional, criminal justice contact and attitudinal measures, Rossi and Berk (1997) report that respondents who would prefer "fewer civil rights for minorities" were more punitive toward all crimes, including drug trafficking and white-collar crime, and were more supportive of the death penalty.

Finally, Leiber and Woodrick (1997) interviewed juvenile court personnel about their beliefs in racial differences. Specifically they asked whether black families were more distrustful than other families and whether black youth have "poorer attitudes" and are less willing to acknowledge guilt. An index was constructed from the responses. The

---

7. The authors also looked at a model with regional interaction terms for the full sample and in that estimate, both racial antipathy and racial stereotyping were statistically significant.

368   CHIRICOS, WELCH AND GERTZ

authors report that the belief in racial differences significantly predicted support for the death penalty being applied to a juvenile in a hypothetical situation, but not support for stricter courts or a general endorsement of the need for stricter punishment in relation to juvenile offenders.

In sum, while there is no research linking punitiveness to the racial typification of crime, the findings we have reviewed here may be indirectly relevant to that question. Most germane is that negative perceptions of blacks and minorities are in most instances related to punitive attitudes. The racial typification of crime can be considered a similar negative perception. Almost all the significant race effects on punitiveness involve whites and this would be relevant if one could assume that whites are more likely to see blacks as criminally threatening. This study will directly address that question.

RESEARCH METHODOLOGY

We conducted a telephone survey of a national random sample (N=885) of adults, 18 years and older, in households accessed by random digit dialing.[8] The calls were made between January and April, 2002. The final sample was 56.5 percent female; 79.8 percent white; 11.4 percent black and 7.5 percent Hispanic. Forty-four percent of the sample had graduated from college. The median age was 46 years. The slight overrepresentation of white, female and older respondents is not uncommon in telephone surveys (Lavrakas, 1987).

DEPENDENT VARIABLE:
PUNITIVE ATTITUDES TOWARD CRIME

As noted, the method for assessing punitiveness toward crime has varied considerably. There has been frequent reliance on global assessments of support for the death penalty or whether courts are too harsh or too little is being spent on fighting crime. There has been some use of vignettes that can vary factors that could play into punitive preferences of respondents. Because the vignette option is too complex for telephone surveys and because we wanted to engage some of the specific punitive policies that legislatures and courts have either been using or considering, our survey asked this question:

---

8. The survey was conducted by The Research Network, Inc., a public opinion polling firm in Tallahassee, Florida. A two-stage Mitofsky-Waksberg sampling design was utilized and an eight call-back rule was employed before replacement. Using the definition recommended by the American Association for Public Opinion Research (1998) we obtained a cooperation rate of 40 percent among all contacts with eligible respondents. Ninety-three percent of all surveys initiated were completed.

I am going to read a list of things that have been suggested as ways of dealing with crime in the United States. On a scale from 0 to 10, where 0 is being not at all supportive and 10 is being very supportive, tell me how much you support each of these proposals:

- Making sentences more severe for all crimes
- Executing more murderers
- Making prisoners work on chain gangs
- Taking away television and recreation privileges from prisoners
- Using more mandatory minimum sentencing statutes, like "Three Strikes" for repeat offenders
- Locking up more juvenile offenders
- Using the death penalty for juveniles who murder
- Sending repeat juvenile offenders to adult courts.

Responses to the eight items are aggregated into an index (PUNATT) with an alpha of 0.88. The individual items with the strongest support (means in parentheses) were more mandatory minimum sentencing (7.2), more severe sentencing for all crimes (7.1), and adult court for repeat juvenile offenders (6.9). Those with the lowest support were death penalty for juvenile murderers (4.2) and locking up more juvenile offenders (5.9). The remaining items scored between 6.5 and 6.7.

INDEPENDENT VARIABLES

Our principal independent variable is an index (BLKCRIME) composed of responses to three questions that assess the extent to which respondents typify crime as a disproportionately black phenomenon.[9] The questions were:

- What percent of people who commit violent crimes in this country would you say are black?
- When you think about people who break into homes and businesses when nobody is there, approximately what percent would you say are black?
- When you think about people who rob other people at gunpoint, approximately what percent would you say are black?

Responses to the three questions are aggregated into an index with an alpha of 0.83. Estimates substantially exaggerate black involvement in violent crime, slightly exaggerate black involvement in burglary and

---

9. We also asked respondents what percent of these crimes were committed by whites and Hispanics. The number, of course, frequently did not add to 100 percent.

370   CHIRICOS, WELCH AND GERTZ

underestimate black involvement in robbery. For example, the median respondent perception of black involvement in violent crime is 39.8 percent, but victim surveys put that level at 29.4 percent for completed crimes of violence (U.S. Department of Justice, 2003a). Respondents put black involvement in burglary at 38.3 percent, but blacks comprise 31.6 percent of those arrested for that crime (U.S. Department of Justice, 2002).[10] Survey respondents attribute 39.8 percent of robberies to black offenders, but victim surveys put black involvement in completed robberies at 48.8 percent (U.S. Department of Justice, 2003a).

Other independent variables include several demographic characteristics of respondents. Sex, (FEMALE = 1), race (WHITE = 1) and ethnicity (HISPANIC = 1) are coded dichotomously, and AGE is coded continuously. EDUCATION is coded into seven categories ranging from no high school to postgraduate work. Prior research on punitiveness in relation to these variables has indicated a tendency for punitiveness to be greater for white respondents and for men, but no consistent results in relation to age. The relationship between education and punitiveness appears to be consistently inverse (Welch, 2002). Southern residence[11] (SOUTHERN = 1) is also included as a predictor, in part because rates of incarceration are consistently higher in the south than elsewhere and because religious fundamentalism, which some have found related to punitiveness (Borg, 1997, 1998; Young and Thompson, 1995) is also strong in that region.

A second set of independent variables includes "crime salience" measures, or indicators of how respondents regard crime. It is reasonable to expect that the more salient crime is in one's consciousness, the more punitive toward crime one may be. Our measures of this dimension include fear of criminal victimization (FEARVIC), which is comprised of a six-item index (alpha = 0.92) based on questions assessing how much respondents fear each of six specific crimes.[12] As noted, there has been no consistent relationship between fear and prior assessments of punitiveness. Ferraro (1995), among others, has noted a conceptual distinction between

---

10. Victim identified race of offenders is not available for burglary and it is impossible to know for certain whether the percent of those arrested for burglary who are black is higher or lower than those who may have been involved in that crime.

11. The states included in this region are: Alabama, Arkansas, Delaware, Florida, Georgia, Kentucky, Louisiana, Maryland, Mississippi, North Carolina, Oklahoma, South Carolina, Tennessee, Texas, Virginia, West Virginia.

12. Respondents were asked: "On a scale from 0-10, with 0 being not at all fearful and 10 being very fearful, how much would you say you fear having your car stolen, having someone break into your house, being robbed or mugged on the street, being raped or sexually assaulted, being beaten up or assaulted by strangers, being murdered."

affective responses to crime, such as fear, and cognitive responses, such as the assessment of risk or expressions of "concern." One can be concerned about crime as a general issue, without being particularly fearful, for whatever reasons.

The second measure is concern about crime (CONCERN), which is measured by a single question, with responses ranging from 0 (unconcerned) to 10 (very concerned). Our final crime salience measure taps into an issue that students of crime and the media have frequently noted—the tendency to exaggerate the violent dimensions of crime (Surrette, 1992). We asked respondents to estimate the percent of crimes in the United States that involve violence (PCTVIO). Not surprisingly, the mean of 53.8 percent vastly overstates the violent component of even serious "Index" crimes. We anticipate that punitiveness will be positively related to this perception.

Two final independent variables that we include in our analyses are political conservatism (POLCONS) and racial prejudice (RACEPREJ). The first is measured by respondents' self attribution as conservative (=1) or either moderate or liberal. This approach has been taken by a number of researchers (McCorkle, 1993; Rossi and Berk, 1997; Sandys and McGarrell, 1997) who most often find punitiveness related to "conservatism." Racial prejudice is measured by an index (alpha = 0.77) based on five questions concerned with the acceptability of having someone of a different race in varying contexts of social proximity.[13]

Table 1 describes each of the variables used in these analyses as well as the bivariate correlation of each independent variable with our measure of punitive attitudes. It can be seen that the strongest correlations with punitive attitudes involve the percent of crime that is perceived to be violent (0.34), concern about crime (0.31), conservatism (0.24), racial prejudice (0.24) and the racial typification of crime (0.22). The net effect of each remains to be seen when other factors are controlled.

RESEARCH FINDINGS

The data are analyzed using ordinary least squares (OLS) regression. There are no apparent problems of multicollinearity, with tolerance levels consistently above 0.73 and no bivariate correlations between independent

---

13. These contexts included "live nearby," "marry into my family," "join a social club or organization of which I was a member," "home for dinner" and "a job in which my supervisor was a different race." Responses ranged from strongly agree to strongly disagree and means were computed because not all questions were responded to. Respondents were dichotomized at the mean to designate "higher" and "lower" levels of prejudice.

372   CHIRICOS, WELCH AND GERTZ

Table 1. Variables Used in the Analysis

Variable Name	Description and Coding	Mean	S.D.	r PUNATT	
Dependent variable					
PUNATT	Index—R's overall attitudes toward punishing adult and juvenile offenders. Scale 0-10 (most punitive)	6.3208	2.3595	—	
Independent variables					
BLKCRIME	Index—R's perception of the percent of crime committed by blacks	43.3592	13.9872	.22	**
FEMALE	Sex of respondent 1 = Female, 0 = Male	.56	.50	.03	
AGE	Age of respondent	46.80	16.03	-.02	
WHITE	Race of respondent—White 1 = White, 0 = All others	.8087	.3935	.00	
HISPANIC	Ethnicity of respondent— Hispanic 1 = Hispanic/Latino, 0 = All others	.0753	.26	.07	*
EDUCATION	R's highest level of schooling 0 = No high school 1 = Some high school 2 = High school graduate 3 = Vocational or trade school graduate 4 = Some college 5 = College graduate 6 = Post graduate work or degree	4.14	1.43	-.29	**
POLCONS	Political ideology of respondent 0 = Moderate/Liberal 1 = Conservative	.3627	.4811	.24	**
CONCERN	R's concern about crime. Scale 0-10 (most concerned)	7.64	2.50	.31	**
PCTVIO	Perceived percent of crimes with violence	53.82	24.73	.34	**
FEARVIC	Index—R's overall fear of victimization. Scale 0-10 (most fearful)	3.3468	2.4861	.22	**
RACEPREJ	R's overall level of racial prejudice 0 = Less racially prejudiced 1 = More racially prejudiced	.4955	.5003	.24	**
SOUTHERN	R's region of residence 1 = Southern, 0 = All others	.3654	.4818	.14	**

*   p<.05
**   p<.01

variables in excess of 0.35 (CONCERN and FEARVIC). Modified Glesjer tests indicate that the assumption of homoskedasticity is not violated. Because much of our analysis will involve subsample comparisons, we report unstandardized (*b*) as well as standardized (Beta) coefficients throughout. Table 2

Table 2. Regression of Punitive Attitudes on Racial Typification of Blacks as Criminals

Variable	PUNATT b (Beta)
FEMALE	-.239
	(-.051)
AGE	-.0119*
	(-.080)
WHITE	.566**
	(.095)
HISPANIC	.689*
	(.078)
EDUCATION	-.215**
	(-.130)
POLCONS	.731**
	(.150)
CONCERN	.158**
	(.165)
PCTVIO	.01997**
	(.208)
FEARVIC	.05483
	(.057)
RACEPREJ	.630**
	(.134)
SOUTHERN	.399**
	(.082)
BLKCRIME	.01373**
	(.081)
N	748
Constant	3.688
R-squared	.282
Adjusted R-squared	.271

* p<.05
** p<.01

Table 2 reports the results of regressing punitive attitudes on the set of independent variables described above for the full sample. The adjusted

R^2 (0.27) is relatively strong for research involving punitiveness[14] and all coefficients (except for FEMALE) are statistically significant. Support for punitive measures is lower for those who are older and better educated. Punitive sentiments are stronger for southerners, self-identified conservatives, those who are racially prejudiced, white and Hispanic respondents, for those who are concerned about or fearful of crime, or perceive crime to be more often violent. Most notable for our purpose is that when each of these factors is controlled, the racial typification of crime has a significant effect on punitiveness ($p<.01$) apparently as strong or stronger than the effects of fear, age, gender and Hispanic ethnicity.

CONTEXTUAL ANALYSES

Racial threat has most often been taken to be an experience of whites threatened by the presence of minorities (Blalock, 1967; Liska, 1992; Taylor, 1998). In addition, negative racial attitudes (Carmines and Layman, 1998; Hurwitz and Peffley, 1998) and to a lesser extent punitiveness (Borg, 1997; Britt, 1998; Cohn, 1991) have been linked to whites. So we first examine whether the relationship between punitiveness and racial typification is similarly concentrated. We have noted that the consequences of racial threat vary by region (Corzine et al., 1983; Emerson, 1994; Jackson, 1989) and it is recognized that punitiveness is generally higher in the South (Rossi and Berk, 1997).[15] For this reason we also examine region.

Also as noted, some related research makes it reasonable to anticipate that the effects of racial typification of crime may be weakest where punitiveness is already high. Table 2 has shown that concern about crime, the perception that it is disproportionately violent, political conservatism and racial prejudice are to this point, the strongest predictors of punitiveness. On that account, these factors will be used to further refine our assessment of racial typification. To do this, we estimate its influence on punitive attitudes for respondents who are above ("high") and below ("low") the median values for CONCERN, PCTVIO and RACEPREJ. We also estimate the relationship separately for southern and nonsouthern as well as conservative and nonconservative respondents.[16] Tests for the

---

14. For example, Rossi and Berk (1997:201) report adjusted R^2 values between .03 and .08 for their fullest models, and Applegate, et al., (2000:734) report values between .03 and .19.

15. Rates of incarceration in the south are 29 percent higher than in western states, 44 percent higher than in the midwest and 76 percent higher than in the northeast (U.S. Department of Justice, 2003b).

16. The mean levels of punitiveness for the contextual categories are as follows: Whites / Minorities (6.33 / 6.30); High / Low CONCERN (7.08 / 5.78); High / Low PCTVIO

significance of difference in slope coefficients for BLKCRIME use the methodology suggested by Paternoster et al. (1998).

Table 3. Estimates for Whites and Minorities		Table 4. Estimates Disaggregated by Level of Concern			
	PUNATT b (Beta)		PUNATT b (Beta)		
Variable	Whites	Minorities	Low CONCERN	High CONCERN	Low PCTVIO	High PCTVIO
FEMALE	-.376*	.456	-.230	-.516*	-.200	-.309
	(-.081)	(.087)	(-.050)	(-.124)	(-.040)	(-.079)
AGE	-.0191**	.006699	-.0156*	-.0224**	-.0192*	-.0203**
	(-.128)	(.041)	(-.103)	(-.169)	(-.114)	(-.178)
EDUCATION	-.222**	-.157	-.276**	-.194*	-.210*	-.251**
	(-.134)	(-.094)	(-.158)	(-.134)	(-.111)	(-.188)
POLCONS	.772**	.779*	.990**	.503*	1.305**	.168
	(.163)	(.145)	(.198)	(.125)	(.251)	(.045)
CONCERN	.138**	.215**			.153**	.183**
	(.145)	(.215)			(.151)	(.208)
PCTVIO	.01937**	.01913*	.01351**	.2617**		
	(.205)	(.186)	(.136)	(.289)		
FEARVIC	.08841**	-.00391	.215**	.006169	.142*	.0631
	(.088)	(-.004)	(.184)	(.008)	(.111)	(.086)
RACEPREJ	.599**	.803*	.660**	.469*	.704**	.475*
	(.130)	(.159)	(.139)	(.115)	(.139)	(.130)
SOUTHERN	.599**	-.591	.564**	.728**	.792**	.249
	(.125)	(-.116)	(.115)	(.178)	(.150)	(.066)
BLKCRIME	.01583**	.01126	.02899**	.005384	.02311**	.009988
	(.093)	(.068)	(.156)	(.039)	(.123)	(.074)
N	606	144	359	247	318	288
Constant	4.634	2.721	4.720	6.730	4.002	6.563
R-squared	.309	.257	.279	.230	.301	.168
Adjusted R-squared	.297	.201	.260	.201	.280	.141
* p<.05			* p<.05			
** p<.01			** p<.01			
a. p-value for PUNATT slope difference is .375			a. p-value for PUNATT slope difference is .025 for CONCERN, and .335 for PCTVIO			

(7.08 / 5.80); High / Low RACEPREJ (6.93 / 5.73); Southern / nonsouthern (6.90 / 6.01); Conservative / non-Conservative (7.11 / 5.85). With the exception of the Whites / Minorities comparison, all values are for whites only and all differences are statistically significant (p < .01).

Table 3 shows separate estimates for whites (N = 606) and minorities (N=144). Because of the small numbers involved, it is not as reliable to look at black and Hispanic respondents separately. Several variables significantly predict punitiveness for both whites and minorities. Specifically, punitive attitudes are harsher for those concerned about crime, politically conservative, racially prejudiced and perceiving a greater proportion of crime to be violent. But education, age, sex, southernness and fear of crime are related to punitiveness only among whites. More important, the racial typification of crime significantly predicts punitiveness (p<.01) among whites but not among racial or ethnic minorities. However, as indicated in the table, the difference in slopes for the two is not statistically significant. Because racial typification is consequential for punitiveness only among whites, our subsequent contextual analyses are limited to white respondents.

Table 4 reports the results of estimating the effects of racial typification on punitiveness for the white subsample, disaggregated by levels of concern about crime and the perception that it is disproportionately violent. It appears that racial typification of crime interacts similarly with both measures of crime salience. Specifically, the perception that crime is disproportionately committed by blacks significantly predicts punitiveness only among those whose concern about crime is relatively low. Similarly, racial typification of crime is a significant predictor of punitive attitudes only among respondents who perceive crime in less violent terms. These interactions suggests that perhaps when the salience of crime is particularly high—as measured by concern and the equation of crime with violence—there may be something of a "ceiling effect" created in relation to punitive attitudes. That is, crime salience may be such a strong predictor of punitiveness that for those who are "high" on the indicators of this factor, there is less opportunity for the effects of racial typification to be expressed. The conclusiveness of these findings are tempered by the fact that slope differences are significant only for the concern context.

A similar interaction is shown in Table 5, which examines the effects of the racial typification of crime in the contexts of low and high racial prejudice as well as nonsouthern and southern residence of white respondents. The significant effects of racial typification are limited to those who are below the median level of prejudice and to those who do not live in the south, though the difference between regression coefficients is not statistically significant. As with the crime salience indicators, there may be something of a ceiling effect in terms of punitiveness among those who are racially prejudiced and live in the south. That is, for southerners and those expressing higher levels of racial prejudice there may be little opportunity for variation in racial typification to influence punitive attitudes.

RACIAL TYPIFICATION OF CRIME   377

Table 5. Effects of the racial typification of crime

Variable	PUNATT b (Beta)			
	Low RACEPREJ	High RACEPREJ	Non-SOUTHERN	SOUTHERN
FEMALE	-.442*	-.310	-.399*	-.305
	(-.090)	(-.079)	(-.085)	(-.072)
AGE	-.0215**	-.0180**	-.0162*	-.0260**
	(-.126)	(-.141)	(-.108)	(-.188)
EDUCATION	-.252**	-.168*	-.197*	-.244**
	(-.136)	(-.116)	(-.116)	(-.163)
POLCONS	1.082**	.462*	.751**	.699**
	(.201)	(.117)	(.152)	(.167)
CONCERN	.167**	.116*	.144**	.137*
	(.164)	(.139)	(.151)	(.151)
PCTVIO	.02327**	.01288**	.02161**	.01511**
	(.237)	(.154)	(.228)	(.171)
FEARVIC	.07363	.101*	.08891*	.08198
	(.064)	(.125)	(.085)	(.093)
SOUTHERN	.794**	.397*		
	(.151)	(.100)		
RACEPREJ			.736**	.409
			(.155)	(.098)
BLKCRIME [a]	.02031*	.0108	.01860*	.01043
	(.107)	(.076)	(.106)	(.068)
N	315	291	384	222
Constant	4.231	5.901	4.074	6.247
R-squared	.326	.182	.300	.256
Adjusted R-squared	.307	.156	.284	.224

* p<.05
** p<.01
a. p-value for PUNATT slope difference is .215 for RACEPREJ, and .25 for SOUTHERN

It is interesting that among self-described conservative respondents, as shown in Table 6, the effects of gender, fear, racial prejudice and the perception that crime is violent are reduced to nonsignificance. Moreover, among conservatives, the perception that crime is disproportionately a black phenomenon is not only a significant predictor of punitiveness, but by standardized coefficients, it is the strongest predictor in the model. The racial typification of crime has no significant effect on punitiveness for liberal and moderate respondents, even though all of the other predictors are significant.

378   CHIRICOS, WELCH AND GERTZ

Table 6. Regression of Punitive Attitudes of Whites on Racial Typification of
         Blacks as Criminals by Conservative

Variable	PUNATT b (Beta)	
	Not Conservative	Conservative
FEMALE	-.424*	-.185
	(-.085)	(-.051)
AGE	-.0184**	-.0227**
	(-.114)	(-.192)
EDUCATION	-.275**	-.145*
	(-.156)	(-.111)
CONCERN	.176**	.09378
	(.175)	(.120)
PCTVIO	.02494**	.005127
	(.255)	(.065)
FEARVIC	.09809*	.05861
	(.091)	(.074)
SOUTHERN	.623**	.488*
	(.120)	(.133)
RACEPREJ	.765**	.326
	(.153)	(.088)
BLKCRIME *	.009515	.02459**
	(.049)	(.194)
N	377	229
Constant	4.457	6.201
R-squared	.325	.185
Adjusted R-squared	.308	.152

*   p<.05
**   p<.01
a. p-value for PUNATT slope difference is .105

In sum, our analyses have shown that racial typification of crime is a
significant predictor of punitive attitudes toward crime, even with controls
for various demographic factors, crime salience variables and attitudinal
dimensions. In addition, we have found that this relationship exists only
for white respondents, and more particularly, whites who are less
concerned about crime, perceive crime to be less often violent, live outside
of the south, are less racially prejudiced and are politically conservative.
Though racial typification is significant in some contexts and not others,
the fact that differences between coefficients are not significant tempers
the conclusiveness of our results.

DISCUSSION

Between 1980 and 2002, the rate of incarceration in the United States
increased 242 percent—from 139 per 100,000 to 476. In 2002, the rate for
black men (3,437) was 6.6 times as high as for white (450) (U.S.

Department of Justice, 2003b). These extraordinary levels of punitiveness, unprecedented in our history and in the history of other Western democracies (Beckett and Sasson, 2000; Garland, 2001; Irwin and Austin, 2001), are clearly not being driven by crime since index crime rates have dropped by 30 percent .

Why then are so many people being locked up for what have become longer and longer periods? There is certainly no single or simple answer. Garland (2001) has suggested that it may be the result of both the increasing salience of crime and a variety of social and economic insecurities. Young (1999) similarly points to "ontological insecurities" of late modern society, which include the risk of crime and promote social processes that "essentialize" and "demonize" others, making social exclusion and the "criminology of intolerance" more likely.

The present results certainly support the relevance of crime salience, inasmuch as the perception that crime is violent and both concern about and fear of crime significantly predict support for punitiveness in many of our estimates. But our results linking punitive attitudes to the racial typification of crime suggest that there may be a racial overlay to the crime salience issue. Indeed, it is when concern about crime and the perception that crime is violent are "low" that racial typification of crime is a significant predictor of punitiveness. In these contexts a racialized crime threat may be substituting for a generalized threat that is presumed by crime salience.

The relationship demonstrated here between the racial typification of crime and punitiveness is consistent with the mechanism of "essentialism" that Young (1999) has shown to be an instrumental moment in the politics of "exclusion." The belief that "others" are essentially different from oneself or one's own group "allows people to believe in their own superiority while being able to demonize the other, as essentially wicked, stupid or criminal". (Young, 1999:109). Indeed, the racial typification of crime essentializes race in terms of crime and crime in terms of race, thereby "demonizing" blacks as the locus of threat. In other historical contexts, such demonizing has been a precursor to the most extraordinary atrocities (Cohen, 1995). Today, it energizes the mechanisms of social exclusion that include, but are surely not limited to, what Young has called "the great penal gulag" (1999:190) that has been created in this country during the past twenty years.

As noted, the mobilization of social controls in response to racialized crime threat has, for some time, been the subject of much research interest. To date, that research has focused on the racial composition of place as a presumed basis of "social threat" (Liska, 1992) and has shown that racial composition is related both to the fear of crime that could animate controls and to such indices of control as rates of arrest, levels of police funding and rates of incarceration. Our research provides an alternative direct measure of how race and threat can potentially energize social control. The fact that the typification of crime as a black phenomenon is consistently related to support for punitive measures to deal with crime is further evidence of how racialized crime threat can help to mobilize punitive control. It suggests as well that "social threat" may be activated not only by the residential proximity of racial minorities, but by the conflation of race and crime that exists in the minds of many, regardless of where they live. It could be argued that the racial typification of crime is a more direct measure of racial crime threat than racial composition, inasmuch as the second implies or assumes that the first is true—otherwise the proximity of blacks would not equate to a threat of crime.

These data, which demonstrate just one of the consequences of the racial typification of crime, may underscore the relevance of what Entman (1990) and Sears (1988), have described as a new form of racism— "modern racism"—that has evolved in the United States. This form of racism eschews overt expressions of racial superiority and hostility but instead sponsors a broad "anti-black affect" that equates blacks with a variety of negative traits, and crime is certainly one of those. In some ways "modern racism" may be more pernicious than the "traditional" overt expressions of racial antipathy, because of its oblique character. Consider James Q. Wilson's assertion that "it is not racism that makes whites uneasy about blacks moving into their neighborhoods... it is fear. Fear of crime, of drugs, of gangs, of violence" (1992:A-16). Such an assertion, in one short sentence, simultaneously disavows white racism while equating blacks with a list of negative attributes. There may be no more apposite expression of what has been called "modern racism" than the simple equation of violence, gangs, drugs and crime with blacks.

Finally, this study demonstrates that the equation of race and crime is a significant sponsor of the punitive attitudes that are given material substance in the extraordinary rates of incarceration now found in this country. In short, these data are consistent with Miller's conjecture (Szykowny, 1994) that initially prompted this research.

REFERENCES

Aguire, Adalberto and David V. Baker
    1993   Racial prejudice and the death penalty: A research note. Social
           Justice 20:150–155.

RACIAL TYPIFICATION OF CRIME 381

Applegate, Brandon K., Francis T. Cullen, Bruce G. Link, Pamela J. Richards and Lonn Lanza-Kaduce
  1996 Determinants of public punitiveness toward drunk driving: A factorial survey approach. Justice Quarterly 13:57–79.

Applegate, Brandon K., Francis T. Cullen, Bonnie S. Fisher and Thomas Vander Ven
  2000 Forgiveness and fundamentalism: Reconsidering the relationship between correctional attitudes and religion. Criminology 38:719–753.

Applegate, Brandon K., Francis T. Cullen and Bonnie S. Fisher
  2002 Public views toward crime and correctional policies: Is there a gender gap? Journal of Criminal Justice 30:89–100.

Barak, Gregg
  1994 Between the waves: Mass-mediated themes of crime and justice. Social Justice 21:133–147.

Barkan, Steven E. and Steven F. Cohn
  1994 Racial prejudice and support for the death penalty by whites. Journal of Research in Crime and Delinquency 31:202–209.

Barlow, Melissa Hickman
  1998 Race and the problem of crime in *Time* and *Newsweek* cover stories, 1946 to 1995. Social Justice 25:149–183.

Beckett, Katherine and Theodore Sasson
  2000 The Politics of Injustice: Crime and Punishment in America. Thousand Oaks, CA: Pine Forge Press.

Blalock, Hubert M.
  1967 Toward a Theory of Minority Group Relations. New York: John Wiley and Sons Publishers.

Blumstein, Albert and Jacqueline Cohen
  1980 Sentencing of convicted offenders: An analysis of the public's view. Law and Society Review 14:223–261.

Borg, Marian J.
  1997 The southern subculture of punitiveness?: Regional variation in support for capital punishment. Journal of Research in Crime and Delinquency 34:25–45.
  1998 Vicarious homicide victimization and support for capital punishment: A test of Black's theory of law. Criminology 36:537–567.

382   CHIRICOS, WELCH AND GERTZ

Bridges, George S., Robert D. Crutchfield and Edith E. Simpson
1987   Crime, social structure and criminal punishment: White and nonwhite rates of imprisonment. Social Problems 34:345–360.

Britt, Chester L.
1998   Race, religion and support for the death penalty: A research note. Justice Quarterly 15:175–191.

Carmines, Edward G. and Geoffrey C. Layman
1998   When prejudice matters: The impact of racial stereotypes on the racial policy preferences of Democrats and Republicans. In John Hurwita and Mark Peffley (eds.) Perception and Prejudice: Race and Politics in the United States. New Haven: Yale University Press.

Chamlin, Mitchell B.
1989   A macro social analysis of change in police force size, 1972–1982: Controlling for static and dynamic influences. The Sociological Quarterly 30:615–624.

Chiricos, Ted, Michael Hogan and Marc Gertz
1997   Racial composition of neighborhood and fear of crime. Criminology 35: 107–129

Chiricos, Ted, Ranee McEntire and Marc Gertz
2001   Perceived racial and ethnic composition of neighborhood and perceived risk of crime. Social Problems 48:322–340.

Chua–Eoan, H.
2000   Black and blue. *Time*, March 6, p.24.

Cohen, Richard
1993   Common ground on crime. Washington Post, December 21:A2.

Cohn, Steven F. Steven E. Barkan and William A. Halteman
1991   Punitive attitudes toward criminals: Racial consensus or racial conflict? Social Problems 38:287–296

Combs, Michael W. and John C. Comer
1982   Race and capital punishment: A longitudinal analysis. Phylon 43:350–359.

Corzine, Jay, James Creech and Lin Corzine
1983   Black concentration and lynchings in the South: Testing Blalock's power-threat hypothesis. Social Forces 61: 774–796.

Covington, Jeanette and Ralph B. Taylor
1991 Fear of crime in urban residential neighborhoods: Implications of between and within neighborhood sources for current models. The Sociological Quarterly 32:231–249.

Drummond, William J.
1990 About face: blacks and the news media. The American Enterprise 1:23–29.

Durham, Alexis M., H. Preston Elrod and Patrick T. Kinkade
1996 Public support for the death penalty: Beyond Gallup. Justice Quarterly 13:705–730.

Emerson, Michael O.
1994 Is it different in dixie?: Percent black and residential segregation in the south and nonsouth. The Sociological Quarterly 35: 571–580.

Entman, Robert M.
1990 Modern racism and the images of blacks in local television news. Critical Studies in Mass Communication 7:332–345.
1992 Blacks in the news: Television, modern racism and cultural change. Journalism Quarterly 69:341–361.

Fishman, Laura T.
1998 The black bogeyman and white self-righteousness. In Coramae Richey Mann and Marjorie S. Zatz (eds.) Images of Color, Images of Crime. Los Angeles: Roxbury Publishing Company.

Garland, David
2001 The Culture of Control. Chicago: University of Chicago Press.

Grasmick, Harold G., Elizabeth Davenport, Mitchell B. Chamlin and Robert J. Bursik Jr.
1992 Protestant fundamentalism and the retributive doctrine of punishment. Criminology 30:21–45.

Grasmick, Harold G., John K. Cochran, Robert J. Bursik, Jr. and M'Lou Kimpel
1993 Religion, punitive justice and support for the death penalty. Justice Quarterly 10:289–314.

Greenberg, David F. Ronald C. Kessler and Colin Loftin
1985 Social inequality and crime control. Journal of Criminal Law and Criminology. 76: 684–704.

384   CHIRICOS, WELCH AND GERTZ

Harer, Miles D. and Darrel Steffensmeier
    1992   The differing effects of economic inequality on black and white
            rates of violence. Social Forces 70:1035–1054.

Harris, Phillip W.
    1986   Over-simplification and error in public opinion surveys on
            capital punishment. Justice Quarterly..3:429–455.

Hawkins, Darnell F.
    1995   Ethnicity, race and crime: A review of selected studies. In
            Darnell Hawkins (ed.) Ethnicity, Race and Crime: Perspectives
            Across Time and Place. Albany, NY: SUNY Press.

Irwin, John and James Austin
    2001   It's About Time: America's Imprisonment Binge, 3rd Edition.
            Belmont, CA: Wadsworth Publishing Company.

Jackson, Pamela Irving
    1985   Ethnicity, region and public fiscal commitment to policing.
            Justice Quarterly 2: 167–194.
    1986   Black visibility, city size and social control. Sociological
            Quarterly 27: 185–203.
    1989   Minority Group Threat: Crime and Policing. New York:
            Praeger.
    1992   Minority group threat, social context and policing. In Allen E.
            Liska (ed.) Social Threat and Social Control. Albany: State
            University of New York Press.

Jacoby, Joseph E.
    1989   The structure of punishment norms. A theoretical integration of
            findings from the 1987 National Punishment Survey. Paper
            presented at the Annual Meetings of the American Society of
            Criminology, November.

Jacobs, David
    1979   Inequality and police strength: Conflict theory and coercive
            control in metropolitan areas. American Sociological Review 44:
            912–925.

Jamieson, Kathleen H.
    1992   Dirty Politics: Deception, Distraction and Democracy. New
            York: Oxford University Press.

Kennedy, Randall
    1997   Race, Crime and the Law. New York: Vintage Books.

Langworthy, Robert H. and John T. Whitehead
  1986 Liberalism and fear as explanations of punitiveness. Criminology 24:575–591.

Lavrakas, Paul J.
  1987 Telephone Survey Methods. Newbury Park, CA: Sage Publications.

Leiber, Michael J. And Anne C. Woodrick
  1997 Religious beliefs, attributional styles and adherence to correctional orientations. Criminal Justice and Behavior 24:495–511.

Liska, Allen E.
  1992 Introduction to the study of social control. In Allen E. Liska (ed.) Social Threat and Social Control. Albany, NY: SUNY Press.

Liska, Allen E., Joseph J. Lawrence and Andrew Sanchirico
  1981 Perspectives on the legal order: The capacity for social control. American Journal of Sociology 87:413–426.

Liska, Allen E. and Mitchell B. Chamlin
  1984 Social structure and crime control among macrosocial units. American Journal of Sociology 90:383–395.

Liska, Allen E., Mitchell B. Chamlin and Mark D. Reed
  1985 Testing the economic production and conflict models of crime control. Social Forces 64:119–138.

Liska, Allen E., Joseph J. Lawrence and Andrew Sanchirico
  1982 Fear of crime as a social fact. Social Forces 60:761–770.

Mauer, Marc
  1999 Race to Incarcerate. New York: The Free Press.

McConahay, John
  1986 Modern racism, ambivalence and the modern racism scale. In John Dovidio and Samuel Gaertner (eds.) Prejudice, Discrimination and Racism: Theory and Research. New York: Academic Press.

McCorkle, Richard C.
  1993 Research note: Punish and rehabilitate? Public attitudes toward six common crimes. Crime and Delinquency 39:240–252.

Mendelberg, Tali
  1997 Executing the Hortons: Racial crime in the 1988 presidential campaign. Public Opinion Quarterly 61:134–157.

386   CHIRICOS, WELCH AND GERTZ

Miller, J. L., Peter Rossi and Jon E. Simpson
  1986 Perceptions of Justice: Race and gender differences in judgments of appropriate prison sentences. Law and Society Review 20:313–334.

Miller, J. L., Peter Rossi and Jon E. Simpson
  1991 Felony punishments: A factorial survey of perceived justice in criminal sentencing. The Journal of Criminal Law and Criminology 82:396–422.

Moeller, Gertrude L.
  1989 Fear of criminal victimization: The effect of neighborhood racial composition. Sociological Inquiry 59:208–221.

Myers, Martha A. and Susette Talarico
  1986 The social contexts of racial discrimination in sentencing. Social Problems 33:236–251.
  1987 The Social Contexts of Criminal Sentencing. New York: Springer-Verlag.

Padgett, Kathy
  2002 Racial Threat and Social Control: An Examination of the Racial/Ethnic Composition-Incarceration Linkage in Florida. Unpublished Doctoral Dissertation, Florida State University.

Paternoster, Raymond, Robert Brame, Paul Mazerolle and Alex Piquero
  1998 Using the correct statistical; test for the equality of regression coefficients. Criminology 36: 859–866.

Roberts, Dorothy E.
  1993 Crime, race and reproduction. Tuland Law Review 67:1945–1977.

Rossi, Peter H. and Richard A. Berk
  1997 Just Punishments: Federal Guidelines and Public Views Compared. New York: Aldine De Gruyter.

Russell, Katheryn K.
  1998 The Color of Crime. Yew York: New York University Press.

Sandys, Marla and Edmund F. McGarrell
  1995 Attitudes toward capital punishment: Preference for the penalty or mere acceptance? Journal of Research in Crime and Delinquency 32:191–213.
  1997 Beyond the bible belt: The influence (or lack thereof) of religion on attitudes toward the death penalty. Journal of Crime and Justice 20:179–190.

Schwartz, Ira M. Shenyang Guo and John J. Kerbs
   1993   The impact of demographic variables on public opinion regarding juvenile delinquency: Implications for public policy. Crime and Delinquency 39:5–28.

Sears, David
   1988   Symbolic racism. In Phyllis Katz and Dalmas Taylor (eds.) Eliminating Racism: Profiles in Controversy. New York: Plenum.

Secret, Philip E. and James B. Johnson
   1989   Racial differences in attitudes toward crime control. Journal of Criminal Justice 17:361–375.

Skogan, Wesley G.
   1995   Crime and the racial fears of white Americans. Annals of the American Academy of Political and Social Science 539:59–71.

Skovron, Sandra E., Joseph E. Scott and Francis T. Cullen
   1988   Prison crowding: Public attitudes toward strategies of population control. Journal of Research in Crime and Delinquency 25:150–169
   1989   The death penalty for juveniles: An assessment of public support. Journal of Research in Crime and Delinquency 35:546–561.

Sniderman, Paul M., Thomas Piazza and Hosea Harvey
   1998   Prejudice and politics: An intellectual biography of a research project. In Jon Hurwitz and Mark Peffley (eds.) Perception and Prejudice. New Haven: Yale University Press.

Sprott, Jane B.
   1999   Are members of the public tough on crime?: The dimensions of public "punitiveness." Journal of Criminal Justice 27:467–474.

Surrette, Ray
   1992   Media, Crime and Criminal Justice. Pacific Grove, CA: Brooks/Cole Publishing Company.

Szykowny, Rick
   1994   No justice, no peace: An interview with Jerome Miller. The Humanist January/February: 9–19.

Taylor, Marylee C.
   1998   How white attitudes vary with the racial composition of local populations: Numbers count. American Sociological Review 63:512–535.

388   CHIRICOS, WELCH AND GERTZ

Taylor, Ralph B. and Jeanette Covington
   1993   Community structural change and fear of crime. Social
          Problems 40:374–395.

Taylor, Garth D., Kim Lane Schepelle and Arthur L. Stinchcombe
   1979   Salience of crime and support for harsher criminal sanctions.
          Social Problems 26:413–424.

Thomas, Charles W., Robin J Cage and Samuel C. Foster
   1976   Public opinion on criminal law and legal sanctions: An
          examination of two conceptual models. The Journal of Criminal
          Law and Criminology 67:110–116.

Tolnay, Stewart E., E.M. Beck and James L. Massey
   1992   Black competition and white vengeance: Legal execution of
          blacks as social control in the cotton south, 1890 to 1929. Social
          Science Quarterly 73: 627–644.

Tyler, Tom R. and Renee Weber
   1982   Support for the death penalty: Instrumental response to crime
          or symbolic attitude? Law and Society Review 17:21–44.

U.S. Department of Justice
   2002a Crime in the United States 2001. Washington, D.C.: U.S.
          Government Printing Office.
   2003a Criminal Victimization in the United States, 2001, Statistical
          Tables.   Available   online: (http://www.ojp.gov/bjs/pub/pdf/
          cvus0102.pdf).
   2003b Prisoners in 2002. Bureau of Justice Statistics Bulletin. NCJ
          200248 (July).

Ward, Russel A., Mark LaGory and Susan R. Sherman
   1986   Fear of crime among the elderly as person/environment
          interaction. The Sociological Quarterly 27: 327–341.

Warner, Barbara D.
   1992   The reporting of crime: A missing link in conflict theory. In
          Allen Liska (ed.) Social Threat and Social Control. Albany, NY:
          SUNY Press.

Welch, Kelly
   2001   Punitive Attitudes: A Review of Prior Research and Analysis of
          Racial Typification. Unpublished Masters Thesis. Florida State
          University.

West, Cornel
   1994   Race Matters. New York: Vintage Books.

Wilson, James Q.
1992 To prevent riots, reduce black crime. The Wall Street Journal 6, May:A16.

Young, Jock
1999 The Exclusive Society. London: Sage Publications, Ltd.

Young, Robert L.
1992 Religious orientation, race and support for the death penalty. Journal for the Scientific Study of Religion 31:76–87.

Young, Robert L. And Carol Y. Thompson
1995 Religious fundamentalism, punitiveness and firearms ownership. Journal of Crime and Justice 18:81–98.

Ted Chiricos is professor of Criminology and Criminal Justice at Florida State University. His current research examines the effects of economic insecurity on punitiveness toward criminals, immigrants and welfare recipients, as well as the relationship between environmental threat and punitive responses to environmental crime. He is also studying the effects of race on the withholding of adjudication, and with it, the legal label of felon for those actually convicted of felony crimes as well as the effect of this judicial decision on the subsequent life chances of criminal offenders.

Kelly Welch is joining the faculty as an assistant professor in the Department of Sociology at Villanova University. Her research interests include race and crime, social justice, public opinion and policy, the sociology of punishment and victimology.

Marc Gertz is a professor of Criminology and Criminal Justice at Florida State University. His current research interests include comparative criminal justice systems, courts and social policy and the consequences of the fear of crime. His recent publications include the 9th edition of The Criminal Justice System: Politics and Policies (edited with George F. Cole and Amy Bunger.

Part III
The Incarceration Explosion

[11]

Ballot Manipulation and the "Menace of Negro Domination": Racial Threat and Felon Disenfranchisement in the United States, 1850–2002[1]

Angela Behrens and Christopher Uggen
University of Minnesota

Jeff Manza
Northwestern University

Criminal offenders in the United States typically forfeit voting rights as a collateral consequence of their felony convictions. This article analyzes the origins and development of these state felon disenfranchisement provisions. Because these laws tend to dilute the voting strength of racial minorities, we build on theories of group threat to test whether racial threat influenced their passage. Many felon voting bans were passed in the late 1860s and 1870s, when implementation of the Fifteenth Amendment and its extension of voting rights to African-Americans were ardently contested. We find that large nonwhite prison populations increase the odds of passing restrictive laws, and, further, that prison and state racial composition may be linked to the adoption of reenfranchisement reforms. These findings are important for understanding restrictions on the civil rights of citizens convicted of crime and, more generally, the role of racial conflict in American political development.

Punishment for felony-level crimes in the United States generally carries collateral consequences, including temporary or permanent voting restric-

[1] This material is based upon work supported by the National Science Foundation (grant 9819015), the Individual Project Fellowship Program of the Open Society Institute, and the University of Minnesota UROP program. We thank Jack Chin, Doug Hartmann, Bert Kritzer, Susan Olzak, Joachim Savelsberg, Sara Wakefield, and the AJS reviewers for helpful comments, and Kendra Schiffman and Melissa Thompson for research assistance. Direct correspondence to Christopher Uggen, Department of Sociology, University of Minnesota, 267 19th Avenue South 909, Minneapolis, Minnesota 55455. E-mail: uggen@atlas.socsci.umn.edu

American Journal of Sociology

tions. These felon disenfranchisement provisions have a significant collective impact. In the most recent presidential election, for example, an estimated 4.7 million people were disenfranchised owing to a felony conviction (Uggen and Manza 2002), representing "the largest single group of American citizens who are barred by law from participating in elections" (Keyssar 2000, p. 308).

If citizenship and the right to vote are truly "the essence of a democratic society," as the Supreme Court once declared (*Reynolds v. Sims*, 377 U.S. 533, 555 [1964]), then the forces driving adoption of disenfranchisement laws take on great importance for understanding the limits of citizenship rights in America. Voting rights in the United States before the Civil War had generally been limited to white males. The struggle to extend the franchise to all citizens, most notably to racial minorities and women, was a contested and protracted process (McCammon, Campbell, Granberg and Mowery 2001). By the mid-1960s, most of the legal barriers to political participation for U.S. citizens had fallen (Keyssar 2000). As one of the few remaining restrictions on the right to vote, felon voting bans stand out; indeed, the rapid *increase* in felon disenfranchisement rates since the early 1970s constitutes a rare example of significant disenfranchisement in an era of worldwide expansion of democratic rights (Uggen and Manza 2002). Today, the United States is conspicuous among advanced industrial societies for its unusually restrictive voting rules for felons (Allard and Mauer 1999; Demleitner 2000; Ewald 2003; Fellner and Mauer 1998).

Felon disenfranchisement laws are "race neutral" on their face, but in the United States race is clearly tied to criminal punishment: African-American imprisonment rates have consistently exceeded white rates since at least the Civil War era (U.S. Department of Commerce 1882) and remain approximately seven times higher than rates among whites today (U.S. Department of Justice 2002). Given the pronounced racial disparities in criminal justice, some legal theorists have offered race as a factor driving the initial adoption and unusual persistence of felon voting bans (e.g., Fletcher 1999; Harvey 1994; Hench 1998; Shapiro 1993). In particular, the prospective enfranchising of racial minorities during the Reconstruction period (with the adoption of the Fourteenth and Fifteenth amendments in 1868 and 1870) threatened to shift the balance of power among racial groups in the United States, engendering a particularly strong backlash not only in the South (see Foner 1988; Kousser 1974) but in the North as well (see Mendelberg 2001, chap. 2). One instance of this backlash, as established by a long line of research, is the connection that lynching and racial violence has to political and economic competition during this period (Olzak 1990; 1992, chap. 7; Soule 1992; Tolnay and Beck 1995). The simultaneous expansion of voting restrictions for criminal offenders in the period following the Reconstruction amendments may thus provide an important clue to the origins of these laws, but this idea has not yet been subject to systematic examination.

Most studies of felon disenfranchisement laws address either their current impact or their moral and philosophical underpinnings (e.g., Allard and Mauer 1999; Clegg 2001; Ewald 2002; Fellner and Mauer 1998; Manfredi 1998; Pettus 2002; Uggen and Manza 2002). While many have noted the unusual origins and historical trajectories of these laws, virtually no empirical research has attempted to identify the conditions—whether racial or nonracial—that have driven their passage (see Keyssar [2000, pp. 62–63, 162–63] for a brief and rare exception). In general, we lack both case studies and comparative-historical analyses of the adoption of disenfranchisement laws.[2] This article begins to fill the void, developing the first systematic analysis of the origins and evolution of felon disenfranchisement laws across the states. We begin with an overview of the history of felon disenfranchisement and introduce results of a historical survey of laws passed by each state. We then outline the three varieties of racial-threat theory that we test in the article. The next part describes our measurement and modeling strategy. Subsequently we present our substantive results, including analyses of both the adoption of disenfranchisement laws throughout the entire period under consideration and the sources of the liberalization of state laws since 1940. The final part discusses the scientific and policy implications of these findings.

CITIZENSHIP, RACE, AND THE LAW

The United States Constitution of 1787 neither granted nor denied anyone the right to vote. Over time, states granted suffrage to certain groups and erected barriers to prevent other groups from voting. African-Americans were not considered legal citizens of the United States until 1868, when the Fourteenth Amendment defined a "national citizenship" (Wang 1997, p. 28). Two years later, the Fifteenth Amendment prohibited the denial of suffrage to citizens "on account of race, color, or previous condition of servitude," thus extending the franchise to black men. Nevertheless, violent suppression of the black vote during Reconstruction combined with weak federal enforcement thereafter, and the eventual adoption of a variety of disenfranchising measures by Southern states after 1890, prevented most African-Americans from voting in the South. It was not until

---

[2] Others have observed this large hole in the existing literature. Ewald (2002, p. 1065), e.g., notes, "There is very little scholarship on the practice [of felon disenfranchisement] in the late nineteenth and early twentieth centuries," while Shapiro (1993, p. 146) asserts "studies of state legislatures' reform and/or repeal of criminal disenfranchisement laws do not exist."

American Journal of Sociology

the 1965 passage of the Voting Rights Act (which effectively eliminated state voting restrictions that undermined the Fifteenth Amendment with the intent to diminish the voting rights of African-Americans) that near universal suffrage was finally assured (Keyssar 2000; Kousser 1999).

Even as the pool of eligible voters expanded after the Civil War to include a wider range of people—women with the passage of the Nineteenth Amendment in 1920 and people ages 18 to 20 with the passage of the Twenty-sixth Amendment in 1971—criminal offenders have generally been excluded. Section 2 of the Fourteenth Amendment, which was passed in 1868, specified that states would lose congressional representation if they denied males the right to vote, "except for participation in rebellion, or other crime." In light of this phrase, the U.S. Supreme Court upheld felon disenfranchisement measures in *Richardson v. Ramirez* (418 U.S. 24 [1974]), interpreting such voting bans as an "affirmative sanction" (p. 54) consistent with the intent of the Fourteenth Amendment. While offenders retain their status as U.S. citizens, they cannot vote, and they forfeit many other civil rights as collateral consequences of their felony conviction (Mauer and Chesney-Lind 2002; Olivares, Burton, and Cullen 1997). States thus exercise a form of internal closure (Booth 1997) against felons, distinguishing those "fit to possess the rights of citizenship" from other members of society (Keyssar 2000, p. 163).

Criminal disenfranchisement has an extensive history in English, European, and Roman law, where it was thought to offer both retribution and a deterrent to future offending (see, e.g., Ewald 2002; Itzkowitz and Oldak 1973; Pettus 2002). Nevertheless, no other contemporary democracy disenfranchises felons to the same extent, or in the same manner, as the United States (Fellner and Mauer 1998).[3] Currently, 48 U.S. states disenfranchise incarcerated felons and 14 states disenfranchise at least some ex-felons who have completed their sentences (Fellner and Mauer 1998; Uggen and Manza 2002). Table 1 shows a summary of state laws passed as of December 31, 2002.

---

[3] Most countries have more narrowly tailored disenfranchisement laws. To our knowledge, the United States is the only nation with broad ex-felon voting bans that extend to all former felons in several states. A few nations, such as Finland and New Zealand, disenfranchise for a few years beyond completion of sentence but only for election offenses (Fellner and Mauer 1998). In Germany, a judge may impose disenfranchisement for certain offenses, such as treason, but only for a maximum of five years (Demleitner 2000). France excludes from suffrage only those convicted of election offenses and abuse of public power. Ireland and Spain both allow prisoners to vote, and in Australia a mobile polling staff visits prisons so that inmates may vote (Australian Electoral Commission 2001). In 1999, South Africa's highest court ruled that prison inmates had the right to vote (Allard and Mauer 1999), and in October 2002 the Supreme Court of Canada ruled that prison inmates may vote in federal elections (*Sauvé v. Canada*, 2002 S.C.C. 68 [2002]).

Ballot Manipulation

TABLE 1
SUMMARY OF STATE FELON DISENFRANCHISEMENT LAWS AT YEAR'S END, 2002

Felons Disenfranchised	N	States
None	2	Maine, Vermont
Prison inmates	14	Hawaii, Illinois, Indiana, Louisiana, Massachusetts, Michigan, Montana, New Hampshire, North Dakota, Ohio, Oregon, Pennsylvania, South Dakota, Utah
Prison inmates and parolees	5	California, Colorado, Connecticut,* Kansas, New York
Prison inmates, parolees, and probationers	15	Alaska, Arkansas, Georgia, Idaho, Minnesota, Missouri, New Jersey, New Mexico,† North Carolina, Oklahoma, Rhode Island, South Carolina, Texas, West Virginia, Wisconsin
Prison inmates, parolees, probationers, and some or all ex-felons‡	14	Alabama, Arizona, Delaware, Florida, Iowa, Kentucky, Maryland, Mississippi, Nebraska, Nevada, Tennessee, Virginia, Washington, Wyoming

* Connecticut changed its law in 2001 to allow felony probationers to vote.
† New Mexico changed its law in 2001 to automatically restore voting rights upon completion of sentence.
‡ While many states have clemency procedures to restore voting rights, most are cumbersome and infrequently used (Fellner and Mauer 1998, p. 5).

American disenfranchisement laws date to colonial times; some states began writing restrictive provisions into their constitutions in the late 18th century. Most state constitutions explicitly gave their legislatures the power to pass laws disenfranchising criminals. Early U.S. disenfranchisement laws drew upon European models and were generally limited to a few specific offenses (Ewald 2002). Over time, states expanded the scope of such laws to include all felonies, often citing a rationale to "preserve the purity of the ballot box" (*Washington v. State*, 75 Ala. 582, 585 [1884]). Many states enacted felon disenfranchisement provisions in the aftermath of the Civil War. Such laws diluted the voting strength of newly enfranchised racial minority groups, particularly in the Deep South but in the North as well (Fellner and Mauer 1998; Harvey 1994; Hench 1998). Felon voting restrictions were the first widespread set of legal disenfranchisement measures that would be imposed on African-Americans, although violence and intimidation against prospective African-American voters were also common (Kousser 1974). Other legal barriers, such as poll taxes, literacy tests, "grandfather" clauses, discriminatory registration requirements, and white-only primaries, would follow at a later date. (Most of these measures were not adopted until after 1890 [Perman 2001; Redding 2003].)

American Journal of Sociology

Table 2 details the key legal changes in state disenfranchisement laws.[4] We gathered information about these laws by examining the elector qualifications and consequences of felony convictions as specified in state constitutions and statutes. We located the information by first examining the state constitutions and legislative histories reported by those states that incorporate such information into their statutory codebooks. For other states, we consulted earlier codebooks that referred specifically to voting laws, all of which are archived at the University of Minnesota and Northwestern University law libraries.

Figure 1 provides a visual display of the broad historical pattern of felon disenfranchisement, showing the percentage of states with any felon voting restriction and the percentage of states disenfranchising ex-felons at the end of each decade (adapted from survival distributions available from the authors). Whereas only 35% of states had a broad felon disenfranchisement law in 1850, fully 96% had such a law by 2002, when only Maine and Vermont had yet to restrict felon voting rights. As the figure shows, the 1860s and 1870s are marked by greater disenfranchisement as well as by the adoption of the Fourteenth and Fifteenth amendments. A period of fewer changes followed before another wave of restrictions began in 1889. After the turn of the century, there were fewer restrictive changes, although a number of newer states adopted disenfranchisement measures with their first state constitution.

The most restrictive form of felon disenfranchisement a state can adopt is that which disenfranchises *ex*-felons. These laws ban voting, often indefinitely, even after successful completion of probation, parole, or prison sentences. Over one-third of states disenfranchised ex-felons in 1850 and, as figure 1 illustrates, three-fourths of states disenfranchised ex-felons by 1920. This level of ex-felon disenfranchisement changed little throughout the next half century until many states removed these restrictions in the 1960s and 1970s, restoring voting rights to some or all ex-felons. No state has passed a broad ex-felon disenfranchisement law since Hawaii did so with statehood in 1959 (later amended to disenfranchise only prison inmates).[5]

---

[4] See Keyssar (2000, pp. 376–86) for a slightly different, independently developed analysis of state felon disenfranchisement laws, and criminal disenfranchisement in general, for the period from 1870 to 1920. We are indebted to Kendra Schiffman for research assistance in tracking down these often difficult to locate legal details.

[5] For a short time in the 1990s, Pennsylvania instituted a five-year waiting period before prison releasees were permitted to register to vote.

TABLE 2
ORIGINS OF AND CHANGES TO STATE FELON DISENFRANCHISEMENT LAWS*

State	Year of Statehood	Year of First Felon Disenfranchisement Law[††]	Major Amendments[‡‡]
Alabama	1819	1867[‖]	
Alaska	1959	1959[*]	1994
Arizona	1912	1912[*]	1978
Arkansas	1836	1868	1964
California	1849	1849[*]	1972
Colorado	1876	1876[*]	1993, 1997
Connecticut	1788	1818	1975, 2001
Delaware	1787	1831	2000
Florida	1845	1868[‖]	1885
Georgia	1788	1868	1983
Hawaii	1959	1959[*]	1968
Idaho	1890	1890[*]	1972
Illinois	1818	1870[‖]	1970, 1973
Indiana	1816	1852[‖]	1881
Iowa	1846	1846[*]	
Kansas	1861	1859[*]	1969
Kentucky	1792	1851[‖]	
Louisiana	1812	1845[‖]	1975, 1976
Maine	1820		
Maryland	1788	1851	1957, 2002
Massachusetts	1788	2000	
Michigan	1837	1963	
Minnesota	1858	1857[*]	
Mississippi	1817	1868	
Missouri	1821	1875[‖]	1962
Montana	1889	1909	1969
Nebraska	1867	1875	
Nevada	1864	1864[*]	
New Hampshire	1788	1967	
New Jersey	1787	1844	1948
New Mexico	1912	1911[*]	2001
New York	1788	1847	1976
North Carolina	1789	1876	1970, 1971, 1973
North Dakota	1889	1889[*]	1973, 1979
Ohio	1803	1835[‖]	1974
Oklahoma	1907	1907[*]	
Oregon	1859	1859[*]	1961, 1975, 1999
Pennsylvania	1787	1860	1968, 1995, 2000
Rhode Island	1790	1841	1973
South Carolina	1788	1868	1895, 1981
South Dakota	1889	1889[*]	1967
Tennessee	1796	1871	1986
Texas	1845	1869[‖]	1876, 1983, 1997
Utah	1896	1998	
Vermont	1791		
Virginia	1788	1830[‖]	

American Journal of Sociology

TABLE 2 (*Continued*)

State	Year of Statehood	Year of First Felon Disenfranchisement Law[††]	Major Amendments[‡‡]
Washington	1889	1889[*]	1984
West Virginia	1863	1863[*]	
Wisconsin	1848	1848[*]	1947
Wyoming	1890	1890[*]	

    * Based on authors' canvass of state constitutional and statutory histories through 2002; full details available upon request.
    † Many states disenfranchised for specific crimes before amending laws to disenfranchise for all felony convictions.
    ‡ Years listed are according to the year of legal change rather than to the year the change became effective.
    § "Major" amendments are those that have changed which groups of felons are disenfranchised. Most states have changed the wording of disenfranchisement laws in ways that generally do not affect who is disenfranchised.
    ‖ The first state constitution gave the state legislature the power to restrict suffrage for criminal activity.
    * Disenfranchisement of felons was instituted at time of statehood.

How Might Race Affect the Adoption of Felon Disenfranchisement Laws?

Drawing from the literatures on ethnic competition and criminal justice, we consider several possible ways in which racial factors, especially perceived racial threat from African-Americans, may be associated with felon voting law changes. Two questions are especially important. First, felon disenfranchisement laws are formally race neutral: all felons, or those falling into certain offense categories, are disenfranchised, not only African-Americans. Does the historical record suggest a plausible link between the laws and racial concerns at *any* point in time? Second, the politics of race have shifted drastically during the past 150 years. Can a single model of racial conflict account for political change over the entire period?

In the wake of the Civil War, states and municipalities enacted a wide range of Black Codes and later Jim Crow laws to minimize the political power of newly enfranchised African-Americans (Woodward 2001). While existing scholarship has rarely addressed the origins of felon voting bans, there are extensive literatures on the origins of general disenfranchisement measures. One classical debate has concerned the social forces driving the legal disenfranchisement of African-Americans after 1890 in the South. The predominant interpretation has been that white Democrats from "black belt" regions with large African-American populations led the fight for systematic disenfranchisement in the face of regional political threat (Key [1949] 1964; Kousser 1974; Woodward 1951), although more recent examinations have identified a number of cases that do not fit this pattern (Perman 2001). Racial violence, in particular the factors driving lynching,

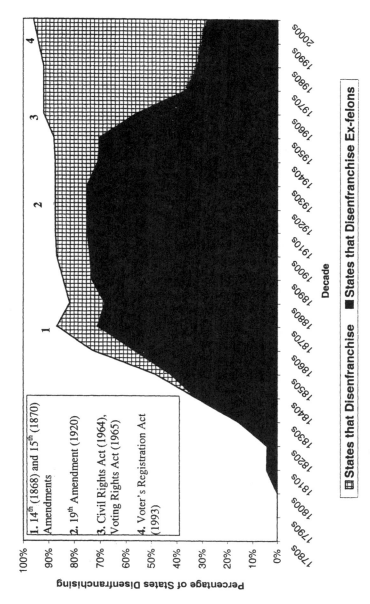

FIG. 1.—Percentage of states disenfranchising felons and ex-felons, 1788–2002

American Journal of Sociology

has also been the subject of thorough investigation. For example, some national-level studies report links between lynching and racial competition over political power (e.g., Olzak 1992, chap. 7), although other investigations (using county-level information) have not found the same effects (see Soule 1992; Tolnay and Beck 1995, chap. 6). Most of these studies have also found important impacts of general political-economic conditions, such as the dynamics of the Southern cotton economy, on racial violence and related outcomes (Tolnay and Beck 1995; see also James 1988).

The existing social science literature on the politics of criminal justice has produced conflicting results about the role of race in driving policy change. Research by Jacobs and Helms (1996, 1997) on prison admissions and police strength finds little racial impact, while the same authors' recent study of overall spending on social control finds that criminal-justice-system expenditures are responsive to racial threat (Jacobs and Helms 1999). Several city-level studies of police strength also report race effects (e.g., Jackson 1989; Liska, Lawrence, and Benson 1981). Myers's (1990, 1998) examination of racial disparities in prison admissions, sentencing, and release rates in Georgia between 1870 and 1940 finds modest support for racial competition explanations, in addition to the effects of economic factors such as cotton prices and industrialization. Overall, the existing research provides at best a mixed picture about the role of racial threat in shaping criminal justice policy. Most studies with appropriate statistical controls, however, focus on recent years rather than on the long historical period covered by this article.

Of course, racism and racial threats change shape over time. During the 19th and first half of the 20th centuries, advocacy of racial segregation and the superiority of whites was both widespread and explicit (see Mendelberg 2001, chap. 2). The Civil Rights Act of 1964 and the Voting Rights Act of 1965, however, served as an "authoritative legal and political rebuke of the Jim Crow social order" (Bobo and Smith 1998, p. 209) and fundamentally reshaped the law of democracy in the United States (Issacharoff, Karlan, and Pildes 1998; Kousser 1999). Nevertheless, in spite of the changes inaugurated by the "second reconstruction" of the 1960s, a number of scholars have argued that racial influence on policy making persists (see, e.g., Gilens 1999; Manza 2000). The institutional legacies of slavery and Jim Crow reverberate to the present in a decentralized polity and through path-dependent and policy feedback processes (see, e.g., Brown 1999; Goldfield 1997; Lieberman 1998; Quadagno 1994). Whereas structural and economic changes have reduced the social acceptability of explicit racial bias, current "race-neutral" language and policies remain socially and culturally embedded in the discriminatory actions of the past (Gilens 1999; Mendelberg 2001; Quadagno 1994).

Ballot Manipulation

Bobo and Smith (1998) characterize this historical process as a shift from "Jim Crow racism" to "laissez-faire racism." The latter is based on notions of cultural rather than biological inferiority, illustrated by persistent negative stereotyping, a tendency to blame African-Americans for racial gaps in socioeconomic standing (and, arguably, criminal punishment), and resistance to strong policy efforts to combat racist social institutions (see also Bobo, Kluegel, and Smith 1997; Kinder and Sanders 1996; Mendelberg 2001; Schuman, Steeh, Bobo, and Krysan 1997). In the case of race and crime, the institutionalization of large racial disparities in criminal punishment both reflects and reinforces tacit stereotypes about young African-American men that are intensified through media coverage (Entman and Rojecki 2000, chap. 5; Hurwitz and Peffley 1997; cf. Gilens 1999 and Quadagno 1994 on welfare).

The transition from the racism evident in the Jim Crow era to more modern forms can be seen in the discourse surrounding suffrage and the disenfranchisement of felons. Table 3 provides examples of the two modes of racial framing. The left side of the table presents examples of rhetoric on race and disenfranchisement in the Jim Crow era. Although the 1894 excerpt from a South Carolina newspaper does not specifically address felon disenfranchisement, it makes a clear racial appeal for suffrage restrictions. As Tindall (1949, p. 224) points out, South Carolina's Democratic leadership spread word that "the potential colored voting population of the state was about forty thousand more than the white" to push for a state constitutional convention to change the state's suffrage laws. When the convention was held in 1895, South Carolina expanded its disenfranchisement law to include ex-felons.

The 1896 excerpt is taken from the Supreme Court of Mississippi, which upheld the state's disenfranchisement law (*Ratliff v. Beale*, 74 Miss. 247 [1896]) while acknowledging the racist intent of its constitutional convention. The state obstructed exercise of the franchise by targeting "certain peculiarities of habit, of temperament, and of character" thought to distinguish African-Americans from whites. The U.S. Supreme Court later cited this Mississippi decision, maintaining that the law only took advantage of "the alleged characteristics of the negro race" and reached both "weak and vicious white men as well as weak and vicious black men" (*Williams v. Mississippi*, 170 U.S. 213, 222 [1898]).

The other excerpts from the Jim Crow era are taken from Alabama's 1901 Constitutional Convention, which altered that state's felon disenfranchisement law to include all crimes of "moral turpitude," applying to misdemeanors and even to acts not punishable by law (*Pippin v. State*, 197 Ala. 613 [1916]). In his opening address, John B. Knox, president of the all-white convention, justified "manipulation of the ballot" to avert "the menace of negro domination" (Alabama 1901, p. 12). John Field

TABLE 3

RACIAL THREAT AND JUSTIFICATIONS FOR FELON DISENFRANCHISEMENT

Jim Crow Era	Modern Era
1894: "Fortunately, the opportunity is offered the white people of the State in the coming election to obviate all future danger and fortify the Anglo-Saxon civilization against every assault from within and without, and that is the calling of a constitutional convention to deal with the all important question of suffrage."—*Daily Register*, Columbia, South Carolina, October 10, 1894.	**1985:** "Felons are not disenfranchised based on any immutable characteristic, such as race, but on their *conscious decision to commit an act for which they assume the risks of detection and punishment.* The law presumes that all men know its sanctions. Accordingly, the performance of a felonious act carries with it the perpetrator's *decision to risk disenfranchisement* in pursuit of the fruits of his misdeed"—U.S. District Court in Tennessee (*Wesley v. Collins*, 605 F. Supp. at 813) upholding the state's disenfranchisement law.
1896: "The [constitutional] convention swept the circle of expedients to obstruct the exercise of the franchise by the negro race. By reason of its previous condition of servitude and dependence, *this race had acquired or accentuated certain peculiarities of habit, of temperament and of character, which clearly distinguished it, as a race, from that of the whites*—a patient docile people, but careless, landless, and migratory within narrow limits, without aforethought, and its criminal members given rather to furtive offenses than to the robust crimes of the whites. Restrained by the federal constitution from discriminating against the negro race, *the convention discriminated against its characteristics and the offenses to which its weaker member were prone.*"—Mississippi Supreme Court (*Ratliff v. Beale*, 74 Miss. at 266–67) upholding the state's disenfranchisement law.	**2001:** *"If it's blacks losing the right to vote, then they have to quit committing crimes. We are not punishing the criminal. We are punishing conduct. . . . You need to tell people to stop committing crimes and not feel sorry for those who do."*—Rep. John Graham Altman (R-Charleston) advocating a more restrictive felon disenfranchisement provision in South Carolina (Wise 2001a).

1901: "[In 1861], as now, the negro was the prominent factor in the issue. . . . And what is it that we want to do? Why it is within the limits imposed by the Federal Constitution, to establish white supremacy in this State. . . . The justification for whatever manipulation of the ballot that has occurred in this State has been the *menace of negro domination*. . . . These provisions are justified in law and in morals, because it is said that the negro is not discriminated against on account of his race, but on account of his intellectual and moral condition."—John B. Knox, president of the Alabama Constitutional Convention of 1901, in his opening address. (See Alabama [1901], pp. 9–15.)

1901: "The crime of *wife-beating alone would disqualify sixty percent* of the Negroes."—John Field Bunting (Shapiro 1993, p. 541), who introduced the ordinance at the Constitutional Convention to change Alabama's disenfranchisement law.

2002: "States have a significant interest in reserving the vote for those who have abided by the social contract. . . . Those who break our laws, should not *dilute the vote of law-abiding citizens*."—Senator Mitch McConnell (R-Ky.) opposing a bill to enfranchise all ex-felons for federal elections (U.S. Congress 2002, p. S802).

2002: "I think this Congress, with this little debate we are having on this bill, ought not to step in and, with a big sledge hammer, *smash something we have had from the beginning of this country's foundation*—a set of election laws in every State in America—and change those laws. To just up and do that is disrespectful to them. . . . *Each State has different standards based on their moral evaluation*, their legal evaluation, their public interest in what they think is important in their States."—Senator Jeff Sessions (R-Ala.) agreeing with McConnell (U.S. Congress 2002, p. S803).

NOTE.—All emphases added.

American Journal of Sociology

Bunting, who introduced the new disenfranchisement law, clearly envisioned it as a mechanism to reduce African-American political power, estimating that "the crime of wife-beating alone would disqualify sixty percent of the Negroes" (Shapiro 1993, p. 541).

With the historical shift away from such overtly discriminatory laws and discourse, felon disenfranchisement laws are now defended on race-neutral grounds. A United States District Court in Tennessee (noted in table 3 under "Modern Era") explicitly rejected race as a criterion, but justified felon disenfranchisement based on individual criminal choice, or the "conscious decision to commit an act for which they assume the risks of detection and punishment" (*Wesley v. Collins*, 605 F. Supp. 802, 813 [M.D. Tenn. 1985]).[6]

In 2001, the South Carolina House of Representatives confronted the issue of race directly in debating a bill to disenfranchise all felons for 15 years beyond their sentence—a proposed expansion of the current law, which restores voting rights upon completion of sentence. After an opponent introduced an African-American ex-felon who would be harmed by the change, one of the bill's sponsors, John Graham Altman, distributed an old newspaper article detailing the man's crime, labeled "Democratic poster boy for murderers' right to vote." One representative likened the act to "Willie Horton race-baiting." Altman, however, denied any racist intent, stating, "If it's blacks losing the right to vote, then they have to quit committing crimes" (Wise 2001*a*, p. A3; Wise 2001*b*, p. B1).

A recent U.S. Senate measure to restore the ballot to all ex-felons in federal elections also met opposition and was ultimately voted down in February 2002. In opposing the bill, Republican Senator Mitch McConnell—himself a likely beneficiary of Kentucky's strict disenfranchisement law in his first Senate election victory in 1984 (Uggen and Manza 2002)—invoked imagery of the most heinous criminals. McConnell stated that "we are talking about rapists, murderers, robbers, and even terrorists or spies," before declaring that "those who break our laws should not

---

[6] Courts have generally upheld state felon disenfranchisement laws, adhering to the U.S. Supreme Court's *Ramirez* decision (418 U.S. 24 [1974]). In a rare case acknowledging racist legislative intent, the Supreme Court struck down Alabama's "moral turpitude" law in 1985 (*Hunter v. Underwood*, 471 U.S. 222 [1985]). Of course, even when a law has a disproportionately adverse effect on a racial group, intent of racial discrimination is difficult to establish. To date, courts have rejected disparate impact arguments that criminal justice system disparities alone constitute impermissible vote dilution (*Farrakhan v. Locke*, 987 F. Supp. 1304 [E.D. Wash. 1997]; *Wesley v. Collins*, 605 F. Supp. 802 [M.D. Tenn. 1985]).

Ballot Manipulation

dilute the vote of law-abiding citizens" (U.S. Congress 2002, p. S802).[7] Arguments such as these shift the focus from historical efforts to dilute the voting strength of racial minority groups to a concern with the vote dilution of "law-abiding citizens." Senator Jeff Sessions drew upon a traditional states' rights discourse—long associated with implicit racial appeals—in defending ex-felon disenfranchisement: "Each State has different standards based on their moral evaluation, their legal evaluation, their public interest" (U.S. Congress 2002, p. S803). Many interpret such statements as representing modern or laissez-faire racism; they appear to accept a legacy of historical racial discrimination uncritically and to oppose reforms by appealing to the legal and popular foundations of a system devised to benefit whites during the slavery and Jim Crow eras (see, e.g., Mendelberg 2001).

Conceptual Models of Racial Threat and Ballot Restrictions on Criminal Offenders

Sociological theories of racial or ethnic threat (Blalock 1967; Blumer 1958; Bonacich 1972) provide one avenue for explaining how racial dynamics shape policy-making processes, such as those surrounding felon disenfranchisement. There are several distinct conceptions of racial threat emphasizing, to varying degrees, economic competition, relative group size, and political power. Each has implications for operationalizing and testing the influence of racial threat on felon disenfranchisement laws.

Most generally, conceptions of "racial" threat are a particular application of group threat theories, which suggest that in situations where subordinate groups gain power at the expense of a dominant group, they will be perceived as a threat by that group (Blalock 1967; Blumer 1958; Bobo and Hutchings 1996; Olzak 1992; Quillian 1996). Actions against minority groups may be triggered by the majority group perception that a "sphere of group exclusiveness," such as the political sphere, has been broached (Blumer 1958, p. 4). In reaction, the majority group seeks to diminish the threat. For example, whites may push for political restrictions on racial minorities if they are concerned that these groups may mobilize and take action against them. The response to perceived threat may be to erect legal barriers, such as Jim Crow laws, and to institute other forms of racial discrimination. By strategically narrowing the scope of the elec-

---

[7] Offenders convicted of these crimes comprise a minority of the total felon population. Based on correctional data for 2000, we estimate that approximately 22% of the total state and federal prison population, and a far smaller share of the probation, parole, and ex-felon populations, would fall into these offense categories (U.S. Department of Justice 2000).

American Journal of Sociology

torate, a dominant majority can use disenfranchisement to sap the political
strength of a minority group and diminish its threat to established social
structures.

   Social psychological aspects of group threat may also be linked to felon
disenfranchisement. Race prejudice operates as a collective process,
whereby racial groups project negative images onto one another that
reinforce a sense of exclusiveness (Blumer 1958; Quillian 1996; Sears,
Sidanius, and Bobo 2000). One particularly salient image that may be
projected onto an ethnic or racial group is that of "criminal," linking race
and crime in public consciousness. Regardless of the actual crime rate,
for example, the percentage of young African-American males in an area
is directly related to fear of crime among white residents, particularly
when whites perceive themselves to be racial minorities in their own
neighborhoods (Chiricos, Hogan, and Gertz 1997; Quillian and Pager
2001). Because such fears may trigger repressive or coercive responses
(Blumer 1958), some suggest that the disproportionate criminal punishment of nonwhites constitutes, in part, a reaction to racial threat (Heimer,
Stucky, and Lang 1999; Myers 1998). Currently, about 10% of the African-
American voting-age population is under correctional supervision, compared to approximately 2% of the white voting-age population (U.S. Bureau of Census 2001; U.S. Department of Justice 2001, 2002). Felon
disenfranchisement thus remains a potentially effective means to neutralize political threats from African-American voters.

   Within the existing literature on racial group threat, two distinct theses
can be identified, and we advance a third, synthetic version. The most
common formulation traces racial threat to *economic* relationships between racial (or ethnic) groups (Bobo and Hutchings 1996; Bonacich 1972;
Giles and Evans 1985; Olzak 1992; Quillian 1995; Tolnay and Beck 1995).
Groups compete for material resources and the growth of a subordinate
group potentially threatens the economic positions of those in the dominant group. Levels of racial hostility may therefore be greater in places
where a dominant group has higher levels of economic marginality (e.g.,
Oliver and Mendelberg 2000; Quillian 1995).

   Economic threat models, however, are potentially problematic in explaining the rise of felon voting restrictions. Disenfranchisement is situated
within the *political* realm, an area that has received comparatively little
attention in models of group threat. General models of racial antagonism
that emphasize a political power threat highlight the importance of the
size of subordinate groups within specific geographical contexts (see Fossett and Kiecolt 1989; Giles and Evans 1985; Quillian 1996; Taylor 1998).
As subordinate groups grow in (relative) size, they may be able to leverage
democratic political institutions to their advantage. Racial threats in the
political realm are potentially devastating to existing power relations be-

Ballot Manipulation

cause the extension of suffrage formally equalizes individual members of dominant and subordinate racial groups with respect to the ballot. Yet racial threats in this domain are also more easily subdued by those in positions of power. Legal disenfranchisement and informal barriers to political participation offer a clear mechanism to neutralize racial threats and maintain a racially stratified electorate.[8]

The findings of a number of studies are also consistent with the more general view that the size of the racial minority population in a region heightens white concerns. As noted above, research on perceptions of crime has established a link to the perceived racial composition of neighborhoods and cities (see esp. Quillian and Pager 2001). When former Ku Klux Klan leader David Duke sought one of Louisiana's U.S. Senate seats in 1990, white support for his campaign was greatest in parishes with the largest African-American populations (Giles and Buckner 1993). Similarly, the proportion of African-Americans in each parish heavily influenced white registration with the Republican Party in Louisiana from 1975 and 1990 (Giles and Hertz 1994). Taylor (1998, 2000) also finds that traditional white prejudice, and white opposition to public policies seeking to enhance racial equality, swells with the proportion of the African-American population.

In applying racial threat theories to the specific case of felon disenfranchisement, however, a third operationalization can also be considered: the racial composition of the convicted felon population. Incarceration may be considered a response to racial threat, in that consigning a high proportion of African-Americans and other racial minorities to prison reduces their imminent economic threat to whites (Heimer, Stucky, and Lang 1999). Unless those imprisoned are also disenfranchised, however, a political threat remains. Moreover, because felon voting laws only affect those convicted of crime, prison racial composition is more proximally related to felon disenfranchisement than is the racial distribution of the general population. Thus, there may be a connection between the racial composition of state prisons and state felon voting bans not captured by the proportion of nonwhites in the total state population.

---

[8] A second, more general problem with economic threat models is that they may overgeneralize from the economic to the political and cultural. Theories of *symbolic racism* (Sears 1988; Sears and Funk 1991) or *racial resentment* (Kinder and Sanders 1996), e.g., suggest that racial antagonisms toward blacks among white Americans are deeply held and not simply reducible to economic conflict. Though these attitudes may remain latent, they can be triggered by events such as the invocation of the name Willie Horton by George Bush in the 1988 Presidential campaign (Mendelberg 2001).

American Journal of Sociology

DATA, METHODS, AND MEASURES

To test whether, and how, racial threat influences the passage of restrictive state felon disenfranchisement laws, we undertake an event history analysis that considers how the racial composition of state prisons and other measures of racial threat affect these voting bans, net of timing, region, economic conditions, political party power, and other state characteristics. We use decennial state-level data taken primarily from historical censuses from 1850 to 2000 (U.S. Department of Commerce 1853–1992; U.S. Bureau of Census 2001). We then conduct a parallel analysis of reenfranchisement to determine whether racial threat has played a continuing role in the recent movement toward restoring the vote to ex-felons, using annual state-level data from 1940 to 2002.

Independent Variables

We test all three of the racial threat models described above, within the limits of the available data for this lengthy time period. To assess the possibility that economic competition affects adoption of felon disenfranchisement laws, we include a measure of the rate of white male idleness and unemployment in each state, drawing upon U.S. Census data from the Integrated Public Use Microdata Series, or IPUMS (Ruggles and Sobek 1997) for the years 1850 to 1990. We derived this measure by dividing the number of unemployed or idle (neither attending school nor participating in the labor force) white males ages 15–39 by the total white male population ages 15–39. Because this indicator is subject to inconsistent measurement over the long observation period, we also operationalize economic conditions with a national economic contraction or recession indicator, which we derived from the National Bureau of Economic Research's series *Business Cycle Expansions and Contractions* (Moore 1961, pp. 670–71; NBER 2003; Stock and Watson 1993). Consistent with the ethnic competition literature (Olzak 1990; Olzak and Shanahan 2002), the latter measure captures cyclical economic fluctuations that may activate feelings of "economic threat."

Second, to capture the possibility that political threat in the general population drives disenfranchisement laws, we consider the impact of variation in the size of the African-American and non-African-American population across the states and years. Some research suggests that minority *male* populations pose a larger threat than the total nonwhite population (Myers 1990), so we also computed a measure based on the number of nonwhite males as a percentage of the total state population in historical censuses. Finally, we consider the percentage of nonwhite inmates in state prisons. We rely on Census Bureau "institutional population" and "group

Ballot Manipulation

quarters" subject reports to obtain state-level decennial information on the racial composition of prisons. Although an indicator of the racial composition of all convicted felons would be preferable to a prison-based indicator, the former is unavailable over the long historical period of our study. Fortunately, the two measures are highly correlated across space and time, at least for recent years when both data series are available (U.S. Department of Justice 2000). Because data on the race of prisoners are unavailable between 1900 and 1920, we interpolated estimates for these years based on data from 1890 and historical correctional statistics from 1926–30 (U.S. Department of Justice 1991). A summary of the key independent and dependent variables we use, and a brief description of their measurement, is presented in table 4.

In addition to racial threat, we also expect factors such as region, partisan control, and criminal justice punitiveness to affect passage of laws restricting the voting rights of felons. Regional effects are especially important in this context. While many states passed ballot restrictions following the Civil War, Southern states generally adopted more comprehensive and detailed laws (Keyssar 2000, p. 162). Although legally enfranchised after the Civil War, African-Americans in many parts of the South remained practically disenfranchised by barriers such as poll taxes and literacy tests well into the 20th century.[9] While Southern states have historically been especially restrictive, many Northern states have also been reluctant to enfranchise minority populations; between 1863 and 1870, 15 Northern states rejected giving African-Americans the right to vote (Keyssar 2000, p. 89). We use Census Bureau categories to represent region, coding northeast, midwest, south, and west as separate indicator variables.

Partisan politics are also tied to legal change, because state politicians ultimately introduce and amend felon disenfranchisement laws.[10] Before and after the Reconstruction period, Republicans were generally more supportive of African-American suffrage than were Democrats, even outside the South. These roles, however, gradually shifted as Northern Democrats became increasingly reliant on black votes and the Northern wing of the party shifted toward a pro–civil rights position (cf. Frymer 1999; Piven 1992; Weiss 1983). The conflicts over the Civil Rights Act of 1964 and the Voting Rights Act of 1965, as well as the virtual disappearance

[9] A 1961 report by the Commission on Civil Rights found that nearly 100 counties in eight Southern states were effectively denying black citizens the right to vote. Following the Voting Rights Act of 1965, nearly 1 million new voters registered in the South (Keyssar 2000, pp. 262–65).

[10] The state electorate sometimes makes the final decision regarding state disenfranchisement laws, as with the recent referenda in Utah in 1998 and Massachusetts in 2000.

TABLE 4
SUMMARY OF DEPENDENT AND INDEPENDENT VARIABLES, 1850–2002

Variable	Description	Coding	Mean
Disenfranchisement law:			
First law	Passage of first felon disenfran-chisement law.	0 = no, 1 = yes	
Ex-felon law	Passage of first ex-felon disenfran-chisement law.	0 = no, 1 = yes	
Racial threat:			
Nonwhite prison	Percentage of prison population that is nonwhite.	Percentage	30.2
Nonwhite males	Percentage of male population that is nonwhite.	Percentage	6.8
Nonwhite population ...	Percentage of total population that is nonwhite.	Percentage	13.6
Black population	Total African-American population.	100,000s	3.1 (4.7)
Nonblack population ...	Total non-African-American population.	100,000s	24.4 (32.6)
Economic competition:			
Idle white males	Percentage of white males, ages 15–39, unemployed or both not in the labor force and not in school.	Percentage	7.4
National recession	Proportion of decade in business contraction (NBER 2003).	Proportion	.33
Region:			
Northeast	Dichotomous Northeastern state indicator (Connecticut, Maine, Massachusetts, New Hampshire, New Jersey, New York, Pennsylvania, Rhode Island, Vermont).	0 = no, 1 = yes	.196
Midwest	Dichotomous Midwestern state indicator (Illinois, Indiana, Iowa, Kansas, Michigan, Minnesota, Missouri, Nebraska, North Dakota, Ohio, South Dakota, Wisconsin).	0 = no, 1 = yes	.251
South	Dichotomous Southern state indicator (Alabama, Arkansas, Delaware, Florida, Georgia, Kentucky, Louisiana, Maryland, Mississippi, North Carolina, Oklahoma, South Carolina, Tennessee, Texas, Virginia, West Virginia).	0 = no, 1 = yes	.341

Ballot Manipulation

TABLE 4 *(Continued)*

Variable	Description	Coding	Mean
West	Dichotomous Western state indicator (Alaska, Arizona, California, Colorado, Hawaii, Idaho, Montana, Nevada, New Mexico, Oregon, Utah, Washington, Wyoming).	0 = no, 1 = yes	.211
State punitiveness:			
Incarceration rate	State incarceration rate per 100,000 population.	Per 100,000	134.3 (114.4)
Political power:			
Pre-1870 Democrat	Dichotomous Democratic governor indicator, pre-1870.	0 = no, 1 = yes	.057
1870–1959 Democrat ...	Dichotomous Democratic governor indicator, 1870–1959.	0 = no, 1 = yes	.269
1960–2002 Democrat ...	Dichotomous Democratic governor indicator, post-1959.	0 = no, 1 = yes	.172
Timing:			
Time since statehood ...	Number of years since statehood.	Years	103.9 (56.4)
Time:			
Decade	Individual decade indicator variables (1850–59, 1860–69, etc.).	0 = no, 1 = yes	

NOTE.—Total state-years covered by this study is 733. Numbers in parentheses are standard deviations.

of black electoral support for the Republican Party, consolidated this new racial cleavage in the party system (Carmines and Stimson 1989; Huckfeldt and Kohfeld 1989).

Data limitations and these numerous historical turning points complicate efforts to assess the role of partisan influence on the passage of felon disenfranchisement laws. Because data on the party affiliations of state legislators are not available for the entire period, we represent political power in the decennial analysis with gubernatorial partisanship. Of course, political affiliations hold different meanings in the early years of our study than they do in the later years. To account for these changes, and for potential interactions between region and partisanship, we specified a series of models using various periodizations. Because we found no statistically significant interactions with time or region, we adopt a reasonably parsimonious specification, based on gubernatorial partisanship prior to 1870, from 1870 to 1960, and from 1960 to the present. This periodization captures the shift of racially conservative southern Democrats to the Republican Party beginning in the early 1960s.

Our sources for political data include the Council of State Governments' *Book of the States* series (1937–87), the Census Bureau's *Statistical Ab-*

American Journal of Sociology

stract series (1980–2001), and the Inter-University Consortium for Political and Social Research's "Candidate Name and Constituency Totals, 1788–1990" (1995). We also include incarceration rate indicators in multivariate models to assess the effects of punitiveness (U.S. Department of Justice 1987). Finally, we use a measure of the years since statehood to account for the likelihood that new states will adopt felon disenfranchisement provisions as part of their constitutions. Each decade does not have 50 potential cases because states do not enter the data set until the decade of official statehood, regardless of the state's status as a recognized territory preceding statehood.

Dependent Variables

The length of time an offender is disenfranchised varies by state, with states generally falling into one of four regimes: disenfranchisement only during incarceration; during parole and incarceration; during sentence (until completion of probation, parole, and incarceration); and after completion of sentence (ex-felons). A law was considered a restrictive change only if it disenfranchised a new category of felons.[11] States that disenfranchised only upon conviction for a few narrowly defined offenses, such as treason or election crimes, were not considered to have a felon disenfranchisement law until the scope of the law reached felony convictions in general. Details of state-level changes are presented in table 2.

Statistical Models

We model changes to felon disenfranchisement laws using event history analysis because this method appropriately models censored cases and time-varying predictors (see, e.g., Allison 1984; Yamaguchi 1991). To correctly model censored cases, states are only included in the analysis when they are at risk of changing their felon disenfranchisement regime. For example, Alaska and Hawaii were not at risk of passing a restrictive law until they attained statehood in 1959. If a state was not at risk of restrictive changes because it had already disenfranchised ex-felons, the most severe voting ban, that state was excluded until it repealed its ex-felon disenfranchisement law. Time-varying independent variables are important for this study because it would be unrealistic to assume stability over 150 years in key predictors such as imprisonment and racial composition. States that passed more restrictive felon disenfranchisement laws within

---

[11] For example, some states that disenfranchise ex-felons routinely change their clemency eligibility criteria. These administrative changes generally affect few ex-felons and were not considered new laws in this analysis.

Ballot Manipulation

the decade were coded "1"; if no change occurred, states were coded "0." These state-years comprise the unit of analysis for this study.

We estimate the effects of racial threat and other factors using a discrete-time logistic regression model (Allison 1984, 1995; Yamaguchi 1991):

$$\log[P_{it}/(1 - P_{it})] = \alpha_t + \beta_1 X_{it1} + \cdots + \beta_k X_{itk}.$$

P_{it} represents the probability that a law is passed in state i in time interval t, β signifies the effect of the independent variables, $X_1, X_2 \ldots X_k$ denote k time-varying explanatory variables, and α_t represents a set of constants corresponding to each decade or discrete-time unit. While we have complete information on state felon disenfranchisement law changes spanning from 1788 to 2002, the time-varying explanatory variables are limited to the period from 1850 to 2002.[12]

To identify the factors responsible for changes in state felon disenfranchisement laws, we first chart historical changes in these laws. We then examine the bivariate relationship between the independent variables and passage of a first restrictive law. Next, we fit multivariate models to show the effects of racial threat, region, economic competition, political power, punitiveness, and time on the passage of laws disenfranchising felons and ex-felons between 1850 and 2002. We also specify piecewise models to estimate the effects of racial threat and other independent variables before and after passage of the Fifteenth Amendment in 1870. Finally, we present an analysis of ex-felon reenfranchisement for the more recent period from 1940 to 2002.

RESULTS

We compiled demographic life tables to identify periods of stability and change in felon disenfranchisement provisions. Figure 2 plots the hazard functions of restrictive (or disenfranchising) changes and liberal (or enfranchising) changes from 1850 to 2002. The solid line represents states passing more restrictive felon voting laws, and the dashed line indicates passage of more liberal laws. The first peak of activity, in the 1860s and

---

[12] Unfortunately, four states are *left censored* (see, e.g., Yamaguchi 1991) because they passed restrictive laws prior to 1840, when data on key independent variables are unavailable. Seven states passed a first restrictive law between 1841 and 1849. We estimated models that applied 1850 data to the 1840 period (assuming stability on the values of independent variables, except gubernatorial partisanship), as well as models that treated these states as left censored. To show regional effects, we present results from the former models (only three Northeastern states adopted a felon disenfranchisement law for the first time after 1847). Aside from region, the effects of racial threat and other independent variables are very similar to those reported below in analyses that omit the 1840 changes (tables available from authors).

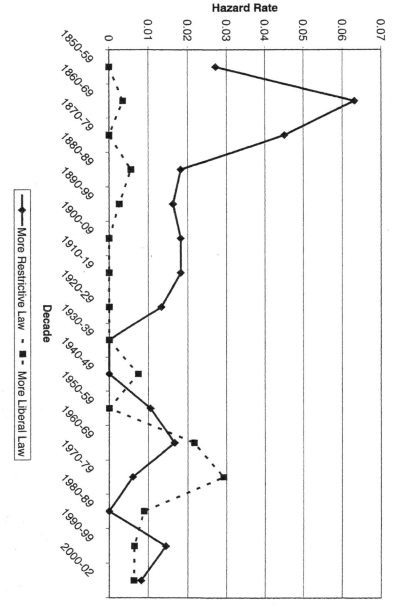

FIG. 2.—Hazard plots for restrictive and liberal changes to state felon disenfranchisement laws, 1850–2002

Ballot Manipulation

1870s, represents predominantly restrictive changes whereas the second peak, occurring 100 years later, is comprised of liberal legal changes. Until the 1930s, the rate of restrictive changes exceeded the rate of liberal changes in each decade. From the 1960s to the 1980s, this trend reversed and the hazard of liberalizing changes to felon disenfranchisement laws surpassed the hazard of restrictive changes until the 1990s. Many of these liberal changes involved the repeal of laws that disenfranchised ex-felons, as states shifted to less restrictive regimes. In the 1960s and 1970s combined, 17 states repealed ex-felon disenfranchisement laws.[13] Although recent history suggests a general trend toward liberalization, most changes in the 1990s were once again restrictive rather than liberal.

First State Felon Disenfranchisement Law

Bivariate analysis.—We next examine the state-level predictors of these laws. Table 5 presents the results of 26 separate discrete-time logistic event history models predicting the passage of states' *first* restrictive felon disenfranchisement law. These models do not include statistical controls for other independent variables, except for time. The first column shows the relation between each predictor and passage of the first restrictive law while controlling for time as a set of dummy variables for each decade. The second column shows coefficients from similar models that represent time as a single linear variable measured in years.

The bivariate results in table 5 show that racial threat, as measured by the percentage of nonwhite prisoners, is associated with restrictive changes to state felon disenfranchisement laws in both models. Since Blalock hypothesized a curvilinear relationship between minority group size and discrimination under some conditions (1967, pp. 148–49), we also fit models with both linear and quadratic terms. Although the squared term is not statistically distinguishable from zero in these models, a positive linear effect and negative second-order effect are consistent with the idea that the odds of disenfranchisement may diminish as the percentage of nonwhite prisoners reaches very high levels. The relative size of the nonwhite male population and nonwhite population and the absolute size of the African-American population also approach significance ($P < .10$).

---

[13] In 2000, Delaware abandoned its requirement of a pardon to restore voting rights, though offenders must still wait five years after completion of sentence to vote. Since July 1, 2001, New Mexico has automatically restored voting rights to felons upon completion of sentence. As of January 1, 2003, Maryland requires a three-year waiting period before restoring the franchise to most recidivists, liberalizing its former law that permanently disenfranchised recidivists. Similarly, Nevada liberalized its law in 2003 and now restores voting rights to nonviolent first-time felons upon completion of sentence.

TABLE 5

BIVARIATE PREDICTORS OF FIRST FELON DISENFRANCHISEMENT LAW

Variable	Model	Dummy Decade	Linear Year	Events	Cases
Racial threat:					
% nonwhite prison	1	.091***	.088***	42	160
		(.019)	(.017)		
% nonwhite prison	2	.119***	.115***	42	160
		(.041)	(.038)		
% nonwhite prison^2	2	−.001	−.001		
		(.001)	(.001)		
% nonwhite males	3	.045*	.041*	42	159
		(.025)	(.022)		
% nonwhite population	4	.021*	.019*	44	162
		(.012)	(.011)		
Black population (100,000s)	5	.233	.251*	44	162
		(.149)	(.135)		
Nonblack population (100,000s)	5	−.011	−.010		
		(.016)	(.016)		
Economic competition:					
% idle white males age 15–39	6	.066	.067	44	162
		(.060)	(.051)		
National recession	7	1.007	.789	45	163
		(.711)	(.625)		
Region (vs. South):					
Northeast	8	−1.314**	−1.665***	48	277
		(.571)	(.562)		
Midwest	8	.408	.297		
		(.512)	(.461)		
West	8	2.122***	.931		
		(.767)	(.595)		
State punitiveness:					
Incarceration rate (per 100,000)	9	.004	.006*	42	160
		(.004)	(.003)		
Political partisanship (vs. other):					
Democratic governor (DG)	10	−.042	−.270	44	162
		(.405)	(.371)		
DG pre-1870	11	−.027	−.255	44	162
		(.555)	(.465)		
DG 1870–1959	11	.248	−.249		
		(.685)	(.574)		
DG 1960–present	11	−.991	−.440		
		(1.277)	(1.195)		
Timing:					
Time since statehood	12	−.022***	−.025***	48	277
		(.006)	(.005)		
Time:					
1860s (vs. 1850)	13	2.320***		48	277
1870s	13	2.407***			
1880s	13	1.531**			

Ballot Manipulation

TABLE 5 (*Continued*)

Variable	Model	Dummy Decade	Linear Year	Events	Cases
1890s	13	.972			
1900s	13	1.126			
1910–49	13	−.260			
1950s	13	1.126			
1960–89	13	.433			
1990s	13	1.126			
2000s	13	1.531			
Linear year only	14		.007**	48	277

NOTE.—Nos. in parentheses are SEs; authors will supply SEs for time dummies on request. Results of 26 separate discrete-time event history models predicting the timing of passage of the first felon disenfranchisement law. Region and timing models span the period from 1780 to 2002 rather than 1850 to 2002.
* $P < .10$.
** $P < .05$.
*** $P < .01$.

Regionally, Northeastern states are less likely to pass punitive felon disenfranchisement laws than Southern states, whereas Western states are more likely to pass such laws relative to Southern states. Democratic state governors have only a marginal impact on the likelihood of felon ballot restrictions in any of the three periods (two- and four-period models yielded similar results). Finally, state incarceration rates have a modest positive effect on passage of disenfranchisement laws in models with a linear time trend.

We observe timing effects consistent with other models of legal diffusion (Edelman 1990; Grattet, Jenness, and Curry 1998; McCammon et al. 2001). First, states are most likely to adopt restrictive laws with statehood or in the years immediately thereafter. Second, in models that treat time as a single linear variable, the positive effect of year indicates that restrictive changes have become somewhat more likely since 1850. Finally, when time is modeled as individual decade dummy variables, we again note that many states passed their first restrictive law in the Reconstruction and Redemption eras following the Civil War—the 1860s, 1870s, and 1880s (see Keyssar 2000, pp. 105–16, on Southern redemption and the right to vote). The Depression and World War II eras had no restrictive changes and are coded as part of the immediately preceding interval (e.g., the 1930s are considered within the 1910–49 period), following Allison (1995, p. 226). Although we estimated all models with both a linear time trend and separate dummy variables for each decade, a likelihood-ratio test established that the full set of time indicators improves the fit of the models. Therefore, all subsequent tables are based on the more conservative dummy variable specification.

American Journal of Sociology

Multivariate analysis.—Building upon the racial threat arguments outlined above and the observed bivariate relationships, table 6 presents
discrete-time logistic regression models predicting passage of states' first
felon disenfranchisement laws. Model 1 considers regional effects, relative
to the Northeast, on a first restrictive change while controlling for time.
All regions are significantly more likely to pass a felon disenfranchisement
law than the Northeast. Model 2 tests one version of the racial threat
hypothesis by introducing the nonwhite prison population. The observed
bivariate effect remains positive and significant after statistically controlling for the effects of state racial composition, region, incarceration
rate, and time. Each 1% increase in the percentage of prisoners who are
nonwhite increases the odds by about 10% that a state will pass its first
felon disenfranchisement law $(100[e^{.094} - 1] = 9.86)$.

Note that the Midwest and the West retain their positive effects in
model 2, but the South effect diminishes when controlling for the nonwhite
prison population, implying that the restrictiveness of Southern states may
be linked to racial composition. Net of the other independent variables,
state incarceration rates are not strongly associated with passage of disenfranchisement laws. This suggests that while felon disenfranchisement
is closely tied to the racial composition of the incarcerated population, it
is not a simple product of rising punitiveness.[14] The effects of race and
region remain robust in models 3 and 4 after adding economic competition
and political partisanship variables. In contrast to their more modest
effects in the bivariate analysis, indicators of national recession years and
gubernatorial partisanship emerge as stronger predictors in the multivariate models, with restrictive changes most likely during times of economic recession and least likely during times of Democratic political control. We model Democratic control as a single variable in table 6, in
contrast to the periodization shown in table 5, because the sign of each
period indicator is negative in the full model and because few states have
passed restrictive disenfranchisement laws in the recent 1960–2002 period.
Finally, time since statehood is a strong negative predictor in model 5,
suggesting that the likelihood of states adopting felon disenfranchisement
provisions declines precipitously with time. Because of their mutual association, the addition of the time-since-statehood indicator produces instability in estimates of time, region, and recession effects (and inflates
their standard errors). The key nonwhite prison effect is robust, though

[14] It is difficult to estimate the independent effects of racial composition, prison racial
composition, and region because these variables are closely correlated (a complete
correlation matrix is available from the authors). Nevertheless, with the exceptions
noted below, the estimates reported in tables 6–9 are generally robust under alternative
specifications.

TABLE 6
PREDICTORS OF FIRST FELON DISENFRANCHISEMENT LAW, 1850–2002
(Discrete-Time Logistic Regression)

	MODELS				
VARIABLE	1	2	3	4	5
Racial threat:					
% nonwhite prison ……		.094***	.093***	.098***	.108***
		(.024)	(.024)	(.025)	(.028)
Black population					
(100,000s) …………		−.012	.033	.140	.428
		(.282)	(.287)	(.298)	(.347)
Nonblack population					
(100,000s) …………		−.004	−.001	−.011	−.012
		(.027)	(.028)	(.029)	(.032)
Region (vs. Northeast):					
South …………………	1.222**	.193	.324	.497	−1.530
	(.552)	(1.015)	(1.032)	(1.049)	(1.355)
Midwest ………………	1.595***	1.268*	1.254*	1.350**	−.612
	(.568)	(.651)	(.671)	(.688)	(1.019)
West …………………	3.158***	2.432**	2.708**	2.796***	−.315
	(.684)	(.975)	(1.053)	(1.050)	(1.625)
State punitiveness:					
Incarceration rate/					
100,000 ……………		.002	.003	.004	.003
		(.005)	(.005)	(.005)	(.006)
Economic competition:					
Idle/unemployed white					
males ages 15–39 ……			.019	.008	.068
			(.119)	(.119)	(.121)
National recession ……			2.033**	2.186**	1.476
			(.898)	(.937)	(1.035)
Political power:					
Democratic governor ….				−1.006*	−1.192**
				(.585)	(.603)
Timing:					
Time since statehood ….					−.037**
					(.015)
Time (vs. 1850):[a]					
1860s …………………	2.260***	.435	.615	.536	.582
1870s …………………	2.412***	.900	.325	−.133	.886
1880s …………………	1.130	.346	.728	.456	.864
1890s …………………	−.160	−.826	−1.463	−1.833	−.585
1900s …………………	.647	−.370	−.328	−.414	.835
1910–49 ………………	−.983	−2.331	−2.552*	−2.528*	−.762
1950–2002 ……………	.550	−1.703	−1.234	−1.144	2.132
	−3.264***	−2.875***	−4.173***	−3.804***	−1.337
Constant …………………	(.500)	(.677)	(1.240)	(1.264)	(1.565)
−2 log likelihood …………	193.80	117.14	111.505	108.368	101.480

American Journal of Sociology

TABLE 6 (*Continued*)

VARIABLE	MODELS				
	1	2	3	4	5
χ^2 (*df*)	61.63***	61.65***	67.283***	70.420***	77.308***
	(10)	(14)	(16)	(17)	(18)
Events	48	40	40	40	40
N	277	158	158	158	158

NOTE.—Nos. in parentheses are SEs.
ᵃ Authors will supply SEs for time variables on request.
* *P* < .10.
** *P* < .05.
*** *P* < .01.

somewhat larger in magnitude in the final model, with respect to the bivariate and multivariate specifications in tables 5 and 6.

Laws Disenfranchising Former Felons

Table 7 shows the effects of the same independent variables upon the passage of a state's first *ex-felon* disenfranchisement law, the most severe ballot restriction. The results in table 7 again reveal a positive and significant effect of the nonwhite prison population. In model 4, for example, a 10% increase in a state's nonwhite prison population raises the odds of passing an ex-felon disenfranchisement law by almost 50% $(10[100(e^{.048} - 1)])$. Moreover, we find greater evidence of a curvilinear relation between the percentage of racial minorities in prison and ex-felon disenfranchisement, net of population composition and the other independent variables. Taken together, tables 5, 6, and 7 show a strong and consistent relationship between racial threat as measured by the percentage of nonwhite state prisoners and laws restricting felon voting rights. States in the Midwest, the South, and the West are also more likely to pass felon disenfranchisement laws than states in the Northeast. The effect of the Southern region, however, again diminishes when controlling for the nonwhite prison population, indicating that race is particularly important in the South. Again, none of the region indicators are statistically significant in models that include time since statehood, and racial threat effects are more pronounced in the final model.

Piecewise Specifications

The preceding analysis has shown the average effect of selected racial threat indicators and other characteristics, measured over a long historical period. We next examine the robustness of these findings in a piecewise

TABLE 7

PREDICTORS OF FIRST LAW DISENFRANCHISING EX-FELONS, 1850–2002 (Discrete-Time Logistic Regression)

VARIABLE	MODELS				
	1	2	3	4	5
Racial threat:					
% nonwhite prison		.048***	.049***	.048***	.130***
		(.016)	(.017)	(.017)	(.045)
Nonwhite prison^2					−.001*
					(.001)
Black population		−.055	−.076	−.035	.552*
(100,000s)		(.258)	(.267)	(.268)	(.294)
Nonblack population		−.044	−.040	−.043	−.063
(100,000s)		(.038)	(.038)	(.037)	(.039)
Region (vs. Northeast):					
South	1.188**	.211	.145	.334	−1.922
	(.603)	(.981)	(1.029)	(1.047)	(1.329)
Midwest	1.621**	1.413*	1.273*	1.331*	−.133
	(.643)	(.759)	(.768)	(.780)	(1.092)
West	3.417***	2.361**	2.491**	2.490**	−.177
	(.813)	(1.064)	(1.095)	(1.090)	(1.572)
State punitiveness:					
Incarceration rate (per		−.001	−.002	−.001	−.001
100,000)		(.004)	(.004)	(.004)	(.004)
Economic competition:					
Idle/unemployed white			.059	.046	.034
males 15–39			(.086)	(.088)	(.116)
National recession			1.089	1.104	.521
			(.782)	(.793)	(.854)
Political power:					
Democratic governor				−.582	−.643
				(.573)	(.591)
Timing:					
Time since statehood					−.030*
					(.016)
Time:[a]					
1860s	1.355**	.161	.145	−.106	−.314
1870s	1.667***	.311	.024	−.336	.197
1880s	.262	−.723	−.481	−.647	−.066
1890s	−.159	−.807	−.874	−1.136	−.125
1900s	−1.153	−1.513	−1.232	−1.416	−.713
Post-1910	−2.500***	−3.591***	−3.649***	−3.658***	−2.823**
Constant	−3.335***	−2.182***	−3.104***	−2.775***	−.841
	(.556)	(.750)	(1.030)	(1.078)	(1.600)
−2 log likelihood	189.355	122.853	120.468	119.421	110.348
χ^2 (*df*)	53.60***	62.13***	64.511***	65.559***	74.631***
	(9)	(13)	(15)	(16)	(18)
Events	38	31	31	31	31
N	361	241	241	241	241

NOTE.—Nos. in parentheses are SEs.

[a] Authors will supply SEs on request.

* $P < .10$.

** $P < .05$.

*** $P < .01$.

American Journal of Sociology

model that considers additional indicators of racial threat and allows effects to vary across historical periods. States were free to impose racial suffrage requirements until passage of the Fourteenth and Fifteenth amendments, such that many nonwhite citizens were already disenfranchised regardless of whether they had committed felonies (Foner 1988; Kousser 1974; Keyssar 2000). We therefore expect the effects of racial threat on felon disenfranchisement to increase after 1868 when states could lose representation if they denied suffrage based on race. Because there are relatively few events to predict, we are limited to two-period models, using the passage of the Fifteenth Amendment in 1870 as a historical cutpoint. We consider the influence of several racial threat indicators across these periods in table 8, including nonwhite population, nonwhite male population, nonwhite prison population, and the idle and unemployed white male population.

Table 8 shows the results for the piecewise models, divided into two time periods: before 1870 and 1870–2002. For each indicator we report a trimmed model that controls only for individual decades and a full model that controls for the effects of region, gubernatorial partisanship, idle or unemployed white males, population, incarceration rate, and time since statehood. In the earlier period, only the nonwhite prison population is a significant predictor of passage of a felon disenfranchisement law. In fact, the other models generally provide a poor fit to the data in the pre-1870 period. As expected, however, each racial threat coefficient is stronger in magnitude and significance after the passage of the Fifteenth Amendment. The nonwhite population, the nonwhite male population, and the nonwhite prison population are all significant positive predictors. The indicator of idle and unemployed white males is not statistically significant (nor is the national recession measure, in analyses not shown), though it is positive in sign, as theories of economic threat would predict.

Consistent with our expectations, racial threat has more pronounced and consistent effects in the post-1870 period. Yet the nonwhite prison population remains a strong predictor in the earlier period. This is perhaps not surprising in models predicting *felon* disenfranchisement, since the racial composition of state prisons likely represents the most proximal measure of racial threat. Though racial challenges to political power were much more visible during and after Reconstruction, it is important to note that they predated 1870. For example, several state provisions allowed for nonwhite suffrage prior to the Reconstruction amendments. When Rhode Island passed its first felon disenfranchisement law, for example, it had no race requirement for voting, and Indiana and Texas excluded African-Americans from the ballot but not other nonwhites. It is also likely that racial threat played an important role in the brief period

Ballot Manipulation

between the adoption of the Fourteenth and Fifteenth amendments, when six states passed their first felon disenfranchisement law.

The Reenfranchisement of Ex-Felons, 1940–2002

As figures 1 and 2 make clear, many states have reconsidered felon disenfranchisement in the past four decades and have repealed restrictions on ex-felons in whole or in part. The 1960s and 1970s, in particular, were periods of relative liberalization. Since 1947, 23 states have repealed ex-felon disenfranchisement altogether, 5 additional states have partially repealed their bans for some categories of ex-felons, and a total of 30 states have liberalized their laws to some degree. For example, North Carolina passed an ex-felon voting ban in 1876, liberalized this law in 1971, by permitting ex-felons to vote after a two-year waiting period, and completely repealed ex-felon disenfranchisement in 1973 by providing for automatic restoration of voting rights upon completion of sentence.

To identify the determinants of these liberalizing trends, we again use a discrete-time logistic event history procedure. Since no state completely repealed ex-felon disenfranchisement until the 1940s, we begin the analysis in 1940. As opposed to the decennial analysis of the passage of disenfranchisement laws from 1850 to 2002, the reenfranchisement analysis is based on an annual data set of 3,112 state-years (48–50 states over 63 years), approximately 1,600 of which were at risk of repealing ex-felon disenfranchisement. States with no history of ex-felon disenfranchisement are thus excluded from this analysis and states are censored for all years following repeal because they are no longer at risk of rescinding an ex-felon ban.

Paralleling the analysis of disenfranchisement, we again consider the effects of racial threat, region, economic competition, political power, timing, and punitiveness. In this case, we expect a negative relationship between the proportion of prisoners who are African-American and the likelihood of reenfranchising ex-felons. We take advantage of the greater availability of data in recent years to refine measures of racial composition, economic conditions, and partisan political strength. We measure Democratic power as the percentage of state legislators that are Democratic multiplied by an indicator variable for the presence of a Democratic governor, coded "1" if Democrat and "0" otherwise. We measure racial threat by the percentage of prison inmates who are African-American and by the number of African-Americans and non-African-Americans in the general population.[15] Economic conditions are indexed by the state unem-

---

[15] Annual data on prison racial composition are taken from Bureau of Justice Statistics publications, including *Correctional Populations in the United States* and the *Source-*

TABLE 8

RACIAL AND ECONOMIC THREAT AND PASSAGE OF FIRST FELON DISENFRANCHISEMENT LAW

	Trimmed	Full	Trimmed	Full	Trimmed	Full	Trimmed	Full
Before 1870:								
% nonwhite population	.001	−.023						
	(.013)	(.029)						
% nonwhite males			.003	−.049				
			(.028)	(.059)				
% nonwhite prison					.070***	.108***		
					(.023)	(.033)		
% idle/unemployed white males							.102	.097
							(.075)	(.089)
−2 log-likelihood	83.27	75.77	81.25	75.108	65.58	57.53	81.37	76.44
χ^2	5.37	12.87	4.36	10.504	18.49***	26.54***	7.27*	12.20
df	3	10	3	10	3	10	3	9
Events	23	23	22	22	21	21	23	23
N	70	70	68	68	68	68	70	70

1870–2002:

	(1)	(2)	(3)	(4)	(5)	(6)	(7)	(8)
% nonwhite population	.585*** (.163)	1.579*** (.557)						
% nonwhite males			1.123*** (.290)	4.44*** (1.69)				
% nonwhite prison					.118*** (.031)	.195** (.094)		
% idle/unemployed white males							.010 (.106)	.287 (.175)
−2 log likelihood	50.61	26.52	47.59	24.83	63.87	43.93	88.81	54.61
χ^2	48.23***	66.25***	48.26***	64.79***	34.97***	48.85***	10.03	38.17***
df	6	13	6	13	6	13	6	12
Events	21	21	20	18	21	19	21	19
N	92	90	91	89	92	90	92	90

NOTE.—Nos. in parentheses are SEs. Trimmed models include only decade dummy variables (1850s, 1860s, 1870s, 1880s, 1890s, 1900s, 1910–49, and 1950–2002) while full models additionally control for region, Democrat governor, idle or unemployed white males, state population, incarceration rate, and time since statehood.

* $P < .10$.
** $P < .05$.
*** $P < .01$.

American Journal of Sociology

ployment rate as well as by the national recession indicator discussed above.[16]

Table 9 presents results of the reenfranchisement analysis. Model 1 shows that the southern and western regions have been slow to repeal disenfranchisement laws. In model 2, the percentage of African-American prison inmates is a negative predictor of repeal, net of population composition, region, and punitiveness.[17] In contrast, states with greater numbers of African-American residents evince a greater likelihood of abolishing ex-felon voting bans. Whereas states with a greater proportion of nonwhite prisoners and states with large African-American populations were most likely to disenfranchise, states with fewer African-American prisoners and states with more African-American residents have been quickest to restore voting rights to former felons.[18]

The effects of economic conditions and partisan political control are comparatively modest in models 3 and 4, though states appear somewhat more likely to repeal ex-felon voting bans in years of national recession. We split Democratic power into two periods to reflect the party's stronger and more consistent support for civil rights after 1964. Neither indicator is statistically significant in model 4, although the direction of these partisan effects is consistent with the idea that the Democratic Party may have favored reenfranchisement in the later period. Finally, the time since statehood added little explanatory power to the final model, nor did inclusion of an indicator for the time since passage of a restrictive law (not shown).

---

book of Criminal Justice Statistics (1982–2001). For 1940 to 1948, we computed state-specific estimates based on race-specific prisons admission data (U.S. Department of Justice 1991).

[16] State-level unemployment data are taken from the U.S. Census Bureau's *Statistical Abstract* series and the U.S. Department of Labor's *Manpower Report of the President* (1957–75). For 1940 and 1950, we use U.S. Census unemployment figures. Data for 1941–49 and 1951–56, periods of little change in disenfranchisement law, are interpolated based on 1940, 1950, and 1957 information. Data for 2002 were obtained directly from the U.S. Department of Labor's *Regional and State Employment and Unemployment: January 2002* (2002).

[17] In contrast to the disenfranchisement analysis, there is only a modest, nonsignificant bivariate association between prison racial composition and reenfranchisement. We therefore place somewhat less confidence in the findings reported in the complex multivariate model of reenfranchisement, in contrast to the more robust and consistent results found in our analysis of restrictive changes. A full bivariate table for the reenfranchisement analysis, similar to that shown in table 5, is available from the authors.

[18] We used product terms to model the interaction of prison racial composition with population racial composition and Democratic power but found no statistically significant effects for these interactions. In light of the small number of events being predicted, however, the failure to detect such interactions at standard significance levels is perhaps unsurprising.

594

TABLE 9

PREDICTORS OF REPEAL OF EX-FELON DISENFRANCHISEMENT, 1940–2002 (Discrete-Time Logistic Regression)

	MODELS				
VARIABLE	1	2	3	4	5
Racial threat:					
% black prison		−.053**	−.055**	−.056**	−.069**
		(.024)	(.024)	(.024)	(.029)
Black population					
(100,000s)		.003**	.003**	.003**	.003**
		(.001)	(.001)	(.001)	(.001)
Nonblack population					
(100,000s)		.000	.000	.000	.000
		(.000)	(.000)	(.000)	(.000)
Region (vs. Northeast):					
South	−1.744**	−2.448***	−2.438***	−2.688***	−2.476**
	(.682)	(.951)	(.951)	(1.007)	(1.015)
Midwest	−.434	−.318	−.213	−.217	.236
	(.658)	(.828)	(.849)	(.853)	(.958)
West	−1.125*	−1.454	−1.468	−1.573	−.835
	(.682)	(.985)	(.983)	(.989)	(1.252)
State punitiveness:					
Incarceration rate/					
100,000		.004	.004	.005	.005
		(.004)	(.004)	(.004)	(.004)
Economic competition:					
State unemployment					
rate			.053	.056	.052
			(.068)	(.066)	(.066)
National recession			.672	.846*	.862*
			(.449)	(.464)	(.466)
Political power:					
Democratic power					
(pre-1964)				−.017	−.018
				(.017)	(.017)
Democratic power					
(1964 or later)				.009	.009
				(.008)	(.008)
Timing:					
Time since statehood					.010
					(.011)
Time (vs. 1940–59):[a]					
1960s	2.087***	2.141***	2.249***	2.049**	1.996**
1970s	3.015***	3.166***	3.145***	2.543***	2.415***
1980s	1.833*	1.779	1.680	1.117	.920
1990s	1.163	.632	.609	.194	.003
2000s	2.446**	1.750	1.364	.886	.629
	−4.952***	−4.284***	−4.958***	−4.746***	−5.987***
Constant	(.838)	(1.091)	(1.209)	(1.238)	(1.836)
−2 log-likelihood	211.25	202.69	199.91	196.47	195.63
	29.82***	38.38***	41.16***	44.60***	45.45***
χ^2 (df)	(8)	(12)	(14)	(16)	(17)

NOTE.—Nos. in parentheses are SEs.

[a] Authors will supply SEs for time variables on request. For all models, events = 23; $N = 1,609$.

* $P < .10$.

** $P < .05$.

*** $P < .01$.

American Journal of Sociology

In recent years, there is some evidence that African-American legislators may play a key role in the passage of reenfranchisement provisions. At the national level, John Conyers, an African-American U.S. representative from Michigan, has unsuccessfully introduced legislation that would permit all ex-felons to vote in federal elections. In Connecticut, the state legislature's Black and Puerto Rican Caucus was instrumental in passage of a 2001 law that reenfranchised probationers (Rapoport 2001). In Maryland, removing ballot restrictions for ex-felons became "a top priority among black lawmakers," in a hard-fought debate between African-American state senators and "tough-on-crime conservatives" (Montgomery and Mosk 2002, p. B2). It therefore seems likely that African-American legislators will be at the forefront of future repeal efforts.

DISCUSSION AND CONCLUSIONS

Our key finding can be summarized concisely and forcefully: the racial composition of state prisons is firmly associated with the adoption of state felon disenfranchisement laws. States with greater nonwhite prison populations have been more likely to ban convicted felons from voting than states with proportionally fewer nonwhites in the criminal justice system. This finding extends and reinforces previous theory and research on the significance of race and group position in the United States (Olzak 1992; Quillian 1996), the racial state (Goldfield 1997; Quadagno 1994), and the impact of racial threat on criminal justice policy (Heimer et al. 1999; Jacobs and Carmichael 2001; Jacobs and Helms 1999, 2001). With the steep increase in citizens disenfranchised by felony convictions in recent years, felon disenfranchisement laws have taken on great significance in contemporary U.S. electoral politics (Fellner and Mauer 1998; Uggen and Manza 2002). Our findings help provide a baseline for understanding the origins and development of these laws that may be relevant to ongoing debates about their merits.

With respect to theories of racial threat, our findings suggest that the racial dynamics of incarceration outweigh other sources of racial threat, at least for the case of felon disenfranchisement. Even while controlling for timing, region, economic competition, partisan political power, state population composition, and state incarceration rate, a larger nonwhite prison population significantly increases the odds that more restrictive felon disenfranchisement laws will be adopted. By contrast, the two other specifications of racial threat we considered—economic competition and demographic composition—had less consistent influence on the likelihood that states would adopt strict felon voting bans. Nevertheless, felon disenfranchisement laws were most likely to be passed in national recession

Ballot Manipulation

years, and the economic threat represented by white male idleness is also a positive (though nonsignificant) predictor of disenfranchisement laws in several models. Moreover, state population composition and all other measures of racial threat became much more closely correlated with passage of felon voting restrictions after the passage of the Fifteenth Amendment.

States were particularly likely to pass punitive felon disenfranchisement laws in the Reconstruction period following the Civil War and through the 1870s. During this time, the threats posed by the possible incorporation of African-American men into the political system were ardently debated. In 1868 the Fourteenth Amendment declared that African-Americans born in the United States are indeed citizens of the country, contradicting the U.S. Supreme Court's ruling a decade earlier in the famous Dred Scott decision (*Scott v. Sandford*, 60 U.S. 393 [1856]). In 1870 the Fifteenth Amendment guaranteed these citizens (albeit only males) the right to vote. In this period, explicit racial appeals were common in political campaigns, as the Democratic and Republican parties diverged on the question of enfranchising black voters (see Mendelberg 2001, chap. 2). The contest was not limited to the South: a number of Northern states (including Democrat-controlled New York, New Jersey, and Delaware, along with California and most other Western states) initially refused to ratify the amendment (Southern states were forced to do so as a condition of readmission to the Union). By the 1868 election, only 11 of the 21 Northern states permitted black men to vote (Frymer 1999, chap. 3; Kennedy 2002). Northern support for the two amendments was due in part to a desire to punish the South, and substantive racial equality was not assured in any region (cf. Mendelberg 2001, chap. 2).

During Reconstruction (ca. 1867–75), the Democratic Party's ability to win elections in the South often hinged on outright intimidation of African-American voters (for details, see, e.g., Foner [1988, pp. 424–35], who described the 1868–71 backlash against black civil rights as a "counterrevolutionary terror"). Although federal authorities could block explicit legal restrictions on African-American suffrage—and the full battery of disenfranchisement measures implemented around the turn of the century were not yet in play—state governments under Democratic control during Reconstruction did move to disenfranchise felons. All nine of the Southern states that restricted felon voting rights in the 10 years following the Civil War were governed by Democrats (with the two non-Southern states adopting restrictive laws in this period, Illinois and Nebraska, governed by Republicans).[19] The historiography of Reconstruction

---

[19] The Democratic states are Alabama, Arkansas, Florida, Georgia, Mississippi, Missouri, South Carolina, Tennessee, and Texas.

American Journal of Sociology

has not generally focused on this important precursor to the later legal strategy of disenfranchisement (see, e.g., Perman 2001).

The expansion of citizenship to racial minorities, and the subsequent extension of suffrage to all citizens, threatened to undermine the political power of the white majority. By restricting the voting rights of a disproportionately nonwhite population, felon disenfranchisement laws offered one method for states to avert "the menace of negro domination" (Alabama 1901, p. 12). The sharp increase in African-American imprisonment goes hand-in-hand with changes in voting laws. In many Southern states, the percentage of nonwhite prison inmates nearly doubled between 1850 and 1870. Whereas 2% of the Alabama prison population was nonwhite in 1850, 74% was nonwhite in 1870, though the total nonwhite population increased by only 3% (U.S. Department of Commerce 1853, 1872). Felon disenfranchisement provisions offered a tangible response to the threat of new African-American voters that would help preserve existing racial hierarchies.

Of course, racial threat and felon disenfranchisement are not solely Southern phenomena directed against African-Americans. Several Western states had larger nonwhite populations than the Midwest and Northeast throughout the observation period, since much of the West was a part of Mexico until 1848 and many Asian immigrants settled in the West. As in the South, new Western states struggled to sustain control "under conditions of full democratization" and a changing industrial and agricultural economy (Keyssar 2000, p. 169; see also Glenn 2002). Racial and ethnic divisions thus led to similar attempts to limit suffrage of the nonwhite population, although Western states were among the first to extend voting rights to women (McCammon and Campbell 2001). With the exception of Montana and Utah, every Western state adopted a felon disenfranchisement law within a decade of statehood. The rapid diffusion of restrictive voting bans across the West and the strong effects of the timing of statehood suggest that felon disenfranchisement law offered a "timely model" for addressing racial threats in the political realm (Eyestone 1977, p. 441; see also Grattet, Jenness, and Curry 1998).

Our results suggest that one of the reasons that felon disenfranchisement laws persist may be their compatibility with modern racial ideologies. The laws are race neutral on their face, though their origins are tainted by strategies of racial containment. Felon disenfranchisement laws have historically found support from both political parties and today reflect the convergence of political agendas around crime in the late 20th century (Beckett 1997). A strong anticrime consensus allows contemporary political actors to disenfranchise racial minorities without making explicit the implications for minority suffrage. Indeed, although the Democratic Party stands to gain when voting rights are restored to ex-felons (Uggen and

Ballot Manipulation

Manza 2002), we find only weak effects of political partisanship in our reenfranchisement analysis. States with a small proportion of African-American prisoners are most likely to abolish ex-felon voting restrictions, though the absolute size of the African-American population base has an independent *positive* effect on repeal in multivariate models. The latter finding suggests an important difference between the pre–World War II period and afterward, when blacks were incorporated into the polity and could thus exercise important political leverage.

Felon disenfranchisement, like racial threat, takes a different form in the United States than in other nations, with the United States maintaining the most restrictive rules in the democratic world (Fellner and Mauer 1998). Felon voting bans impose a "shadowy form of citizenship" (*McLaughlin v. City of Canton*, 947 F. Supp. 954, 971 [S.D. Miss. 1995]) as punishment for criminal behavior. Racial threat theories predict that such shadows may be intentionally cast to dilute the voting strength of minority groups, and our event history analysis of felon disenfranchisement laws offers general support for this view. We conclude that racial threat is reflected in the composition of state prisons and find that such racial disparities in punishment drive voting restrictions on felons and ex-felons.

EPILOGUE

Although we have focused on the long history of felon disenfranchisement laws, we should note that this is an ongoing, dynamic political contest. Indeed, Connecticut, New Mexico, Nevada, and Maryland have all liberalized their felon voting laws since 2001, and laws in New York and Florida currently face legal challenges. At the national level, pressure for a nationwide ban on ex-felon restrictions garnered enough adherents to push a reenfranchisement bill to the floor of the U.S. Senate in February 2002 (where it was defeated 63–31). Recent opinion polls show that the American public is generally supportive of allowing probationers and parolees the right to vote, while even greater numbers favor allowing all ex-felons to vote—even those convicted of violent crimes (Manza, Brooks, and Uggen 2003). Still, it is a striking historical fact that while some states have liberalized their provisions, no state has ever completely abolished a felon disenfranchisement law.

APPENDIX

Legal cases cited in this article are listed below.
   Hunter v. Underwood, 471 U.S. 222 (1985)

American Journal of Sociology

Farrakhan v. Locke, 987 F. Supp. 1304 (E.D. Wash. 1997)
McLaughlin v. City of Canton, 947 F. Supp. 954 (S.D. Miss. 1995)
Pippin v. State, 197 Ala. 613 (1916)
Ratliff v. Beale, 74 Miss. 247 (1896)
Reynolds v. Sims, 377 U.S. 533 (1964)
Richardson v. Ramirez, 418 U.S. 24 (1974)
Sauvé v. Canada, 2002 S.C.C. 68 (2002)
Scott v. Sandford, 60 U.S. 393 (1856)
Washington v. State, 75 Ala. 582 (1884)
Wesley v. Collins, 605 F. Supp. 802 (M.D. Tenn. 1985)
Williams v. Mississippi, 170 U.S. 213 (1898)

REFERENCES

Alabama. 1901. *Journal of the Proceedings of the Constitutional Convention of the State of Alabama*. Montgomery, Ala.: Brown Printing Co.
Allard, Patricia, and Marc Mauer. 1999. *Regaining the Vote: An Assessment of Activity Relating to Felon Disenfranchisement Laws*. Washington, D.C.: Sentencing Project.
Allison, Paul. 1984. *Event History Analysis: Regression for Longitudinal Event Data*. Beverly Hills, Calif.: Sage.
———. 1995. *Survival Analysis Using the SAS System: A Practical Guide*. Cary, N.C.: SAS Institute.
Australian Electoral Commission. 2001. *Frequently Asked Questions: Voting*. Canberra, ACT: Commonwealth of Australia.
Beckett, Katherine. 1997. *Making Crime Pay: The Politics of Law and Order in the Contemporary United States*. New York: Oxford University Press.
Blalock, Hubert M. 1967. *Toward a Theory of Minority-Group Relations*. New York: John Wiley & Sons.
Blumer, Herbert. 1958. "Race Prejudice as a Sense of Group Position." *Pacific Sociological Review* 1:3–7.
Bobo, Lawrence, and Vincent L. Hutchings. 1996. "Perceptions of Racial Group Competition: Extending Blumer's Theory of Group Position to a Multiracial Social Context." *American Sociological Review* 61:951–72.
Bobo, Lawrence D., James R. Kluegel, and Ryan A. Smith. 1997. "Laissez Faire Racism: The Crystallization of a 'Kinder, Gentler' Anti-Black Ideology." Pp. 15–44 in *Racial Attitudes in the 1990s: Continuity and Change*, edited by S. A. Tuch and J. K. Martin. Westport, Conn.: Praeger.
Bobo, Lawrence D., and Ryan A. Smith. 1998. "From Jim Crow Racism to Laissez-Faire Racism: The Transformation of Racial Attitudes." Pp. 182–220 in *Beyond Pluralism: The Conception of Groups and Group Identities in America*, edited by W. F. Katkin, N. Landsman, and A. Tyree. Chicago: University of Illinois Press.
Bonacich, Edna. 1972. "A Theory of Ethnic Antagonism: The Split Labor Market." *American Sociological Review* 37:547–59.
Booth, William James. 1997. "Foreigners: Insiders, Outsiders and the Ethics of Membership." *Review of Politics* 59:259–92.
Brown, Michael K. 1999. *Race, Money, and the American Welfare State*. Ithaca, N.Y.: Cornell University Press.
Carmines, Edward G., and James A. Stimson. 1989. *Issue Evolution: Race and the Transformation of American Politics*. Princeton, N.J.: Princeton University Press.
Chiricos, Ted, Michael Hogan, and Marc Gertz. 1997. "Racial Composition of Neighborhood and Fear of Crime." *Criminology* 35:107–31.

Ballot Manipulation

Clegg, Roger. 2001. "Who Should Vote?" *Texas Review of Law and Politics* 6:159–78.

Council of State Governments. 1937–87. *The Book of the States*. Lexington, Ky.: Council of State Governments.

Demleitner, Nora V. 2000. "Continuing Payment on One's Debt to Society: The German Model of Felon Disenfranchisement as an Alternative." *Minnesota Law Review* 84: 753–804.

Edelman, Lauren B. 1990. "Legal Environments and Organizational Governance: The Expansion of Due Process in the American Workplace." *American Journal of Sociology* 95:1401–40.

Entman, Robert M., and Andrew Rojecki. 2000. *The Black Image in the White Mind: Media and Race in America*. Chicago: University of Chicago Press.

Ewald, Alec C. 2002. "'Civil Death': The Ideological Paradox of Criminal Disenfranchisement Law in the United States." *University of Wisconsin Law Review* 2002:1045–1137.

———. 2003. "Of Constitutions, Politics, and Punishment: Criminal Disenfranchisement Law in Comparative Context." Manuscript. University of Massachusetts at Amherst, Department of Political Science.

Eyestone, Robert. 1977. "Confusion, Diffusion, and Innovation." *American Political Science Review* 71:441–47.

Fellner, Jamie, and Marc Mauer. 1998. *Losing the Vote: The Impact of Felony Disenfranchisement Laws in the United States*. Washington, D.C.: Human Rights Watch' and the Sentencing Project.

Fletcher, George. 1999. "Disenfranchisement as Punishment: Reflections on the Racial Uses of *Infamia*." *UCLA Law Review* 46:1895–1908.

Foner, Eric. 1988. *Reconstruction: America's Unfinished Revolution, 1863–1877*. New York: Harper & Row.

Fossett, Mark A., and Jill K. Kiecolt. 1989. "The Relative Size of Minority Populations and White Racial Attitudes." *Social Science Quarterly* 70:820–35.

Frymer, Paul. 1999. *Uneasy Alliances: Race and Party Competition in America*. Princeton, N.J.: Princeton University Press.

Gilens, Martin. 1999. *Why Americans Hate Welfare*. Chicago: University of Chicago Press.

Giles, Michael W., and Melanie A. Buckner. 1993. "David Duke and Black Threat: An Old Hypothesis Revisited." *Journal of Politics* 55:702–13.

Giles, Michael W., and Arthur S. Evans. 1985. "External Threat, Perceived Threat, and Group Identity." *Social Science Quarterly* 66:50–66.

Giles, Michael W., and Kaenan Hertz. 1994. "Racial Threat and Partisan Identification." *American Political Science Review* 88:317–26.

Glenn, Evelyn Nakano. 2002. *Unequal Freedom: How Race and Gender Shaped American Citizenship and Labor*. Cambridge, Mass.: Harvard University Press.

Goldfield, Michael. 1997. *The Color of Politics: Race and the Mainsprings of American Politics*. New York: New Press.

Grattet, Ryken, Valerie Jenness, and Theodore R. Curry. 1998. "The Homogenization and Differentiation of Hate Crime Law in the United States, 1978 to 1995: Innovation and Diffusion in the Criminalization of Bigotry." *American Sociological Review* 63: 286–307.

Harvey, Alice. 1994. "Ex-Felon Disenfranchisement and Its Influence on the Black Vote: The Need for a Second Look." *University of Pennsylvania Law Review* 142: 1145–89.

Heimer, Karen, Thomas Stucky, and Joseph B. Lang. 1999. "Economic Competition, Racial Threat, and Rates of Imprisonment." Paper presented at the Annual Meeting of the American Society of Criminology, Toronto.

Hench, Virginia E. 1998. "The Death of Voting Rights: The Legal Disenfranchisement of Minority Voters." *Case Western Law Review* 48:727–98.

American Journal of Sociology

Huckfeldt, Robert, and Carol W. Kohfeld. 1989. *Race and the Decline of Class in American Politics*. Urbana: University of Illinois Press.

Hurwitz, Jon, and Mark Peffley. 1997. "Public Perceptions of Race and Crime: The Role of Racial Stereotypes." *American Journal of Politics* 41:375–401.

Inter-University Consortium for Political and Social Research. 1995. "Candidate Name and Constituency Totals, 1788–1990" (MRDF). 5th ICPSR ed. Ann Arbor, Mich.: Inter-University Consortium for Political and Social Research.

Issacharoff, Samuel, Pamela S. Karlan, and Richard H. Pildes. 1998. *The Law of Democracy: Legal Structure of the Political Process*. Westbury, N.Y.: Foundation Press.

Itzkowitz, Howard, and Lauren Oldak. 1973. "Restoring the Ex-Offender's Right to Vote: Background and Development." *American Criminal Law Review* 11:721–70.

Jackson, Pamela I. 1989. *Minority Group Threat, Crime, and Policing: Social Context and Social Control*. Westport, Conn.: Praeger.

Jacobs, David, and Jason T. Carmichael. 2001. "The Politics of Punishment across Time and Space: A Pooled Time-Series Analysis of Imprisonment Rates." *Social Forces* 80:61–89.

Jacobs, David, and Ronald E. Helms. 1996. "Toward a Political Model of Incarceration: A Time-Series Examination of Multiple Explanations for Prison Admission Rates." *American Journal of Sociology* 102:323–57.

———. 1997. "Testing Coercive Explanations for Order: The Determinants of Law Enforcement Strength over Time." *Social Forces* 75:1361–92.

———. 1999. "Collective Outbursts, Politics, and Punitive Resources: Toward a Political Sociology of Spending on Social Control." *Social Forces* 77:1497–1523.

———. 2001. "Racial Politics and Redistribution: Isolating the Contingent Influence of Civil Rights, Riots, and Crime on Tax Progressivity." *Social Forces* 80:91–121.

James, David R. 1988. "The Transformation of the Southern Racial State: Class and Race Determinants of Local-State Structures." *American Sociological Review* 53: 191–208.

Kennedy, Robert C. 2002. "On This Day: March 12, 1870." *Harper's Monthly*, accessed at http://www.nytimes.com/learning/general/onthisday/harp/0312.html, on July 18, 2003.

Key, V. O. (1949) 1964. *Southern Politics in State and Nation*. New York: Vintage Books.

Keyssar, Alexander. 2000. *The Right to Vote: The Contested History of Democracy in the United States*. New York: Basic Books.

Kinder, Donald, and Lynn Sanders. 1996. *Divided by Color*. Chicago: University of Chicago Press.

Kousser, J. Morgan. 1974. *The Shaping of Southern Politics: Suffrage Restriction and the Establishment of the One-Party South, 1880–1910*. New Haven, Conn.: Yale University Press.

———. 1999. *Colorblind Injustice: Minority Voting Rights and the Undoing of the Second Reconstruction*. Chapel Hill: University of North Carolina Press.

Lieberman, Robert C. 1998. *Shifting the Color Line*. Cambridge, Mass.: Harvard University Press.

Liska, Allen E., Joseph J. Lawrence, and Michael Benson. 1981. "Perspectives on the Legal Order: The Capacity for Social Control." *American Journal of Sociology* 87: 413–26.

Manfredi, Christopher. 1998. "Judicial Review and Criminal Disenfranchisement in the United States and Canada." *Review of Politics* 60:277–305.

Manza, Jeff. 2000. "Race and the Underdevelopment of the American Welfare State." *Theory and Society* 30:819–32.

Manza, Jeff, Clem Brooks, and Christopher Uggen. 2003. "'Civil Death' or Civil

Rights? Public Attitudes towards Felon Disenfranchisement in the United States." Working paper. Northwestern University, Institute for Policy Research.

Mauer, Marc, and Meda Chesney-Lind, eds. 2002. *Invisible Punishment: The Collateral Consequences of Mass Imprisonment.* New York: New Press.

McCammon, Holly J., and Karen E. Campbell. 2001. "Winning the Vote in the West: The Political Successes of the Women's Suffrage Movement, 1866–1919." *Gender and Society* 15:56–83.

McCammon, Holly J., Karen E. Campbell, Ellen M. Granberg, and Christine Mowery. 2001. "How Movements Win: Gendered Opportunity Structures and U.S. Woman's Suffrage Movements, 1866 to 1919." *American Sociological Review* 66:49–70.

Mendelberg, Tali. 2001. *The Race Card: Campaign Strategy, Implicit Messages, and the Norm of Equality.* Princeton, N.J.: Princeton University Press.

Montgomery, Lori, and Matthew Mosk. 2002. "Md. Bill Advances to Let Ex-Criminals Vote." *Washington Post*, March 30, p. B2.

Moore, Geoffrey H., ed. 1961. *Business Cycle Indicators.* Princeton, N.J.: Princeton University Press.

Myers, Martha A. 1990. "Black Threat and Incarceration in Postbellum Georgia." *Social Forces* 69:373–93.

———. 1998. *Race, Labor, and Punishment in the New South.* Columbus: Ohio State University Press.

National Bureau of Economic Research. 2003. *Business Cycle Expansions and Contractions.* Accessed at http://www.nber.org/cycles.html on July 18, 2003.

Olivares, Kathleen M., Velmer S. Burton, and Francis T. Cullen. 1997. "The Collateral Consequences of a Felony Conviction: A National Study of State Legal Codes 10 Years Later." *Federal Probation* 60:10–17.

Oliver, J. Eric, and Tali Mendelberg. 2000. "Reconsidering the Environmental Determinants of White Racial Attitudes." *American Journal of Political Science* 44: 574–89.

Olzak, Susan. 1990. "The Political Context of Competition: Lynching and Urban Racial Violence, 1882–1914." *Social Forces* 69:395–421.

———. 1992. *The Dynamics of Ethnic Competition and Conflict.* Stanford, Calif.: Stanford University Press.

Olzak, Susan, and Suzanne Shanahan. 2002. "Racial Conflict and Racial Policy in the Urban United States, 1889–1924." Manuscript. Stanford University, Department of Sociology.

Perman, Michael. 2001. *Struggle for Mastery: Disenfranchisement in the South, 1888–1908.* Chapel Hill: University of North Carolina Press.

Pettus, Katherine. 2002. "Felony Disenfranchisement in the Contemporary United States: An Ancient Practice in a Modern Polity." Ph.D. thesis, Department of Political Science, Columbia University, New York.

Piven, Frances F. 1992. "Structural Constraints and Political Development: The Case of the American Democratic Party." Pp. 235–64 in *Labor Parties in Postindustrial Societies*, edited by F. Piven. New York: Oxford University Press.

Quadagno, Jill. 1994. *The Color of Welfare.* New York: Oxford University Press.

Quillian, Lincoln. 1995. "Prejudice as a Response to Perceived Group Threat: Population Composition and Anti-Immigrant and Racial Prejudice in Europe." *American Sociological Review* 60:586–611.

———. 1996. "Group Threat and Regional Change in Attitudes toward African Americans." *American Journal of Sociology* 102:816–60.

Quillian, Lincoln, and Devah Pager. 2001. "Black Neighbors, Higher Crime? The Role of Racial Stereotypes in Evaluations of Neighborhood Crime." *American Journal of Sociology* 107:717–67.

Rapoport, Miles S. 2001. "Restoring the Vote." *American Prospect* 12:14.

American Journal of Sociology

Redding, Kent. 2003. *Making Race, Making Power: North Carolina's Road to Disenfranchisement*. Urbana: University of Illinois Press.

Ruggles, Steven, and Matthew Sobek. 1997. *Integrated Public Use Microdata Series*, ver. 2.0. University of Minnesota, Historical Census Projects.

Schuman, Howard, Charlotte Steeh, Lawrence Bobo, and Maria Krysan. 1997. *Racial Attitudes in America: Trends and Interpretations*, rev. ed. Cambridge, Mass.: Harvard University Press.

Sears, David O. 1988. "Symbolic Racism." Pp. 53–84 in *Eliminating Racism: Profiles in Controversy*, edited by P. A. Katz and D. A. Taylor. New York: Plenum.

Sears, David O., and Carolyn L. Funk. 1991. "The Role of Self-Interest in Social and Political Attitudes." *Advances in Experimental Social Psychology* 24:1–91.

Sears, David O., Jim Sidanius, and Lawrence Bobo, eds. 2000. *Racialized Politics*. Chicago: University of Chicago Press.

Shapiro, Andrew L. 1993. "Challenging Criminal Disenfranchisement under the Voting Rights Act: A New Strategy." *Yale Law Journal* 103:537–66.

Soule, Sarah. 1992. "Populism and Black Lynching in Georgia, 1890–1900." *Social Forces* 71:431–49.

Stock, James H., and Mark W. Watson, eds. 1993. *Business Cycles, Indicators and Forecasting*. Chicago: University of Chicago Press.

Taylor, Marylee C. 1998. "How White Attitudes Vary with the Racial Composition of Local Populations: Numbers Count." *American Sociological Review* 63:512–35.

———. 2000. "The Significance of Racial Context." Pp. 118–36 in *Racialized Politics: The Debate about Racism in America*, edited by D. O. Sears, J. Sidanius, and L. Bobo. Chicago: University of Chicago Press.

Tindall, George B. 1949. "The Campaign for the Disenfranchisement of Negroes in South Carolina." *Journal of Southern History* 15:212–34.

Tolnay, Stewart E., and E. M. Beck. 1995. *A Festival of Violence: An Analysis of Southern Lynchings, 1882–1930*. Urbana: University of Illinois Press.

Uggen, Christopher, and Jeff Manza. 2002. "Democratic Contraction? The Political Consequences of Felon Disenfranchisement in the United States." *American Sociological Review* 67:777–803.

U.S. Bureau of Census. 1975–2001. *Statistical Abstract of the United States*. Washington, D.C.: Government Printing Office.

U.S. Congress. 2002. *Congressional Record*. 107th Congress, 2d Sess. S. 565, pp. S797–S809.

U.S. Department of Commerce, Bureau of the United States. 1853–1992. *Census of the United States*. Washington, D.C.: Government Printing Office.

U.S. Department of Justice, Bureau of Justice Statistics. 1982–2001. *Sourcebook of Criminal Justice Statistics*. Washington, D.C.: Government Printing Office.

———. 1987. *Historical Corrections Statistics in the United States, 1850–1984*. Washington, D.C.: Government Printing Office.

———. 1991. *Race of Prisoners Admitted to State and Federal Institutions, 1926–1986*. Washington, D.C.: Government Printing Office.

———. 2000. *Correctional Populations in the United States*. Washington, D.C.: Government Printing Office.

———. 2001. *Probation and Parole in the United States, 2000—Press Release*. Washington, D.C.: Government Printing Office.

———. 2002. *Prison and Jail Inmates at Midyear 2001*. Washington, D.C.: Government Printing Office.

U.S. Department of Labor. 1957–75. *Manpower Report of the President*. Washington, D.C.: Government Printing Office.

———. 2002. *Regional and State Employment and Unemployment: January 2002*. Washington, D.C.: Government Printing Office.

Ballot Manipulation

Wang, Xi. 1997. *The Trial of Democracy: Black Suffrage and Northern Republicans, 1860–1910*. Athens: University of Georgia Press.

Weiss, Nancy. 1983. *Farewell to the Party of Lincoln*. Princeton, N.J.: Princeton University Press.

Wise, Warren. 2001a. "House Doesn't Kill Bill to Delay Felons Voting." *Charleston (South Carolina) Post and Courier*, February 16, p. A3.

————. 2001b. "Criminal Example Upsets Lawmakers." *Charleston (South Carolina) Post and Courier*, February 15, p. B1.

Woodward, C. Vann. 1951. *Origins of the New South, 1877–1913*. Baton Rouge: Louisiana State University Press.

————. (1955) 2001. *The Strange History of Jim Crow*, 3d ed. New York: Oxford.

Yamaguchi, Kazuo. 1991. *Event History Analysis*. Newbury Park, Calif.: Sage Publications.

[12]

THE IMPACT OF INCARCERATION ON WAGE MOBILITY AND INEQUALITY

BRUCE WESTERN
Princeton University

A life course perspective on crime indicates that incarceration can disrupt key life transitions. Life course analysis of occupations finds that earnings mobility depends on stable employment in career jobs. These two lines of research thus suggest that incarceration reduces ex-inmates' access to the steady jobs that usually produce earnings growth among young men. Consistent with this argument, evidence for slow wage growth among ex-inmates is provided by analysis of the National Longitudinal Survey of Youth. Because incarceration is so prevalent—one-quarter of black non-college males in the survey were interviewed between 1979 and 1998 while in prison or jail—the effect of imprisonment on individual wages also increases aggregate race and ethnic wage inequality.

PENAL POPULATION growth during the 1980s and 1990s made incarceration a common life event for disadvantaged and minority men. In the 13 years from 1985 to 1998, the prison and jail population grew by 7.3 percent, numbering 1.8 million by 1998 (Gilliard 1999). Penal expansion significantly affected unskilled African American youth. On an average day in 1996, more black male high school dropouts aged 20 to 35 were in custody than in paid employment (Western and Pettit 2000). By 1999, over one-fifth of black noncollege men in their early thirties had prison records (Pettit and Western 2001). Although historically a rare event reserved for violent or incorrigible offenders, during recent years incarceration has become pervasive among socially marginal men.

The prison boom of the 1980s and 1990s coincided with growing polarization of the American labor market. Wage inequality increased during these decades, and wage de-

Direct correspondence to Bruce Western, Department of Sociology, Princeton University, Princeton, NJ 08544 (western@princeton.edu). This research was supported by Princeton University, the Russell Sage Foundation, and by National Science Foundation grant SES-0004336. I gratefully acknowledge the helpful advice of Jeff Kling, the *ASR* Editors and reviewers, and numerous seminar participants.

clines were particularly large among men with little education (Bernhardt et al. 2001). Wage decline or stagnation was especially marked among black and Hispanic men (Morris, Bernhardt, and Handcock 1994; Wright and Dwyer 2000).

The relationship between prison growth and falling wages among low-skill and minority men might be interpreted in several ways. Men with felony records have difficulty finding good jobs. A small research literature thus finds that incarceration reduces earnings (see the review by Western, Kling, and Weiman 2000). Given increases in wage inequality through the 1980s and 1990s, however, the low earnings of ex-convicts may be an artifact of widespread wage stagnation among men with little schooling.

A strong causal inference about the negative effect of imprisonment on wages is also threatened by the fact that men with few economic opportunities may turn to crime. This link between crime and economic disadvantage has been shown in many ways. At the aggregate level, unemployment rates are found to drive variation in crime rates (Land, Cantor, and Russell 1995; also see the review by Chiricos 1987). At the individual level, unemployed men are more likely to engage in crime (Rossi, Berk, and Lenihan 1980). Conversely, desistance from crime is associated with the social attachments and the normative bonds of regular employment (Crutchfield and Pitchford 1997; Hagan 1993; Sampson and Laub 1990; Uggen 2000).

Although high crime rates among disadvantaged men partly explains their high risk of incarceration, increasing imprisonment rates in the 1980s and 1990s is not closely associated with crime trends (Boggess and Bound 1997). Instead, shifts in criminal justice policy fueled penal system growth by intensifying the punishment of drug and violent offenders, and recidivists (Blumstein and Beck 1999; Mauer 1999; Tonry 1996). The policy-driven rise in incarceration motivates a reexamination of the economic effects of imprisonment.

I examine the effect of incarceration on wages in the context of growing inequality in the U.S. labor market. My analysis departs from earlier research by treating incarceration as a key life event that triggers a cumulative spiral of disadvantage (Sampson and Laub 1993). In this approach, incarceration reduces not just the level of wages but also the rate of wage growth over the life course. The life path of ex-inmates diverges from the usual employment trajectory in which earnings mobility for young men is generated by steady jobs with regular career ladders (Spilerman 1977). Combining life course perspectives on crime and employment, I use data from the National Longitudinal Survey of Youth (NLSY), 1983–1999, to estimate the wage trajectory of ex-convicts. Unlike earlier research studying this time period, my analysis also controls for declining wages among men with little schooling.

If incarceration slows wage growth at the individual level, the prison boom may have increased wage inequality in the aggregate. Was the growth in wage inequality in the 1980s and 1990s due to the poor labor market performance of low-skill and minority ex-convicts? Although some claim that—"mass imprisonment" has significant aggregate effects (Garland 2001; Wacquant 2000), the size of these effects has not been systematically studied. Pervasive incarceration among low-skill minority men may increase wage inequality within and across racial and ethnic groups. I investigate this question by calculating the effects of incarceration on

wage inequality using estimates of the impact of incarceration on individual earnings. By focusing on the life course and aggregate effects of imprisonment on wages, I aim to draw the penal system into an institutional account of economic inequality.

INCARCERATION AND EARNINGS

Most research relating the criminal justice system to wages focuses on estimating a main effect—a constant decrement in wages attributed to, say, criminal conviction or incarceration. A common design links arrest records to earnings data from unemployment insurance reports (Grogger 1995; Kling 1999; Lott 1990; Waldfogel 1994a). Research with this design finds transitory effects of arrest or conviction, but persistent effects for prison time: The earnings loss associated with imprisonment is found to range between 10 and 30 percent. A few analyses of survey data find that youth detained in correctional facilities before age 20 have higher unemployment rates and receive lower wages a decade or more after incarceration (Freeman 1992; Western and Beckett 1999; also see Sampson and Laub 1993:162–68).

INCARCERATION AND DISRUPTED CAREERS

Previous research on incarceration neglects the tendency of earnings to grow over the life course. Longitudinal studies of careers find that internal labor markets in large firms, public sector pay schedules, on-the-job training, and union seniority provisions all contribute to job continuity and earnings growth among young men (DiPrete 1989; Spilerman 1977; also see the review by Rosenfeld 1992:45–50). If ex-convicts ultimately recover their pre-incarceration wage level, the life course perspective suggests they may still be worse off because wages would have grown even higher without incarceration.

While life course research on occupations ties earnings growth to employment in career jobs, a life course perspective on crime treats incarceration as a turning point that disrupts key transitions, restricting access to such jobs (Sampson and Laub 1993). If imprisonment redirects the usual employment trajectory, the main effect of incarceration will be supplemented by an interaction effect in which wages grow more slowly with age for ex-convicts.

Three mechanisms explain why prison or jail time is linked to slow wage growth. Incarceration is stigmatizing, and it erodes human and social capital. The negative relationship between crime and earnings is usually attributed to the stigma of criminal conviction. A criminal record signals to employers that a potential employee might be untrustworthy. Thus, employers are less likely to hire ex-offenders than comparable job applicants without criminal records (Holzer 1996:59; Schwartz and Skolnick 1962). The stigma of conviction is especially prohibitive of entry into high-status or career jobs. Men in trusted or high-income occupations before conviction experience especially large earnings losses after release from prison (Lott 1990; Waldfogel 1994a). Similar observations are reported for white-collar offenders (Kling 1999). The stigma of conviction also has legal consequences that mostly affect career jobs. A felony record can temporarily disqualify an individual from employment in licensed or professional occupations, skilled trades, or in the public sector (Office of the Pardon Attorney 1996). The stigma of conviction thus reduces ex-convicts' access to jobs characterized by trust and continuity of employment.

Incarceration also erodes job skills. Time out of employment prevents the acquisition of skills gained through work experience. As a result, for some categories of federal prison inmates, earnings decrease as sentence length increases (Kling 1999). Besides limiting work experience, incarceration may exacerbate pre-existing mental or physical illnesses. Furthermore, behaviors that are adaptive for survival in prison are likely to be inconsistent with work routines on the outside (Irwin and Austin 1997:121). For these reasons, ex-inmates are likely to be less productive than are similar workers who have not served time in prison or jail. The effects of incarceration on skills also has implications for wage mobility: Most employers will be unwilling to invest in the firm-specific skills of workers with criminal records, and thus ex-offenders are relegated to spot markets with little prospect for earnings growth (Nagin and Waldfogel 1998).

Finally, the social contacts that provide information about job opportunities may be eroded by incarceration. Hagan (1993) argues that juvenile delinquency weakens social connections to stable employment opportunities. If prisons are criminogenic, adult incarceration may have a similar negative effect on job referral networks. Sánchez-Jankowski (1991:272–76) finds ethnographic evidence for this effect, reporting that incarceration can deepen ex-inmates attachments to gangs (Venkatesh 2000:133). The disruptive impact of imprisonment on social capital is also found in family relationships where ex-inmates share a low likelihood of marriage or cohabitation (see the review by Hagan and Dinovitzer 1999:131–40). Entry to trades and public sector employment also depends strongly on referral networks (Granovetter 1995:173–74). To the extent that incarceration undermines social networks, ex-inmates will have limited access to apprenticeships and careers in crafts and the public sector.

Although most research focuses on the average earnings loss associated with incarceration, a few studies observe that the penal system channels ex-inmates into unsteady jobs with little wage growth. Thus Sampson and Laub (1993:153–68) found that time served in prison by youths aged 17 to 25 was negatively related to continuity of employment and work commitment at ages 25 to 32. Urban ethnographers similarly report that the prison system provides a pathway to secondary labor markets and informal economies (Duneier 1999; Sánchez-Jankowski 1991:281; Sullivan 1989; Hagan 1993). For Sullivan's (1989) subjects in a New York City neighborhood,

> . . . participation in income-producing crime and the resulting involvement in the criminal justice system in turn kept them out of school and forced them to abandon their occupational goals. . . . By the end of their teens most of these youths had found and lost several jobs. . . . Wages, though irregular, replaced theft as their major source of income. . . . They were still frequently unemployed and generally made low wages when they did work. (Pp. 64, 72)

Evans's (1968) sample of parolees had a similar experience:

> Obtaining employment was not a real problem; instead it was the character and quality of the jobs that was the problem. (P. 208)

In short, although ex-inmates regularly find employment, their jobs often provide little secure wage growth.

Theories linking incarceration to wages have two main empirical implications. First, incarceration has a main effect, reducing the level of earnings. And second, ex-inmates experience slower wage growth than men without prison records. Because they are seldom hired in primary sector jobs with strongly age-graded pay scales, ex-inmates follow the low-wage trajectories common among day laborers and other kinds of "flexible" or contingent workers. Other researchers similarly argue that career jobs are inaccesible to ex-offenders, and this is reflected in large earnings penalties for those arrested or convicted relatively late in life (Bushway 1996; Nagin and Waldfogel 1998; cf. Kling 1999). However, incarceration is not observed in this earlier research, and the NLSY data used here are more extensive than those analyzed earlier.

EARNINGS INEQUALITY AND MASS IMPRISONMENT

The penal system's production of large numbers of marginal workers suggests a provocative account of the increase in men's wage inequality in the 1980s and 1990s. During these decades, increasing inequality was produced by the emergence of a flat wage trajectory among men with little education (Bernhardt et al. 2001). Evidence of racial and ethnic division is given by the growing employment share of black and Hispanic workers in low-paying, low-quality jobs (Wright and Dwyer 2000). In light of these trends, the prison boom may have increased inequality by supplying the labor market with low-skill minority ex-inmates who remain mired at the bottom of the wage distribution.

The collective effect of the penal system is captured by Garland's (2001:2) term "mass imprisonment." In his formulation, the incarceration rate is so high for some groups that its influence is felt not just by individuals, but by broad demographic groups. A few researchers have connected the polarization of the American labor market to mass imprisonment. In an early statement of the broad influence of the criminal justice system, Freeman (1991) observes that "the magnitudes of incarceration, probation, and parole among black drop outs, in particular, suggest that crime has become an intrinsic part of the youth unemployment and poverty problem, rather than deviant behavior on the margin" (p. 1). Wacquant (2000) argues that the prison, alongside the ghetto, has become a system of forced confinement that marginalizes minority communities from mainstream economic life. Along similar lines, the U.S. penal system in the 1980s and 1990s has been described as a state intervention in the labor market that increased race and class inequalities in earnings and employment (Western and Beckett 1999; Western and Pettit 2000).

Despite claims for the effects of mass imprisonment, there are few estimates of the effects of incarceration on aggregate labor market outcomes. The disruption of careers by incarceration, however, has clear implications for patterns of wage inequality. If the prison boom is producing a generation of men stuck in low-wage jobs in the secondary labor market, mass imprisonment has likely increased economic inequality by reducing the wages of low-skill and minority men.

MEASURING INCARCERATION IN THE NLSY

Most research on the economic effects of contact with the criminal justice system uses administrative data on arrests, corrections, and earnings. Although this research has produced valuable findings, the reliance on arrest records is restrictive. Most research evaluates federal defendants who tend to be older and more educated than the state inmates who account for 90 percent of the prison population (Kling 1999; Lott 1990; Nagin and Waldfogel 1998; Waldfogel 1994a, 1994b). Even when state offenders are analyzed (Grogger 1992, 1995), earnings data from unemployment insurance records understate the incomes of those in day labor or other informal work (Kornfeld and Bloom

Table 1. Percentage of Male Respondents Providing Interviews While in Correctional Facilities, by Race and Ethnicity: NLSY Men, 1979 to 1998

Interview Status	All	Whites	Blacks	Hispanics
Percentage imprisoned by age 40	7.8	3.5	26.6	12.7
All Respondents				
Prison/jail interviews, 1998 (%)	3.2	.9	7.0	3.4
Prison/jail interviews, 1979 to 1998 (%)	9.2	4.8	18.7	10.7
Mean number of prison/jail interviews	3.5	2.8	4.1	3.2
Median number of prison/jail interviews	2.0	2.0	3.0	2.0
Sample size	5,824	3,430	1,444	950
Respondents with No College Education				
Prison/jail interviews, 1998 (%)	4.6	1.4	9.0	4.7
Prison/jail interviews, 1979 to 1998 (%)	12.9	7.3	23.3	14.2
Mean number of prison/jail interviews	3.5	2.8	4.0	3.3
Median number of prison/jail interviews	2.0	2.0	3.0	2.0
Sample size	3,574	1,971	985	626

Note: Imprisonment by age 40 is estimated by Bonczar and Beck (1997) using 1991 incarceration data. The mean and median number of interviews completed at correctional facilities is reported for respondents providing at least one interview while incarcerated.

1999:194; Rossi et al. 1980:182–83). Several biases may result. If earnings are only observed for ex-inmates who get jobs in the formal economy, analysis may include just those with successful experiences of re-integration. The negative post-release effect of incarceration on earnings would be underestimated with such data. Alternatively, if ex-convicts with off-the-books incomes are assumed to have no earnings, incarceration effects will be over-estimated (Grogger 1992:101). Finally, administrative data provide little information beyond the race and age of offenders. Analyses of these data often cannot control for offender characteristics like schooling or work history that influence the risk of incarceration and low earnings.

Survey data are rarely used because few surveys include institutionalized respondents or ask about imprisonment. However, a few studies do analyze the NLSY (Grogger 1992; Freeman 1992; Western and Beckett 1999; Bushway 1996 analyzes the National Youth Survey). The NLSY reports on youth detention and adult incarceration, in addition to providing detailed data on employment and earnings. The NLSY (Center for Human Resource Research 2000) began in 1979, interviewing a national sample of young men and women aged 14 to 21 at the end of 1978. The respondents were interviewed each year until 1994, and then again in 1996 and 1998.

The main source of time-varying data on adult incarceration is provided by an annual residence item that identifies respondents interviewed in prison or jail. Correctional residence measures incarceration with error because the respondent's status is only obtained at the time of interview. As a result, prison or jail spells shorter than 12 months are underobserved. Barring survey nonresponse, prison sentences (which typically exceed 12 months) are observed with certainty. Error due to survey nonresponse is likely to be small because response rates do not differ greatly by incarceration status.

In addition to residence in a correctional facility, the NLSY contains two other useful measures of contact with the criminal justice system. First, a crime module in the 1980 survey asked respondents if they had ever been sentenced to a correctional facility. The crime module also recorded other contacts with the justice system including police stops, criminal charges, convictions, and probation. Second, a series of employment items, fielded from 1989 to 1993, listed jail

Crime and Criminal Justice

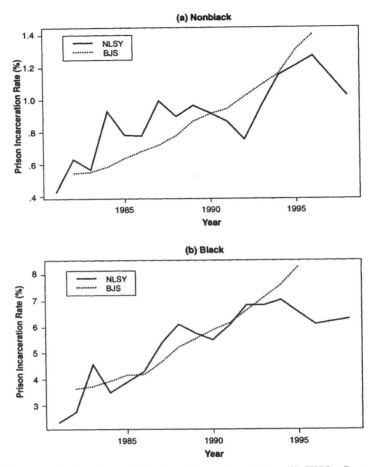

Figure 1. Rate of Interviews Completed at Correctional Facilities among NLSY Men Compared with Prison Incarceration Rates for Black and Nonblack Males, Aged 20 to 35

Note: Prison incarceration rates are calculated from aggregate Bureau of Justice Statistics (BJS) data and other sources (see Western and Pettit 2000).

incarceration as a reason for not seeking work. Because the employment and crime items are only asked in a few surveys, they are less helpful for studying earnings mobility over a long time period. Still, I use the crime module and jail incarceration data to construct a subsample of respondents who have a high risk of criminal behavior. The subsample is used to form a comparison group for the analysis of incarceration effects.

Table 1 reports descriptive statistics for the correctional residence variable. Figures

published by the Bureau of Justice Statistics (BJS) indicate that black men are about seven times more likely and Hispanic men three times more likely to be incarcerated than white men (Blumstein and Beck 1999:22). The NLSY shows similar differences. In the 1998 survey, 3.2 percent of all interviews with men were conducted in correctional facilities. More than 3 percent of Hispanic male respondents and 7 percent of black male respondents were in custody during their 1998 interview compared with less than 1 percent of white men. The distribution of the number of interviews in correctional institutions is highly skewed. Most incarcerated respondents are only interviewed once or twice while in prison or jail. Just 18 percent of those ever interviewed while incarcerated gave five or more interviews in prison or jail. Table 1 also indicates the stratification of incarceration by education: At least 23.3 percent of black respondents and 14.2 percent of Hispanic noncollege respondents were incarcerated at some time before ages 34 to 41. These figures are also comparable to lifetime risks of imprisonment calculated from 1991 correctional survey data (Bonczar and Beck 1997).

The accuracy of incarceration as measured in the NLSY can be assessed by comparing trends in incarceration rates in the survey data with imprisonment trends estimated from aggregate data. Figure 1 plots trends in prison incarceration rates for black men and nonblack (white and Hispanic) men aged 20 to 35, and for male NLSY respondents. Aggregate incarceration rates are taken from estimates combining labor force data from the Current Population Survey, BJS administrative data on the incarcerated population, and correctional microdata (Western and Pettit 2000). NLSY incarceration rates track the aggregate (BJS) data well until the mid-1990s when survey respondents begin to age out of the penal system. We can thus be confident that the NLSY correctional residence item provides reasonable coverage of prison inmates.

DATA AND MODEL

I conducted a regression analysis of wage mobility in a sample of young men. To trace mobility in earnings, data on log hourly wages, y_{it}, is analyzed for respondent i in year t for the period 1983–1998. The hourly wage rate is measured for the respondent's current or most recent main job. The wage data are standardized by the consumer price index deflator to obtain earnings in constant 1984 dollars. Like other work on the NLSY, I discard observations with zero wages and a few outliers greater than five times the median wage (see Bernhardt et al. 2001). Unlike administrative records on earnings, the NLSY wage captures temporary and part-time work, and work for small and public

sector employers. Because illegal earnings are likely missed, the analysis provides information about the effects of incarceration on ex-inmates' legitimate economic opportunities.

The regression models are built around three main predictors. First, the log of respondent's age, A_{it}, captures the nonlinear age-earnings profile. The age effect in earnings models is often specified to be quadratic (Murphy and Welch 1990:203). For simplicity, I allow the age effect to be nonlinear but monotonic. This functional form fits well for this young cohort of workers.

Second, a dummy variable, P_{it}, records whether the respondent previously served time in prison or jail. The prior incarceration variable scores 1 if the respondent recorded a correctional interview in year $t - 1$ or earlier, and 0 otherwise. This prior incarceration variable provides the key information needed to estimate the effect of incarceration after release.[1]

Third, another dummy variable, C_{it}, measures current incarceration status. For C_{it}, respondents score 1 if interviewed in prison or jail in year t, and 0 otherwise. Many respondents report earnings while interviewed in prison. These earnings may come from prison work programs or, if admission is recent, from the open labor market just prior to incarceration. Current incarceration status provides no information about the post-release effect of incarceration. It captures the earnings loss while in prison or jail or an earnings dip just before incarceration. Controlling for C_{it} prevents confounding the post-release effect of P_{it} with lost earnings during incarceration.[2]

---

[1] I also experimented with a quantitative code that counted the number of prior correctional interviews. The count of prior correctional interviews might identify serious offenders who serve several years or multiple spells in prison or jail. Results for this quantitative indicator were slightly more uneven, perhaps because there were few respondents with multiple correctional interviews. Estimates for the simpler binary measurement of prior incarceration are reported below. Estimates for the binary P_{it} variable can be interpreted as the average effect of prior incarceration across offenders who differ in severity.

[2] Current incarceration status could also be controlled by simply dropping observations

The analysis fits main effects and interaction models. The main effect model is written:

$$y_{it} = \alpha_0 + \alpha_1 A_{it} + \alpha_2 P_{it} + \alpha_3 C_{it}$$
$$+ \mathbf{x}'_{it}\beta + \varepsilon_{it}, \qquad (1)$$

where $\mathbf{x}_{it}$ is a vector of other covariates, and ε_{it} is an error term. For this model, incarceration produces a shift in log wages of size α_2. The career disruption theory suggests that incarceration also influences wage growth after release. This effect is described by equation 2, the interaction model:

$$y_{it} = \alpha_0 + \alpha_1 A_{it} + \alpha_2 P_{it} + \gamma A_{it} P_{it}$$
$$+ \alpha_3 C_{it} + \mathbf{x}'_{it}\beta + \varepsilon_{it}, \qquad (2)$$

The interaction model estimates the age-earnings profile of noninmates and ex-inmates by adding an interaction between log age and prior incarceration. If ex-inmates have limited access to primary sector jobs with age-graded pay scales, γ will be negative. A negative coefficient indicates that the earnings profile of ex-inmates is flat compared to that of noninmates. Throughout the analysis, log age is written in mean deviation form so the main effect, α_2, gives the wage gap between noninmates and ex-inmates at average age.

Although mass imprisonment may explain some of the polarization of the American labor market, the analysis must also confront the rival explanation that declining wages among ex-convicts results from the general decline in wages among low-education men in the 1980s and 1990s. To model this period effect, the covariate vector contains terms for year of interview (t), years of education (E_{it}), and the interaction $E_{it}t$. This model captures the fall in earnings among low-education men, independently of any effect of imprisonment. As shown below, the age-earnings profiles of nonconvicts and ex-convicts are highly sensitive to these period effects.

Without further specification, models portrayed in equations 1 and 2 provide poor estimates of the causal effects of incarceration. Characteristics of criminal offenders that

place them at high risk of incarceration may also reduce their wages. Consequently, the low wages attributed to incarceration may really be due to the weak earnings capacity of offenders. The endogeneity of prison time to worker productivity is the key methodological challenge for research on the labor market effects of incarceration (Rossi et al. 1980). Instrumental variables, difference-of-difference estimates, and fixed- and random-effects models have been used to adjust for the unobserved heterogeneity of prison inmates (Freeman 1992; Kling 1999; Western and Beckett 1999).

In this analysis, I adopt three different strategies to control for the nonrandom selection of men into prison and jail. First, several sources of selectivity are explicitly controlled (Table 2 lists the control variables). Criminal offenders tend to have little human capital (Caspi et al. 1998; Moffit 1993; Sullivan 1989), and this is controlled in the regressions by years of schooling and work experience. Some models below also include a standardized test score to measure cognitive ability. In addition, offenders who are highly impulsive or who lack self-control may have trouble holding steady employment (Gottfredson and Hirschi 1990:165). Social attachments of marriage and family relationships are important for promoting self-control and criminal desistance (Laub, Nagin, and Sampson 1998; Sampson and Laub 1993). Low self-control and social attachment are measured by variables for drug use and marital status. Some models also measure self-control with individual-level variables capturing delinquency before age 18. In addition, the regressions include variables for industry, region, public sector employment, and union membership to capture other determinants of earnings associated with respondent characteristics.

Second, a more general model of respondent characteristics introduces fixed effects to capture the influence of time-invariant, observed and unobserved characteristics. With the fixed-effects model, the errors in equations 1 and 2 decompose into two terms:

$$\varepsilon_{it} = u_i + v_{it},$$

where u_i captures the impact of stable respondent characteristics, and v_{it} is random error. The fixed effect, u_i, describes the in-

---

where $C_{it} = 1$. This approach yields substantively identical results to those reported below.

534 AMERICAN SOCIOLOGICAL REVIEW

Table 2. Description of Additional Predictors for Regressions of Wages on Incarceration: NLSY, 1983 to 1998

Variable	Description	Year Measured
Race/ethnicity	Dummy variables for non-Hispanic blacks, and Hispanics.	1979
Human Capital		
Education	Years of schooling completed.	All years
Work experience	Cumulative mean of weeks per year spent in paid employment up to interview year.	All years
Cognitive ability	Percentile score on the Armed Forces Qualifying Test.	1980
Self-Control and Social Attachments		
Drug use	Dummy for those recently using marijuana, cocaine or other drugs (interpolated for missing years).	1984, 1988, 1992, 1994, and 1998
Married	Dummy for married respondents.	All years
Charged, under age 18	Dummy for those charged with an offense before age 18.	1980
Incarcerated, under age 18	Dummy for those sentenced to a correctional facility before age 18.	1980
Job and Labor Market Characteristics		
Enrolled	Dummy for school or college enrollment.	All years
Union	Dummy for union members or wages set by collective bargaining.	All years
Industry	Six category code: (1) construction and manufacturing (reference category), (2) agriculture and mining, (3) transport and utilities, (4) sales, (5) miscellaneous services, (6) professional, financial and public administration services.	All years
Public sector	Dummy for public sector employment.	All years
Urban	Dummy if county of residence is 50-100 percent urban.	All years
Unemployment	Local area unemployment rate coded from 6-category classification.	All years
Region	Four category code: (1) Northeast (reference category), (2) West, (3) South, and (4) Midwest.	All years

fluence of omitted variables that may be correlated with the observed predictors. Traits like cognitive ability or impulsivity (Caspi et al. 1998), or fixed demographic characteristics like race and ethnicity, are absorbed by the fixed effects. Although the main effects of race and ethnicity are not identified in the fixed-effects model, covariate effects may differ across blacks, whites, and Hispanics. Separate models are estimated for the three racial and ethnic groups.

Finally, the selectivity of inmates is also examined by restricting the comparison group against which the incarceration effect is evaluated. Studies of training programs

involving ex-offenders find that comparison groups drawn from the general population often yield inaccurate causal inferences about program effects (Lalonde 1986). Restricting comparison to people similar to the treatment group—prison and jail inmates in our case—can significantly reduce bias in the estimation of causal effects. In the analysis below, results are presented for the full sample of NLSY men and a subsample of men at high risk of crime or delinquency. The at-risk subsample includes those who (1) are interviewed in prison, (2) report jail incarceration in the 1989–1993 employment supplements, or (3) report contact with the

Table 3. Descriptive Statistics for Hourly Wage and Selected Independent Variables Used in the Regression Analyses: NLSY Men, 1990

Variable	Never Incarcerated	Not Yet Incarcerated	Currently or Previously Incarcerated
Whites			
Hourly wage (in dollars)	8.92	5.84	5.77
Age (in years)	29.40	28.65	28.88
Education (in years)	13.10	11.10	10.07
Work experience (in weeks)	40.55	41.10	26.16
Married	.58	.40	.36
Enrolled	.06	.05	.03
Drug use	.31	.55	.65
Union job	.16	.05	.06
Number of respondents	2,205	20	78
Blacks			
Hourly wage (in dollars)	7.01	4.92	5.33
Age (in years)	29.23	28.90	29.38
Education (in years)	12.56	11.26	11.10
Work experience (in weeks)	37.38	32.19	25.80
Married	.37	.18	.13
Enrolled	.04	.00	.03
Drug use	.28	.41	.27
Union job	.24	.14	.21
Number of respondents	780	49	97
Hispanics			
Hourly wage (in dollars)	8.03	6.18	5.33
Age (in years)	29.31	28.70	27.94
Education (in years)	12.04	10.73	10.69
Work experience (in weeks)	40.59	35.09	25.48
Married	.57	.30	.26
Enrolled	.06	.00	.00
Drug use	.27	.43	.46
Union job	.22	.19	.09
Number of respondents	597	23	35

Note: Statistics are not reported for the variables urban, industry, public sector, or region.

criminal justice system in the 1980 crime module. The subsample likely includes a large share of nonincarcerated felons. Estimated incarceration effects may be small for this subsample as wages for the nonincarcerated comparison group will reflect the penalty of arrest or conviction shared by the treatment group of ex-inmates.

Data for analysis are drawn from nonmilitary men interviewed between 1983 and 1998. By 1998, the NLSY respondents were aged 34 to 41. Illustrative statistics for one year, 1990, are reported for men who are never incarcerated, men who are not yet incarcerated, and those who are or have been incarcerated (Table 3). The wage gap between inmates and noninmates varies from about $1.70 for blacks to $3.15 for whites. Much of the gap is likely explained by large differences in education and work experience. Among men interviewed in prison, the earnings differential before and after incarceration is small. Only Hispanic ex-inmates show significantly lower wages than Hispanics who have not yet been to prison or jail. Still, the small age difference between the pre- and post-incarceration samples provides some preliminary cross-sectional evidence of weak wage growth among ex-inmates.

I tried a variety of other specifications in addition to the reported models. One alternative includes random intercepts and random effects for time-varying predictors like age or prior incarceration. Prior incarceration may also interact with education or work experience. These alternatives all yield substantively identical results for the main effects of prior incarceration and the age-earnings profile of ex-inmates.

Nonrandom sample attrition can bias the analysis of panel data covering a long time period. Between 1983 and 1998, 14 interviews were scheduled and in the data analyzed, respondents missed an average of 2.01 interviews. (Sample sizes for regression analysis reflect higher nonresponse because unemployed workers may not report wages.) Response rates are nearly identical for noninmates and inmates. Some attrition is produced by design because a supplementary sample of poor whites was dropped in 1990. The results are unaffected by excluding the supplementary sample. The tables below are based on the complete sample. The NLSY also provides weights to adjust for over-sampling and differential attrition. Weighted and unweighted analyses yield substantively identical results; I report unweighted results below.

RESULTS

The main effects results show that estimates are robust across different models and subsets of the data (Table 4). The simplest model estimated with ordinary least squares (OLS) includes just age, prior and current incarceration status, and time-varying and individual-level control variables. The OLS estimates of Model 1 indicate that ex-inmates earn about 7 percent less than men who have not been incarcerated. Model 1 neglects unobserved variables that differ across individuals. Once individual-level fixed effects are

controlled, incarceration is estimated to reduce earnings by 19 percent (Model 2).

Including work experience reduces the OLS coefficient to less than half the fixed-effect estimate. The fixed-effect and OLS incarceration effects are nearly equal when work experience is excluded. OLS attributes most of the gap between pre- and post-incarceration wages to differences in work experience. In effect, most of the sample who are never incarcerated (who have high experience and pay) are in the same pre-incarceration comparison group as men who are later incarcerated (who have low experience and pay). The fixed-effects models (Models 2, 3, and 4) remove large differences in work experience between never-incarcerated and pre-incarcerated men as a confounding source of variation. The fixed-effects models thus attribute much less of the gap between pre- and post-incarceration wages to differences in work experience. Adding period effects reduces the estimated incarceration penalty slightly to 16 percent, but the coefficient remains statistically significant (Table 4, Model 3). The size of the incarceration effect is unchanged by restricting analysis to the at-risk subsample of men reporting crime or delinquency (Table 4, Model 4).

WAGE GROWTH AND INCARCERATION

If ex-prisoners have trouble getting career jobs, incarceration should also reduce wage growth. Estimates of the *age × incarceration* interaction are reported in Table 5. For all models, estimated interaction effects are negative and statistically significant. In the simplest model (Model 5)—which controls just for human capital, job, and personal characteristics—the interaction effect exceeds the main effect of age. This estimate suggests that incarceration eliminates all wage growth among ex-convicts. Introducing fixed effects (Model 6) yields similar results. Adding the main effect of age to the interaction effect $(.53 - .72 = -.19)$ shows that the wages of ex-inmates declined through their twenties and thirties.

The results are sensitive to period effects in which the effect of education grows between 1983 and 1998 (Table 5, Model 7). The time counter starts in 1979 $(t = 0)$, the year of the first NLSY interview. In 1983,

Table 4. Unstandardized Coefficients from the Regression of Log Hourly Wages on Incarceration, Main Effects Model: NLSY Men, 1983 to 1998

Independent Variable	Model 1	Model 2	Model 3	Model 4
Intercept	1.04**	.71**	2.23**	2.23**
	(.02)	(.05)	(.09)	(.14)
Was incarcerated (P)	−.07**	−.19**	−.16**	−.16**
	(.01)	(.02)	(.02)	(.02)
Now incarcerated (C)	−.23**	−.24**	−.23**	−.23**
	(.02)	(.02)	(.02)	(.02)
Log age (A)	.42**	.50**	2.27**	2.05**
	(.02)	(.02)	(.13)	(.21)
Education (E) × 10	.43**	.65**	−.05	−.15
	(.01)	(.03)	(.05)	(.08)
Year (t)	—	—	−.11**	−.10**
			(.01)	(.01)
(Education × year) × 100	—	—	.41**	.38**
			(.02)	(.03)
Fixed effects	No	Yes	Yes	Yes
Sample	Full	Full	Full	At-risk
R^2	.34	.61	.62	.60
Number of observations	47,616	51,424	51,424	18,923
Number of respondents	4,953	5,438	5,438	2,092

Note: Standard errors are in parentheses. Model 1 includes controls for juvenile contact with the criminal justice system, cognitive ability, race, and ethnicity. All models control for work experience, enrollment status, drug use, marital status, union membership, industry, and region. The full sample includes all respondents. The at-risk subsample includes respondents who report crime, delinquency or any incarceration. Results for control variables are reported in Appendix A.

*$p < .05$ **$p < .01$ (two-tailed tests)

the first year for the regression analysis, the education coefficient equals (4 × .0039) ≈ .016. By 1998, the education effect had grown to .074, reflecting the decline in earnings among low-skill men. When the effect of education on earnings is allowed to grow, the *age × incarceration* interaction declines by about one-third. The age coefficient also increases substantially with Model 7. As a result, the age-earnings profile of ex-inmates is much steeper when period effects are included. Essentially the same results are given by the subsample of men at high risk of crime (Model 8).

The sensitivity of results can be studied by plotting the age-earnings profile of ex-convicts and nonconvicts (Figure 2). The age-earnings profiles are based on the estimates of Models 6 and 7 in Table 5. To estimate wages, all covariates except age and incarceration status are set to zero. When period effects are omitted, ex-convicts' wages ex-

ceed those of nonconvicts in their early twenties, but ex-convicts' pay declines over the next two decades. Controlling for wage losses among low-skill men in the 1980s and 1990s, the wages of ex-convicts' increase through their twenties and thirties, although more slowly than their counterparts who are not incarcerated. The top panel of Figure 2 provides an accurate empirical description of wage growth among ex-convicts. The lower panel of Figure 2 indicates, however, that wage decline results mostly from the broad decline in wages among workers with little education.

Results from the interaction models are reported separately for blacks, whites, and Hispanics in Table 6. I can assess the magnitude of the interaction effect in relation to the main effect of age. Across the three groups, the interaction effects are about 30 percent smaller than the age main effect, indicating that incarceration reduces wage

538 AMERICAN SOCIOLOGICAL REVIEW

Table 5. Unstandardized Coefficients from the Regression of Log Hourly Wages on Incarceration, Interaction Model: NLSY Men, 1983 to 1998

Independent Variable	Model 5	Model 6	Model 7	Model 8
Intercept	1.03**	.71**	2.15**	2.03**
	(.02)	(.05)	(.09)	(.14)
Was incarcerated (P)	−.02	−.10**	−.10**	−.09**
	(.01)	(.02)	(.02)	(.02)
Now incarcerated (C)	−.23**	−.23**	−.23**	−.22**
	(.02)	(.02)	(.02)	(.02)
Log age (A)	.44**	.53**	2.18**	1.80**
	(.02)	(.02)	(.13)	(.21)
Was incarcerated × log age	−.68**	−.72**	−.50**	−.55**
	(.07)	(.07)	(.07)	(.07)
Education (E) × 10	.43**	.65**	−.02	−.07
	(.01)	(.03)	(.05)	(.08)
Year (t)	—	—	−.10**	−.08**
			(.01)	(.01)
(Education × year) × 100	—	—	.39**	.34**
			(.02)	(.03)
Fixed effects	No	Yes	Yes	Yes
Sample	Full	Full	Full	At-risk
R²	.34	.61	.62	.60
Number of observations	47,616	51,424	51,424	18,923
Number of respondents	4,953	5,438	5,438	2,092

Note: Standard errors are in parentheses. Model 5 includes controls for juvenile contact with the criminal justice system, cognitive ability, race, and ethnicity. All models control for work experience, enrollment status, drug use, marital status, union membership, public sector employment, industry, and region. The full sample includes all respondents. The at-risk subsample includes respondents who report crime, delinquency, or any incarceration. Results for control variables are reported in Appendix A.

*$p < .05$ **$p < .01$ (two-tailed tests)

growth by almost one-third. The coefficient for the *age × incarceration* interaction is roughly the same for Hispanics and whites, but is smaller for blacks. Wages grow slowly for blacks, and the relative decline in wage growth among black ex-convicts is about 25 percent (.20/.77), slightly smaller than the relative decline for whites.

These findings point to the persistent effects of adult incarceration on wages: The wage gap between nonconvicts and ex-convicts grows as workers age. Contrast with this the research on employment, which finds that the effects of adult incarceration decay after several years (Western and Beckett 1999). Other analysis (not shown), using a more elaborate model of wage dynamics, supports the interpretation of the persistent effects of incarceration on wages over the life course. This divergence in find-ings between results on employment and wages is consistent with the idea that ex-convicts are ultimately able to find employment after their release, but the jobs they get offer little wage growth.

WAGE INEQUALITY AND INCARCERATION

Because incarceration is common among minority and low-skill men, the earnings penalty experienced by ex-convicts may influence aggregate wage inequality. To test this mass imprisonment hypothesis, I predict wages using a pooled version of the regressions reported in Table 6. In the pooled analysis, the coefficients for the *age × incarceration* interactions vary by race and ethnicity. Because interest centers on the entire wage distribution, estimation is based on the full NLSY sample. Two sets of predicted

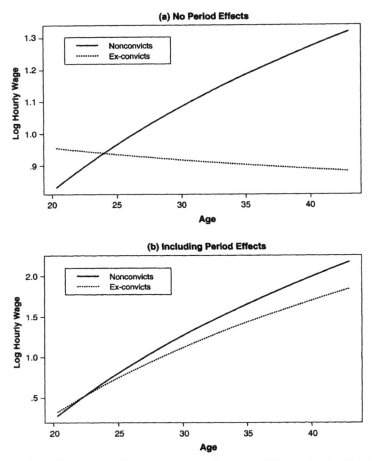

Figure 2. **Estimated Log Hourly Wages by Age for Ex-Convicts and Nonconvicts for Models with and without Period Effects: NLSY Men, 1983 to 1998**

wages are calculated: The first is based on the observed predictors; the second uses all the observed predictors, except the incarceration variables, which are set to zero, $C_{it} = P_{it} = 0$. The second series of predictions estimates the wages we would observe if none of the NLSY respondents went to prison or jail between 1979 and 1998.

Two kinds of inequality are examined. First, we might expect incarceration to increase inequality within racial/ethnic groups by lowering earnings among low-education men. We estimate this effect by calculating the coefficient of variation (standard deviation divided by the mean) of log wages at observed and zero incarceration. Second, incarceration will likely increase inequality between whites and blacks, and between whites and Hispanics, because minority incarceration rates are relatively high. This effect is estimated by calculating the white-minority differences in mean log wages. Predicted inequality is reported for models with and without period effects.

The measures of hypothetical wage inequality take no account of the spillover effect of decarcerated workers on the earnings of noninmates. An increase in the supply of low-skill workers through decarceration may drive down wages among low-skill workers

Table 6. Unstandardized Coefficients from the Regression of Log Hourly Wages on Incarceration, by Race and Ethnicity, Interaction Models: NLSY Men, 1983 to 1998

Independent Variable	Whites		Blacks		Hispanics	
	Model 1	Model 2	Model 3	Model 4	Model 5	Model 6
Intercept	2.53**	2.61**	1.39**	1.05**	2.32**	1.98**
	(.12)	(.19)	(.18)	(.32)	(.19)	(.32)
Was incarcerated (P)	−.11**	−.11**	−.06	−.05	−.15**	−.15**
	(.04)	(.04)	(.03)	(.03)	(.05)	(.05)
Now incarcerated (C)	−.24**	−.24**	−.23**	−.22**	−.19**	−.19**
	(.04)	(.04)	(.03)	(.03)	(.05)	(.05)
Log Age (A)	2.79**	2.56**	.77**	.05	2.36**	2.27**
	(.17)	(.28)	(.25)	(.45)	(.29)	(.45)
Was incarcerated × log age	−.85**	−.87**	−.20*	−.27*	−.72**	−.75**
	(.12)	(.12)	(.10)	(.12)	(.16)	(.16)
Education (E) × 10	−.13*	−.31**	.13	.10	−.06	.21
	(.06)	(.10)	(.11)	(.20)	(.11)	(.21)
Year (t)	−.13**	−.12**	−.04**	.00	−.10**	−.08**
	(.01)	(.01)	(.01)	(.02)	(.01)	(.02)
(Education × year) × 100	.47**	.48**	.24**	.09	.30**	.20*
	(.03)	(.05)	(.04)	(.08)	(.04)	(.08)
Fixed effects	Yes	Yes	Yes	Yes	Yes	Yes
Sample	Full	At-risk	Full	At-risk	Full	At-risk
R^2	.63	.61	.59	.55	.58	.59
Number of observations	29,433	10,327	12,958	5,129	9,033	3,467
Number of respondents	3,198	1,171	1,352	576	888	345

Note: Standard errors are in parentheses. All models control for work experience, enrollment status, drug use, marital status, union membership, public sector employment, industry, and region. The full sample includes all respondents. The at-risk subsample includes respondents who report crime, delinquency, or any incarceration. Results for control variables are reported in Appendix A.

*$p < .05$ **$p < .01$ (two-tailed tests)

who have not been to prison or jail. The net impact of spillover effects on inequality is unclear. Given the capacity of the U.S. labor market to absorb new entrants in the 1990s, however, the spillover effect may not be large.

Table 7 reports wage inequality estimated at observed and zero incarceration for men interviewed between 1994 and 1998. If we ignore period effects, in which the earnings of low-education men decreased through the 1980s and 1990s, wage inequality among whites would be about 5.3 percent lower if the incarceration rate were zero between 1979 and 1998. The effect of incarceration on inequality is twice as large for blacks and Hispanics. The largest effects are for white versus Hispanic inequality, which would be 15 percent lower but for the effects of incarceration.

As in the regression reported above, incarceration effects are reduced if period effects are considered. If the effect of education on earnings is allowed to become larger over time, incarceration is estimated to have increased wage inequality among blacks and Hispanics and between blacks and whites by 8 to 9 percent. Again, the largest incarceration effect is found for white-Hispanic inequality. The estimates show that the difference in mean log wages of whites and Hispanics would be 12.2 percent lower in the absence of incarceration. The impact of period effects on estimates of inequality underlines the result that a significant part of the the low earnings of ex-convicts is due to wage stagnation among low-education men.

Analysis of the effects of incarceration on inequality might be elaborated in several ways. One might focus on groups, like non-

Table 7. Estimated Inequality in Log Hourly Wages Assuming Actual and Zero Incarceration, 1994 to 1998

Measure	Assumed Incarceration		Percent Difference
	Observed	Zero	
No Period Effects			
White coefficient of variation	.192	.182	5.3
Black coefficient of variation	.254	.227	10.5
Hispanic coefficient of variation	.222	.199	10.5
White vs. black mean difference	.318	.285	10.4
White vs. Hispanic mean difference	.168	.141	15.7
Period Effects			
White coefficient of variation	.205	.196	4.3
Black coefficient of variation	.267	.244	8.6
Hispanic coefficient of variation	.235	.214	8.8
White vs. black mean difference	.332	.306	8.1
White vs. Hispanic mean difference	.196	.172	12.2

Note: Respondents include all those interviewed between 1994 and 1998.

college men, whose incarceration rates are higher. One might also consider the indirect effects of incarceration on the acquisition of work experience (employment). I studied these other incarceration effects in supplementary analyses, but the results were not dramatically different from those reported. Results for noncollege men were similar to those calculated for the full sample, and indirect effects of incarceration on wage inequality through employment tended to be small. (These results are available on request.)

DISCUSSION

This analysis has reported evidence for the hypothesis that incarceration is a turning point that reduces the earnings mobility of young men. The analysis also considered whether the individual-level effects of incarceration on earnings summed to a large aggregate effect on wage inequality. Analysis of the NLSY provided mixed support for these claims. There is strong evidence that incarceration reduces the wages of ex-inmates by 10 to 20 percent. More relevant for the idea of imprisonment as a turning point, incarceration was also found to reduce the rate of wage growth by about 30 percent. Indeed, ex-inmates experienced marked declines in real wages as they moved through

the life course in the 1980s and 1990s. Much of this decline, however, resulted from an increasing penalty for low education, widely experienced by men without a college education. The aggregate effects of incarceration on wage inequality were relatively small. Differential incarceration accounts for almost 10 percent of the mean difference in wages across race and ethnic groups. In sum, the analysis provides strong evidence for slow wage growth among ex-inmates. The effects of incarceration on aggregate wage inequality are more modest.

Although the effects of incarceration on wage inequality were relatively small, the true effect in the population may be larger. Because of the way incarceration is measured in the NLSY, the proportion of men with prison records is somewhat underestimated and the underestimate is larger for blacks than for whites. If the NLSY accurately captured the true prevalence of imprisonment in the population, estimated black-white inequality due to incarceration would be higher. In addition, with very high incarceration rates among some groups like low-education black men, the stigma of imprisonment may attach to the group as a whole rather than to individuals. This effect would be reflected in the overall wage disadvantage of black noncollege men, rather than the estimated effect of incarceration.

Relatively small incarceration effects for blacks hint at this process, in which the labor market does not differentiate so strongly between black noninmates and ex-inmates. Further analysis would examine how black-white wage differentials among noncollege men have changed over time as the incarceration rate has increased.

The findings here can also be placed in the wider context of research on crime and inequality. Research relating crime to labor market outcomes views stable employment as an important source of criminal desistance (Crutchfield and Pitchford 1997; Sampson and Laub 1993). These effects appear strongest for men in their late twenties and thirties (Uggen 2000). The low wages earned by ex-inmates may thus be associated with further crime after release from prison. The causal path from incarceration to irregular employment to crime may be especially damaging because the economic pain of incarceration is largest for older men—precisely the group that benefits most from stable employment. This analysis also supports the claim by Sampson and Laub (1993) that incarceration adds to an accumulation of disadvantage. Although Sampson and Laub (1993) focus on the long-term effects of juvenile incarceration, the evidence presented here indicates that adult incarceration can further limit economic mobility in later life.

The effects of incarceration on economic mobility challenge our general understanding of the influence of institutions on economic opportunity. Research on American racial inequality views institutional change as a progressive influence, but the evidence here indicates that penal expansion has deepened racial inequality. Many researchers attribute improvements in black earnings and employment to school desegregation, affirmative action, and equal employment policies (Card and Krueger 1992; Heckman 1989). The growth of the black middle class is rooted in many of these policies (Wilson 1978). However, expanding imprisonment has increased racial inequality in earnings and in lifelong careers. Although racial differences in incarceration may not result in a straightforward way from racial bias in policing or the courts (Tonry 1996), the penal system has influenced the relative distribution of life chances among young poorly educated black men over the last two decades of the twentieth century.

More generally, the penal system has never occupied a central place in the study of American inequality and has been relegated instead to a specialty interest among criminologists. Low incarceration rates throughout most of the twentieth century placed prisons at the distant fringes of the stratification system, far behind the institutional influence of families, schools, labor unions, and the military. By the 1990s, around one-fifth of minority men and a comparable proportion of those with only a high school education will pass through prison at some point in their lives. Under these conditions, it appears that the U.S. penal system has grown beyond disciplining the deviant few, to imposing a systemic influence on broad patterns of social inequality.

Bruce Western is Professor of Sociology at Princeton University. He has research interests in the political and economic sociology of labor markets and statistical methods. His paper, "Bayesian Thinking about Macrosociology," recently appeared in the American Journal of Sociology *(2001, vol. 107, pp. 353–79).*

APPENDIX A. REGRESSION RESULTS FOR CONTROL VARIABLES

Table A-1. Regression Results for the Control Variables in the Models Reported in Table 4

Control Variable	Model 1	2	3	4	Control Variable	Model 1	2	3	4
Charged, under 18	−.01 (.01)	—	—	—	Cognitive ability test score	.30 (.01)	—	—	—
Incarcerated, under 18	.01 (.01)	—	—	—	Black	−.05 (.01)	—	—	—

(Continued on next page)

(Talbe A-1 continued)

Control Variable	Model 1	2	3	4	Control Variable	Model 1	2	3	4
Hispanic	−.01 (.01)	—	—	—	Agriculture, mining	−.21 (.01)	−.09 (.01)	−.09 (.01)	−.07 (.02)
Experience	.01 (.00)	.01 (.00)	.01 (.00)	.01 (.00)	Transportation, utilities	.00 (.01)	.00 (.01)	.00 (.01)	−.02 (.02)
Married	.13 (.00)	.07 (.01)	.05 (.01)	.05 (.01)	Sales	−.23 (.01)	−.14 (.01)	−.14 (.01)	−.15 (.01)
Enrolled	−.18 (.01)	−.17 (.01)	−.14 (.01)	−.12 (.02)	Miscellaneous services	−.10 (.01)	−.10 (.01)	−.10 (.01)	−.15 (.01)
Local unemployment	−.01 (.00)	−.01 (.00)	−.01 (.00)	−.01 (.00)	Professional, financial	−.18 (.01)	−.11 (.01)	−.11 (.01)	−.11 (.01)
Urban	.09 (.01)	.04 (.01)	.04 (.01)	.05 (.01)					
Drug use	−.01 (.00)	−.01 (.01)	−.01 (.01)	.01 (.01)	West	.00 (.01)	.05 (.02)	.04 (.02)	−.02 (.04)
Union	.20 (.01)	.15 (.01)	.14 (.01)	.17 (.01)	South	−.11 (.01)	−.05 (.02)	−.05 (.02)	−.05 (.03)
Public sector	−.08 (.01)	−.05 (.01)	−.05 (.01)	−.12 (.02)	Midwest	−.11 (.01)	−.07 (.02)	−.07 (.02)	−.08 (.04)

Note: Standard errors are in parentheses.

Table A-2.   Regression Results for the Control Variables in the Models Reported in Table 5

Control Variable	Model 5	6	7	8	Control Variable	Model 5	6	7	8
Charged, under 18	−.01 (.01)	—	—	—	Union	.20 (.01)	.15 (.01)	.14 (.01)	.16 (.01)
Incarcerated, under 18	.00 (.01)	—	—	—	Public sector	−.08 (.01)	−.05 (.01)	−.05 (.01)	−.12 (.02)
Cognitive ability test score	.30 (.01)	—	—	—	Agriculture, mining	−.22 (.01)	−.09 (.01)	−.09 (.01)	−.07 (.02)
Black	−.05 (.01)	—	—	—	Transportation, utilities	.00 (.01)	.00 (.01)	.00 (.01)	−.01 (.02)
Hispanic	−.01 (.01)	—	—	—	Sales	−.23 (.01)	−.14 (.01)	−.14 (.01)	−.15 (.01)
Experience	.01 (.00)	.01 (.00)	.01 (.00)	.01 (.00)	Miscellaneous services	−.10 (.01)	−.10 (.01)	−.10 (.01)	−.15 (.01)
Married	.13 (.00)	.07 (.01)	.05 (.01)	.05 (.01)	Professional, financial	−.17 (.01)	−.11 (.01)	−.11 (.01)	−.11 (.01)
Enrolled	−.18 (.01)	−.17 (.01)	−.14 (.01)	−.12 (.02)					
Local unemployment	−.01 (.00)	−.01 (.00)	−.01 (.00)	−.01 (.00)	West	.00 (.01)	.04 (.02)	.04 (.02)	−.02 (.04)
Urban	.09 (.01)	.04 (.01)	.04 (.01)	.05 (.01)	South	−.10 (.01)	−.04 (.02)	−.04 (.02)	−.05 (.03)
Drug use	−.01 (.00)	−.01 (.01)	−.01 (.01)	.01 (.01)	Midwest	−.11 (.01)	−.07 (.02)	−.07 (.02)	−.08 (.04)

Note: Standard errors are in parentheses.

Table A-3. Regression Results for the Control Variables in the Models Reported in Table 6

Cointrol Variable	Whites		Blacks		Hispanics	
	Model 1	Model 2	Model 3	Model 4	Model 5	Model 6
Experience	.01	.01	.01	.01	.01	.01
	(.00)	(.00)	(.00)	(.00)	(.00)	(.00)
Married	.05	.04	.06	.08	.04	.03
	(.01)	(.01)	(.01)	(.02)	(.01)	(.02)
Enrolled	−.15	−.12	−.13	−.11	−.07	−.11
	(.01)	(.02)	(.02)	(.04)	(.02)	(.04)
Local unemployment	−.01	−.01	−.01	.00	.00	−.01
	(.00)	(.00)	(.00)	(.00)	(.00)	(.00)
Urban	.04	.04	.07	.08	−.02	.07
	(.01)	(.02)	(.02)	(.04)	(.03)	(.04)
Drug use	−.01	.00	−.01	.02	−.02	.00
	(.01)	(.01)	(.01)	(.02)	(.01)	(.02)
Union	.16	.17	.13	.17	.14	.14
	(.01)	(.01)	(.01)	(.02)	(.01)	(.02)
Public sector	−.06	−.07	−.04	−.19	−.03	−.07
	(.01)	(.02)	(.02)	(.03)	(.02)	(.04)
Agriculture, mining	−.11	−.08	−.05	−.04	−.07	−.06
	(.01)	(.02)	(.02)	(.04)	(.03)	(.04)
Transportation, utilities	−.02	−.06	.02	.02	.00	.04
	(.01)	(.02)	(.02)	(.03)	(.02)	(.03)
Sales	−.13	−.14	−.17	−.19	−.12	−.13
	(.01)	(.01)	(.01)	(.02)	(.02)	(.03)
Miscellaneous services	−.08	−.14	−.16	−.22	−.05	−.09
	(.01)	(.02)	(.01)	(.03)	(.02)	(.03)
Professional, financial	−.10	−.11	−.15	−.15	−.08	−.06
	(.01)	(.01)	(.01)	(.02)	(.02)	(.03)
West	.06	.02	.11	.17	−.11	−.21
	(.03)	(.04)	(.05)	(.09)	(.06)	(.08)
South	.01	.00	−.06	.01	−.23	−.22
	(.02)	(.04)	(.03)	(.05)	(.05)	(.07)
Midwest	−.07	−.10	.06	.11	−.08	−.02
	(.03)	(.04)	(.04)	(.08)	(.07)	(.11)

Note: Standard errors are in parentheses.

REFERENCES

Bernhardt, Annette, Martina Morris, Mark Handcock, and Marc Scott. 2001. *Divergent Paths: Economic Mobility in the New American Labor Market.* New York: Russell Sage.

Blumstein, Alfred and Allen J. Beck. 1999. "Population Growth in U.S. Prisons, 1980–1996." Pp. 17–62 in *Crime and Justice: Prisons*, vol. 26, edited by M. Tonry and J. Petersilia. Chicago, IL: University of Chicago Press.

Boggess, Scott and John Bound. 1997. "Did Criminal Activity Increase During the 1980s? Comparisons across Data Sources." *Social Science Quarterly* 78:725–39.

Bonczar, Thomas P. and Allen J. Beck. 1997. *Lifetime Likelihood of Going to State or Fed-eral Prison.* Bureau of Justice Statistics Bulletin, NCJ 160092. Washington, DC: U.S. Department of Justice.

Bushway, Shawn David. 1996. "The Impact of a Criminal History Record on Access to Legitimate Employment." Ph.D. dissertation, School of Public Policy and Management, Carnegie Mellon University, Pittsburgh, PA.

Caspi, Avshalom, Bradley R. Entner Wright, Terrie E. Moffit, and Phil A. Silva. 1998. "Early Failure in the Labor Market: Childhood and Adolescent Predictors of Unemployment in the Transition to Adulthood." *American Sociological Review* 63:424–51.

Card, David and Alan B. Krueger. 1992. "School Quality and Black-White Relative Earnings: A

Direct Assessment." *Quarterly Journal of Economics* 107:151–200.

Center for Human Resource Research. 2000. *National Longitudinal Study of Youth, 1979–1998* [MRDF]. University of Chicago, Chicago, IL: National Opinion Research Center [producer]. Ohio State University, Columbus, OH: Center for Human Resources [distributor].

Chiricos, Theodore G. 1987. "Rates of Crime and Unemployment: A Review of Aggregate Research Evidence." *Social Problems* 34:187–212.

Crutchfield, Robert D. and Susan R. Pitchford. 1997. "Work and Crime: The Effects of Labor Stratification." *Social Forces* 76:93–118.

DiPrete, Thomas A. 1989. *The Bureaucratic Labor Market: The Case of the Federal Civil Service.* New York: Plenum.

Duneier, Mitchell. 1999. *Sidewalk.* New York: Farrar, Strauss, Giroux.

Evans, Robert. 1968. "The Labor Market and Parole Success." *Journal of Human Resources* 3:201–12.

Freeman, Richard B. 1991. "Crime and the Employment of Disadvantaged Youths." Working Paper No. 3875, National Bureau of Economic Research, Cambridge, MA.

———. 1992. "Crime and the Employment of Disadvantaged Youth." Pp. 201–37 in *Urban Labor Markets and Job Opportunity*, edited by G. Peterson and W. Vroman. Washington, DC: Urban Institute Press.

Garland, David. 2001. "Introduction: The Meaning of Mass Imprisonment." Pp. 1–3 in *Mass Imprisonment: Social Causes and Consequences*, edited by D. Garland. London, England: Sage.

Gilliard, Darrell K. 1999. *Prison and Jail Inmates at Midyear, 1998.* Bureau of Justice Statistics Bulletin, NCJ 173414. Washington, DC: U.S. Department of Justice.

Gottfredson, Michael R. and Travis Hirschi. 1990. *A General Theory of Crime.* Stanford, CA: Stanford University Press.

Granovetter, Mark. 1995. *Getting a Job: A Study of Contracts and Careers.* 2d ed. Chicago, IL: University of Chicago Press.

Grogger, Jeffrey. 1992 "Arrests, Persistent Youth Joblessness, and Black/White Employment Differentials." *Review of Economics and Statistics* 74:100–106.

———. 1995 "The Effect of Arrests on the Employment and Earnings of Young Men." *Quarterly Journal of Economics* 110:51–71.

Hagan, John. 1993. "The Social Embeddedness of Crime and Unemployment." *Criminology* 31:465–91.

Hagan, John and Ronit Dinovitzer. 1999. "Collateral Consequences of Imprisonment for Children Communities and Prisoners." Pp. 121–62 in *Crime and Justice: Prisons*, vol. 26, edited by M. Tonry and J. Petersilia. Chicago, IL: University of Chicago Press.

Heckman, James. 1989. "The Impact of Government on the Economic Status of African Americans." Pp. 50–80 in *The Question of Discrimination*, edited by S. Shulman, W. Darity, and R. Higgs. Middletown, CT: Wesleyan University Press.

Holzer, Harry J. 1996. *What Employers Want: Job Prospects for Less-Educated Workers.* New York: Russell Sage.

Irwin, John and James Austin. 1994. *Its About Time: America's Imprisonment Binge.* Belmont, CA: Wadsworth.

Kling, Jeffrey R. 1999. "The Effect of Prison Sentence Length on the Subsequent Employment and Earnings of Criminal Defendants." Discussion Paper in Economics No. 208, Woodrow Wilson School, Princeton University, Princeton, NJ.

Kornfeld, Robert and Howard S. Bloom. 1999. "Measuring Program Impacts on Earnings and Employment: Do Unemployment Insurance Wage Reports from Employers Agree with Surveys of Individuals?" *Journal of Labor Economics* 17:168–97.

LaLonde, Robert J. 1986. "Evaluating Econometric Evaluations of Training Programs with Experimental Data." *American Economic Review* 76:604–20.

Land, Kenneth C., David Cantor, and Stephen T. Russell. 1995. "Unemployment and Crime Rate Fluctuations in the Post-World War II United States: Statistical Time-Series Properties and Alternative Models." Pp. 55–79 in *Crime and Inequality*, edited by J. Hagan and R. Peterson. Stanford, CA: Stanford University Press.

Laub, John H., Daniel S. Nagin, and Robert J. Sampson. 1998. "Trajectories of Change in Criminal Offending: Good Marriages and Desistance Process." *American Sociological Review* 63:225–38.

Lott, John R. 1990. "The Effect of Conviction on the Legitimate Income of Criminals." *Economics Letters* 34:381–85.

Mauer, Marc. 1999. *Race to Incarcerate.* New York: New Press.

Moffit, Terrie E. 1993. "Adolescence-Limited and Life-Course-Persistent Antisocial Behavior: A Developmental Taxonomy." *Psychological Review* 100:674–701.

Morris, Martina, Annette D. Bernhardt, and Mark S. Handcock. 1994. "Economic Inequality: New Methods for New Trends." *American Sociological Review* 59:205–19.

Murphy, Kevin M. and Finis Welch. 1990. "Empirical Age-Earnings Profiles." *Journal of Labor Economics* 8:202–29.

546 AMERICAN SOCIOLOGICAL REVIEW

———. 1998. "The Effect of Conviction on Income Through the Life Cycle." *International Review of Law and Economics* 18:25–40.

Office of the Pardon Attorney. 1996. *Civil Disabilities of Convicted Felons: A State-by-State Survey.* Washington, DC: U.S. Department of Justice.

Pettit, Becky and Bruce Western. 2001. "Inequality in Lifetime Risks of Incarceration." Paper presented at the annual meeting of the Population Association of America, Washington, DC.

Rosenfeld, Rachel A. 1992. "Job Mobility and Career Processes." *Annual Review of Sociology* 18:39–61.

Rossi, Peter H., Richard A. Berk, and Kenneth J. Lenihan. 1980. *Money, Work, and Crime: Experimental Evidence.* New York: Academic.

Sampson, Robert J. and John H. Laub. 1990. "Crime and Deviance over the Life Course: The Salience of Adult Social Bonds." *American Sociological Review* 55:609–27.

———. 1993. *Crime in the Making: Pathways and Turning Points Through Life.* Cambridge, MA: Harvard University Press.

Sánchez-Jankowski, Martín. 1991. *Islands in the Street: Gangs and American Urban Society.* Berkeley, CA: University of California Press.

Schwartz, Richard D. and Jerome H. Skolnick. 1962. "Two Studies of Legal Stigma." *Social Problems* 10:133–42.

Spilerman, Seymour. 1977. "Careers, Labor Market Structure, and Socioeconomic Achievement." *American Journal of Sociology* 83:551–93.

Sullivan, Mercer. 1989. *"Getting Paid": Youth Crime and Work in the Inner City.* Ithaca, NY: Cornell University Press.

Tonry, Michael. 1995. *Malign Neglect.* New York: Oxford University Press.

Uggen, Christopher. 2000. "Work as a Turning Point in the Life Course of Criminals: A Duration Model of Age, Employment, and Recidivism." *American Sociological Review* 65:529–46.

Venkatesh, Sudhir Alladi. 2000. *American Project: The Rise and Fall of a Modern Ghetto.* Cambridge, MA: Harvard University Press.

Wacquant, Loïc. 2000. "The New 'Peculiar Institution': On the Prison as Surrogate Ghetto." *Theoretical Criminology* 4:377–89.

Waldfogel, Joel. 1994a. "The Effect of Criminal Conviction on Income and the Trust 'Reposed in the Workmen.'" *Journal of Human Resources* 29:62–81.

———. 1994b. "Does Conviction Have a Persistent Effect on Income and Employment?" *International Review of Law and Economics* 14:103–19.

Western, Bruce and Katherine Beckett. 1999. "How Unregulated Is the U.S. Labor Market: The Penal System as a Labor Market Institution." *American Journal of Sociology* 104:1030–60.

Western, Bruce, Jeffrey R. Kling, and David F. Weiman. 2001. "The Labor Market Consequences of Incarceration." *Crime and Delinquency* 47:410–27.

Western, Bruce and Becky Pettit. 2000. "Incarceration and Racial Inequality in Men's Employment." *Industrial and Labor Relations Review* 54:3–16.

Wilson, William Julius. 1978. *The Declining Significance of Race: Blacks and Changing American Institutions.* Chicago, IL: University of Chicago Press.

Wright, Erik Olin and Rachel Dwyer. 2000. "The American Jobs Machine: Is the New Economy Creating Good Jobs?" *Boston Review* 25:6.

[13]

The Mark of a Criminal Record[1]

Devah Pager
Northwestern University

With over 2 million individuals currently incarcerated, and over half a million prisoners released each year, the large and growing number of men being processed through the criminal justice system raises important questions about the consequences of this massive institutional intervention. This article focuses on the consequences of incarceration for the employment outcomes of black and white job seekers. The present study adopts an experimental audit approach—in which matched pairs of individuals applied for real entry-level jobs—to formally test the degree to which a criminal record affects subsequent employment opportunities. The findings of this study reveal an important, and much underrecognized, mechanism of stratification. A criminal record presents a major barrier to employment, with important implications for racial disparities.

While stratification researchers typically focus on schools, labor markets, and the family as primary institutions affecting inequality, a new institution has emerged as central to the sorting and stratifying of young and disadvantaged men: the criminal justice system. With over 2 million individuals currently incarcerated, and over half a million prisoners released each year, the large and growing numbers of men being processed through the criminal justice system raises important questions about the consequences of this massive institutional intervention.

This article focuses on the consequences of incarceration for the em-

[1] Support for this research includes grants from the National Science Foundation (SES-0101236), the National Institute of Justice (2002-IJ-CX-0002), the Joyce Foundation, and the Soros Foundation. Views expressed in this document are my own and do not necessarily represent those of the granting agencies. I am grateful for comments and suggestions from Marc Bendick, Jr., Robert M. Hauser, Erik Olin Wright, Lincoln Quillian, David B. Grusky, Eric Grodsky, Chet Pager, Irving Piliavin, Jeremy Freese, and Bruce Western. This research would not have been possible without the support and hospitality of the staff at the Benedict Center and at the Department of Sociology at the University of Wisconsin—Milwaukee. Direct correspondence to Devah Pager, Department of Sociology, Northwestern University, 1810 Chicago Avenue, Evanston, Illinois 60208. E-mail: pager@northwestern.edu

American Journal of Sociology

ployment outcomes of black and white men. While previous survey research has demonstrated a strong *association* between incarceration and
employment, there remains little understanding of the mechanisms by
which these outcomes are produced. In the present study, I adopt an
experimental audit approach to formally test the degree to which a criminal record affects subsequent employment opportunities. By using
matched pairs of individuals to apply for real entry-level jobs, it becomes
possible to directly measure the extent to which a criminal record—in the
absence of other disqualifying characteristics—serves as a barrier to employment among equally qualified applicants. Further, by varying the
race of the tester pairs, we can assess the ways in which the effects of
race and criminal record interact to produce new forms of labor market
inequalities.

TRENDS IN INCARCERATION

Over the past three decades, the number of prison inmates in the United
States has increased by more than 600%, leaving it the country with the
highest incarceration rate in the world (Bureau of Justice Statistics 2002*a*;
Barclay, Tavares, and Siddique 2001). During this time, incarceration has
changed from a punishment reserved primarily for the most heinous offenders to one extended to a much greater range of crimes and a much
larger segment of the population. Recent trends in crime policy have led
to the imposition of harsher sentences for a wider range of offenses, thus
casting an ever-widening net of penal intervention.[2]

While the recent "tough on crime" policies may be effective in getting
criminals off the streets, little provision has been made for when they get
back out. Of the nearly 2 million individuals currently incarcerated,
roughly 95% will be released, with more than half a million being released
each year (Slevin 2000). According to one estimate, there are currently
over 12 million ex-felons in the United States, representing roughly 8%
of the working-age population (Uggen, Thompson, and Manza 2000). Of
those recently released, nearly two-thirds will be charged with new crimes
and over 40% will return to prison within three years (Bureau of Justice
Statistics 2000). Certainly some of these outcomes are the result of desolate
opportunities or deeply ingrained dispositions, grown out of broken fam-

---

[2] For example, the recent adoption of mandatory sentencing laws, most often used for
drug offenses, removes discretion from the sentencing judge to consider the range of
factors pertaining to the individual and the offense that would normally be taken into
account. As a result, the chances of receiving a state prison term after being arrested
for a drug offense rose by 547% between 1980 and 1992 (Bureau of Justice Statistics
1995).

Criminal Record

ilies, poor neighborhoods, and little social control (Sampson and Laub 1993; Wilson 1997). But net of these contributing factors, there is evidence that experience with the criminal justice system in itself has adverse consequences for subsequent opportunities. In particular, incarceration is associated with limited future employment opportunities and earnings potential (Freeman 1987; Western 2002), which themselves are among the strongest predictors of recidivism (Shover 1996; Sampson and Laub 1993; Uggen 2000).

The expansion of the prison population has been particularly consequential for blacks. The incarceration rate for young black men in the year 2000 was nearly 10%, compared to just over 1% for white men in the same age group (Bureau of Justice Statistics 2001). Young black men today have a 28% likelihood of incarceration during their lifetime (Bureau of Justice Statistics 1997), a figure that rises above 50% among young black high school dropouts (Pettit and Western 2001). These vast numbers of inmates translate into a large and increasing population of black ex-offenders returning to communities and searching for work. The barriers these men face in reaching economic self-sufficiency are compounded by the stigma of minority status and criminal record. The consequences of such trends for widening racial disparities are potentially profound (see Western and Pettit 1999; Freeman and Holzer 1986).

PRIOR RESEARCH

While little research to date has focused on the consequences of criminal sanctions, a small and growing body of evidence suggests that contact with the criminal justice system can lead to a substantial reduction in economic opportunities. Using longitudinal survey data, researchers have studied the employment probabilities and income of individuals after release from prison and have found a strong and consistent negative effect of incarceration (Western and Beckett 1999; Freeman 1987; Nagin and Waldfogel 1993).

This existing research has been instrumental in demonstrating the possible aggregate effects of incarceration on labor market outcomes. Unfortunately, however, there are several fundamental limitations of survey data that leave the conclusions of this research vulnerable to harsh criticism. First, it is difficult, using survey data, to rule out the possibility that unmeasured differences between those who are and are not convicted of crimes may drive the observed results. Figure 1 presents one possible model of the relationship between incarceration and employment outcomes, with a direct causal link between the two. In this model, an individual acquires a criminal record, which then severely limits his later

American Journal of Sociology

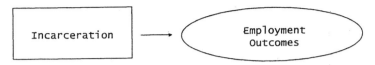

FIG. 1.—Model of direct causation

employment opportunities. But what evidence can we offer in support of this causal relationship? We know that the population of inmates is not a random sample of the overall population. What if, then, the poor outcomes of ex-offenders are merely the result of preexisting traits that make these men bad employees in the first place? Figure 2 presents a model of spurious association in which there is no direct link between incarceration and employment outcomes. Instead, there are direct links between various preexisting individual characteristics (e.g., drug and alcohol abuse, behavioral problems, poor interpersonal skills), which increase the likelihood of both incarceration and poor employment outcomes.[3] In this model, the association between incarceration and employment is entirely spurious—the result of individual predispositions toward deviance.

Consistent with figure 2, Kling (1999), Grogger (1995), and Needels (1996) have each argued that the effect of incarceration on employment is negligible, at an estimated 0%–4%. Using administrative data from unemployment insurance (UI) files matched with records from various state departments of corrections, these authors contend that the observed association is instead largely determined by unmeasured individual characteristics.[4] The findings of these authors stand in stark contrast to the majority of literature asserting a strong link between incarceration and employment (Western and Beckett 1999; Bushway 1998; Sampson and Laub 1993; Freeman 1987; Grogger 1992). While it remains an open question as to whether and to what extent incarceration causes employ-

[3] The variables listed here are just a few of the many potential sources of spuriousness that are virtually untestable using survey data.

[4] Studies using administrative data have the advantage of analyzing large samples of ex-offenders over extended periods of time, before and after incarceration. However, this line of research also suffers from several important limitations: First, employment and wage data from UI administrative records are available only for those jobs covered by and in compliance with unemployment insurance laws, thus excluding many temporary, contingent, or "grey-market" jobs, which may be more likely held by ex-offenders. Second, administrative data are typically limited to one state or jurisdiction; individuals who move to other states during the period of observation are thus mistakenly coded as unemployed or as zero-earners. And finally, missing social security numbers or difficulties in matching records often results in fairly substantial reduction in sample representativeness. See Kornfeld and Bloom (1999) for an in-depth discussion of these issues.

Criminal Record

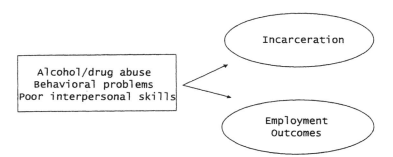

FIG. 2.—Model of spurious effects

ment difficulties, survey research is poorly equipped to offer a definitive answer. The Achilles heel of the survey methodology is its inability to escape from the glaring problems of selection that plague research in this field (see Winship and Morgan 1999; Rubin 1990; Heckman et al. 1998).[5]

A second, related limitation of survey research is its inability to formally identify mechanisms. From aggregate effects, we can infer plausible causal processes, but these are only indirectly supported by the data. Because numerous mechanisms could lead to the same set of outcomes, we are left unable to assess the substantive contribution of any given causal process. Survey researchers have offered numerous hypotheses regarding the mechanisms that may produce the observed relationship between incarceration and employment. These include the labeling effects of criminal stigma (Schwartz and Skolnick 1962), the disruption of social and familial ties (Sampson and Laub 1993), the influence on social networks (Hagan 1993), the loss of human capital (Becker 1975), institutional trauma (Parenti 1999), legal barriers to employment (Dale 1976), and, of course, the possibility that incarceration effects may be entirely spurious (Kling 1999; Grogger 1995; Needels 1996). Without direct measures of these variables, it is difficult, using survey data, to discern which, if any, of these causal explanations may be at work.

The uncertainty surrounding these mechanisms motivates the current project. Before addressing some of the larger consequences of incarcer-

[5] Researchers have employed creative techniques for addressing these issues, such as looking at pre- and postincarceration outcomes for the same individuals (e.g., Grogger 1992; Freeman 1991), comparing ex-offenders to future offenders (e.g., Waldfogel 1994; Grogger 1995), estimating fixed- and random-effects models (Western 2002), and using instrumental variables approaches to correct for unmeasured heterogeneity (e.g., Freeman 1994). There remains little consensus, however, over the degree to which these techniques effectively account for the problems of selection endemic to this type of research.

American Journal of Sociology

ation, it is essential to first establish conclusively the mechanism—or at least one of the mechanisms—driving these results. In the present study, I focus on the effect of a *criminal record* on employment opportunities. This emphasis directs our attention to the stigma associated with criminal justice intervention and to the ways in which employers respond to this stigma in considering applicants. While certainly there are additional ways in which incarceration may affect subsequent employment, this focus allows us to separate the institutional effect from the individual (or from the interaction of the two) and to directly assess one of the most widely discussed—but rarely measured—mechanisms of carceral channeling (Wacquant 2000). While incarceration may in fact additionally transform individuals (and/or their social ties) in ways that make them less suited to work, my interest here is in what might be termed the "credentialing" aspect of the criminal justice system. Those sent to prison are institutionally branded as a particular class of individuals—as are college graduates or welfare recipients—with implications for their perceived place in the stratification order. The "negative credential" associated with a criminal record represents a unique mechanism of stratification, in that it is the state that certifies particular individuals in ways that qualify them for discrimination or social exclusion.[6] It is this official status of the negative credential that differentiates it from other sources of social stigma, offering greater legitimacy to its use as the basis for differentiation. (See Pager [2002] for a more extensive discussion of negative credentials and their implications for stratification).

In order to investigate this question, I have chosen an experimental approach to the problem, a methodology best suited to isolating causal mechanisms. There have, in the past, been a limited number of studies that have adopted an experimental approach to the study of criminal stigma. These studies have relied on a "correspondence test" approach, whereby applications are submitted by mail with no in-person contact. The most notable in this line of research is a classic study by Schwartz and Skolnick (1962) in which the researchers prepared four sets of resumes to be sent to prospective employers, varying the criminal record of applicants. In each condition, employers were less likely to consider appli-

---

[6] Numerous opportunities become formally off-limits to individuals following a felony conviction, including (depending on the state of residence) access to public housing, voting rights, and employment in certain occupational sectors (e.g., health care occupations, public sector positions, child and elder care work). In addition, the widespread availability of criminal background information allows for the information to be further used as the basis for allocating opportunities not formally off-limits to ex-offenders, as studied here.

cants who had any prior contact with the criminal justice system.[7] Several later studies have verified these findings, varying the types of crimes committed by the hypothetical applicant (Finn and Fontaine 1985; Cohen and Nisbett 1997) or the national context (Boshier and Johnson 1974; Buikhuisen and Dijksterhuis 1971). Each of these studies reports the similar finding that, all else equal, contact with the criminal justice system leads to worse employment opportunities.

Unfortunately, the research design of Schwartz and Skolnick and others using this approach has several limitations. First, Schwartz and Skolnick's study, while clearly demonstrating the substantial effect of criminal stigma, is limited to one job type only (an unskilled hotel job). It remains uncertain how these effects generalize to the overall population of entry-level jobs. Ex-offenders face a diverse set of job openings, some of which may be more or less restricted to applicants with criminal records.

Second, correspondence tests are poorly equipped to address the issue of race. While it is possible to designate national origin using ethnic names (see, e.g., Riach and Rich 1991), it is much more difficult to clearly distinguish black and white applicants on paper.[8] Given the high rates of incarceration among blacks and the pervasive media images of black criminals, there is good reason to suspect that employers may respond differently to applicants with criminal records depending on their race (see discussion below). Prior research using correspondence tests to study the effect of criminal records, however, has not attempted to include race as a variable.

Finally, the type of application procedure used in correspondence tests—sending resumes by mail—is typically reserved for studies of administrative, clerical, and higher-level occupations. The types of job openings ex-offenders are most likely to apply for, by contrast, typically request in-person applications, and a mailed resume would therefore appear out of place.

The present study extends the work of Schwartz and Skolnick to include a more comprehensive assessment of the hiring process of ex-offenders across a full range of entry-level employment. By using an experimental audit design, this study effectively isolates the effect of a criminal record, while observing employer behavior in real-life employment settings. Fur-

---

[7] The four conditions included (1) an applicant who had been convicted and sentenced for assault, (2) an applicant who had been tried for assault but acquitted, (3) an applicant who had been tried for assault, acquitted, *and* had a letter from the judge certifying the applicant's acquittal and emphasizing the presumption of innocence, and (4) an applicant who had no criminal record. In all three criminal conditions—even with a letter from the judge—applicants were less likely to be considered by employers relative to the noncriminal control.

[8] For an excellent exception, see Bertrand and Mullainathan (2002).

American Journal of Sociology

ther, by using in-person application procedures, it becomes possible to simulate the process most often followed for entry-level positions, as well as to provide a more direct test of the effects of race on hiring outcomes.

RESEARCH QUESTIONS

There are three primary questions I seek to address with the present study. First, in discussing the main effect of a criminal record, we need to ask whether and to what extent employers use information about criminal histories to make hiring decisions. Implicit in the criticism of survey research in this area is the assumption that the signal of a criminal record is not a determining factor. Rather, employers use information about the interactional styles of applicants, or other observed characteristics—which may be correlated with criminal records—and this explains the differential outcomes we observe. In this view, a criminal record does not represent a meaningful signal to employers on its own. This study formally tests the degree to which employers use information about criminal histories in the absence of corroborating evidence. It is essential that we conclusively document this effect before making larger claims about the aggregate consequences of incarceration.

Second, this study investigates the extent to which race continues to serve as a major barrier to employment. While race has undoubtedly played a central role in shaping the employment opportunities of African-Americans over the past century, recent arguments have questioned the continuing significance of race, arguing instead that other factors—such as spatial location, soft skills, social capital, or cognitive ability—can explain most or all of the contemporary racial differentials we observe (Wilson 1987; Moss and Tilly 1996; Loury 1977; Neal and Johnson 1996). This study provides a comparison of the experiences of equally qualified black and white applicants, allowing us to assess the extent to which direct racial discrimination persists in employment interactions.

The third objective of this study is to assess whether the effect of a criminal record differs for black and white applicants. Most research investigating the differential impact of incarceration on blacks has focused on the differential *rates* of incarceration and how those rates translate into widening racial disparities. In addition to disparities in the rate of incarceration, however, it is also important to consider possible racial differences in the *effects* of incarceration. Almost none of the existing literature to date has explored this issue, and the theoretical arguments remain divided as to what we might expect.

On one hand, there is reason to believe that the signal of a criminal record should be less consequential for blacks. Research on racial stere-

Criminal Record

otypes tells us that Americans hold strong and persistent negative stereotypes about blacks, with one of the most readily invoked contemporary stereotypes relating to perceptions of violent and criminal dispositions (Smith 1991; Sniderman and Piazza 1993; Devine and Elliott 1995). If it is the case that employers view all blacks as potential criminals, they are likely to differentiate less among those with official criminal records and those without. Actual confirmation of criminal involvement then will provide only redundant information, while evidence against it will be discounted. In this case, the outcomes for all blacks should be worse, with less differentiation between those with criminal records and those without.

On the other hand, the effect of a criminal record may be worse for blacks if employers, already wary of black applicants, are more hesitant when it comes to taking risks on blacks with proven criminal tendencies. The literature on racial stereotypes also tells us that stereotypes are most likely to be activated and reinforced when a target matches on more than one dimension of the stereotype (Quillian and Pager 2002; Darley and Gross 1983; Fiske and Neuberg 1990). While employers may have learned to keep their racial attributions in check through years of heightened sensitivity around employment discrimination, when combined with knowledge of a criminal history, negative attributions are likely to intensify.

A third possibility, of course, is that a criminal record affects black and white applicants equally. The results of this audit study will help to adjudicate between these competing predictions.

THE AUDIT METHODOLOGY

The method of audit studies was pioneered in the 1970s with a series of housing audits conducted by the Department of Housing and Urban Development (Wienk et al. 1979; Hakken 1979). Nearly 20 years later, this initial model was modified and applied to the employment context by researchers at the Urban Institute (Cross et al. 1990; Turner, Fix, and Struyk 1991). The basic design of an employment audit involves sending matched pairs of individuals (called testers) to apply for real job openings in order to see whether employers respond differently to applicants on the basis of selected characteristics.

The appeal of the audit methodology lies in its ability to combine experimental methods with real-life contexts. This combination allows for greater generalizability than a lab experiment and a better grasp of the causal mechanisms than what we can normally obtain from observational data. The audit methodology is particularly valuable for those with an interest in discrimination. Typically, researchers are forced to infer dis-

American Journal of Sociology

crimination indirectly, often attributing the residual from a statistical model—which is essentially all that is not directly explained—to discrimination. This convention is rather unsatisfying to researchers who seek empirical documentation for important social processes. The audit methodology therefore provides a valuable tool for this research.[9]

Audit studies have primarily been used to study those characteristics protected under Title VII of the Civil Rights Act, such as race, gender, and age (Ayres and Siegelman 1995; Cross et al. 1990; Turner et al. 1991; Bendick, Brown, and Wall 1999; Bendick 1999; Bendick, Jackson, and Reinoso 1994; Neumark 1996). The employment of ex-offenders, of course, has not traditionally been thought of as a civil rights issue, but with the rapid expansion of the criminal justice system over the past three decades, there has been heightened concern over the growing population of men with criminal records. Recognizing the increasing importance of this issue, several states (including Wisconsin) have passed legislation expanding the fair employment regulations to protect individuals with criminal records from discrimination by employers. Employers are cautioned that crimes may only be considered if they closely relate to the specific duties required of the job, however "shocking" the crime may have been. If anything, then, this study represents a strong test of the effect of a criminal record. We might expect the effect to be larger in states where no such legal protection is in place.[10]

STUDY DESIGN

The basic design of this study involves the use of four male auditors (also called testers), two blacks and two whites. The testers were paired by race; that is, unlike in the original Urban Institute audit studies, the two black testers formed one team, and the two white testers formed the second

---

[9] While the findings from audit studies have produced some of the most convincing evidence of discrimination available from social science research, there are specific criticisms of this approach that warrant consideration. Heckman and Siegelman (1993) identify five major threats to the validity of results from audit studies: (1) problems in effective matching, (2) the use of "overqualified" testers, (3) limited sampling frame for the selection of firms and jobs to be audited, (4) experimenter effects, and (5) the ethics of audit research. For a useful discussion of these concerns, see the series of essays published in Fix and Struyk (1993). See also app. A below.

[10] Indeed, in a survey of employer attitudes, Holzer, Raphael, and Stoll (2002) found that Milwaukee employers were significantly more likely to consider hiring ex-offenders than were employers in Boston, Atlanta, Los Angeles, or Detroit, suggesting that Wisconsin may represent a best case scenario for the employment outcomes of ex-offenders relative to other major metropolitan areas (see also Holzer and Stoll 2001).

Criminal Record

team (see fig. 3).[11] The testers were 23-year-old college students from Milwaukee who were matched on the basis of physical appearance and general style of self-presentation. Objective characteristics that were not already identical between pairs—such as educational attainment and work experience—were made similar for the purpose of the applications. Within each team, one auditor was randomly assigned a "criminal record" for the first week; the pair then rotated which member presented himself as the ex-offender for each successive week of employment searches, such that each tester served in the criminal record condition for an equal number of cases. By varying which member of the pair presented himself as having a criminal record, unobserved differences within the pairs of applicants were effectively controlled. No significant differences were found for the outcomes of individual testers or by month of testing.

Job openings for entry-level positions (defined as jobs requiring no previous experience and no education greater than high school) were identified from the Sunday classified advertisement section of the *Milwaukee Journal Sentinel*.[12] In addition, a supplemental sample was drawn from *Jobnet*, a state-sponsored web site for employment listings, which was developed in connection with the W-2 Welfare-to-Work initiatives.[13]

The audit pairs were randomly assigned 15 job openings each week. The white pair and the black pair were assigned separate sets of jobs, with the same-race testers applying to the same jobs. One member of the pair applied first, with the second applying one day later (randomly varying whether the ex-offender was first or second). A total of 350 employers were audited during the course of this study: 150 by the white pair and 200 by the black pair. Additional tests were performed by the black pair because black testers received fewer callbacks on average, and there were thus fewer data points with which to draw comparisons. A larger sample

[11] The primary goal of this study was to measure the effect of a criminal record, and thus it was important for this characteristic to be measured as a within-pair effect. While it would have been ideal for all four testers to have visited the same employers, this likely would have aroused suspicion. The testers were thus divided into separate teams by race and assigned to two randomly selected sets of employers.

[12] Occupations with legal restrictions on ex-offenders were excluded from the sample. These include jobs in the health care industry, work with children and the elderly, jobs requiring the handling of firearms (i.e., security guards), and jobs in the public sector. An estimate of the collateral consequences of incarceration would also need to take account of the wide range of employment formally off-limits to individuals with prior felony convictions.

[13] Employment services like *Jobnet* have become a much more common method of finding employment in recent years, particularly for difficult-to-employ populations such as welfare recipients and ex-offenders. Likewise, a recent survey by Holzer and Stoll (2001) found that nearly half of Milwaukee employers (46%) use *Jobnet* to advertise vacancies in their companies.

American Journal of Sociology

White   Black

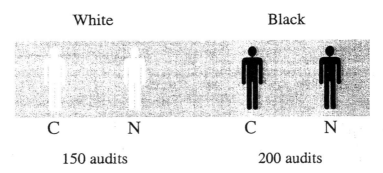

C   N   C   N

150 audits   200 audits

FIG. 3.—Audit design: "C" refers to criminal record; "N" refers to no criminal record

size enables me to calculate more precise estimates of the effects under investigation.

Immediately following the completion of each job application, testers filled out a six-page response form that coded relevant information from the test. Important variables included type of occupation, metropolitan status, wage, size of establishment, and race and sex of employer.[14] Additionally, testers wrote narratives describing the overall interaction and any comments made by employers (or included on applications) specifically related to race or criminal records.

One key feature of this audit study is that it focuses only on the first stage of the employment process. Testers visited employers, filled out applications, and proceeded as far as they could during the course of one visit. If testers were asked to interview on the spot, they did so, but they did not return to the employer for a second visit. The primary dependent variable, then, is the proportion of applications that elicited callbacks from employers. Individual voicemail boxes were set up for each tester to record employer responses. If a tester was offered the job on the spot, this was also coded as a positive response.[15] The reason I chose to focus only on this initial stage of the employment process is because this is the stage likely to be most affected by the barrier of a criminal record. In an audit study of age discrimination, for example, Bendick et al. (1999) found that 76% of the measured differential treatment occurred at this initial stage of the employment process. Given that a criminal record, like age,

[14] See Pager (2002) for a discussion of the variation across each of these dimensions.
[15] In cases where testers were offered jobs on the spot, they were instructed to tell the employer that they were still waiting to hear back from another job they had interviewed for earlier. The tester then called the employer back at the end of the same day to let him or her know that the other job had come through and he was therefore no longer available.

Criminal Record

is a highly salient characteristic, it is likely that as much, if not more, of the treatment effect will be detected at this stage.

TESTER PROFILES

In developing the tester profiles, emphasis was placed on adopting characteristics that were both numerically representative and substantively important. In the present study, the criminal record consisted of a felony drug conviction (possession with intent to distribute, cocaine) and 18 months of (served) prison time. A drug crime (as opposed to a violent or property crime) was chosen because of its prevalence, its policy salience, and its connection to racial disparities in incarceration.[16] It is important to acknowledge that the effects reported here may differ depending on the type of offense.[17]

In assigning the educational and work history of testers, I sought a compromise between representing the modal group of offenders, while also providing some room for variation in the outcome of the audits. Most audit studies of employment have created tester profiles that include some college experience, so that testers will be highly competitive applicants for entry-level jobs and so that the contrast between treatment and control group is made clear (see app. B in Cross et al. 1989). In the present study, however, postsecondary schooling experience would detract from the representativeness of the results. More than 70% of federal and nearly 90% of state prisoners have no more than a high school degree (or equivalent).

---

[16] Over the past two decades, drug crimes were the fastest growing class of offenses. In 1980, roughly one out of every 16 state inmates was incarcerated for a drug crime; by 1999, this figure had jumped to one out of every five (Bureau of Justice Statistics 2000). In federal prisons, nearly three out of every five inmates are incarcerated for a drug crime (Bureau of Justice Statistics 2001). A significant portion of this increase can be attributed to changing policies concerning drug enforcement. By 2000, every state in the country had adopted some form of truth in sentencing laws, which impose mandatory sentencing minimums for a range of offenses. These laws have been applied most frequently to drug crimes, leading to more than a fivefold rise in the number of drug arrests that result in incarceration and a doubling of the average length of sentences for drug convictions (Mauer 1999; Blumstein and Beck 1999). While the steep rise in drug enforcement has been felt across the population, this "war on drugs" has had a disproportionate impact on African-Americans. Between 1990 and 1997, the number of black inmates serving time for drug offenses increased by 60%, compared to a 46% increase in the number of whites (Bureau of Justice Statistics 1995). In 1999, 26% of all black state inmates were incarcerated for drug offenses, relative to less than half that proportion of whites (Bureau of Justice Statistics 2001).

[17] Survey results indicate that employers are substantially more averse to applicants convicted of violent crimes or property crimes relative to those convicted of drug crimes (Holzer et al. 2002; Pager 2002).

American Journal of Sociology

The education level of testers in this study, therefore, was chosen to represent the modal category of offenders (high school diploma).[18]

There is little systematic evidence concerning the work histories of inmates prior to incarceration. Overall, 77.4% of federal and 67.4% of state inmates were employed prior to incarceration (Bureau of Justice Statistics 1994). There is, however, a substantial degree of heterogeneity in the quality and consistency of work experience during this time (Pager 2001). In the present study, testers were assigned favorable work histories in that they report steady work experience in entry-level jobs and nearly continual employment (until incarceration). In the job prior to incarceration (and, for the control group, prior to the last short-term job), testers report having worked their way from an entry-level position to a supervisory role.[19]

DESIGN ISSUES

There are a number of complexities involved in the design and implementation of an audit study.[20] Apart from the standard complications of carrying out a field experiment, there were several specific dilemmas posed in the development of the current study that required substantial deliberation. First, in standard audit studies of race or gender, it is possible to construct work histories for test partners in such a way that the amount of work experience reported by each tester is identical. By contrast, the present study compares the outcome of one applicant who has spent 18 months in prison. It was therefore necessary to manipulate the work histories of both applicants so that this labor market absence did not bias the results.[21] The solution opted for here was for the ex-offender to report six months of work experience gained while in prison (preceded by 12

[18] In 1991, 49% of federal and 46.5% of state inmates had a high school degree (or equivalent; Bureau of Justice Statistics 1994).

[19] Testers reported working either as an assistant manager at a national restaurant chain or as a supervisor at a national home retail store. While it is unlikely that the modal occupational attainment for high school graduates (with or without criminal records) would be a supervisory position, this feature was added to the tester profiles in order to make them more competitive applicants. The solid job histories of these applicants should affect the results in a conservative direction, offering cues about the tester's reliability and competence, which may offset some of the negative associations with a criminal background.

[20] See app. A for a discussion of additional methodological concerns.

[21] Though time out of the labor market is in fact one component of the total impact of incarceration, this study sought to isolate the effect of criminal stigma from other potential consequences of incarceration. Again, an estimate of the total effect of incarceration would also need to take account of employment difficulties resulting from a prolonged labor market absence.

Criminal Record

months out of the labor force, representing the remainder of the total prison time). The nonoffender, on the other hand, reported graduating from high school one year later (thereby accounting for 12 months) and, concurrent to his partner's six months of prison work time, worked for a temporary agency doing a similar kind of low-skill work. Thus, the actual amount of work experience was equivalent for both testers. The effect of having the noncriminal graduate from high school one year later should impose a conservative bias, as graduating from high school late may indicate less motivation or ability.

A second major difference between audit studies of race or gender and the present study is that criminal status is not something that can be immediately discerned by the employer. The information had to be explicitly conveyed, therefore, in order for the interaction to become a "test." In most cases, the tester was given the opportunity to communicate the necessary information on the application form provided, in answer to the question "Have you ever been convicted of a crime?"[22] However, in the 26% of cases where the application form did not include a question about criminal history, it was necessary to provide an alternate means of conveying this information. In the present study, testers provided two indirect sources of information about their prior criminal involvement. First, as mentioned above, the tester in the criminal record condition reported work experience obtained while in the correctional facility. Second, the tester listed his parole officer as a reference (calls to whom were recorded by voicemail). These two pieces of evidence provided explicit clues to employers that the applicant had spent time in prison; and both of these strategies are used by real ex-offenders who seek to account for empty time by reporting work experience in prison or who wish to have their parole officer vouch for their successful rehabilitation.[23] Pilot tests with employers in a neighboring city suggested that this strategy was an effective means of conveying the criminal record condition without arousing suspicion.

STUDY CONTEXT AND DESCRIPTIVES

The fieldwork for this project took place in Milwaukee between June and December of 2001. During this time, the economic condition of the met-

---

[22] To the extent that real ex-offenders lie about their criminal record on application forms, this approach may lead to an overestimate of the effect of a criminal record. See app. A for a discussion of this issue.

[23] This approach was developed in discussion with several Milwaukee employment counselors and parole officers and is based on a composite profile of resumes belonging to real ex-offenders.

American Journal of Sociology

ropolitan area remained moderately strong, with unemployment rates ranging from a high of 5.2% in June to a low of 4% in September.[24] It is important to note that the results of this study are specific to the economic conditions of this period. It has been well-documented in previous research that the level of employment discrimination corresponds closely with the tightness of the labor market (Freeman and Rodgers 1999). Certainly the economic climate was a salient factor in the minds of these employers. During a pilot interview, for example, an employer reported that a year ago she would have had three applications for an entry-level opening; today she gets 150.[25] Another employer for a janitorial service mentioned that previously their company had been so short of staff that they had to interview virtually everyone who applied. The current conditions, by contrast, allowed them to be far more selective. Since the completion of this study, the unemployment rate has continued to rise. It is likely, therefore, that the effects reported here may understate the impact of race and a criminal record in the context of an economic recession.

As mentioned earlier, the job openings for this study were selected from the Sunday classified section of the *Milwaukee Journal Sentinel* and from *Jobnet*, a state-sponsored Internet job service. All job openings within a 25-mile radius of downtown Milwaukee were included, with 61% of the resulting sample located in the suburbs or surrounding counties, relative to only 39% in the city of Milwaukee. Because a limited boundary was covered by this project, the distribution of jobs does not accurately represent the extent to which job growth has been concentrated in wider suburban areas. According to a recent study of job growth in Milwaukee, nearly 90% of entry-level job openings were located in the outlying counties and the Milwaukee county suburbs, with only 4% of full-time openings located in the central city (Pawasarat and Quinn 2000).

The average distance from downtown in the present sample was 12 miles, with a substantial number of job openings located far from reach by public transportation. Again, testers in this study represented a best case scenario: all testers had their own reliable transportation, allowing them access to a wide range of employment opportunities. For the average entry-level job seeker, by contrast, the suburbanization of low wage work can in itself represent a major barrier to employment (Wilson 1997).

---

[24] Monthly unemployment rates followed a U-shaped pattern, with higher levels of unemployment in the first and last months of the study. Specifically: June (5.4%), July (5.2%), August (4.8%), September (4.4%), October (4.7%), November (4.9%), December (4.5%). National unemployment rates were nearly a point lower in June (4.6%), but rose above Milwaukee's unemployment rate to a high of 5.8% in December (Bureau of Labor Statistics 2002).

[25] The unemployment rate in Milwaukee had been as low as 2.7% in September of 1999 (Bureau of Labor Statistics 2002).

Criminal Record

Similar to other metropolitan labor markets, the service industry has been the fastest growing sector in Milwaukee, followed by retail and wholesale trade, and manufacturing (Pawasarat and Quinn 2000). Likewise, the sample of jobs in this study reflects similar concentrations, though quite a range of job titles were included overall (table 1).

The most common job types were for restaurant workers (18%), laborers or warehouse workers (17%), and production workers or operators (12%). Though white collar positions were less common among the entry-level listings, a fair number of customer service (11%), sales (11%), clerical (5%), and even a handful of managerial positions (2%) were included.[26]

Figure 4 presents some information on the ways employers obtain background information on applicants.[27] In this sample, roughly 75% of employers asked explicit questions on their application forms about the applicant's criminal history. Generally this was a standard question, "Have you ever been convicted of a crime? If yes, please explain."[28] Even though in most cases employers are not allowed to use criminal background information to make hiring decisions, a vast majority of employers nevertheless request the information.

A much smaller proportion of employers actually perform an official background check. In my sample, 27% of employers indicated that they would perform a background check on all applicants.[29] This figure likely represents a lower-bound estimate, given that employers are not required to disclose their intentions to do background checks. According to a national survey by Holzer (1996), 30%–40% of employers perform official background checks on applicants for noncollege jobs. The point remains,

---

[26] As noted above, this sample excludes health care workers—which represented the largest category of entry-level job openings—and other occupations with legal restrictions on ex-felons (see app. A).

[27] These are nonexclusive categories and are thus not meant to sum to 100.

[28] An overwhelming proportion of employers used generic questions about criminal backgrounds (with the only major source of variation stemming from an emphasis on all prior convictions vs. felonies only). A handful of large national companies, however, used questions that reflected a more nuanced understanding of the law. One company, e.g., instructed applicants *not* to answer the question if they were a resident of certain specified states; another asked only about prior convictions for theft and burglary, ignoring all other possible offenses.

[29] The issue of official background checks raises some concern as to the validity of the experimental condition, given that the information provided by testers can be (dis)confirmed on the basis of other sources of information available to employers. In cases where employers in this study did perform background checks on testers, the check would come back clean (none of the testers in this study actually had criminal records). It is my expectation that because employers would not expect someone to lie about *having* a criminal record, and because employers know that criminal history databases are fraught with errors, they would be inclined to believe the worst case scenario—in this case, the self-report.

American Journal of Sociology

TABLE 1
OCCUPATIONAL DISTRIBUTION

Job Title	%
Waitstaff	18
Laborer/warehouse	17
Production/operators ...	12
Service	11
Sales	11
Delivery driver	9
Cashier	7
Cook/kitchen staff	5
Clerical	5
Managerial	2

NOTE.—An excluded "other" category combines the remaining 3% of job titles.

however, that fewer than half of all employers check criminal background information through official sources.[30]

Finally, reference checks were included as an outcome in this study with the belief that, for applicants with criminal records, having former employers or a parole officer willing to vouch for the reliability and competence of the individual would be critical. Additional voicemail boxes were set up for references, such that each application could provide numbers for two functioning references. As it turns out, however, employers seemed to pay virtually no attention to references whatsoever. Over the course of the 350 audits completed, only four separate employers checked references.[31] Employers would frequently tell testers, "I'll just check your references and then give you a call," or leave messages saying, "I'm going to call your references, and then I'd like you to come in for a training [session]," and yet no calls were registered.[32]

This finding emphasizes the point that employers do not go out of their way to solicit nuanced information about applicants for entry-level jobs. Rather, it is up to the applicant to convey the important information on

[30] There is some indication that the frequency of criminal background checks has increased since September 11, 2001. First Response Security, Inc., for example, saw a 25% increase in employers conducting background checks since that time (see http://www.maine.rr.com/Around_Town/features2001/jobsinme/11_01/default.asp [last accessed March 1, 2003]).

[31] Two additional employers made calls to the number listed for the parole officer on the testers' applications. These calls, however, were not for the purpose of obtaining additional background information about the candidate. Rather, in both cases, employers had made several calls to the tester about the job opening and, reaching only his voicemail, were thus looking for an alternative way to track down the applicant.

[32] The voicemail system was set up in such a way that even hang-ups could be detected.

Criminal Record

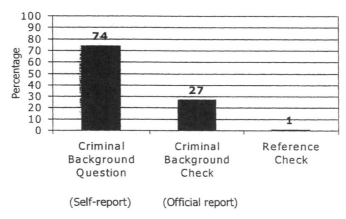

FIG. 4.—Background checks

the written application or during a brief interview. It is possible that a larger number of employers do check references at a later stage of the employment process (see Pager 2002). By this point, however, the ex-offender has already likely been weeded out of the pool under consideration.

The question now becomes, To what extent are applicants with criminal records weeded out of the process at this initial stage? To answer this question, I turn to the results of the audit study.

THE EFFECT OF A CRIMINAL RECORD FOR WHITES

I begin with an analysis of the effect of a criminal record among whites. White noncriminals can serve as our baseline in the following comparisons, representing the presumptively nonstigmatized group relative to blacks and those with criminal records. Given that all testers presented roughly identical credentials, the differences experienced among groups of testers can be attributed fully to the effects of race or criminal status.

Figure 5 shows the percentage of applications submitted by white testers that elicited callbacks from employers, by criminal status. As illustrated below, there is a large and significant effect of a criminal record, with 34% of whites without criminal records receiving callbacks, relative to only 17% of whites with criminal records. A criminal record thereby reduces the likelihood of a callback by 50% (see app. B for coefficients from the logistic regression model).

There were some fairly obvious examples documented by testers that illustrate the strong reaction among employers to the signal of a criminal

American Journal of Sociology

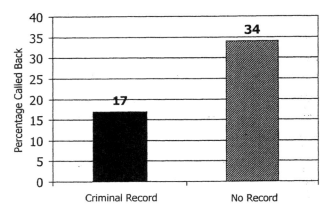

FIG. 5.—The effect of a criminal record on employment opportunities for whites. The effect of a criminal record is statistically significant $(P < .01)$.

record. In one case, a white tester in the criminal record condition went to a trucking service to apply for a job as a dispatcher. The tester was given a long application, including a complex math test, which took nearly 45 minutes to fill out. During the course of this process, there were several details about the application and the job that needed clarification, some of which involved checking with the supervisor about how to proceed. No concerns were raised about his candidacy at this stage. When the tester turned the application in, the secretary brought it into a back office for the supervisor to look over, so that an interview could perhaps be conducted. When the secretary came back out, presumably after the supervisor had a chance to look over the application more thoroughly, he was told the position had already been filled. While, of course, isolated incidents like this are not conclusive, this was not an infrequent occurrence. Often testers reported seeing employers' levels of responsiveness change dramatically once they had glanced down at the criminal record question.

Clearly, the results here demonstrate that criminal records close doors in employment situations. Many employers seem to use the information as a screening mechanism, without attempting to probe deeper into the possible context or complexities of the situation. As we can see here, in 50% of cases, employers were unwilling to consider equally qualified applicants on the basis of their criminal record.

Of course, this trend is not true among all employers, in all situations. There were, in fact, some employers who seemed to prefer workers who had been recently released from prison. One owner told a white tester in the criminal record condition that he "like[d] hiring people who ha[d] just

Criminal Record

come out of prison because they tend to be more motivated, and are more likely to be hard workers [not wanting to return to prison]." Another employer for a cleaning company attempted to dissuade the white non-criminal tester from applying because the job involved "a great deal of dirty work." The tester with the criminal record, on the other hand, was offered the job on the spot. A criminal record is thus not an obstacle in all cases, but on average, as we see above, it reduces employment opportunities substantially.

THE EFFECT OF RACE

A second major focus of this study concerns the effect of race. African-Americans continue to suffer from lower rates of employment relative to whites, but there is tremendous disagreement over the source of these disparities. The idea that race itself—apart from other correlated characteristics—continues to play a major role in shaping employment opportunities has come under question in recent years (e.g., D'Souza 1995; Steele 1991). The audit methodology is uniquely suited to address this question. While the present study design does not provide the kind of cross-race matched-pair tests that earlier audit studies of racial discrimination have used, the between-group comparisons (white pair vs. black pair) can nevertheless offer an unbiased estimate of the effect of race on employment opportunities.[33]

Figure 6 presents the percentage of callbacks received for both categories of black testers relative to those for whites. The effect of race in these findings is strikingly large. Among blacks without criminal records, only 14% received callbacks, relative to 34% of white noncriminals ($P <$

---

[33] Between-pair comparisons provide less efficient estimators, but they are nevertheless unbiased, provided that there are no systematic differences between the sample of jobs assigned to each pair or between the observed characteristics of the black and white pair (apart from race). In this study, jobs were randomly assigned to tester pairs such that no systematic differences should be observed between samples. Of course, it is impossible, even in an experimental design, to rule out the possibility that unmeasured differences between the black testers and the white testers systematically bias the results (see Heckman and Siegelman 1993). This problem is one of the key limitations of the audit design. In the present study, several attempts were made to minimize this source of bias: first, testers were chosen based on similar physical and dispositional characteristics to minimize differences from the outset; second, testers participated in an extensive training (including numerous role plays) in which they learned to approach employers in similar ways; third, testers used identical sets of resumes to ensure their comparability on objective dimensions; and finally, the fact that this study tests only the first stage of the employment process means that testers had little opportunity to engage in the kind of extensive interaction that might elicit systematic differences in treatment (based on factors other than race).

American Journal of Sociology

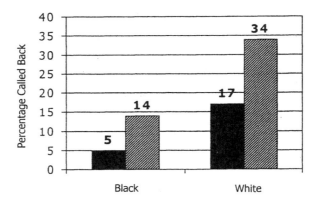

FIG. 6.—The effect of a criminal record for black and white job applicants. The main effects of race and criminal record are statically significant ($P < .01$). The interaction between the two is not significant in the full sample. Black bars represent criminal record; striped bars represent no criminal record.

.01). In fact, even whites *with* criminal records received more favorable treatment (17%) than blacks *without* criminal records (14%).[34] The rank ordering of groups in this graph is painfully revealing of employer preferences: race continues to play a dominant role in shaping employment opportunities, equal to or greater than the impact of a criminal record.

The magnitude of the race effect found here corresponds closely to those found in previous audit studies directly measuring racial discrimination. Bendick et al. (1994), for example, find that blacks were 24 percentage points less likely to receive a job offer relative to their white counterparts, a finding very close to the 20 percentage point difference (between white and black nonoffenders) found here.[35] Thus in the eight years since the last major employment audit of race was conducted, very

[34] This difference is not significantly different from zero. Given, however, that we would expect black noncriminals to be *favored* (rather than equal) relative to criminals of any race, the relevant null hypothesis should be positive rather than zero, thus generating an even larger contrast.

[35] Here, I am relying on percentage point differences in order to compare equivalent measures across studies. As I discuss below, however, I find it useful to rather calculate relative differences (ratio tests) when comparing the magnitude of an effect across two groups with different baseline rates. Unfortunately, the Bendick et al. (1994) study does not include the raw numbers in its results, and it is thus not possible to calculate comparative ratios in this case. Note also that the Bendick et al. (1994) study included an assessment of the full hiring process, from application to job offer. The fact that the racial disparities reported here (at the first stage of the employment process) closely mirror those from more comprehensive studies provides further reassurance that this design is capturing a majority of the discrimination that takes place in the hiring process.

Criminal Record

little has changed in the reaction of employers to minority applicants. Despite the many rhetorical arguments used to suggest that direct racial discrimination is no longer a major barrier to opportunity (e.g., D'Souza 1995; Steele 1991), as we can see here, employers, at least in Milwaukee, continue to use race as a major factor in hiring decisions.

RACIAL DIFFERENCES IN THE EFFECTS OF A CRIMINAL RECORD

The final question this study sought to answer was the degree to which the effect of a criminal record differs depending on the race of the applicant. Based on the results presented in figure 6, the effect of a criminal record appears more pronounced for blacks than it is for whites. While this interaction term is not statistically significant, the magnitude of the difference is nontrivial.[36] While the ratio of callbacks for nonoffenders relative to ex-offenders for whites is 2:1, this same ratio for blacks is nearly 3:1.[37] The effect of a criminal record is thus 40% larger for blacks than for whites.

This evidence is suggestive of the way in which associations between race and crime affect interpersonal evaluations. Employers, already reluctant to hire blacks, appear even more wary of blacks with proven criminal involvement. Despite the face that these testers were bright articulate college students with effective styles of self-presentation, the cursory review of entry-level applicants leaves little room for these qualities to be noticed. Instead, the employment barriers of minority status and criminal record are compounded, intensifying the stigma toward this group.

The salience of employers' sensitivity toward criminal involvement among blacks was highlighted in several interactions documented by testers. On three separate occasions, for example, black testers were asked in person (before submitting their applications) whether they had a prior

[36] This interaction between race and criminal record becomes significant when estimated among particular subsamples (namely, suburban employers and employers with whom the testers had personal contact). See Pager (2002) for a discussion of these results.

[37] Previous audit studies, focusing on one comparison only, have often relied on net differences in percentages as the primary measure of discrimination. Extending this approach to the present design, it would likewise be possible to compare the percentage point difference in treatment among white nonoffenders relative to offenders and that of blacks (a difference in differences approach). Given that the baseline rate of callbacks is substantially different for blacks and whites, however, this measure would be misleading. In an absolute sense, whites have greater opportunity overall and thus have more to lose. Taking into account this differential baseline, we see that the *relative* effect of a criminal record is in fact smaller among whites than it is among blacks.

criminal history. None of the white testers were asked about their criminal histories up front.

The strong association between race and crime in the minds of employers provides some indication that the "true effect" of a criminal record for blacks may be even larger than what is measured here. If, for example, the outcomes for black testers *without* criminal records were deflated in part because employers feared that they may nevertheless have criminal tendencies, then the contrast between blacks with and without criminal records would be suppressed. Evidence for this type of statistical discrimination can be found in the work of Bushway (1997) and Holzer, Raphael, and Stoll (2001).

DISCUSSION

There is serious disagreement among academics, policy makers, and practitioners over the extent to which contact with the criminal justice system—in itself—leads to harmful consequences for employment. The present study takes a strong stand in this debate by offering direct evidence of the causal relationship between a criminal record and employment outcomes. While survey research has produced noisy and indirect estimates of this effect, the current research design offers a direct measure of a criminal record as a mechanism producing employment disparities. Using matched pairs and an experimentally assigned criminal record, this estimate is unaffected by the problems of selection, which plague observational data. While certainly there are additional ways in which incarceration may affect employment outcomes, this finding provides conclusive evidence that mere contact with the criminal justice system, in the absence of any transformative or selective effects, severely limits subsequent employment opportunities. And while the audit study investigates employment barriers to ex-offenders from a microperspective, the implications are far-reaching. The finding that ex-offenders are only one-half to one-third as likely as nonoffenders to be considered by employers suggests that a criminal record indeed presents a major barrier to employment. With over 2 million people currently behind bars and over 12 million people with prior felony convictions, the consequences for labor market inequalities are potentially profound.

Second, the persistent effect of race on employment opportunities is painfully clear in these results. Blacks are less than half as likely to receive consideration by employers, relative to their white counterparts, and black nonoffenders fall behind even whites with prior felony convictions. The powerful effects of race thus continue to direct employment decisions in ways that contribute to persisting racial inequality. In light of these find-

Criminal Record

ings, current public opinion seems largely misinformed. According to a recent survey of residents in Los Angeles, Boston, Detroit, and Atlanta, researchers found that just over a quarter of whites believe there to be "a lot" of discrimination against blacks, compared to nearly two-thirds of black respondents (Kluegel and Bobo 2001). Over the past decade, affirmative action has come under attack across the country based on the argument that direct racial discrimination is no longer a major barrier to opportunity.[38] According to this study, however, employers, at least in Milwaukee, continue to use race as a major factor in their hiring decisions. When we combine the effects of race and criminal record, the problem grows more intense. Not only are blacks much more likely to be incarcerated than whites; based on the findings presented here, they may also be more strongly affected by the impact of a criminal record. Previous estimates of the aggregate consequences of incarceration may therefore underestimate the impact on racial disparities.

Finally, in terms of policy implications, this research has troubling conclusions. In our frenzy of locking people up, our "crime control" policies may in fact exacerbate the very conditions that lead to crime in the first place. Research consistently shows that finding quality steady employment is one of the strongest predictors of desistance from crime (Shover 1996; Sampson and Laub 1993; Uggen 2000). The fact that a criminal record severely limits employment opportunities—particularly among blacks—suggests that these individuals are left with few viable alternatives.[39]

As more and more young men enter the labor force from prison, it

---

[38] In November 1996, California voters supported Proposition 209, which outlawed affirmative action in public employment, education, and contracting. In the same year, the Fifth Circuit Court of Appeals suspended affirmative action in Texas in the case of *Hopwood vs. University of Texas Law School.*

[39] There are two primary policy recommendations implied by these results. First and foremost, the widespread use of incarceration, particularly for nonviolent drug crimes, has serious, long-term consequences for the employment problems of young men. The substitution of alternatives to incarceration, therefore, such as drug treatment programs or community supervision, may serve to better promote the well-being of individual offenders as well as to improve public safety more generally through the potential reduction of recidivism. Second, additional thought should be given to the widespread availability of criminal background information. As criminal record databases become increasingly easy to access, this information may be more often used as the basis for rejecting otherwise qualified applicants. If instead criminal history information were suppressed—except in cases that were clearly relevant to a particular kind of job assignment—ex-offenders with appropriate credentials might be better able to secure legitimate employment. While there is some indication that the absence of official criminal background information may lead to a greater incidence of statistical discrimination against blacks (see Bushway 1997; Holzer et al. 2001), the net benefits of this policy change may in fact outweigh the potential drawbacks.

American Journal of Sociology

becomes increasingly important to consider the impact of incarceration on the job prospects of those coming out. No longer a peripheral institution, the criminal justice system has become a dominant presence in the lives of young disadvantaged men, playing a key role in the sorting and stratifying of labor market opportunities. This article represents an initial attempt to specify one of the important mechanisms by which incarceration leads to poor employment outcomes. Future research is needed to expand this emphasis to other mechanisms (e.g., the transformative effects of prison on human and social capital), as well as to include other social domains affected by incarceration (e.g., housing, family formation, political participation, etc.);[40] in this way, we can move toward a more complete understanding of the collateral consequences of incarceration for social inequality.

At this point in history, it is impossible to tell whether the massive presence of incarceration in today's stratification system represents a unique anomaly of the late 20th century, or part of a larger movement toward a system of stratification based on the official certification of individual character and competence. Whether this process of negative credentialing will continue to form the basis of emerging social cleavages remains to be seen.

APPENDIX A

Methodological Concerns

Below I discuss some of the limitations of the audit methodology and ways in which findings from an experimental design may conflict with real-life contexts.

Limits to Generalizability

Reporting criminal backgrounds.—In the present study, testers in the criminal record condition were instructed to provide an affirmative answer to any question about criminal background posed on the application form or in person. Employers are thus given full information about the (fictional) criminal record of this applicant. But how often do real ex-offenders offer such complete and honest information? To the extent that ex-offenders lie about their criminal background in employment settings, the results of this study may overestimate the effect of having a criminal record. If employers do not know about an applicant's criminal record, then surely it can have no influence on their hiring decisions.

[40] For promising work in these areas, see Uggen and Manza (2002), Western and McLanahan (2000), and Travis, Solomon, and Waul (2001).

Criminal Record

Before starting this project, I conducted a number of interviews with parolees and men with criminal records. When asked how they handled application forms, the majority of these men claimed to report their criminal record up front. There are a number of reasons motivating this seemingly irrational behavior. First, most men with criminal records believe that the chances of being caught by a criminal background check are much higher than they actually are. While a majority of employers do not perform background checks on all applicants, there is the perception that this practice is widespread. Second, most men coming out of prison have a parole officer monitoring their reintegration. One of the most effective mechanisms of surveillance for parole officers is to call employers to make sure their parolees have been showing up for work. If the individual has not reported his criminal history, therefore, it may soon be revealed.[41] There is thus a strong incentive for parolees to be up front in their reporting.

A second source of information on this issue comes from interviews with employers. In a second stage of this project, the same sample of employers were interviewed about their hiring practices and experiences (see Pager 2002). During these conversations, the employers were asked to report what percentage of applicants over the past year had reported a prior conviction and, among those employers who performed official criminal background checks, what percentage were found to have criminal records. According to the employers, roughly 12% of applicants over the past year reported having a prior record on their application form. Of those employers who perform official background checks, an average of 14% of applicants were found to have criminal records. The disparity between self-reports and official records, therefore, is a minimal 2%. In fact, one manager of a national restaurant chain mentioned that sometimes applicants report *more* information than they need to. While the question on the application form only asked about felony convictions over the past year, this employer revealed that some applicants report misdemeanors or felony convictions from several years back. Whatever the reason, there seems to be evidence that far more ex-offenders report their prior convictions than "rational actor" models might predict. While surely some ex-offenders do lie on their applications, there is reason to believe this is far from the norm.

A related issue of study design concerns the reporting of criminal background information even when not solicited by the employer. Recall that roughly one-quarter of employers did not ask explicit questions on their

[41] This is particularly consequential for employees in states such as Wisconsin, where employers are not allowed to fire someone for *having* a criminal record, but they are allowed to fire him for *lying* about his record.

American Journal of Sociology

application forms about an applicant's criminal history. In order to make sure the experimental condition was known to all employers, testers also reported work experience in the correctional facility and listed their parole officers as references. While this strategy was based on a composite profile of a number of real ex-offenders, in no way does it represent a modal application procedure. In most cases, if employers do not ask about (or check) criminal histories, they will never know. It is possible that in conveying the information artificially, the level of measured discrimination is inflated. To address this concern, a direct test is possible. Figure A1 presents the callback rate for employers who did and did not solicit information about prior convictions.[42]

As is clear from this graph, employers who did not solicit information about criminal histories were much less likely to use the information in their hiring decisions. The disparity in treatment of ex-offenders relative to nonoffenders among employers who did request the information (12% vs. 35%) is more than twice as large as that among employers who did not ask (25% vs. 33%). In terms of its correspondence to the "real world," therefore, providing unsolicited information about criminal backgrounds did little to affect employer responses.

Representativeness of testers.—The testers in this study were bright, articulate college students with effective styles of self-presentation. The interpersonal skills of the average inmate, by contrast, are likely to be substantially less appealing to employers. The choice of testers in this respect was deliberate, as a means of fully separating the signal of a criminal record from other correlated attributes to which employers may also respond. It is nevertheless important to consider the extent to which these testers can be considered accurate representatives of the ex-offender experience. On one hand, it may be the case that the testers in this study represent a best case scenario. Because their interactional style does not correspond to that of a stereotypical criminal, employers may be more willing to consider them as viable candidates, despite their criminal background. In this case, the present study design would underestimate the true effect of a criminal record. On the other hand, for individuals with poor interpersonal skills, a criminal record may represent just one additional—but less consequential—handicap to the already disadvantaged candidate. If this is the case, the effect of a criminal record may be overestimated by the testers in the present study.

One approach to investigating this problem is to analyze those applications submitted with no personal contact with the employer.[43] In these

---

[42] This figure presents the results for white testers only. Similar patterns are found for black testers, not shown here.

[43] Over 75% of applications were submitted with no personal contact with the employer.

Criminal Record

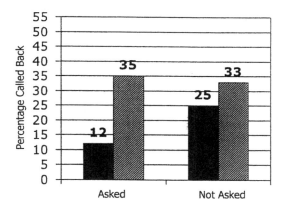

FIG. A1.—Differences by whether criminal history information was solicited: black bars represent criminal record; striped bars represent no criminal record.

cases, the interpersonal skills of the testers should have no influence on the employer's consideration of the applicant. In the analysis reported in figure A2, I find that the effect of a criminal record is even greater in the absence of personal contact, relative to the overall findings reported earlier.[44] Personal contact appears to mediate the effect of a criminal record, reducing its negative impact. These results are suggestive of the former hypothesis: the interpersonal skills of testers in the present study, to the extent that they are noticed by employers, serve to weaken the effect of a criminal record. The estimates reported here, therefore, likely represent a lower-bound estimate of the true effect of a criminal record.

The case of Milwaukee.—One key limitation of the audit study design is its concentration on a single metropolitan area. The degree to which the findings of each study can be generalized to the broader population, therefore, remains in question. In the present study, Milwaukee was chosen for having a profile common to many major American cities, with respect to population size, racial composition, and unemployment rate. There are, however, two unique features of Milwaukee that limit its representativeness of other parts of the country. First, Milwaukee is the second most segregated city in the country, implying great social distance between blacks and whites, with possible implications for the results of the audit study. If race relations are more strained in Milwaukee than in other parts of the country, then the effects of race presented in this study may be larger than what would be found in other urban areas. Second, Wisconsin had the third largest growth in incarceration rates in the coun-

---

[44] This figure presents the callback rates for white testers only.

American Journal of Sociology

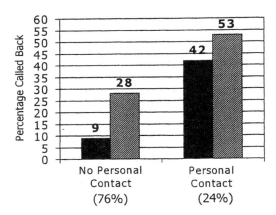

FIG. A2.—The effect of personal contact: black bars represent criminal record; striped bars represent no criminal record.

try (Gainsborough and Mauer 2000) and currently has the highest rate of incarceration for blacks in the country (Bureau of Justice Statistics 2002*b*). If the statewide incarceration rates are reflective of an especially punitive approach to crime, this could also affect the degree to which a criminal record is condemned by employers, particularly among black applicants.

Of course, the only way to directly address these issues is through replication in additional areas. With respect to the main effect of race, previous audit studies have been conducted in Washington, D.C., Chicago, and Denver, confirming the basic magnitude of the effects reported here (Bendick et al. 1994; Turner et al. 1991; Culp and Dunson 1986). Likewise, a recent correspondence of the effects of race on a more restrictive sample of occupations in Boston and Chicago produced strikingly similar estimates (Bertrand and Mullainathan 2002). These results, therefore, provide some indication that Milwaukee is not a major outlier in its level of racial discrimination in hiring.

In the case of the criminal record effect, only future studies can confirm or contradict the results presented here. As the first study of its kind, it is impossible to assess the degree to which these findings will generalize to other cities. Looking to existing survey research, however, we can gain some leverage on this issue. According to a recent survey conducted by Holzer and Stoll (2001), employers in Milwaukee reported substantially greater openness to considering applicants with criminal records relative to their counterparts in Chicago, Los Angeles, and Cleveland. If these self-reports accurately reflect employers' relative hiring tendencies, then we would expect the results of this audit study to provide conservative

Criminal Record

estimates of the barriers to employment faced by ex-offenders in other metropolitan areas.

Sample restrictions.—The present study was intended to assess the effect of a criminal record on employment in entry-level jobs. In order to obtain a sample of such positions for use in this study, however, it was necessary to impose certain sample restrictions on the categories of entry-level employment to be included. The degree to which these restrictions affect the generalizability of these findings to real employment searches therefore warrants careful consideration.

Virtually all employment audits have relied on samples of job openings identified through ads in metropolitan newspapers. Though want ads provide an easily accessible listing of job vacancies, research on actual job search behavior demonstrates that only a minority of jobs are found through this source. Holzer (1988) estimates that roughly 20%–25% of search time is spent on contacts generated by newspaper advertising; friends and relatives and direct contact of firms by applicants represent a much more common sources of new employment.

Though it would preferable to include job vacancies derived from representative sources, it is difficult if not impossible to map the network of informal contacts that lead to most job opportunities. Instead, researchers have relied upon sources that allow for systematic and consistent sampling schemes, despite the reduction in representativeness. Following previous research, the present study relies upon a random sample of job openings from advertised sources (the *Milwaukee Journal Sentinel* and *Jobnet*). Fortunately, there is compelling research to suggest that the restricted sample provides a more conservative estimate of racial discrimination. Firms who wish to discriminate, it is argued, are more likely to advertise job openings through more restrictive channels than the metropolitan newspaper, such as through referrals, employment agencies, or more selective publications (Fix and Struyk 1993, p. 32). Indeed, this argument is indirectly supported by research showing that minorities are more successful in job searches generated by general newspaper ads than through other means (Holzer 1987). Further, pilot audits conducted by the Fair Employment Council in Washington, D.C., also indicate lower rates of discrimination against minorities in jobs advertised in metropolitan newspapers than those advertised in suburban newspapers or through employment agencies (Bendick et al. 1991, 1994).

In the case of ex-offenders, personal networks may represent a more important source of employment. Though there have been few systematic investigations of the search methods of individuals coming out of prison, small-scale case studies indicate that personal referrals can be extremely important for the job placement of this population (Nelson, Deess, and Allen 1999; Sullivan 1989). Because of the pervasive discrimination faced

American Journal of Sociology

by ex-offenders in the labor market as a whole, personal networks can direct individuals to specific employers who are willing to hire applicants with criminal records. In this case, ex-offenders may be likely to queue for lower-quality jobs that accept applicants with criminal histories rather than applying for the wider range of (higher-quality) employment among which they are likely to face more severe discrimination. If this is the case, incarceration effects would be more likely to show up in estimates of earnings and job security, rather than employment probabilities as measured here (see Western 2002). Future research mapping the search patterns of ex-offenders would provide useful information with which to evaluate the types of jobs in which ex-offenders are most at risk of discrimination.

It is important to note, however, that the importance of social networks for ex-offenders seeking employment may differ across racial groups. Sullivan (1989), for example, reports that, among juvenile delinquents, whites and Hispanics were readily placed in employment through relatives or extended networks following release from incarceration; blacks, by contrast, benefited much less from social networks in finding work. These informal methods of job search behavior, therefore, may in fact result in greater evidence of racial disparities in employment following incarceration than what is reported here.

Prior to sampling, the following additional restrictions were imposed (for reasons discussed below): not hiring through employment agency, no more than high school degree required, no public sector positions, no health care positions, no jobs related to the care of children or the elderly, and no jobs whose announcements explicit stated security clearance required.

The restrictions with the largest effect on my sample are those related to employment agencies and the health care industry. Employment agencies are becoming increasingly dominant in regulating the market for entry-level labor. Between 35% and 40% of jobs advertised through *Jobnet* (the Internet employment bulletin) were temporary to permanent positions through an employment agency. There exists quite a bit of literature on the quality of temporary employment and the treatment of workers hired through employment agencies (Henson 1996). An audit of employment agencies, however, warrants an independent study, given the very different hiring processes operating in such establishments.

The elimination of health care positions from my sample was due to the extensive legal restrictions in this sector barring the employment of individuals with criminal records.[45] This sample constraint eliminated a

[45] Such restrictions also apply to occupations involving care for children or the elderly and many public sector positions.

Criminal Record

huge number of jobs otherwise available to entry-level job seekers without criminal records. The health services sector represents 8.3% of total employment in the Milwaukee region (COWS 1996), and a much larger share of new employment. Hospitals alone were the fourth largest employers in Milwaukee in 1995 (COWS 1996). These are some of the highest-wage jobs in the service sector (COWS 1996).

Other occupations were likewise eliminated from the sample, not because of blanket legal restrictions, but because their job announcements explicitly stated that applicants must pass a criminal background check or that security clearance was required. While it is not clear that blanket exclusion of all criminal convictions in these cases was defensible under the law, the employers' policies were made explicit. While one cannot always assume that stated policies will be enforced, in the case of criminal records, these jobs are unlikely to demonstrate much variance.

A true estimate of the collateral consequences of a criminal record on employment opportunities would take into account the large number of jobs formally closed to ex-offenders (rather than just those demonstrating a preference for or against applicants with criminal records). The estimates produced from the audits, therefore, represent only part of the total effect of a criminal record of the likelihood of finding employment.

Experimenter Effects

One potential weakness of the audit study methodology is that the expectations or behaviors of testers can influence the outcome of results in nonrandom ways. In the course of this research, it became apparent that testers may in fact (unconsciously) behave differently depending on the experimental condition. With respect to the criminal record condition, several testers commented that they felt irrationally bad about themselves when presenting themselves as ex-offenders. If it is the case that these feelings made them more self-conscious or more reticent or nervous when speaking with employers, then this behavior in itself may lead to spurious outcomes. These psychological reactions may be even more pronounced in the case of black testers. One tester early on reported feelings of discouragement and frustration that he had received very few responses from employers. As a successful, bright college student, the change in status to a young black criminal was extreme, and the difference in treatment he received seemed to take a toll. Fortunately, after gaining more experience with the project, this tester (and others) seemed to feel more comfortable in their interactions and better able to perform in their assigned roles.

It is certainly the case that the psychological experiences of testers can influence the outcome of audit studies in nontrivial ways. It is unlikely, however, that these internal dynamics are the driving force behind the

American Journal of Sociology

results reported from this study. As noted earlier, in a vast majority of cases, testers had little if any contact with employers. Given that a majority of callbacks were made on the basis of applications submitted with little or no personal contact, the internal disposition of the tester is unlikely to exert much influence. The finding that personal contact actually served to weaken the effect of a criminal record (see fig. A2 above) provides further evidence that the friendly, appealing qualities of the testers were apparent to employers, even among applicants in the criminal record condition.

APPENDIX B

TABLE B1
LOGISTIC REGRESSION OF THE EFFECTS OF CRIMINAL RECORD
AND RACE ON APPLICANTS' LIKELIHOOD OF RECEIVING A
CALLBACK

	Coefficient	Robust SE
Criminal record	−.99	.24***
Black	−1.25	.28***
Criminal record × black ...	−.29	.38

NOTE.—SEs are corrected for clustering on employer ID in order to account for the fact that these data contain two records per employer (i.e., criminal record versus no criminal record). This model also controls for location (city vs. suburb) and contact with the employer, variables that mediate the relationship between race, crime, and employer responses.
*** $P < .001$.

REFERENCES

Ayres, Ian, and Peter Siegelman. 1995. "Race and Gender Discrimination in Bargaining for a New Car." *American Economic Review* 85 (3): 304–21.
Barclay, Gordon, Cynthia Tavares, and Arsalaan Siddique. 2001. "International Comparisons of Criminal Justice Statistics, 1999." U.K. Home Office for Statistical Research. London.
Becker, Gary. 1975. *Human Capital.* New York: Columbia University Press.
Bendick, Marc, Jr. 1999. "Adding Testing to the Nation's Portfolio of Information on Employment Testing." Pp. 47–68 in *A National Report Card on Discimrination in America: The Role of Testing*, edited by Michael Fix and Margery Turner. Washington, D.C.: Urban Institute.
Bendick, Marc, Jr., Lauren Brown, and Kennington Wall. 1999. "No Foot in the Door: An Experimental Study of Employment Discrimination." *Journal of Aging and Social Policy* 10 (4): 5–23.
Bendick, Marc, Jr., Charles Jackson, and Victor Reinoso. 1994. "Measuring Employment Discrimination through Controlled Experiments." *Review of Black Political Economy* 23:25–48.
Bendick, Marc, Jr., Charles Jackson, Victor Reinoso, and Laura Hodges. 1991. "Discrimination against Latino Job Applicants: A Controlled Experiment." *Human Resource Management* 30:469–84.

Criminal Record

Bertrand, Marianne, and Sendhil Mullainathan. 2002. "Are Emily and Brendan More Employable than Lakisha and Jamal? A Field Experiment on Labor Market Discrimination." Working paper, University of Chicago.

Blumstein, Alfred, and Allen J. Beck. 1999. "Population Growth in U.S. Prisons, 1980–1996." Pp. 17–62 in *Prisons: Crime and Justice: A Review of Research*, vol. 26. Edited by Michael Tonry and J. Petersilia. Chicago: University of Chicago Press.

Boshier, R., and Derek Johnson. 1974. "Does Conviction Affect Employment Opportunities?" *British Journal of Criminology* 14:264–68.

Buikhuisen, W., and F. P. H. Dijksterhuis. 1971. "Delinquency and Stigmatisation." *British Journal of Criminology* 11:185–87.

Bureau of Justice Statistics. 1994. *Comparing Federal and State Prison Inmates 1991*, by Caroline Harlow. Washington, D.C.: NCJ-145864.

———. 1995. *Prisoners in 1994*, by Allen J. Beck and Darrell K. Gilliard. Special report. Washington, D.C.: Government Printing Office.

———. 1997. *Lifetime Likelihood of Going to State or Federal Prison*, by Thomas P. Bonczar and Allen J. Beck. Special report, March. Washington, D.C.

———. 2000. Bulletin. *Key Facts at a Glance: Number of Persons in Custody of State Correctional Authorities by Most Serious Offense 1980–99*. Washington, D.C.: Government Printing Office.

———. 2001. *Prisoners in 2000*, by Allen J. Beck and Paige M. Harrison. August. Bulletin. Washington, D.C.: NCJ 188207.

———. 2002a. *Sourcebook of Criminal Justice Statistics*. Last accessed March 1, 2003. Available http://www.albany.edu/sourcebook/

———. 2002b. Bulletin. *Prison and Jail Inmates at Midyear 2001*, by Allen J. Beck and Paige M. Harrison. August. Washington, D.C.: NCJ 191702.

Bureau of Labor Statistics. 2002. "Local Area Unemployment Statistics." Last accessed March 1, 2003. http://www.blr.gov/lan/home.htm

Bushway, Shawn D. 1997. "Labor Market Effects of Permitting Employer Access to Criminal History Records." Working paper. University of Maryland, Department of Criminology.

———. 1998. "The Impact of an Arrest on the Job Stability of Young White American Men." *Journal of Research in Crime and Delinquency* 35 (4): 454–79.

Cohen, Dov, and Richard E. Nisbett. 1997. "Field Experiments Examining the Culture of Honor: The Role of Institutions in Perpetuating Norms about Violence." *Personality and Social Psychology Bulletin* 23 (11): 1188–99.

COWS (Center on Wisconsin Strategy). 1996. "Milwaukee Area Regional Economic Analysis." Unpublished report. University of Wisconsin—Madison.

Cross, Harry, Genevieve Kenney, Jane Mell, and Wendy Zimmerman. 1989. *Differential Treatment of Hispanic and Anglo Job Seekers: Hiring Practices in Two Cities*. Washington, D.C.: Urban Institute Press.

———. 1990. *Employer Hiring Practices: Differential Treatment of Hispanic and Anglo Job Seekers*. Washington, D.C.: Urban Institute Press.

Culp, Jerome, and Bruce Dunson. 1986. "Brothers of a Different Color: A Preliminary Look at Employer Treatment of White and Black Youth." Pp. 233–60 in *The Black Youth Employment Crisis*, edited by Freeman, Richard B., and Harry J. Holzer. Chicago: University of Chicago Press for National Bureau of Economic Research.

Dale, Mitchell. 1976. "Barriers to the Rehabilitation of Ex-Offenders." *Crime and Delinquency* 22:322–37.

Darley, J. M., and P. H. Gross. 1983. "A Hypothesis-Confirming Bias in Labeling Effects." *Journal of Personality and Social Psychology* 44:20–33.

Devine, P. G., and A. J. Elliot. 1995. "Are Racial Stereotypes Really Fading? The Princeton Trilogy Revisited." *Personality and Social Psychology Bulletin* 21 (11): 1139–50.

American Journal of Sociology

D'Souza, Dinesh. 1995. *The End of Racism: Principles for a Multiracial Society.* New York: Free Press.

Finn, R. H., and P. A. Fontaine. 1985. "The Association between Selected Characteristics and Perceived Employability of Offenders." *Criminal Justice and Behavior* 12:353–65.

Fiske, Susan, and Steven Neuberg. 1990. "A Continuum of Impression Formation, from Category-Based to Individuating Processes." Pp. 1–63 in *Advances in Experimental Social Psychology*, vol. 23. Edited by Mark Zanna. New York: Academic Press.

Fix, Michael, and Raymond J. Struyk, eds. 1993. *Clear and Convincing Evidence: Measurement of Discrimination in America.* Washington, D.C.: Urban Institute Press.

Freeman, Richard B. 1987. "The Relation of Criminal Activity to Black Youth Employment." *Review of Black Political Economy* 16 (1–2): 99–107.

———. 1991. "Crime and the Employment Problems of Disadvantaged Youths." NBER Working Paper no. 3875. Cambridge, Mass.: National Bureau of Economic Research.

———. 1994. "Crime and the Job Market." NBER Working Paper no. 4910. Cambridge, Mass.: National Bureau of Economic Research.

Freeman, Richard B., and Harry J. Holzer, eds. 1986. *The Black Youth Employment Crisis.* Chicago: University of Chicago Press for National Bureau of Economic Research.

Freeman, Richard B., and William M. Rodgers III. 1999. "Area Economic Conditions and the Labor Market Outcomes of Young Men in the 1990s Expansion." NBER Working Paper no. 7073. Cambridge, Mass.: National Bureau of Economic Research.

Gainsborough, Jenni, and Marc Mauer. 2000. *Diminishing Returns: Crime and Incarceration in the 1990s.* Washington, D.C.: The Sentencing Project.

Grogger, Jeffrey. 1992. "Arrests, Persistent Youth Joblessness, and Black/White Employment Differentials." *Review of Economics and Statistics* 74:100–106.

———. 1995. "The Effect of Arrests on the Employment and Earnings of Young Men." *Quarterly Journal of Economics* 110:51–72.

Hagan, John. 1993. "The Social Embeddedness of Crime and Unemployment." *Criminology* 31 (4): 465–91.

Hakken, Jon. 1979. *Discrimination against Chicanos in the Dallas Rental Housing Market: An Experimental Extension of the Housing Market Practices Survey.* Washington, D.C.: U.S. Department of Housing and Urban Development.

Heckman, James, Hidehiko Ichimura, Jeffrey Smith, and Petra Todd. 1998. "Characterizing Selection Bias Using Experimental Data." *Econometrica* 6:1017–99.

Heckman, James, and Peter Seligman. 1993. "The Urban Institute Audit Studies: Their Methods and Findings." Pp. 187–258 in *Clear and Convincing Evidence: Measurement of Discrimination in America*, edited by Michael Fix and Raymond J. Struyk. Washington, D.C.: Urban Institute Press.

Henson, Kevin D. 1996. *Just a Temp.* Philadelphia: Temple University Press.

Holzer, Harry. 1987. "Informal Job Search and Black Youth Unemployment." *American Economic Review* 77 (3): 446–52.

———. 1988. "Search Methods Used by Unemployed Youth." *Journal of Labor Economics* 6 (1): 1–20.

———. 1996. *What Employers Want: Job Prospects for Less-Educated Workers.* New York: Russell Sage Foundation.

Holzer, Harry, Steven Raphael, and Michael Stoll. 2001. "Perceived Criminality, Criminal Background Checks and the Racial Hiring Practices of Employers." Discussion Paper no. 1254–02. University of Wisconsin—Madison, Institute for Research on Poverty.

———. 2002. "Employer Demand for Ex-Offenders: Recent Evidence from Los

Criminal Record

Angeles." Paper presented at the Association of Public Policy and Management Conference, Dallas.

Holzer, Harry, and Michael Stoll. 2001. *Employers and Welfare Recipients: The Effects of Welfare Reform in the Workplace*. San Francisco: Public Policy Institute of California.

Kling, Jeffrey. 1999. "The Effect of Prison Sentence Length on the Subsequent Employment and Earnings of Criminal Defendants." Discussion Paper no. 208. Princeton University, Woodrow Wilson School.

Kluegel, James, and Lawrence Bobo. 2001. "Perceived Group Discrimination and Policy Attitudes: The Sources and Consequences of the Race and Gender Gaps." Pp. 163–216 in *Urban Inequality: Evidence from Four Cities*, edited by Alice O'Connor, Chris Tilly, and Lawrence D. Bobo. New York: Russell Sage Foundation.

Kornfeld, Robert, and Howard S. Bloom. 1999. "Measuring Program Impacts on Earnings and Employment: Do Unemployment Insurance Wage Reports from Employers Agree with Surveys of Individuals?" *Journal of Labor Economics* 17 (1): 168–97.

Loury, Glenn C. 1977. "A Dynamic Theory of Racial Income Differences." Pp. 153–86 in *Women, Minorities, and Employment Discrimination*, edited by P. A. Wallace and A. M. La Mond. Lexington, Mass.: Heath.

Mauer, Marc. 1999. *Race to Incarcerate*. New York: New Press.

Moss, Philip, and Chris Tilly. 1996. "'Soft Sills' and Race: An Investigation of Black Men's Employment Problems." *Work and Occupations* 23 (3): 256–76.

Nagin, Daniel, and Joel Waldfogel. 1993. "The Effect of Conviction on Income through the Life Cycle." NBER Working Paper no. 4551. Cambridge, Mass.: National Bureau of Economic Research.

Neal, Derek, and William Johnson. 1996. "The Role of Premarket Factors in Black-White Wage Differences." *Journal of Political Economy* 104 (5): 869–95.

Needels, Karen E. 1996. "Go Directly to Jail and Do Not Collect? A Long-Term Study of Recidivism, Employment, and Earnings Patterns among Prison Releases." *Journal of Research in Crime and Delinquency* 33:471–96.

Nelson, Marta, Perry Deess, and Charlotte Allen. 1999. *The First Month Out: Post-Incarceration Experiences in New York City*. New York: Vera Institute of Justice.

Neumark, David. 1996. "Sex Discrimination in Restaurant Hiring: An Audit Study." *Quarterly Journal of Economics* 3 (3): 915–41.

Pager, Devah. 2001. "Criminal Careers: The Consequences of Incarceration for Occupational Attainment." Paper presented at the annual meetings of the American Sociological Association, Anaheim, August.

———. 2002. "The Mark of a Criminal Record." Doctoral dissertation. Department of Sociology, University of Wisconsin—Madison.

Parenti, Christian. 1999. *Lockdown America: Police and Prisons in the Age of Crisis*. New York: Verso.

Pawasarat, John, and Lois M. Quinn. 2000. "Survey of Job Openings in the Milwaukee Metropolitan Area: Week of May 15, 2000." University of Wisconsin—Milwaukee, Employment and Training Institute, University Outreach.

Pettit, Becky, and Bruce Western. 2001. "Inequality in Lifetime Risks of Imprisonment." Paper presented at the annual meetings of the American Sociological Association. Anaheim, August.

Quillian, Lincoln, and Devah Pager. 2002. "Black Neighbors, Higher Crime? The Role of Racial Stereotypes in Evaluations of Neighborhood Crime." *American Journal of Sociology* 107 (3): 717–67.

Riach, Peter B., and Judith Rich. 1991. "Measuring Discrimination by Direct Experimentation Methods: Seeking Gunsmoke." *Journal of Post-Keynesian Economics* 14 (2): 143–50.

American Journal of Sociology

Rubin, Donald B. 1990. "Formal Modes of Statistical Inference for Causal Effects." *Journal of Statistical Planning and Inference* 25:279–92.

Sampson, Robert J., and John H. Laub. 1993. *Crime in the Making: Pathways and Turning Points through Life.* Cambridge, Mass.: Harvard University Press.

Schwartz, Richard, and Jerome Skolnick. 1962. "Two Studies of Legal Stigma." *Social Problems* 10:133–42.

Shover, Neil. 1996. *Great Pretenders: Pursuits and Careers of Presistent Thieves.* Boulder, Colo.: Westview.

Slevin, Peter. 2000. "Life after Prison: Lack of Services Has High Price." *Washington Post,* April 24.

Smith, Tom W. 1991. *What Americans Say about Jews.* New York: American Jewish Committee.

Sniderman, Paul M., and Thomas Piazza. 1993. *The Scar of Race.* Cambridge, Mass.: Harvard University Press.

Steele, Shelby. 1991. *The Content of Our Character: A New Vision of Race in America.* New York: Harper Perennial.

Sullivan, Mercer L. 1989. *"Getting Paid": Youth Crime and Work in the Inner City.* Ithaca, N.Y.: Cornell University Press.

Travis, Jeremy, Amy Solomon, and Michelle Waul. 2001. *From Prison to Home: The Dimensions and Consequences of Prisoner Reentry.* Washington D.C.: Urban Institute Press.

Turner, Margery, Michael Fix, and Raymond Struyk. 1991. *Opportunities Denied, Opportunities Diminished: Racial Discrimination in Hiring.* Washington, D.C.: Urban Institute Press.

Uggen, Christopher. 2000. "Work as a Turning Point in the Life Course of Criminals: A Duration Model of Age, Employment, and Recidivism." *American Sociological Review* 65 (4): 529–46.

Uggen, Christopher, and Jeff Manza. 2002. "Democratic Contradiction? The Political Consequences of Felon Disfranchisement in the United States." *American Sociological Review* 67 (6): 777–803.

Uggen, Christopher, Melissa Thompson, and Jeff Manza. 2000. "Crime, Class, and Reintegration: The Socioeconomic, Familial, and Civic Lives of Offenders." Paper presented at the American Society of Criminology meetings, San Francisco, November 18.

Wacquant, Loïc. 2000. "Deadly Symbiosis: When Ghetto and Prison Meet and Mesh." *Punishment and Society* 3 (1): 95–134.

Waldfogel, J. 1994. "Does Conviction Have a Persistent Effect on Income and Employment?" *International Review of Law and Economics,* March.

Western, Bruce. 2002. "The Impact of Incarceration on Wage Mobility and Inequality." *American Sociological Review* 67 (4): 526–46.

Western, Bruce, and Katherine Beckett. 1999. "How Unregulated is the U.S. Labor Market? The Penal System as a Labor Market Institution." *American Journal of Sociology* 104 (4): 1030–60.

Western, Bruce, and Sara McLanahan. 2000. "Fathers behind Bars: The Impact of Incarceration on Family Formation." *Contemporary Perspective in Family Research* 2:309–24.

Western, Bruce, and Becky Pettit. 1999. "Black-White Earnings Inquality, Employment Rates, and Incarceration." Working Paper no. 150. New York: Russell Sage Foundation.

Wienk, Ronald E., Clifford E. Reid, John C. Simonson, and Frederick J. Eggers. 1979. *Measuring Discrimination in American Housing Markets: The Housing Market Practices Survey.* Washington, D.C.: U.S. Department of Housing and Urban Development.

Criminal Record

Wilson, William Julius. 1987. *The Truly Disadvantaged: The Inner City, the Underclass, and Public Policy.* Chicago: University of Chicago Press.

———. 1997. *When Work Disappears: The World of the New Urban Poor.* New York: Vintage Books.

Winship, Christopher, and Stephen L. Morgan. 1999. "The Estimation of Causal Effects from Observational Data." *Annual Review of Sociology* 25:659–706.

[14]

COERCIVE MOBILITY AND CRIME: A PRELIMINARY EXAMINATION OF CONCENTRATED INCARCERATION AND SOCIAL DISORGANIZATION*

TODD R. CLEAR**
City University of New York

DINA R. ROSE***
Women's Prison Association

ELIN WARING****
City University of New York

KRISTEN SCULLY*****
Florida State University

This article explores how incarceration affects crime rates at the neighborhood level. Incarceration is analyzed as a form of residential mobility that

---

* This research was supported by a grant from the Center for Crime, Communities, and Culture of the Open Society Institute. The opinions, findings, and conclusions, or recommendations expressed herein are those of the authors and do not necessarily represent the official position of the Open Society Institute. The authors thank Ken Land, Gary Kleck, and Darren Sherkat for their comments on an earlier version of the article. A previous version of this article was presented at the annual meeting of the Southern Sociological Society, April 8-11, 1999. Address all correspondence to Todd R. Clear, Doctoral Studies, John Jay College of Criminal Justice, 899 10th Avenue, New York, NY 10019; e-mail: tclear@jjay.cuny.edu.

** Todd R. Clear is Distinguished Professor, John Jay College of Criminal Justice, City University of New York. He is currently involved in studies of religion and crime, the criminological implications of "place," and the concept of "community justice," including a recent book, *Community Justice* (with Eric Cadora). He serves as editor of *Criminology & Public Policy*, published by the American Society of Criminology.

*** Dina R. Rose is director of research at the Women's Prison Association. She has a B.S. in journalism from Boston University and a M.A. and PhD in sociology from Duke University. Her research interests include the impact of crime and criminal justice on communities, the concept of parochial social control and social networks, and policy considerations of women and families in criminal justice. Her articles have appeared in *Criminology, Crime and Delinquency, Sociological Forum*, and other journals.

**** Elin Waring is associate professor of sociology and social work at Lehman College, City University of New York. Her research focuses on co-offending, white-collar crime, and organized crime. She has recently edited (with David Weisburd) *Crime and Social Organization*, Vol. 10 *of Advances in Criminological Theory*. Her book, *White-Collar Crime and Criminal Careers* (with David Weisburd) was published in 2001 by Cambridge University Press.

***** Kristen Scully is a doctoral candidate in the department of Criminology and Criminal Justice at Florida State University. Her current research focuses on attitudes toward the justice system and how both neighborhood residence and experience with the justice system influence those attitudes.

may damage local network structures and undermine informal control. Ge-ocoded data are combined with census data, data on incarceration convic-tions and releases, and crime data for Tallahassee, Florida. The results show a positive relationship between the rate of releases one year and the community's crime rates the following year. They also show that low rates of admissions to prison have an uncertain impact on crime rates, moderate rates reduce crime, and higher rates increase crime. Implications for crimi-nal justice policies are discussed.

Theorists working in the social disorganization tradition have long focused on three ecological predictors of crime: poverty, ethnic heterogeneity, and residential mobility (Shaw & McKay, 1942). Contemporary researchers have expanded that list to examine the impact of additional factors, such as single-parent families, struc-tural density, and urbanization (Bursik, 1986, 1988; Bursik & Grasmick, 1993; Sampson, 1985; Sampson & Groves 1989). These forces are thought to promote crime through the way they increase social disorganization, reduce social integration, increase isolation and anonymity, and reduce informal social control. Advances in so-cial disorganization theory have helped to update our understand-ing of the ways in which urban areas have changed since the first exposition of these ideas in the 1940s. Other studies (Bursik & Grasmick 1993; Morenoff, Sampson, & Raudenbush, 2001; Roun-tree & Warner, 1999; Sampson & Groves, 1989; Sampson, Raudenbush, & Earles, 1997) have attempted to specify the mediat-ing factors of disorganization. Taken as a body, social disorganiza-tion theory has an extraordinarily rich conceptual and empirical heritage, and a broad literature has developed regarding the sources of social disorganization.

Rose and Clear (1998a) hypothesized that high concentrations of incarceration may be another disorganizing factor. They put forth the idea that incarceration, especially at high rates, could dis-rupt social networks by damaging familial, economic, and political sources of informal social control. The consequence of this damage, they theorized, would be more, not less, crime. From their review of the literature, Rose and Clear first showed how high rates of incar-ceration may be expected to damage fragile social networks that constitute the basis for informal social control. They also argued that prison releasees, many of whom have deviant orientations, fur-ther exacerbate problems of normative heterogeneity. Using Bursik and Grasmick's (1993) systemic reformulation of social disorganiza-tion theory as a framework, Rose and Clear described a nonrecur-sive model of the effects of incarceration. Essentially, their hypothesis defined incarceration as "coercive mobility," in which the effects of formal social-control efforts at Time 1 produce neighborhood dynamics at Time 2 that are similar to those resulting from the voluntary mobility typically modeled by theorists of social disorganization.

Until recently, theorists of social disorganization have not regarded the effects of public policies as important considerations for their models of public safety. Public policies were generally thought of as responses to crime, not antecedents of it, so these theorists tended to concentrate on informal social control, rather than formal social control.

It is clear from a string of studies that informal social control has important impacts on crime rates at the neighborhood level. To illustrate, Bellair (1997) analyzed the influence of the frequency of neighbors' interactions on crime in 60 urban neighborhoods, finding that "getting together with neighbors" had a negative impact on burglary, auto theft, and robbery. A related analysis (Bellair, 2000) found that neighbors' "informal" surveillance of one another's property had a negative affect on some types of crime, but not on others. Markowitz, Bellair, Liska, and Liu's (2001) analysis of the British Crime Survey found that decreases in neighborhood cohesion resulted in greater crime and disorder. The preponderance of evidence indicates that informal social control has engendered a new theoretical specification of neighborhood-level crime, "collective efficacy," positing that social cohesion and informal social control reduce crime (Sampson et al., 1997). Data from Chicago suggest that informal social controls—voluntary associations, kin/friend networks, and local organizations—can be the source of greater collective efficacy that, in turn, reduces crime (Morenoff et al., 2001).

In their important clarification of the systemic nature of social ecological models, however, Bursik and Grasmick (1993) noted that social disorganization theory may be specified as a theory both of formal and informal social control. They pointed out that mechanisms of social disorganization blunt the capacities of both formal and informal social control and thereby contribute to the occurrence of crime. There is evidence to support the converse of this argument; Velez (2001) showed that poor neighborhoods with strong ties to local government and good relations with the police suffer less crime than do those that lack that access to resources of public social control. But the relationship between formal social control and crime at the neighborhood level has not been the subject of much previous study.

Rose and Clear's (1998a) hypothesis is that incarceration as a formal social control can, after a certain level or "tipping point," become a source of social disorganization. This article provides a partial test of their hypothesis. In our study, we used two measures of incarceration (admission rates and release rates) while controlling for the traditional variables of social disorganization to test whether incarceration, conceptualized as "coercive mobility," leads to higher levels of crime. Although the model that Rose and Clear proposed is a nonrecursive one, in which there is a feedback loop between policy responses to crime and the ecological factors that lead to crime, we tested a recursive model, in which we investigated the impact of a neighborhood's incarceration rates in one year on crime rates the following year. Nonetheless, by incorporating a variable (incarceration) typically thought of as a response to crime as an independent variable modeled to influence crime, this study is conceptually consistent with their work.

INCARCERATION, MOBILITY, AND CRIME

A central tenet of social disorganization theory is that mobility is a powerful ecological-level criminogenic factor. High rates of residential mobility are thought to contribute to crime in three different ways. First, mobility produces residential areas in which neighbors are isolated from one another and therefore are constrained from engaging in the collective action that undergirds self-regulation (Sampson, 1991). Second, a residential area that has high rates of newcomers will have a low degree of social integration among residents, contributing to the anonymity that impedes social cohesion (Crutchfield, 1989; Crutchfield, Geerken, & Gove, 1982). Third, mobility reduces the sense of commitment to a neighborhood that makes those who live there feel they have a stake in collective action to achieve shared aims—an atmosphere of anonymity impedes informal social control (Warner & Pierce, 1993). Thus, an area's level of mobility is an important feature of social stability, a factor that influences the link between neighborhood disorder and crime (Skogan, 1990) and the community's capacity for collective efficacy (Sampson & Raudenbush 1999; Sampson et al., 1997).

These various conceptualizations of mobility present it as a source of instability in local neighborhood life. The perspective is intuitively appealing. In a place where one's neighbors turn over rapidly, there is less incentive to get to know them and more disincentive to rely on them in times of need. When one lives in an area with a sense of being there only temporarily, one has little reason to join local social groups or develop interdependent ties to others. The friendships among people become strained by transience, and the capacity of parochial social control (Hunter, 1985) suffers from a dearth of committed participants in the groups that form the basis for those controls (Putnam, 1993).

Mobility is typically thought of as voluntary movement from one place to another. In some communities, however, involuntary or coercive mobility may be the dominant force of movement in and out of a neighborhood. This may be particularly true in opportunity-starved locations, in which voluntary relocation is a rare option and the forces of residential segregation are difficult to overcome (Massey, 1990; Massey & Denton, 1993). In these areas, coercive relocation may be common: Many residents may be removed from the neighborhood for incarceration, and others may return to the neighborhood after incarceration.

The importance of incarceration as a form of mobility is a relatively new phenomenon. Since the 1970s, incarceration rates nationally have risen 500%. In 1997, an estimated 7.5 million people were removed from their communities to serve sentences in prison or jail, and an equivalent number were returned to their communities from prison or jail (Hammett, 2000). This outward mobility is matched by an equivalent inward mobility, since by far, most of those who are incarcerated are eventually released to be reintegrated into a community. Nationally, it was estimated that in 2002, about 600,000 (Petersilia, 2000) people were released from prison and upward of 10 million were released from jail (Hammett, 2000).

Most of the impact of this growth has been concentrated among inner-city residents and those of color. It is estimated that the lifetime probability of a black male going to prison is now 28% (Bonczar & Beck, 1997). This racial concentration further clusters in particular inner-city neighborhoods. Lynch and Sabol (1992, 1996) estimated that in some sections of Washington, DC, for example, as many as 25% of black men aged 20-45 are locked up on any given day. Incarceration rates in the Brownsville neighborhood of Brooklyn are 150 times that of another Brooklyn neighborhood, a few blocks away. In Brownsville, it has been estimated that about 3% of the men went to prison in 1996 alone (Center for Alternative Sentencing and Employment Services, 1998).

It is easy to see how coercive mobility in these locations could play a destabilizing role in community life that is similar to that of voluntary mobility (independent of the direct effects of incarceration itself). Residents who go into and out of neighborhoods because of prison would be as likely to exhibit some of the same lack of interest in the long-term interests of those places as those who are transient for other reasons. But coercive mobility is also thought to have an impact on the people who remain in the neighborhood.

38   COERCIVE MOBILITY AND CRIME

Some researchers have explored the destabilizing impacts of incarceration on familial, political, and economic systems (Meares, 1998a, 1998b; Rose & Clear, 1998a). For instance, although attempts to identify the contribution of incarceration to single-parent families (Lynch & Sabol, 2002; Myers, 2000) have produced inconclusive results, the removal of men is likely to be associated with higher levels of unsupervised youths, one of the principal characteristics of disorder. In a study of two high-incarceration neighborhoods, Rose, Clear, and Ryder (2000) found that while residents benefited from the incarceration of family members and neighbors who were committing crimes, they suffered many losses as well. For instance, family members had to absorb the additional financial burden of paying for phone calls from inmates, traveling to visit them, and financially supporting them on their return to the community. Residents suffered from other effects, such as problems associated with the stigma of incarceration in the family and the neighborhood, in addition to problems with self-esteem and attenuated social relationships. Many residents reported withdrawing from community life in the aftermath of a family member's incarceration. Thus, it seems likely that high incarceration rates concentrated in certain communities could increase social disorganization by depleting the already limited resources of community members and by damaging the social networks that serve as the basis for social capital and ultimately promote private and parochial social control.

There is an additional problem with coercive mobility: It negatively affects family and friends and their attitudes toward the criminal justice system. Rose and Clear (1998b) found that knowing someone who has been incarcerated influences people's attitudes about formal and informal social control. They noted that for people who are exposed to incarceration, either by having been to prison or by knowing someone who has, a low opinion about formal control was associated with a low opinion of informal control. (They found the opposite relationship for these who were not exposed to incarceration.) Thus, high levels of incarceration may undermine the efficacy of informal social control.

Coercive and voluntary mobility, then, should have parallel effects on community stability because they both represent a kind of population churning that inhibits integration and promotes isolation and anonymity. At the same time, coercive mobility is different from voluntary mobility because incarceration removes people from the community who commit crimes. As a result, removing offenders from the community is commonly thought to promote community cohesion by reducing both the fear of crime and the existence of disorder that contribute to isolation and anonymity (Kelling & Coles, 1997).

Rose and Clear (1998a) recognized the dual impact that coercive mobility may have on the community. To address this impact, they proposed a tipping point of effects, at which low concentrations of incarceration may indeed enhance community stability and high concentrations may diminish it. The idea of a social-effects tipping point, at which a few people, coercively moved out of one neighborhood, affect the entire neighborhood, is not obvious on its face. Even in high-incarceration neighborhoods, for example, only 2%-3% of the population get removed for imprisonment in a given year, with a roughly equivalent number returned annually. As a cross-sectional measure of mobility, the numbers seem low. But for high-incarceration neighborhoods, one year's sample of disruptions represents a pattern of disruption over time: Over a four- or five-year period, a 2% disruption rate becomes 10%-15% of coercive residential mobility. When this figure is disaggregate by sex and age groups, the proportion of parent-aged men affected by coercive mobility can be high. Moreover, the impact of this pattern is felt not just on the individuals who are removed or returned, but on the kinship and community networks associated with each case.

The theory, then, is that coercive mobility effects those who remain through networks of associations. For example, Rose et al. (2000) interviewed over 120 people (snowball sampled using multiple entry points) in two high-incarceration neighborhoods in Tallahassee and reported that every respondent identified at least one family member who had been to prison. Across time and through interwoven networks of association, the impact of imprisonment in high-incarceration neighborhoods can spread widely. Rose and Clear's (1998a) hypothesis is that these impacts, after a certain level of incarceration, damage the capacity of informal social control.

In this study, we sought to clarify the ways in which coercive mobility affects community stability. As a result, we disaggregated coercive mobility into its components, admissions and releases. Although we typically might expect to see a decrease in crime with increases in prison admissions and an increase in crime with increases in prison releases, what the preceding discussion shows is that the relationship between admissions and crime may be different in high-incarceration neighborhoods than it is in low-incarceration neighborhoods. Thus, while we hypothesized a positive relationship between releases and crime, we hypothesized a curvi-linear relationship (first negative, then positive) between admis-sions and crime.

DATA, MEASURES, AND METHODS

This neighborhood-level study was conducted in Tallahassee, Florida (Leon County), a moderate-sized southern city and the capi-tal of the state. For each neighborhood, we collected three types of data: Florida Department of Corrections (DOC) prison admissions from Leon County and prison releases to Leon County, 1996; Talla-hassee Police Department crimes known to the police, 1996 and 1997; and U.S. census data, 1990.

Construction of Tallahassee Neighborhoods

Tallahassee has many neighborhoods and active neighborhood associations, but we know of no prior attempt to delineate neighbor-hoods and establish their boundaries formally. As a result, our first task was to define as many neighborhoods as possible. We began by contacting the Tallahassee Leon County Planning Commission, which provided current maps of Tallahassee city limits, census tracts, and block groups.

We mapped Tallahassee neighborhoods in three steps. In the first step, completed in early 1997, we conducted a survey of all lo-cal neighborhood associations registered with the city of Tallahas-see Neighborhood Services, asking each to identify the boundaries of their association. Responses were mapped and coded and, as a validity check, were compared with the boundaries determined by the Tallahassee Neighborhood Services. Where exact neighborhood boundaries were problematic, a second step involved a case-by-case review of substantive geographic features, such as roads, railroad tracks, and land uses. The final step, completed with the assistance of the Tallahassee Police Department, compared neighborhood boundaries to established police crime-reporting areas and U.S. census block groups. The result was a total of 103 Tallahassee neighborhoods, each of which was defined by boundaries cotermi-nous to both police reporting areas and to data on the U.S. census block groups. In 23 neighborhoods, the census block group spanned across the county boundary; thus, while the neighborhood we iden-tified was wholly in the city, the census data covered a larger area.

So as not to attribute noncity census demographics to these neighborhoods, we excluded them from the analysis, leaving a total sample of 80 for subsequent analysis.[1] These neighborhoods range from a population of 249 to a population of 4,538.

Sources of Data

Crimes known to the police, 1996 and 1997. The Tallahassee Police Department provided crime statistics by geographic location that were based on Tallahassee Police Department reporting areas. All 1996 and 1997 offenses reported within Tallahassee's city limits, including homicide, sexual battery, other sex offenses, strong-arm robbery, armed robbery, commercial burglary, residential burglary, auto burglary, auto theft, aggravated battery with firearm only, aggravated assault with firearm only, loitering and prowling, and suspicious incident, were mapped by neighborhood.

Florida DOC admissions. The Florida DOC provided two data files for all offenders admitted in 1996 to serve prison sentences who listed Leon County as their place of residence. The first file contained address records for all Leon County offenders. These records, obtained from the DOC original arrest reports filed by the arresting officers, listed 465 offenders admitted to prison in 1996. Twelve records were duplicates and were dropped from the study. Of the remaining 453 records, 201 (44%) had no address and thus were also dropped from the study. The remaining 252 addresses were mapped, indicating that 97 (38%) were outside the city of Tallahassee. The total number of offenders admitted to prison in our sample was 155. There were 146 admissions to prison in 1996 in the 80 neighborhoods used in this analysis.

The second file provided by the DOC contained demographic data on the total sample of 462 offenders; 93% were male and 7% were female, and 76% are black and 22.7% were white.[2] The most frequent offenses these offenders were convicted for were cocaine-related (possession and sale) robbery and burglary. Although most

---

[1] All 23 excluded neighborhoods occupy the perimeter of the city and thus have overlapping police-reporting districts with the county sheriff. Our crime data were from the Tallahassee Police Department. Crimes reported at locations within these neighborhoods but outside the city of Tallahassee are not recorded by the Tallahassee Police Department and thus were unavailable to us. Crime was our dependent variable, so we did not estimate models using cases for which we had incomplete crime data. Because these are perimeter neighborhoods, they are different in several respects from the remaining Tallahassee neighborhoods that fall fully within the city boundaries, including prison admissions rates, release rates, poverty, and public assistance. Excluding these cases means that the pattern we report does not include some of the city's perimeter locations, nearly all of which are low on the coercive mobility measures. The loss of these locations is a constraint on our models.

[2] For both admissions and releases, no common field linked the demographic data to the address files.

of the offenses were committed before 1996 (70%), most of the offenders were convicted sometime during 1996.

Florida DOC releases. The Florida DOC provided two data files for all offenders who were released in 1996 back into Leon County. The first data file contained 417 records obtained from Inmate Release Plans. Of the 417 records, 12 (3%) contained no addresses and were dropped from the study. The remaining 405 records were mapped, indicating 115 addresses (28%) outside the city of Tallahassee. The total number of released offenders in our data set was 290. There were 253 released offenders in the 80 neighborhoods used in this analysis.

The second file contained demographic data provided by the DOC on all 417 releases, showing that 77% of the releasees that year were black and 23% were white. The most frequent offenses these offenders were convicted for were burglary, cocaine related (possession and sale). Information on gender was not provided.

1990 U.S. census data. Demographic information was drawn from 1990 U.S. census block groups (U.S. Bureau of the Census, n.d.), aggregated to the neighborhood level. Census variables included in our analysis were population, race-ethnicity, residents not living in their same house since 1985 (residential mobility), and residents living below the poverty level.[3]

Measures

Crime and corrections variables. The dependent variable was crime in each neighborhood in 1997. The number of crimes per neighborhood ranged from 5 to 260, with a mean of 62. The crime rate, measured as crime per 100 residents, ranged from .36 to 30.92, with a mean of 5.54.

Two independent variables were used to tap the level of coercive mobility: admissions to prison in 1996 and releases from prison

---

[3] We attempted to find supplementary data to measure residential mobility because the data provided by the census made it impossible to distinguish between interneighborhood moves and intraneighborhood moves. Potentially, this is an important distinction, since it may be argued that intraneighborhood moves would be less disruptive for the community because the population base would be stable even if residents moved around within the neighborhood. In addition, the census measure of residential mobility does not measure equally well the stability of neighborhoods that lost population and those that gained population during the previous five years and thus may seriously underestimate the instability in neighborhoods with significant outward mobility but no significant inward mobility—precisely those neighborhoods that are the least desirable. We also attempted to locate supplementary data on the size of neighborhood populations in an effort to measure population gains and losses as a way to capture differences between inter- and intraneighborhood mobility. Unfortunately, we were unable to correct these problems because the city of Tallahassee does not collect these neighborhood-level data.

in 1996. The number of offenders per community admitted to prison ranged from 0 to 15, with a mean of 1.8 offenders per neighborhood. However, only 42 of the neighborhoods had offenders admitted to prison in 1996. Of these neighborhoods, the mean number of offenders per neighborhood was 3.5. The rate of admissions, the number of admissions per 100 residents, ranged from 0 to 2.00, with a mean of .16. The mean admission rate for neighborhoods with at least 1 admission was .31 ($n = 42$). The full model includes a third-order polynomial for centered percentage of admissions to capture the hypothesized curvilinear relationship between the rate of admissions and crime. Centering prior to the calculation of the polynomials helps alleviate computational difficulties created by the multicollinearity of the three terms (Neter, Kutner, Nachtsheim, & Wasserman, 1996).

The number of releases per community ranged from 0 to 22, with a mean of 3.2 releases back into each neighborhood. However, 24 of the communities had no releases. Of the group that did have releases, the mean number of releases per neighborhood was 4.5. The release rate, calculated per 100 residents, ranged from 0 to 1.61, with a mean of .26. For the neighborhoods with at least 1 release, the mean was .37 ($n = 56$).

Social disorganization variables. The three primary social disorganization variables originally suggested by Shaw and McKay (1942) were poverty, residential mobility, and ethnic heterogeneity. Most contemporary scholars who have used the social disorganization framework (see, e.g., Bursik, 1988; W. J. Wilson, 1987) have argued for a reconceptualization of the original Shaw-McKay variables as suggesting a new construct, often called "concentrated disadvantage," which is meant to reflect the fact that some urban areas are afflicted by multiple problems that place them at a disadvantage with regard to other areas nearby. Several different strategies have been used to model concentrated disadvantage.[4] We followed the strategy of Morenoff et al. (2001), who combined the z-scores of the percentage of families receiving public assistance, percentage of individuals who are unemployed, percentage of female-headed households with children, and percentage of residents who

---

4 The resuscitation of interest in social disorganization has been led by Sampson and his colleagues, who have used various measures of concentrated disadvantage. Sampson and Groves (1989) used measures of divorced parents and single parents with children; Sampson and Raudenbush (1999) used an index of factor loadings of poverty, public assistance, unemployment, female-headed households, density of children, and percentage black; Morenoff and Sampson (1997) used factor loadings of public assistance, poverty, unemployment, and single-parent families; Raudenbush and Sampson (1999) used poverty and ethnic isolation; and Morenoff et al. (2001) used z-scores for public assistance, unemployment, female-headed households, and percentage black.

are black. The Concentrated Disadvantage Index has a mean of zero and a standard deviation of .767.

Our main interest was to test the impact of coercive mobility, measured as removals to and returns from prison. We thus retained residential mobility, measured as the number of residents in the neighborhood older than age 5 who did not live in the same house five years earlier in 1985, to distinguish this form of residential flux from coercive mobility of the criminal justice system. Residential mobility ranged from 19.68 to 96.03, with a mean of 65.13.[5] (Correlations and descriptive statistics for all variables are presented in Appendix A.)

Methods

The data were analyzed using the generalized linear model with a negative binomial response function. This model is appropriate for the prediction of positive integers and, as Osgood (2000) showed, can be applied to the prediction of crime rates by incorporating the logged population as an independent variable. Osgood indicated that the negative binomial is a substantially better model than ordinary least-squares (OLS) regression and has the advantage of constraining predicted values to positive numbers. Because it incorporates a dispersion term, the negative binomial is more appropriate for many situations than a Poisson model.

Our general strategy was to construct multivariate social disorganization models of crime in Tallahassee in 1997 in which the effects of coercive mobility—prison admissions and releases—were included as terms. Coercive mobility, in turn, was modeled as an effect of 1996 releases and three effects of 1996 admissions denoted as a polynomial (raw, squared, and cubed). Modeling admissions in this way directly tested Rose and Clear's (1998a) hypothesis because it enabled us to separate the effects of low levels of incarceration from moderate and higher levels, which are thought to be different.

Because of the nature of the data, extensive diagnostics were completed to test for the presence of multicollinearity.[6] As expected, the percentage of residents admitted to prison and the percentage of residents released from prison are highly correlated (.83). Two typical solutions to this level of multicollinearity are to use one term only or to combine the two variables into a new construct. We

---

[5] Some analysts have modeled the impact of heterogeneity by using a direct measure of normative consensus, following Sampson and his colleagues' practice of operationalizing collective efficacy as "shared expectations for social control" (Morenoff et al., 2001, p. 526). This direct measure was unavailable to us.

[6] We also examined the data carefully, using variograms and mixed models, for evidence of spatial autocorrelation, but found none.

considered combining the two measures to tap the joint effects of incarceration on the community but ultimately decided that admissions and releases were different dimensions and that we wanted to capture this difference, rather than mute it with one construct.[7] Therefore, we chose a two-step strategy. First, we examined models that contained the third-order polynomial for either admissions rate or release rate and compared these two models. Then we conducted analyses using both measures simultaneously. OLS variance inflation factors (VIF) and eigenvalues were analyzed for all the models. The relationship between the admissions and release rates did not have severe multicollinearity using standard cutoffs of 10 for VIF and 45 for the condition index (Neter et al., 1996). As would be expected, the analysis showed substantial multicollinearity among the three terms of the polynomial for admissions rate. Sequential tests of significance (based on the improvement of fit associated with the addition of each polynomial term) were used to evaluate the impact of each of the terms (Neter et al., 1996).

In small samples, statistical outliers are often a concern. We therefore performed extensive analyses of influential observations. The problem of influence can occur for cases with extreme values on the dependent variable or for cases that exert an undue influence on covariance estimates, often assessed using Cook's Distance (hereafter Cook's D). An examination of the dependent variable (crime97) revealed a skewed distribution with three neighborhoods having outlying high values. An approximation of Cook's D was calculated for each observation in the full model. A value with an associated F percentile of greater than 50 almost certainly should lead to the use of remedial measures, while values between 20 and 50 should be further investigated to determine whether such measures should be used (Neter et al., 1996). In addition, there were two neighborhoods with Cook's Ds percentiles between 20 and 30. One neighborhood, which had the highest Cook's D value and one of the highest crime rates, was therefore in both outlier groups.[8]

---

[7] An exploratory analysis revealed that this combined construct was significantly, positively related to crime.

[8] Of the influential observations, the DFBETAS indicate that two neighborhoods, South Monroe and Tennessee Strip, had a sizable influence on the estimates of the nonlinear terms for admissions. These two neighborhoods had the highest scores on admissions and were two of the three highest on the 1997 crime rate. In addition, they were both among the top four neighborhoods in terms of the percentage of releases and the percentage who were poor. Overall, this pair of neighborhoods represents a cluster of observations with high values of crime, rather than two distinctive profiles. Indeed, although the two neighborhoods are separated by the city center (Tennessee Strip to the north and South Monroe to the south), they are similar types of areas in that both are characterized by a combination of commercial and transitory residential usage. In addition, both are adjacent to relatively stable, noncommercial neighborhoods populated by moderate-income African Americans.

46   COERCIVE MOBILITY AND CRIME

We should note that there is some controversy regarding the problem of influential observations in neighborhood data. Some scholars have argued that the analysis of data using a theory thought to apply to residential areas only ought to exclude "downtown" areas (see Crutchfield, 1989) or, it follows, other areas that do not fit the theory. Others have noted the obvious point that excluding certain cases because they influence the statistical result has a flavor of "cooking the books." This problem is made even more difficult by the mathematical conundrum: To include these cases may produce results that suggest an overall relationship in neighborhood data that is actually driven by one or two extreme cases, while excluding the cases tends to remove the variance needed for meaningful significance testing (especially in small samples). In this article, we opt for a conservative approach, in which we report the results for all cases as a test of the theory and then report the results for subsamples after influential cases were omitted from the analysis to investigate the importance of these influential cases.

RESULTS

Figure 1 is a map of the 80 Tallahassee neighborhoods showing the pattern of admissions, releases, and crime. Each star represents one admission to prison from that neighborhood; each circle represents one release. Both admissions and releases are clustered primarily in the center of town, near the two universities and the poorer neighborhoods. The more affluent communities in the northeast section of Tallahassee have only a few releases and admissions. It is important to note is that admissions and releases are not concentrated in only the highest crime areas. Indeed, they tend to be concentrated adjacent to these areas.

In Table 1, we estimate five different negative binomial models[9] of the 1997 crime rates in Tallahassee. Model 1 is the baseline model, in which we test the effects of concentrated disadvantage and mobility on the crime rate in 1997, controlling for the neighborhood population and crime rate in 1996. Both terms are significant in the direction predicted by social disorganization theory.

Model 2 tests Rose and Clear's (1998a) hypothesis. In this model, we add release rate and the polynomial for admission rate to Model 1. While mobility remains statistically significant, concentrated disadvantage loses its significance.[10] Neighborhood releases

---

[9] Because the dependent variable is logged, the coefficients should be interpreted as the proportional change in predicted crime owing to a one-unit change in the independent variable.

[10] The Index of Concentrated Disadvantage is correlated more highly with the two measures of coercive mobility, releases (.66) and admissions (.55), than with the dependent variable, logged crime97 (.42).

**Figure 1.   80 Tallahassee Neighborhoods with Prison
Admissions and Releases Shaded by
Neighborhood Crime Rate**

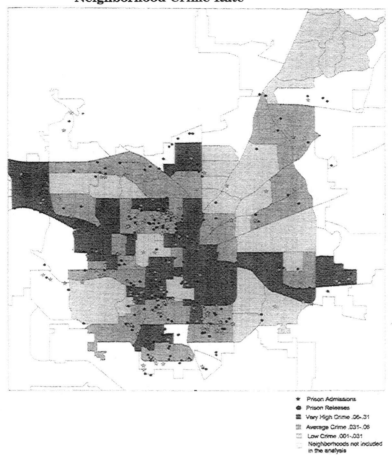

★   Prison Admissions
●   Prison Releases
▓   Very High Crime .06-.31
▒   Average Crime .031-.06
░   Low Crime .001-.031
    Neighborhoods not included
    in the analysis

do not have a significant relationship to crime, nor is there a linear
relationship between admissions to prisons and logged crime97.
But the quadratic (squared) prison admissions term has a significant, *negative* impact on the amount of crime, and the cubic admissions rate has a significant, but *positive*, impact on crime ($p < .10$; a
discussion of significance testing levels is presented later). This result is partly consistent with Rose and Clear's prediction that admissions would be related to crime in a curvilinear fashion.

Table 1. Negative Binomial Regressions Estimating the Effects of Incarceration on Crime Rates in 1997, Tallahassee, Florida

Independent Variable	(1) Estimate Model Without Coercive Mobility	(2) Estimate Full Model	(3) Estimate with the Influential and Outlying Observation Removed	(4) Estimate with the Two Most Influential Observations Removed	(5) Estimate with Observations with the Three Highest Crime Rates Removed
Intercept					
b	-2.23	-2.08	-2.74	-2.90	-3.09
Chi-square	5.89	5.54	11.53	13.49	15.04
p	.015	.019	<0.001	<.001	<.001
Ln population					
b	.729	.692	.762	.769	.800
Chi-square	31.69	31.28	46.30	49.84	52.97
p	<.001	<.001	<.001	<.001	<.001
Crime rate 1996					
b	6.28	6.62	11.19	10.42	13.36
Chi-square	26.09	21.43	48.13	43.02	56.92
p	<.001	<.001	<.001	<.001	<.001
Concentrated disadvantage					
b	0.232	.087	0.011	.021	-.002
Chi-square	8.27	0.63	0.01	0.05	0.00
p	.004	.437	0.915	.830	.985
Percentage mobility					
b	0.010	.012	0.009	.011	.008
Chi-square	9.54	12.5	8.10	12.07	7.74
p	.002	<.001	0.004	<.001	.005
Release rate					
b		.361	.835	.828	.802
Chi-square		1.31	6.96	7.22	6.97
p		.253	.008	.007	.008

Table 1. Negative Binomial Regressions Estimating the Effects of Incarceration on Crime Rates in 1997, Tallahassee, Florida (continued)

Independent Variable	(1) Estimate Model Without Coercive Mobility	(2) Estimate Full Model	(3) Estimate with the Influential and Outlying Observation Removed	(4) Estimate with the Two Most Influential Observations Removed	(5) Estimate with Observations with the Three Highest Crime Rates Removed
Admissions rate (centered) polynomial					
Admissions rate					
b		.879	0.307	.499	-.021
Chi-square		1.75	0.26	0.70	0.00
p		.186	.613	.404	.972
Sequential chi-square		1.59	9.19	7.90	1.04
p		.208	.002	.005	.307
Admissions rate^2					
b		-2.41	-2.89	-3.11	-4.86
Chi-square		4.64	7.83	9.49	2.81
p		.031	0.005	.002	.094
Sequential chi-square		3.40	6.85	7.32	3.10
p		.065	.009	.007	.078
Admissions rate^3					
b		.854	.997	1.094	4.76
Chi-square		2.85	4.49	5.70	1.59
p		.031	0.034	.002	.208
Sequential chi-square		2.72	4.23	5.32	1.55
p		.099	.040	.021	.213
Dispersion	.218	.195	.154	.145	.143
N	80	80	79	78	77
Deviance	83.62	83.28	82.01	80.63	79.66
Log likelihood	16710	16714	16247	16089	15560

Our concern about influential observations led us to replicate this model in three subsamples in which certain cases were excluded from the analysis. We had to be cautious, of course, in dropping cases from the analysis merely because they were in some way extreme. For one thing, the theory we tested predicts a curvilinear relationship, and extreme cases may be necessary to capture the pattern. For another, these neighborhoods represent real conditions in Tallahassee and are not an artifact of sampling. Finally, in small samples, much of the variance to be analyzed is produced by these cases. Thus, not only is it practically prudent to retain as many cases as possible in the analysis, but in small samples it is important not to drop cases when they are both theoretically and statistically important. Nonetheless, influential cases raise concerns that relationships reported in the aggregate are actually being produced by happenstance patterns in a handful of cases, and this possibility is particularly strong in small samples. We therefore report the results for three additional models.

Model 3 eliminates the most influential observation (the downtown Tallahassee area with a low residential population and a high crime rate, arguably not subject to coercive mobility effects). This model provides even stronger support for Rose and Clear's (1998a) hypothesis. All the coercive mobility terms are statistically significant ($p < .05$), with concentrated disadvantage remaining nonsignificant.

Model 4 was estimated omitting the two cases identified as potentially influential using Cook's D (see footnote 8). The removal of these observations has only a marginal impact on the estimates compared to Model 3 and provides support for Rose and Clear's (1998a) hypothesis.

Model 5 was estimated eliminating the three neighborhoods with the highest crime rates. In this model, the quadratic (squared) and cubic terms have larger estimates than in the other models, but only the former is significant ($p < .10$), although all the coefficients are in the direction predicted by Rose and Clear (1998a). The loss of significance is likely due to the loss of covariance (in relation to the standard error) that resulted from dropping the high-crime neighborhoods.

In sum, Models 2-5 provide consistent (though not uniform) support for Rose and Clear's (1998a) hypothesis. Releases predict increases in crime in three of the four models. The admissions quadratic, representing a moderate level of removals to prison, is associated with a reduction in crime in all four models. The cubic term of the polynomial is associated with an increase in crime in three of the four models.[11]

Figure 2 shows the relationship between the percentage of admissions and the predicted value of the logged number of crimes for Models 2-5. (Caution should be taken in interpreting this figure because the actual size of the impact of change in the independent variable on a logged dependent variable depends on the values of the other independent variables.) Model 2 elicits a curvilinear pattern, in which the suppression effect on crime occurs in the quadratic but changes to an aggravation effect in the cubic. An interpretation of this curve is that the cumulative effect of admissions on crime continues to be negative at the higher levels of admissions, but the cumulative negative impact begins to wane because the additional removals are increasing, rather than decreasing, crime. This pattern occurs for all four models, and notably the elimination of influential observations, Model 4, yields curves in which the impact of the higher admissions rate on crime is stronger, not weaker. (Model 5, in which high-crime neighborhoods are eliminated, exhibits a similar, but exaggerated version of that pattern.)

Figure 2 provides evidence that the impact of incarceration changes as the rate of prison admissions increases. Estimates of the precise turning points can be obtained by using the power rule to take the derivative of the regression equation with respect to the admissions rate; these estimates are presented in Table 2.[12] For Model 2, for example, setting the derivative equal to zero and solving using the quadratic equation yields the two turning points (local minima or maxima): .20 and 1.68. Evaluating the second derivative at these points indicates that the first is a maximum and the second is a minimum, as is clear in Figure 2. Table 2 also shows the turning-point estimates for other models, which are similar, with the change to a positive effect occurring earlier in the admission rate's growth when influential cases are removed. To approximate a rough confidence interval for these turning points, we reestimated them eliminating one neighborhood at a time. We found that 90% of these estimates fell between 1.65 and 1.73.

---

[11] Rose and Clear's argument is silent on the impact of small rates of coercive mobility. We found that the linear effect, controlling for the other terms of the polynomial, is an increase in crime for two of the four models, a result that has no obvious logical relationship to the standard crime-control theory or Rose and Clear's alternative theory of coercive mobility.

[12] The derivative provides a formula for the slope of a function. Using the power rule, we find that the derivative of an expression of the form cx^n is ncx^{n-1}. The slope of a horizontal line equals 0; a local maximum or minimum will, by definition, have a tangent that is a horizontal line. For a nonlinear function, points that are local maxima or minima can be determined by setting the derivative equal to 0 and solving for x (see any basic calculus book, e.g., Iverson, 1996).

52   COERCIVE MOBILITY AND CRIME

Figure 2:   **Relationship between Admissions Rates and ln (Crime)**

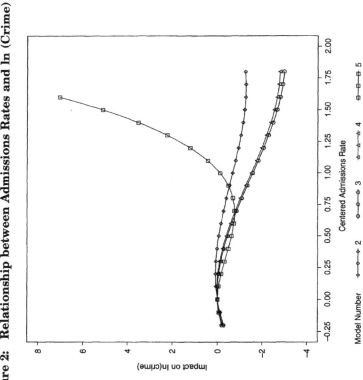

Table 2. Estimates of the Points at Which Slopes Change Signs (Local Maxima and Minima) for the Nonlinear Relationship Between Prison Admissions and Crime (Adjusted for Centering)

	Local Maximum (Immediately above this point the slope becomes negative)	Local Minimum (Immediately above this point, the slope becomes positive)
Model 2: All observations	0.20	1.68
Model 3: Delete influential observation with an outlying value of crime rate	0.05	1.88
Model 4: Delete the two most influential observations	0.08	1.81
Model 5: Delete three observations with outlying values of crime rate	−0.00	0.68
Analysis of results for 80 models estimated by deleting one observation at a time		
Mean	0.21	1.64
Median	0.21	1.67
Maximum	0.34	2.02
Minimum	0.05	−1.20
5th percentile	0.19	1.63
95th percentile	0.22	1.71

Taken as a whole, both the direction of the effects of coercive mobility and the nature and location of changes in its effects are all consistent with Rose and Clear's (1998a) predictions. Some of these effects fail to rise to a level of statistical significance, although, in general, the effects are significant ($p < .10$). Some aspects of our data make significance testing problematic: small sample sizes, multicollinearity, and limited covariance. Maltz (1994) pointed out that significance testing in circumstances such as ours can be misleading, since the chances of a Type II error are high unless the effects being studied are dominant.

Given the limits of significance testing in data such as ours, it is advisable to investigate confidence intervals in addition to point estimates (Maltz, 1994). Figure 3 shows the 95% Wald confidence intervals for the four sets of estimates for the admissions polynomial. Model 2—all neighborhoods—and Model 3—with Downtown excluded—show a likely curvilinear effect. Model 4—influential observations excluded—is less conclusive regarding the cubic term. Model 5—with the high crime neighborhoods excluded—is similar to Models 2 and 3, although with larger confidence intervals because of the loss of covariance. Overall, despite the differences in the estimates associated with the removal of various observations,

54   COERCIVE MOBILITY AND CRIME

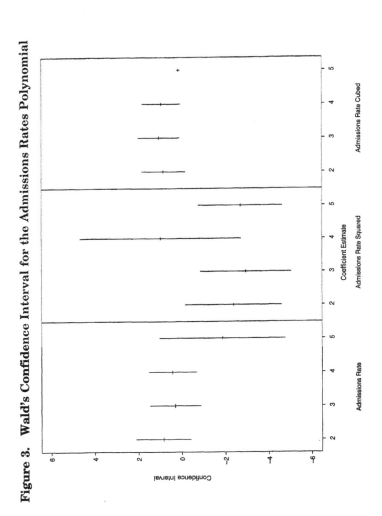

Figure 3. Wald's Confidence Interval for the Admissions Rates Polynomial

the possibility of a curvilinear effect of admissions to prison, in which increases in crime result from higher levels of incarceration, is consistently supported by these data. We found no evidence that high levels of incarceration suppress crime.

DISCUSSION AND CONCLUSION

Our purpose in this analysis was to investigate Rose and Clear's (1998a) hypothesis of the neighborhood-level impact of high rates of incarceration on crime. Our data are insufficient to provide a complete test of the model. To do so would require data from multiple time points (not currently available to us) tested in a causal model.[13] We believe, however, that the models we present are conceptually consistent with Rose and Clear's nonrecursive model because they include a variable commonly thought of as a policy response to crime rather than as an indicator of crime.

Given our data, we chose a partial test of the model, in which we investigated the effect of admissions and releases on crime, net of some of the other factors that are thought to influence crime at the ecological level. This approach enabled us to provide a conservative appraisal of the argument that high incarceration rates may contribute to crime. Our test is conservative in the sense that if incarceration *does not* behave in the way Rose and Clear proposed, then our models would find no impact of incarceration, after appropriate statistical controls. Our analysis revealed that increasing admissions to prison in one year have a negligible effect on crime at low levels and a negative effect on crime the following year when the rate is relatively low, but, after a certain concentration of residents is removed from the community through incarceration, the effect of additional admissions is to increase, not decrease, crime. This finding lends support to Rose and Clear's hypothesis that removing a high concentration of offenders from the community has a destabilizing effect on the community's level of social disorganization. It also lends support to the idea of a tipping point, at which the size and direction of effects change.

The analysis also showed a strong, positive effect of releasing offenders into the community in one year on crime the following year. Undoubtedly, one interpretation of this finding would follow routine-activities theory (Cohen & Felson, 1979), that releasing ex-

---

[13] Data limitations make it impossible to estimate either structural equation models or 2SLS models, since both would require having incarceration data that precede the census variables in time. It is not consistent with the proposed theory to model incarceration as a mediating factor between the ecological variables (poverty, mobility, ethnic heterogeneity) and crime. The addition of 2000 census data would more closely fit the current demographics of the neighborhood, but would be measures that follow, not precede, the data on incarceration and crime.

offenders into the community increases the number of offenders in the community and that an increase in crime is, therefore, not surprising. Another interpretation, consistent with the social disorganization framework we used, is that releases are people whose arrival in the community constitutes a challenge to the community's capacity for self-regulation. Taken together, the combined effects of coercive mobility, concentrated at high levels within certain neighborhoods, constitutes a potentially profound challenge to public safety.

Although tentative, we believe our findings have important implications both for theorists and policy makers. Hence, we discuss these implications separately.

Implications for Theory

Recent advances in social disorganization theory have helped to update our understanding of the contemporary components of social disorganization and the ways in which urban areas have changed since the first exposition of these ideas in the 1940s. With few exceptions, however, researchers have conceptualized the social disorganization model as recursive, that is, ecological factors influence disorganization, which, in turn, influences crime. Public policies, when they are entertained, are thought of as responses to crime.

Social disorganization theorists have overlooked the effects of public policies on community life. Our data suggest that those who are interested in testing social disorganization theory should consider more closely the impact of public policies on community structure. In particular, we believe that including the effects of coercive mobility produced by state policy will help theorists better understand mechanisms of disorganization working in the community by providing a deeper appreciation of the ways in which concentrated mobility destabilizes community life.

Indeed, recent studies that have tested social disorganization theory have highlighted why it is essential to consider the importance of public policies, in general, and the policy on incarceration, in particular. First, Silver (2000) showed that community context is important in explaining the variation in violence among people with mental illnesses because neighborhood disadvantage is positively related to violence for mentally ill people. His study, following the work of Cullen (1994) and Lin (1986), considered the importance of social supports and assessed how social disorganization may condition the availability of those supports. Although he found that individual social supports did not mediate the impact of neighborhood disadvantage on violence, Silver did find that neighborhood disadvantage was negatively related to the number of social supporters available and was positively related to individual violence.

In a direct test of the impact of high levels of criminal justice activity on a neighborhood's capacity for informal social control, Lynch, Sabol, Planty, and Shelley (2001) found that upper ranges of arrest and incarceration seemed to decrease confidence in formal criminal justice and adversely affect elements of collective efficacy, leading to higher rates of crime. Their results for a national sample of census areas are consistent with the data we presented here for Tallahassee. If the results of these studies withstand replication, incarceration will be shown to be a significant factor that increases neighborhood disadvantage, thereby potentially indirectly influencing violence. In addition, incarceration is a factor that directly influences both the quality of social supports and the level of anger and violence in the community (Rose et al., 2000).

That levels of public social control may be important in their own right was suggested by the results of a study by Wikstrom and Loeber (2000) that the level of neighborhood disadvantage was not, in itself, a determinant of age of onset or level of delinquent offending, once individual risk factors (especially protective factors, such as parental supervision) were controlled. Yet the results of this and other studies of the impact of formal social control on children (for reviews, see Eddy & Reid, 2002; Parke & Clarke-Stewart, 2002) suggest that the criminal justice system may be one of the very forces that, in high quantities, destabilizes some of the protective factors available to young people in poor communities.

The concept of tipping points also has important theoretical implications. Social disorganization theorists have generally assumed a linear relationship between the ecological factors that influence disorganization and the effects of disorganization. This study has shown that, at least with regard to admissions to prisons, the effects on the community at low levels are different from the effects at high levels. Although policy would theorize a linear negative relationship between admissions and crime, a simple linear term in the model would have indicated a strong, positive relationship between the two variables because of the strength of the positive effect in high-incarceration neighborhoods. This study has shown that a linear model would have been incorrect. A nonlinear approach may be appropriate for modeling other ecological determinants of disorganization, too.

The tipping point shows that there may well be a qualitative difference between highly disorganized areas and other areas with

58   COERCIVE MOBILITY AND CRIME

lower levels of disorganization. In this case, neighborhoods with high levels of admissions and high levels of releases were significantly more likely to suffer from crime because at high levels, both variables had a strong positive effect on crime, whereas at lower levels, the two variables had opposing effects. Thus, high-incarceration neighborhoods are different from low-incarceration neighborhoods. The concept of a tipping point may help incorporate work on social disorganization with that being done on the urban underclass.

Implications for Policy

One of the most important advances in work on poverty and crime has been the identification and exploration of the urban underclass (W. J. Wilson, 1987, 1996). This group is depicted as living amid multigenerational, entrenched poverty and in isolation from standard economic, political, and social forces. Most large cities in the United States have residential areas that are almost wholly occupied by the urban underclass. These places tend to be comprised of concentrations of people of color living in subsidized housing on chaotic, tough streets dominated by high levels of unemployment. In these areas, many of the basic institutions have failed: Families are broken and residents are often isolated from mainstream social institutions. Those who live in these areas are stuck in their locations, unable to relocate because of abject poverty and residential segregation (Massey, 1990; Massey & Denton, 1993).

The result of an emergent underclass is a kind of permanent system of urbanized social disorganization for the most destitute areas of inner-city life. In today's world of entrenched poverty, the processes of heterogeneity and mobility may no longer work as they once did. It is not surprising that empirical tests of social disorganization theory bear this point out when they find inconsistent support for the main tenets of the theory. The inner-city areas that are dominated by the underclass have the greatest levels of crime, as well as little racial heterogeneity and little outward mobility. They also have the greatest concentrations of cycling into and out of prison, and our data suggest that these processes of coercive mobility compound problems of informal social control for the neighborhoods that start out with depleted collective efficacy.

The implications of this situation for policy makers and practitioners are troubling. There is broad familiarity with and popular support for the conventional argument that increases in imprisonment lead to decreases in crime through incapacitation and deterrence (DiIulio & Piehl, 1991; Reynolds, 1991). Recently, a softer version of this argument has received attention, that increases in formal social control that are directed at reducing "incivilities" and "broken windows" disorder result in reduced criminality because residents are encouraged to "take control" of public space and join together to regulate the places where they live (Kelling & Coles, 1997; Skogan, 1990; J. Q. Wilson & Kelling, 1982). This stream of research tends to support the contemporary policy of growth in formal social control as a means of augmenting informal social control, for it has as the centerpiece the removal of offenders from their neighborhoods. Although this line of argument enjoys considerable popular appeal and policy support, studies of neighborhoods in Baltimore (Taylor, 2000) and Chicago (Sampson and Raudenbush, 1999) have questioned the role of incivilities and broken-windows factors in crime rates and found considerable support for structural factors, including traditional social disorganization factors, instead. Regarding incivilities and broken windows, the jury is still out.

Our data are in accord with the contrasting body of research that shows that growing formal social control has a negative impact on the capacity for informal social control, especially when that growth is concentrated among certain groups. For example, Sampson and Bartusch (1999) found that blacks were more likely than whites to view legal norms as not legally binding and to be dissatisfied with the police. These differences disappeared when community context was taken into account. It follows, then, that this attitude among blacks arises because they are more likely to live in places where disadvantage is concentrated and where the growth in formal social control has been most apparent. These neighborhoods, in turn, produce high levels of legal cynicism and dissatisfaction with the police. It seems fair to conclude that those who are cynical about the law and the police will be less inclined to perform effective roles of informal social control. Another study found that among those who personally know someone who has been incarcerated, a negative attitude toward formal control is associated with a negative attitude toward informal social control, as well (Rose & Clear, 1998b).

The concentration of growing formal social control has ripple effects not just for peoples' attitudes, but for their life prospects. Western and Becket's (1999) study of incarceration and unemployment found that although growing levels of incarceration initially resulted in lower rates of conventional measures of unemployment, the recycling of these ex-offenders back into the job market with reduced job prospects had the effect of increasing unemployment in the long run. The concentration of residents with poor job prospects in certain high-unemployment areas has been shown to correlate with higher crime in these areas (Crutchfield & Pitchford, 1997).

These residents, many of whom may be hampered by criminal records, struggle to obtain good jobs. But they have a leg up compared to recently released offenders, for whom employment is typically a crucial concern. Seen in this context, it is easy to understand why our data show that *both* removal and return rates are hazards for these communities. Those in reentry need to be reintegrated somehow into the community, but the strains they pose for resources of informal social control, such as family or employment, constitute a force that tends to increase social disorganization. Even if these offenders are disinclined to commit crimes, there may still be a destabilizing effect from their mobility that increases the crime rate even further.

Thus, policy makers who are used to thinking about ways to expand the potency of the state in these multiproblem communities must consider the long-term implications of this trend. If we are correct that coercive mobility in and out of prison is disorganizing at the community level when it occurs at high rates, then today's penal policy that emphasizes ever-increasing rates of incarceration can be counterproductive. We do not pretend that there are no benefits to removing criminally active residents from their neighborhoods. But our data are consistent with the growing literature that has found that an overuse of incarceration can pose problems for those neighborhoods and leave deficits that are experienced by those who remain in them. And whatever the effects of the removal of offenders, the offenders eventually return, and their return poses a set of problems at the neighborhood level that is the natural consequence of their removal in the first place (Travis, Solomon, & Waul, 2001). The problem of concentrated criminal-justice effects has led some observers (Clear & Cadora, 2003) to argue for neighborhood-based community-justice strategies that focus on building collective efficacy and community capacity, rather than merely arresting and processing residents through the criminal justice system.

There is, of course, a need for further research. Our data about Tallahassee challenge the typical conceptions of social disorganization theory and social control policy. But the sample was small and limited to a small number of neighborhoods in one city, and the statistical analysis was complex. New studies in additional areas will help to clarify the problematic nature of the impact of coercive mobility on crime and, ultimately, on neighborhood life.

REFERENCES

Bellair, P. E. (1997). Social interaction and community crime: Examining the importance of neighbor networks. *Criminology, 35,* 677-704.

Bellair, P. E. (2000). Informal surveillance and street crime. *Criminology, 38,* 137-170.

Bonczar, T. P., & Beck, A. J. (1997). *Lifetime likelihood of going to state or federal prison.* Washington, DC: Bureau of Justice Statistics.

Bursik, R. J., Jr. (1986). Ecological stability and the dynamics of delinquency. In A. J. Reiss, Jr., & M. Tonry (Eds.), *Communities and crime* (pp. 35-66). Chicago: University of Chicago Press.

Bursik, R. J., Jr. (1988). Social disorganization and theories of crime and delinquency: Problems and prospects. *Criminology, 26,* 519-551.

Bursik, R. J., Jr., & Grasmick, H. G. (1993). *Neighborhoods and crime: The dimensions of effective community control.* Lexington, MA: Lexington Books.

Center for Alternative Sentencing and Employment Services. (1998). *Community justice centers: A proposal to the Open Society Institute.* New York: Author.

Clear, T. R., & Cadora, E. (2003). *Community justice.* Belmont, CA: Wadsworth.

Cohen, L., & Felson, M. (1979). Social change and crime rate trends. *American Sociological Review, 44,* 588-605.

Crutchfield, R. D. (1989). Labor stratification and violent crime. *Social Forces, 68,* 489-512.

Crutchfield, R. D., Geerken, M. R., & Gove, W. R. (1982). Crime rate and social integration: The impact of metropolitan mobility. *Criminology, 20,* 467-478.

Crutchfield, R. D., & Pitchford, S. R. (1997). Work and crime: The effects of labor stratification. *Social Forces, 76,* 93-118.

Cullen, F. T. (1994). Social support as an organizing concept for criminology: Presidential address to the Academy of Criminal Justice Sciences. *Justice Quarterly, 11,* 527-559.

DiIulio, J., & Piehl, A. M. (1991, Fall). Does prison pay? *The Brookings Journal,* 28-35.

Eddy, M., & Reid, J. (2002, January 30). *Adolescent children of incarcerated parents.* Paper presented to the National Policy Conference, From Prison to Home: The Effect of Incarceration and Reentry on Children, Families, and Communities, U.S. Department of Health and Human Services and the Urban Institute, Bethesda, MD.

Hammett, T. M. (2000, October 13). *Health-related issues in prisoner reentry to the community.* Paper presented to the Urban Institute Reentry Roundtable, Washington, DC.

Hunter, A. J. (1985). Private, parochial and public social orders: The problem of crime and incivility in urban communities. In G. D. Suttles & M. N. Zald (Eds.), *The challenge of social control: Citizenship and institution building in modern society* (pp. 230-242). Norwood, NJ: Ablex.

Iverson, G. (1996). *Calculus* (Quantitative Applications in the Social Sciences, Vol. 110). Newbury Park, CA: Sage.

Kelling, G. L., & Coles, C. B. (1997). *Fixing broken windows.* New York: Free Press.

Lin, N. (1986). Conceptualizing social support. In N. Lin, A. Dean, & W. M. Ensel (Eds.), *Social support, life events and depression* (pp. 153-170). Orlando, FL: Academic Press.

Lynch, J. P., & Sabol, W. J. (1992, November 5). *Macro-social changes and their implications for prison reform: The underclass and the composition of prison populations.* Paper presented to the American Society of Criminology, New Orleans.

Lynch, J. P., & Sabol, W. J. (1996, August). *Did getting tougher on crime pay?* (Crime policy report). Washington, DC: Urban Institute State Policy Center.

Lynch, J. P., & Sabol, W. J. (2002). Assessing the longer-run consequences of incarceration: Effects on families and employment. In D. F. Hawkins, S. Myers, & R. Stone (Eds.), *Crime control and criminal justice: The delicate balance.* Westport, CT: Greenwood Press.

Lynch, J. P., Sabol, W. J., Planty, M., & Shelley, M. (2001). *Crime, coercion and community: The effects of arrest and incarceration policies on informal social*

62   COERCIVE MOBILITY AND CRIME

control (report to the National Institute of Justice). Washington, DC: Urban Institute Justice Policy Center.

Maltz, M. (1994). Deviating from the mean: The declining significance of significance. *Journal of Research in Crime and Delinquency, 31,* 434-463.

Markowitz, F., Bellair, P., Liska, A., & Liu, J. (2001). Extending social disorganization theory: Modeling the relationship between cohesion, disorder and fear. *Criminology, 39,* 293-320.

Massey, D. S. (1990). American apartheid: Segregation and the making of the underclass. *American Journal of Sociology, 96,* 329-357.

Massey, D. S., & Denton, N. (1993). *American apartheid: segregation and the making of the underclass*: Cambridge, MA: Harvard University Press.

Meares, T. L. (1998a). Place and crime. *Chicago Kent Law Review, 73,* 669-705.

Meares, T. L. (1998b). Social disorganization and drug law enforcement. *American Criminal Law Review, 35,* 191-227.

Morenoff, J. D. & Sampson, R. J. (1997). Violent crime and the spatial dynamics of neighborhood transition: Chicago, 1970-1990. *Social Forces, 76,* 31-64.

Morenoff, J. D., Sampson, R. J., & Raudenbush, S. W. (2001). Neighborhood inequality, collective efficacy, and the spatial dynamics of urban violence. *Criminology, 39,* 7-560.

Myers, S. L. (2000, August 12). *The unintended impacts of sentencing guidelines on family structure.* Paper presented at the annual meeting of the American Sociological Association, Washington, DC.

Neter, J., Kutner, M. H., Nachtsheim, C., & Wasserman, W. (1996). *Applied linear statistical models* (4th ed). Homewood, IL: Richard D. Irwin.

Osgood, W. (2000). Poisson-based regression analysis of aggregate crime rates. *Journal of Quantitative Criminology, 16,* 21-43.

Parke, R., & Clarke-Stewart, A. (2002, January 30). *Effects of parental incarceration on young children.* Paper presented to the National Policy Conference, From Prison to Home: The Effect of Incarceration and Reentry on Children, Families, and Communities, U.S. Department of Health and Human Services and the Urban Institute. Bethesda, MD.

Petersilia, J. (2000, October 12). *Prisoners returning to communities: Political, economic, and social consequences.* Paper presented at the Urban Institute Reentry Roundtable, Washington, DC.

Putnam, R. D. (1993). *Making democracy work: Civic tradition in modern Italy.* Princeton, NJ: Princeton University Press.

Raudenbush, S., & Sampson, R. J. (1999). "Ecometrics": Toward a science of assessing ecological settings, with applications to the systematic observation of neighborhoods. *Sociological Methodology, 29,* 1-41.

Reynolds, M. (1991, February). *Crime in Texas* (NCPA policy report 102). Dallas: National Center for Policy Analysis.

Rose, D. R., & Clear, T. R. (1998a). Incarceration, social capital, and crime: Implications for social disorganization theory. *Criminology, 36,* 441-480.

Rose, D. R., & Clear, T. R. (1998b, April 2-4). *Who doesn't know someone in jail? The impact of exposure to prison on attitudes of public and informal control.* Paper presented at the annual meeting of the Southern Sociological Society, Atlanta.

Rose, D. R., Clear, T. R., & Ryder, J. A. (2000, September). *Drugs, incarceration and neighborhood life: The impact of reintegrating offenders into the community* (Final report to the National Institute of Justice). New York: John Jay College of Criminal Justice.

Rountree, P. W., & Warner, B. D. (1999). Social ties and crime: Is the relationship gendered? *Criminology, 37,* 789-814.

Sampson, R. J. (1985). Neighborhoods and crime: The structural determinants of personal victimization. *Journal of Research in Crime and Delinquency, 22,* 7-40.

Sampson, R. J. (1991). Linking the micro- and macro-level dimensions of community social organization. *Social Forces, 70,* 43-64.

Sampson, R. J., & Bartusch, D. J. (1999, June). Attitudes toward crime, Police, and the law: Individual and neighborhood differences. *National Institute of Justice Research Preview.*

Sampson, R. J. & Groves, W. B. (1989). Community structure and crime: Testing social-disorganization theory. *American Journal of Sociology, 94,* 774-802.

Sampson, R. J., & Raudenbush, S. (1999). Systematic social observation of public spaces: A new look at disorder in urban neighborhoods. *American Journal of Sociology, 105,* 603-651.

Sampson, R. J., Raudenbush, S., & Earls, F. B. (1997). Neighborhoods and violent crime: A multilevel study of collective efficacy. *Science, 277,* 918-924.

Shaw, C. R., & McKay, H. D. (1942). *Juvenile delinquency and urban areas.* Chicago: University of Chicago Press.

Silver, E. (2000). Extending social disorganization theory: A multilevel approach to the study of violence among persons with mental illnesses. *Criminology, 38,* 1043-1074.

Skogan, W. (1990). *Disorder and decline: Crime and the spiral of decay in American neighborhoods.* New York: Free Press.

Taylor, R. B. (2000). *Breaking away from broken windows: Baltimore neighborhoods and the nationwide fight against crime, grime, fear and decline.* Boulder, CO: Westview Press.

Travis, J., Solomon, A. L., & Waul, M. (2001). *From prison to home: The dimensions and consequences of prisoner reentry.* Washington, DC: Urban Institute.

U.S. Bureau of the Census. (n.d.). *1990 census summary tape file 1 (STF1a).* Washington, DC: Author.

Velez, M. B. (2001). The role of public social control in urban neighborhoods: A multilevel analysis of victimization risk. *Criminology, 39,* 837-864.

Warner, B. D., & Pierce, G. L. (1993). Reexamining social disorganization theory using calls to the police as a measure of crime. *Criminology, 31,* 493-517.

Western, B., & Beckett, K. (1999). How unregulated is the U.S. labor market? The penal system as a labor market institution. *American Journal of Sociology, 104,* 1030-1060.

Wikstrom, P. H., & Loeber, R. (2000). Do disadvantaged neighborhoods cause well-adjusted children to become adolescent delinquents? A study of male juvenile serious offending, individual risk and protective factors, and neighborhood context. *Criminology, 38,* 1109-1142.

Wilson, J. Q., & Kelling, G. L. (1982). Broken windows: The police and neighborhood safety. *Atlantic Monthly, 249,* 29-48.

Wilson, W. J. (1987). *The truly disadvantaged: The inner city, the underclass, and public policy.* Chicago: University of Chicago Press.

Wilson, W. J. (1996). *When work disappears: The world of the new urban poor.* New York: Alfred A. Knopf.

Appendix. Correlations, Means, and Standard Deviations for all Variances

	1.	2.	3.	4.	5.	6.	7.	8.	9.	Mean	Standard Deviation
1. Crime rate 97	1.00									5.554	5.160
2. Concentrated disadvantage	.335**	1.00								0.00	
3. % mobility	.238*	.115	1.00							65.126	19.352
4. Admissions	.610***	.552***	-.107	1.00						0.164	0.319
5. Admissions²	.628***	.265*	.019	.907***	1.00					0.127	0.499
6. Admissions³	.614***	.180	-.004	.802***	.975***	1.00				0.163	0.931
7. Releases	.609***	.658***	-.089	.834***	.660***	.537***	1.00			0.261	0.383
8. Crime rate 96	.420***	.325***	.171	.568***	.535***	.508***	.574***	1.00		0.065	46.36
9. Ln population	.322**	.080	.175	.029	-.352**	-.355**	-.186	-.456***	1.00	7.069	0.528
10. Ln crime rate 97	.659***	.416***	.271*	.446***	.333**	.311**	.513***	.712***	-.361	-3.238	0.880

* $p < .05$, ** $p < .01$, *** $p < .001$.

[15]

Why Are U.S. Incarceration Rates So High?

Michael Tonry

Most explanations of the unprecedented increase in American incarceration rates are inadequate. Crime rate increases, more punitive public attitudes, postmodernist angst, and cynical politics are all only part of the explanation. Those things characterize all Western countries; in some of these countries, imprisonment rates have long been stable or declining, and, where they are rising, absolute levels and rates of increase are dwarfed by those in America. The scale of the phenomenon is distinctly American. It arises partly from American moralism and partly from structural characteristics of American government that provide little insulation from emotions generated by moral panics and long-term cycles of tolerance and intolerance.

American imprisonment rates, 668 per 100,000 residents behind bars in mid-1998, have reached unprecedented levels compared with other times in United States history or with current times in other Western democracies. In other Western countries, between 50 and 135 residents per 100,000 are in prison or jail on an average day. In Sweden, 1 resident per 2,000 is locked up; that is the lowest rate. In England, where the rate is the highest, 1 resident per 800 is imprisoned. By contrast, in the United States, 1 resident per 150 is imprisoned; that is 6 to 12 times the rate in other Western countries (Bureau of Justice Statistics 1999; Kuhn 1998).

American punishment policies are especially severe in respects other than imprisonment rates. Only in the United States are constitutional and other safeguards of criminal defendants systematically being reduced; throughout Europe, under the influence of the European Human Rights Convention and Court, defendants' procedural protections have steadily been expanding for the last 20 years (Kurki forthcoming). Among advanced Western countries, only the United States retains and uses the death penalty, and the United States does so with increasing frequency. Only the United States has adopted three-strikes and extensive mandatory minimum-sentencing laws. Only in the United States is the civil service job category prison gerontologist imaginable. Only the United States uses life-without-possibility-of-parole sentences; elsewhere, even murderers sentenced to life terms are eligible for parole or executive-branch commutation, and they are typically released after

MICHAEL TONRY: Director, Institute of Criminology, Cambridge University, and Sonosky Professor of Law and Public Policy, University of Minnesota.

8 to 12 years. Only in the United States are prison sentences longer than 1 or 2 years common; in most countries, fewer than 5 percent of sentences are for a year or longer. In the United States, in 1994, the average sentence among people sent to state prisons for felonies was 71 months. Among those in prison, more than half were serving terms exceeding 10 years (Bureau of Justice Statistics 1998, table 1.3:9).

All of this is a drastic change from earlier times. In the 1930s, for example, the United States had incarceration rates comparable to or lower than European countries such as England, France, Switzerland, and Finland (Tonry and Hatlestad 1997, chap. 3).

More recently, in the 1960s, the United States was in the mainstream. The death penalty was withering away, the incarceration rate was dropping and comparable to those in other Western countries (Blumstein and Cohen 1973; Zimring and Hawkins 1991), the courts were establishing and refining defendants' procedural protections, and crime control was not generally viewed as a partisan or ideological issue.

Now, of course, the United States is unique. The aim of this article is to offer and assess alternate explanations for why American policies have diverged so far from our own past practices and from the practices of other Western countries. To avoid having to use longer-winded phrases repeatedly, I refer to this in shorthand as the problem of "American exceptionalism." I discuss five explanations of increasing complexity for American exceptionalism, and conclude a bit pessimistically that we know why our policies are as they are, but that acting on that knowledge requires qualities of political maturity and public civility that do not now characterize U.S. politics.

The first of the five explanations is crudely empirical. American crime rates are higher or have increased more than other countries', and punishment patterns and policies are no more than a reflection of that reality. The second is psephological. No matter what the crime rates and trends, opinion surveys show that the public has demanded tougher penalties, and elected officials have bowed to that demand. The third is journalistic. Conservative politicians have cynically used crime, as they have used welfare, immigration, and affirmative action, as wedge issues designed to separate White working-class voters from the Democratic Party, and current policies are the result. The fourth is political. American social developments in the past quarter century have fragmented the electorate into a mélange of single-issue political groups, and politicians have had to seek broad-based support around emotional issues like crime, welfare, and immigration that would offend no politically powerful groups. The fifth is historical. Complex and regularly recurring, but poorly understood, interactions among crime trends, public attitudes, and policy making shape our thoughts, our policy debates, and our policies, and current policies are a predictable result.

No single factor could cause so massive a change in policy (Garland 1990). The five explanations do not exhaust the possibilities. Other explanations include widespread public anxieties associated with economic restructuring, the civil rights and feminist movements and increased population diversity, ubiquitous violence in the mass media, the angst associated with postmodernism, and other major social changes (Caplow and Simon 1999; Garland forthcoming). However, all of these, in various forms, affect every Western country and therefore cannot explain why U.S. policies have become so much more severe than elsewhere.

CRUDE EMPIRICISM

The first explanation for why so many Americans are in prison, that our crime rates are higher or faster rising than other countries', has virtually no validity. Crime rates in the United States in the 1990s are, for the most part, no higher than in other Western countries. We know this from the International Crime Victimization Survey, which has been conducted by national governments in most major Western countries since 1989 (e.g., Mayhew and van Dijk 1997). For property crimes, the United States is in the middle of the pack. Chances of being burglarized, having your pocket picked, or having your car stolen are considerably higher in England and several other European countries. For most violent crimes, American rates are among the highest, along with Australia, Canada, Spain, and France, but not the highest. Chances of being robbed, being assaulted, or being a victim of a stranger rape are higher in several other Western countries. Where the United States stands out is in gun violence; our rates of robberies and assaults involving guns, and of gun homicides, are substantially higher than elsewhere (Zimring and Hawkins 1997). Gun violence is important; however, fewer than a fourth of those sentenced to prison are convicted of violent crimes of any type, so this cannot be why U.S. prison patterns and penal policies are so different.

If higher crime rates do not explain American exceptionalism, perhaps crime trends do. Perhaps there is a necessary connection between crime rates and imprisonment rates. When crime rates rise, imprisonment rates follow, and that is why the number of people locked up has increased by five times in the past quarter century, from about 300,000 in 1972 to 1,802,496 in mid-1998.

Figure 1 shows trends in American imprisonment, homicide, and violent crime rates from 1960 to 1993, and the patterns suggest that violent crime and imprisonment at least initially rose together (more recently, however, imprisonment rates have continued their steep climb whereas violence rates have dropped sharply). However, Figure 2 and Figure 3, which show comparable data for Finland and Germany during the same period, indicate that there is no such necessary connection. Other countries could have been used for the comparison, but the United States would still be an exceptional case (Kuhn 1997). Although the homicide and violent crime curves in Finland and Germany rose as steeply as the U.S. curves shown in Figure 1, the imprisonment rate in Germany fell throughout the 1960s and remained roughly level thereafter, and the incarceration rate in Finland fell sharply and steadily throughout the entire period. The reasons for those two countries' patterns are somewhat different (Lappi-Seppälä forthcoming; Weigend forthcoming), but the important point is that they reflect policy decisions that are based on the belief that increased incarceration is neither an appropriate nor an effective response to rising crime rates. American politicians decided otherwise. American imprisonment rates did not rise simply because crime rates rose. They rose because American politicians wanted them to rise.

Something was not working, and deterrence and incapacitation were chosen as strategies to lower crime rates. The only problem with this is that the most drastic such strategies were adopted long after crime rates began to fall. As Figure 4 shows, crime rates for most crimes peaked around 1980, fell through the mid-1980s, rose for awhile for reasons largely associated with the crack cocaine epidemic, and have since fallen sharply. However, the first three-strikes law was enacted in 1993, and the federal truth-in-sentencing law, which authorized $8 billion for state prison construction, was passed in 1994. The meanings of these data are complex, but whatever else they show, they do not show any simple interaction between crime trends and imprisonment patterns.

PUBLIC OPINION

The second explanation for the high imprisonment rate is that public opinion survey results sometimes show that crime and drugs come in first as America's most pressing problem, that large majorities often express the view that sentencing is too lenient, and that people demand that criminal punishment be made tougher. On this account, elected officials have merely respected the public will, and imprisonment rates have risen as a result.

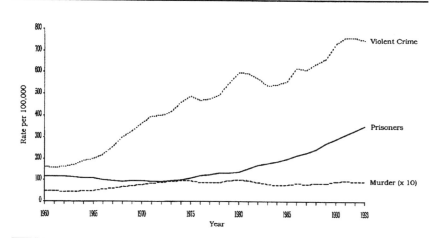

**Figure 1:   Imprisonment, Violent Crime, and Murder Rates per 100,000 Popula-
tion, United States, 1960 to 1993**
SOURCES: Bureau of Justice Statistics. 1962-1994. *Prisoners in the United States.*
Washington, DC: Author. Federal Bureau of Investigation. 1962-1994. *Crime in the
United States.* Washington, DC: Government Printing Office.
NOTE: Violent crime and murder rates are calculated somewhat differently than in Fin-
land and Germany; imprisonment rates do not include jail inmates.

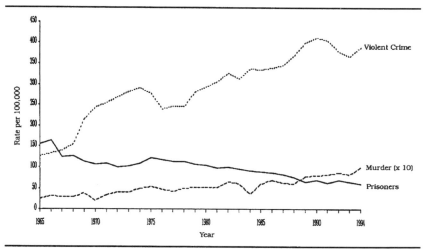

**Figure 2:   Imprisonment, Violent Crime, and Murder Rates per 100,000 Popula-
tion, Finland, 1965 to 1994**
SOURCE: Finnish Ministry of Justice. Available from the National Institute for Legal
Research in Helsinki, Finland.
NOTE: Violent crime and murder rates are calculated somewhat differently than in the
United States; imprisonment rate includes pretrial detainees.

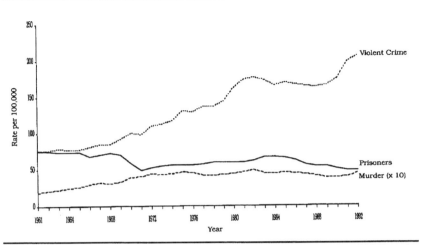

**Figure 3:   Imprisonment, Violent Crime, and Murder Rates per 100,000 Popula-
tion, Germany, 1961-1992**
SOURCE: German Ministry of Justice. Offense data are available from the Bun-
deskriminalamt [Federal Bureau of Criminal Investigation] in Bonn, Germany. Prisoner
data are available from the Statistiches Bundesamt [Office of Federal Statistics] in
Bonn, Germany.
NOTE: Violent crime and murder rates are calculated somewhat differently than in the
United States; imprisonment rate excludes pretrial detainees.

There are two serious deficiencies in this story. The first is that a mountain
of public-opinion scholarship and research shows that the findings I have
reported are fundamentally misleading (Roberts 1992; Roberts and Stalans
1997). We know that ordinary citizens base their opinions on what they know
about crime from the mass media. Consequently, they regard heinous crimes
and bizarre sentences as the norms, they believe sentences are much softer
than they are, and they believe crime rates are rising when they are falling. As
a result, majorities nearly always report that judges' sentences are too lenient;
yet, when they are asked to propose sentences appropriate for individual
cases, they generally propose sentences that are shorter than those actually
imposed (Hough and Roberts 1997). A different body of public opinion
research, using more complex methods than telephone calls at dinnertime,
shows that ordinary people have the same complex and ambivalent attitudes
to criminals that judges and lawyers do—simultaneously wanting offenders
punished and rehabilitated, willing to see taxes increased to pay for treatment
programs but not for prison building, and being insistent on prison sentences
only for the most violent crimes (Roberts and Stalans 1997). Thus, the opin-

ion research findings do not actually support policies of unyielding and ever harsher severity.

The second point is more important. Public nomination of crime as the nation's most pressing problem and public support for harsh laws typically follow, not precede, media and political preoccupation with crime. Although politicians who attempt to win favor by demonstrating their toughness nearly always say that they are honoring citizens' wishes, the evidence is that harping by politicians and the media on crime issues is what causes citizens to become concerned. This is best shown in a recent book by Katherine Beckett (1997), who analyzed interactions among media attention to crime and drug issues, politicians' relative emphasis on those issues, and the results of opinion surveys. She did this in relation to crime policy in the 1970s and drug policy in the 1980s. Content analyses of newspaper and television coverage, when compared with public opinion survey results, showed a recurring pattern: politicians focus on crime policy, or the media increase their crime coverage, or both, and afterward, opinion surveys begin to show heightened public concern about crime or drugs, and heightened support for tough policies.

So public support for harsh policies has coincided with their adoption. However, it is not public opinion per se that leads to harsher policies, but politicians' proposals and posturing that lead to changes in public opinion. This leads to the third explanation for American exceptionalism—politicians for partisan advantage have persistently banked the fires of public fear of crime, and then offered harsh policies to dampen those fires. Assessing that explanation requires a look back at how and why crime control became a focal issue in American politics.

PARTISAN POLITICS

Crime and punishment have been high on American political agendas since the late 1960s. Before Republican presidential candidate Barry Goldwater raised crime in the streets as a partisan issue in his unsuccessful 1964 campaign, public safety was generally seen as one among several important, but unglamorous, core functions of government, like public health, public transit, and public education. Public officials were expected to do their work conscientiously and well, and systematic knowledge was widely seen as relevant to the formulation of policies and the improvement of institutions and practices. Reasonable people differed over the best approaches for addressing particular problems, but the debates were seldom partisan or ideological. Criminal justice policy was a subject for practitioners and technocrats, and

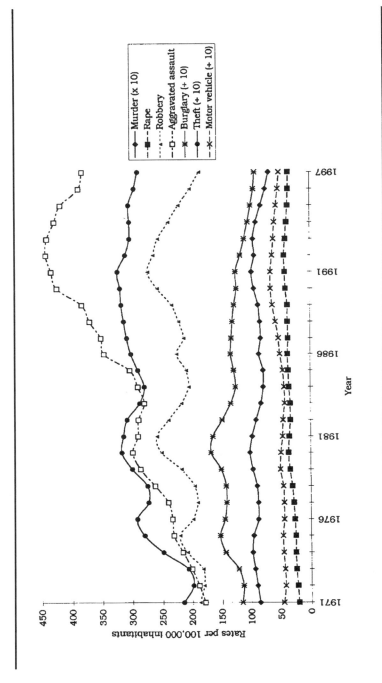

Figure 4:   Offenses Known to Police, Rates per 100,000 Inhabitants, 1971-1997
SOURCE: Federal Bureau of Investigation. 1972-1998. *Crime in the United States*. Washington, DC: Government Printing Office.
NOTE: Murder rates are multiplied by 10 and burglary, theft, and motor vehicle theft rates are divided by 10 for purposes of presentation.

sentencing was the specialized case-by-case business of judges and corrections officials.

In recent decades, however, crime control has been at the center of partisan politics, and policies have been shaped more by symbols and rhetoric than by substance and knowledge. Political scientists and journalists tell the story of how that happened. Until the 1960s, in most of the South, the Democratic Party had dominated electoral politics since the end of Reconstruction. Although many southern voters held conservative views on social and racial issues, policy differences were fought out within a state's Democratic Party rather than between parties. The civil rights movement, however, created a fissure within the Democratic Party between racial and social policy liberals and racial and social policy conservatives. This occurred initially in the South, and eventually nation wide. Republican strategists seized the opportunity to appeal to Nixon (later Reagan) Democrats by defining sharp differences between the parties on three wedge issues: crime control, welfare, and affirmative action. On crime control, conservatives blamed rising crime rates on lenient judges and soft punishments, and demanded toughness. On welfare, conservatives blamed rising welfare rolls on welfare cheats and laziness, and demanded budget cuts. On affirmative action, conservatives blamed White unemployment and underemployment on quotas, and urged elimination of affirmative action (Applebome 1996; Edsall and Edsall 1991).

Crime's role as a wedge issue has had important consequences. Issues that are debated on television and examined in 15- and 30-second commercials necessarily are presented in simplistic and emotional terms. Matters judges and prosecutors agonize over in individual cases are addressed in slogans and symbols, which often leads to the adoption of ham-fisted and poorly considered policies. Notable recent examples include widespread adoption of broadly defined three-strikes laws, mandatory minimum-sentence laws, sexual psychopath laws, and the federal sentencing guidelines. Few corrections executives, judges, or informed scholars support such laws in the forms that are typically adopted, principally for practical reasons: They are too rigid and often result in unjustly harsh penalties, they result in circumvention by judges and lawyers who believe that their application is inappropriate in individual cases, and they are often redundant because serious cases nearly always result in severe penalties anyway (Tonry 1996, chap. 4). Many more practitioners and scholars would support such laws if they were narrowly drawn and carefully crafted to encompass only genuinely serious crimes and genuinely threatening offenders. However, in a "sound-bite politics" era, few politicians are prepared to act as voices of moderation and parsimony, and, as a result, new sentencing laws often lack those qualities.

428   CRIME & DELINQUENCY / OCTOBER 1999

As important, when crime control became one of the central issues in American politics, it ceased being a specialized policy subject, and became instead a symbol or metaphor for broad concepts like personal responsibility and vindication of victims' interests and for more focused ideas such as criminals' immorality and irresponsibility. A broadly defined sexual psychopath law, three-strikes law, or mandatory minimum-sentence law may be ineffective, cruel, or costly, but none of that may matter. If the law's proponents and voters view it as a symbol of revulsion with crime and outrage toward criminals, whether it works or achieves just results in individual cases is often politically irrelevant. When issues are defined in polar terms of morality and immorality, or responsibility and irresponsibility, few elected officials are prepared to be found at the wrong pole.

Few informed people will disagree with the broad outlines of this account. Many liberals might say that the conservative emphasis on toughness was cynical and intellectually dishonest. Many conservatives might respond that they believe that tougher penalties reduce crime rates and, through public opinion polls and electoral support for tough-on-crime candidates, citizens have shown that they support such policies. What better basis for policy making can there be?

In any case, the Right won, and many Democratic politicians have concluded that the only way to defend against sound-bite law-and-order politics, as Bill Clinton is often complimented for having done, is to "get to the right of the Republicans" (Friedman 1993; Walker 1998).

Of all the explanations offered so far, this is the most plausible. It is possible that current American imprisonment policies, and the avoidable damage that they do to prisoners, their families, and their communities; and the fiscal and opportunity costs that they impose on governments (Hagan and Dinovitzer 1999), are merely by-products of an effective political strategy for winning elections. However, that the Right won, whether cynically or honestly motivated, does not fully explain American exceptionalism. It does not explain why such policies were adopted here and not in other countries, and now and not at other times.

POLITICAL FRAGMENTATION

What is needed is an explanation for why crime and punishment served so nicely as a wedge issue, and why so many elected officials were prepared, in recent decades, to behave in ways that their opponents and many observers often perceived as demagogic. Social scientists have offered analyses of political and governmental trends of recent decades that attempt to explain why crime has received so much more sustained attention from governments and politicians than other equally important public policy issues.

Sociologists Theodore Caplow and Jonathan Simon (1999) offer two interconnected reasons (among others) for why U.S. crime policy developed as it did during the past quarter century. One relates to the anomaly that the role of government, particularly the federal government, has broadened greatly in the last 30 years at a time when public confidence in the capacity of government to achieve public purposes has declined. The second relates to the decline of broad-based political coalitions and the development of single-issue politics.

The scope of federal government activity has expanded greatly. For example, the following subjects were largely outside the reach of federal law before the 1960s but are within it today (these are not controversial in principle but very controversial in detail): health care; education; street crime; consumer protection; occupational safety; employment practices; infant and child care; environmental protection; sponsorship of the arts and humanities; and discrimination on grounds of age, race, sex, and disability. Whatever the merits of these changes, they have transformed American politics.

The result, Caplow and Simon (1999) argue, has been a spiral of governmental failure. A whole series of related social problems from disorderly schools to illegitimacy have come to be seen as products of failed governmental programs and as sources of crime. The most visible evidence that they cite is the massive escalation of costs for virtually all major federal government programs without corresponding increases in benefits. Between 1970 and 1995, federal expenditures for health care outpaced inflation by 5 to 1, for education by 3.5 to 1, for Aid to Families with Dependent Children (AFDC) by 3 to 1, and for criminal justice by 6 to 1. Although none of these systems is widely regarded as conspicuously successful, they are interconnected in many ways, and their defects are mutually reinforcing. The extraordinary costs of the health care system prevent any serious effort to alleviate poverty. The deficiencies of the antipoverty programs undermine the public schools. The failures of the schools pour into the criminal justice system.

All of this has led to a remarkable collapse of confidence in government. In response to the survey question, "How much of the time do you trust the government in Washington to do the right thing," Caplow and Simon (1999) reported that 75 percent of a representative national sample in 1964 answered "just about always" or "most of the time." When the same question was put to a similar sample in 1995, only 25 percent gave those answers.

Caplow and Simon's (1999) second observation is that, for unrelated reasons, American politics have moved away from traditional class and regional divisions, and toward a range of single-issue movements. Political campaigns are won by means of overriding themes that link minorities with strong value-based identities. Public discourse is dominated by culture wars, including controversies over abortion, affirmative action, gun control, school prayer, gay rights, capital punishment, animal rights, and assisted suicide.

These controversies, Caplow and Simon (1999) note, do not lend themselves to the log-rolling and bargaining characteristic of traditional American politics. New political movements invite people to join the side of good against evil. To antiabortion activists, abortion is cold-blooded murder. To their adversaries, the right to abortion secures women's ownership of their own bodies. To advocates of strict gun control, the private possession of firearms is foolish and dangerous; to their adversaries, it is the keystone of liberty. The well-organized pressure groups that represent such interests have few means of achieving their goals outside of federal courts, Congress, and the state legislatures. These groups do not have many incentives to cooperate in making government more effective. This makes coalition building difficult and effective implementation of policies even harder.

Until the 1960s, the federal government took no position on most of these issues. Since then, as the result of political balkanization, the balance of power in close elections is likely to be held by single-issue constituencies. Consequently, Congress has increasingly placed the federal government in favor of minority positions on many contested issues. Faced with voters who split on so many issues and who are profoundly skeptical about the ability of government to improve their lives, policy initiatives that command the broadest support—such as harsh crime, welfare, and immigration policies—are understandably important to elected politicians. The important point is that harsh policies on crime and welfare can be debated in moral terms, respond to broad-based anxieties and empathies, and affront no powerful constituency.

By this point, the explanation for American exceptionalism has gotten complicated. Crime rate levels and changes do not have much explanatory power by themselves. Rising crime rates do provide a plausible basis for heightened public concern about crime, but the best evidence is that ordinary people's views are much more complex, ambivalent, and temperate than is widely recognized. Frightening stereotypes and valid fears provide an intelligible reason why voters respond to tough-on-crime rhetoric and appeals, but they do not explain why politicians in our time choose to campaign on those issues rather than others. The account of structural changes in American politics is part of the explanation—there is little support in the late 1990s for ambitious broad-based policy initiatives by government, and it is often easier to mobilize support against something than for something. All of these things provide points of understanding like the dots in a pointillist painting, but they lack a pattern that provides an intelligible picture. That pattern comes from the work of historian David Musto (1987), which suggests that crime policies, political sensibilities, and the nature of public attitudes about crime are determined by cyclical trends in criminality and responses to it.

HISTORICAL CYCLES

Historians have long known that crime rates rise and fall over extended periods for reasons that have little to do with crime control policies. The three most influential scholars of the subject—historian Roger Lane (1989, 1992, 1999) and political scientists Ted Robert Gurr (1989) and James Q. Wilson (Wilson and Herrnstein 1985)—concur in the view that crime rates in the United States, England, Germany, France, and other Western countries have followed a U-shaped or a backwards J-shaped curve, falling from the second quarter of the nineteenth century through the middle of the twentieth century and rising until late in the twentieth century. They disagree as to why that happened. Gurr and Lane argue that the century-long decline is primarily associated with the emergence of the industrial economy and the development of bureaucratic institutions like schools, factories, and the military, which socialized people into patterns of behavioral conformity, rule observance, and deference to authority. Wilson assigns a major role to religious revivalism in the nineteenth century and a related moral awakening that enhanced character-building processes and law-abiding characteristics. However, none of them attributes the decline primarily to changes in criminal justice system agencies or policies. Many of the major institutions of modern criminal justice systems—professional police, the penitentiary, probation, parole, the reformatory, and the juvenile court—were first established during the long period when crime rates were falling, but neither then nor now has the fall been attributed to them (e.g., Friedman 1993; Walker 1998).

More recently, there is evidence that crime rates in Western countries may be in another long-term decline. In the United States, for example, data from the National Crime Victimization Survey show that rates for many crimes fell steadily from 1973 to the 1980s, after which, they increased or stabilized for a few years and resumed a downward path (Kurki 1999). Police data from the Federal Bureau of Investigation's Uniform Crime Reports show a somewhat different (but reconcilable) pattern of crime rates that rose through 1981, fell through 1986, rose again through 1991, and have plummeted since then to levels that, for some crimes, have not been seen since the 1960s. English (Home Office 1998), Dutch (Tak forthcoming), Swedish (Kyvsgaard 1998), and

Norwegian (Larsson 1999) data likewise show significant victimization-rate declines in the 1990s as do data from many countries that participate in the International Crime Victimization Survey (Mayhew and van Dijk 1997).

Drug use and drug policies also exhibit long-term trends with periods of prohibitionism in the 1850s, 1890 to 1930, and 1980 to the present alternating with periods of greater tolerance. Yale historian David Musto (1987) has shown that antidrug policies interact in predictable ways with patterns of drug use. Seemingly perverse but, on reflection understandable, the harshest policies are adopted and the most vigorous prosecutions are carried out after drug use has begun to decline. In our era, for example, self-reported use of marijuana, heroin, and amphetamines peaked for every age group in 1979 to 1980 (for cocaine, in 1984 to 1985) and fell steadily thereafter (Tonry 1996, chap. 3), but the harshest federal antidrug laws were not enacted until 1986 and 1988, and the first federal drug czar was not named until 1989. If reduced drug use was its aim, the war was being won a decade before it was declared.

The reason all this is understandable is that recreational drug use during prohibitionistic periods is widely seen as immoral and socially destructive. Such attitudes explain why an increasing number of people stop using and experimenting with drugs and why, after drug use begins falling, comparatively few voices are raised in opposition to harsh policies. Few people, especially elected public officials, are comfortable speaking out on behalf of immorality. After a while, psychological processes well understood as cognitive dissonance cause many people, perhaps most, to decide that drug use is immoral and threatening and that there is little to be said in favor of classical liberal values of tolerance. In more tolerant periods, by contrast, many more people celebrate Enlightenment ideals of moral autonomy and individuals' rights to make choices about their own lives, and comfortably oppose harsh laws and policies on those grounds.

I mention the recurrent interaction between drug-use patterns and drug-abuse policy because similar patterns may characterize interactions between contemporary crime patterns and crime-control policies. Three similarities stand out. First, the harshest crime control policies—three-strikes laws; lengthy mandatory minimum sentence laws; truth-in-sentencing laws; and increased use of the death penalty—date from the early and mid-1990s, long after crime rates began their steep decline.

Second, few elected officials have been prepared to oppose proposals for harsher laws. Few politicians happily risk being labeled "soft on crime" or "for criminals" rather than for victims. But that is a disparaging account—cowardly, pusillanimous, unprincipled politicians who are unwilling to stand up for what they believe in the face of cynical and demagogic appeals by their political opponents. Some of that disparagement may be warranted, but it is equally likely that, in periods just after crime rates have peaked and begun falling, many more people come to believe that harsh measures are called for and will be effective, even if a few years earlier, their beliefs were very different.

Moreover, enhancing people's predisposition to believe that harsh measures work, harsh laws are often enacted when crime rates are already falling. People who want to make year-to-year comparisons can easily show that the new, tougher policies have worked, because crime rates have fallen in the years immediately after the change when compared with the year immediately before. This happened in relation to New York City's adoption in the early 1990s of zero-tolerance policing, California's adoption in 1994 of a broadly defined three-strikes law, and many states' passage in the mid 1990s of truth-in-sentencing laws. These may be plausible claims on the part of people who are unaware of long-term crime trends, but for people who are, they are disingenuous. The year-to-year crime-rate declines are at least as likely merely to be a continuation of long-term trends as they are to be effects of policy changes. Nonetheless, such patterns bedevil efforts to devise rational and humane public policies for crime (and for drugs), because they provide plausible support for claims that harsh policies work.

Scholars have, in recent years, been trying to make sense of the seeming anomaly that public receptivity to proposals for harsh crime and drug policies remained high in the late 1990s, even in the face of substantial and long-term drops in crime rates and drug use (e.g., Caplow and Simon 1999; Garland forthcoming). A cynical explanation mentioned earlier, and for which there is some evidence, is that conservative politicians found it in their interest to keep voters' attention focused on an issue about which liberals are reluctant to disagree, and public attitudes are simply a predictable response in an era of declining crime rates and moralized policies.

A related explanation is that the mass media have learned that crime pays because of the mass public fascination with the darker sides of life, and that the fears vicariously enjoyed in front of the television or the movie screen are generalized to life outside the home.

A third explanation, consistent with Musto's account of drug policy history and its extension to crime, is that, in the 1990s, people do not really care about the effectiveness of crime and drug-abuse policies but, instead, support harsh policies for expressive reasons. The argument, for which there is some confirmatory public-opinion survey evidence (Doob and Marinos 1995; Tyler and Boeckmann 1997), is that people in our time value the denunciatory qualities of harsh laws.

434   CRIME & DELINQUENCY / OCTOBER 1999

UNDERSTANDING THE FUTURE

As a hypothesis, Musto's paradigm provides a richer account of American exceptionalism in the past quarter century than do any of the other accounts that I have attempted. It explains why public attitudes are harsher when crime rates are falling than when they are rising and, consequently, why law-and-order appeals fell on fertile electoral ground. It explains why politicians feel comfortable appealing to base instincts and proposing policies that, in other times, would have seemed demagogic and cruel. It explains not only why so few voices were raised in opposition to those policies but also why few people felt a need to speak out in opposition. It explains why people were inclined to believe that declining crime and drug-use rates showed that harsh policies worked.

There is really nothing unusual about Musto's account of drug policy history and my extension of it to crime policy generally. Historian John Boswell's celebrated history of homosexuality (1980) shows similar cycles of live-and-let-live tolerance and lethal intolerance of homosexuality, and historians of religion and of the arts have documented similarly cyclical patterns. Grant Gilmore (1974) has written of the alternation of classical and romantic periods in the arts:

> During classical periods, which are, typically, of short duration, everything is neat, tidy, and logical; theorists and critics reign supreme; formal rules of structure and composition are stated to the general acclaim. . . . But the classical period, once it has been formulated, regularly breaks down in a protracted agony. The romantics spurn the exquisitely stated rules of the preceding period; they experiment, they improvise; they deny the existence of any rules; they churn around in an ecstasy of self-expression . . . then, the romantic energy having spent itself—there is a new classical formulation—and so the rhythms continue. (P. 112)

Nor is there anything unusual in the claim that where we stand, and when, influence what we think and what we believe. The where we stand part is something we all recognize in day-to-day life. Wealthy people are more likely to favor low taxes and Republicans than are poor people, who are more likely to favor generous social welfare programs and Democrats. Usually, however, we convince ourselves that we have good reasons other than our self-interest for believing what we believe.

The when we stand part is the same. People in intolerant times are more likely to believe that drug use is immoral and threatening, or that homosexuality is decadent and dangerous, than in tolerant times. Likewise in the arts: during classical periods, people believe that they like tradition, regularity, and formalism; and in romantic times, they do not.

Here, again, historians have things to teach us. Yale's Jaroslav Pelikan (1985), the greatest church historian of our time, in a wonderful book called *Jesus Through the Centuries*, showed how each era reinvents or reinterprets the historical Jesus. Sometimes he is the messianic figure, sometimes the social and political reformer, sometimes the founder of the church, sometimes the charismatic leader, and sometimes the spiritual ascetic whom St. Francis might have imagined. The historic Jesus was who he was, but people in different times saw what they wanted or needed to see.

What has any of this to do with understanding American exceptionalism? Everything, for it shows that America's unprecedented and unmatched taste for imprisonment and harsh criminal justice policies has little to do with them—the offenders who get dealt with one way or another—and everything to do with us.

If we took the historical lessons to heart, we might be less quick to adopt harsh crime policies. In our private lives, we know these things, and our folk wisdom celebrates it—do not strike in anger; sit down and count to 10; do not take your frustrations out on your child, your spouse, or your employee; and write the angry letter, but put it aside until tomorrow and see if you still want to send it. Whether those private insights will soon shape our public policies remains to be seen.

So, actually, we do know a good bit about why our prisons are so full and our policies are so harsh. Unfortunately, it is always easier to see clearly with hindsight to other times, or from afar to other places. Only time will tell whether American crime policies can be made more effective and more humane, more like those of America in other times or those of other Western countries today, or whether the United States will long remain trapped in Musto's paradigm. Until fundamental policy changes are made, the seemingly inexorable increases in incarceration will continue, and American penal policy will retain a severity unknown in other Western countries.

REFERENCES

Applebome, Peter. 1996. *Dixie Rising: How the South Is Shaping American Values, Politics and Culture*. New York: Times Books.

Beckett, Katherine. 1997. *Making Crime Pay: Law and Order in Contemporary American Politics*. New York: Oxford University Press.

Blumstein, Alfred and Jacqueline Cohen. 1973. "A Theory of Stability of Punishment." *Journal of Criminal Law and Criminology* 64:198-201.

Boswell, John. 1980. *Christianity, Social Tolerance, and Homosexuality*. Chicago, IL: University of Chicago Press.

Bureau of Justice Statistics. 1998. *State Court Sentencing of Convicted Felons, 1994*. Washington, DC: Author.

————. 1999. *Prisoners and Jail Inmates at Mid-Year 1998.* Washington, DC: Author.

Caplow, Theodore and Jonathan Simon. 1999. "Understanding Prison Policy and Population Trends." In *Prisons*, edited by M. Tonry and J. Petersilia, vol. 26, *Crime and Justice: A Review of Research*, edited by M. Tonry. Chicago, IL: University of Chicago Press.

Doob, Anthony and Voula Marinos. 1995. "Reconceptualizing Punishment: Understanding the Limitations on the Use of Intermediate Punishments." *University of Chicago Law School Roundtable* 2:413-33.

Edsall, Thomas and Mary Edsall. 1991. *Chain Reaction: The Impact of Race, Rights, and Taxes on American Politics.* New York: Norton.

Friedman, Lawrence. 1993. *Crime and Punishment in American History.* New York: Basic Books.

Garland, David. 1990. *Punishment and Society.* Oxford: Clarendon.

————. Forthcoming. "The Culture of High Crime Societies: The Social Precondition of the New Politics of Crime Control." *British Journal of Criminology.*

Gilmore, Grant. 1974. *The Death of Contract.* Columbus: Ohio State University Press.

Gurr, Ted Robert. 1989. "Historical Trends in Violent Crime: England, Western Europe, and the United States." Pp. 21-54 in *Violence in America*, vol. 1, *The History of Crime*, edited by T. R. Gurr. Newbury Park, CA: Sage.

Hagan, John and Ronit Dinovitzer. 1999. "Collateral Consequences of Imprisonment for Children, Communities, and Prisoners." In *Prisons*, edited by M. Tonry and J. Petersilia, vol. 26, *Crime and Justice: A Review of Research*, edited by M. Tonry. Chicago, IL: University of Chicago Press.

Home Office. 1998. *Criminal Statistics for England and Wales.* London: H.M. Stationery Office.

Hough, Mike and Julian Roberts. 1997. *Attitudes to Punishment: Findings from the British Crime Survey.* Home Office Research Study No. 179. London: Home Office.

Kuhn, André. 1997. "Prison Populations in Western Europe." Pp. 124-33 in *Sentencing Reform in Overcrowded Times—A Comparative Perspective*, edited by M. Tonry and K. Hatlestad. New York: Oxford University Press.

————. 1998. "Sanctions and Their Severity." Pp. 115-43 in *Crime and Criminal Justice Systems in Europe and North America 1990-1994*, edited by K. Kangasunta, M. Joutsen, and N. Ollus. Helsinki, Finland: European Institute for Crime Prevention and Control (HEUNI).

Kurki, Leena. 1999. "United States Crime Rates Keep Falling." *Overcrowded Times* 10(1):1, 6-10.

————. Forthcoming. "International Standards and Limits on Sentencing and Punishment." In *Punishment and Penal Systems in Western Countries*, edited by M. Tonry and R. Frase. New York: Oxford University Press.

Kyvsgaard, Britta. 1998. "Penal Sanctions and the Use of Imprisonment in Denmark." *Overcrowded Times* 9(6):1, 9-10.

Lane, Roger. 1989. "On the Social Meaning of Homicide Trends in America." Pp. 55-79 in *Violence in America*, vol. 1, *The History of Crime*, edited by T. R. Gurr. Newbury Park, CA: Sage.

————. 1992. "Urban Police and Crime in Nineteenth-Century America." Pp. 1-50 in *Modern Policing*, edited by M. Tonry and N. Morris, vol. 15, *Crime and Justice: A Review of Research*, edited by M. Tonry. Chicago, IL: University of Chicago Press.

————. 1999. "Murder in America: A Historian's Perspective." Pp. 191-224 in *Crime and Justice: A Review of Research*, vol. 25, edited by M. Tonry. Chicago, IL: University of Chicago Press.

Lappi-Seppälä, Tapio. Forthcoming. "Sentencing and Punishment in Finland: The Decline of the Repressive Ideal." In *Punishment and Penal Systems in Western Countries*, edited by M. Tonry and R. Frase. New York: Oxford University Press.

Larsson, Paul. 1999. "Norway Prison Use Up Slightly, Community Penalties Lots." *Overcrowded Times* 10(1):1, 11-13.

Mayhew, Pat and Jan van Dijk. 1997. *Criminal Victimisation in Eleven Industrialized Countries: Key Findings from the 1996 International Crime Victims Survey*. The Hague: Dutch Ministry of Justice.

Musto, David. 1987. *The American Disease: Origins of Narcotic Control*. Rev. ed. New Haven, CT: Yale University Press.

Pelikan, Jaroslav. 1985. *Jesus Through the Centuries: His Place in the History of Culture*. New Haven, CT: Yale University Press.

Roberts, Julian V. 1992. "Public Opinion, Crime, and Criminal Justice." Pp. 99-180 in *Crime and Justice: A Review of Research*, vol. 16, edited by M. Tonry. Chicago, IL: University of Chicago Press.

Roberts, Julian V. and Loretta Stalans. 1997. *Public Opinion, Crime, and Criminal Justice*. Boulder, CO: Westview.

Tak, Peter. Forthcoming. "Sentencing and Punishment in the Netherlands." Pp. in *Punishment and Penal Systems in Western Countries*, edited by M. Tonry and R. Frase. New York: Oxford University Press.

Tonry, Michael. 1996. *Sentencing Matters*. New York: Oxford University Press.

Tonry, Michael and Kathleen Hatlestad, eds. 1997. *Sentencing Reform in Overcrowded Times—A Comparative Perspective*. New York: Oxford University Press.

Tyler, Tom and Robert Boeckmann. 1997. "Three Strikes and You're Out, But Why?" *Law and Society Review* 31:237-65.

Walker, Samuel. 1998. *Popular Justice: A History of American Criminal Justice*. Rev. ed. New York: Oxford University Press.

Weigend, Thomas. Forthcoming. "Sentencing Policy in Germany." In *Punishment and Penal Systems in Western Countries*, edited by M. Tonry and R. Frase. New York: Oxford University Press.

Wilson, James Q. and Richard Herrnstein. 1985. *Crime and Human Nature*. New York: Simon & Schuster.

Zimring, Franklin E. and Gordon Hawkins. 1991. *The Scale of Imprisonment*. Chicago, IL: University of Chicago Press.

———. 1997. *Crime Is Not the Problem: Lethal Violence in America*. New York: Oxford University Press.

Part IV
Political Challenges

[16]

The Politics of Punishment across Time and Space: A Pooled Time-Series Analysis of Imprisonment Rates*

DAVID JACOBS, *Ohio State University*
JASON T. CARMICHAEL, *Ohio State University*

Abstract

Despite considerable theoretical interest, little is known about the political determinants of punishment. This study uses a pooled time-series design to fill this gap by examining political and other determinants of state imprisonment rates. The presence of Republican elected officials is used to assess the strength of the law-and-order political party. Ethnic threat theories suggest that imprisonments will be more likely in jurisdictions with the most blacks or Hispanics, while economic threat theories suggest that the imprisoned population will be greater where economic stratification is most pronounced. After controlling for social disorganization, religious fundamentalism, political conservatism, and violent crimes, the results show that Republican strength and minority threat lead to higher imprisonment rates. Statistical interactions support predictions that these relationships became stronger after greater Republican stress on law and order. The latter findings confirm theoretical expectations that these relationships are historically contingent.

What factors account for shifts in the imprisoned population? Theoretical explanations for the incidence of punishment are fundamental to an understanding of social order. Many theorists (Collins 1975; Goode 1972; Lenski 1966; Tilly 1992; Weber 1968) claim that sanctions must be used to insure internal stability even in

* We thank Joan Huber, Lisa Keister, and Edward Crenshaw for their comments on prior drafts. Bob Kaufman and Jim Zilliak helped us with statistical advice. All unreported analyses referred to in the text and the data are avialable on request. Direct correspondence about this manuscript to David Jacobs, Department of Sociology, 300 Bricker, 190 N. Oval Mall, Ohio State University, Columbus, Ohio 43210. E-mail jacobs.184@osu.edu.

the most progressive societies. As Weber pointed out long ago, the crucial defining element of the state is its ability to punish domestic dissidents. Although domestic order in advanced societies is based on more than the state's ability to sanction, without this power governments cease to exist.

The classical theorists who followed Hobbes and asked how social order is possible went to great lengths to account for the amount of formal punishment under various conditions. Durkheim and Weber help us understand how states employ legal sanctions to control their populations, while recent scholars have used neo-Marxist perspectives to explain the incidence and severity of punishment. A better understanding of the determinants of imprisonments should increase our knowledge about the punitive foundations of social order.

The popular wisdom views fluctuations in imprisonments as a natural response to changes in crime. Yet there is little recent correspondence between yearly shifts in the crime and imprisonment rates in the U.S. From 1947 until the early 1970s the imprisonment rates remained almost constant (see Figure 1). After 1980 the total crime rates stopped growing and after 1990 these rates fell, yet Figure 1 shows that the proportion of the population that was imprisoned grew dramatically throughout this period. The absence of a positive relationship between the crime and the imprisonment rates suggests a need for other explanations.

Many theorists see incarceration as intensely political (Chambliss 1994; Foucault 1977; Garland 1990; Savelsberg 1994). Garland (1990:134) justifies a political approach when he writes that punishment should be seen "not in the narrow terms of the "crime problem" but instead as one of the mechanisms for managing the underclass" Because the punishments administered by the state are a fundamental component of political authority (Foucault 1977; Garland 1990), a well developed political sociology of sanctions should deepen our understanding about how this authority is created and sustained. A better understanding of these relationships also should help explain the puzzling discrepancy between the stability or the recent reduction in street crime and the sharp growth in the imprisonment rates. All of these considerations suggest that research that focuses on the political determinants of imprisonments should be theoretically productive.

Only a few quantitative studies examine the political determinants of punishment. Beckett (1997) holds both the crime rates and media coverage constant and finds that statements of national politicians magnify public perceptions about the salience of street crime. Her results suggest that the law and order appeals that some politicians use to gain office amplify public anxieties and resentments about these offenses. Jacobs and Helms (1996) analyze yearly shifts in prison admissions and find that growth in the strength of the law-and-order Republican party produces a subsequent expansion in these rates. Caldeira and Cowart (1980) find that in contrast to Democrats, Republican presidents since Truman increased spending on corrections and other criminal justice programs.

Politics of Punishment across Time and Space / 63

FIGURE 1:   Shifts in the Prison Population per 100,000 and Crime Rates
            Using Differing Scales

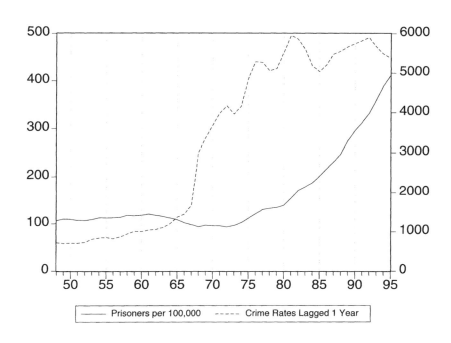

Note: Crime rates graphed on right axis

Although state officials are responsible for most of the decisions about sentencing, time served, and prison capacity, these three longitudinal investigations of yearly outcomes in the entire U.S. could not isolate state-level effects. Because the available pooled time-series studies of state imprisonment rates (Carroll & Cornell 1985; Greenberg & West 1998; Parker & Horwitz 1986; Wallace 1981) have not given much attention to political explanations, we employ this useful estimation procedure to assess the influence of politics on state incarceration rates.

A panel design offers many advantages. Perhaps the influence of the political or other determinants of imprisonments is historically contingent. Some explanations may be more influential in one period than others (Isaac & Griffin 1989). We therefore use a panel design that is sensitive to historical shifts in the strength of relationships. Such an estimation approach is advantageous because it takes into account both cross-sectional variation and changes in imprisonments over time. Yet single factor explanations are suspect, so we must examine many hypotheses in this analysis, but this means the next section cannot focus on just a few accounts.

State agencies have the most influence on correctional outcomes. It would be surprising if these administrative units are not governed by the same political factors that account for the behavior of other state bureaucracies. While we do not believe that politics is the only explanation for jurisdictional differences in imprisonment rates, various considerations suggest that these underresearched explanations should be subjected to additional study.

Theoretical Explanations for Imprisonments

Three approaches inform our understanding of state behavior. The most recent, exemplified by Evans et al. (1984), suggests that parochial interests determine political outcomes. Office holders and candidates strategically chose issues that increase their support at the expense of their rivals. A second tradition treats public policy as the result of external social forces that act on the state. This explanatory approach leads to hypotheses about the effects of social divisions on political outcomes. A third approach stresses ideology because citizen political values may best determine which policies they will support.

We first present explanations for imprisonments based on the strategic behavior of political entrepreneurs. We go on to discuss the effects of minority and economic threat. After presenting rationales for political ideology and fundamentalist religious beliefs, we present the logic for the controls used in this analysis.

POLITICAL ENTREPRENEURS AND PUNITIVE OUTCOMES: BRINGING THE STATE BACK IN

State officials often stress issues that help them overcome electoral handicaps. An anti-crime agenda can be extremely useful in this endeavor. Conservative parties generally support economic policies that help the affluent at the expense of the least affluent. Hibbs (1987) and Blank and Blinder (1986), for example, show that conservative parties chose macroeconomic policies that help their prosperous constituents at the expense of the poor. Allen and Campbell (1994) show that regressive tax policies that benefit the rich and hurt the poor are more likely when Republicans hold office. Yet economic resource distributions are skewed so the affluent are in the minority. This makes the electoral base of more conservative parties smaller than the base of moderate left parties.

While their support for regressive policies makes electoral success more difficult for conservative parties, an emphasis on street crime helps to overcome this disadvantage. Conservative candidates use law and order appeals to attract less affluent voters who are more likely to be crime victims and who are more likely to live in or near to areas where violent crime is problematic. Officials in the Nixon administration have acknowledged that they deliberately used the law and order issue to appeal to anti-minority sentiments (Edsal & Edsal 1991). By emphasizing street crime and other social problems readily blamed on a racial underclass, parties closer to the right can win elections by attracting votes from the less prosperous (Beckett 1997) and still pursue economic policies that help their affluent core supporters (Hibbs 1987).

Instead of highlighting social arrangements that close off law abiding alternatives for the poor, conservatives see reprehensible individual choices as the primary explanation for street crime (Burnham 1970; Thorne 1990). If this view is correct, increases in the expected costs of illegal acts should be effective. Republicans often claim that deterrence is the best remedy for these offenses. The core support for conservative parties comes from the prosperous who are well served by existing arrangements, so appeals for law and order will not offend this constituency. In part because Democrats and their liberal supporters are likely to see street crime as the result of unfortunate social circumstances, it has been more difficult for Democrats to adopt a political strategy that emphasizes deterrence and retribution. In any case, claims that the Democrats are "soft on crime" became a major part of Republican campaigns at both the national and the state levels since the 1964 presidential election (Chambliss 1994; Davey 1998).

After they were elected, Republican incumbents did not disregard their promises. Caldeira and Cowart (1980) find that Republican presidents since 1935 spent greater amounts on various criminal justice policies more than their Democratic counterparts. State level Republican officials also allocated more tax dollars to law enforcement and corrections than their Democratic counterparts (Scheingold 1991; Davey 1998). Both federal and state Republican officials vigorously supported longer sentencing provisions and increased the number of crimes punishable by imprisonment.

If Beckett's (1997) findings are correct and political rhetoric enhances public fear of and resentments against street crime, successful law and order campaigns should increase political support for harsh punishment. Imprisonment rates therefore should be more substantial in jurisdictions where the law and order Republican party has been most successful for two reasons. First, according to Beckett, Republican rhetoric magnifies public demands for severe penalties. Second, after they gain office Republican officials can follow their predilections and make imprisonment and longer sentences more likely by increasing the penalties for various offenses and by expanding prison capacity. Both accounts suggest that *jurisdictions with more Republicans in important political offices and a politically stronger Republican party should have higher imprisonment rates.*

Beckett's findings that claims of national politicians create anxieties about street crime suggest that these relationships may be historically contingent. After a tentative use of this issue in the 1964 election, subsequent Republican presidential candidates increased their emphasis on law and order. Nixon ran on riots and street crime in 1968, while Reagan used the same rhetoric in 1980 (Beckett 1997; Edsal & Edsal 1991). Yet the Bush campaign against Dukakis in 1988 reached new heights in the weight given to this issue. Bush supporters ran vivid advertisements implying that when Dukakis was governor of Massachusetts, he was responsible for the violent crimes committed by a black inmate on temporary furlough from prison. Davey (1998) provides evidence that these contrasts in Republican and Democratic rhetoric about punitive reactions to crime expanded throughout the 1980s.

Beckett's results about the relationship between political rhetoric about law and order and the salience of crime and Davey's evidence about the growth in partisan differences on this issue lead to a historically contingent hypothesis. If political rhetoric about street crime increases public demands for harsh punishments, *the relationships between Republican political strength and incarcerations should become more substantial during the latter part of the analysis period during a time when both state and national Republicans placed greater emphasis on law and order.* Tests for the presence of interactive relationships between Republican strength and time should show if these expectations about the presence of historically contingent relationships are correct.

SOCIAL DIVISIONS WITH POLITICAL IMPLICATIONS: MINORITY PRESENCE AND ECONOMIC INEQUALITY

Social divisions that are external to the state should explain imprisonment rates as well. The threat posed by a large racial underclass should produce enhanced incarceration rates. Substantial gaps in the economic resources of the rich and the poor may have the same effect because repressive measures may be particularly likely in the most unequal jurisdictions where the affluent feel menaced by an economic underclass with much to gain from violence that takes resources from the rich.

Minority Threat

Blumer (1958) and Blalock (1967) claim that dominant groups are threatened by growth in minority populations. Fossett and Kiecolt (1989), and Bobo and Hutchings (1996) show that negative attitudes about blacks are more likely in areas with the most blacks. Liska, Lawrence, and Sanchirico (1982) hold the crime rate constant and find that fear of crime is greater in cities with more African-Americans. Perceptions about the menace of a potentially violent, expanding racial underclass should increase the likelihood that dominant whites will successfully demand harsh punishments and increased incarceration rates.

Additional findings support these threat expectations about social control. Studies of the determinants of police strength show that cities with more minorities have larger numbers of police officers relative to their population (Jackson 1989; Liska et al. 1981). Jacobs and Helms (1999) find that a growth in the percentage of nonwhites led to greater spending on prisons and jails. These results suggest that whites successfully demand severe penalties for crime in areas where minority presence is greatest. If this threat hypothesis is correct, *we can expect that imprisoned populations should be larger in jurisdictions with the most blacks*. Because Hispanics occupy a role similar to that of blacks in many states, it is equally plausible that *states with more substantial Hispanic populations will have higher imprisonment rates as well.*

The same logic leads to additional hypotheses about historically contingent relationships. While the relative presence of African-Americans stayed almost constant, the percentage of Hispanics increased substantially during the analysis period. *If the Hispanic version of the ethnic threat account is correct, the relationship between Hispanic presence and imprisonments should become stronger with the passage of time.*

Another historically contingent hypothesis about minority threat seems equally plausible. Perhaps the covert racial elements in the increasingly strident Republican appeals for law and order (Davey 1998) accentuated public fear of violent black criminals. If this hypothesis is correct, we can expect other period contrasts in the results. *If the sharp growth in Republican rhetoric about law and order magnified fears of a violent black underclass, the relationship between African American presence and the imprisonment rates also should become stronger near the end of the analysis period.* We therefore estimate contingent relationships between ethnic threat and imprisonments by testing for interactions between period and the presence of two minorities. This approach will tell us if relationships between ethnic threat and imprisonments became stronger after expansions in political emphasis on law and order.

Economic Threat

Many scholars (Garland 1990; Chambliss & Seidman 1980), have argued that rates of punishment are shaped by the menace of an economic rather than a racial or ethnic underclass. Both Weberians and neo-Marxists claim that disparities in economic resources create a potentially unstable social order that must be sustained by repression. Chambliss and Seidman (1980:33), for example, write that "the more economically stratified a society becomes, the more it becomes necessary for dominant groups to enforce through coercion the norms of conduct that guarantee their supremacy."

A growing economic underclass with an interest in the use of violence to redistribute resources and little to lose should threaten economically influential groups. The privileged may respond to increased inequality by calling for heightened punishment. The menace of an economic underclass is best thought of as a relational concept (Jacobs 1979), so increased differences in the resources of the affluent and the least affluent should magnify this threat. If the economic version

Crime and Criminal Justice

68 / *Social Forces* 80:1, September 2001

of the threat hypothesis is correct, *enhanced economic inequality should produce more substantial imprisonment rates*. Because disputes about the relative importance of minority threat or economic inequality remain unresolved, we test both of these versions of threat theory.

POLITICAL IDEOLOGY AND RELIGIOUS FUNDAMENTALISM

The prior explanations have emphasized explanations that stress political and social arrangements. Yet public belief systems may provide more powerful explanations for punitive outcomes especially in a relatively populistic, direct democracy like the U.S. where public opinion can be such an important determinant of symbolic policies like punishment.

Political Ideology

While expansions in the strength of the more conservative Republican party may lead to higher imprisonment rates because strategically acute Republicans can reap substantial political gains by emphasizing street crime, an equally plausible alternative explanation focuses on ideology. Perhaps the Republican party does best in jurisdictions where conservative values are strongest. Instead of being imposed from above by political leaders, it is equally plausible that higher incarceration rates are the result of demands for harsh punishment by a conservative citizenry.

An emphasis on punishment is consistent with conservative beliefs about individual accountability. Conservatives see criminals as autonomous, rational individuals who are responsible for their acts and therefore deserve to be punished (Lacey 1988). Conservative thought about crime relies on other concepts borrowed from the marketplace. According to this view "punishment should be equivalent to the offense, so that justice consists in a kind of equity or fair trading that exchanges one harmful act for another which equals it" (Garland 1990:113).

Because they believe that individuals deliberately choose to disobey the law (Burnham 1970; Thorne 1990), conservatives often hold that deterrence is the best remedy for lawless behavior. Molnar (1976:47), for example, claims that "if those who deserve it are not appropriately penalized, then the so-far guiltless tend to fall, by a kind of social gravitational pull, to lower levels of discipline and civilization." Studies indicate that respondents with liberal values are far less likely to support punitive reactions to crime (Taylor, Scheppele, & Stinchcombe 1979; Langworthy & Whitehead 1986; Van Dijk & Steinmetz 1988). All of these considerations suggest that *the imprisonment rates should be most substantial in jurisdictions where conservative values are strongest and support for liberal views is least substantial.*

Religious Fundamentalism

In part because they follow their political counterparts and give little weight to environmental factors that mitigate culpability, religious conservatives stress retribution. Historical research suggests that religious views influenced punishment (Erikson 1966; Ignatieff 1978; McGowen 1995). Survey research (Grasmick et al. 1992; Grasmick & McGill 1994; Curry 1996) shows that fundamentalist Protestant values are associated with greater support for harsh reactions to crime. According to this retaliatory outlook, the state is obligated to make those who are guilty of grievous social harms pay for what they have done.

Where such values are prevalent, we can expect increased demands for severity. In states where membership in fundamentalist Protestant churches and traditional religious views are most common, public officials should face heightened pressures to sentence offenders to prison and increase sentence length. Because these demands should increase prison admissions and time served, we expect that *states with the largest membership in fundamentalist Protestant churches will have higher incarceration rates.*

Unemployment and Additional Controls

Most empirical work on imprisonment rates focused on the neo-Marxist hypothesis that imprisonment is used to control the excess supply of labor in capitalist societies (Rusche & Kirchheimer 1939). Many studies have examined the links between unemployment and subsequent imprisonments, but investigators do not find consistent results (Melossi 1989; Michalowski & Pearson 1990). A literature review conducted by sympathetic scholars (Chiricos & Delone 1992) concludes that only 60% of the 147 reported relationships between unemployment and imprisonments are positive. Despite these discrepancies, the attention given to this hypothesis in the literature suggests unemployment should be investigated.

Because we must limit this research to relationships of theoretical interest, the administrative procedures that states use to control the size of their incarcerated population are not at issue. Policies such as determinate sentencing laws can be viewed as part of the dependent variable. Yet there is considerable interest in the influence of these laws, so we assess their independent effects on imprisonments. The standard assumption is that such provisions increase the incarcerated population. In what is probably the most carefully done study, however, Marvell and Moody (1996) find that the great majority of states with determinate sentencing laws have smaller prison populations. Because there is disagreement about the direction of this relationship, we use two-tailed significance tests to evaluate this effect.

Jurisdictions with greater percentages of their population living in larger communities may have higher imprisonment rates because large cities are notoriously difficult to police. Officials in these jurisdictions may be more likely to invoke severe penalties for street crimes. Studies of public policy often find that the presence of economic resources required to support expensive programs is an important explanatory factor (Dye 1966; Hofferbert 1966), so we see if the tax base matters. Regional effects that capture unmeasured cultural and other differences should be held constant as well. Finally, incarcerations should be most likely in states with the greatest amount of lawless behavior, so we include serious crime rates in all analyses.

Summary

This study focuses on political effects and ethnic or economic divisions that should be reflected in the politics of punishment. Because local Republican officials should be likely to support severe punishments, we see if states where the Republican party is strongest have larger incarcerated populations. Minority threat hypotheses suggest that states with the most blacks or Hispanics will have higher imprisonment rates, while an economic threat hypothesis suggests that economic inequality will produce more incarcerations. We also see if political ideology and religious fundamentalism explain state imprisonment rates, and we include controls for the amount of serious crime, and unemployment as well.

Methods

RESEARCH DESIGN, THE DEPENDENT VARIABLE, AND ESTIMATION

We follow Greenberg and West (1998) and use data from the 50 states largely taken from the 1970, 1980, and 1990 Census. If the analysis is not confined to census years, the values of critical explanatory variables such as the percentage of blacks or Hispanics and economic inequality must be estimated for the nine years between each census. To avoid measurement error in such important explanatory variables and results that would automatically favor some hypotheses over others, we study imprisonment in these three periods and analyze 150 state-years. The sample starts in 1970 because the census does not report Hispanic presence or economic inequality before then.[1]

We analyze prisoners per hundred thousand because this outcome is a more comprehensive indicator of total punitive responses than admission rates or sentences. When admissions or the length of sentences increase, prison officials can use early releases to create space for new inmates. Prison admissions or sentence length therefore could expand even when total imprisonments stay constant or decline. Imprisonment rates are a more exhaustive measure than sentence length or admission rates because they capture the probability of imprisonment, time served, early releases, and the state provisions about parole violation reincarcerations.[2]

Because prison terms often are longer than a year, we borrow a method used in time-series research when investigators are unsure about the time needed for relationships to be completed and use two-year averages of the imprisonment rates. The dependent variable therefore is constructed by calculating the natural log of the mean of per capita imprisonments in 1971-72, 1981-82, and 1991-92 (variables are logged to the base e to create unskewed distributions and multivariate normality). When we analyze prison populations limited to just the first year after each census in unreported equations, the point estimates are similar and the significance tests remain identical to those we report.

There are two standard ways to estimate panel models with more cases than periods. Fixed-effects models automatically hold constant all unchanging case attributes that are not included in models, so stronger claims can be made that unmeasured effects are not biasing the results. Because the alternative random-effects procedure does not automatically eliminate all case attributes that remain constant over time, the effects of theoretically interesting time-invariant explanatory variables can be estimated with this approach. Each procedure has advantages and disadvantages, so we present results based on both.[3]

We estimate shifts in the strength of relationships at different times by breaking some explanatory variables by year and by including interactions with time and the main effects in the models (Hsiao 1986; McDowell, Singell & Zilliak 1999). This use of period-specific interactions will show how relationships shift over time. In addition to their substantive advantages, such specifications should increase model explanatory power because the coefficients on the periodized variables will not be forced to be equal. To promote comparisons, we report results from both unperiodized and periodized equations, but we include uninteracted period dummies in all models to control for the sharp expansions in imprisonments. The use of these period dummies in all analyses means we use either two-factor fixed-effects or mixed fixed-effects, random-effects estimation.

MEASUREMENT OF EXPLANATORY VARIABLES

We measure Republican strength with an index created by multiplying a dummy coded 1 for the presence of a Republican governor with the percentage of Republicans in state legislatures. Minority presence is assessed with the percentage of blacks and with the natural log of the percentage of Hispanics.[4] We assess economic inequality with a Gini index calculated by the Census on family incomes, while the unemployment rates are taken from the same source. We assess poverty with the log of the percentage of families below the poverty line.

Berry et al. (1998) view citizen ideology as the mean position on a liberal-conservative continuum. To construct a measure that varies over time, they identify the ideological position of each member of Congress from a state with interest group ratings by the Americans for Democratic Action and COPE. These pressure groups computed each representative's liberalism-conservatism score from their voting record. Berry et al. estimate citizen ideology within each congressional district in a state with the ideology score for district incumbents and an estimated score for each incumbent's last challenger. Incumbent ideology scores are combined with estimated challenger ideology scores weighted by within district vote margins to measure congressional district ideology. Berry et al. then compute state scores on liberalism-conservatism with the mean scores for all congressional districts in a state.

Following a useful innovation in Greenberg and West (1998), we measure religious fundamentalism in the states with the natural log of a scale created by Morgan and Watson (1991) based on state religious affiliations enumerated by Quinn et al. (1982). This variable is measured only in 1980, although Newport (1979) suggests that church membership is extremely stable. Finally, the regional dummies are coded from census definitions. Because religious fundamentalism and the regional dummies do not change from one period to the next, we must use random-effects models to assess their effects.[5]

The degree to which state populations live in large communities of 50,000 or more is measured with the percentage living in MSAs. A state's tax base is operationalized with the log of mean incomes in 1987 dollars. Although we tried other crime rate combinations, the natural log of the violent crime rates is the most effective measure. We follow Greenburg and West (1998) and use a dummy variable coded "1" if a state had determinate sentencing provisions based on the codes in Marvell and Moody (1996).[6]

SPECIFICATION

Except for regional dummies and the political ideology measure (which assigns higher scores to more liberal states), the coefficients on all explanatory variables should be positive. One of the more general specifications of the fixed-effects panel models that do not include interactions with time therefore is:

$$
\begin{aligned}
Prison\ population = &\ b_0 + b_1 Repub + b_2 Ideology + b_3 Black + b_4 Hispanics \\
&+ b_5 Inequal + b_6 Unemployment + b_7 Metro + b_8 Violent\ crime + b_9 Tax\ base \\
&+ b_{10} DSL + b_{11} Yr_{1980} + b_{12} Yr_{1990}
\end{aligned}
\tag{1}
$$

where *Prsion population* is the natural log of the mean number of prisoners per 100,000 population in the two years after a census, *Repub* is a dummy coded 1 if a state had a Republican governor times the percentage of Republicans in the legislature, *Ideology* is the Berry et al. measure of political ideology, *Black* is the percentage of blacks, *Hispanics* is the natural log of the percentage of Hispanics, *Inequal* is a Gini index computed on income, *Unemployment* is the unemployment rate, *Metro* is the percentage of state residents living in metropolitan areas, *Violent*

TABLE 1: The Means and Standard Deviations Over Time and Across States.

	Mean 1970	Mean 1980	Mean 1990	Overall Standard Deviation	Cross State Standard Deviation	Over Time Standard Deviation
Ln Prisoners per capita	4.239	4.840	5.471	.684	.437	.529
Republican Strength	21.520	19.794	17.435	24.637	16.694	18.222
Ln percent Hispanic	.388	.784	.976	1.161	1.125	.316
Percent black	8.778	9.182	9.612	9.200	9.235	.710
Ln violent crime rate	5.384	5.964	6.110	.692	.603	.347
Percent unemployed	4.874	6.786	6.366	1.716	1.270	1.164
Economic enequalty (Gini)	.359	.360	.395	.027	.020	.019
Percent residents in MSAs	61.488	61.364	66.914	22.661	22.525	3.599
Ln percent poor families	.823	.818	.792	.149	.140	.055
Tax base (Ln mean income)	10.289	10.218	10.362	.163	.146	.075
Determinate sentencing laws	.000	.140	.200	.318	.239	.212
Political ideology	44.589	42.406	48.222	15.980	14.761	6.356
Ln fundamentalism	-2.222	-2.222	-2.222	1.295	1.295	.000

crime is the natural log of the violent crime rate, *Tax base* is the natural log of real mean household incomes, *DSL* is a dummy scored 1 if a state had a determinate sentencing law, and *Yr* is a dummy is coded 1 for that year.

In additional fixed-effects models we estimate the period-specific effects of some explanatory variables by testing for interactions between these variables and the two period dummies. A general specification of these models is:

$$\begin{aligned}
\textit{Prison population} &= b_0 + b_1 \left(Repub \times Yr_{1990} \right) + b_2 \left(Repub \times Yr_{1980} \right) + b_3 Repub \\
&+ b_4 Ideology + b_5 \left(Hisp \times Yr_{1990} \right) + b_6 \left(Hisp \times Yr_{1980} \right) + b_7 Hisp \\
&+ b_8 \left(Black \times Yr_{1990} \right) + b_9 \left(Black \times Yr_{1980} \right) + b_{10} Black + b_{11} \text{ Violent crime} \\
&+ b_{12} Unemp + b_{13} Inequality + b_{14} Yr_{1980} + b_{15} Yr_{1990}
\end{aligned} \tag{2}$$

where all variables are defined as above, and b_3, b_7, b_{10}, b_{14} and b_{15} are the coefficients on all required main effects. Because their scores do not change from one period to the next, we conclude the analyses by using three regional dummies and religious fundamentalism in random-effects models that use specifications otherwise similar to those in equation 2.

74 / *Social Forces* 80:1, September 2001

TABLE 2: Fixed-Effects Estimates of the Determinants of U.S. State Imprisonment Rates[a]

	1	2	3	4
Intercept	2.8268***	2.4537*	-.7324	-2.6174
	(.7782)	(1.0406)	(3.8786)	(3.8437)
Republican srength[b]	.1369	.1428	.1407	.1236
	(.0879)	(.0889)	(.0891)	(.0869)
Political ideology	-.0047*	-.0045*	-.0047*	-.0056*
	(.0027)	(.0028)	(.0028)	(.0027)
Ln percent Hispanic	.1164	.1224	.1080	.0736
	(.0807)	(.0817)	(.0835)	(.0823)
Percent black	.0455*	.0399	.0392	.0378
	(.0262)	(.0283)	(.0283)	(.0275)
Ln violent crime rate	.1693	.1588	.1541	.1430
	(.1116)	(.1137)	(.1140)	(.1108)
Percent unemployed	.0199	.0174	.0155	.0160
	(.0200)	(.0206)	(.0208)	(.0202)
Percent residents in MSAs	.0023	.0029	.0025	.0037
	(.0064)	(.0065)	(.0066)	(.0064)
Economic inequalty (Gini)	—	1.2187	1.5820	2.9084
		(2.2457)	(2.2891)	(2.2868)
Tax base (Ln mean income)	—	—	.3047	.4471
			(.3573)	(.3518)
Determinate sentencing laws	—	—	—	-.2067**
				(.0827)
1 if 1980	.3948***	.4040***	.4370***	.4912***
	(.0924)	(.0943)	(.1021)	(.1015)
1 if 1990	.9881***	.9516***	.9343***	.9420***
	(.1084)	(.1280)	(.1296)	(.1260)
R^2	.795***	.803***	.804***	.807***
(N = 150)				

Note: Standard errors are in parentheses.
[a] State fixed effects are not included in the R^2
[b] To facilitate comparisons, all coefficients on Republican Strength have been multiplied by 100.

* p ≤ .05   ** p ≤ .01   *** p ≤ .001 (one-tailed tests except for determinate sentencing)

TABLE 3: Fixed-Effects Models of the Relationships between Explanatory Variables and U.S. State Imprisonment Rates that Test for Time-Varying Relationships[a]

	1	2	3	4
Intercept	3.6107***	3.6453***	3.8325***	3.6126***
	(.6847)	(.7289)	(1.0111)	(.9805)
Republican strength $_{1990}$	.5823***	.5866***	.5920***	.6088***
	(.1837)	(.1871)	(.1892)	(.1829)
Republican strength $_{1980}$	.4065*	.4155*	.4215*	.4403**
	(.1726)	(.1844)	(.1868)	(.1806)
Republican strength [b]	-.1269	-.1302	-.1359	-.1544
	(.1230)	(.1258)	(.1282)	(.1241)
Political ideology	-.0103***	-.0103***	-.0103***	-.0109***
	(.0032)	(.0032)	(.0033)	(.0032)
Ln percent Hispanic $_{1990}$	.0599*	.0597*	.0638*	.0729*
	(.0328)	(.0330)	(.0366)	(.0356)
Ln percent Hispanic $_{1980}$	.0071	.0070	.0075	.0189
	(.0356)	(.0358)	(.0360)	(.0351)
Ln percent Hispanic	.0986	.1004	.0974	.0713
	(.0774)	(.0788)	(.0801)	(.0780)
Percent black $_{1990}$	.0149**	.0151**	.0151**	.0150**
	(.0050)	(.0052)	(.0052)	(.0050)
Percent black $_{1980}$	.0153***	.0155**	.0153**	.0151**
	(.0049)	(.0051)	(.0051)	(.0049)
Percent black	.0129	.0125	.0151	.0131
	(.0254)	(.0256)	(.0275)	(.0266)
Ln violent crime rate	.1786	.1755	.1789	.1725
	(.1080)	(.1107)	(.1120)	(.1083)
Percent unemployed	—	-.0029	-.0017	.0004
		(.0202)	(.0208)	(.0201)
Economic inequality (Gini)	—	—	-.6364	.2043
			(2.3686)	(2.3106)
Determinate sentencing laws	—	—	—	-.2013**
				(.0759)
1 if 1980	.2036*	.2070*	.2035*	.2289*
	(.1107)	(.1137)	(.1151)	(.1116)
1 if 1990	.7652***	.7685***	.7826***	.8016***
	(.1094)	(.1124)	(.1246)	(.1206)
R^2	.852***	.850***	.851***	.862***
(N = 150)				

Note: Standard errors are in parentheses.

[a] State fixed effects are not included in the R^2

[b] To facilitate comparisons, all coefficients on Republican Strength have been multiplied by 100.

* p ≤ .05   ** p ≤ .01   *** p ≤ .001 (one-tailed tests except on determinate sentencing)

Analyses

Summary Statistics and the Fixed-Effects Results

Table 1 shows the means and the standard deviations over time and across states.[7] Because they provide an informative contrast with subsequent results, Table 2 presents the findings from fixed-effects models that ignore period-specific interactions. In addition to Republican strength and political ideology, the first model includes conventional sociological indicators such as Hispanic and black presence, the percentage living in MSAs, plus the unemployment and the violent crime rates. We add economic inequality in model 2 and assess two policy measures by including the tax base measure in model 3 and determinate sentencing in the final model.

The results support expectations that conservative states have higher imprisonment rates, but the relationship between racial threat and imprisonments is more inconsistent. The percentage of blacks matters only in the first analysis while the percentage of Hispanics never has a positive influence on the size of the incarcerated population. We find that states with determinate sentencing laws have reduced incarceration rates, but the amount of unemployment and violent crime in the states does not predict these rates.

These initial analyses suggest that more conservative views produce larger prison populations, but the remaining relationships are negligible. Yet we do not know what will happen if these relationships are not forced to remain constant over time. The next section describes findings from fixed-effects models that test for historically contingent associations.

Estimating Period-Specific Relationships

Table 3 shows the results when the coefficients on three explanatory variables are not forced to be equal across periods. We test Republican strength, Hispanic presence, and the percentage of blacks for interactions with time, since (in unreported analyses that are available on request) *we find no differences when we test for period interactions between imprisonments and all remaining variables.* Recall that period interaction terms are created by multiplying the explanatory variables in question with dummies coded 1 for year and then including these interacted explanatory variables and all main effects in models. If an interaction between an explanatory variable and time is significant after main effects are held constant, we can conclude that a particular explanatory variable had different relationships in different periods.

We again begin with a simple specification. Model 1 includes the violent crime rates, Republican strength interacted with the 1990 and the 1980 year dummies and the relevant main effects (the year dummies and Republican strength in all years), political ideology, percent Hispanic interacted with the 1990 and the 1980 dummy plus its main effects, and the percentage of blacks interacted with these

Politics of Punishment across Time and Space / 77

TABLE 4: Random-Effects Models — Relationships between Variables and Imprisonment Rates[a]

	1	2	3	4
Intercept	2.9292***	3.6932***	2.9011***	2.8170***
	(.3153)	(.6937)	(.3330)	(.2965)
Republican strength $_{1990}$	.4794**	.4989**	.4992**	.4921**
	(.1717)	(.1734)	(.1743)	(.1683)
Republican strength $_{1980}$	.4007**	.4104**	.4388**	.4145**
	(.1627)	(.1685)	(.1670)	(.1626)
Republican strength	-.0605	-.0873	-.0649	-.0643
	(.1103)	(.1131)	(.1112)	(.1076)
Political ideology	-.0073***	-.0075***	-.0076***	-.0076***
	(.0021)	(.0022)	(.0022)	(.0020)
Ln percent Hispanic $_{1990}$	.0609*	.0756*	.0613*	.0814**
	(.0324)	(.0346)	(.0327)	(.0324)
Ln percent Hispanic $_{1980}$	.0098	.0131	.0106	.0297
	(.0339)	(.0343)	(.0342)	(.0338)
Ln percent Hispanic	.0161	.0204	.0126	.0059
	(.0341)	(.0351)	(.0381)	(.0322)
Percent black $_{1990}$	.0119**	.0116**	.0123**	.0109**
	(.0044)	(.0045)	(.0045)	(.0043)
Percent black $_{1980}$	.0157***	.0145***	.0163***	.0144***
	(.0045)	(.0046)	(.0046)	(.0045)
Percent black	.0020	.0044	-.0006	.0008
	(.0055)	(.0061)	(.0063)	(.0051)
Fundamentalism	.0903**	.1038***	.0835*	.0902***
	(.0300)	(.0342)	(.0411)	(.0278)
Ln violent crime rate	.3390***	.3263***	.3472***	.3565***
	(.0636)	(.0728)	(.0647)	(.0596)
Percent unemployed	—	.0081	—	.0094
		(.0152)		(.0142)
Percent residents in MSA	—	.0000	—	—
		(.0019)		
Economic inequality (Gini)	—	-1.9878	—	—
		(1.6200)		
North East	—	—	-.0229	—
			(.1209)	
Midwest	—	—	-.0534	—
			(.0959)	
South	—	—	.0522	—
			(.1177)	
Determinate sentencing laws	—	—	—	-.2377***
				(.0618)
1 if 1980	.1505*	.1481	.1335	.1524*
	(.0868)	(.0918)	(.0884)	(.0852)
1 if 1990	.7427***	.7926***	.7341***	.7589***
	(.0816)	(.0937)	(.0828)	(.0805)
R^2	.891***	.894***	.894***	.905***
(N = 150)				

[a] To facilitate comparisons, all coefficients on Republican Strength have been multiplied by 100.

*p ≤ .05   ** p ≤ .01   *** p ≤ .001 (one-tailed tests except on determinate sentencing) two years plus its main effects. In model 2 we add the unemployment rate. In model 3 we add economic inequality, while in the last model we add the presence of determinate sentencing laws to the prior explanatory variables.

These periodized results are far more interesting than the time invariant findings reported in Table 2. Significant interactions between Republican strength and period after the sharp increase in Republican rhetoric about law and order appear in all four models. We find historically contingent evidence for threat effects as well. After the substantial growth in the Hispanic population, the percentage of Hispanics had more substantial relationships with the imprisonment rates in 1990. The percentage of blacks now matters in all four analyses, but the evidence from these superior specifications shows that this explanatory variable's relationship with the incarceration rates also becomes stronger with the passage of time. When the coefficients on these explanatory variables are not forced to be identical in different periods, we find substantial increases in the explanatory power of the models.

The controls in these fixed-effects models are extensive. As a result of these more extensive controls, a comparison of the coefficients across rows in Table 3 shows that the point estimates are similar, while the results of the significance tests are virtually identical. Because unmeasured time-invariant state differences and over-time variation are held constant in these two-factor fixed-effects models, it is not easy to argue that these findings are spurious.

Compared to the prior analyses that ignored historical contingency, these results offer much stronger support for theoretical predictions based on political perspectives about punishment.[8] In accord with expectations, after the increased emphasis on law and order by the Republican party, the relationship between imprisonments and Republican strength becomes much stronger. Period-specific interactions also suggest that the relationship between the presence of two minority groups and the incarceration rates intensifies with the passage of time. Yet we still do not know if religious fundamentalism or region explain punitive reactions to crime.

ESTIMATING THE INFLUENCE OF FUNDAMENTALISM AND REGION WITH RANDOM EFFECTS

Random-effects panel models can assess the effects of time-invariant explanatory variables. This estimation procedure will let us estimate the influence of religious fundamentalism and region even though their scores do not vary over time. When these time-invariant indicators are included in random-effects models, the Hausman test for differences in the coefficients estimated by random- and fixed-effects procedures can tell us if these time-invariant explanatory variables capture the omitted effects that were automatically held constant by the state dummies in the fixed-effects models.

The random-effects analyses reported in Table 4 use specifications that are almost identical to those employed in the fixed-effects models in Table 3. In model 1 we enter the same interactions and main effects used in model 1 of Table 3, but we now can include religious fundamentalism. In model 2 we again add the unemployment rate, economic inequality, and the percentage living in MSAs. In model 3 we drop ineffective controls and add dummies for region. In the last model we revert to the baseline specification in model 1, but we add the dummy scored 1 for the presence of determinate sentencing legislation.

The findings are similar to those reported inTable 3 with one theoretically important exception. The results invariably suggest that imprisonment rates are higher in jurisdiction where religious fundamentalism is most prevalent. Model 2 shows that this result and the other findings persist after three standard controls are added. In model 3 we find no evidence that regional differences matter. Chi-square tests show that the joint effects of these regional dummies are insignificant. If we instead use eight dummies to represent the nine census subregions, we find the same negligible relationships. The last model shows that sentencing legislation reduces the relative size of the incarcerated population. The findings in these analyses persist if other mixes of the explanatory variables are used. For example, adding the three regional variables to the longer list of variables in model 2 or using the determinate sentencing indicator in other (unreported) models leaves the theoretical implications intact.

Hausman tests that gauge whether there are significant differences between coefficients from fixed- and random-effects models suggest that the coefficients estimated by these two statistical procedures do not differ *as long as religious fundamentalism is included in the random-effects models*. These repeated findings give us reason to believe that the religious fundamentalism variable captures most of the time-invariant state attributes that are automatically controlled by state dummies in the fixed-effects models.[9]

We again find that Republican strength and minority group presence explain the imprisonment rates with relationships that become stronger over time. Yet these random-effects analyses produce one additional theoretically interesting relationship that could not be investigated with a fixed-effects approach. The findings reported in Table 4 suggest that greater religious fundamentalism leads to higher incarceration rates.

ADDITIONAL METHODOLOGICAL CONSIDERATIONS

We tried other variables in unreported analyses. Including the tax base measure in the models that test for statistical interactions does not alter the results. State divorce rates, density, the percentage of residents 15 to 24, and the poverty rates or separate black and white poverty rates do not matter, and their inclusion does not alter the theoretical implications. Replacing violent crime rates with murder rates or with combined murder and robbery rates as well as using the total crime or the property crime rates does not change the findings, but these alternative crime measures reduce explanatory power. When we use the presence of self-identified Republicans

80 / *Social Forces* 80:1, September 2001

in the equations, this common measure of partisanship in political science (Miller 1991) has no discernable effects. Narrow majorities in the legislature also do not matter.

We reestimated the models in Table 4 with a population averaged approach (Liang & Zeger 1986). This procedure lets us correct for potential heteroskedasticity with White's (1980) adjustment, but the results do not change. AR1 corrections for autocorrelation when the models are estimated this way give results with identical implications. Correcting the standard errors for within region interdependence and spatial propinquity produces only minor changes in the significance tests, so we conclude that spatial autocorrelation probably is not biasing the results.

The results remain stable when we use diverse specifications and different estimation procedures.[10] Because we include dummies for both time and states in the fixed-effects models and hold constant multiple explanations, it is difficult to believe that omitted variables are distorting the findings. These considerations suggest that we have isolated the major social and political processes that produce state differences in imprisonment rates.

Discussion

FINDINGS

With many explanations held constant, the results show that expansions in the strength of the Republican party and stronger conservative values produce subsequent increases in the prison population. Despite the theoretical interest in this relationship, few statistical findings show a connection between politics and formal punishment. The stronger relationships between Republican strength and incarcerations in different periods provide added support for expectations based on the history of recent political events.

While this analysis focuses on direct measures of political effects, we find evidence for alternative explanations about ethnic divisions that are indirectly political. These threat explanations are political because effective demands for harsh punishments that result from shifts in minority presence must be directed at the political officials who can alter the criminal codes or sentence offenders. As threat theorists would expect, the results show that states with the largest black populations have higher incarceration rates after violent crime and other explanations have been held constant. The tests for period-specific relationships confirm expectations that the increased political emphasis on black street crime led to stronger relationships between African American presence and the incarceration rates.

The period specific relationship between Hispanic presence and imprisonments provides added evidence for such indirect political threat explanations. In contrast to blacks, the Hispanic population increased substantially during the analysis period. If ethnic threat theories are correct, the recent sharp growth in Hispanic presence should lead to stronger relationships between the percentage of Hispanics and the imprisonment rates during the period near the end of the analysis. The results invariably support this expectation, but they also suggest that black threat has a more substantial influence on U.S. imprisonment rates. Such contrasts in minority threat effects should not be surprising given the intense political disputes about race throughout the history of the U.S. While these threat effects are robust, they do not appear to be as strong as the relationships between the strength of the Republican party and state imprisonment rates.

We also find that states where membership in fundamentalist churches is greatest are likely to imprison larger percentages of their population. It is unfortunate that the only available measure does not capture shifts in religious fundamentalism over time. Yet researchers claim that church membership is largely inherited (Newport 1979), so changes in fundamentalist strength in large aggregates like states should be modest. Our results suggest that findings about the relationship between fundamentalist views and punitive attitudes (Curry 1996; Grasmick et al. 1992; Grasmick & McGill 1994) have wider consequences. Religious fundamentalism evidently provides an important macro level explanation for punitive outcomes as well.

The results show that determinate sentencing legislation reduces the size of incarcerated populations. This finding should not be surprising for several reasons. First, the history of this legislation shows that these provisions often were deliberately adopted to control costs by limiting prison populations (Marvel & Moody 1996). Second, even though Marvel and Moody use a different pooled-time series design than the one used in this study, they find equivalent negative relationships. Studies of public policy often reveal unintended effects. Once a determinate sentencing law is in place and not readily altered, the evidence in both this and the Marvel and Moody study suggests that such laws place limits on the forces that would have produced higher incarceration rates if such laws had not been present. Perhaps the limits on incarcerations imposed by determinate sentencing laws prevail even in jurisdictions where officials did not intend this result when these laws were enacted.

Prior research based on a time-series analysis of national data shows that increased Republican strength at the national level led to expansions in prison admissions (Jacobs & Helms 1996), but these relationships were not examined in the states where most of these decisions are made. Table 1 shows that variation in the imprisonment rates across states and over time is almost equal, so these substantial contrasts in cross jurisdictional incarceration rates should not be ignored.

Their highly aggregated time-series data did not let Jacobs and Helms detect the effects of two kinds of ethnic threat. This analysis of national level data also obscured the theoretically interesting historically contingent shifts in the strength of political and ethnic relationships, and this choice meant that Jacobs and Helms

82 / *Social Forces* 80:1, September 2001

could not assess the influence of political ideology or religious fundamentalism. The absence of these disadvantages together with the inferential benefits conferred by fixed-effects estimation and the larger number of cases in this study probably make the findings in this investigation more definitive.

WIDER IMPLICATIONS

Claims that political factors influence punishments are common in the theoretical literature (Foucault 1977; Garland 1990), but little empirical work has been done on this issue. As one would expect from this emphasis and from the Republican party's increasing stress on law and order, our findings suggest that growth in the political strength of this party produce higher incarceration rates. A claim that Republican political strength leads to harsh reactions to street crime is supported by additional findings. One objection to this conclusion runs that Republican political strength may be based on preexisting conservative views that are the primary cause of punitive reactions. Yet we find that the strength of the Republican party continues to explain the imprisonment rates after citizen ideology and membership in fundamentalist Protestant churches have been held constant.

Such results help us understand the puzzling sharp increases in imprisonments during a time when the crime rates stayed constant or fell. More conservative political parties in two party systems face a persistent dilemma because their electoral base is smaller than their rival's. Because the less affluent outnumber the prosperous, parties whose economic policies primarily help the prosperous (Blank & Blinder 1986; Hibbs 1987) will find that electoral success is problematic. One solution is to stress social issues like law and order to capture increased support from working and lower middle class voters who have greater reasons than the affluent to resent street crime. The results suggest that the Republican party's reliance on such tactics explains a substantial part of the great expansion in imprisonments from the early 1970s until 1990.

Repeated findings that Republican political strength produces increased incarceration rates after indicators of public conservatism have been held constant support a strategic explanation. While a law and order strategy does not contradict Republican views, the persistent relationship between Republican strength and incarceration rates after public ideology is controlled implies that this law and order emphasis was not imposed on Republicans by the public. Instead, perhaps Republican political strategists found that campaigns based on law and order would create a wedge issue that could be used to break the rival Democratic voting coalition apart (Edsal & Edsal 1991).

It is plausible that in order to win elections, Democrats have been forced to match the Republican emphasis on law and order. Yet such a matching effect would reduce the coefficients on Republican strength. If differences between Republicans and Democrats in the emphasis they placed on law and order substantially diminished toward the end of the years in our sample, we should *not* find that Republican strength is an increasingly strong predictor of the incarceration rates especially after so many other effects have been held constant, yet that is exactly what we find. Claims that the Democrats have matched Republican tendencies to emphasize harsh reactions to street crime have not been supported in this study. A national analysis by Jacobs and Helms (2001) suggests that after 1990 some important Democrats began to adopt Republican tactics and emphasize punitive reactions to crime, but we find no evidence for this before 1990.

More generally, the findings show that political relationships that explain incarceration rates operate on three levels. The Republican political strength results support state theories about the entrepreneurial activities of political officials. Because two ethnic divisions account for differences in the incarceration rates, we find that more conventional hypotheses that stress social cleavages explain the imprisonment rates as well although these political threat effects are not as strong as the direct political relationships. Finally, the influence of political ideology and religious fundamentalism suggests that differences in public values also help account for jurisdictional differences in the proportion of the population that is incarcerated.

Yet the historically contingent relationships uncovered in this study probably are the most theoretically noteworthy. Because theorists claim that a political emphasis on crime increases punishment (Garland 1990; Savelsberg 1994), we see if the political relationships are strengthened after Republican candidates increased their rhetoric about law and order (Davey 1998). The results support these contingent expectations. The associations between Republican strength and imprisonments become stronger at the end of the analysis period. Such results do not contradict findings (Beckett 1997) that pronouncements by public officials about law and order create a political climate that encourages harsh measures. The results also suggest that those who have criticized statistical research because it ignores the contingent nature of historical process may have overstated their case.

But there may be limits on the generality of these findings. In comparison to the European democracies, the U.S. has an exceptional political system with comparatively frail parties, nominations determined by primary elections, and a relatively weak bureaucracy. Such conditions probably give U.S. voters greater influence over decisions that are largely made by bureaucratic experts in other advanced democracies. Perhaps the political factors that explain imprisonment rates so well in a populistic democracy like the U.S. have less effect on this outcome in the more bureaucratic European states (Savelsberg 1994; Windlesham 1998).

This study nevertheless has isolated historically contingent associations that lead to two theoretically informative generalities about the determinants of the imprisonment rates in one advanced democracy. First, the results support those theorists who claim that incarceration is one method the modern state uses to manage latent political conflicts created by racial and ethnic divisions. Second, we

84 / *Social Forces* **80:1, September 2001**

find robust evidence that conservative shifts in political climate are likely 'to strengthen punitive reactions to crime. More generally, the findings suggest that research that makes a concerted effort to assess diverse political and economic explanations will provide a better understanding of how historical forces combine to shape the primary punishment used in advanced states.

Notes

1. In addition to its other advantages, using periods separated by multiple years in a pooled time-series design reduces serial correlation and the biases created by measurement errors in explanatory variables (Johnston & DiNardo 1997). We acknowledge, however, that the decennial census years we are forced to use may not exactly correspond to peaks in Republican rhetoric about law and order.

2. Northern and less populated Midwestern states had the fewest prisoners relative to their population. In 1971-1972 the five states with the lowest imprisonment rates were North Dakota with the least, New Hampshire, Massachusetts, Hawaii, and Minnesota. In 1991-92 states with the fewest prisoners (again starting with the lowest score) were North Dakota, Minnesota, West Virginia, Maine, and Vermont. States with the most prisoners tended to be in the South or West. In the early 1970s the five states with the highest incarceration rates were Florida, Texas, Oklahoma, North Carolina, and Georgia with the highest rate. In 1991-92 Arizona had the most prisoners per capita followed by Oklahoma, Nevada, Louisiana, and South Carolina. It remains to be seen if region accounts for these contrasts after we use theoretically derived hypotheses to explain incarcerations.

3. Fixed-effects models automatically correct for any unmeasured state attributes that do not vary over time by including dummies for all states but one in the model. This makes estimates from fixed-effects models robust when unmeasured time-invariant case attributes that are correlated with explanatory variables influence the dependent variable. Random-effects models assume normal error terms and correct for the reduced information given by scores for the same state at different times by weighting with residuals produced by fixed-effects and between regressions (or OLS models estimated using the mean of each variable's three yearly scores for each state). Estimates from random-effects models are more efficient than fixed-effects counterparts, and random-effects estimates are more robust when measurement error is present. Both procedures require standard assumptions about the absence of omitted variables and correlated errors, but this claim is more likely to be true when relationships are estimated with fixed-effects (for more discussion see in rough order of difficulty, Pindyck & Rubinfeld 1998; Johnston & DiNardo 1997; Baltagi 1995; Greene 1997). We use the fixed- and random-effects routines in Stata version 6, but Limdep version 7 produces theoretically equivalent results.

4. We use separate indicators for these concepts because these two minority groups differ substantially in their presence in different states and because adding these two measures together would require the implausible assumption that the coefficients on both indicators are identical.

Politics of Punishment across Time and Space / 85

5. The information required to assess additional theoretically interesting explanations either is unavailable for the entire analysis period or it cannot be obtained at all. For example, an attempt to isolate determinants of state imprisonments of African-Americans must be limited to the years after 1980. The primary goal of this analysis is to see if political explanations matter. Because the three periods we analyze are best suited for this purpose, but information about black prisoners is not available in the first period, the determinants of black incarcerations should be the subject of a different study perhaps undertaken after the necessary information in the 2000 census becomes available.

6. Some researchers try to assess the influence of drug crimes with arrests for drug offenses. Yet research suggests that drug arrest rates in a city fluctuate substantially after shifts in internal departmental directives about the crimes that should be given the most attention (Rubenstein 1973). Drug arrest rates seem to respond to both the political environment of law enforcement agencies and the resulting pressures on officers as well as the number of drug crimes in a city, but the exact weighting of these factors is unclear. Because we do not know what drug arrest rates measure, they should not be included in an analysis like this.

7. Percentage change scores calculated on the two minority presence variables contrast sharply. The mean percentage of blacks across states grew by only 4.6% from 1970 to 1990, but the unlogged percentage of Hispanics expanded by 47.9% during this period. Across state means for percent Hispanic before it is logged are: 1970-3.56%, 1980-4.30%, and 1990-5.27%. The yearly means for Republican strength are well below 50%, but many states are scored "0" on this index because they did not have a Republican governor. The mean tax base diminished in 1980 because across-state mean income *corrected for inflation* fell from its value in 1970. The standard deviations across time and space are calculated with the XTSUM procedure in Stata version 6.

8. The contrasting results in these two tables let us make another important distinction. In an inventive paper that used a similar research design to address related issues, Greenberg and West (1998) report results much like those in Table 2. It is unfortunate that Greenberg and West did not use interactions that let their coefficients vary by period. Other methodological differences between this study and theirs include their use of a less comprehensive measure of Republican strength and a political ideology indicator that is time-invariant and measured after 1977. The latter difficulty meant Greenberg and West had to assume that state ideologies did not change. Greenberg and West apparently find that only African American presence is a consistent predictor of state imprisonment rates, but the improved design used in this study lets us detect many other theoretically important relationships. We nevertheless acknowledge an important dept to Greenberg and West because they provide such a useful literature review and some innovative methods that helped us resolve vexing problems.

9. Sociologists may question the number of regressors in these models, but Johnston (1984) states that exhaustive specifications are preferable, while Blalock (1979) says we should dramatically increase the number of regressors in our equations. The ratio of explanatory variables to cases in many econometric studies is far greater than it is in this analysis. Johnston (1984:262) is worth quoting on this issue. He says "it is more serious to omit relevant variables than to include irrelevant variables since in the former case the coefficients will be biased, the disturbance variance overestimated, and

86 / *Social Forces* 80:1, September 2001

conventional inference procedures rendered invalid, while in the latter case the coefficients will be unbiased, the disturbance variance properly estimated, and the inference procedures properly estimated. This constitutes a fairly strong case for including rather than excluding relevant variables in equations. There is, however, a qualification. Adding extra variables, be they relevant or irrelevant, will lower the precision of estimation of the relevant coefficients." It follows that inclusive specifications will lead to more conservative significance tests.

10. This stability suggests that collinearity does not seem to be distorting these findings. The similarity of the coefficients and the identical significance test results for the models within each table despite extreme changes in the specifications supports this conclusion.

References

Allen, Michael P., and John L. Campbell. 1994. "State Revenue Extraction from Different Income Groups: Variations in Tax Progressivity in the United States, 1916-1986." *American Sociological Review* 59:169-86.

Baltagi, Badi H., 1995. *Econometric Analysis of Panel Data*. Wiley.

Beckett, Katherine. 1997. *Making Crime Pay: Law and Order in Contemporary American Politics*. Oxford.

Berry, William D., Evan J. Ringquist, Richard C. Fording, and Russell L. Hanson. 1998. "Measuring Citizen and Government Ideology in the States." *American Journal of Political Science* 42: 327-48.

Blalock, Hubert. 1967. *Towards a Theory of Minority Group Relations*. Capricorn Books.

Blalock, Hubert M. 1979. "Measurement and Conceptualization Problems: The Major Obstacle to Integrating Theory and Research." *American Sociological Review* 44:881-94.

Blank, Rebecca, and Alan Blinder. 1986. "Macroeconomics, Income Distribution, and Poverty." Pp. 180-208 in *Fighting Poverty*, edited by Sheldon Danzinger and Daniel Weinberg. Harvard University Press.

Blumer, Herbert. 1958. "Race Prejudice as a Sense of Group Position." *Pacific Sociological Review* 1:3-7

Bobo, Lawrence, and Vincent Hutchings. 1996. "Perceptions of Racial Group Competition: Extending Blumer's Theory of Group Position in a Multiracial Social Context." *American Sociological Review* 61:951-72.

Burnham, James. 1970. "Notes on Authority, Morality, Power." *The National Review* 123:283-89.

Caldeira, Greg A., and Andrew T. Cowart. 1980. "Budgets, Institutions, and Change: Criminal Justice Policy in America." *American Journal of Political Science* 24:413-38.

Carroll, Leo, and Claire P. Cornell. 1985. "Racial Composition, Sentencing Reforms, and Rates of Incarceration, 1970-1980." *Justice Quarterly* 2:475-90.

Chambliss, William J. 1994. "Policing the Ghetto Underclass: The Politics of Law and Law Enforcement." *Social Problems* 41:177-94.

Chambliss, William J., and R. Seidman. 1980. *Law, Order, and Power*. Addison-Wesley.

Politics of Punishment across Time and Space / 87

Chiricos, Theodore G., and Miriam Delone. 1992. "Labor Surplus and Punishment: A Review and Assessment of Theory and Evidence." *Social Problems* 39:421-46.

Collins, Randall. 1975. *Conflict Sociology*. Academic Press.

Curry, Theodore R. 1996. "Conservative Protestantism and the Perceived Wrongfulness of Crimes: A Research Note." *Criminology* 34:453-64.

Davey, Joseph D. 1998. *The Politics of Prison Expansion: Winning Elections by Waging War on Crime*. Praeger.

Dye, Thomas R. 1966. *Politics, Economics, and the Public: Policy Outcomes in the American States*. Rand McNally.

Edsal, Thomas B., and Mary D. Edsal. 1991. *Chain Reaction: The Impact of Race, Rights, and Taxes on American Politics*. Norton.

Erikson, Kai. 1966. *Wayward Puritans*. Wiley.

Evans, Peter B., Dietrich Rueschemeyer, and Theda Skocpol. 1984. *Bringing the State Back In*. Cambridge.

Fossett, Mark A., and K. Jill Kiecolt. 1989. "The Relative Size of Minority Populations and White Racial Attitudes." *Social Science Quarterly* 70:820-35.

Foucault, Michel. 1977. *Discipline and Punish: The Birth of the Prison*. London:

Garland, David. 1990. *Punishment and Modern Society: A Study in Social Theory*. University of Chicago Press.

Goode, William J. 1972. "The Place of Force in Modern Society." *American Sociological Review* 37:507-19.

Grasmick, Harold G., Elizabeth Davenport, Mitchell B. Chamlin, and Robert Bursik. 1992. "Protestant Fundamentalism and the Retributive Doctrine of Punishment." *Criminology* 30:21-45.

Grasmick, Harold G., and Ann McGill. 1994. "Religion, Attribution Style, and Punitiveness toward Juvenile Offenders." *Criminology* 32:23-46.

Greenberg, David F., and Valerie West. 1998. "The Persistent Significance of Race: Growth in State Prison Populations, 1971-1991." Paper presented to the American Sociological Association meetings in San Francisco, August 1998.

Greene, William H. 1997. *Econometric Analysis*. Macmillan.

Hibbs, Douglas. 1987. *The American Political Economy*. Harvard University Press.

Hofferbert, Richard L. 1966. "The Relation between Public Policy and Some Structural and Environmental Variables in the American States." *American Political Science Review* 60: 73-82.

Hsiao, Chang. 1986. *The Analysis of Panel Data*. Cambridge University Press.

Ignatieff, Michael. 1978. *A Just Measure of Pain: The Penitentiary in the Industrial Revolution, 1750-1850*. Pantheon.

Isaac, Larry W., and Larry J. Griffin. 1989. "Ahistoricism in Time-Series Analyses of Historical Process: Critique, Redirection, and Illustrations in U.S. Labor History." *American Sociological Review* 54:873-90.

Jackson, Pamela Irving. 1989. *Minority Group Threat, Crime, and Policing: Social Context and Social Control*. Praeger.

88 / *Social Forces* 80:1, September 2001

Jacobs, David. 1979. "Inequality and Police Strength: Conflict Theory and Coercive Control in Metropolitan Areas." *American Sociological Review* December 44:913-25.

Jacobs, David, and Ronald E. Helms. 1996. "Towards A Political Model of Incarceration: A Time-Series Examination of Multiple Explanations For Prison Admission Rates." *American Journal of Sociology* 102:323-57.

————. 1999. "Collective Outbursts, Politics, and Punitive Resources: Toward a Political Sociology of Spending on Social Control." *Social Forces* 77:1497-1524.

————. 2001. "Towards a Political Sociology of Punishment: Politics and Changes in the Incarcerated Population." *Social Science Research* 30:171-94.

Johnston, Jack. 1984. *Econometric Methods*. McGraw-Hill.

Johnston, Jack, and John DiNardo. 1997. *Econometric Methods*. McGraw-Hill.

Lacey, Nicola. 1988. *State Punishment: Political Principles and Community Values*. Routledge.

Langworthy, Robert H., and John T. Whitehead. 1986. "Liberalism and Fear as Explanations for Punitiveness." *Criminology* 24:575-91.

Lenski, Gerhard. 1966. *Power and Privilege*. McGraw-Hill.

Liang, K.Y., and L. Zeger. 1986. "Longitudinal Data Analysis Using Generalized Linear Models." *Biometrika* 73:13-22.

Liska, Allen E., J.J. Lawrence, and M. Benson. 1981. "Perspectives on the Legal Order: The Capacity for Social Control." *American Journal of Sociology* 87:412-26.

Liska, Allen E., J.J. Lawrence, and A. Sanchirico. 1982. "Fear of Crime as a Social Fact." *Social Forces* 60:760-71.

Marvell, Thomas B., and Carlisle E. Moody. 1996. "Determinate Sentencing and Abolishing Parole: The Long-Term Impacts on Prisons and Crime." *Criminology* 34:107-28.

McDowell, John M., Larry D. Singell, and James P. Zilliak. 1999. "Cracks in the Glass Ceiling: Gender and Promotion in the Economics Profession." *American Economic Review: Papers and Proceedings* 89:392-96.

McGowen, Randall. 1995. "The Well-Ordered Prison: England, 1780-1865." Pp. 79-105 in *The Oxford History of the Prison*, edited by Norval Morris and David J. Rothman. Oxford University Press.

Melossi, Dario. 1989. "An Introduction: Fifty Years Later, *Punishment and Social Structure* in Comparative Perspective." *Contemporary Crises* 13:311-26.

Michalowski, Raymond, and Michael Pearson. 1990. "Punishment and Social Structure at the State Level: A Cross-Sectional Comparison of 1970 and 1980." *Journal of Research on Crime and Delinquency* 27:52-78.

Miller, Warren E. 1991. "Party Identification, Realignment, and Party Voting: Back to the Basics." *American Political Science Review* 85:557-68.

Molnar, Thomas. 1976. *Authority and Its Enemies*. Arlington House.

Morgan, David R., and Sheilah S. Watson. 1991. "Political Culture, Political System Characteristics, and Public Policies among the American States." *Publius* 21:31-48.

Newport, Frank. 1979. "The Religious Switcher in the United States." *American Sociological Review* 44:528-52.

Politics of Punishment across Time and Space / 89

Parker, Robert Nash, and Allan V. Horwitz 1986. "Unemployment, Crime, and Imprisonment: A Panel Approach." *Criminology* 24:751-73.

Pindyck, Robert S., and Daniel L. Rubinfeld. 1998. *Econometric Models and Economic Forecasts.* Irwin/McGraw-Hill.

Quinn, Bernard, Herman Anderson, Martin Bradley, Paul Goetting, and Peggy Shriver. 1992. *Churches and Church Membership in the United States 1980.* Atlanta: Glenmary Research Center for the National Council of Churches.

Rubenstein, Jonathan. 1973. *City Police.* Farrar, Straus & Giroux.

Rusche, Georg, and Otto Kirchheimer. 1939. *Punishment and Social Structure.* Russell & Russell.

Savelsberg, Joachim J. 1994. "Knowledge, Domination, and Criminal Punishment." *American Journal of Sociology* 99:911-43.

Scheingold, Stuart A. 1991. *The Politics of Street Crime.* Temple University Press.

———. 1984. *The Politics of Law and Order.* Longman.

Taylor, Douglas, Kim Lane Schepele, and Arthur L. Stinchcombe. 1979. "Salience of Crime and Support for Harsher Criminal Sanctions." *Social Problems* 46:413-24.

Thorne, Melvin J., 1990. *American Conservative Thought Since World War II: The Core Ideas.* Greenwood Press.

Tilly, Charles. 1992. *Coercion, Capital, and European States, AD 990-1992.* Blackwell.

Wallace, Don. 1981. "The Political Economy of Incarceration: Trends in Late Capitalism, 1971-1977." *Insurgent Sociologist* 10:59-66.

Weber, Max. 1968. *Economy and Society.* University of California Press.

White, Halbert. 1980. "A Heteroskedasticity-Consistent Covariance Matrix and a Direct Test for Heteroskedasticity." *Econometrica* 48:817-38.

Windlesham, Lord. 1998. *Politics, Punishment, and Populism.* Oxford University Press.

[17]
'The Politics of Punishing: Building a State Governance Theory of American Imprisonment Variation'

Vanessa Barker

This article asks why some American states are more likely to rely on imprisonment in response to crime while others are not. By employing comparative historical methodology, it brings news kinds of data to address contested questions in the field. In three case studies, it examines archival material, including citizens' letters to political leaders, transcripts from townhall meetings, internal government reports, public testimony; and it uses extensive secondary sources, including statistical data and political histories to tease out complex causal processes of crime control policy formation and its impact on imprisonment patterns. Analyzing evidence both temporarily and spatially, the paper introduces a new account of American imprisonment variation based on the democratic process itself.

Today the United States imprisons more people than ever before, particularly people of color, outpaces all other democracies, and continues to expand reliance on confinement despite the recent drop in crime. Yet, many American states diverge from this national trend. Minnesota, for example, imprisons 150 inmates per 100,000 population, New York imprisons 343 inmates per 100,000 population, both below the national rate of 429 inmates per 100,000 population and well below Texas' 692 inmates per 100,000 population or Louisiana's 803 inmates per 100,000 population (Bureau of Justice Statistics [BJS] 2004: 3). The American states use confinement differently. This difference is significant and we do not quite understand it. This article seeks to explain why the American states use confinement differently in response to crime.

I argue that sub-national imprisonment variation is fundamentally a story about American democracy in all its variation and complexity. The U.S. is not a coherent or singular state but rather made up of mixed democratic practices, a rich political imagination, and varying sub-national polities – polities responsible for the creation, enactment, and implementation of nearly all criminal justice policy (Stuntz 2001) among other important policy areas (e.g., state budgets, education, land use). This article builds on scholarship that shows how punishment is fundamentally linked to the ways in which states exercise power in order to maintain legitimacy (Foucault 1977; Garland 1996 and 2001; Savelsberg 1994; Simon 1997; Beckett and Western 2001; Sutton 2000; Greenberg and West 2001; Jacobs and Carmichael 2001; Jacobs and Helms 1996). Like Savelsberg's (1994) political institutionalist approach, this article argues that differences in the ways in which states exercise, organize, and institutionalize power will have differential impacts on state reliance on confinement. Advancing a new perspective, this article theorizes that differences in the ways in which citizens participate in political life will significantly influence the ways in which states use confinement. The democratic process itself may help to explain how much or how little punishment states are likely to use in response to crime in order to maintain legitimacy.

By following the logic and methods of a comparative historical approach, this article closely examines how three American states with significant political differences responded to the common condition of increased crime beginning in the mid 1960s. To date, this article is the first to employ such methods in the case of American imprisonment. Based on the case studies presented here and developed elsewhere (Barker 2004), the findings suggest, somewhat counter-intuitively, American states with widespread citizen participation tend to keep imprisonment relatively low even in the face of high crime. The case studies suggest that when citizens participate in public life, they may be more likely to keep a check on the repressive powers of the state. And conversely, when citizens withdraw from public life, we are more likely to see increased imprisonment, a crude policy response to high crime. The case studies also suggest that a centralized state while somewhat insulated from public demands does not necessarily lead to lower imprisonment rates. Instead, it is likely to lead to a differentiated use of imprisonment – higher imprisonment rates for certain kinds of crimes but lower imprisonment rates for others. We should note here that the small number of cases limits our ability to generalize the findings. Yet, we should also note that the small number of cases analyzed comparatively and historically provides us with rich empirical detail, a move that can strengthen and refine our explanatory accounts. By doing so, this article contributes to the ongoing project of theory-building.

By focusing on political structures and political practices, under-developed factors in the literature, this article seeks to incorporate current scholarship on imprisonment into a broader account based on the democratic process. Current scholarship has done much to advance our understanding of how various *social* factors (e.g., racial demographics, economic marginality, crime patterns) effect imprisonment rates (see Blumstein and Beck 2000; Zimring and Hawkins 1991; Tonry 1995; Western and Beckett 1999; Greenberg and West 2001; Sutton 2000; Wacquant 2001). Yet, we still need to account for how and why these social factors may vary in different political contexts with varying effects on imprisonment. I argue that the structures of state governance and practices of civic engagement significantly shape how states understand and respond to crime and other perceived problems of order in the first place. Race and economic marginality may indeed influence the extent to which states rely on confinement in response to complex social problems, but these social factors may matter differently in different political contexts with varying effects on imprisonment (for discussion of these accounts and others, see Barker 2004). This article suggests that we gain explanatory power when we take into account how the political process translates social pressures into particular courses of state action. We gain explanatory power when we take into account how states and civil society struggle over how much or how little force to use in response to crime.

2

The Durée of Governance: Comparative Historical Methodology

The political process approach shifts our understanding of causality itself, especially the temporality of causality. Consider, for example, that the work of governance is made up of ongoing activity, small moments, small movements, repetitious and mundane. These small actions exert their causal influence gradually, slowly over time, and do so in cumulative ways. I call this kind of causal process the *durée of governance* where the continuous work and enduring features of governance result in particular outcomes over time (on cumulative causes, see Pierson 2003; on the *longue durée*, see Annales École; on *durée* of human action, see Giddens 1993). In this kind of causal process, institutionalized power arrangements, for example, can result in outcomes at times other than their apparent proximity to the events under investigation (Pierson 2003; Putnam 2000). Natural scientists call attention to the long-term and sometimes delayed effects of colder and deeper ocean currents on much warmer southern seas, great distances away. We can think of causality in social and political life in much the same way.

A state's prison population is the result of continuous rather than discrete actions. No one, not even the most powerful state official, can round up an entire prison population in one fell swoop since the population is the cumulative outcome of millions of arrest, charging, sentencing, plea-bargaining, and release decisions by thousands of actors, made over long periods of time (Tonry 1996; Stunz 2001). We make a mistake if we give too much causal weight to single events or particular pieces of legislation. Three strikes laws, for example, can only impact the prison population slowly over time as admissions gradually increase and release dates slow down. In order to fully explain a state's reliance on confinement, we need to examine causal processes over time rather than single moments.

This article employs such research strategies to develop an explanatory approach based on the causal effects of state governance over time. By working in the political and socio-logical tradition of Max Weber and Alexis de Tocqueville, I specifically rely on the logic and methods of the comparative historical approach (Mahoney and Rueschemeyer 2003; Skocpol and Finegold 1986). First, I make ideal typical comparisons of three American states, California, Washington, and New York, 1965–present. This thirty-five year plus period allows me to investigate the long-term causal dynamics that produced contemporary imprisonment populations and it covers the major transformations of American punishment in the late 20th century. By following the small-*n* approach (Rueschemeyer 2003), I limited the case selection to three states. The smaller sample allows me to study the cases in richer detail and investigate intricate causal processes in a much more refined way.

I selected the cases, California, Washington, and New York, because these states are representative of broader patterns in politics and punishment. The cases represent major democratic practices and governing styles present in American political life (Putnam 2000; Elazar 1966; Bellah et al. 1985). And perhaps most importantly, the cases diverge on state governance features, namely political structures and political practices, seriously under-explored and under-researched factors in the literature.

Washington State, for example, an open-polity with decentralized power, has consistently maintained higher than national average voter participation rates (51 per cent) with nearly 57 per cent of registered voters voting in 2000 (US Census Bureau 2003, Statistical Abstract of the United States: No. 420). Washington ranks 10th in terms of Robert Putnam's social

3

capital index, scoring 0.65 (Putnam 2000). We should note here that in *Bowling Alone*, Robert Putnam (2000:19) defines 'social capital' as social networks that tend to bring about increased reciprocity and trust among individuals. In Putnam's conceptualization, the rate of civic engagement in public life provides a useful indicator of social capital. In contrast to Washington, California has maintained lower than the national average voter participation rates in spite of its direct democracy measures with roughly 44 per cent of registered voters voting in 2000 and ranks 28th in terms of social capital, scoring –0.18 (US Census Bureau 2003; Putnam 2000). New York, a much more closed polity with its high degree of centralization, has maintained average voter participation rates (49 per cent) but ranks 34th in terms of social capital, scoring –0.36 (US Census Bureau 2003; Putnam 2000). I discuss these variations in detail in the next section.

The cases also changed modes of state governance at least twice since the turn of the 20th century, providing additional variation and insight into the processes of state formation.[1] During the fertile and sometimes violent protest period of the Progressive era, each state turned away from patronage politics, the purportedly corrupt mode of governance dominant throughout the U.S. (e.g., Tammany Hall, 'Boss Tweed'). California and Washington both created populist modes of governance while New York formed its enduring pragmatic and activist mode of governance (see Peirce and Hagstrom 1983). With the rise of the New Deal, California formed a pragmatic mode governance which lasted until 1965 when populism resurfaced. In the post war period, Washington developed a participatory and activist mode of governance, linking its populist roots with the pragmatic influence of the New Deal.

I also selected California, Washington, and New York because crime and violence reached extraordinary levels by the early 1970s, but each state pursued different imprisonment policies, policies that did not mimic shifts in crime patterns. For over thirty years, these states experienced unprecedented levels of crime, but each maintained varying levels of imprisonment. While Washington does have lower violent crime rates than California and New York, Washington, like almost all other American states, experienced a significant increase in violent crime in the late 1960s when states began major punishment policy reform. Between 1965 and 1975, for example, violent crime more than doubled in Washington, California, and New York (Uniform Crime Reports 2003).

Recent imprisonment rates show that California imprisons 455 inmates per 100,000 population, a rate higher than the national average of 429 inmates per 100,000 population; Washington imprisons 262 inmates per 100,000 population, a rate significantly lower than the national average; and New York imprisons 343 inmates per 100,000 population, a rate under the national average (BJS 2004: 3). None of these states reach the very highest or very lowest imprisonment rates. Instead they represent the common patterns of American imprisonment variation. The patterns of imprisonment in the cases pose certain puzzles that cannot be explained by previous research. And they allow us to address questions about the dynamics of punishment in ways that do not reduce them to instrumental crime control.

This article introduces new kinds of data to answer contested questions in the field. It uses a wide range of archival material and secondary sources including: transcripts from townhall meetings; letters to public and political leaders; public hearing testimony; state constitutions; penal codes; legislative bill files; governors papers; state agency reports and memos; legislative committee reports; oral histories; newspaper clippings; statistical information; state histories, social and political histories. The data show how decision making is organized, how key players participate and want they might want, and show the substance and what trajectory of key policy areas such as crime and punishment.

Differentiated State Governance and Imprisonment Variation

Political Structures and Political Practices

Perhaps no one has done more to advance our understanding of the causal effects and organizational features of state governance than Alexis de Tocqueville whose observations about American political culture, particularly civic engagement, continue to influence how scholars think about American democracy. And perhaps no one has done more to connect the exercise of state power to punishment than Michel Foucault (1977), David Garland (1985 and 1996) and Joachim Savelsberg (1994). These scholars all persuasively show that punishment is necessarily linked to the foundation and maintenance of social order. This section explicitly builds on these important sociological contributions by taking into account how institutionalized power arrangements and political practices shape and are shaped by social and cultural conditions in ways that account for shifts in state policy, particularly imprisonment practices.

The state governance approach, based on the causal effects of political structures and political practices on state policy, effectively captures the heart of democracy – that is to say, people (*demos*) and power (*kratos*). Specifically, political structures refer to how power is exercised in a particular political system, usually institutionalized in state constitutions and routinized in the practices of politics. Because democratic states developed in different ways (e.g., revolution, bureaucratization, people's protests, technocratic reform) and at different times under various historical conditions (e.g., 17th century New England religious settlements, 18th century mid Atlantic seaboard commercial enterprises, 19th century western territorial expansion and colonization), we see significant variation rather than uniformity in the very organization of state sovereignty across nation-states and within sub-national polities over time. Following political scientists and political sociologists, I map the exercise of state power in terms of variation in political authority (e.g., how decision making power is organized and distributed) in terms of the degree of centralization (Weber 1978; Amenta and Young 1999; McGovern 1998).

A model of state policy based on political structures offers a tremendous amount of explanatory power (Skocpol 1992; Ertman 1997). Yet, I think that we can increase the efficacy of political institutionalist models by incorporating political practices into our approach. We can think of political practices as the ways in which actors understand the very possibilities of action and how they take action in the political field. In other words, we need to take into account how actors conceptualize the role of governance, how they understand the nature of the state, particularly the state's relationship with civil society, and how actors make governance meaningful through habitual and routinized activities, particularly through political participation (Tocqueville 1955 and 1990; Sewell 1999; Friedland and Alford 1991; Swidler 1986; Bourdieu 1996; McGovern 1998; Polletta 1997). It matters to the creation and substance of state policy whether actors think the state itself is indeed activist, a useful and effective instrument of governing, or whether actors are anti-statist,

5

openly hostile to the very idea of a strong state and seek to limit governance to the most basic functions, internal order and national defense. I map variation in political practices in terms of the degree of state activism (e.g., a broad or narrow view of government) and the degree of civic engagement – that is to say, how often and how many people participate in local or community affairs vis à vis town meetings, civic and social organizations and how many registered voters vote (Putnam 2000; McGovern 1998).

Taken together, the two analytical dimensions yield four ideal types of governance: Populist, Participatory Democracy, Pragmatic, and Patronage. We should note that the empirical cases will approximate rather than mirror these ideal types. We should also note that even though states tend to form stable configurations, states are not immune from change, especially since the meaning of governance is rarely permanent and hardly universal. Instead, the diversity of American democratic practices encourages actors to think about the wide range of possibilities for changing existing states and building new ones (Swidler 1986; Clemens 1997). The inherent instability of political practices can lead to intense, sometimes unreconcilable and violent conflict which under certain historical conditions leads to increased state repression rather than reform.

Table 1:   State Governance by Political Structures and Political Practices

Political Practices:	Political Authority: Degree of Centralization	
Degree of Activism	Low	High
Low	Populist	Patronage[*]
High	Participatory democracy	Pragmatic

[*] Patronage is presented here simply as a theoretical example and not discussed in the case studies. More research is needed to assess crime control policies in a patronage mode of governance.

Political practices are often related to particular kinds of political structures, but one type does not necessarily cause the other. We see elective affinities between political structures and political practices where one type influences and is shaped by the other, re-enforcing particular alignments over time. For example, American states that centralize decision making tend to discourage widespread citizen participation as executive officials and technocrats dominate the business of governing. It is not all that surprising to see lower voter turnout and lower participation in civic affairs in this pragmatic mode of governance with highly centralized political authority where 'the few' make decisions.

In the American context, we also see states with a low degree of centralization and high political participation where citizens actively engage in the ongoing business of governing either through town meetings, volunteer associations, and citizen advisory boards. This kind of republican style governance, also referred to as participatory democracy, less recognized and often underestimated, still exists and exerts causal influence on American political life and public policy across a wide range of states. We may be more familiar with populist modes of governance, a somewhat paradoxical arrangement. In a populist mode of governance, political authority is highly fragmented, opening up the possibilities for widespread participation, but citizen participation is quite low and often left to extremists.

Particular understandings of governance take shape and are made meaningful through various habitual and ritualized practices. We are likely to see specific kinds of routines and habitual practices correspond to particular meanings of governance and institutionalized power arrangements. For example, in pragmatic governance (e.g., highly centralized political authority and activist state), we are likely to see the extensive use of expert knowledge, executive appointed special commissions, and collective inquiry rather than unfiltered public opinion to solve context specific problems. In populist governance (decentralized power and limited view of governance), we see the use of initiative process where citizens create legislation and policy that bypasses the state legislature; initiatives tend to operate as critical statements against the state, an ineffective state that cannot be trusted to do the right thing for 'the people'. In participatory democracies (decentralized power and activist governance), we are likely to see the extensive use of citizen participation in town meetings, citizen councils, and voluntary associations where citizens collaborate with state actors to create legislation and policy; here citizen participation operates to increase cooperation, trust in governance, and submerge conflict.

We can think of political structures and political practices, both historically contingent and mutually constitutive, as a *logic of action* of the political field (Friedland and Alford 1991). As a logic of action, these basic elements not only help to produce and reproduce particular patterns of action, they simultaneously make action meaningful (Giddens 1993; Sewell 1992). As a logic of action, these basic elements shape action in the political field. As such, I suggest that types of governance, guided by a certain logic and structure of action, will share elective affinities with types of punishment regimes. Based on the above discussion of different democratic state processes, we can expect to see relatively lower imprisonment rates in a participatory democracy, average imprisonment rates in pragmatic governance, higher imprisonment rates in a populist mode of governance, and the highest imprisonment rates in a patronage mode of governance. I explore these linkages in more detail in the case studies below and elsewhere (Barker 2004).

Empirical Cases: How Populist, Participatory, and Pragmatic Modes of Governance Impact State Reliance on Confinement

Given the space constraints, this article cannot provide a thick description of each case study. Instead, this paper focuses on key moments in each state's political history, democratic process, and crime control policy in order to illustrate the elective affinities between the type of governance and imprisonment patterns. I have chosen to highlight exemplary moments rather than provide a strict historical narrative of each case (for historical narrative, see Barker 2004).

California: populism, the rise of retribution and high imprisonment rates By the late 1960s, within the context of rising crime, white resistance towards black civil rights gains, and challenges to New Deal pragmatism, California introduced a more retributive approach to crime. By emphasizing mandatory penalties and stiff prison sentences, California began to de-emphasize the goals and practices of rehabilitation and began to emphasize straight up punishment. The 1976 Uniform Determinate Sentencing Act proclaimed: 'Imprisonment is to be for punishment' (in Parnas and Salerno 1978: 31). By mandating imprisonment for all kinds of crimes, burglary, carjacking, drug dealing, and murder alike, California gradually increased its reliance on confinement. These early shifts in crime control created long lasting policy legacies that continue to impact California's imprisonment rate. Today, California imprisons 455 inmates per 100,000 population, a four-fold increase since 1971, and a rate just above the national rate of 429 inmates per 100,000 (BJS 2004: 3; BJS 1990:605). Across the American states, California's imprisonment rate ranks 16th in the nation, far outpacing New York and Washington, ranking 30th and 40th, respectively.

To explain why California developed these kinds of policies, we need to understand how California's patterns of imprisonment are deeply embedded in its particular political and historical context. I suggest that California's political context encourages a particular way of doing politics that tends to intensify conflict instead of compromise and it tends to encourage simple responses to complex policy problems. As a consequence, in the areas of crime and punishment, the state has tended to develop quick fixes in response to the social complexities of crime. High reliance on imprisonment, a rather crude policy instrument, is one such example.

California's political context: re-emergent populism   By the late 1960s, populism resurfaced in California. A populist mode of governance is a set of political structures and political practices based on decentralized power, anti-statist views of government, and lower levels of civic engagement, trust and reciprocity. As noted earlier, in terms of social capital, a useful indicator of civic engagement, trust and reciprocity, California ranks 28th in the nation (Putnam 2000) and ranks below the national average in terms of voter participation in state and national elections held since the mid 1970s (US Census Bureau 2003; Gray et al, 1983 and 1990). Californians exhibit low levels of civic engagement despite the state's open and decentralized political structures represented in part by the initiative, referendum, and recall measures.

Populism, dormant throughout the 1940s and 1950s under the dominance of New Deal pragmatism and centralization of Governors Earl Warren and Pat Brown (Sabato, Ernst and Larson 2001; Allswang 2000), has deep roots in California politics. California populism is intertwined in the struggles of the Farmers' Alliances and progressive movement at the turn of the 20th century. Farmers, progressive reformers, along with other disempowered social groups challenged high finance, bankers, monopolistic railroads, agribusiness, and Eastern political and economic dominance for more control over the state's political and economic resources (Goodwyn 1978; Clemens 1997; McGirr 2001; Thomas 1991). After much struggle, this coalition pushed for and won direct democracies measure such as the initiative, referendum and recall. Reformers won direct access to government decision making through the ballot box, a move that would help 'the people' circumvent the state, perceived to be dominated by corrupt politicians and special interests. Populist challengers created a new form of politics – direct democracy (California State Constitution; Allswang 2000; Sabato et al., 2001). But they also left a legacy of anti-statism – that is to say, a hostile view of the state, perceived as a hungry Leviathan taking advantage of 'the people'.

In the 1960s, we see a more conservative strand of populism emerge in California politics. Polity members tapped into the state's deep roots in anti-statism, a move that paradoxically expanded the state's role in maintaining law and order and paved the way for an increased use of the initiative process, enabling citizens to bypass state legislators to write their own anti-crime legislation. For example, in 1964, California voters used the initiative process to block the Rumford Fair Housing Act, an act that would have protected African Americans against housing discrimination.

This particular populist challenge emerged out of the lived experience of cold war politics. In *Suburban Warriors*, Lisa McGirr (2001) explains how California's defense industry professionals lived day to day with a heightened sense of paranoia, insecurity, and fear of communism, especially its big state and collectivist social organization. McGirr explains how these feelings of paranoia were intensified by the new American experience of suburban living – an experience that left many residents feeling alienated and alone. These cold war insecurities were compounded by rising crime rates in the 1960s, the apparent expansion of the state, especially through social welfare, and the perceived immorality of an unruly youth culture protesting authority (Garland 2001). These 'suburban warriors' looked to the odd mix of libertarianism and social conservatism brought to life by Barry Goldwater in 1964 and Ronald Reagan in 1966 to restore some sense of security to their daily lives (McGirr 2001; Berlet and Lyons 2000; Klatch 1987; Diamond 1995).

We should note here that this type of anti-statism with its critique of big government (implicated in command economies and infringements upon individual liberties), is a somewhat inconsistent view of the state since California, like nearly all western states, is heavily dependent upon the federal government for employment and economic development – more so than any other region in the U.S. (Thomas 1991:14). Nevertheless, populism as it reemerged in California in the1960s sought to limit state governance to its most basic functions – internal security and national defense.

Populism's effect on crime control policies and imprisonment   It is in this context, we see a shift in California's crime control responses with its heightened emphasis on retribution. Already in 1967, the California State Legislature passed and Governor Ronald Reagan signed State Senator George Deukmejian's anti-crime penalty package, Senate Bill 85–87 (SB 85–87). SB 85–87 significantly increased penal sanctions for certain crimes of violence. Specifically, it increased the minimum penal sanction from five years to fifteen years to life imprisonment for offenders who injured crime victims (Berk, Brackman, and Lesser 1977; Cannon 2003). Offenders who inflicted 'great bodily harm' on victims while committing other crimes such as burglary, robbery, and rape were now subject to much lengthier prison terms. In a transformative move, the anti-crime bill introduced the pain and suffering of crime victims as a rationale for increasing penal sanctions and punishing offenders.

By incorporating the pain of victims into the calculus of punishment, the Reagan-Deukmejian 'penalty package' signaled a more emotive response to crime than had been previously practiced under California's more clinical treatment approach. The penalty package represented a more intuitive mode of punishment, a mode directly tied to the insecurities and concerns of 'the people' rather than to the dispassionate treatment models espoused by the state's technocrats and criminological experts (also see Savelsberg 1994). At this moment, we see how crime victims come to represent or stand in for everyday people (Garland 2001; Simon n.d.). By following a more intuitive sense of justice, retribution does not depend on technocratic knowledge, state elites or in Governor Reagan's words, a 'self-

9

appointed group of experts' and sociologists' 'pretentious double talk' about the root causes of crime (Reagan 1968a and 1968b).

This policy shift laid the groundwork for future crime control policies that would increase penal sanctions in the name of crime victims, the 1982 Proposition 8 'Victims Bill of Rights' and the 1993 Initiative in particular. In the name of victims' rights, Proposition 8 linked bail decisions to public safety, limited plea bargaining, and eased rules about the use of illegally seized evidence – moves that eased the prosecution of criminal defendants (see McCoy 1993). Three Strikes significantly increased prison terms for repeat felony offenders (for more on Three Strikes, see Zimring, Hawkins and Kamin 2001; Shichor and Sechrest 1996). This series of anti-crime legislation coupled with a multitude of less dramatic changes to the state penal code and penal practices (e.g., slow rates of parole release, high rates of parole revocation) over time led to California's relatively high imprisonment rate.

The Proposition 8 campaign illustrates not only how anti-crime measures conflate crime control with victims rights, but it also illustrates how the initiative process itself tends to exacerbate this type of zero-sum politics. As an example of California's populist govern-ance, the initiative process tends to reduce complex policy issues into simple 'yes or no' formulas where voters must choose one side over another. If voters vote 'yes' for victims' rights, they are voting against criminal defendants. If they vote 'no' for victims rights, they are apparently endorsing unsanctioned criminal violence. In addition, the initiative process tends to dampen political participation. Apart from the initiatives' acrimonious campaigns that pitch one side fiercely against the other, many voters with mixed policy preferences may not find a reasonable policy choice in the 'yes or no' formulation and consequently, they may not vote at all. Political scientists Cain and Miller (2001) also point to the fundamentally anti-democratic nature of the initiatives process. Since no one is actually held accountable for the initiative, voters cannot vote authors of initiatives out of office if they disapprove of the outcomes. Instead, disgruntled citizens must start the initiative process all over again to override the previous initiative.

The initiative process not only reflects but it tends to reproduce distrust in state officials and politicians. Consider, for example, prior to and during the Proposition 8 campaign, citizens wrote letters to Paul Gann, a grassroots activist heading up the Victims Bill of Rights and leader of the 1970s tax revolt, Proposition 13. The Paul Gann Archive, housed at the California State Library, provides a rich source of primary data on Gann and his supporters' concerns about crime, victims, and views on state government. These letters express exasperation, frustration, and anger with state government, perceived to be ineffec-tive and unresponsive to their concerns, especially their feelings of insecurity.

For example, one such letter writer, Thad Przybycien, wrote: 'Judges don't give a damn for the honest citizen and rule in favor of the criminal' (Przybycien letter to Gann, Novem-ber 29, 1981). Echoing these sentiments, Gann warned that the 'real terror' in California was not the escapee child molester but 'impotent politicians' who failed to follow the 'will of the people'. Another Gann supporter, Mrs. Mays, wrote about her disgust and distrust of politi-cians. She blamed these untrustworthy politicians for California's crime problem. She wrote:

> The politicians and their attitudes in government and lack of respect for the tax payers money and how they spend it is still another and the appalling lack of doing the bidding of their constituency

is also a factor and their example to the people proving this by ghost voting and switching is causing the people to give up and lose interest in elected officials which in turn promotes more crime against people from within as they follow their own interests and not the best interest of the general public and their wishes (Mays letter to Gann n.d.).

In these letters and other memos, Paul Gann and his supporters expressed a recurring sense of embattlement from various directions, the state, an apathetic public, and 'elitists' which tends to exacerbate mistrust and alienation (Gann 1980 and 1981). These kinds of conflict ridden interactions, routines, and practices tend to encourage ideological battles rather than a politics of compromise and coalition. For example, potential allies such as the ACLU actively opposed Proposition 8 and called the initiative a 'flawed piece of garbage' (Barnhart quoted in Ellison 1982). Rather than work with these grassroots activists who were also critical of state power in a way that could have changed the direction of the reform initiative, the ACLU refused to align themselves with Proposition 8. Proposition 8 resonated deeply with ordinary people, afraid of crime and feeling abandoned by state officials, who found meaning in the victims rights movement. Proposition 8 passed despite its narrow gains for victims.

California summary   Taken together, California's populist mode of governance creates a political context that encourages conflict rather than compromise, counter-posing one social group against another, counter-posing one policy plan against another, and counter-posing the state against citizen. By doing so, California's political practices tend to intensify alienation and antipathy among many parts of the population, further exacerbating citizens' withdrawal from public life. Civic disengagement subsequently weakens civil society and dampens citizens' sense of common purpose (see Tocqueville in Bellah et al. 1985; Barber 1984). As a consequence, citizens, in what Benjamin Barber might call a 'thin democracy', not only fail to keep a check on state repression, they often demand it. They demand that force be used against perceived threats to their own security.

At the same time, decentralized power and distrust of government can hinder the development of more sophisticated policy instruments, limiting the state's response to crime. In this political context, the prison, a comparatively crude and blunt policy instrument (especially when oriented towards punishment and incapacitation rather than active rehabilitation or training), becomes the obvious response to crime. Imprisonment (based on retribution) fits nicely with populism's common sense approach to social problems. That is to say, retribution – in other words, making lawbreakers suffer for the harm done to society – is grounded in common sense rather than in expert knowledge.

By responding to crime with high rates of imprisonment, California tends to maintain its legitimacy at the expense of one social group, the socially and economically marginalized. Yet, because the state relies on a repressive exercise of power that is internally directed, this crime control strategy fails to promote trust and reciprocity, let alone social cohesion or social solidarity. As a consequence, California returns to imprisonment again and again as it can not get out of this policy loop. It cannot imagine another way to respond to crime. It cannot imagine another way to respond to social conflict and other perceived problems of order.

Washington State: participatory democracy, the practice of parsimony and low imprison-ment rates   By the late1960s, within the context of rising crime, Washington State began its long-term effort to restrict the use of confinement and expand non-carceral sanctions. In the realm of penal sanctions, Washington began to emphasize what the late Norval Morris called 'the principle of parsimony'. That is to say, the state tends to punish offenders with the 'least restrictive (punitive) sanction' possible (Morris 1974: 59).

From the late 1960s onwards, Washington has consistently turned convicted offenders away from prison by using First Time Offender Waivers, probation, and other diversionary mechanisms. By 1980, 75 per cent of all felony defendants received probation (Washington Association of Prosecuting Attorneys 1980: 2). In the early 1980s, the state adopted sentenc-ing guidelines and explicitly directed the Sentencing Guidelines Commission to come up with alternatives to incarceration (Boerner 1985). By 2002, Washington ranked first in the nation with the highest percentage of its overall correctional population in community supervision (BJS 2003a: 2). Today, despite a net increase in imprisonment since the early 1970s, Washington ranks 40th in the nation, imprisoning 262 inmates per 100,000 popula-tion, a rate well below the national rate of 429 inmates per 100,000 population (BJS 2004: 3).

To explain these policies, we need to locate Washington's penal patterns within its particular political context with a focus on the nature of the democratic process in the state. I suggest that Washington's political context encourages a particular way of doing politics that tends to defuse conflict. Through a deliberative democratic process, polity members debate differing policy responses in open forums – forums that emphasize compromise rather than winner-take all politics. By doing so, this style of politics tends to promote empathy rather than antipathy between different social groups and defuses rather than exacerbates social conflicts and social divisions (see Barber 1984). As a consequence, in the areas of crime and punishment, polity members, state officials and citizens have tended to prioritize non-carceral sanctions, seeking to limit the state's repressive force.

Washington's political context: participatory democracy   By the late 1960s, a participatory mode of governance took hold in Washington State. During this turbulent time of rising crime, anti-war, civil rights and environmental protest, Washington officials feared and documented their own citizens' declining 'faith in government' (Evans 1966 and 1975). Faced with similar historical conditions as California, Washington polity members did not resort to populism's paranoia and insecurity nor co-opt citizens' concerns about crime and poverty, for example, to justify increased state repression. Instead, state officials, under the strong leadership of then Governor Daniel Evans, tried to incorporate citizens into decision making and promote activist governance.

To do so, Washington tapped its deep roots in progressive politics, particularly its roots in the cooperative practices of the farmers' Grange and other 'producerist associations' influ-ential in transforming Washington's political institutions at the turn of the 20th century (Clemens 1997: 260). Washington carried these legacies of cooperation, shared power and decision making, and citizen participation in political life into the contemporary era (Evans 1964; Washington State Constitution; Elazar 1966; Barber 1984; Putnam 2000).

Taken together, we see how Washington approximates a participatory mode of govern-ance. A participatory mode of governance is a set of political structures and political

12

practices based on decentralized power, activist views of government, and high levels of civic engagement in political life. In addition to direct democracy measures, citizens participate in political life vis à vis townhall meetings, hybrid citizen-state councils and commission, and the state's extensive volunteer program. Washington ranks 10th in the nation in terms of social capital with particularly strong participation in town meetings and civic associations (Putnam 2000) and consistently ranks above national average in voter participation rates in state and national elections held since the mid 1970s (US Census Bureau 2003; Gray and Hanson 2004). These political practices and political structures, particularly the routines of debate, discussion, open exchange of ideas and opinions – in other words, the habits of communicative action – tend to strengthen reciprocal and trusting networks. By doing so, these habits encourage compromise and collaboration between the state and civil society in matters of governance (see Putnam 2000; Barber 1984).

Participatory democracy's effect on crime control policies and imprisonment   It is in this context, we see Washington's crime control policies emphasize the 'principle of parsimony'. We see an emphasis on non-carceral sanctions and the state's overall resistance to the use of confinement as a response to crime and other signs of social disorder and social conflict.

Like other American states, Washington faced high crime rates in the 1960s (Uniform Crime Reports 2003). Unlike most other states, Washington came up with street lighting rather than the prison to deal with it. A hybrid citizen-state council, the Washington Citizen Council, proposed these 'situational' crime control techniques to transform the environment rather than reform or punish criminals to decrease opportunities for crime (e.g., car alarms, credit cards, motion detectors) (Clarke 1997; Washington State Citizens Council on Crime February 22, 1966).

Consider another example. In the 1960s, when faced with rising crime the Central District, a predominantly poor black neighborhood in Seattle, the state sought ways to improve the living conditions of black and other minority communities rather than criminalize poverty. The state established a hybrid citizen-state commission, the Washington State Commission on Causes and Prevention of Civil Unrest, to discuss, debate, and come up with solutions to race discrimination, crime, residential segregation, poor housing, and economic marginality. The Commission set up a 'multi-service center' that provided 'outreach, counseling, basic education, vocational and job training, and job placement' (Washington State Commission on the Causes and Prevention of Civil Unrest 1968). We should note here that unlike California's tendencies towards racial exclusion (as partially evidenced by the rejection of Fair Housing in the mid 1960s), Washington tried to address potential racial conflict with acts of political and economic integration. Here we can see how the state's democratic processes may have redirected potentially explosive race relations away from social conflict and towards political integration. Given Washington's much smaller black population, it is still crucial to note how these early acts may have provided a buffer against the use of imprisonment as a blunt instrument of racial social control.

Consider another significant example. In the mid 1980s, after nearly twenty years of debate, discussion, and extensive public hearings among political figures, professionals, and ordinary citizens, Washington adopted Sentencing Guidelines. Washington's Sentencing Reform Act (1983) phased in presumptive sentencing, explicitly linked sentencing to prison capacity, and charged the Sentencing Guidelines Commission to come up with alternatives

13

to incarceration. By doing so, Washington emphasized proportionate sentences, non-carceral sanctions, and created an institutionalized mechanism to control and limit prison growth.

By turning to Washington's democratic process, we see how citizen participation, the deliberative process, and the open forums of the townhall meetings and public hearings, may have influenced the substance and trajectory of the state's policy priorities. Washington held extensive hearings around the state to find out how the public felt about the Sentencing Guidelines Commissions report on sentencing reform. Space constraints do not allow a full accounting of citizens' comments and policy suggestions, but we can see from a few poignant examples, citizens overwhelming favored non-carceral sanctions.

Of course, many participants favored stiff penalties, victims' advocates such as Family and Friends of Missing Persons and Violent Crime Victims in particular. Yet, by the end of this long term process, a consensus emerged that favored alternatives to imprisonment as the main penal sanction for all sorts of crime categories. In her testimony, Margaret Casey of the Washington State Catholic Conference argued that prison should be the 'last resort'. Jonathan C. Nelson, former inmate and Lutheran pastor, agreed and described prison and jails as 'vile septic system' where 'a-social people' are made worse by 'the acid that prison represents'. Bart Haggin, a citizen, captured the dominant sentiment expressed at public hearings: 'I hate to see concrete and steel as the answer rather than reform'. Kitty Gillespie, citizen, testified that it was a 'myth that prison construction will decrease crime'; Tina Peterson, citizen, argued that the 'state can't afford to imprison all offenders' and so 'alternatives are needed' (Washington State Sentencing Guidelines Commission Public Hearings and Written Comments, 1981–1983).

Mary Ann Connelly of the League of Women Voters, Janet Rice of the King County Public Defenders, Donna Schram of the Sentencing Guidelines Commission and Washington Council on Crime and Delinquency, Maria Lindsey, a citizen, Gerard Sheehan of the ACLU, Margaret Casey of the Washington State Catholic Conference, Lamont Smith, a criminologist, and associates of the Catholic Prison Jail Ministry and Unitarian Universalist Service Committee all testified and advocated for alternatives to incarceration, proposing community sanctions and increased use of probation instead of confinement (Washington State Sentencing Guidelines Public Hearings and Written Comments, 1981–1983).

Washington summary   For well over thirty years, Washington has maintained relatively low reliance on confinement by pursuing non-carceral sanctions such as probation, waiver programs, and alternatives to imprisonment, and has limited growth by linking sentencing to prison capacity. While Washington has in recent years created stiffer penalties, passed three strikes legislation and tough sex offender legislation, this legislation has been drawn quite narrowly and has not significantly impacted the prison population (Sentencing Guidelines Commission 2003; Washington State Public Policy Institute 2003; Austin et al. 1999).

I suggest that Washington's participatory mode of governance has created a way of doing politics that prioritizes low reliance on confinement even in the face of increased crime rates and racial unrest. Increased civic engagement, decentralized power, and activism have encouraged a more deliberative policy making process based on participation and compromise rather than winner take all politics. Citizens and civic groups have been incorporated into long-term decision making. I suggest that these acts of political integration encourage actors to take one another seriously, make compromises, diffuse conflict, and express empathy rather than antipathy (Barber 1984; Putnam 2000). By doing so, this style of governance facilitates networks of trust and reciprocity not only among social groups but between the state and civil society (Putnam 2000).

Participatory democracy tends to promote empathy rather than antipathy between different social groups and defuses rather than exacerbates social conflicts and social divisions. In this context, citizens are less willing to incarcerate one another because incarceration implies that the state and civil society cares little for the social groups who will suffer under it. Additionally, Washington's mode of governance creates a permeable boundary between the state and civil society best exemplified by the state's extensive reliance on the hybrid citizen-state councils and commissions. This permeability can dampen actors' willingness to incarcerate because imprisonment, understood as raw form of state power, amplifies the colonizing and repressive powers of the state – practices that infringe upon individual liberty and quite possibly break trust.

New York: pragmatism, managerialism and medium imprisonment rates From the mid 1960s onwards, New York pursued a managerial response to crime and other perceived problems of order. Unlike California's more indiscriminate use of imprisonment, locking up petty thieves and parole violators alongside muggers and murderers, and unlike Washington's more restrictive use of imprisonment, New York tends to use imprisonment strategically, imprisoning certain classes of offenders and uses non-custodial sanctions for others. In other words, New York tends to be choosy but not shy about sending criminals to prison. Specifically, New York fills its prisons with violent felony and drug offenders, particularly drug dealers, rather than property offenders, parole violators, and other low level offenders.

In 2000, for example, violent and drug offenders made up over 83 per cent of New York's prison population, 53.4 per cent and 30 per cent respectively, whereas property offenders made up 15 per cent (New York State Department of Correctional Services).[2] These figures contrast with the national average of 48 per cent violent offenders, 20 per cent property offenders, and 20 per cent drug offenders in U.S. prisons (BJS 2003b). At the same time, despite its notoriously stiff drug penalties, New York has maintained a medium rate of imprisonment. The state falls below the national average for 22 of the 33 years under study between 1971 and 2004 (BJS 1990 and 2004). Today, New York's imprisonment rate, 343 inmates per 100,000 population, currently ranks 30th in the nation, a figure below the national average of 429 inmates per 100,000 population (BJS 2004).

New York's political context encourages a particular way of doing politics that tends to emphasize pragmatic responses to conflict and prioritize managerial responses to complex policy problems. Here the state's legitimacy hinges upon its ability to appear useful and responsive to context-specific problems rather than as a carrier of a particular ideology. As a consequence, the state has tended to develop a managerial cost-benefit approach to crime control. That is to say, the state tries to calculate the appropriate degree of force to use in response to crime based on the perceived risk and estimated cost of the response (Feeley and Simon 1992; Bottoms 1995; Garland 2001). In this context, drug crimes necessitate an extreme response as they are perceived to be highly contagious, breeding more crime, infecting entire communities whereas lower level offenses are considered fairly innocuous and do not require the use of custodial resources. Bypassing concerns about moral depravity and social deprivation, New York tends to use more or less confine-

15

ment to quarantine perceived contagions rather than to strictly punish wrongdoers or rehabilitate incorrigibles.

New York's political context: elitist pragmatism   By the late 1960s, New York's pragmatic governance was in full swing under the strong leadership of Governor Nelson A. Rockefeller. A pragmatic mode of governance is a set of political structures and political practices based on a high degree of centralized power, a high degree of state activism, and lower levels of civic engagement. As noted, New Yorkers do not vote as often as the national average (US Census Bureau 2003; Gray et al., 1983, 1990, 1999), nor participate as much in town meetings and civic associations (Putnam 2000). New York ranks 34th in the nation in terms of social capital (Putnam 2000). Without direct democracy measures and without much civic engagement in political life, New York governance is dominated instead by state elites, government officials, technocrats, and elected officials. Decision making power tends to be concentrated in the executive branch as governors, without term limits, can maximize their high degree of institutional control over the budget, appointments, and vetoes to shape the substance and trajectory of public policy (Beyle 2004: 212).

New York's pragmatic mode of governance emerged out of the Progressive Era. Inspired by the momentum of social reformers and state builders, New York progressives such as Theodore Roosevelt, Charles Evans Hughes and Alfred Smith and other state actors, challenged the dominance of patronage politics, partly suppressing the politics of cronyism, corruption, private interest, and other abuses of power (Peirce and Hagstrom 1983). In order to reclaim decision making power and regain control of the state, New York concentrated power in the executive branch, centralizing political authority (New York State Constitution; Liebschultz et al., 1998; Beyle 2004; Schneier and Murtaugh 2001). We should note that in contrast to California and Washington, states that decentralized power in response to patronage politics, New York centralized decision making. Within a decade, New York had established its enduring pragmatic governance and subsequently laid the foundation for New Deal politics, a mode of governance that would eventually transform national state policy and politics (see Skocpol and Finegold 1986; Amenta 1998; Clemens 1997).

New York's pragmatic governance is made up of a high degree of state activism. In other words, the state is considered legitimate to the extent it is considered useful. Rather than an entity to be feared or scaled back, a utilitarian state can be put to work to solve emergent social problems and at times, improve social conditions (Nichols 2001). Informed by Progressive sensibilities of efficiency and rationality, New York has developed a more regulatory and interventionist style state based on technical and practical responses to emergent social problems (McGovern 1998). Over time, New York has created a fairly extensive state apparatus but created one that is oriented towards the public welfare rather than personal gain. As a result, the state has tended to provide public policies that are fairly generous by American standards. New York consistently outspends the national average on general expenditures which include education, social services, and public safety spending. For example, in 2000, New York spent over $7.4 million per capita on general expenditures, a rate much higher than the $5.3 million per capita national average, California's $5.8 million per capita and Washington's $5.7 million per capita (US Census Bureau 2004). As a pragmatic state, New York has tended to provide fairly generous public services not so much for a great love of 'the people', but because it is more efficient to bring the poor along than let them sink the economy.

16

Taken together, these kinds of habits and routines – centralization, low civic engagement, technical analysis, state activism – exemplify a style of politics that seeks to manage and control conflict rather than facilitate winner-take-all or zero-sum politics. At the same, this mode of governance, dominated by state insiders, insulated from public pressure, can also lead to a slow, laborious policy process, deadlock, and inaction.

Pragmatism's effect on crime control and imprisonment   In this context, high crime rates are particularly threatening to the state's legitimacy as they point to the state's inefficacy – its inability to provide internal security and public safety, the state's most basic duties. In the words of Governor Rockefeller, New Yorkers expect their 'hard-earned tax dollars' to 'produce a correspondingly high level of efficient and economical public services' (Rockefeller 1973a: 10). To shore up the state's legitimacy and do so quickly, state elites such as the governor, the state legislators, and expert driven commissioners, try to find ways to maximize the state's public impact and do so efficiently.

By the mid 1960s, as crime rates dramatically increased, New York had already turned its attention to crime victims. But it did so with financial aid rather than increased penal sanctions. By 1966, New York State, led by a series of expert commissions such as the New York Commission on the Revision of the Penal Law, created the Crime Victims Board, created a new state agency that would administer the new crime victims compensation program (*New York Times* October 23, 1965). Within a year, victims compensation increased five times, from awarding 43 victims $55,665 to awarding 220 victims a total of $386,585 (New York Statistical Yearbook 1979, Table L-9). Today, New York maintains one of the most generous compensation programs in the country.[3] I suggest that New York's early efforts to incorporate victims into the business of governing may have averted victims' moral protests against an unresponsive state. I also suggest that the state's generous financial response, instead of a punitive response, may have defused some of the victims' anger and resentment. In contrast, in California, victims' feelings of anger and resentment had been legislated into California's 1967 'great bodily harm' penalty as justification for stiffer penalties.

By the early 1970s, New York state elites turned their attention to criminal offenders but did so in a characteristically managerial fashion. Governor Rockefeller, a series of expert commissions and state insiders such as the New York Temporary Commission on Revision of the Penal Law and Criminal Code, the New York State Commission on Management and Productivity in the Public Sector, the Bellacosa-Feinberg Committee, and the Black and Puerto Rican Legislative Caucus developed and pushed for differentiated penal sanctions – sanctions that included prison sentences for the most violent offenders and alternatives to incarceration for low level offenders (Griset 1991). With the Second Felony Law (1973), New York institutionalized its differentiated crime control response by sorting repeat and violent offenders into prison and diverting low level offenders away from prison with its 'alternative definite sentence' – a provision that enabled judges to sentence low level felony offenders to fixed short prison terms of less than one year (New York Consolidated Laws 2004).

Consider another example. The 1973 Rockefeller drug laws, often characterized as a conservative and punitive 'law and order' campaign, I think are better understood as the result of pragmatic governance. The drugs laws exemplify a pragmatic state's persistent attempt to solve a rather narrow policy problem (heroin drug addiction) and do so with restrained force. The drug laws also exemplify a pragmatic state's managerial response to conflict. Like its technical approach to crime victims, New York sought ways to manage and appease potential sources of conflict, to appear responsive to demands, and defuse sources of discontent. Governor Rockefeller in particular tried to enlist the support of African Americans into his anti-drug efforts.

Throughout his fourteen year tenure as governor (1959–1973), Nelson A. Rockefeller mobilized the power of the centralized executive branch in order to redirect massive state and private resources towards drug addiction. He considered drug addition a serious social problem that was 'akin to cancer in spreading deadly disease among us' and 'deserving all the brain power, manpower, and resources to overcome it' (quoted in Underwood and Daniels 1982: 140). Rockefeller called for a national effort to end drug addiction on the scale of the Manhattan Project. In 1959, he urged the federal government to police international drug traffic to stop the flow of drugs into the country. In the early 1960s, he poured millions of dollars and other state resources into the nation's largest drug treatment program, the Narcotics Addiction Control Commission and continued throughout his administration to expand drug treatment, including methadone programs, drug research, and preventive education (Rockefeller 1971). Through various committees, commissions, task forces, and surveys, his administration (with financial aid from Rockefeller's personal estate) continually proposed possible solutions to drug addiction and fulfilled its obligations as an activist state, taking action with concrete programs and policies.

Then in 1973, after a decade long battle, Rockefeller acknowledged that the state had failed to eliminate drug abuse: 'whole neighborhoods have been effectively destroyed by addicts as by invading army'(Rockefeller 1973a: 21). So in order to stop the supply of drugs into neighborhoods, a practical way to prevent addiction and its associated crime, Rockefeller went after drug pushers. Reversing much of his own and long-time treatment oriented approach to drug addition, the new drug laws mandated prison terms for felony drug offenses. Criticized for their severity, Rockefeller eventually toned down some of the harshest elements. After extensive discussion with various staff members, administrators, and other state insiders, he restored plea bargaining and parole, sentencing practices he had originally eliminated (Rockefeller 1973a).

At the same time, many African Americans, the social group most adversely affected by crime and the drug trade, supported Rockefeller's anti-drug efforts. Since the late 1960s, many black activists pushed the state to take a tougher stand against lawlessness in their communities. African Americans wanted the state to fulfill its responsibility and provide protection. Black residents wanted to 'escape the reign of criminal terror' (*New York Times* January 8, 1969a). In the late 1960s, for example, the NAACP Citizens' Mobilization Against Crime advocated stronger law enforcement presence in black neighborhoods and lobbied Governor Rockefeller for stiffer penalties against violent offenders. In 'Harlem Likened to the Wild West', the *New York Times* reported that African American activists sent Governor Rockefeller and the New York State Legislature telegrams supporting increased police presence and minimum prison terms, including five years for muggers (*New York Times* January 8, 1969a).

Well into the late 1960s, many black activists continued to patrol their own neighborhoods in an effort to root out drug dealers. For example, John Shabazz, leader of the Harlem based

Black Citizens Patrol, an organization made up of 155 reported members, explained that his voluntary association would try to root out drug dealers from the city's public schools:

> We have the names and photographs of pushers...and we have people inside the schools to turn over the names to the proper authorities. If they [the police] don't deal with the problem, we will have to deal with it our own way (*New York Times* September 23, 1969b).

By the early 1970s, African American community groups, social activists, church leaders, and ordinary residents wanted more state action, they want the state to intervene in the drug trade and its associated violence and crime. In support of the stiffer penalties, Reverend Oberia Dempsey of Harlem argued: 'Citizens have a right to be protected. We're being punished [by drug pushers] punishment is being meted against you, me, our children' (Rockefeller, January 22, 1973b). Mrs. Spring Anne Bell, a Bronx resident, explained her support: 'What is being done to our youth who fall prey to some unscrupulous pusher is awful ... our children are dying on rooftops, in dirty basements and hallways' (January 13, 1973a). Similarly, the *Amsterdam News*, the major black newspaper in New York City argued that 'Aggressive state action against narcotics addiction is long overdue' (editorial January 13, 1973b). The *Amsterdam News* supported mandatory life sentences for the 'non-addict drug pusher of hard drugs' because as the editors explained, this kind of drug dealing 'is an act of cold calculated, pre-meditated, indiscriminate murder of our community' (editorial January 13, 1973b). However, the *Amsterdam News* like many African Americans opposed any attempts to criminalize addicts or low level addict-pushers.

As the above example suggests, I think it is too crude to characterize the drug laws as a blunt instrument of racial social control. Many African Americans, activists, community leaders, and ordinary urban residents, wanted more state protection against the perceived threat of drug offenses, particularly against its associated crimes of violence. Unlike California, in New York throughout the 1960s, African Americans were incorporated into polity as the state adopted integrative civil rights policies, pro-black community programs, and strengthened anti-discrimination in housing and employment (Lockard 1968). In New York, African Americans were not passive victims to a repressive state unconcerned about their fate. That said, we should note that African Americans provided legitimating support for the drug laws but many of their specific concerns about drug addicts were ignored. Neither Governor Rockefeller nor the New York State Legislature altered the drug laws to ensure that drug addicts would not be swept up into the prison alongside drug dealers. Inside a centralized state, insulated to a certain degree from public demands, New York state elites may have used black support to their own advantage. By including the social group most likely to be impacted by the drug laws but without fully incorporating their demands into policy, state elites still gained strategic support for the drug laws. They sought to manage the problem by minimizing opposition. By taking into account the political context in New York, we gain a richer understanding of the complex racial dynamics involved in crime control policies – an understanding that is grounded in empirical realities.

New York summary Taken together, New York's pragmatic governance – that is to say, its high degree of centralization, activist political practices, dampened civic participation, heavy reliance on expert knowledge and scientific inquiry, and dominance of state elites in deci-

19

sion making – creates a political context within which the state pursues technical or managerial approaches to policy problems. In this context, the pragmatic state shrewdly calculates the degree of responsiveness and compromise necessary to maintain legitimacy. In other words, the pragmatic state seeks to use state power efficiently and deliberately. Because of which, the state is less likely to overindulge in democratic participation and it is less likely to overindulge in repressive exercises of state force. Since the state does not pursue democracy for its own sake the state must show itself to be useful to maintain legitimacy. With its strong activist component, the pragmatic state seeks to intervene in and respond to crime and other perceived problems of order with technical rather than crude or vulgar responses. The state prides itself on its expertise and scientific engagement with social problems and is therefore less likely to pursue strictly punitive responses, considered crass and unscientific. As a result, we see a highly differentiated response to crime and differentiated penal sanctions.

In contrast to mass imprisonment, an indiscriminate use of state power, New York's differentiated use of confinement is a highly disciplined use of state power. The removal of violent and drug offenders from the community is an immediate display of state action and state competence. The state moves quickly to remove contagious threats from communities. Violent and drug offenders are quarantined (but not cured) to maintain the health and viability of surrounding communities. Rather than invest in long term social engineering, rehabilitation, or even crime prevention, imprisonment is a visible and quite dramatic expression of state action. Without delay, the state tells its citizens that it takes its duties and obligations seriously. Differentiated imprisonment efficiently provides internal security, reenforcing the legitimacy of the state.

Conclusions

By the late 1960s, the American states faced some of the most difficult governing conditions of the 20th century – high crime rates, contentious racial politics, and challenges to New Deal pragmatism – conditions that challenged the meaning and practices of democratic governance. Rising crime became particularly troublesome to American state governments since it undermined their authority. High rates of crime questioned the states' competence and willingness to provide internal order and security, the most basic duty of governance. In this moment of political turmoil, American states transformed the nature of governance, changes that had ongoing and lasting effects on state imprisonment policies.

Some states like California turned to populism, specifically anti-statism, and intensified reliance on confinement in order to bring about a new social order based on exclusion. Other states like New York clung to pragmatism, stretched activist governance to its limits, and deployed a strategic use of confinement to restore social order with minimal force and maximum legitimacy. In contrast, Washington solidified its tendencies towards participatory governance, gave up state power, and tightly linked active citizen participation to the maintenance of social order which subsequently led to low reliance on confinement.

The findings complicate conventional accounts of American imprisonment. Like the work of Garland (2001), Beckett and Western (2001), Wacquant (2001), the paper has suggested that crime rates, contentious racial politics, and state regulation of social marginality do

20

indeed matter to the rise and fall of American imprisonment. But a close examination of California, Washington and New York has also shown that these social forces – crime rates and racial politics, for example – matter differently in different political contexts with varying effects on imprisonment. Like the work of Savelsberg (1994) and Simon, this paper suggests that the state, political institutions and practices of governance are *necessary* components to our explanations of punishment patterns. However, this article has suggested that is not the state alone that accounts for imprisonment variation, but rather the dynamic interaction between the state and civil society. In other words, this article claims that the democratic process itself must be incorporated into our accounts of punishment. Civic engagement, the intensity and its character, has consequences for how and why states use confinement against their own citizens. Increased citizen participation can actually set limits to state reliance on confinement. Increased democratization does not necessarily lead to mass imprisonment as Zimring, Hawkins and Kamin (2001) have argued.

The findings suggest that how states responded to black civil rights has had a lasting effect on the use of imprisonment. Space constraints do not allow for a full account, but the Civil Rights Movement has had a profound effect on American social and political life. Activist states like Washington and New York formulated pro-civil rights policies which tend to keep imprisonment rates lower than states that continued to exclude blacks from full citizenship. New York and Washington, for example, integrated blacks both politically and economically through a wide range of state policies (e.g., anti-discrimination laws, education, employment). Over time, these incorporative measures can defuse periodic racial conflict and latent hostilities. Black political participation in state governance provides a crucial buffer against the use of imprisonment as a blunt instrument of racial social control.

More research, especially cross-national comparison, is needed to further develop the point that higher levels of civic engagement may lead to lower imprisonment rates. It is possible that additional comparative historical research in other political contexts may lead to contradictory findings. But at this point in time, we simply do not know enough about how democratic states rely on confinement differently and how variations in institutionalized power, activist governance, and citizen participation, may actually explain those differences. Additional research can only help us refine our understanding and explanation of causal processes that lead democratic states to solve problems of order with imprisonment.

Notes

1   A proper analysis and explanation of state formation is well beyond the scope of this article, but I mention these transformations in order to call attention to: (1) the rich variation of democratic practices in the U.S., often overlooked in the literature; (2) the ongoing nature of state-building; (3) and to challenge the common perception of state structures as highly static variables. Although states tend to form stable and long-term configurations, they rarely submerge past policies or past structures (Pierson 2003), and they are open and quite vulnerable at times to major change (Clemens 1997; Amenta 1998), especially since the meaning of democracy itself is not settled, fixed or universal.

2   We should note here that while the New York State Department of Correctional Services classifies burglary as a violent felony offense, for comparative purposes, I have calculated burglary under property offenses. I have done so in order to make more meaningful comparisons across cases and

across offense type with data from the California's Department of Corrections, Washington's Department of Corrections, and the US Bureau of Justice Statistics.

3   We should note that even though it was an innovator in compensation, California maintains one of the stingiest victims compensation programs in the country–California caps awards at $6000 whereas Washington caps at $20,000 and New York does not cap awards (Marion 2002, pg. 117).

References

Allswang, John M. (2000), *The Initiative and Referendum in California, 1898–1998*, Stanford, CA: Stanford University Press.

Amenta, Edwin (1998), *Bold Relief: Institutional politics and the origins of modern American social policy*, Princeton, NJ: Princeton University Press.

Amenta, Edwin and Michael P. Young (1999), 'Democratic States and Social Movements: Theoretical Arguments and Hypotheses', *Social Problems*, 46.2 pp. 153–168.

Amsterdam News (1973a), 'Governor Rockefeller proposes new laws that impose mandatory life sentences for hard core drug pushers and on addicts who commit serious crimes while under the influence...What are your views?', January 13, *Amsterdam News*, New York.

———— (1973b), 'Rockefeller and Narcotics', Editorial, January 13, *Amsterdam News*, New York.

Austin, James, John Clark, Patricia Hardyman and D. Alan Henry (1999), 'The Impact of "Three Strikes and You're Out"', *Punishment and Society*, 1.2 pp. 131–62.

Barber, Benjamin (1984), *Strong Democracy: Participatory Politics for a New Age*, Berkeley, Los Angeles and London: University of California Press.

Barker, Vanessa (2004), *The Politics of Punishing: A Comparative Historical Analysis of American Democracy and Imprisonment Variation, 1965–present*, Ph.D. Thesis. New York, New York University.

Beckett, Katherine and Bruce Western (2001), 'Governing Social Marginality: Welfare, Incarceration, and the Transformation of State policy', in David Garland (ed.), *Mass Imprisonment: Social Causes and Consequences*, London: Sage, pp. 43–60.

Bellah, Robert, Richard Madsen, William Sullivan, Ann Swidler and Steven Tipton (1985), *Habits of the Heart: Individualism and Commitment in American Life*, Berkeley: University of California Press.

Berk, Richard, Harold Brackman and Selma Lesser (1977), *A Measure of Justice: An Empirical Study of Changes in the California Penal Code, 1955–1971*, New York: Academic Press.

Berlet, Chip and Matthew Lyons (2000), *Right-Wing Populism in America: Too Close for Comfort*, New York: Guilford Press.

Beyle, Thad (2004), 'Governors', in Virginia Gray and Russell Hanson (eds) *Politics in the American States: A Comparative Analysis, 8th edition*, Washington DC: CQ Press.

Blumstein, Alfred and Allen J. Beck (2000), 'Population growth in the US prisons, 1980–1996', in Michael Tonry and Joan Petersilia (eds), *Crime and Justice: 26*, Chicago and London: University of Chicago Press, pp. 17–61.

Boerner, David (1985), *Sentencing in Washington: A Legal Analysis of the Sentencing Reform Act of 1981*, Seattle, Washington: Butterworth Legal Publishers.

Bottoms, Anthony (1995), 'The Philosophy and Politics of Punishment and Sentencing', in Chris and Rod Morgan Clarkson (eds) *The Politics of Sentencing Reform*, pp. 17–49. Oxford: Clarendon Press.

Bourdieu, Pierre (1996), *Distinction: a Social Critique of the Judgment of Taste*, Cambridge, Mass: Harvard University Press.

Bureau of Justice Statistics (1990), 'Table 6.56. Rate (per 100,000 resident population) of Sentenced Prisoners in State and Federal Institutions, December 31. By Region and Jurisdiction, 1971–1989', in *Sourcebook of Criminal Justice Statistics*, US Department of Justice.

———— (2003a), 'Prisoners in 2002'. Washington DC: US Department of Justice.

22

——— (2003b), 'Felony Sentences in State Courts, 2000', June. Washington DC: Department of Justice, Office of Justice Programs.

——— (2004), 'Prison and Jail Inmates at Midyear 2003'. Washington DC: US Department of Justice.

Cain, Bruce and Kenneth Miller (2001), 'The Populist Legacy: Initiatives and Undermining of Representative Government', in Larry and Howard R. Ernst and Bruce Larson Sabato (eds) *Dangerous Democracy? The Battle over Ballot Initiatives in America*, pp. 33–61. Lanham, NJ: Rowman & Littlefield Publishers.

California State Constitution, n.d. available at: http://www.leginfo.ca.gov/consttoc.html (retrieved January 25, 2002).

Cannon, Lou (2003), *Governor Reagan: His Rise to Power*, New York: Public Affairs.

Chiricos, Ted and Miriam Delone (1992), 'Labor surplus and punishment: A review and assessment of theory and evidence', *Social Problems*, 39.4 pp. 421–46.

Clarke, Ronald V. (ed.) (1997), *Situational Crime Prevention: Successful Case Studies, 2nd edition*, Guilderland, N.Y. : Harrow and Heston.

Clemens, Elizabeth (1997), *The People's Lobby: Organizational Innovation and the Rise of Interest Group Politics in the United States, 1890–1925*, Chicago, IL: University of Chicago Press.

Diamond, Sara (1995), *Roads to Dominion: Right-wing Movements and Political Power in the United States*, New York: Guilford Press.

Elazar, Daniel (1966), *American Federalism: A View from the States*. New York: Thomas Y. Crowell.

Ellison, Katherine (1982), 'New Crusaders Fight Zealously Against Crime'. News-clippings. General Criminal. Governors' Office. Legal Affairs. Allen Sumner. Box 7 A.5.6. Brown Collection. Regional History Collection, University of Southern California.

Ertman, Thomas (1997), *Birth of the Leviathan: Building States and Regimes in Medieval and Early Modern Europe*, Cambridge: Cambridge University Press.

Evans, Daniel (1964), 'A Blue Print for Progress'. Campaign Speeches. Evans gubernatorial papers, 2S-4–37. Olympia Washington, Washington State Archive.

——— (1966), Speech to Citizens Conference on Washington's Courts. November. Evans gubernatorial papers. 2S-4–38. Olympia Washington, Washington State Archive.

——— (1975), *Address to Joint Session, Washington State Legislature*, January 13, Evans gubernatorial papers. Olympia, Washington, Washington State Archive.

Feeley, Malcolm and Jonathan Simon (1992), 'The New Penology: Notes on the Emerging Strategy of Corrections and its Implications', *Criminology*, 30.4 pp. 449–74.

Foucault, Michel (1977), *Discipline and Punish: The Birth of the Prison*, New York: Pantheon.

Friedland, Roger and Robert R. Alford (1991), 'Bringing Society Back In: Symbols, Practices, and Institutional Contradictions', in Walter W. Powell and Paul J DiMaggio (eds) *The New Institutionalism in Organizational Analysis*, pp. 232–66. Chicago: University of Chicago Press.

Gann, Paul Archive (1980), 'A Proposal Citizens Committee to Stop Crime', Drafts. Box 1393 Folder 7. Paul Gann Archive, Sacramento, California, California History Section, California State Library.

——— (1981), 'Proposition 8: Victims Bill of Rights', Box 1392. Paul Gann Archive. Sacramento, California, California History Section, California State Library.

Garland, David (1985), *Punishment and Welfare: A History of Penal Strategies*. Aldershot, England: Gower.

——— (1996), 'Limits of the sovereign state: strategies of crime control in contemporary society', *British Journal of Criminology*, 36 p. 445.

——— (2001), *The Culture of Control: Crime and Social Order in Late Modernity*, Chicago: Chicago University Press.

Giddens, Anthony (1993), 'Problems of Action and Structure', in Philip Cassell (ed.) *The Giddens Reader*, Stanford, CA: Stanford University Press, pp. 88–175.

Goodwyn (1978), *The Populist Moment*, Oxford: Oxford University Press.

Gray, Virginia, Herbert Jacob and Kenneth N. Vines (eds) (1983), 1990 and 1999, *Politics in the American States: A Comparative Analysis*, Boston: Little, Brown and Company.

Gray, Virginia and Russell Hanson (2004), *Politics in the American States*. Washington D.C.: CQ Press.

Greenberg, David and Valerie West (2001), 'State Prison Populations and Their Growth, 1971–1991'. *Criminology*, 39.3 pp. 615–54.

Griset, Pamala (1991), *Determinate Sentencing: The Promise and the Reality of Retributive Justice*, Albany: State University of New York.

Jacobs, David and Jason T. Carmichael (2001), 'The Politics of Punishment Across Time and Space: A Pooled Time-Series Analysis of Imprisonment Rates', *Social Forces*, 80.1 pp. 61–91.

Jacobs, David and Ronald Helms (1996), 'Toward a Political Model of Incarceration: A Time-Series Examination of Multiple Explanation for Prison Admission Rates', *American Journal of Sociology*, 102 pp. 323–57.

King, Gary, Robert O. Keohane, and Sidney Verba (1994), *Designing Social Inquiry: Scientific Inference in Qualitative Research*, Princeton, NJ: Princeton University Press.

Klatch, Rebecaa (1987), *Women of the New Right*, Philadelphia: Temple University Press.

Kramer, Daniel C. (1997), *The Days of Wine and Roses Are Over: Governor Hugh Carey and New York State*, Lantham, New York and London: University Press of America, Inc.

Liebschultz, Sarah with Robert Bailey, Jeffrey Stonecash, Jane Shapiro Zacek and Joseph Zimmerman (1998), *New York Politics and Government: Competition and Compassion*. Lincoln, Nebraska: University of Nebraska Press.

Lockard, Duane (1968), *Toward Equal Opportunity: A Study of State and Local Anti-Discrimination Laws*, New York: MacMillan.

Mahoney, James and Dietrich Rueschemeyer (eds) (2003), *Comparative Historical Analysis in the Social Sciences*, Cambridge: Cambridge University Press.

Mays, Mrs. (n.d.) Letter to Paul Gann, Box 1393 Folder 6. Analyses and Correspondence Received. Paul Gann Archive. Sacramento, California, California History Section, California State Archive.

McCoy, Candace (1993), *Politics and Plea Bargaining: Victims Rights in California*, Philadelphia: University of Pennsylvania Press.

McGirr, Lisa (2001), *Suburban Warriors: The Origins of the New American Right*, Princeton and Oxford: Princeton University Press.

McGovern, Stephen J. (1998), *The Politics of Downtown Development: Dynamic Political Cultures in San Francisco and Washington, D.C.*, Lexington, KY: University Press of Kentucky.

Morris, Norval (1974), *The Future of Imprisonment*. Chicago and London: University of Chicago Press.

New York State Constitution (n.d.) Available at http://www.assembly.state.ny.us/leg//co=0 (retrieved January 25, 2003).

New York State Consolidated Laws, (2004), Available at http://assembly.state.ny.us/leg

New York State Department of Correctional Services, 'Inmates Under Custody: By Crime, 1975–1979; 1980–1989; 1987–1992; 1991–2000'. Albany, New York.

New York State Statistical Yearbook (1979), Albany: New York State Division of the Budget.

New York Times (1965), 'Rockefeller Seeks State Fund to Aid Victims of Crime'. *New York Times*. October 23:1.

———— (1969a), 'Harlem Likened to Wild West'. *New York Times*, January 8: 48.

———— (1969b), 'Addicts' Victims Turn Vigilante'. *New York Times*, September 23:1.

Nichols, James H. (2001), 'Pragmatism', in Seymour Martin Lipset (ed.), *Political Philosophy: Theories, Thinkers, Concepts*, Washington D.C.: CQ Press, 145–49.

Peirce, Neal R. and Jerry Hagstrom (1983), *The Book of America: Inside the 50 States Today*, 1st edition, New York: Norton.

Pierson, Paul (2003), 'Big, Slow-Moving, and Invisible: Macrosocial Processes in the Study of Comparative Politics', in James and Dietrich Rueschemeyer Mahoney (eds), *Comparative Historical Analysis in the Social Sciences*, pp. 177–207, Cambridge, UK: Cambridge University Press.

Polletta, Francesca (1997), 'Culture and Its Discontents: Recent Theorizing on the Cultural Dimensions of Protest'. *Sociological Inquiry*, 67 4 pp. 431–50.

Przybycien, Thad (1981), Letter to Gann November 29. Box 1393 Folder 6, Analyses and Correspondence Received. Paul Gann Archive, Sacramento, California, California History Section, California State Archive.

Putnam, Robert (2000), *Bowling Alone: The Collapse and Revival of American Community*, New York: Simon and Schuster.

Reagan, Ronald (1968a), *The Creative Society: Some Comments on Problems Facing America*, New York: Devin-Adair Co.

———— (1968b), 'Joint Conference of California School Boards Association and California Association of School Administrators'. F3869:106: CCCJ Governor Speeches.

Rockefeller, Nelson A. (1971), 'Annual Message to the Legislature', in *Public Papers of Nelson A. Rockefeller 53rd Governor of the State of New York*, State of New York.

———— (1973a), 'Annual Message to the Legislature', in *Public Papers of Nelson A. Rockefeller 53rd Governor of the State of New York*, State of New York.

———— (1973b), 'News Conference with Governor Nelson A. Rockefeller, January 22, 1973'. Press Office, Box 89 F 1837, Rockefeller Archive Center, Sleepy Hollow, New York.

Rueschemeyer, Dietrich (2003), 'Can One or a Few Cases Yield Theoretical Gains?', in James Mahoney and Dietrich Rueschemeyer (eds) *Comparative Historical Analysis in the Social Sciences*, pp. 305–36. Cambridge: Cambridge University Press.

Rusche, Georg and Otto Kirchheimer (1939), *Punishment and Social Structure*, New York: Russell and Russell.

Sabato, Larry, Howard R. Ernst and Bruce Larson (eds) (2001), *Dangerous Democracy? The Battle over the Ballot Initiatives in America*. New York: Rowman and Littlefield.

Savelsberg, Joachim (1994), 'Knowledge, Domination and Criminal Punishment'. *American Journal of Sociology*, 97 pp. 1346–81.

———— (1999), 'Knowledge, Domination and Criminal Punishment Revisited: Incorporating State Socialism', *Punishment and Society*, 1.**1** pp. 45–70.

Schneier, Edward and John Brian Murtaugh (2001), *New York Politics: A Tale of Two States*, Armonk, New York and London: M.E. Sharpe.

Sewell, William H. (1999), 'The Concept(s) of Culture', in Victoria E. Bonnell and Lynn Hunt (eds) *Beyond the Cultural Turn: New Directions in the Study of Society and Culture*, Berkeley, CA: University of California Press, pp. 35–61.

Shichor, David and Dale K. Sechrest (1996), *Three Strikes and You're Out: Vengeance as Public Policy*, Thousand Oaks, CA: Sage.

Simon, Jonathan (1993), *Poor Discipline: Parole and the Social Control of the Underclass, 1890–1990*, Chicago and London: University of Chicago Press.

———— n.d. *Governing Through Crime*, Unpublished manuscript.

Skocpol, Theda (1992), *Protecting Soldiers and Mothers*, Cambridge, MA: Harvard University Press.

Skocpol, Theda and Kenneth Finegold (1986), 'State Capacity and Economic Intervention in the Early New Deal'. *Political Science Quaterly*, (97) 2 pp. 255–78.

Stuntz, William J. (2001), 'The Pathological Politics of Criminal Law'. 100 *Michigan Law Review*, 505.

Sutton, John (2000), 'Imprisonment and Social Classification in Five Common Law Countries, 1955–1985'. *American Journal of Sociology*, 106.2 pp. 350–86.

Swidler, Ann (1986), 'Culture in Action: Symbols and Strategies'. *American Sociological Review*, 51 pp. 273–86.

Thomas, Clive S. (ed.) (1991), *Politics and Public Policy in the Contemporary American West*, Albuquerque, New Mexico: University of New Mexico Press.

Tocqueville, Alexis (1990), *Democracy in America, Volumes 1 and 2*, The Henry Reeve text, New York: Vintage.

———— (1955), *The Old Regime and the French Revolution*, trans. Stuart Gilbert, New York: Anchor Books.

Tonry, Michael (1995), *Malign Neglect: Race, Crime and Punishment in America*, New York: Oxford University Press.

———— (1996), *Sentencing Matters*, New York: Oxford University Press.

Underwood, James and William Daniels (1982), *Governor Rockefeller in New York: the Apex of Pragmatic Liberalism in the United States*, Westport, Connecticut: Greenwood Press.

25

Uniform Crime Reports (2003), 'California Crime Rates per 100,000, 1965–2000', available at: http://www.disastercenter.com/crime/cacrime.htm (retrieved February 7, 2003).
——— (2003), 'New York Crime Rates per 100,000, 1965–2000', available at: http://www.disastercenter.com/crime/nycrime.htm (retrieved February 7, 2003).
——— (2003), 'Washington Crime Rates per 100,000, 1965–2000', available at: http://www.disastercenter.com/crime/wacrime.htm (retrieved February 7, 2003).
US Census Bureau (2000), 'State Profiles'. U.S. Census Bureau, available at: http://www.census.gov/stabab/www/states.
——— (2003), 'Persons Reported Registered and Voted by State: 2000, No. 420', available at: http://www.census.gov/statab.
——— (2004), 'State Rankings: State Government Revenue per Capita 2001', available at: http://www.census.gov/statab/ranks.
Wacquant, Loic (2001), 'Deadly Symbiosis: When Ghetto and Prison Meet and Mesh', in David Garland (ed.), *Mass Imprisonment: Social Causes and Consequences*, London: Sage, pp. 95–134.
Washington State Constitution, available at: http://www.courts.wa.gov/education/constitution (retrieved January 25, 2003).
Washington Association of Prosecuting Attorneys (1980), 'Justice in Sentencing'. Olympia, Washington: House of Representatives, Committee on Institutions.
Washington State Citizens Council on Crime (1966), Council Minutes February 22, Governor Evans gubernatorial papers. Olympia Washington, Washington State Archive.
Washington State Commission on The Causes and Prevention of Civil Unrest (1968), 'Report on Race and Violence in Washington'. Governor Evans gubernatorial papers. Olympia Washington, Washington State Archive.
Washington State Sentencing Guidelines Commission (2003), 'Two-Strikes and Three Strikes: Persistent Offender Sentencing Law in Washington State through June 2003', Washington Sentencing Guidelines Commission.
——— (1981–82), Sentencing Guidelines Commission Public Hearings and Written Comments, in Governor Jonathan Spellman papers, Issues. Sentencing Guidelines Commission. 2U-08-045. Olympia Washington, Washington State Archive.
——— (2004), 'Statistical Summary of Adult Felony Sentencing Fiscal Year 2003'. Olympia, Washington: Sentencing Guidelines Commission.
Washington State Institute for Public Policy (2003), 'The Criminal Justice System in Washington State: Incarceration Rates, Taxpayer Costs, Crime Rates and Prison Economics', Olympia, Washington.
Weber, Max (1978) [1922] *Economy and Society: An Outline of Interpretive Sociology*, Berkeley, CA: University of California Press.
Western, Bruce and Katherine Beckett (1999), 'How Unregulated is the US Labor Market? The Penal System as a Labor Market Institution', *American Journal of Sociology*, 104 pp. 1135–72.
Zimring, Franklin and Gordon Hawkins (1991), *The Scale of Imprisonment*, Chicago: University of Chicago Press.
Zimring, Frank, Gordon Hawkins and Sam Kamin (2001), *Punishment and Democracy: Three Strikes and You're Out in California*, Oxford: Oxford University Press.

26

[18]

The Political Response to Black Insurgency: A Critical Test of Competing Theories of the State

RICHARD C. FORDING *University of Kentucky*

Although empirical studies have concluded that political leaders in democratic systems often respond to mass unrest by expanding the welfare state, most of this research fails to explain adequately why the state responds as it does. I test the validity of pluralist and social control theories of state response by examining black insurgency in the United States during the 1960s and 1970s. Using pooled time-series analysis, I estimate the relationship between state AFDC recipient rates, state incarceration rates, and black political violence, testing a series of specific hypotheses that distinguish between these two competing theories. The results lend much support to the social control characterization of state response and may help explain trends in welfare and criminal justice policies over the last two decades.

There has been considerable debate among social scientists concerning the role of violent protest in the politics and policies of modern democracies. Much of the discussion centers on the consequences of mass violence and, in particular, whether the state responds by providing benefits to the insurgent group. Contrary to classic pluralist accounts of group influence and public policymaking in modern democracies, most empirical work concludes that mass political violence often results in a favorable response from the state, usually in the form of welfare state expansion. This research includes studies of state response to unrest among the unemployed and labor during the Great Depression (e.g., Goldfield 1989; Jenkins and Brents 1989; Piven and Cloward 1971, 1977), to black violence during the 1960s and 1970s (e.g., Fording 1997; Hicks and Swank 1983; Isaac and Kelly 1981; Piven and Cloward 1971), and to labor insurgency in Western Europe (Swank 1983).

Despite the evidence of a relationship between mass insurgency and welfare state expansion, there is little information about the process by which this occurs or the state's motivation. A favorable response to unrest by the state might plausibly result from one of two processes. On the one hand, the state may respond favorably as a strategy to control unrest. For example, transfer payments might be increased to pacify the insurgents, thus resulting in demobilization and cessation of violence. This is often labeled the social control perspective and has been put forth by neomarxists to explain the development and evolution of the welfare state as well as the survival of capitalism (e.g., Offe 1974; Poulantzas 1973).

On the other hand, a somewhat modified form of pluralist theory views collective violence as a strategy employed by otherwise powerless groups to achieve access to the policymaking agenda. Presumably, they gain sympathy and support through increased visibility and then can effectively compete and bargain with other interests to obtain policy changes favorable to their interests (e.g., Cobb, Ross, and Ross 1976; Lipsky 1970).

The two models describe very different processes by which social and political change occur. More important, perhaps, they suggest vastly different roles for the state in policymaking and depict contrasting power relationships between aggrieved groups and policymakers. The purpose of this research is to determine which of these processes most accurately characterizes the response to insurgency in the United States.

First, I specify more fully the alternative theories of state response and explain why the literature does not distinguish between them. Next, I develop a series of hypotheses that seek to determine which of the theoretical models is most accurate. I then present the results of an empirical analysis that distinguishes between these competing explanations by estimating the relationship among state rates for recipients of Aid to Families with Dependent Children (AFDC), state incarceration rates, and black political violence.

ALTERNATIVE MODELS OF STATE RESPONSE TO INSURGENCY

The Social Control Perspective

A key insight of social control theory is that influence may be exerted in one of two general ways.[1] First, behavior may be controlled by threats of negative sanctions in the event of noncompliance. Some theories refer to this as coercive control. Alternatively, influence may be exerted by offering incentives or rewards in exchange for compliance, which is often labeled beneficent control. In the context of mass insurgency, the social control perspective posits that the state, acting in the long-term interest of elites, will seek to minimize the effect of insurgency by increasing the level of social control, whether it be coercive, beneficent, or some combination of the two.

Although the most visible form of control is coercive, many theorists suggest that the state is not likely to rely

---

Richard C. Fording is Assistant Professor of Political Science, University of Kentucky, Lexington, KY 40506-0027.

I am grateful to Paul Brace, William Claggett, Larry Isaac, Evan Ringquist, and especially William Berry for their comments and suggestions at various stages of this research.

[1] "Social control" is used across several fields in the social sciences. My use of the term most closely resembles that emerging from the conflict perspective, the theoretical origins of which can be traced to Marx. See Liska (1997) for a review of this literature.

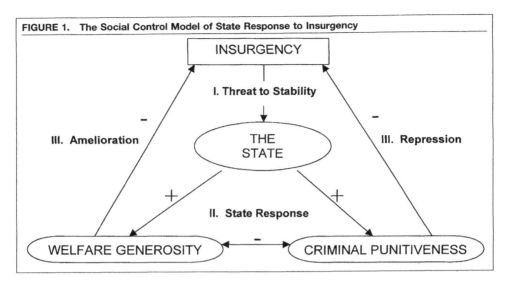

FIGURE 1.   The Social Control Model of State Response to Insurgency

upon it exclusively in managing insurgency. One of the most controversial applications of this theory is put forth by Piven and Cloward (1971). Consistent with more general arguments of some neomarxists (e.g., Offe 1975; Poulantzas 1973), Piven and Cloward argue that an important means by which the state maintains political stability, and thus preserves capitalism, is through periodic expansion of the welfare state. More specifically, during periods of mass insurgency, the state expands the relief rolls. This serves the dual function of addressing the grievances of the poor and restoring legitimacy to the incumbent government. When disorder subsides, the state slowly contracts the welfare rolls to keep labor markets competitive. This historical dynamic, they argue, was manifested most recently by the "relief explosion" that began during the late 1960s. Piven and Cloward claim that it was due in large part to the threat posed by widespread black violence that started with a wave of riots in 1964, followed by the insurgency of the (mostly black) poor throughout the remainder of the decade.

The role of beneficent control in quelling insurrection is clear enough, but social control theories are often rather vague about the role of coercive control, or repression. Most scholars who address this subject suggest that the state will respond to social unrest by an increase in both beneficent and coercive controls. Piven and Cloward (1971) perceive a mixed strategy, even in the absence of democratic political institutions, in their historical account of European relief systems during the sixteenth century. Since "penalties alone" were not adequate to maintain order, "some localities began to augment punishment with provisions for the relief of the vagrant poor" (p. 8).

In developing a more general model of social control, Quinney (1974) explicitly recognizes the role of both coercive and social welfare bureaucracies in the

control of threatening classes. When this model is extended to the case of black insurgency, it suggests that the response may be an expansion of welfare coupled with an increase in coercive control, as reflected by more punitive criminal justice policies. This process is represented graphically in Figure 1.

The Neopluralist Perspective

At the heart of the classic pluralist interpretation of democratic politics are three assumptions. First, the means by which groups may communicate preferences to leaders are effective and accessible to all groups should they wish to use them. Second, sufficient competition among all groups exists so that no single group has a policymaking monopoly. Third, policymakers are open to demands put forth by any group that gains access to the policy arena (e.g., Dahl 1961).

An important corollary of this model with respect to social movements is that the use of unconventional political tactics is thus unnecessary and even pathological. The plausibility of this conclusion, as well as the adequacy of the classic pluralist model more generally, is perhaps most clearly questioned by the emergence and success of the civil rights movement in the United States, which effectively challenged the pluralist assumption that available (legal) means of political participation are available to all groups. This case led to new approaches to explain the use of unconventional political strategies and the rise of social movements. Modifications of the pluralist model concerning the origins of protest have become known as the resource mobilization and political process approaches to the study of social movements (e.g., Jenkins 1985; McAdam 1982; McCarthy and Zald 1973; Tilly 1978). According to these neopluralist models, the infrequent and often unexpected occurrence of insurgency is due

American Political Science Review   Vol. 95, No. 1

to insufficient resources and opportunities for success-ful mobilization, which counters the classic pluralist position that insurgency is unnecessary.

The success of the civil rights movement in achieving its goals also led to a revision of the pluralist model regarding the consequences of protest. By the late 1960s, a number of modifications attempted to account for the rationality and effectiveness of unconventional politics but retained many of the model's core assumptions. Among the earliest and most influential of these was Lipsky's (1970) study of protest by the poor in New York. Consistent with neopluralist critiques, Lipsky saw the problem of powerless groups to be a lack of bargaining resources. The role of protest is to "activate third parties to enter the implicit or explicit bargaining arena in ways favorable to the protesters" (p. 2). The key to reaching these third parties, which Lipsky called "reference publics," is the mass media. Backed by the financial and organizational resources of reference publics, powerless groups may then be able to influence policy.

The role of protest, and more specifically that of political violence, has been incorporated into broader theoretical models of policymaking, which is clearly seen in the literature on agenda setting. Cobb, Ross, and Ross (1976) identify several stages of the agenda-building process, along with characteristics of policies and groups that lead to different strategies for achieving access to the formal agenda. One particular strategy of agenda building is likely, they argue, when the relevant group originates from outside the government structure. In their outside initiative model, access to the formal agenda is achieved indirectly through issue expansion and eventual inclusion on the public agenda. At that point, access to the formal agenda is relatively easy, due to the interest aroused in a larger number of voters, and policymakers are likely to be inclined to act. The most critical stage for groups pursuing this strategy is issue expansion: "In order to be successful in getting on the formal agenda, outside groups need to create sufficient pressure or interest to attract the attention of decision makers" (p. 128). A common tactic, particularly among groups that are large in number but have few financial resources, is through "violence and threats of violence" (p. 131).[2]

Similar attempts to specify the potential outcomes of insurgency abound in the more recent literature on social movements. Generally speaking, these theories predict that insurgency may or may not be successful, depending upon a number of movement characteristics and/or environmental factors. Like Lipsky (1970) and Cobb, Ross, and Ross (1976), many of these scholars cite the importance of third-party support (e.g., Jenkins and Perrow 1977; McAdam 1982). Other works cite such factors as the "strength" of insurgent forces (Tilly 1978), the nature of movement goals (e.g., Gamson 1975), and the ability of insurgent groups to combine violence with conventional modes of participation (Gamson 1975).

Despite differences, all these approaches share im-

portant features. First, the use of violence by aggrieved groups is assumed to be due to their inability to influence policymaking through conventional forms of participation. Second, success is thought to be contingent upon the nature of the political environment, most notably the level of public support for the insurgent group. Finally, and most important, although each of these models differs with the classic pluralist model regarding the utility of insurgency, all agree with it that the role of the state is to mediate among competing interests. In other words, although protest may be necessary for aggrieved groups to obtain access to the policy arena and the resources to compete effectively, once they reach the arena, the policymaking process is still a pluralist one. In the case of black insurgency, the specific implications are that any success in achieving issue expansion, gaining agenda access, and obtaining sufficient bargaining resources should have resulted in a favorable state response in one or more of the policy areas with which the insurgents were most concerned.

Black violence can be linked to a host of grievances, but two categories dominated the responses of insurgents to surveys conducted in the aftermath of major riots in 1967 (National Advisory Commission on Civil Disorders 1968). These were impoverishment in urban ghettos, including poor housing and unemployment, and harsh treatment by the criminal justice system. These concerns also were emphasized by protest leaders in negotiations with white officials after many riots and were reflected in press coverage of the events. Thus, to the extent that insurgency was successful, neopluralist theory predicts that it should have resulted in an expansion of the welfare state and a less punitive criminal justice system. This model is displayed in Figure 2.

Distinguishing between Models of Response

Despite the extensive empirical literature on the response to insurgency, work thus far has not distinguished between the models described above. This is due to the fact that the vast majority of these studies have only examined the relationship between black insurgency and welfare expansion. Most find that a relationship exists, but both the social control and the neopluralist theories predict such a relationship. Inherently, then, studies that examine a beneficent response alone cannot distinguish between the two models.

This problem does not exist with respect to research that examines the relationship between insurgency and criminal justice policy. Indeed, as can be seen by comparing figures 1 and 2, the competing theories suggest an opposite relationship between insurgency and criminal punitiveness. Very little research falls in this category, however. Welch (1975) examined city-level responses to riots across several local expenditure categories. Based on a sample of all cities with more than 50,000 in population, she found the number of riots to be positively related to expenditures for police and fire protection but unrelated to expenditures for public welfare. The only research on the federal response to insurgency is by Button (1978), who exam-

---

[2] Similar models can be found in Cobb and Elder (1983) and especially in Baumgartner and Jones (1993), who specifically address the role of the 1960s riots in moving urban issues to the public agenda.

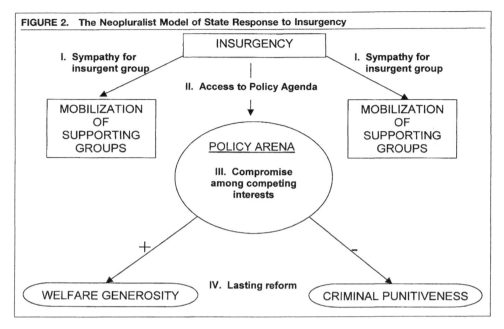

FIGURE 2.   The Neopluralist Model of State Response to Insurgency

ined how urban riots affected the targeting of a variety of federal programs that represented both beneficent responses (Office of Equal Opportunity; Department of Health, Education, and Welfare; and Department of Housing and Urban Development) and coercive responses (Department of Justice). Based on data from 40 cities, Button found that urban riots were positively related to both types of responses, to which he referred respectively as the "carrot" and the "stick."

The only other study to examine both forms of response (Iris 1983) used interrupted time-series analysis for a sample of 35 large metropolitan areas to examine the effect of urban rioting on both AFDC and police expenditures. Like Button, Iris found that the response to disorder could be characterized as beneficent, because rioting was related to AFDC expansion. Unlike Welch and Button, however, Iris found no evidence of a coercive response, as rioting was unrelated to police expenditures. That finding is supported by two city-level studies that examine the law enforcement response to urban unrest (Jackson and Carroll 1981; Jacobs 1979). In sum, the paucity of research and the inconsistent findings provide little guidance as to which of the competing theories of state response may be correct.

In an effort to distinguish between the two models, I employ several modifications to the studies described above. Although I analyze the response to insurgency with respect to both welfare and criminal justice policy, I examine responses at the state rather than the city level. States are the most important actors in the

American federal system, at least with respect to these two policy areas. States are generally responsible for about half the welfare expenditures in the country. In the case of criminal justice, most arrests are made by local law enforcement agencies, but criminal courts are under state control, and nearly all convicted offenders are sent to state prisons. In addition, annual data for all states are available for nearly all the variables in this study, which is not the case at the city or county level. This permits a pooled cross-section time-series design, which has important inferential advantages over the designs used in previous studies. The period 1962–80 was chosen to include the entire span of black insurgency and yields an N of 912 cases.

Even with these modifications, it is possible that the findings across both types of response will be inconclusive. Consider the following. If a positive relationship were found between insurgency and welfare generosity, as empirical evidence leads us to believe, this would leave us with three possibilities. First, there might also be a positive relationship between insurgency and coercive control (criminal punitiveness), which would support the social control model. Second, there might be a negative relationship between insurgency and criminal punitiveness, which would be consistent with the neopluralist model, as it suggests that blacks were successful with respect to grievances in both policy areas. Third, despite a positive relationship between insurgency and welfare generosity, if insurgency and criminal punitiveness are unrelated, we would still be unable to distinguish between the two theories. This third combination of findings would be consistent with a social control response and might be expected when elites fear the electoral costs of coercion are too great. Yet, this situation also would be consistent with a neopluralist model, as the lack of a coercive response could be interpreted as a victory for insurgent blacks.

In the third combination of relationships we would be able to distinguish between the two models by examining two additional hypotheses. The first rests on assumptions of the two models regarding the relationship between welfare and criminal justice policy. According to the social control model, both policies perform the same function, that is, social control. Assuming cost constraints and a fixed demand for social control, we should expect investment in these two areas to be negatively and reciprocally related (Inverarity and Grattet 1989; Liska 1997; Spitzer 1975). In other words, there should be a tradeoff between welfare and criminal justice expenditures as policymakers seek to maintain a desired level of social control at the lowest possible cost. In the neopluralist model, however, such a relationship should not exist. Policymakers are expected to approach each policy area separately, responding only to the preferences and resources of the groups in the arena. These alternative relationships are represented in figures 1 and 2.

The second distinguishing hypothesis concerns the expected duration of the various responses to insurgency. According to the neopluralist perspective, a favorable state response represents an exercise of power by the insurgent group in the bargaining arena, and therefore policy changes can be seen as genuine reform. If so, we should expect these changes to be relatively permanent, ceteris paribus. To use the language of Tilly (1978), the successful insurgent group, once a challenger from outside the polity, now becomes a member of the polity and henceforth has more or less direct access to the policy agenda. If the neopluralist model is correct, increases in welfare and decreases in criminal justice punitiveness should continue beyond the period of insurgency. In contrast, the social control model assumes that response to insurgency is driven by the need to reestablish order at the lowest possible cost. We should expect the state to reduce the overall level of social control investment once disorder subsides. Piven and Cloward (1971, 3) conclude with respect to a welfare response: "As turbulence subsides, the relief system contracts, expelling those who are needed to populate the labor market." Similarly, to the extent that the state responds with coercive controls, we should expect decreased investment in this strategy once disorder subsides.

AN EMPIRICAL MODEL OF STATE RESPONSE TO BLACK INSURGENCY

I rely on insurgency data originally reported in Fording (1997), where I defined insurgency as "any act of violence on behalf of blacks or minorities, either spontaneous or planned, which is either framed as or can be construed as politically motivated" (p. 11). The data cover collective acts of political violence (i.e.,

riots) as well as activities that involve fewer people, such as arson and sniping attacks, which were carried out by various black revolutionary groups. Violent acts are defined as rock throwing, vandalism, arson, looting, sniping, or beating of whites. Consistent with past research, insurgency is measured as the number of incidents. Data were collected for 923 events.[3]

A Model of State Welfare Generosity

Consistent with past research, welfare generosity is measured as the annual growth (change) in the number of AFDC recipients per one million state population in each state. This measure, as opposed to benefit levels or expenditures, is chosen due to the emphasis given this dimension of welfare policy by social control explanations (Piven and Cloward 1971). Although the social control approach does not preclude the possibility that insurgency may be related to AFDC benefit levels as well, Piven and Cloward argue that the effect on recipient rates should be strongest, since it is presumed that the primary source of insurgency, and thus the target of state control, is the unruly poor who are not currently receiving government aid.

Exogenous variables for this model are suggested in past research on AFDC growth and on the growth of social welfare programs generally. Broadly conceptualized, several of these approaches to explaining welfare policy comprise what Rochefort (1986) has termed the progressive perspective. Other explanations focus on changes in welfare programs originating at the federal level, the characteristics of state political institutions, and the extension and expansion of political rights for the poor.

The Progressive Perspective. Within this general approach, different theorists have stressed various factors, but all the explanations share the position that welfare policy is primarily driven by the benevolent motives of policymakers and the needs of poor. To the extent that at least some motivation is humanitarian, we should expect change in AFDC rolls to be related to the size of the needy population, as measured by the annual change in the number of female-headed households in poverty and by the annual change in the level of unemployment in a state (e.g., Fording 1997; Isaac and Kelly).

Theorists also have linked welfare expansion to increased capacity to afford social welfare and to the increase in social pathologies caused by urbanization (e.g., Wilensky and Lebeaux 1965). To capture these effects, I include *Per Capita Income* and *Per Capita State Revenue* as measures of economic capacity (each measured as the annual change) as well as the annual change in the level of urbanization in a state *(Urban-*

---

[3] Another form of insurgency potentially relevant here are the relatively disruptive yet nonviolent protests by various welfare rights groups, many organized under the leadership of the National Welfare Rights Organization. Because these protests were nonviolent, they did not receive much attention from the major news media, and they are not included in this analysis.

ization). Each of these variables is expected to be positively related to AFDC expansion.[4]

Federal Changes. According to some analysts, important changes in welfare policy, particularly the introduction of Medicaid in 1965 and the abolition of residency requirements by the Supreme Court in 1969, have altered the incentives of the poor and caused significant changes in AFDC participation (Durman 1973). To capture the effect of the Medicaid program, I include *Medicaid*, a dummy variable with the value of 1 in the year that the program was introduced in a state, 0 otherwise.[5] The effect of residency requirements is captured by *Residency Requirements*, a dichotomous variable that equals 1 in 1969 for states affected by the Court's decision, 0 for all other states and years.[6] Both variables are expected to be positively related to AFDC growth.[7]

State Political Institutions. Ideological differences between the major political parties as well as the level of competition between them are accounted for by *Democratic Control*, a variable measuring Democratic control of state government (e.g., Dye 1984; Erikson, Wright, and McIver 1993), and *Interparty Competition*, which measures the annual change in interparty competition (Key 1949). The ideology of state electorates (measured as the change in ideology), which is presumed to influence the decisions of state policymakers (Erikson, Wright, and McIver 1993), is captured by *Ideology*, a measure of liberalism constructed by Berry et al. (1998). Each of these variables is hypothesized to affect AFDC growth positively.

Political Citizenship. Some theorists suggest that welfare expansion is associated with periodic expansion of "citizenship," that is, the evolution and extension of social and political rights (e.g., Gronbjerg 1977). One of the most important periods in this regard was the

1960s, and two dimensions of this expansion are incorporated into the analysis.

First, due to significant changes in voting qualifications that affected both blacks and whites (e.g., abolition of poll tax), masses of poor people were effectively enfranchised for the first time during the 1960s, which presumably altered the class composition of the electorate. Therefore, *Class Bias* is adopted from Husted and Kenny (1997), a measure that captures the expansion of the electorate during the 1960s as well as variation in the relative participation of the poor over the period of this analysis. Because it reflects the degree to which the poor are underrepresented in the electorate, class bias (measured as the annual change) is expected to have a negative effect on AFDC expansion.

Second, important court decisions ended decades (in some cases) of extreme malapportionment and gave densely populated poorer districts more power, which may have contributed to welfare expansion. I include *Reapportionment* and model this process as an intervention, that is, the variable has a nonzero value only for the first year after the first significant reappointment was implemented in a state.[8] The variable is not dichotomous, however, because the intervention value represents the magnitude of malapportionment (alternatively, the extent of reapportionment) that existed previously. Reapportionment is expected to result in greater representation for the urban poor, so it is expected to be positively related to AFDC growth.

A Model of State Criminal Punitiveness

The criminal justice response to insurgency is hypothesized to be reflected by the change in incarceration rates and is measured as the annual change in the number of prisoners in state prisons per one million population. In addition to black insurgency, several other variables are hypothesized to influence growth in state incarceration rates.

Criminal Involvement. Many criminologists cite the stability of punishment thesis, that is, incarceration rates remain relatively stable over time and change in response to society's tolerance for crime, rather than in response to crime itself. Several studies have found crime to be an important determinant of incarceration rates (e.g., Carroll and Cornell 1985; Garofalo 1980), but others have found little if any relationship (e.g., Carrol and Doubet 1983; Joubert, Picou, and McIntosh 1981). Given these mixed findings, I include *Crime*, measured as the annual change in crime rates, which is expected to be positively related to incarceration.

Economic Characteristics. Rusche and Kirchheimer (1939) argue that incarceration rises with unemployment due to the potential threat to the social order from the unemployed. The issue of threat aside, Cappel and Sykes (1991) point out that employment status

---

[4] For specific sources and details about how all the variables in this analysis were constructed, see the Appendix.

[5] In an earlier analysis (Fording 1997), I used the annual change in the Medicaid recipient rate to represent the effect of Medicaid on AFDC expansion. Although I found a significant relationship between the two, we might alternatively expect AFDC expansion to cause an increase in the Medicaid recipient rate, which suggests that the causal arrow runs in the opposite direction. To determine which is the case, I conducted Granger causality tests. The results provide strong evidence that increases in the Medicaid recipient rate are caused by AFDC expansion ($F = 21.56$, $p = .000$ at five lags). I use a dummy variable representing the introduction of the Medicaid program to avoid potential simultaneity bias.

[6] Since the dependent variable is measured as the *change* in AFDC recipient rates, I code this variable (as well as the Medicaid variable) as 1 in the year of the intervention (i.e., when a residency requirement was dropped, or when the Medicaid program was introduced), 0 in all other years. This is equivalent to modeling an intercept change in the level of the dependent variable.

[7] One of the anonymous reviewers suggested that federal court decisions handed down in 1967 that increased access to welfare for the black poor in the South could be an additional source of the "relief explosion." Yet, inclusion of a dummy variable for 1967 to control for this factor failed to reach statistical significance ($t = 1.14$) and did not significantly affect any of the results reported below. As this variable contributes to multicolinearity problems, I do not include it in the models estimated in tables 1 and 2.

---

[8] Because the dependent variable is measured as the change in AFDC, this is equivalent to modeling an intercept change in the level of the dependent variable.

is an important determinant of sentencing outcomes because it indicates the likelihood that the defendant will continue to commit crime. Based on both of these hypotheses, the annual change in a state's unemployment rate is included in the incarceration model. *Unemployment* is expected to be positively related to incarceration.

In similar vein, many researchers posit a direct relationship between level of poverty and incarceration (e.g., Taggert and Winn 1993). Consistent with the threat hypothesis for unemployment, states with a higher level of inequality might be subject to greater potential threat from the lower classes, which could result in a greater level of incarceration. As with unemployment, however, an alternative explanation can be given for a positive relationship between inequality and incarceration. Defendants with sufficient financial resources can purchase competent defense and can sustain numerous appeals upon conviction, which increases the probability that they will not be incarcerated for very long, if at all. Consistent with other studies, I include *Poverty*, measured as the annual change in state poverty rates, as a measure of inequality.[9]

Finally, as noted earlier, two indicators of a state's economic capacity, per capita state income and per capita state revenue, are included. The direction of their effect on incarceration is not entirely clear. On the one hand, wealthy states may be able to afford more prisons, so economic prosperity should be positively related to incarceration. On the other hand, for the same reasons we expect poverty to be positively related to incarceration, we might expect per capita state income and revenue to be negatively related to incarceration.

State Political Institutions. As with welfare policies, several features of state political institutions and ideology are hypothesized to affect state incarceration rates. Relatively liberal voters, Democratic control of state government, competitive party systems, reapportionment, and extensive political participation by the poor and blacks are all expected to contribute to more lenient sentencing and parole policies, more alternatives to imprisonment, and hence lower incarceration rates, ceteris paribus. Although political variables have not been incorporated into many studies of incarceration rates in the past, recent research finds that political forces are an important determinant (e.g., Taggert and Winn 1993).

Military Mobilization Rates. Many studies have noted a negative correlation between military participation rates and incarceration rates. This is not surprising, given a presumed indirect influence of military participation rates through some of the variables discussed above (e.g., unemployment and poverty). A direct relationship also may exist; Inverarity and Grattet (1989, 357) note the "legal folklore" that, during times

of war, "judges commonly offer young miscreants a choice between jail and enlistment." In any case, a direct relationship is supported to some extent by empirical research that controls for some of the variables (but not all) through which military mobilization might influence incarceration indirectly (e.g., Cappell and Sykes 1991). Based on this possibility, I include *Military*, measured as the annual change in the number of individuals in the state in the armed forces (active duty).

The Conditional Effect of Insurgency

The strength of the relationship between insurgency and welfare depends on two important contextual factors (Fording 1997). First, presumably due to electoral incentives of policymakers, a welfare response only occurs when the insurgent group achieves effective electoral access (defined as both voting right *and* electoral systems that are not malapportioned). Second, as suggested by Keech (1968), during periods of effective electoral access, the influence of insurgency on AFDC growth is strongest in states with a relatively small black population (presumably due to a low level of white resistance) and in states with a relatively large black population (presumably due to black electoral influence). In other words, the insurgency effect is curvilinear (U-shaped) over the black population range of values and is weakest in the middle range (Fording 1997, 21). Based on this finding, a similar interactive specification is applied to the welfare model in this research.[10]

With respect to insurgency and incarceration, two curvilinear interactions are possible in the context of black electoral access. In a neopluralist model, a generally negative relationship would be expected between insurgency and incarceration across the range of black population size, as this is representative of a beneficient response. Consistent with the pattern of response found for AFDC, however, we would expect states in the middle range of black population size to show a relatively weak beneficient response, as blacks in these states simultaneously experience a relatively high level of white resistance and a low level of black electoral strength (Keech 1968). In a social control model, however, a generally positive relationship would be expected between insurgency and incarceration, as this is representative of a coercive response. Moreover, in this case the magnitude of the relationship should be strongest in the middle range, again due to the (presumed) combination of white resistance and weak black electoral influence.

For each dependent variable, the conditional relationship is incorporated by estimating a model in which insurgency is hypothesized to interact with black electoral access and the size of the black population. To capture the effect of black electoral access, I adopt a dichotomous measure from Fording (1997), which I label *Power*. It has a value of 1 for a state in which the following two conditions are satisfied for all years: (1) blacks have effective voting rights (based on implementation of the Voting Rights Act of 1965 in certain

---

[9] Although poverty rates are not perfect measures of income inequality, better measures (such as Gini coefficients) are not readily available for the period analyzed here. Recently, Langer (1999) computed state-level Gini coefficients beginning in 1976 and reports sufficient correlation with state poverty rates to provide some confidence that poverty rates are a reasonable surrogate (>.70).

[10] For a thorough derivation of this specification in the context of a welfare model, see Fording 1997, 25–6.

states), and (2) electoral districts are not malapportioned (for states in which more than 90% of blacks resided in heavily populated urban areas). Otherwise, its value is 0. This implicitly assumes that both dimensions of access are essential to black interests being translated through electoral mechanisms.

Additional Hypotheses

The Welfare-Incarceration Tradeoff. As discussed previously, a crucial distinguishing feature of the social control model is the welfare-incarceration tradeoff. Although the model seems to rest heavily on this hypothesis (e.g., Liska 1997; Spitzer 1975), few empirical studies have tested it. In what appears to be the only research of its kind, Inverarity and Grattet (1989) used time-series analysis at the national level to test for a tradeoff between incarceration rates and the number of AFDC recipients, but they found no relationship. Aggregation is a potential source of problems in their analysis, however, and they failed to use an estimation technique that explicitly allows for reciprocal causation. Both problems are avoided in the present research, which posits a direct contemporaneous relationship between AFDC and incarceration. If the social control model is correct, the tradeoff should lead to a negative relationship between the two.

The Durability of Response. Another distinguishing hypothesis necessitates modeling both the short- and long-term effects of insurgency. Here it is important to consider the way in which the dependent variables, AFDC and incarceration, as well as insurgency are measured. The dependent variables are measured as changes (first-differences), whereas insurgency is measured simply as the number of incidents of political violence. Therefore, if insurgency is found to have an effect on either dependent variable for a particular lag length, the effect is assumed to result in a permanent increase in the level of that variable; in the language of time-series analysis, an intercept change in the level of the dependent variable occurs. This is consistent with the notion of lasting reform posited by the neopluralist model but inconsistent with the social control model, which suggests that welfare and incarceration levels will decline once disorder subsides. In order to test both models simultaneously, it is necessary to include multiple lags of insurgency. According to social control theory, a significant positive effect (for either dependent variable) eventually will be followed by a negative effect as the state readjusts the level of assistance/incarceration necessary to achieve social control. To accomplish this, I examine the effect of insurgency for up to seven lags. Lags lengths for other variables are determined by theory or, when theory is ambiguous, empirically (*t*-values). The entire model to be estimated, along with hypothesized relationships for both the welfare model and the incarceration model, is presented in Figure 3.

ESTIMATION AND RESULTS

The framework for this analysis is a pooled cross-sectional time-series design. Due to the hypothesized

reciprocal effect between AFDC and incarceration, I employ two-stage least-squares (2SLS) to generate coefficient estimates. To deal with likely violations of error assumptions, I follow Beck and Katz (1995), who recommend calculating standard errors (panel corrected standard errors, or PCSEs) that are consistent in the presence of heteroskedasticity and spatial autocorrelation. To handle serial correlation, they recommend a lagged dependent variable (LDV) rather than a traditional generalized least squares (GLS) correction. As they argue, the LDV approach explicitly brings the dynamics into the model and, based on Monte Carlo tests, appears to provide more efficient parameter estimates (compared to GLS) for typical pooled data sets. Thus, the final estimation strategy used here integrates 2SLS with PCSEs.[11]

To arrive at the final set of results, I engaged in three rounds of estimation. The first used an iterative process to determine the proper lags for the effect of insurgency, beginning with a strictly additive model that contained lags of up to seven years, and the lags that exhibited the strongest effects were retained.[12] The second round introduced interaction terms for the insurgency variables, dropped any interactions that did not appear significant (based on joint *F*-tests) or theoretically plausible, and reestimated. These results are presented as model 1 in tables 1 and 2 for both AFDC and incarceration. Based on these results, the third round estimated a final parsimonious model, retaining all variables that exhibited both the correct sign and a *t*-value of at least 1.0 in absolute value. These final results are presented as model 2 in tables 1 and 2.

Explaining State Welfare Generosity

Many scholars refer to the late 1960s as the "relief explosion," due to the innovation and expansion that occurred across a variety of public assistance programs, especially AFDC. What was responsible for this massive increase in welfare participation? The answer may be at least partially provided in Table 1, which displays regression results for AFDC. Consistent with my earlier analysis (Fording 1997), unemployment, residency requirements, and state ideology were all significant factors. In addition, urbanization and female poverty are positively related to AFDC growth. My earlier analysis failed to account for urbanization, and the significance of female poverty (which was insignificant earlier) is likely explained by the improved specification of the model.

The influence of insurgency on AFDC growth is strong and appears to be conditional upon electoral access and the size of the black population. This can be seen from examining the coefficients for the first set of insurgency variables in model 2 of Table 1 (i.e., where

---

[11] As Figure 2 indicates, the model is clearly overidentified, assuming the hypothesized relationships between the exogenous variables unique to each model and the endogenous variables do in fact exist. Identification is also significantly aided (at least for the AFDC model) by the inclusion of state dummy variables in the incarceration model.

[12] It is possible to include all the interactive terms up to seven lags in one model, but it would be unwieldy and likely suffer crippling multicollinearity problems.

American Political Science Review   Vol. 95, No. 1

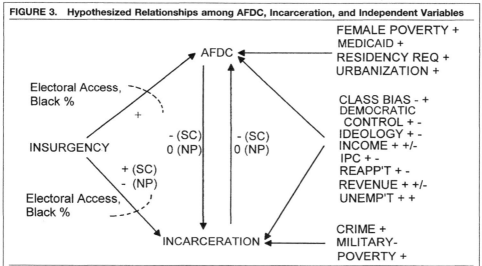

FIGURE 3. Hypothesized Relationships among AFDC, Incarceration, and Independent Variables

Note: Dashed lines denote conditional relationships. Hypothesized signs of relationships are given for each independent variable. For exogenous variables (other than insurgency) hypothesized to affect both AFDC and incarceration, the two signs listed denote hypothesized effects on AFDC and incarceration, respectively. For relationships serving as critical tests of the social control (SC) and neopluralist (NP) models, hypothesized signs are listed for each of these competing theories.

insurgency is lagged two years). As in my 1997 analysis, the effect of insurgency is near zero when blacks did not have electoral access. Once they achieved electoral power, however, the effect indeed appears to be strong and varies significantly across the black population range in a curvilinear manner. Using slope coefficient estimates from Table 1, and setting the contextual variables of power and black to the desired values, the effect of insurgency when access has been achieved can be estimated for the range of values of the black population observed throughout the 1962–80 period.

These estimated effects, depicted graphically in Figure 4, generally reflect the curvilinear pattern reported in my earlier analysis (Fording 1997). At a two-year lag and in states where blacks comprise less than 3% of the population, each incident of insurgency is predicted to cause an increase in AFDC growth of 250–300 recipients per million population. When the black population is larger, the effect of insurgency diminishes, although not as significantly as my original results suggest. In states in which at least 30% of the population is black, each episode of insurgency is estimated to produce an increase in AFDC growth of at least 500 recipients per million population.

Explaining State Criminal Punitiveness

The results for the incarceration model are presented in Table 2, which reveals that the strongest effects originate from state economic conditions. Unemployment and poverty both exhibit relatively strong positive relation-

ships with incarceration rates, whereas higher state revenue is associated with a reduction. As with welfare generosity, the influence of political variables is significant but not especially striking. Both Democratic control and interparty competition are negatively related to incarceration, which is consistent with hypotheses that liberal control of political institutions or competitive party systems in the state produces more liberal policies. The other political variables—ideology, reapportionment, and class bias—all proved insignificant.

The effect of insurgency on incarceration was estimated in the same manner as for AFDC, by an iterative procedure that isolated the potentially significant lags and then determined the significance of the various interactions. The results clearly demonstrated that the effect of insurgency is not conditional as hypothesized, so an additive specification was used to generate the final results presented in Table 2. This is not to say that insurgency is unrelated to incarceration, however, as can be seen by examining the coefficient value for the two-year lag of insurgency, which indicates a positive and significant relationship. According to the results, each act of insurgency is predicted to increase incarceration by about 23 prisoners (per million population), holding other variables constant.

These results have two important theoretical implications. First, they provide support for the social control theory of state response, in particular a model in which the state increases both coercive and beneficent types of controls when threatened. Second, the

TABLE 1. Two-Stage Least-Squares Regression Results for AFDC Growth					
	Model 1		Model 2		
Independent Variable	β	PCSE	β	PCSE	β*
Progressive Perspective					
Female poverty$_{i,t}$	471.97**	190.00	491.13**	181.45	.08
Unemployment$_{i,t}$	861.96**	137.82	842.43**	138.87	.28
Revenue$_{i,t-1}$	−3,652.96	8,962.03	—	—	—
Income$_{i,t-1}$	−.04	1.29	—	—	—
Urbanization$_{i,t-1}$	193.30**	54.05	212.19**	56.41	.12
Federal Changes					
Medicaid$_t$	−125.13	385.83	—	—	—
Residency requirement$_{i,t}$	1,639.53*	831.89	1,863.59*	814.39	.09
State Institutions					
Democratic control$_{i,t-1}$	−282.69	462.28	—	—	—
Interparty competition$_{i,t-1}$	8.27	20.71	—	—	—
Ideology$_{i,t-1}$	44.93**	17.99	42.62*	18.90	.08
Political Citizenship					
Reapportionment$_{i,t}$	42.93	109.44	—	—	—
Class bias$_{i,t-3}$	−1,154.66	1,463.94	—	—	—
Insurgency: Lag of Two Years					
Insurgency$_{i,t-2}$	−45.16	240.40	−25.62	241.99	—
Power$_{i,t}$	342.81	531.60	668.80	486.34	—
Insurgency$_{i,t-2}$ × Power$_{i,t}$	352.93	266.53	321.16	267.49	—
Insurgency$_{i,t-2}$ × Power$_{i,t}$ × Black$_{i,t}$	−20.92	14.68	−19.58	15.02	—
Insurgency$_{i,t-2}$ × Power$_{i,t}$ × Black$^2_{i,t}$	.94**	.36	.89*	.38	.29/.21
Insurgency: Lag of Five Years					
Insurgency$_{i,t-5}$	332.87	250.90	356.25	252.60	—
Power$_{i,t-3}$	−1,042.09*	441.32	−1,200.81**	425.15	—
Insurgency$_{i,t-5}$ × Power$_{i,t-3}$	−567.47*	278.18	−743.28**	294.04	—
Insurgency$_{i,t-5}$ × Power$_{i,t-3}$ × Black$_{i,t}$	15.73	14.95	—	—	—
Insurgency$_{i,t-5}$ × Power$_{i,t-3}$ × Black$^2_{i,t}$	−.19	.38	—	—	—
Insurgency$_{i,t-5}$ × ln(Black)$_{i,t}$	—	—	125.73	67.34	−.37/−.06
Welfare-Incarceration Tradeoff					
Incarceration$_{i,t}$	−1.14**	.37	−1.09**	.35	−.29
AFDC$_{i,t-1}$	.30**	.06	0.29**	.06	.30
Constant	750.51*	369.17	668.65*	321.09	—
Number of cases	912		912		
Adjusted R^2	.43		.44		

Note: Column entries are unstandardized slope estimates (β), PCSEs, and for model 2, standardized slope estimates (β*). The standardized effects reported for insurgency are calculated by setting the variable *Black* (percentage black) at the values represented by the 25th and 75th percentiles (1.44% and 13.78%, respectively, based on the full sample). A joint F-test indicated that the inclusion of unit effects (i.e., state dummies) was not warranted. An LM (language modifier) test demonstrates that the inclusion of the lagged dependent variable sufficiently eliminates serial correlation. All estimates were generated by RATS (regression analyses of time series), using a two-stage least-squares PCSE procedure written by Nathaniel Beck. Significance tests are two-tailed for insurgency variables, one-tailed for all other variables. *$p < .05$, **$p < .01$.

insignificance of insurgency for welfare generosity when blacks do not have electoral access suggests that, in the absence of electoral power, insurgency is likely to receive only a coercive response from the state.

Additional Hypotheses

Despite the initial support for the social control model, it is useful to examine hypotheses concerning other aspects of state response that help distinguish between the neopluralist and social control models. The first concerns the durability or permanency of the response. If the direct (positive) effect of insurgency on AFDC growth is relatively permanent, then the lasting reform posited by the neopluralist model is supported, and the findings concerning incarceration are contradicted. An

additive model of AFDC growth was estimated with a series of insurgency variables lagged up to seven years.[13] The values of the coefficients obtained from this regression display a relatively clear pattern over time. The initial response to insurgency is positive, with the first significant coefficient value seen at a lag of two years. Beyond this point, the coefficient value becomes negative, although only significantly so at a lag of five years, that is, three years after the initial positive response.[14] A similar pattern can be observed

---

[13] Additive models were used in these diagnostic regressions because seven lags of interaction terms are extremely cumbersome, and the multicolinearity problem would be severe.

[14] For the effect of insurgency on AFDC, the coefficient values for seven lags were −34.3, 247.4*, −21.0, 7.7, −83.1*, 9.3, −53.8 (*$p < .05$). For incarceration, they were 17.9*, 7.0, −13.8, −11.5, 4.2, 5.6,

TABLE 2. Two-Stage Least-Squares Regression Results for Incarceration

Independent Variable	Model 1		Model 2		
	β	PCSE	β	PCSE	β^*
Crime$_{i,t-1}$	.20	.14	.26*	.13	.10
Unemployment$_{i,t}$	156.64**	36.73	159.29**	37.35	.20
Poverty$_{i,t}$	483.80**	94.51	491.63**	90.13	.32
Revenue$_{i,t-1}$	−4,071.37*	2,405.72	−4,259.44*	2,410.08	−.06
Income$_{i,t-1}$	−.36	.37	—	—	—
Democratic control$_{i,t-1}$	−234.38*	124.49	−221.33*	126.59	−.07
Interparty competition$_{i,t-1}$	−13.28*	6.00	−13.77**	6.13	−.09
Ideology$_{i,t-1}$	9.09	5.48	—	—	—
Reapportionment$_{i,t}$	−.27	26.49	—	—	—
Class bias$_{i,t-3}$	127.54	359.25	—	—	—
Military$_{i,t}$	−.09	.23	—	—	—
Insurgency$_{i,t-2}$	23.92**	8.69	24.31**	9.20	.10
Insurgency$_{i,t-3}$	−16.03	8.92	−16.85	9.41	−.07
AFDC$_{i,t}$	−.06**	.02	−.06**	.02	−.24
Constant	642.34	427.57	621.35	426.48	—
Number of cases	912		912		
Adjusted R^2	.20		.20		

Note: Column entries are unstandardized slope estimates (β), PCSEs, and for model 2, standardized slope estimates (β^*). A joint *F*-test indicated that the inclusion of unit effects (i.e., state dummies) was necessary for both first- and second-stage regressions (results not reported). Diagnostic tests reveal an absence of serial correlation, which is reflected by the insignificance of the coefficient for a lagged dependent variable when included in the model (results not reported). All estimates were generated by RATS, Version 4.2, using a two-stage least-squares PCSE procedure written by Nathaniel Beck. Significance tests are two-tailed for insurgency, one-tailed for all other variables. *$p < .05$, **$p < .01$.

for the effect of insurgency on incarceration. In Table 2, we see that the positive effect of insurgency at a lag of two years is matched by a negative effect at a lag of three years.[15] This temporal pattern across the two dimensions of response provides additional support for the social control model: The levels of social control increase in response to insurgency and then decline when disorder subsides.

Returning to the dynamics of the welfare response, since it was found that AFDC expansion is contingent upon electoral considerations represented by size of the black population, we might expect the extent of AFDC contraction to be conditional upon the electoral context as well. Based on the coefficient estimates in model 2 of Table 1, this appears to be the case to some degree.[16] The dashed line in Figure 4 displays the predicted effect of insurgency at a lag of five years across the range of values for the black population. As we can see, the picture that emerges here is somewhat different from that for AFDC expansion with the two-year lag. At lower levels of black population, the AFDC rolls appear to contract somewhat after order is

restored, which does not appear to be the case at higher population levels. It seems that black electoral strength helps protect concessions made during disorder from being lost over time.

Thus far, the results across the two dimensions of response provide strong support for the social control model. Further support would be gained if it were found that AFDC and incarceration are reciprocally related, indicating that the two policy dimensions at least partly serve the same function of social control. This hypothesis is supported in tables 1 and 2, where coefficient estimates for the effect of incarceration on AFDC and for the effect of AFDC on incarceration are both negative and significant.

The Cumulative Effect of Insurgency

In combination with the direct influence of insurgency and the conditional nature of both the long- and short-term effects, a welfare-incarceration tradeoff would suggest that the overall effect of insurgency may be quite complex. As the cumulative effect of insurgency is not easily discernible from tables 1 and 2, I present Figure 5, which displays predicted levels of AFDC recipient rates and incarceration rates for two hypothetical states. To generate these estimates, predicted values for changes in AFDC and incarceration were first calculated, holding the values of all exogenous noninsurgency variables constant at representative values, which allowed the total effect of insurgency (direct and indirect effects combined) to be isolated. These predicted change values (i.e., first differences) were then converted to levels for ease of interpretation

---

1.8 (*$p < .05$). Moving to the reduced model (models 1 and 2, as reported in Table 2), however, a lag of two years proved to be significant, whereas a lag of one year did not.

[15] The coefficient estimate for the lag of insurgency at three years is not quite significant at the .05 level ($p = .06$), but given the inherent multicolinearity in distributed lag models, I treat it as such.

[16] In estimating the interactive effect of insurgency in the case of AFDC contraction, the results in Table 1 (model 1) indicate that coefficient values for the interaction terms are not significant. As this result may be due to multicolinearity, and given the shape of the curve in Figure 4 representing a lag of two years, I used the natural log of black population, rather than black population and its square, to model the conditional effect of insurgency in model 2. This specification shows a larger effect ($p = .07$).

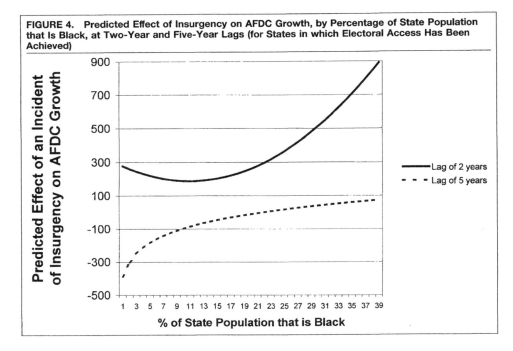

FIGURE 4.   Predicted Effect of Insurgency on AFDC Growth, by Percentage of State Population that Is Black, at Two-Year and Five-Year Lags (for States in which Electoral Access Has Been Achieved)

and plotted in Figure 5.[17] The hypothetical state in panel A experienced relatively little black violence (six incidents) during 1967–68, and black population size was rather small (3%). States that fit this description include Colorado, Iowa, Kansas, Massachusetts, and Nebraska. In this case the initial response to insurgency is heavier reliance on beneficent control, but eventually both AFDC and incarceration return to levels close to those before unrest (holding other variables constant).

A much different picture emerges for the hypothetical state in panel B of Figure 5, where there was considerable black insurgency (23 incidents), and black population size was large (30%). In this category are most of the states in the Deep South. Due to the relatively strong expansive effect of insurgency on welfare generosity, coupled with the durability of this policy in the years following unrest, the long-term influence of insurgency is quite significant. There is a relatively permanent increase in AFDC levels, and the predicted tradeoff between social control strategies contributes to a relatively permanent decrease in the level of incarceration.

Figure 5 depicts two very different scenarios, and we are left to wonder whether and how these effects might have combined into a national picture over the same period. This can be seen in Figure 6, which plots observed AFDC recipients rates, incarceration rates, and levels of insurgency during 1962–80. There is

evidence of the pronounced inverse relationship between AFDC and incarceration found in the state-level analyses presented above. In addition, the national trends resemble the pattern in Figure 5A more than the pattern in Figure 5B. This is not surprising, because the values of black population size and the level of violence used to calculate panel A are more typical across states than those used to generate panel B.

CONCLUSION

Although a relationship between mass unrest and welfare expansion has been established in several contexts, relatively little effort has been applied by social scientists to uncover the causal mechanisms. This research indicates that the social control perspective may provide the most valid explanation for this relationship in the case of black insurgency. Further work is necessary to determine whether these findings are applicable to other democratic systems, but this analysis may help explain important policy developments both past and present within the United States.

A widely debated historical question concerns the motivation behind New Deal legislation during the Great Depression, a period of unprecedented welfare state expansion to address the needs of the poor, the unemployed, labor, and the aged (e.g., Ametha, Dunleavey, and Bernstein 1994; Goldfield 1989; Piven and Cloward 1977; Quadango 1984; Skocpol 1980). A key

---

[17] Predicted AFDC and incarceration changes were converted by assuming representative levels for the initial year of each series.

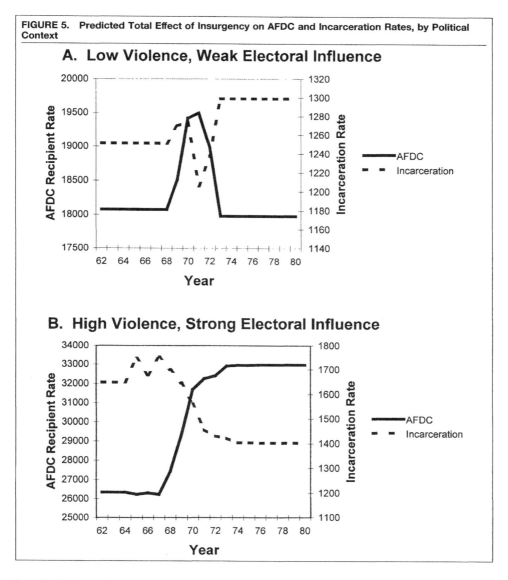

FIGURE 5. Predicted Total Effect of Insurgency on AFDC and Incarceration Rates, by Political Context

issue in this debate is the role of insurgency versus reform-minded politicians and parties in promoting reform. To the extent that the state functioned similarly during the 1930s and the 1960s, this research provides some support for the view that extrainstitutional politics have been important in the development of the American welfare state.

This conclusion is not without qualification, however, as conventional electoral channels appear not only to condition the response to insurgency but also can contribute to reform independently. With respect to AFDC, this is evident by the direct influence of state ideology on welfare expansion (Table 1). For incarceration, the effects of party control and interparty competition also provide evidence of the importance of conventional politics in the area of criminal justice

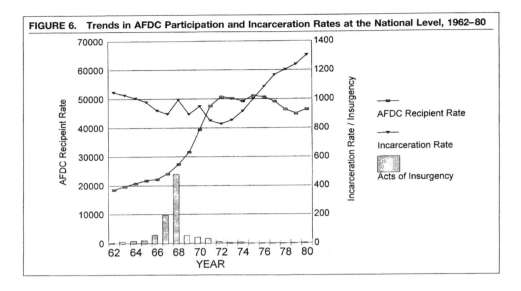

FIGURE 6.   Trends in AFDC Participation and Incarceration Rates at the National Level, 1962–80

policy (Table 2). Even if Marxists are correct regarding the role of the state, one should not ignore the relevance of other political and social constraints on state behavior. This seems to be the conclusion reached by Ametha, Dunleavey, and Bernstein (1994) in their analysis of Huey Long's followers. Their political mediation theory suggests that evolution of the welfare state is due to, and often conditional upon, a number of traditional economic and conventional political factors, and unconventional politics is only one (albeit the strongest) determinant. The results of my research fit nicely with such an interpretation, as conventional political institutions appear to operate as important constraints on state behavior and sometimes have significant effects in and of themselves.

Perhaps of more interest to students of contemporary welfare policy is the extent to which these findings, and the social control perspective more generally, can explain welfare trends since 1980. It appears that many states were unsuccessful in reducing AFDC in the years immediately after unrest subsided. If the social control model is correct, however, labor market imperatives, coupled with a mobilization of the business community, eventually would motivate policymakers to reduce welfare generosity throughout the 1980s and 1990s. According to Piven and Cloward (1982, 13), this was an important motivation for President Reagan's attack on public assistance programs, as AFDC served to "limit profits by enlarging the bargaining power of workers with employers." This thesis is echoed by Noble (1997, 107) who maintains that "generous public assistance programs made it harder for employers to cut labor costs because they cushioned workers from the shock

of unemployment." He concludes that the political mobilization of the American business community played an important role in the contraction of the welfare state over the last two decades, perhaps culminated by national legislation in 1996. On the surface these developments appear to represent merely an ideological swing to the right that began in the 1980s, but this research suggests that the continued effort by states to reduce AFDC might best be seen as part of the historical dynamic of welfare expansion and contraction first identified by Piven and Cloward in *Regulating the Poor*.

If this dynamic at least partly explains recent contraction of the welfare rolls, then this research may explain a second important policy trend in recent years. If a welfare-incarceration tradeoff exists, then efforts to reduce welfare throughout the 1980s and 1990s should have been matched by some increase in incarceration. This seems to correspond with what we know about the aggregated national level trends, but it is not necessarily the case at the state level. Some evidence is provided, however, by recent state-level analyses of AFDC caseload reductions and AFDC waiver adoptions (Fording 1998), and an analysis of state welfare reform provisions under the Temporary Assistance to Needy Families Program (Soss et al. n.d.). Each of these studies reports that a decline in welfare generosity by states is related to an increase in incarceration levels. More research is needed to determine exactly why this relationship exists, but it appears that the utility of the social control perspective in explaining policymaking may extend beyond the period of black insurgency.

American Political Science Review Vol. 95, No. 1

APPENDIX: DEFINITION OF VARIABLES AND DATA SOURCES

Insurgency: From Fording (1997, 11), defined as "any act of violence on behalf of blacks or minorities, either spontaneous or planned, which is either framed as, or can be construed as politically motivated." Data were originally obtained from several sources, including the *New York Times*; the *Report of the National Advisory Commission on Civil Disorders; Riot Data Review*, published by the Lemberg Center for the Study of Violence; *Facts on File*; and *Congressional Quarterly*.

AFDC: Change in the number of AFDC recipients per one million population, for December of each year. These data are available from *Social Security Bulletin*, various years.

Incarceration: Change in the number of adults incarcerated per one million population. Data are published by the Department of Justice in *Prisoners in State and Federal Institutions on December 31* and are reprinted in *Statistical Abstract of the United States*.

Per Capita State and Local Government Tax Revenue, Per Capita Income (1967 dollars): Measured as the first difference. Published yearly in *Statistical Abstract of the United States*.

Interparty Competition: A yearly measure was computed by averaging the majority vote for governor and the average majority percentage within the state legislature (% of majority in House/2 + % majority in Senate/2). This value was subtracted from 100 to yield a measure of competition that ranges from zero (no competition) to 50 (perfect competition). Interparty competition is measured as the change (first difference) in competition. All component variables are available from *Statistical Abstract of the United States* and the *Book of the States*.

Democratic Control of State Government: Measured as the *change* in Democratic control, so that state-years in which Democratic control replaces Republican or divided control receive a value of 1, state-years in which Republican or divided control replaces Democratic control receive a value of −1, and all other state-years receive a value of 0. Relevant data are available from *Statistical Abstract of the United States* and the *Book of the States*.

Crime: Change in the yearly crime rate (number of offenses per 100,000 population). Crime data are published by the Federal Bureau of Investigation in *Uniform Crime Reports for the United States* (reprinted in *Statistical Abstract of the United States*). Part I and II offenses are included.

Urbanization: Annual change in the percentage of state population that resides in metropolitan areas. Data were obtained for decennial years from the U.S. Census and for intervening years from the Bureau of Census, *Current Population Reports* (P-25).

Poverty Data: Annual change in the number of female-headed families below poverty per 1,000 population (AFDC model) and in the percentage of individuals below poverty (for incarceration). Available for 1959, 1969, 1975, and 1979 (intervening years interpolated) in *State and Metropolitan Area Data Book, 1979, 1982*, and *Statistical Abstract of the United States*.

Unemployment: Annual change in state unemployment rate (yearly average). State data were obtained for every year and are published by the U.S. Department of Labor, *Employment and Training Report of the President*.

Class Bias: From Husted and Kenny (1997), measured as the annual change. This variable is constructed by (1) obtaining yearly income per capita for each state, (2) obtaining an alternative version of state income per capita by computing a weighted average of county-level income per capita, with weights based on turnout in the most recent federal election, and (3) calculating the final measures as the ratio of the turnout-adjusted measure created in step 2 to the statewide average published by the U.S. Department of Commerce.

Reapportionment: Modeled as an intervention; the value represents the magnitude of malapportionment (i.e., the extent of reapportionment (i.e., the extent of reapportionment) that existed before the properly apportioned system was implemented. This value is calculated as follows: (Maximum District Size − Minimum District Size)/(Average District Size). The measure is based on detailed accounts of state reapportionment efforts reported by the National Municipal League in *Apportionment in the Nineteen Sixties* and the *Book of the States*, published by the Council of State Governments.

Black Electoral Access (Power): From Fording (1997), a dummy variable taking on a value of 1 when two conditions are satisfied: (1) blacks have effective voting rights (based on implementation of the Voting Rights Act [VRA] of 1965 in certain states) and (2) districts are properly apportioned (for states in which more than 90% of blacks reside in urban areas); 0 otherwise. Data are from the National Municipal League, *Apportionment in the Nineteen Sixties*, and the *Book of the States* as well as targeting of VRA enforcement.

Black Population: Data are available for black population at the state level for 1960 from the U.S. Census and 1970–80 from the Bureau of the Census, *Intercensal Estimates of the Population of Counties by Age, Sex, and Race: 1970–80* (ICPSR #8384). Values for intervening years were interpolated between 1960 and 1970.

Medicaid: A dichotomous variable that takes on a value of 1 in the first year a state implemented the Medicaid program, 0 otherwise. Implementation dates for the Medicaid program are reported in Table 7 of National Center for Social Statistics (NCSS) report B-5, *Medicaid Statistics, FY 1971*.

AFDC Residency Requirements: Detailed data for various characteristics of state AFDC programs are published by the U.S. Department of Health, Education, and Welfare in *Characteristics of State Public Assistance Plans under the Social Security Act*.

Military Data: Total number of active-duty military personnel (Army, Navy, Marine Corps, and Air Force). Published by the Department of Defense, available at http://web1.whs.osd.mil/mmid/military/trends.htm.

REFERENCES

Amenta, Edwin, Kathleen Dunleavey, and Mary Bernstein. 1994. "Stolen Thunder? Huey Long's 'Share Our Wealth,' Political Mediation, and the Second New Deal." *American Sociological Review* 59 (October): 678–702.

Baumgartner, Frank R., and Bryan D. Jones. 1993. *Agendas and Instability in American Politics*. Chicago: University of Chicago Press.

Beck, Nathaniel, and Jonathan Katz. 1995. "What to Do (and Not to Do) with Time-Series Cross-Section Data." *American Political Science Review* 89 (September): 634–47.

Berry, William D., Evan J. Ringquist, Richard C. Fording, and Russell L. Hanson. 1998. "Measuring Citizen and Government Ideology in the American States, 1960–93." *American Journal of Political Science* 42 (January): 327–48.

Button, James W. 1978. *Black Violence: The Political Impact of the 1960's Riots*. Princeton, NJ: Princeton University Press.

129

Cappell, Charles L., and Gresham Sykes. 1991. "Prison Commitments, Crime and Unemployment: A Theoretical and Empirical Specification for the United States, 1933–85." *Journal of Quantitative Criminology* 7 (June): 155–99.

Carroll, Leo, and Claire P. Cornell. 1985. "Racial Composition, Sentencing Reforms, and Rates of Incarceration, 1970–80." *Justice Quarterly* 2 (August): 473–90.

Carroll, Leo, and M.B. Doubet. 1983. "U.S. Social Structure and Imprisonment." *Criminology* 21 (August): 449–56.

Cobb, Roger W., and Charles D. Elder. 1983. *Participation in American Politics: The Dynamics of Agenda Building.* Baltimore, MD: Johns Hopkins University Press.

Cobb, Roger, Jennie-Keith Ross, and Marc Howard Ross. 1976. "Agenda Building as a Comparative Political Process." *American Political Science Review* 70 (March): 126–38.

Dahl, Robert. 1961. *Who Governs?* New Haven, CT: Yale University Press.

Durman, Eugene. 1973. "Have the Poor Been Regulated: Toward a Multivariate Understanding of Welfare Growth." *Social Service Review* 47 (September): 339–59.

Dye, Thomas R. 1984. "Party and Policy in the States." *Journal of Politics* 46 (November): 1097–116.

Erikson, Robert S., Gerald C. Wright, Jr., and John McIver. 1993. *Statehouse Democracy.* Cambridge: Cambridge University Press.

Fording, Richard C. 1997. "The Conditional Effect of Violence as a Political Tactic: Mass Insurgency, Electoral Context and Welfare Generosity in the American States." *American Journal of Political Science* 41 (January): 1–29.

Fording, Richard C. 1998. *The Political Response to Black Insurgency: A Test of Competing Images of the Role of the State.* Ph.D. diss. Florida State University.

Gamson, William A. 1975. *The Strategy of Social Protest.* Homewood, IL: Dorsey.

Garofalo, James. 1980. "Social Structure and Rates of Imprisonment: A Research Note." *Justice Systems Journal* 5 (June): 299–305.

Goldfield, Michael. 1989. "Worker Insurgency, Radical Organization, and New Deal Labor Legislation." *American Political Science Review* 83 (December): 1257–82.

Gronbjerg, Kirsten A. 1977. *Mass Society and the Extension of Welfare, 1960–1970.* Chicago: University of Chicago Press.

Hicks, Alexander, and Duane H. Swank. 1983. "Civil Disorder, Relief Mobilization, and AFDC Caseloads: A Reexamination of the Piven and Cloward Thesis." *American Journal of Political Science* 27 (4): 695–716.

Husted, Thomas A., and Lawerence W. Kenny. 1997. "The Effect of the Expansion of the Voting Franchise on the Size of Government." *Journal of Political Economy* 105 (February): 54–82.

Inverarity, James, and Ryken Grattet. 1989. "Institutional Responses to Unemployment: A Comparison of U.S. Trends, 1948–1985." *Contemporary Crises* 13 (3): 351–70.

Isaac, Larry, and William R. Kelly. 1981. "Racial Insurgency, the State, and Welfare Expansion: Local and National Level Evidence from the Postwar United States." *American Journal of Sociology* 86 (May): 1348–86.

Iris, Mark. 1983. "American Urban Riots Revisited." *American Behavioral Scientist* 26 (3): 333–52.

Jackson, Pamela Irving, and Leo Carroll. 1981. "Race and the War on Crime: The Sociopolitical Determinants of Municipal Police Expenditure in 90 Non-Southern Cities." *American Sociological Review* 46 (June): 290–305.

Jacobs, David. 1979. "Inequality and Police Strength: Conflict Theory and Coercive Control in Metropolitan Areas." *American Sociological Review* 44 (December): 913–25.

Jenkins, J. Craig. 1985. *The Politics of Insurgency: The Farm Worker Movement in the 1960's.* New York: Columbia University Press.

Jenkins, J. Craig, and Barbara G. Brents. 1989. "Social Protest, Hegemonic Competition, and Social Reform: A Political Struggle Interpretation of the Origins of the American Welfare State." *American Sociological Review* 54 (6): 891–909.

Jenkins, J. Craig, and Charles Perrow. 1977. "Insurgency of the Powerless: Farm Worker Movements, 1946–1972." *American Sociological Review* 42 (April): 249–68.

Joubert, Paul E., J. S. Picou, and W. A. McIntosh. 1981. "U.S. Social Structure, Crime and Imprisonment." *Criminology* 19 (November): 344–59.

Keech, William R. 1968. *The Impact of Negro Voting.* Chicago: Rand McNally.

Key, V.O. 1949. *Southern Politics in State and Nation.* New York: Random House.

Langer, Laura. 1999. "Measuring Income Distribution across Space and Time in the American States." *Social Science Quarterly* 80 (March): 55–67.

Liska, Allen E. 1997. "Modeling the Relationships between Macro Forms of Social Control." *Annual Review of Sociology* 23: 39–61.

Lipsky, Michael. 1970. *Protest in City Politics.* Chicago: Rand McNally.

McAdam, Doug. 1982. *Political Process and the Development of Black Insurgency, 1930–70.* Chicago: University of Chicago Press.

McCarthy, John D., and Mayer N. Zald. 1973. *The Trend of Social Movements in America: Professionalization and Resource Mobilization.* Morristown, NJ: General Learning Press.

National Advisory Commission on Civil Disorders. 1968. *Report of the National Advisory Commission on Civil Disorders.* Washington, DC: Government Printing Office.

Noble, Charles. 1997. *Welfare as We Knew It.* New York: Oxford University Press.

Offe, Claus. 1975. "The Theory of the Capitalist State and the Problem of Policy Formation." In *Stress and Contradiction in Modern Capitalism,* ed. Leon Lindberg, Robert Alford, Colin Crouch, and Claus Offe. Lexington, MA: D.C. Heath. Pp. 125–44.

Piven, Frances Fox, and Richard A. Cloward. 1971. *Regulating the Poor: The Functions of Public Welfare.* New York: Vintage.

Piven, Frances Fox, and Richard A. Cloward. 1977. *Poor People's Movements: Why They Succeed, How They Fail.* New York: Vintage.

Piven, Frances Fox, and Richard A. Cloward. 1982. *The New Class War.* New York: Pantheon.

Poulantzas, Nicos. 1973. *Political Power and Social Classes.* London: New Left Books.

Quadagno, Jill S. 1984. "Welfare Capitalism and the Social Security Act of 1935." *American Sociological Review* 49 (October): 632–47.

Quinney, Richard. 1974. *Critique of the Legal Order.* Boston: Little Brown.

Rochefort, David A. 1986. *American Social Welfare Policy.* Boulder, CO: Westview.

Rusche, Georg, and Otto Kirchheimer. 1939. *Punishment and Social Structure.* New York: Columbia University Press.

Skocpol, Theda. 1980. "Political Response to Capitalist Crisis." *Politics and Society* 10 (2): 155–201.

Soss, Joe, Sanford F. Schram, Thomas Vartanian, and Erin O'Brien. N.d. "Setting the Terms of Relief: Political Explanations for State Policy Choices in the Devolution Revolution." *American Journal of Political Science.* Forthcoming.

Spitzer, Steven. 1975. "Toward a Marxian Theory of Deviance." *Social Problems* 22 (5): 638–51.

Swank, Duane H. 1983. "Between Incrementalism and Revolution: Group Protest and the Growth of the Welfare State." *American Behavioral Scientist* 26 (3): 291–310.

Taggart, William A., and Russell G. Winn. 1993. "Imprisonment in the American States." *Social Science Quarterly* 74 (December): 736–49.

Tilly, Charles. 1978. *From Mobilization to Revolution.* Reading, MA: Addison-Wesley.

Welch, Susan. 1975. "The Impact of Urban Riots on Urban Expenditures." *American Journal of Political Science* 19 (November): 741–60.

Wilensky, Harold, and Charles Lebeaux. 1965. *Industrial Society and Social Welfare.* New York: Free Press.

[19]

Megan's Law: Crime and Democracy in Late Modern America

Jonathan Simon

To an unprecedented degree American society at the turn of the twentieth century is governed through crime. Nearly three percent of adults are in the custody of the correctional system. Crime and fear of crime enter into a large part of the fundamental decisions in life: where to live, how to raise your family, where to locate your business, where and when to shop, and so on. The crime victim has become the veritable outline of a new form of political subjectivity. This essay explores the complex entanglements of democracy and governing through crime. The effort to build democratic governance after the American Revolution was carried out in part through the problem of crime and punishment. Today, however, the enormous expansion of governing through crime endangers the effort to reinvent democracy for the twenty-first century.

Crime and punishment have come to play a central role in the ongoing reconstruction of liberal government and its rationalities in the United States and some other postmodern/postindustrial societies (Simon 1997, 1999a).[1] Two of the most visible aspects of this occur in the field of electoral politics and in the correctional population. The centrality of crime to

---

Jonathan Simon is professor of Law, University of Miami. This article is a report of an ongoing investigation to which many people and institutions have contributed. The first version of this article was prepared as a paper for the Law and Society Summer Institute 1996 and revised in response to critical discussion by the other participants in that Institute, including Rob Rosen, Kim Scheppele, Tom Tyler, Mark Galanter, and Jennifer Culbert. Special thanks to Jo Carrillo and Rob Rosen for organizing the institute. Subsequent versions of the article were presented to faculty workshops at NYU and Yale. Special thanks to Bruce Ackerman, Joseph Kennedy, and Reva Siegel for comments on those drafts.

1. A case can be made that this is a wider pattern of the English-speaking postindustrial nations including Australia, Canada, Great Britain, and New Zealand, as well as the United States. Although the U.S. rates are dramatically higher than others in this Anglophone group, the other nations are high in comparison to other regional peers (Currie 1998).

electoral politics and the formal actions of state and federal politicians has long since become conventional wisdom (Wattenburg 1995; Dionne, 1991). When the history of the U.S. party system at the end of the twentieth century is completed, crime may nudge out the Cold War, and earn a place along with the Great Depression, as the issues around which fundamental regime shifts took place.

After two decades or more of a "severity revolution" (Kennedy forthcoming) U.S. prisons and their community adjuncts contain a population unprecedented in the history of the United States or any of our peer societies (Currie 1998; Caplow and Simon 1999). With nearly 3% of the adult population in some form of penal custody (Maguire and Pastore 1998, 464),[2] crime policy has by itself reversed what most people take to be a shrinking of the role of government in society since the late 1970s (Beckett and Western 1999; forthcoming).

Less obvious is the spread of crime as an organizing problem to the actual sites of governing, (e.g., universities, day care centers, factories and shopping centers). The colossal mass of that penal population serves to reorder the lives of those outside the prison walls in complex ways. Of course it is intended to do that. In institutional setting after institutional setting one can spell out the ways that the very real sanctions applicable to conduct described as criminal produce powerful incentives for strategic action by all players. The importance of crime nudges out other kinds of opportunities that a different hierarchy of public problems might produce (e.g., a government obsessed with governing by educating would produce all kinds of incentives to define various people as efficient or deficient in education, capable or incapable, and so on). The economic metaphor of incentive is essential for capturing how basic the appeal of crime is, but as a metaphor it misses important features of the phenomenon. Crime is a genre, in the dramaturgical sense. It comes with certain kinds of roles; vulnerable victims, willing offenders, vigilant prosecutors, and harsh but fair judges (and all the deviant variations those set up). When we govern through crime we pass out these scripts to hundreds if not thousands of real people with little in the way of an audition and no accountability for the consequences.[3]

In introducing the slogan "governing through crime" I have sought to bring together a growing body of literature within political science, critical criminology, and sociology, pointing out the unprecedented growth of the penal state and its adjuncts and seeking to explain the causes and

---

2. This status is not evenly distributed in the population. Those in custody at any given time make up nearly 5% of the male adult population, and almost 10% of the African American adult population (Maguire and Pastore 1998).

3. Crime and punishment are a vast archive of political subjectivities from the formation of a "bad boy" (Deveare-Smith 1993, 100) or "bad ass" (Katz 1988) subjectivity necessary for survival in certain neighborhoods (Anderson 1998), to learning how to be a "confidence man" as a defense lawyer (Blumberg 1967).

consequences (Radzinowicz 1991; Zimring and Hawkins 1995; Scheingold 1991; Christie 1993; Gordon 1994; Kaminer 1995; Tonry 1995; Donziger 1996; Miller 1996; Garland 1996; Beckett 1997; Parenti 1998; Stern 1998; Schlosser 1998; Young 1999; Wacquant 1999; Caplow and Simon 1999) with work on the history of the governmental rationalities through which political authority is realized as a capacity to know and regulate the population (Foucault 1991; Dean 1991; Barry, Osborne, and Rose 1996; Garland 1997; Rose 1999; Simon 2000). I take the return of criminal law to a pivotal role in government as coincident with a profound transformation in the nature of liberal governance, not only in the United States but, in some forms, across most of the postindustrial world.

In all these societies, the basic intellectual "software" (Balkin 1998) of governance has been undergoing change over the past three decades (Rose and Miller 1992; Rose 1999; Procaci 1998). Forms of knowledge associated with "the social" (e.g., sociology, social work, and the close-up study of the lives of the poor) have all experienced downward mobility (Baudrillard 1983; Rose 1996; Simon 1999b). Likewise, technologies of power associated with what some have called the "social activist state" (Garth and Sterling 1998), like social insurance (Ewald 1986, 1991), fiscal stimulus policy, and regulation, have in varying degrees declined.[4] A whole family of rationalities of governing through defining social problems, shifting risks and responsibilities from the individual to the collective level, and empowering governmental organizations to intervene seems to be passing into history.

The political figures most famously associated with the turn away from welfare and regulation, Margaret Thatcher and Ronald Reagan, were figures of the political right. The emerging knowledge and power strategies of governance, however, are best seen as a kind of "advanced liberalism" (Rose and Miller 1992; Rose 1999), where liberalism is understood as a broad family of strategies for governing people through rather than over their freedom (Rose 1999). It is consistent with this view that successors like Tony Blair in Great Britain and Bill Clinton in the United States are considered well to the left of Thatcher and Reagan, but have also embraced many of the same forms of expertise and many of the same technologies of power.

In the United States crime has turned out to be a major platform for reconstructing liberal governance. While not inevitable, this association has roots in American culture, the vicissitudes of crime rates, and memories in the generational pattern of American society. Moreover, it has consequences for the way "advanced liberalism" is being played out in the United States. The penal population is an example of those most thoroughly

---

4. Alternative expertise associated with systems management, risk assessment, and new therapies of self-improvement (Rose and Miller 1992; Cruikshank 1994), among others, have gained prestige and become more central to government. New strategies for governing emphasize disaggregating masses (of consumers, students, workers, etc.), intensifying the responsibility of individuals, and promoting market mechanisms for individual, firm, or family choice.

governed through crime. The past 20 years has seen the correctional subject tied ever more tightly to his or her crime, so that the likelihood of going to prison depends mostly on the crime and the criminal record, and the regime in prison is more defined by the moral status of crime (i.e., punitive). Upon release the prisoners find themselves in a wider correctional population difficult to exit from (Simon 1993). Recent laws aim at making the mark of criminal conviction more consequential for educational opportunities, access to employment, and welfare.

If the correctional population was the central story of governing through crime it would form a disturbing but subordinate element in the construction of an advanced liberal governance in the United States. In fact, this is only the core of a constellation of relationships, including those governed as victims (Madriz 1997), as potential victims, as potential offenders, as people who know and might influence potential victims or potential offenders.[5] Governing through crime in this sense means making crime the defining feature of the subject's relationship to power.

In addition to bringing the full range of truth and power effects of crime into the discussion, a governance perspective requires us to look beyond the model of simple behavioral conformity to consider the ways technologies of power both act on and produce knowledge of the subject. To exercise power is inevitably and sometimes inexorably to alter the governability of the subjects on whom power is being exercised.[6] In a larger project, I am currently seeking to map these changes across a whole set of institutional domains including schools, employment relations, debtor/creditor relations and the family. Here I want to focus on a crucial slice of that landscape, the practices of political freedom we know generally as democracy.

Part 1 discusses crime control as an integral part of three strands of what might be called democratic penal traditions. Part 2 examines three different but related accounts of how the embedding of governing through crime into the new regime of liberal governance taking shape in the United

---

5. This should be distinguished from the narrower concern with governing criminal behavior that has been the traditional function of the criminal justice system. Indeed, once we take this perspective seriously we can see that the vast majority of people governed through crime control are not recalcitrant and oppositional, but in fact are highly motivated to seek out and comply with behavioral controls designed to make them safer. Moreover, these measures can operate to reinforce hierarchies at all sorts of levels.

6. The influence of Foucault on the study of the reciprocal links between penality and governance should not be overstated. Of great value here is the tradition of British Marxist and cultural studies of law and the social order. The role of crime and the criminal justice system in constructing power relations in eighteenth-century England has been the subject of extensive research by E. P. Thompson (1975), Douglas Hay (1975), Peter Linebaugh (1992), and others. A very different and potentially more comparable case is the work of Stuart Hall (Hall et. al. 1979), Paul Gilroy (1987) and others on the intersection of race, class, and crime in England during the long British economic slump of the late 1970s and 1980s. These works form the basis for a comparative study of governing through crime that would yield useful insights.

States might disable a democratic society. Part 3 briefly considers a recent example of penal legislation, the wave of sex-offender notification laws adopted in the mid-1990s under the name "Megan's Law," to suggest how these democratic traditions and dangers intertwine in forms of contemporary governance.

I. DEMOCRATIC PENAL STRATEGIES

Crime and punishment were central concerns of democratizing forces in the United States at the end of the eighteenth century.[7] Even a cursory reading of the U.S. Constitution shows the revolutionary generation's vivid concern with crime control as governance. Cruel and unusual punishments (Eighth Amendment); the right to jury, counsel, and to confront your accusers (Sixth Amendment); freedom from multiple prosecutions and the right not to testify against oneself (Fifth Amendment); the right to be free from unreasonable searches and seizures (Fourth Amendment) all loom large there. For that generation the struggle with monarchy was as much embedded in institutions of criminal justice as it was in the scenes of battle or the radical printing presses also invoked in that document. The theory of American democracy called for the sovereign to give up forms of preventive repression of the population so typical of the monarchical style of rule, but in equal measure it demanded a criminal law able to respond forcefully to the predatory invasion of private rights. Criminal laws in this respect have always served as the definitive grammar of American democratic governance. Reform of the criminal law, preferably into a highly transparent criminal code, and the creation of punishments that would efficiently discourage crime have been constitutive projects for the republic almost from the beginning. Substantive criminal law jurisprudence reflects this relationship to freedom in its traditional requirements that punishment be limited to those subjects sufficiently free of internal delusion or external coercions by some system of regulation other than those of the law itself (Kaplan, Weisberg, and Binder 2000, 687–747).

The ringing condemnation of monarchical procedures set out by the great Enlightenment political theorists left us a tradition of civil liberties that remains integral to liberal politics and government (Dubber 1998, 114). But the other side of this critique was a positive project of managing crime in a democratic way that protected the people from crime and provided even the guilty with treatment appropriate to sovereign self-governing

---

7. In other settings the emergence of the penitentiary had a more problematic relationship to democratization. For example in Latin America the penitentiary was associated with slavery and with modernizing dictatorships as well as with democrats (see Salvatore and Aguirre 1996).

subjects. In what follows I want to briefly canvass some of the main strands of this positive democratic project of penality.

A. Safer Correctives: Democracy and Deterrence

> But we have nothing to fear from the demoralizing reasoning of some, if others are left free to demonstrate their errors. And especially when the law stands ready to punish the first criminal act produced by the false reasoning. These are safer correctives then the conscience of a judge.
>
> —Thomas Jefferson, Letter to Elijah Boardman

> Among free men, the deterrents ordinarily to be applied to prevent crime are education and punishment for violations of the law, not abridgment of the rights of free speech and assembly.
>
> —Louis Brandeis, *Whitney v. California*

A student of American constitutional law will recognize these sentiments (if not the words themselves) as central elements in the tradition of freedom of expression protected by the First Amendment to the U.S. Constitution. For monarchy, crime was the most obvious and dangerous fruit of unregulated speech. Seditious speech above all could destroy the bonds of loyalty and deference that kept colonial society ordered at all levels (state, plantation, family) (Wiebe 1985, 11). As the Supreme Court recognized in its famous *New York Times v. Sullivan* decision, 376 U.S. 254 (1964), the sovereign's renunciation of the authority to punish seditious libel was the core meaning of the First Amendment (Kalven 1965, 57–58).

The above quotes remind us how important an effective governmental response to crime was to the logic of liberalizing preventive controls on provocative behavior. Notice that for each, the governmental tools for responding to the danger of seditious speech is the combination of education and punishment.[8] The central problem for deterrence as a democratic project early on was designing a distribution and publication of punishments just strong enough to outweigh the temptation for crime without producing the surplus pain and violence associated with monarchical punishments (Foucault 1977; Dubber 1998). It was to this end that new codes were rapidly drawn up in the years preceding and following the revolutions, a pattern that has periodically recurred since.[9] Deterrence is both penal and political theory. It is here that penal strategy and liberal governmental

---

8. Interestingly, Brandeis defines both education and punishment for crime as part of deterrence. Deterrence requires both communication of the sanctions for violating a norm and the production of punishment.

9. Foucault (1977, 75) argues that these changes were already taking place under monarchical institutions.

rationality most perfectly correlate. It is here that the penal machinery seems to operate directly on the calculative rationality of the democratic body politic. Deterrence has been the original and most enduring way of governing people through their freedom (i.e., through their capacity to make choices) (Rose 1999).

Perhaps for this reason, deterrence has been so frequently reinvented and rediscovered as a penal rationale. Since the 1960s, libertarian and conservative policy thought has reemphasized the deterrence of the criminal law as the social control appropriate to a society of individual liberty and private property.[10] In a rather striking and self-conscious parallel to the democratic critique of monarchical justice, the neo-liberal/neo-conservative discourse of deterrence condemned liberal government in the 1960s and 1970s for undermining the clarity of deterrent signals with talk of rehabilitation and treatment, and as a result, unleashing a wave of violent crime (Wilson 1983).

The case for deterrence and democracy has also been emphasized recently by outsider jurisprudence that looks to the criminal law to provide a counterbalance to violent forms of domination. One of the most significant examples of this is in the area of domestic violence and particularly violence against women. Feminists have waged a successful struggle in recent years in getting courts, police departments, and state legislatures to recognize domestic violence as a serious crime and to provide commensurate sanctions and enforcement policies (Berk and Loseke 1981). Much of this struggle has implicitly or explicitly accepted the deterrent force of the criminal law as an effective strategy for resisting the continuation of violent male domination within the household. This effort has required feminist legal scholars to engage in a thorough going critique of criminal-law and criminal-procedure constructs, and to identify and replace concepts that embody stereotypes of women which militate against the application of criminal law to violent male dominators (Coombs 1987; Mahoney 1991).

B. Democracy and Discipline

Social history in the 1970s, beginning with the path-breaking work of David J. Rothman, recalled to that time of social upheaval, the importance of the penitentiary and asylum—projects of social control—to the revolutionary generation that had won the war of independence and set out to a life of unprecedented democratic self-government for its preferred class of citizen (white males). The attraction of the prison as a new technology applicable to crime control at the end of the eighteenth century was due in

---

10. This is by now a formidable literature. Some of the most important landmarks are Becker 1968; Posner 1985; J. Q. Wilson 1983.

part to the popularity of deterrence as a democratic theory of crime control (Ignatieff 1978). Deterrence called for a technology of readily divisible sanctions. The prison was such a technology through the seizure of time in the prison.

If deterrence explains the popularity of the prison as governmental technology in revolutionary America, it does not exhaust the possibilities of the prison. Deterrence was soon joined by another program of democratic penality, one drawing on the several centuries of experimentation in the fields of disciplinary training and rooted in the prison itself as transformative technology of power (Rothman 1971; Foucault 1977; Dumm 1987). Prison, in this tradition, was a machinery of reform, the penitentiary, that could transform those too unsettled by the Revolution and its aftermath to fully take up its invitation to self-government (Rothman 1971).

In the twentieth century this tradition reached its peak with formal establishment of rehabilitation as the dominant official ideology of state punishment in the United States and other democratic nations. Taking over in the reduction of penal severity from where the deterrence theorists had left it, rehabilitation promised to reduce punishment to the subtle humiliations of the medical situation in favor of effective methods for addressing criminal deviance at its roots in individual psychology and community disorganization (Rothman 1980; Simon 1993).

The prison as a technology of discipline, and later treatment, represented a fundamentally different way of imagining a democratic response to crime, a shift in the technologies through which power was exercised, and the fundamental terms in which it was rationalized. Deterrence focused on crime and punishment as a semiotic system designed to create the conditions for rational agents to behave cooperatively in a free society. In contrast, the penitentiary as a technology was targeted on specific individuals already identified as dangerously deviant through conviction for a serious crime. Deterrence operated like a communicative system "broadcasting" its message of norm compliance across society as a whole, while disciplinary normalization was rooted in particular locations and depended on its own concentrations of people to operate. For deterrence the punishment need only be reliably disagreeable, and as cheap as possible. For the penitentiary project, the design and method of the prison became of incalculable importance, thus unleashing one of the most heated policy debates of the early republic (Rothman 1971; Foucault 1977; Dumm 1987).[11]

Like deterrence, the rehabilitative project has failed many times without disappearing. Most recently, since the 1970s, rehabilitation has been

---

11. One model, that of Philadelphia, emphasized moral redemption through total isolation in a setting of individual labor and meditation. The second model, that of New York's Auburn prison, emphasized isolation only at night, with days filled with silent labor in common projects. See generally Dumm 1987.

seen as a paradigmatic example of the failures of liberal governance. Despite vigorous efforts in progressive states like California during the 1960s, correctionalists never managed to achieve much in the way of measurable success. More politically damaging, the level and viciousness of crime itself rose measurably during the 1960s, the very period when rehabilitation enjoyed its closest association with the prestige of liberal government. Today disciplinary rehabilitation remains politically suspect, but it is not difficult to imagine its reinvention because its emphasis on technologies of individual transformation remains part of the political subjectivities produced by liberalism.

C. We Feel Your Pain: Crime and Responsive Democracy

In societies as different as Mexico, Trinidad, South Africa, and the United States, expansive electoral democracy has brought crime, fear of crime, and rituals of punishment to the center of electoral politics. Economic and social liberalization almost everywhere seem to yield real increases in crime as new opportunities and temptations are opened up by the ending of formal security states and the maintenance of monstrous levels of inequality. Politicians in liberalizing societies also have incentives to make crime a central focus for campaigning. Promises of sweeping economic reforms could yield immediate problems on the markets. Promising to strike hard against crime is likely to offend no important interests. Criminal laws and prosecutions are exemplary acts of popular will. Whether the subject is alcohol, prostitution, drugs, or pollution, campaigns to criminalize behavior perceived as antisocial, even if not assaultive, have often inspired democratic publics.[12] Governing through crime in this sense is attractive to people because it permits popular fears and experiences to be valorized in the strongest and most public terms (Simon and Spaulding 1999).

We can see a contemporary version of this in the effort of prosecutors in states like Alabama, Mississippi, and Florida to bring prosecutions for violent crimes and murders committed by die-hard defenders of segregation against civil rights workers and ordinary African American citizens during the early 1960s. In most of the original cases charges resulted in acquittals or were never brought at all, as juries, prosecutors, and police seemed to collude in sheltering concededly fringe elements of the white community. Contemporary prosecution efforts have come at a time when these states in many other ways have continued to resist the civil rights revolution, preserving de facto segregated private "academies" and electing conservative

---

12. Of course, populist vengeance can become antidemocratic very quickly indeed if it is not locked into strong procedural restraints. In that sense we might well see the era of liberal due process jurisprudence in the United States as a necessary condition for crime and punishment to become a self-sustaining democratic engine.

1120 LAW AND SOCIAL INQUIRY

Republican legislatures opposed to affirmative action, public schools, and welfare benefits. Against such a background, new prosecutions for these old crimes represent valued gestures of recognition. Just as the violence of the early 1960s, and even more so the lynchings common in those states before the 1920s, represented a clear signal that notwithstanding the formal adoption of the Thirteenth and Fourteenth Amendments, members of the former slave race were not going to be treated as equal citizens, today's prosecutions are a mark of equal citizenship.

D.   Tough on Crime As a Democratic Project

In this section I suggest that governing through crime has an old and deep relationship to democratic governance itself. A rejection of monarchical penality is implicit in our tradition of civil liberties, but several strands of democratic penality also look to the power to punish to help fulfill the promise of self-government. In the course of two centuries during which the real scope of democratic life in the United States has expanded enormously (through, for example, the enfranchisement of women [1917] and African Americans [1950–80]), the meaning of government's commitment to security has expanded as well. Expanding democratization was associated with the declining importance of crime as a defining purpose of government. Indeed, for most of the twentieth century the primary icon of both crime and punishment at the national level was the reactionary image of the American Deep South, framed in acts of official barbarism and injustice and savage racially targeted criminality. The aspirations of progressive government lay elsewhere, in economic management, in education, in military preparedness. Criminal law and punishment were only a small part of this overall effort.

The striking return of crime, criminal law, and punishment to the center of the American political imaginary from 1980 on throws us back onto these strands of democratic penality that have never altogether disappeared but have been minor themes of government for a long time. The historical deposit of power in the scripts and metaphors of crime control has several consequences. It makes crime an enormously attractive site for government at a time when the dominant twentieth-century forms of government are being strongly contested. Just as the individual voter may find in harsh penalties aimed at malevolent violent offenders a sense of renewed solidarity with fellow citizens whose values and objectives have otherwise been problematized by globalization, multiculturalism, and other late-twentieth-century forms of postmodernization (Tyler et al. 1997, 247–48), politicians find in punishment a safe grammar for governing (Caplow and Simon 1999, 78–93). The "tough on crime" posture has served American politicians for almost as long since Nixon's election as the law-and-order candidate in 1968 (an election that would have been a landslide without George Wallace's appeal on many of the same themes) as the "New Deal" did between 1936 and 1968. Its enduring appeal reveals that it provides much more than an issue-specific response to voter concerns about crime. Instead "tough on crime" enables political actors to express commitment to the security of the people while avoiding debate on the difficult questions of how to manage the major forms of modern public security (pensions, insurance, public education). It also makes it possible to criticize more elaborate measures of government social policy (whether funding for the arts or fighting poverty) as undervaluing and even undercutting the strength of government's primary commitment to physical security.

Against this background we should properly hesitate before drawing the most distopian conclusions from the enormous expansion of the government's formal penal effort, or even from the expansion of different dimensions of crime (fear, victims, etc.) as a model for governing in different settings. Even as we appreciate the enduring entanglements between democracy and punishment left by the revolutions of the eighteenth century, we should be wary of taking on their focus on crime control as a tool of monarchical abuse as our primary metaphor for the ways this entanglement may endanger democracy. The real danger is not a return to premodern forms of political authority but the creation of postmodern social formations that are ungovernable democratically.

II. GOVERNING THROUGH CRIME AS A THREAT TO DEMOCRATIC PRACTICE

The philosopher and historian Friedrich Nietzsche was actually writing about the history of punishment when he made one of his most famous and enduring points about the relationship of the past to the present generally.

> The origin of the emergence of a thing and its ultimate usefulness, its practical application and incorporation into a system of ends, are *toto coelo* separate; that anything in existence, having somehow come about, is continually interpreted anew, requisitioned anew, transformed and redirected to a new purpose by a power superior to it; that everything that occurs in the organic world consists of *overpowering, dominating*, and in their turn, overpowering and dominating consist of reinterpretation, adjustment, in the process of which their former 'meaning' [*Sinn*] and 'purpose' must necessarily be obscured or completely obliterated. . . . So people think punishment has evolved for the purpose of punishing. But every purpose and use is just a *sign* that the will to power has achieved mastery over something less powerful, and has impressed upon it its own idea [*Sinn*] of a use function. (1994, 55; emphasis in the original)

The fact that crime control practices have long been central to the democratization project cannot assure that these same technologies and rationalities of power are a viable way to sustain democratic public life in the United States and similarly situated countries. Several recent accounts suggest quite different ways that our growing national commitment to punishment, and the cultural shifts around it, endanger the democratic character of the society. In this section I want to revisit these accounts (which are by no means exclusive) with a focus on the broader constellation of ways of knowing and ways of acting upon the world I call "governing through crime."

A. Racism and Penality

Few things are clearer in the history of the United States than the powerful links between racism and antidemocratic forces. This is especially true of prejudice against African Americans. The constitutional framework, developed to protect the enslavement of Africans at the dawn of our republic, required systematic limitations on the democratic character of the polity created including limitations on speech, franchise, and the right to travel (Foner 1988). Even after the Civil War and Reconstruction, anti-African racism has been a critical force unifying oligarchic elites and dividing the popular classes in American society (Woodward 1966).

In the mid-1990s nearly one in nine young African American males was in prison at least some of the year, and one in three was in prison, on parole or on probation (Miller 1996). However, in big cities with large zones of concentrated poverty, the penal custody rate is closer to half the population of young African American men (Donziger 1996, 102). In the course of a lifetime, nearly one-third of African American men will serve time in jail or prison (Bonczar and Beck 1997, 1). Nearly one in seven African American men have lost the right to vote as a result of a felony conviction (Felner and Mauer 1998). These simple demographic facts speak volumes about the role of criminal justice in undermining the expansion of democratic practice achieved in the third quartile of the twentieth century through the civil rights movement and its victories in education, equal employment opportunity, housing, and suffrage. Just as in Reconstruction, African American citizenship rights in the most punitive states may turn out to have had a historical longevity of only a generation or two. Criminal justice policy at the end of the twentieth century seems to be playing the role for the United States as a whole that segregation did in the "redemption" of the American South for white supremacy at the end of the nineteenth century.

Recent books by Miller (1996); Tonry (1995); Donziger (1996); Hagan and Peterson (1995); and Cole (1999) argue forcefully that U.S. crime control policies since 1980, from police stops to executions, with respect to their consequences for African American and Hispanic communities, reflect governmental attitudes ranging from willful and intentional discrimination to reckless disregard of a well-known risk (but see Kennedy 1997). Few scholarly observers believe that simple bias in the selection and treatment of criminal suspects fully explains the extreme racial skewing evident in incarceration and other forms of punishment. Whatever we ultimately make of the mountain of penal legislation produced by state legislatures and the U.S. Congress over the past quarter century, it was not analogous to the "Black Act" enacted by the eighteenth-century English gentry elite representing a mere fraction of the population (Thompson 1975). Voters have continuously ratified the expanding investment in law enforcement resources against crime. Even most African American elected representatives have supported harsh anti-crime laws until very recently.

While the motives of legislators are rarely simple racial animus, the results have been catastrophic for African Americans and other minorities overrepresented in the economic underclasses of American society (Tonry 1995). The resulting policing and prosecutorial strategies have affected African American communities in a variety of ways. During a period when the economic opportunities open to inner-city residents were at their worst since the Great Depression of the 1930s, the young men providing the major labor force for the illegal drug trade have hardly been the least functional members of the community. Their physical removal may or may not have affected the profits of the drug cartels, but they almost certainly made these communities less rather than more governable by removing young men who are fathers and sometimes breadwinners and exposing them to the hardening effects of incarceration (Meares 1998).

Jerome Miller (1996, 13) argues that crime-control policies have also aggravated racist sentiments in the majority population. The war on drugs and its policing have created a flood of minor convictions that in an earlier era would never have resulted in official action. Many of these arrests are for trivial acts and amount to what John Irwin (1985) called "rabble management." But the nearly endless spectacle of young African American men being led away by police and prison guards feeds the perception that violent crime is spiraling out of control and that African Americans are uniquely responsible for it as a community. Miller points out that the creation of a stereotype of African American crime has also helped facilitate the return of eugenically inclined thought in American political discourse (1996, 233).

The critique of contemporary crime-control policies as a racial strategy is compelling. Even if it does not explain the motives for either politicians or the public to govern through crime, the intersection of America's history of racial domination and its contemporary tendency to govern through crime contain grave threats to democratic order in the United States.

Governing through crime, as simply racism by other means, seems most plausible at the level of electoral politics where crime/race ads have been hot-wire mobilizing issues for white voters since at least the 1950s. This approach to governance is also palpable in the appearance of the penal population itself, which is often a strikingly African American. Thus, it is not impossible to imagine contemporary prisons as the new plantations, or the new segregation. If the prison is the new "ghetto" (Wacquant forthcoming), a space that concentrates subjects by race and invests those racial subjects with social meanings and economic capacities, it functions as no previous racial regime has. For the first time in even the usually sordid racial history of the United States, a substantial racially defined population is being given economic significance primarily as a market for social waste management (profiting the largely white small towns seeking prison construction as employment development).

But if the new prison system has features of the ghetto and earlier forms of race making in the United States, racism is less descriptive of the features of punishment as an institution. Penal management is highly legalistic (Feeley and Rubin 1997).[13] Penal staffs over the past generation have experienced real diversification due to affirmative action policies. Towns that have courted prisons may be white and rural, but because of state efforts to promote minority hiring they may find themselves drawing many more people of color, including families of penal staff and families of inmates. Furthermore, important African American opinion leaders view the war on crime and drugs as a critical feature of improving life for ordinary African Americans.[14]

Framing crime as a kind of modality of government offers an alternative account of the race effects and their consequence for democracy. Since the nineteenth-century American democracy has been anchored to mechanisms of collective opportunity and risk sharing, including public schools, social insurance, government loans, and pension systems. The politics of aggregation in America has always been laden with racial concerns. Indeed, one can look at the original New Deal, the great leap forward for the politics of aggregation in the United States, as a complex political compromise built on the exclusion of African Americans. This traditional and racialized anxiety about risk sharing across ethnic and class lines has taken on a new urgency in part because U.S. society has experienced a widespread rollback in the institutions of collective risk sharing. Beginning in the mid-1970s the political fortunes of unions, regulatory agencies, and most social welfare

---

13. Florida's Secretary of Corrections, himself an African American, was harshly critical of the "chain gang" innovation (Lichtenstein 1996).

14. For some time, Randall Kennedy has offered a powerful critique of law enforcement as underprotective of African Americans against crime (1997). A position that he acknowledges entails a heavy portion of African American defendants, since so much crime is intraracial.

systems have all plummeted. A growing climate of mistrust has grown around even relatively beloved institutions like Social Security. Less beloved systems, like Aid to Families with Dependent Children, have been dismantled.

Rather than trying to bring criminal-justice policy and race politics into direct relationship, it may be more helpful to see their connection within the context of this restructuring of governance. The civil rights movement in the 1950s and 1960s destroyed that political consensus behind which the American version of social democracy was forged, but an emerging post–civil rights consensus is making crime the new logic of exclusion (Kennedy forthcoming). The "deviant other," whose presence endangers collective security, has been officially changed from all African American and other minorities, to an "underclass" largely defined by the criminal justice system. Crime normalizes what remained problematic when framed in explicitly racial terms. White flight to avoid school desegregation was an acknowledged social problem. Twenty years later, recoded as the divide between "high crime areas" and others, a whole set of tactics that remain ones of racial exclusion are being normalized (Davis 1990, 1998). For example, efforts to keep largely minority group city residents out of suburban shopping centers, parks, and residential communities have become commonplace.

Analogies in modern penal history might suggest room for hope. Looking at Edwardian Britain, David Garland (1985) showed how the extension of penal interventions beyond the prison into the community, and beyond crime into deviance, were part of a much larger process of bringing the working classes into governmental oversight and management. This, in turn, was a kind of quid pro quo for the extension of suffrage to the working class; in effect, the disciplinary control of criminal deviants was part and parcel of qualifying the working class for the privileges of self-government. A move from excluding African Americans on the basis of race to excluding many of them on the basis of crime might seem like forward progress toward full citizenship, so long as realistic opportunities enable the vast majority to evade the cycle of crime and punishment.

Today, however, criminalization does not function as a correlate to enhanced citizenship for two reasons. First, as other bases of exclusion have become less sustainable through the expansion of civil rights law, crime is doing a lot of the work of risk segregation today. Criminal conviction may be so disabling and stigmatizing today that few may be able to "requalify" as full citizens. Second, a hardening of criminal penalties has occurred simultaneously with a shrinking of the outlets for legitimate employment available to the inner-city poor (Sampson and Wilson 1995; W. J. Wilson 1996).[15]

---

15. It is a very significant problem that most of our theorizing and much of our empirical work on the links between the penal state and the inner-city poor date from the 1980s and

To be marked as criminal is increasingly coming to function as a general forfeiture of legal rights without any apparent proportionality to the degree of responsibility, harm, or program for social control.

Seen from the governance perspective, this hybrid of race and crime poses a serious threat to democracy in its tendency to intensify the disaggregation of those collective opportunity and risk structures of modern government that American democracy has always relied on to resolve group conflicts within civil society. City limits and public school district lines have been allowed to become barriers more legally significant than those between states when it comes to carving up who shares fortune and danger with whom.[16] Crime is used to justify isolating cities from private-sector investment even as public investment in crime control goes up. The high cost of managing the least manageable populations forces cities to raise taxes to levels that drive out those residents and businesses with the option to move, which in turn raises the tax bill for all remaining. In short, the racial effects of governing through crime may greatly shorten the time before the present governmental structure becomes unworkable.

B.　The Penal-Industrial Complex

The rapid expansion of the penal system has led to the growth of a formidable power block of interest groups with a stake in continued escalation. Some have spoken of a parallel between the older military-industrial complex (Schiraldi 1994; Beckett 1997; Irwin and Austin 1997; Schlosser 1998). Since the end of the cold war in 1989, the overall public and private investment in crime responses now approaches investment in military defense after growing more rapidly for some time (Donziger 1996, 85). Like the military-industrial complex, this alliance crosses classes, enabling a broad coalition of interest to form behind the banner of increasingly severe punishment.

Punishment as a form of governmental power shares many features with the military that undermine democratic accountability. Both are capable of producing strong pressures against civil liberties, including the First Amendment's protections for speech and the Fifth Amendment's

---

early 1990s, before the economic boom of the late 1990s sent unemployment rates down to 1960s levels, even for minorities. It remains to be seen exactly how the boom is producing economic opportunity for the "underclass." Ironically, it may be just as the boom begins to create pathways out for many young workers in the inner city that the social and economic consequences of governing through crime may become most destructive. The stigma of criminal conviction, given business fears of crime and liability, combined with hypermasculine and violent culture of prisons (Silberman 1995), make prisonization one of the worst imaginable labor policies (Beckett and Western 1999). From this perspective state laws extending the scope of prison sentences ought to be considered inflationary.

16. *Milliken v. Bradley*, 418 U.S. 717 (1974) (holding that federal courts lack the power to impose interdistrict remedies for school segregation).

protections of property, as well as traditional criminal-procedure rights like the Fourth Amendment's right to be free of unreasonable searches and seizures. Both punishment and military defense draw on and reproduce powerful images of deviance as the source of collective and individual threat. These can lead to cycles of fear and demonization that are not easily cabined in traditional interest-group politics. Finally, both are highly expansive in that they open up possibilities for intervention along a much broader front of activities than their core functions. Virtually any activity can be seen in relationship to a powerful enough imperative like military defense or social defense against crime. The Cold War famously led to investments in highways, universities, and the Internet, all in the name of military competition with the Soviet Union. Crime spending has thus far been invested most heavily in prisons and the supplies needed to operate them, but crime control more generally can provide an agenda for school reform, urban renewal, architecture, and tax policy among other things.

As in the Cold War, important political-interest groups have formed a prison lobby for more severe punishment. In California, for example, the penal officers' union has emerged as one of the two or three largest contributors to legislative and other statewide campaigns (hugely expensive given the number of media markets in the state) (Donziger 1996, 96–97; Schrag 1998). In alliance with victim groups, other law enforcement lobbies, and key politicians, they have been able to halt internal efforts at slowing incarceration and enact major new expansions (like California's 3-strikes law).

While the comparison between the Cold War and governing through crime is imperfect, the two share some useful features. Both operated as master narratives for government at various levels of the state and in private organizations. Both provided ready motives for political actors, but also certain technologies of power and knowledge easily transferred to other ends. Thus far, however, the Cold War comes off as more helpful to democratic governing (with the possible exception of the nuclear threat that has, in any case, outlived it). The Cold War generated a broad front of governmental investments to enhance the capacities of the population in a whole host of ways functional to democracy (education, steady employment), but the resulting transformations in culture hardly fit a pattern of militarization. The universities expanded in the 1950s under a Cold War imperative, but by the 1960s when the concrete was dry and the classrooms were full, it was not ROTC and nationalist chauvinism that dominated campus life. The National Defense Highway Act (1950) funded the interstate system that in turn transformed American culture in the second half of the twentieth century, but not along recognizably military lines. Once again Nietzsche's warning about origins and functions is appropriate.

Perhaps governing through crime will also produce effects well beyond the specific emotions and meanings that sustain it today. There is, however, less reason to be optimistic that the social payoff from the war on crime will be anything like the Cold War. In the war on crime, investment has overwhelmingly been in assets with little potential to accomplish any other goal than crime suppression.[17] In contrast, the cultural spread of a punitive mentality as an integral feature of governance may be the real contribution of the prison boom. In short, the Cold War built a lot of new hardware for the society while producing relatively little militaristic "software."[18] The war on crime is producing little usable hardware, but it's producing lots of punitive software. In this sense the Cold War analogy is only somewhat helpful in characterizing the punitive turn of governance. It is ultimately the things that governing through crime does not have in common with Cold War government that seem most significant.

C. Victims, Vengeance, and Civic Culture

Crime in this perspective is a potent stimulant to political community, but what kind of political community? It invests individuals with political subjectivity as victims, offenders, prosecutors, and judges. What does it mean for democracies if stakeholders in all kinds of communities begin to view themselves primarily as victims or potential victims? What happens when the most common aspirations for collective welfare are directed primarily to punishing and preventing crime or crime-like conduct? Recent works of political theory (Putnam 1993; Brown 1995) and cultural studies (Kaminer 1995) have begun to shed light on the logic of political relationships forged around crime. While not yet fully directed toward crime as a fulcrum of governance (but see Dumm 1994), this political theorizing suggests that the political solidarities forged through crime may turn out to be very fragile structures for building the effective democratic consensus necessary for taking the hard decisions and renegotiating the social contract of the liberal state as it experiences a reconfiguration of its rationalities of governing.

1. *Vicious Circles of Declining Civic Participation*

In an important study of the social conditions under which democratic governance seems to thrive, Robert Putnam and his colleagues (1993) raised some troubling implications for the growth of governing through crime. Putnam and his associates closely studied the experience of regional governments in Italy from the time they were constitutionally created in the early

---

17. One should say, deliberate goal, since our prisons are obviously quite capable of producing a range of pathologies ranging from violent racism to AIDS victims.

18. Jack Balkin (1998) uses software as a term for cultural programs that complete interpretive grids for subjects in societies.

1970s through the late 1980s. They sought to measure the success of government both in its own terms, and in the view of relevant publics. They found a strongly consistent pattern over the entire period. After assessing various theoretical frameworks to explain the pattern of democratic success, Putnam and his colleagues found that the most important determinant in predicting the governmental effectiveness of a region was the character of its civic culture.

One type of civic culture, associated with a more successful governance, was characterized by cross-cutting horizontal bonds among people in popular associations ranging from sports clubs and bird-watching groups to technical societies. In such regions, democratic governance worked well because these horizontal bonds helped produce coherent objectives around which terms of agreement could be settled by bargaining-oriented institutions. Once objectives were determined, the chances for cooperation in implementation at all levels were also much higher. A second type of civic culture, associated with failed governance, was dominated by vertical ties of patronage linking otherwise inwardly focused individuals and families. In such regions, governance foundered on an absence of trust and the expectation of competent performance. In the absence of horizontal bonds, consensus takes the shape of deals cut among an elite, and implementation is hampered by the usual need in such settings to provide immediate incentives for cooperation.

It was in regions characterized by the second civic culture that Putnam found a tendency for political demands to coalescence around coercive enforcement of repressive norms—that is, strikingly close to what I have called "governing through crime."

> Lacking the confident self-discipline of the civic regions, people in less civic regions are forced to rely on what Italians call "the forces of order," that is, the police. . . . Citizens in the less civic regions have no other resort to solve the fundamental Hobbesian dilemma of public order, for they lack horizontal bonds of collective reciprocity that work more efficiently in the civic regions. In the absence of solidarity and self-discipline, hierarchy and force provide the only alternative to anarchy. (Putnam 1993, 112)

Unfortunately crime control fails in such an environment for many of the same reasons other governmental efforts founder in the absence of civic culture.

> In the less civic regions even a heavy-handed government—the agent for law enforcement—is itself enfeebled by the uncivic social context. The very character of the community that leads citizens to demand stronger government makes it less likely that any government can be

1130 LAW AND SOCIAL INQUIRY

strong, *at least if it remains democratic.* (Putnam 1993, 113; emphasis added)

British criminologists Bill Jordan and Jon Arnold (1995) have suggested that the United States is already an advanced case of just such a vicious circle, and warn that British political culture may be on the same track. Jordan and Arnold see the development of ever-more-severe penal sanctions, like California's 3-strikes law, and the rhetoric of the Republican Party on crime as marks of a virulent populism. The emergence of crime as a central focus of political advantage-seeking both corrodes what remains of civic feeling among the populace and dominates other (presumably) healthier sources of democratic participation. Jordan and Arnold describe the direction in American political culture: "From inclusive to exclusive social interactions, with groups defining themselves in terms of opposition towards the values and goals of others, and recognising no wider (or common) interest, except in punitive enforcement" (1995, 172). Jordan and Arnold see the social effects of conservative social policies in the United Kingdom and the United States as largely to blame. These policies, designed to reward individual enterprise, have had the collateral effect of breaking up the incentive structures for horizontal civic culture. The result at the margins has been to drive more people into resistance strategies of illegality and raise the costs of all forms of governing (1995, 177).

The mobilization of political participation through crime and criminal justice polarizes society further by leading groups to define their relationships with others in extreme terms of moral outrage that make resolution through negotiation less likely. Consider, for example, the different ways of lowering the social cost of drunk driving (Gusfield 1981). A city might use zoning power and negotiation to compel pubs and taverns to locate in areas accessible to public transportation, or choose to subsidize extensive cab service or car pooling. An alternative strategy is to define drunk drivers as moral monsters and then expend significant efforts to catch, prosecute, and punish them. This approach leaves in place structural features that will guarantee a steady flow of drunk driving (i.e., the geographic distribution of taverns and the absence of effective public transportation). It also increases the cost for all kinds of other institutions that now must reassess their relationship to an individual in terms of that kind of status transformation. These measures also contribute to a distorted sense of how threatened people are by deviant others who engage in concededly reckless and irresponsible behavior (whether driving under the influence, smoking crack, or having unprotected sex). They also introduce tremendous sources of strain into the lives of those operating largely in normative conformity but engaging in behavior that puts them at risk of being defined as a moral monster (whether from possessing small amounts of marijuana, or engaging in drinking above the legal limit but below the individual threshold of drunk-enness). Such resistance raises costs of governance, creating a vicious circle in which both punitiveness and dissatisfaction with governance increase together.

The civic culture account focuses on the role of the state in defining and enforcing criminal laws and the consequences for an individual's likeli-hood of cooperation. Missing from this is the significance of crime and fear of crime as "regulators." One can easily agree that it's preferable to have a thriving culture of civic participation that makes all forms of government more effective than a desiccated one in which citizens crouch behind doors, uncertain whether to fear criminals or the police more. That democratic self-government is difficult to sustain in the latter is also a real fear. Less clear is whether crime-control strategies themselves should be seen as exac-erbating such a spiral of civic collapse. For example, crime and fear of crime may independently erode civic participation by causing people to withdraw further and more rapidly from communities that are already experiencing transitional pressures (Skogan 1990). Some have argued that aggressive en-forcement of criminal laws, especially minor public-order norms, will have positive effect on civic participation by drawing people back into the public (Wilson and Kelling 1982). The aggressive use of street stop-and-search tac-tics and enforcement of public-order offenses have been deployed in New York to some recent critical acclaim (Bratton 1996a, 1996b).

In short, from this perspective, it is not always clear whether the prior-ity of crime control in contemporary governance is undermining democratic practice or enhancing it. Crime-prevention strategies often focus directly on the role of participation. The successful movement to intensify the criminal status of drunk drivers has produced a broad set of efforts at valorizing new kinds of responsibility among individuals ("friends don't let friends drive drunk"). More recent advertising efforts are targeted at drinkers themselves to be responsible in using alcohol. Such efforts point to sources of govern-ance other than the state and enhance the importance of the individual as an agent of control over self and others.[19]

2. *Ressentiment*

Political Theorist Wendy Brown (1995) also views the social solidarity based on victim identity as potentially disastrous for a democratic political culture. Brown focuses on the claims of victimization by women and minor-ity groups who have suffered historic and ongoing forms of oppression and domination. She offers an empathetic critique of the dangers of forming political identity around the wounds of oppression. What Brown calls

---

19. It is difficult to know how important such norms are.

"politicized" identity is a potent source of mobilizing political participation, but she argues it also carries a high risk of locking people into the very categories generated by their oppression. The satisfaction that comes from avenging oppression carries the price of reinforcing the very categories of the original victimization. It also tends to reconfigure relationships so that law and the state become inevitable intermediaries (Brown 1995, 27).

Brown's critique can be extended beyond the role of victim identity among feminist and critical race activists to the more general cultural milieu of crime. The point is not that sexism and racism can be reduced to the category of crime anymore than to one another, but that they are linked together through the increasingly politicized identity of the victim. In its own way, the crime-centered "victims' rights movement" has in the 1980s and 1990s usurped the place of feminism and antiracism in articulating the kind of governance that victims demand.[20] Feminism and antiracism, even as they produce the kind of victim identity that Brown addresses, have important self-limiting capacities in this regard. Feminists and antiracists confront the mechanisms of oppression and exploitation on a routine and systematic basis. Crime-victim subjectivity is all too concrete for some, but it has come to function as an all-purpose form of oppression for many whose contact with crime will be mainly through the media. It is perhaps because of this that sociolegal scholars have long observed that those who are the most severely affected victims of sexism and racism (e.g., prostitutes or teenaged black males in the juvenile justice system) qualify least as "genuine" victims of crime.

Brown's analysis helps counterbalance the emphasis on faction implicit in the critique of governing through crime as racism discussed above. No doubt numerous enduring cultural narratives help channel racial animus, especially against African Americans, into demands for security and vengeance against criminals. However, crime victimization is such a powerful basis for identity in contemporary U.S. society partly because it is possible to make it so inclusive. Brown recognizes that the dangers of governing through crime are also those of unification within forms of subjectivity that are themselves too ungrounded in history or politics to generate effective formations of democratic will.

As traditional pluralist competition for state resources comes to focus on crime, groups find strategic reasons to pursue the goods provided by such

---

20. The relationship between feminist work on rape and sexual harassment, and the more general victims' rights movement, has been very complicated. In some countries—England, for example—the problem of women as victims of sexual crimes was the critical crossover issue for involving government administration in building a victim movement (Rock 1990). In the United States there have been symbiotic links but also important tensions. Feminist groups have used their influence to support reform of rape law and domestic violence enforcement in ways that parallel the larger victims' rights struggle and constitute some of its greatest successes. At the same time crime victims who become involved in victims' rights groups are often women who are not attracted to feminism.

a government (Simon and Spaulding 1999). Less clear is how governable the multiple fragmented publics constituted by such politics are, and conversely, how much punishment allows real development of the capacities of these new publics.[21] Identities based on victimization, in Brown's analysis, produce subjects that are increasingly less capable of defining their interests in terms that can be effectively resolved in the boundaries of democratic politics. The astounding political success of recent punitive legislation like 3-strikes and Megan's Law shows that crime is not necessarily a wedge issue. Almost all demographic segments of the population, and both political parties, supported these measures. On the other hand, one may fear that they produce a kind of false unity around narratives whose compelling facts provide potent political mobilization but little mandate to govern.

Governing through crime increasingly includes efforts to govern victims themselves and not just criminals or those suspected of crime. While classical criminal laws placed restrictions on the dangerous in the name of protecting the innocent, sexual offender notification laws like Megan's Law aim at affecting the behavior of the innocent in the name of managing the dangerous. In so doing it redraws the lines of responsibility between family and state. Potential victims are encouraged to take preventive measures in the way they dress, move through the city, and conduct basic economic transactions (Clarke 1995). These measures may in fact be more effective than those directed at potential criminals, since they target obedient citizens and utilize their self-discipline. Indeed, one might think of crime prevention as a way of governing the less controllable (potential criminals) through manipulating the more controllable (potential victims).

Much of this does not conform to either a passive or a submissive role of a victim enthralled by a state. Some crime-prevention techniques skip the subject altogether in favor of governing the environment, but other tactics aim at making the potential victim a manager of their own risks (and those of others). These new technologies of crime prevention create a potentially very different political effect than state-oriented vengeance strategies (Simon 1999c). They are often based in the private sector, encouraged by tort liability, paternalistic concern, and even market forces (Shearing 1996). They emphasize technologies of loss prevention and harm reduction rather than rituals of accusation and punishment (O'Malley 1996). They tend to avoid the identification of specific victims and perpetrators. (Measures can be taken by anyone, and the need to deploy them is typically justified by environment or routine activities than by subjectivity).

---

21. Political scientists and others have observed a trend toward fragmentation of the public (both politically and culturally) since the 1960s (Inglehart 1977, 1990; Jameson 1991) in liberal postindustrial societies. For the argument that this fragmentation helps directly feed the salience of crime and punishment to electoral politics, see Caplow and Simon 1999.

As a result of their private-sector locus, crime-prevention governance tends to be very result oriented and thus less susceptible to the rent-seeking behavior of traditional, modern crime-control bureaucracies. For the same reasons, however, these measures carry a great risk of enhancing the problem of exclusion. Private crime-prevention efforts may or may not consider the runoff effects on other communities (opportunistic crime shifted from one neighborhood to another), or care about protecting potential users from the negative externalities ranging from hostile and suspicious treatment at the hands of private police to the mere inconvenience caused by removing public transportation links to a shopping mall.

These technologies require us to look beyond the relationship of citizen to state in understanding the circumstances of democratic governance. We should not assume punitiveness as a culturally fixed desire exogenous to government. Even opinion-survey data suggest that public expectations about punishment are ambiguous. A recent national survey found that only higher education and gun ownership were consistent predictors of punitiveness (with education tending toward less and guns tending toward more punitiveness) (Flanagan and Longmire 1996, 73). Rather than specific political cultures of punitiveness (Stinchcombe 1980), we might think of a far wider and shallower public culture of crime shaped in quite changeable ways. Indeed, these attitudes may express frustration with government itself as much as with crime. The same survey found that a majority favors early release for prisoners who behave well, but rejects having parole boards with discretion to release prisoners (Flanagan and Longmire 1996, 88). Support for lengthy imprisonment and executions expressed frustration and skepticism about government as well as fear of the offender (Ellsworth and Gross 1994, 42).

III. MEGAN'S LAW

Any attempt to think through the politics of so broad a field as governing through crime must confront the sheer complexity of the penal state (O'Malley 1999, 175–79). This final section takes a closer look at one of the most politically potent examples of recent penal law making, which opens a window into the way governing through crime is being articulated into a reconfiguration of government. In 1994 New Jersey adopted the first of a wave of sexual offender community-notification laws under the name *Megan's Law*. The act was actually a host of measures aimed at the state's treatment of convicted sex offenders.[22] The most widely publicized portion

---

22. Under the name Megan's Law, the New Jersey legislature actually adopted 10 separate measures against sex offenders including extending terms, making the murder of a child under 14 an aggravating circumstance for purposes of New Jersey's death penalty, and intro-

required sex offenders in the state to register with state authorities and authorized the state to assess the risk level of sex offenders and provide notification to families and organizations concerned with children who might be at particular risk because of the residential location of the offender.

The law took its name from a seven-year-old girl, Megan Kanka, murdered near her home in Hamilton Township, New Jersey. The man convicted of her murder, Jesse Timmendequas, was twice convicted of sex offenses against young female children, one of which almost resulted in the death of the victim. Megan's murder became a rallying point for victims' rights activists who attacked the state's efforts at policing sex offenders. These groups, prominently featured by the media, framed the issue as one of the betrayal of parents by a state unable to control predators and unwilling to empower citizens to protect themselves. The movement to require registration and notification of sex offenders swept the country in the 1990s following several well-publicized crimes including the Megan Kanka case (Small 1999, 1458). Today every state has a registration law, and nearly 20 have notification of citizens. Some under the name Megan's Law, while others have attached the name of local child victim.

The issue of child sex abuse had been a growing locus of governmental attention and moral panic (Hall et. al. 1979; Cohen 1972) since the 1980s (Jenkins 1998; Logan 2000a, b). The thrust of Megan's Law was nationalized by the United States Congress in the *Jacob Wetterling Crimes against Children and Sexually Violent Offender Registration Act*, 42 U.S.C. § 14,071 (1994), which required states to maintain registries of convicted sex offenders and release information "necessary to protect the public." These laws reflect a set of somewhat different governance capacities than we associate with the crime-control efforts of the state—for example, the burgeoning prison system, which for all its recent high-tech bells and whistles, at best evidences the continuing ability of state governments (and the federal government) to pour concrete, hire correctional officers, and maintain a larger version of the "carceral archipelago" (Foucault 1977, 298) familiar in the United States since the 1830s. The essential elements of this regime—prisoners, guards, and locked facilities—have existed in easily recognizable form throughout this period. In contrast, the sex offender registration and notification laws model a different picture of governing through crime with quite different elements. Here I want to concentrate on three of them: the constitution of crime victims as the subjects of a democratic polity; the sex offender as a risk to children; and state expertise and power as risk prediction and communication.

---

ducing involuntary civil commitment for "dangerous criminals," lifetime parole supervision, and mandatory DNA sampling for identification procedures (Goodman 1996).

1136 LAW AND SOCIAL INQUIRY

A. The Victim As Sovereign

Megan's Law is a story about the power of a social movement, the victims' rights movement, to command remarkable attention from state legislatures and Congress. Victims' rights has emerged over the past 25 years as one of the most important social movements of our time, comparable in its influence on our political culture to the civil rights movement or feminism. In part because of the enormous appeal of victimization to television media, the victims' rights movement has been able to make visible a whole host of criminal justice decisions that until recently were made with little attention to public justification. The demand for accountability to victims has put new constraints on courts, parole boards, and governors (Shapiro 1997).[23] The recently proposed constitutional amendment on victims' rights promises to embed these influences in unpredictable ways into the criminal process and perhaps beyond.

Beyond its legislative success, the victims' movement has been most important in broadening crime victimization from a social problem requiring government action to a status authorizing one to act virtuously as a citizen. Consider, for example, remarks that Attorney General Janet Reno made in a speech to a victims' rights conference:

> I draw most of my strength from victims, for they represent America to me: people who will not be put down, people who will not be defeated, people who will rise again and stand again for what is right . . . You are my heroes and heroines. You are but little lower than the angels. (Shapiro 1997)

Allowing for the excess that political discourse requires on such occasions, something remaining speaks the truth about victims in contemporary politics. In American history the yeoman farmer and the industrial worker have been among those figures that for a time capture in the broadest possible ways the boundaries of democratic citizenship both in its responsibilities and its needs. In our time the crime victim is emerging as a dominant representation of the governable interests of the population. This is true not only in the relationship of citizen to state but also in the institutional settings of work, family, and education.

This is perhaps the significance of what has been one of the most influential aspects of Megan's Law: its name. Laws named after dead children have become one of the markers of our era replacing earlier traditions of naming laws after legislators (e.g., the Wagner Act or the Volstead Act). Megan's Law demands that we consider Megan's fate. The structure of the

---

23. Bruce Shapiro relates how Penny White, a member of the Tennessee Supreme Court, was removed from office by a campaign mobilized after she concurred in the reversal of one death sentence (Shapiro 1997).

law, shaped around the specific experience of Megan's death, marks Megan's own subject position as the law's coordinates (which is not to say that the actual administration of this law will be able to operate in this way). Megan's Law testifies to the importance of the politics of identity in contemporary political life, and to the importance of victimization to the politics of identity (Rajchman 1995). As a consequence of this monumentalizing of Megan, the law brings us before the specificity of Megan Kanka as a young white female killed near her home in a suburban area coded in popular political geography as safe. Indeed, the only murder (other than celebrity ones) that has attracted this kind of attention before a trial has even taken place is that of Polly Klas, a young white girl from a town in northern California previously best known for being the site of President Reagan's famous "morning again in America" commercials during the 1984 presidential campaign. Klas was literally taken out of her home and murdered by a repeat offender (Schrag 1998, 227–28).

If Wendy Brown (1995) is right that the experience of victimization in contemporary society is replacing the recognition of class solidarities, it is not surprising that it is occurring in the victimization of figures like Megan Kanka and Polly Klas, from white middle- and working-class families (themselves increasingly disempowered by the conditions of late-twentieth-century capitalism).[24] Brown suggests that the tendency of an identity based on victimization is an intensification of the politics of *ressentiment*, which finds its satisfaction most in punishment.

> Politicized identity, premised on exclusion and fueled by the humiliation and suffering imposed by its historically structured impotence in the context of a discourse of sovereign individuals, is as likely to seek its own or collective liberation through empowerment. Indeed, it is more likely to punish and reproach—"punishment is what revenge calls itself; with a hypocritical lie it creates a good conscience for itself"—than to find venues of self affirming action. (Brown 1995, 71, quoting Nietzsche 1954, 242)

In anchoring the law's authority in a deceased child, Megan's Law describes a kind of political community that may incorporate nearly everybody but in an inert and passive form that is anything but self-governing. Ironically, at a time when citizenship is being reinterpreted to demand greater levels of individual responsibility and risk taking, Megan's Law constructs an infantilized political community incapable of formulating interests that are not for protection against others. As Brown (1995) would suggest, in gathering and recognizing people in their vulnerabilities to predatory attack, Megan's Law confines subjects to a narrative with a limited set of objectives, a built

---

24. Part of the dark genius of David Lynch's television series *Twin Peaks* was placing a dead young white girl at the center of its mythic late 1980s exurban community.

in bias toward the state's own most authoritarian agencies for social control, and the risk of pathological overreaction.

B.   Intolerable Risks

If Megan's law helps make victimization into a constitutive experience for the participation of the people in their own government, it also helps constitute another more select group of people as belonging to the class of monsters (i.e., the aforementioned "sexual predators"). New Jersey and most other states have simply placed all convicted sex offenders into the class of predators, leaving it to administrative decisions to sort them for purposes of the law's notification function.[25] The legislature of New Jersey made a finding in Megan's law:

> The danger of recidivism posed by sex offenders and offenders who commit other predatory acts against children, and the dangers posed by persons who prey on others as a result of mental illness, require a system of registration that will permit law enforcement officials to identify and alert the public when necessary for the public safety. (N.J. Stat. Ann. § 2C:7-1[a][West 1996])

In deploying the terms *predatory* and *prey*, Megan's Law invokes nonhuman forms of danger. Over time the law may bequeath us new generations of state-defined "monsters" who can be neither altered or eliminated but only managed.[26] Those who fall under the technical boundaries of Megan's Law will be defined for the rest of their lives as "sexual predators" (Clawges 1996). The law having defined a problem of governance, sexual predators, an administrative process will set to work employing the technologies of power available to it against this political enemy.

The rationality of government associated with the social democratic governments in the United States and western Europe for the first three decades after World War II was best expressed in the great risk-sharing devices like workers' compensation, the pension systems, and the health care systems (Rose 1999). For much of the twentieth century the central questions of domestic politics had to do with managing this social risk sector. Correctionalism in penology, with its emphasis on community corrections,

---

25. The legislation adopts as public policy a set of assumptions about sexual offenders that is part of a highly contested field within criminology and psychology.

26. While there is both popular and scientific support for treating "sex offenders" as a special class, the New Jersey version of Megan's Law sweeps broadly in its registration requirement, including all convicted of aggravated sexual assault, sexual assault, aggravated criminal sexual contact, and certain kinds of kidnapping, and those who attempt these crimes if they are found by the state to be "characterized by a pattern of repetitive, compulsive behavior" (see N.J. Stat. Ann. §§ 2C:7-2[b][1]–[3] [West 1996]).

was a part of this. Even the risks of criminals must be socialized, channeled back into communities whose security is in that sense tied up with its capacity to normalize (including through the development of a specialized rehabilitative sector).

Governing through crime in the United States has run along with moves to scale back this social sector and introduce more principles of disaggregation into it. A zero-sum game model of risk is replacing the social solidarity of the past. We see this expressed throughout the culture and in the everyday choices of the population. The hard time of prison, from this perspective, is an artificially created hyper-risk zone occupied by those whose removal in large enough numbers from society is promised to lower risks somewhat on the outside. Megan's Law and its progeny produce not simply new entitlements or sanctions but a model of the risk relationship in which the terms could hardly be less solidaristic. Beginning on the already charged ground of child sexual abuse, Megan's Law frames the risk as one of assault by strangers. In this space there are few equities upon which to imagine collective forms of risk reduction. The role of government can only be to reduce the risks of the child, regardless of how marginally, at the expense of the convicted sex offenders, regardless of how severely.

Megan's Law has no therapeutic component. Like the new laws aimed at preventively detaining some of the highest-risk sex offenders, the explicit functions is to exclude, to banish. Long before the great confinement associated with the disciplinary regimes of hospital, prison, and schools, the exclusion of lepers, according to Foucault, operated as a form of government by elimination. There is little doubt that if one were looking for modern lepers, repetitive obsessive sex offenders would be high on one's list. But there is little reason to believe that the model of subject formation represented by Megan's Law will be limited to this particular issue.[27]

C. *Megan's Law as Democratic Penality*

Social liberalism made information a critical vehicle for state intervention into the population. Penology was part of this. The capacity to probe the subjectivity of delinquents and criminals was part and parcel of managing social problems through nuanced interventions in families and communities. The emerging features of advanced liberalism suggest that the state, and agencies like the police, increasingly become dealers in information

---

27. Representative Jackson-Lee of Texas spoke in support of the federal Megan's Law by invoking another young female murder victim, Monique Miller of Houston, Texas, who, as Ms. Jackson-Lee put it, "was brutally murdered and sexually abused by a repeat offender" (142 Cong. Rec. H62 [Lexis]). The murderer of Polly Klas was also a repeat offender. Whatever core of reality there may be to the legal definition of sexual predator, repeat offenders, especially in the age of widespread imprisonment, must be a heterogeneous lot (Caplow and Simon 1999).

that constitutes its primary intervention (Ericson and Haggerty 1997) . One of the most unusual features of Megan's Law is its focus on information. In the legislative campaign for Megan's Law, this information logic was framed in populist terms of ineffective elites and ordinary people forced to grapple with menacing evils. As Maureen Kanka put the matter in a letter written to the House Judiciary Committee:

> If pedophiles are going to be out on the street where they can accost children, then parents have the right to know if they live on our streets. My daughter Megan would be alive today if I had known that my neighbor was a twice convicted pedophile. *I had responsibility to protect my daughter.* I have always told my children that I would never let anything happen to them. But I guess I lied. I could not protect my Megan as she was being brutally raped and murdered across the street from my home. I have to live with the fact that she screamed out my name as she was being murdered. (Testimony to the House of Representatives, Judiciary Committee, 1996 WL 117175 [1996 Federal Document Clearing House]; emphasis added)

Although Maureen Kanka may or may not have had it consciously in mind, her testimony provides a critique of the technologies of power associated with the social liberal state and its penality. The traditional answer of state penology to the problem posed by Megan's Law was the creation of parole agents (Simon 1993; Lynch 1998), a hybrid of factory supervisor, therapist, and prison guard who were expected to "supervise" released offenders like Jesse Timmendequas. Had Timmendequas been on parole (he had completed his term of supervision), it is doubtful that a parole agent would have permitted him to live with another sex offender. The agent would also likely have visited with parents of vulnerable-age children in the vicinity. Ironically, the current preference for imprisonment as the penal sanction of choice has left parole little more than a lower-cost prosecutorial function in many states (Simon 1993). In this sense, Megan's Law reflects a model for governance that is becoming a familiar pattern in the advanced liberal state: the centrality of risk to the construction of governable problems; the delegation of responsibility for risk reduction to private and nonspecialized actors often with little political influence; the state little more than a provider of information (Rose 1999).

Risk prediction has become widespread in the criminal justice system (Feeley and Simon 1994). These mechanisms, fitted to the other needs of administrative bureaucracies, now influence decision making at virtually every point in the process from being stopped or interrogated by the police, to bail decisions, to jail and prison custody decisions, to conditions of release. Under Megan's Law the threat of private action is added to this system but remains, in fact, tied to the official control of the risk-evaluation process (Logan 2000). What is interesting about Megan's Law is the degree to which risk assessment has separated itself from other substantive tasks of criminal justice—incapacitating, rehabilitating, and so on—and become an autonomous governmental practice intended to have its own direct effects.

Megan's Law recognizes victims as subjects, but it also brings victims into its object field as targets of power. Megan's Law is a way of governing people through the experience of victimization. Sex offenders are required to submit to certain kinds of reporting, and the guardians of children are promised information on proximate high-risk offenders, but in between, Megan's Law governs through other relations—parents to children, parents to schools and youth centers, all of the above to the police. Megan's Law also affirms community groups involved with religion, schools, and youth generally as elements of a crime-control strategy against sexual abuse. Most institutions involved with children have for some time been under special legal obligations to report signs of child abuse to the state. Megan's Law may be the first statute to make these institutions part of the specific response to offenders (as opposed to victims). It makes these groups part of the state's power to surveil and potentially to punish (although violent actions against the person are not authorized). It does not purport to prescribe all these relationships, but it sets them into motion with its circulation of knowledge. Thus, the experience of victimization, which begins as a kind of denunciation of the liberal state and its failings, becomes a mandate to a set of non-state actors to take part in governing the potential relationship between sex offenders and children.

Along with the victim and the perpetrator, and significantly implied in the valorization of both, is a complicated and contradictory message about state power. The political rhetoric behind Megan's Law has consistently invoked the theme of state failure. Existing laws and the administrative bureaucracies do not adequately protect children from sex offenders because of plea bargaining, deceptive sentencing laws that allow prisoners to earn early release regardless of their treatment, and inadequate post-release preventive supervision. From this perspective, state efforts at crime control actually render citizens more vulnerable by hiding the need for self-defense and creating administrative bodies jealous of their knowledge advantages over the public that pays their salaries. But Megan's Law also redefined the role of state actors in a way that insulates government from failure. If the primary job of government is collecting and dispensing information about sex offenders, and if it is primarily a problem of family and community to effectively use that information to protect children, than the state is vulnerable to certain kinds of mistakes (e.g., failing to classify a particular offender as worthy of notification) but insulated from the ultimate failures of abused and murdered children.

This model can be criticized on a number of grounds. Most especially, it presumes a family that has the resources to protect itself by choosing a location in which the streets are safe and a family structure that allows for the kind of surveillance that Maureen may have been able to provide Megan had she been alerted to that particular threat. The specific slogan of Megan's Law has been "empowering families, women, and children." Its congressional supporters made vague references to how the Megans and Maureen Kankas of this world can seek their own protection "to take the necessary precautions to ensure that there are not second, third or fourth victims" (142 Cong Rec. H4451, 55 [Lexis]). These supporters said much less about what those precautions might be. Others, those whose employment and housing situations make children unprotectable through a strategy of commands to stay away from certain persons, enforced by personal observation, are strangely out of place in the law. Indeed, their plight can now only look more like a kind of irresponsibility on their part. Once the knowledge is provided, those parents who do not act to protect their children personally will have to answer for their dependence on the state.

In promising a direct circuit to state knowledge about offenders in the community Megan's Law repudiates the discretionary, expertise-based control system associated with the social liberal state and its penality. It remains to be seen, of course, what kinds of real circuits of knowledge/power these laws create. The rhetoric of the law invokes the idea of meaningful communities acting in self-defense. In most states, however, the law vests in judges, prosecutors, or a state commission to assess risk and determine at what risk level notification should take place. The parole officer is replaced by the risk-assessment consultant, but the power over the knowledge remains centralized. Indeed, in Florida and California, for example, the state has created a virtual community over the Internet by allowing citizens to search for sex offenders regardless of their own proximity or danger. Also, by defining the large and diverse population of convicted sex offenders as belonging to a unitary class of "sexual predators," these laws actually increase the experience of threat in the community (Small 1999, 1456). To the extent that community really means "local knowledge," these circuits seem likely to intensify mistrust of one's neighbors while building new kinds of dependency on the state.

CONCLUSION

Governing through crime is probably a feature of most societies at most times. During the past quarter century, however, the United States has experienced phenomenal growth in the importance of governing through crime. Because the incarcerated population, despite its unprecedented growth, is still small relative to other sites of governance like schools, businesses, and families, it is tempting to view it as a specialized sector. It is easy to show that incorporation into this sector is most unequally spread among all the most problematic differences in societies. But governing through crime seems to have a broader purchase in a number of ways that are harder to measure than the formal jurisdictional demography of the criminal justice system.

Elsewhere I have offered a richer descriptive account of governing through crime and sought to canvass explanations for why it seems to be undergoing explosive growth (Simon 1997). In this article I have concentrated on what seems one of the most disturbing and paradoxical features of this trend toward governing through crime—its relationship with democracy. Governing through crime has long roots in democratic practice and theory. As James Q. Wilson (1996) has recently reminded us, imprisonment is an almost inevitable response to crime in democracies, which can neither ignore popular discomforts nor brutally "disappear" the enemies of order. One can, in fact, make a strong case within the discourses of mainstream political theory that the criminal law is among the most democratic form, of exercising power, at least when one is focusing on that part of governance characterized as the state.[28] Clearly the current ascendance of governing through crime is supported by substantial majorities participating in electoral politics.[29] But recognizing the profound links between democracy and governing through crime cannot make us sanguine to the growing role of the former. The expansion of governing through crime poses a danger to democratic practices and institutions. These dangers exist regardless of whether the reasons for incarcerating people are sound and the procedures used utterly fair (neither of which can be taken as assumptions in this country).

It is essential to appraising the real stakes in these broad changes in American political and legal culture that they have corresponded to a broad reconfiguration of the rationality of governance in liberal societies. After a century in which the freedom of the liberal subject was secured by socializing risk through large structures of solidarity, and in which the state sought to govern through expert knowledge of population and its social conditions, a fundamental transformation of liberal rule is underway. The reasons why crime has become such a central surface for this transformation are beyond the scope of this article, which identified the consequences of shaping the new terms of risk spreading and management in the context of crime. While fear of crime has eroded the political structures of social liberalism (large cities, public schools, social welfare), the salience of crime is establishing

---

28. That would seem to be the logic of the libertarian position that has recently been so influential in law and politics.

29. One can show how much this support is based on distorted information (see, e.g., Donziger 1996), but this essay argues that it is a mistake to ignore the genealogies that anchor crime in popular thought.

new relations in terms likely to exacerbate racism, promote inequality, and preserve some of the least defensible features of the old regime (patronage government driven by large public unions and election contributions).

Robert Post (1995) has argued that American democracy has historically been a balancing act between tendencies toward communitarian solidarities and engines of managerial power. Post argues that the great challenge of American constitutional law is sustaining a functioning democratic state dependent on both community and bureaucracy, while being colonized by neither. Democracy requires a space of individual choice that is suffocated when community values are rigidly enforced as law. On the other hand, democracies require citizens with values and interests that can only come from the normative creativity of community (Post 1995, 189). Where protecting individual liberty means negating community values, the very source of democratic citizenship may be suffocated. Likewise, democracy is both dependent upon and endangered by managerial practices that make it possible to carry out the democratic will and distort its formation. Where government does not have the organizational strength to carry out the mandates of law, democratic choice ceases to have much meaning (Cover 1986). Yet large and powerful enforcement organizations pose their own threat to democracy, both by the great concentration of human and other capital that can have an undue influence, and by the often stifling pressure of managerial considerations.

Governing through crime threatens to exacerbate this historic tension. First, as communities become more and more defined by the experience of personal victimization—whether real or imagined, firsthand or mediated by television—the criminal law emerges as a tempting way to reaffirm the very existence of community (Kennedy forthcoming). We are fast becoming a society in which we must compete in virtually every aspect of life, while simultaneously reinforcing a public ideology that brooks no real recognition of conflicts other than those inspired by perversity and criminality. Crime control reproduces the community as a series of links running between the state and various intermediate organizations (schools, churches, families). Meanwhile, what we might take as the sociological reality of community (i.e., the realm of more spontaneous interactions structured by shared space and custom) is actually made to appear more dangerous and less worthy of trusting engagement. Megan's Law is touted as community empowerment, but it replaces reliance on the "local knowledge" of neighbors with new forms of dependence on the state. In short, it places management where the gesture of community points.

While the priority of governing through crime control reflects an increasingly desperate attempt to shore up community, the actual expansion of the criminal law goes along with a massive expansion in the managerial functions of government. A larger and larger proportion of the population finds that they are being directly managed by the criminal justice system. An even larger proportion is exposed to this managerial force through policing and community supervision. But while this managerial power may effectively represent majority political support, it also stifles the kinds of interactions and potential solidarities that might form new directives for both social order and governing.

REFERENCES

Anderson, Elijah. 1998. The Social Ecology of Youth Violence. In *Youth Violence: Crime & Justice*, ed. Mark H. Moore and Michael Tonry. Vol. 24. Chicago: University of Chicago Press.

Balkin, J. M. 1998. *Cultural Software: A Theory of Ideology*. New Haven, Conn.: Yale University Press

Barry, Andrew, Thomas Osborne, and Nikolas Rose, eds. 1996. *Foucault and Political Reason: Liberalism, Neo-liberalism, and Rationalities of Government*. Chicago: University of Chicago Press

Baudrillard, Jean. 1983. *In the Shadow of the Silent Majorities or "The Death of the Social."* New York: Semiotext(e).

Beck, Ulrich. 1992. *Risk Society: Towards a New Modernity*, trans. Mark Ritter. London: Sage.

Becker, Gary. 1968. Crime and Punishment: An Economic Approach. *Journal of Political Economy* 76:68–95.

Beckett, Katherine. 1997. *Making Crime Pay: Law & Order in Contemporary American Politics*. New York: Oxford University Press.

Beckett, Katherine, and Bruce Western. 1999. How Unregulated Is the U.S. Labor Market? The Dynamics of Jobs and Jails. *American Journal of Sociology* 104:1030–60.

———. Forthcoming. Social Control, Welfare, and the Transformation of the State. *American Sociological Review*.

Berk, Sarah Fenstermaker, and Donileen R. Loseke. 1981. "Handling" Family Violence: Situational Determinants of Police Arrest in Domestic Disturbances. *Law and Society Review* 15:317–346.

Blumberg, Abraham. 1967. The Practice of Law as a Confidence Game. *Law and Society Review* 1:15–39.

Bonczar, Thomas P., and Allen J. Beck. 1997. *Lifetime Likelihood of Going to State or Federal Prison*. Washington, D.C.: U.S. Department of Justice.

Bratton, William J. 1996a. New Strategies for Combating Crime in New York City. *Fordham Urban Law Journal* 23:781–795.

———. 1996b. How to Win the War Against Crime. *New York Times*, 5 April 1996, A27.

Brown, Wendy. 1995. *States of Freedom: Power and Freedom in Late Modernity*. Princeton, N.J.: Princeton University Press.

Caplow, Theodore, and Jonathan Simon. 1999. Understanding Prison Policy and Population Trends. *Prisons: Crime and Justice: A Review of Research*, ed. Michael Tonry and Joan Petersilia, 63–120. Vol. 26. Chicago: University of Chicago Press.

Christie, Nils. 1993. *Crime Control as Industry*. London: Routledge.

Clarke, Ronald V. 1995. Situational Crime Prevention. In *Building a Safer Society: Crime and Justice*, ed. Michael Tonry and David Farrington. Vol. 19. Chicago: University of Chicago Press.

1146 LAW AND SOCIAL INQUIRY

Clawges, Timothy L. 1996 Political Posturing or Real Change: Analysis of the Legislature's Special Session on Crime. *Pennsylvania Lawyer*, March/April 1996, 20.

Cohen, Stanley. 1972. *Folk Devils and Moral Panics*. Oxford: Blackwell.

Cole, David. 1999. *No Equal Justice*. New York: New Press.

Coombs, Mary I. 1987. Shared Privacy and the Fourth Amendment, or the Rights of Relationships. *California Law Review* 75:1593–1664.

Cover, Robert. 1986. Violence and the Word. *Yale Law Journal* 95:1601–1629.

Cruikshank, Barbara. 1994. The Will to Empower: Technologies of Citizenship and the War on Poverty. *Socialist Review* 23:29–55.

Currie, Elliott. 1998. *Crime and Punishment in America*. New York: Metropolitan Books.

Davis, Mike. 1990. *City of Quartz: Excavating the Future in Los Angeles*. London: Verso.

———. 1998. Ecology of Fear: Los Angeles and the Imagination of Disaster. New York: Metropolitan Books.

Dean, Mitchell. 1991. *The Constitution of Poverty: Towards a Genealogy of Liberal Governance*. London: Routledge.

Deavere-Smith, Anna. 1993. *Fires in the Mirror*. New York: Anchor Books.

Dionne, E. J. Jr. 1991. *Why Americans Hate Politics*. New York: Simon and Schuster.

Donziger, Steven R., ed. 1996. *The Real War on Crime: The Report of the National Criminal Justice Commission*. New York: HarperPerennial.

Dubber, Markus Dirk. 1998. The Right to Be Punished: Autonomy and Its Demise in Modern Penal Thought. *Law and History Review* 16:113–46.

Dumm, Thomas. 1987. *Democracy and Punishment: Disciplinary Origins of the United States*. Madison: University of Wisconsin Press.

———. 1994. *United States*. Ithaca, N.Y.: Cornell University Press.

Ellsworth, Phoebe C., and Samuel R. Gross. 1994. Hardening of Attitudes: Americans' Views on the Death Penalty. *Journal of Social Issues* 20:19–52.

Ericson, Richard V., and Kevin D. Haggerty. 1997. *Policing the Risk Society*. Toronto, Ont.: University of Toronto Press.

Ewald, Francois. 1986. *L'Etat Providence*. Paris: Grasset.

———. 1991. Insurance and Risk. In *The Foucault Effect*, ed. G. Burchell C. Gordon, and P. Miller. Chicago: University of Chicago Press.

Feeley, Malcolm, and Edward Rubin. 1997. *Judicial Policy Making in the Modern State: How the Courts Reformed America's Prisons*. New York: Cambridge University Press.

Feeley, Malcolm, and Jonathan Simon. 1992. The New Penology: Notes on the Emerging Strategy of Corrections and Its Implications. *Criminology* 30: 449–74.

———. 1994. Actuarial Justice: The Emerging New Criminal Law. In *The Futures of Criminology*, ed. David Nelken. London: Sage.

Felner, Jamie, and Marc Mauer. 1998. *Losing the Vote: The Impact of Disenfranchisement Laws in the United States*, 7–8 October. Washington D.C.: The Sentencing Project and Human Rights Watch.

Flanagan, Timothy J., and Dennis R. Longmire, eds. 1996. *Americans View Crime and Justice: A National Opinion Survey*. London: Sage.

Foner, Eric. 1988. *Reconstruction, 1863–1877*. New York: Harper and Row.

Foucault, Michel. 1977. *Discipline and Punish: The Birth of the Prison*, trans. Alan Sheridan. New York: Pantheon.

———. 1991. Governmentality. In *The Foucault Effect: Studies in Governmentality*, ed. Graham Burchell, Colin Gordon, and Peter Miller. Chicago: University of Chicago Press.

Garland, David. 1985. *Punishment and Welfare*. Brookfield, Vt.: Gower.

———. 1996. The Limits of the Sovereign State: Strategies of Crime Control in Contemporary Society. *British Journal of Criminology* 36:445–71.

———. 1997. "Governmentality" and the Problem of Crime: Foucault, Criminology, Sociology. *Theoretical Criminology* 1:173–213.

———. 2000. The Culture of High Crime Societies: The Social Preconditions of the New Politics of Crime Control. *British Journal of Criminology* 40:347–375.

Garth, Bryant, and Joyce Sterling. 1998. From Legal Realism to Law and Society: Reshaping Law for the Last Stages of the Social Activist State. *Law and Society Review* 32:409–772.

Gilroy, Paul. 1987. *"There Ain't No Black in the Union Jack": The Cultural Politics of Race and Nation.* Chicago: University of Chicago Press.

Goodman, Elga A. 1996. Comment: Megan's Law: The New Jersey Supreme Court Navigates Uncharted Waters. *Seton Hall Law Review* 26:764–802.

Gordon, Diana R. 1994. *The Return of the Dangerous Classes: Drug Prohibition and Policy Politics.* New York: Norton.

Gusfield, J. 1981. *The Culture of Public Problems: Drinking-Driving and the Symbolic Order.* Chicago: University of Chicago Press.

Hagan, John, and Ruth D. Peterson. 1995. Criminal Inequality in America: Patterns and Consequences. In *Crime and Inequality,* ed. John Hagan and Ruth D. Peterson, 14–36. Stanford, Calif.: Stanford University Press.

Hall, Stuart, Chas Critcher, Tony Jefferson, John Clarke, and Brian Roberts. 1979. *Policing the Crisis: Mugging, the State, and Law and Order.* London: MacMillan.

Hay, Douglas. 1975. Property, Authority, and the Criminal Law. In *Albion's Fatal Tree: Crime and Society in 18th-Century England, ed.* Hay et. al. New York: Pantheon.

Ignatieff, Michael. 1978. A Just Measure of Pain: The Penitentiary in the Industrial Revolution, *1750–1850.* London: Penguin Books.

Inglehart, Ronald. 1977. *The Silent Revolution: Changing Values and Political Styles Among Western Publics.* Princeton, N.J.: Princeton University Press.

———. 1990. *Culture Shift in Advanced Industrial Society.* Princeton, N.J.: Princeton University Press.

Irwin, John. 1985. *The Jail: Managing the Underclass in American Society.* Berkeley and Los Angeles: University of California Press.

Irwin, John, and James Austin. 1997. *It's About Time: America's Imprisonment Binge.* Belmont, Calif.: Wadsworth.

Jameson, Frederic. 1991. *Postmodernism, or The Cultural Logic of Late Capitalism.* Durham, N.C.: Duke University Press.

Jefferson, Thomas. 1801. Letter of Thomas Jefferson to Elijah Boardman, 3 July 3. Jefferson Papers, Library of Congress, vol. 115, folio 19761.

Jenkins, Philip. 1998. *Moral Panic: Changing Concepts of the Child Molester in Modern America.* New Haven, Conn.: Yale University Press.

Jordan, Bill, and Jon Arnold. 1995. Democracy and Criminal Justice. *Critical Social Policy* 44/45 (Autumn):170–82.

Kalven, Harry. 1965. *The Negro and the 1st Amendment.* Chicago: Phoenix Books.

Kaminer, Wendy. 1995. *It's All the Rage: Crime and Culture.* Chicago: Addison-Wesley.

Kaplan, John, Robert Weisberg, and Guyora Binder. 2000. *Criminal Law: Cases and Materials.* 4th ed. Boston: Little Brown.

Katz, Jack. 1988. *Seductions of Crime: Moral and Sensual Attractions of Doing Evil.* New York: Basic Books.

Kennedy, Joseph. Forthcoming. The Search for Solidarity Through Modern Punishment. *Hastings Law Review.*

Kennedy, Randall. 1997. *Race, Crime, and the Law.* New York: Pantheon.

Lichtenstein, Alex. 1996. Chain Gang Blues. *Dissent,* Fall, 7–10.

1148 LAW AND SOCIAL INQUIRY

Linebaugh, Peter. 1992. *The London Hanged: Crime and Civil Society in the 18th Century.* New York: Cambridge University Press.

Logan, Wayne. 2000a. A Study in "Actuarial Justice": Sex Offender Classification. *Practice and Procedure* 3:593–637.

———. 2000b.Liberty Interests in the Preventive State: Procedural Due Process and Sex Offender Community Notification Laws. *Journal of Criminal Law and Criminology* 89:1167–232.

Lynch, Mona. 1998. Waste Managers? The New Penology, Crime Fighting, and Parole Agent Identity. *Law and Society Review* 32:839–70.

Madriz, Esther. 1997. *Nothing Bad Happens to Good Girls: Fear of Crime in Women's Lives.* Berkeley and Los Angeles: University of California Press.

Maguire, Kathleen, and Ann L. Pastore. 1998. *Sourcebook of Criminal Justice Statistics 1997.* Washington, D.C.: Bureau of Justice Statistics.

Mahoney, Martha R. 1991. Legal Images of Battered Women: Redefining the Issue of Separation. *Michigan Law Review* 90:1–94.

Meares, Tracey. 1998. Race and Place. *Chicago Kent Law Review* 73:669–724.

Miller, Jerome. 1996. *Search and Destroy: African-American Males in the Criminal Justice System.* Cambridge, U.K.: Cambridge University Press.

Nietzsche, Friedrich. 1954. Thus Spake Zarathustra. In *The Portable Nietzsche*, ed. Walter Kaufman. New York: Knopf.

———. 1994. *On the Genealogy of Morals,* trans. Carol Diethe. Cambridge: Cambridge University Press.

O'Malley, Pat. 1996. Consuming Risks: Harm Minimization, Risk Management, and the Government of "Drug Users." Paper presented to the International Conference on New Forms of Government, University of Toronto, October 1996 (copy on file with author).

———. 1999. Volatile and Contradictory Punishment. *Theoretical Criminology.* 3:175–96.

Parenti, Christian. 1998. *Lockdown America: Police and Prisons in the Age of Crisis.* London: Verso.

Post, Robert. 1995. *Community, Management, and Democracy.* Cambridge: Harvard University Press.

Posner, Richard. 1985. An Economic Theory of the Criminal Law. *Columbia Law Review* 85:1193–1257.

Procaci, Giovana. 1998. Poor Citizens: Social Citizenship and the Crisis of the Welfare States. In *Displacement of Social Policy,* ed. S. Hanninen. Jyvaskyla, Finland: University of Jyvaskyla.

Putnam, Robert D. 1993. *Making Democracy Work.* Princeton, N.J.: Princeton University Press.

Radzinowicz, Sir Leon. 1991. Penal Regressions. *Cambridge Law Journal* 50:422–44.

Rajchman, John, ed. 1995. *The Identity Question.* New York: Routledge.

Rock, Paul. 1990. *Helping Victims of Crime: The Home Office and the Rise of Victim Support in England and Wales.* New York: Oxford University Press.

Rose, Nikolas. 1996. Governing "Advanced" Liberal Democracies. In Barry, Osborne, and Rose 1996, 37–64.

———. 1999. *The Powers of Freedom.* Cambridge, U.K: Cambridge University Press.

Rose, Nikolas, and Peter Miller. 1992. Political Power Beyond the State: Problematics of Government. *British Journal of Sociology* 43:172–205.

Rothman, David J. 1971. *The Discovery of the Asylum: Social Order and Disorder in the New Republic.* Toronto: Little Brown.

————. 1980. *Conscience and Convenience: The Asylum and Its Alternatives in Progressive America*. Boston: Little, Brown.

Salvatore, Ricardo D., and Carlos Aguirre. 1996. The Birth of the Penitentiary in Latin America: Toward an Interpretive Social History of Prisons. In *The Birth of the Penitentiary in Latin America: Essays on Criminology, Prison Reform, and Social Control, 1830–1940*, ed. Ricardo D. Salvatore and Carlos Aguirre, 1–43. Austin: University of Texas Press.

Sampson, Robert J., and William Julius Wilson. 1995. Toward a Theory of Race, Crime, and Urban Inequality. In *Crime and Inequality*, ed. John Hagan and Ruth D. Peterson. Stanford, Calif.: Stanford University Press.

Scheingold, Stuart. 1991. *The Politics of Street Crime: Criminal Process and Cultural Obsession*. Philadelphia: Temple University Press.

Schiraldi, Vincent. 1994. *The Undue Influence of California's Prison Guard's Union: California's Correctional-Industrial Complex*. San Francisco: Center on Juvenile and Criminal Justice.

Schlosser, Eric. 1998. The Prison-Industrial Complex. *Atlantic Monthly*, December, 51–77.

Schrag, Peter. 1998. *Paradise Lost: California's Experience, America's Future*. New York: New Press.

Shapiro, Bruce. 1997. Victims and Vengeance: Why the Victims' Rights Amendment Is a Bad idea. *The Nation*, 10 February, p. 13.

Shearing, Clifford. 1996. Public and Private Policing. In *Themes in Contemporary Policing*, ed. William Saulsbury, Joy Mott, and Time Newburn. Plymouth, U.K.: Latimer Trend & Co., Ltd.

Silberman, Mathew. 1995. *A World of Violence: Corrections in America*. Belmont, Calif.: Wadsworth.

Simon, Jonathan. 1993. *Poor Discipline: Parole and the Social Control of the Urban Underclass, 1890–1990*. Chicago: University of Chicago Press.

————.1997. Governing through Crime, in Lawrence Friedman and George Fisher, eds. *The Crime Conundrum: Essays on Criminal Justice*. Boulder: Westview.

————. 1999a. From a Tight Place: Crime, Punishment, and American Liberalism. *Yale Law and Policy Review* 17: 853–76.

————. 1999b. Law after Society. *Law and Social Inquiry* 24:143–94.

————. 1999c. On Their Own: Delinquency without Society. *University of Kansas Law Review* 47:1001–19.

————. 2000. From the Big-House to the Warehouse: Rethinking Prisons and State Government in the 20th Century. *Punishment and Society* 3:213–33.

Simon, Jonathan, and Christina Spaulding. 1999. Tokens of Our Esteem: Aggravating Factors in the Era of Deregulated Death Penalties. In *The Killing State: Capital Punishment in Law, Politics, and Culture*, ed. Austin Sarat, 81–114. New York: Oxford University Press.

Skogan, Wesley G. 1990. *Disorder and Decline: Crime and the Spiral of Decay in American Neighborhoods*. New York: Free Press.

Small, Jane A. 1999. Who Are the People in Your Neighborhood? Due Process, Public Protection, and Sex Offender Notification Laws. *New York University Law Review* 74:1451–93.

Stern, Vivian. 1998. *A Sin Against the Future: Imprisonment in the World*. Boston: Northeastern University.

Stinchcombe, Arthur. 1980. *Crime and Punishment: Changing Attitudes in America*. San Francisco: Josey-Bass.

1150 LAW AND SOCIAL INQUIRY

Tonry, Michael. 1995. *Malign Neglect—Race, Crime, and Punishment in America.* New York: Oxford University Press.

Thompson, E. P. 1975. *Whigs and Hunters: The Origin of the Black Act.* New York: Pantheon.

Tyler, Tom. 1997. *Social Justice in a Diverse Society.* Boulder, Colo.: Westview.

Wacquant, Loïc. 1999. *Les Prisons de la Misere.* Paris. Raison D'Agir Editions.

———. Forthcoming. The Prison as Ghetto. *Punishment and Society.*

Wattenburg, Ben J. 1986. *Values Matter Most: How Republicans or Democrats or a Third Party Can Win and Renew the American Way of Life.* New York: Free Press.

Wiebe, Robert H. 1985. *The Opening of American Society.* New York: Vintage Books.

Wilson. James Q. 1983. *Thinking About Crime.* 2d. ed. New York: Basic Books.

———. 1996. Interview with James Q. Wilson. *Criminal Justice Matters* 25:1–3.

Wilson, James Q., and George C. Kelling. 1982. Broken Windows: The Police and Neighborhood Safety. *Atlantic Monthly,* March, p. 29.

Wilson, William J. 1996. *When Work Disappears: The World of the New Urban Poor.* New York: Knopf.

Woodward, C. Vann. 1966. *Reunion and Reaction, the Compromise of 1877, and the End of Reconstruction.* Boston: Little Brown.

Young, Jock. 1999. Cannibalism and Bulemia *Punishment and Society* 3:387–408.

Zimring, Franklin, and Gordon Hawkins. 1995. Incapacitation: *Penal Confinement and the Restraint of Crime.* New York: Oxford University Press.

[20]

The Politics of Crime and Punishment

by William Lyons and Stuart Scheingold

The underlying thesis of this paper is that crime control policy is politically constructed. In developing our thesis and its implications, we depart from much of the conventional wisdom in three basic ways. First, in demonstrating the political derivations of crime control policy we reveal how, why, and to what extent criminological knowledge is marginalized in the policymaking process. Second, this paper takes issue with what is largely taken for granted by criminologists, criminal process professionals, and the general public as well: the pervasive attractions of a punitive discourse and punitive approaches to crime control. Finally, our exploration of the politics driving crime control policy reveals more complexity, contingency, and variation within the political process than most observers attribute to the politics of crime and punishment.

Many claim that the widespread drop in crime is directly and causally linked to zero-tolerance policing, to extraordinarily high rates of incarceration, to the increasing length of sentences, to harsh conditions of imprisonment, and to the return of capital punishment. Even if these claims are in part true, our counterclaim is that these putative benefits must be weighed against the oppressive costs of overwhelmingly punitive policies. Punitive policies are destructive in a number of ways that will be discussed in this paper—but principally in that

William Lyons is an Assistant Professor in the Department of Political Science at the University of Akron in Ohio. Stuart Scheingold is a Professor in the Political Science Department at the University of Washington in Seattle.

they have exacerbated racial cleavage and, in effect, are shattering communities in order to save them. We argue that regardless of whether or not punishment "works"—itself a contested proposition—it diverts attention, energy, and resources from strategic responses that recognize and respond to the complexity of the crime problem as it is revealed by social inquiry in general and criminological knowledge in particular.

104

THE NATURE OF CRIME: CONTINUITY AND CHANGE

The underlying thesis of this paper is that crime control policy is *politically constituted*: policy choices are driven by, and responsive to, prevailing values and interests rather than criminological knowledge. In developing our thesis and its implications, we depart from much of the conventional wisdom in three basic ways. First, in demonstrating that crime control policy is politically constituted we reveal how, why, and to what extent criminological findings are disregarded in the policymaking process. Second, this paper challenges what is largely taken for granted by criminologists, criminal process professionals, and the general public as well: the pervasive attractions of a punitive discourse and of punitive crime control policies. Finally, our exploration of the politics driving crime control policy reveals more complexity, contingency, and variation within the political process than most observers attribute to the politics of crime and punishment.

Many claim the widespread drop in crime is directly and causally linked to punitive policies—to zero-tolerance policing, to extraordinarily high rates of incarceration, to the increasing length of sentences, to harsh conditions of imprisonment, and to the return of capital punishment. To question, as we do, the advisability of a predominantly punitive policy agenda is not to claim that getting tough with criminals is inappropriate or ineffective. Instead, our objectives are to make the case for a more balanced policy agenda and to explore both the obstacles that stand in the way of balance and the opportunities for it.

Even if the most sweeping claims made on behalf of punitive approaches to crime control are valid, our counterclaim is that these putative benefits must be weighed against the destructive costs of overwhelmingly punitive policies. Punitive policies are destructive in a number of ways that will be discussed in this paper—but principally in that they have exacerbated racial cleavages and contributed to the decomposition of inner-city communities. The manifest costs of the punitive status quo include harming local communities, the broader American polity, and American justice. Less obvious, but equally as telling, are the opportunity costs that are incurred by a fixation on punishment.

For these reasons, we argue at the end of this paper for an approach to crime control that strikes a better balance between punishment and prevention on one hand and that deals with causes as well as symptoms on the other hand. Movement in that direction will be possible only if we understand why punishment has tended to crowd out alternative responses to crime. Perhaps the most telling finding that emerges from our inquiry is that the linkage between crime and the politics of crime and punishment is tenuous and contingent.[1] Research reveals that whether or not punishment works in strictly criminological terms—

> *Recent experience with the war on drugs, determinate sentencing, three strikes laws, and aggressive order maintenance policing all weaken the persuasiveness of the view that too little punishment is a threat to the social order while the costs of too much punishment are borne only by criminals.*

whether or not punishment reduces crime—it serves a mix of other instrumental and expressive purposes. Exploring the configuration of the political, economic, social, and cultural forces that privilege punishment reveals that support for these "other purposes" varies among the relevant constituencies: local, State, and national political leaders; criminal process professionals; and various elements within the general public.

Thus, although the Nation has not stumbled into the punitive mode by accident—but rather in response to a complex convergence of values and interests—the arena in which the politics of crime and punishment play out is neither immutable nor uniform, and the punitive status quo is neither inevitable nor irretrievable. Historically, more enlightened policies have certainly been deployed and even today there are signs of more progressive penology—especially at the local level. If we can clarify the circumstances that sustain alternatives to punishment, the chances for reform will be enhanced—albeit hardly assured.

Punishment, Criminology, and Crime Control

Stated simply, prevailing justifications hold that imprisonment rates rise because crime rates rise and that rising prison rates will mean lower crime rates (Wilson 1985, 1991). This view contains two discrete, but not necessarily congruent, propositions—one political and the other criminological. The criminological claim is that punishment will actually reduce crime, whereas the political claim is that the punitive crime control policies are first and foremost a response to rising crime rates. Our reading of the available data raises serious questions about both of these generalizations and about the way they tend to be inextricably linked in so much of the public discourse about crime.

We will review the relevant data and decouple the criminological case for punishment from the largely separate question of why this polity has so enthusiastically embraced punitive policies. In sum, our criminological arguments, presented in this section of the paper, are that the crime control case for punishment is built on emphatically disputed terrain and should be balanced

THE NATURE OF CRIME: CONTINUITY AND CHANGE

against the heavy collateral damage that has been inflicted by a predominantly punitive approach to crime control. In the next section, we will turn more directly to the politics of punishment and argue that the choice to punish is driven by an extensive array of political, social, economic, and cultural forces that transcend, and are arguably unrelated to, the crime rate and criminal victimization.

The purpose of our review of the criminological findings in this section of the paper is, we repeat, *not* to claim that they conclusively demonstrate that punishment is ineffective or counterproductive. As we read these data, they do, however, cast grave doubt on what, in our judgment, amounts to an excessive reliance on punishment in recent years.

Many years ago, James Q. Wilson gave partial voice to a widely shared view that it is probably better to err on the side of too much, rather than too little, punishment: "If we try to make the penalties for crime swifter and more certain, and it should turn out that deterrence does not work, then all we have done is increase the risks facing persons who commit a crime" (1985, 144).

We strongly disagree. To err in the direction of too much punishment is to incur serious costs that extend beyond the burdens imposed on "persons who commit a crime." Recent experience with the war on drugs, determinate sentencing, three strikes laws, and aggressive order maintenance policing all weaken the persuasiveness of the view that too little punishment is a threat to the social order while the costs of too much punishment are borne only by criminals.[2] It is to the broader costs of punishment that we now turn.

Punishment as contested criminological terrain

The criminological community is, with some exceptions (Currie 1998),[3] increasingly willing to acknowledge a substantial, even a dramatic, reduction in violent crime throughout the course of the 1990s. LaFree, for example, presents data that reveal marked decreases in both violent crimes and property crimes during the current decade (1998, 19–25). There is also general agreement that insofar as punishment has contributed to a reduction in crime, that contribution has come through deterrence and/or incapacitation. Punishment is said to deter crime by increasing its costs and, in this way, reducing the temptation to break the law. Clearly the success of deterrence is dependent, as is widely acknowledged, on offenders and would-be offenders making rational cost-benefit calculations before deciding to commit a crime. Incapacitation, it might be said, picks up where deterrence stops: For the nonrational and incorrigible, incarceration is the only way to prevent them from committing crimes. It is probably also fair to say that criminologists would agree that the fear of punishment does deter some people from committing crimes and that incarceration does prevent some crimes from being committed.

This criminological consensus tends to break down, however, over what relationship, if any, there is between the punitive trajectory of crime control policies and the dramatic decrease in crime in the 1990s. James Q. Wilson, one of the leading proponents of punishment, recently claimed in the *New York Times* that "putting people in prison has been the single most important thing we've done to reduce crime" (Egan 1999). When Wilson published the first edition of *Thinking About Crime*, he saw deterrence as the primary mechanism through which punishment reduced crime. He stressed that deterrence was not dependent on the severity of the sanction, but rather on its certainty—and could indeed include both carrots and sticks (Wilson 1977, 194–204). In the revised edition of *Thinking About Crime*, published almost a decade later, Wilson incorporated incapacitation into his crime control policy agenda and made a strong case for the multiplier effect of incarcerating those likely to commit multiple offenses (Wilson 1985, 145–46). Because incapacitation is premised on keeping repeat offenders off of the streets for as long as possible, severity becomes the key to success—albeit as imposed solely on those who are, or are predicted to be, multiple offenders.

Although Wilson may well be the most prominent figure in the criminological debate, other leading criminologists challenged his claims. They question both the effectiveness of deterrence and incapacitation as tools of crime control and, more generally, the companion claim that incarceration explains the reductions in crime that have been recorded during the 1990s.

Michael Tonry traces the case *against* deterrence to the 1960s and 1970s. The 1967 President's Commission on Law Enforcement and Administration of Justice, he tells us, failed to support deterrence, and the 1978 National Academy of Sciences Panel on Research on Deterrent and Incapacitative Effects concluded that they could not "assert that the evidence warrants an affirmative conclusion regarding deterrence" (Tonry 1995, 19). Additionally, Tonry stated:

> [I]n 1993, after the most exhaustive and ambitious analysis of the subject ever undertaken, the National Academy of Sciences Panel on the Understanding and Control of Violent Behavior concluded that greatly increased use of imprisonment has had little effect on violent crime rates. . . . The clear weight of the evidence in every Western country indicates that tough penalties have little effect on crime rates. (1995, 19)[4]

108

THE NATURE OF CRIME: CONTINUITY AND CHANGE

Consider also Jeffrey Fagan's study of recidivism among 6,800 individuals arrested on drug charges in New York City from 1983 to 1986. He found that "neither the prevalence nor the rates of recidivism were associated with sanction severity" (1994, 188). Instead, he argued that to the extent that there is a deterrent effect, it would vary with the labor market generally. His bottom-line finding is that "the marginal reduction in rearrest rates for those imprisoned, compared to probationers or those not sanctioned at all, suggests little utility in the widespread use of incarceration as a crime control measure for drug offenders" (1994, 205) (see exhibit 1).[5]

Zimring and Hawkins' research in California leads them to be equally skeptical about the impact of incapacitation—particularly its effect on the *violent* crimes of homicide, assault, and robbery (1995, 126). Zimring and Hawkins also make a technical point that is particularly relevant to this era of escalating sentences. They explain that, assuming initial predictions about which offenders are likely

Exhibit 1. Percentage of those rearrested for five offense types by sanction severity (1 or more years at risk)

Sanction	Rearrest offense type				
	Drug sale	Drug possession	Felony violence	Felony property	All offenses
Incarceration>1 year (N=156)	14.1	15.4	10.3	9.0	41.0
Incarceration<1 year (N=1,389)	18.4	26.3	12.4	22.3	56.0
Probation (N=551)	15.6	14.0	6.4	9.6	39.0
Fine continuation (N=2,293)	18.8	30.3	10.0	16.4	52.2
Dismissed/discharged (N=418)	23.4	23.4	9.8	17.0	49.5
Statistics					
X^2	13.47	46.26	16.53	56.76	91.32
P	.097	.000	.035	.000	.000
Gamma	.069	-.0002	-.059	-.047	-.006

Source: Fagan 1994, 202.

to commit multiple crimes are correct, the more or less indiscriminate incarceration of more and more offenders will be subject to the law of diminishing marginal utility (p. 50).[6] It follows, as Currie argues, that at some point increasing incarceration will do more harm then good. "Our failure to match the increasing rates of imprisonment with corresponding increases in programs to reintegrate offenders into productive lives means that we are steadily producing ever-larger armies of ex-offenders whose chances of success in the legitimate world have been diminished by their prison experience. . . ." (1998, 30). Nor can incapacitation prevent the nearly immediate replacement of incarcerated drug dealers by other dealers on the street.[7]

It might seem, at least at first glance, that national data belie these arguments against punishment. After all, the prison population in the United States doubled from 1982 to 1992, while the Bureau of Justice Statistics reported that in 1992 victimization continued a decade-long decline and personal crime dropped 26 percent from 1973 to 1990. Savelsberg (1994, 919–920), however, claims that this linkage is more apparent than real:

> [W]hile increasing punishment in combination with stabilizing crime rates could be perceived as a rational deterrence response, such an interpretation prompts considerable doubt. First, the steepest and steadiest increase in incarceration rates began in 1980, when the crime rate had already been leveling out during the preceding four years. Second, the incarceration rate increased by more than 50 inmates per 100,000 population between 1980 and 1984 without resulting in any change in the crime rate. In the following years (1984–1989) the incarceration rate grew by an additional 50 again without achieving any change in crime rates. Since 1989 the increase in incarceration rate has again been 50, as in the two preceding five-year periods, without changing the trend in crime rates but at considerable expense in times of a sluggish economy, declining budgets, and an eroding public infrastructure.

Thus there are many reasons to be dubious about the privileging of punishment in U.S. crime control policy.

Of late, even longtime conservative supporters of punishment as crime control seem to be reconsidering their position (see Davey 1998, 107). Tonry (1995, 119) tells us that Wilson himself seems to be persuaded that, at least with respect to drugs, we have reached the point of diminishing returns:

> After surveying research and experience through 1990, James Q. Wilson, for two decades the country's leading conservative scholar of crime control policy and research, concluded that "significant reductions in drug use will come only from reducing demand for those drugs . . . the marginal product

110

of further investment in supply reduction is likely to be small." He reports "that I know of no serious law-enforcement official who disagrees with this conclusion. Typically, police officials tell interviewers that they are fighting a losing war or, at best, a holding action."

According to an article in the *New York Times*, national drug czar Gen. Barry McCaffrey has come to much the same conclusion—namely that "we can't incarcerate our way out of the problem" and that drug treatment programs would be more effective and would save a great deal of money (Egan 1999). Note similarly that Margaret Thatcher's conservative government, in a 1990 white paper, concluded that although deterrence was "a principle with much immediate appeal," it was "unrealistic" to assume criminals were rational calculators when the evidence showed that crime was more impulsive. Canada, under the conservative government of Brian Mulroney, in a 1993 report proposed moving away from deterrence and toward prevention (Tonry 1995, 19).

Although there are, in sum, good reasons to be dubious about the effect of punishment on crime, our core claim is that, whether or not punishment actually works as an instrument of crime control, the Nation pays a heavy price for privileging punitive crime control policies. It is to these costs that we now turn.[8]

The costs of punishment

To fully appreciate the costs of punitive policies, it is necessary to factor in some aspects of the prevailing policy matrix that are not, strictly speaking, punitive. Feeley and Simon (1992) call attention to a "new penology" with an extensive impact on politics and culture in the United States. As they see it, the key is not just that sentences are getting longer and punishment practices are becoming harsher and more unforgiving; more insidiously, the United States is confronting crime by an array of public-sector and private-sector *risk reduction* policies. This approach, which Diana Gordon (1994) has dubbed "the return of the dangerous classes" and Mike Davis (1990) has portrayed in his exposé of "fortress LA," puts the emphasis on managing crime by using risk profiles to insulate the law-abiding from the lawbreakers.

This new penology thus fuels, and is fueled by, suspicion and stereotyping that are turning Americans against one another. Among the relevant policies is target hardening, which ranges from putting identification numbers on personal property and creating neighborhood watch groups through using a bewildering variety of home, office, automobile, and personal security devices to building gated communities that literally wall off portions of society from one another. There are also more proactive versions of the new penology. These include offender profiling by street cops, highway patrolmen, and officials monitoring airports or border crossings. Then there are the street cameras, zero-tolerance policing, and the ever-more pervasive presence of metal detectors.

The impact of these policies, while falling most heavily on the marginalized, is diffuse and indiscriminate—altering the nature of society for everyone (Cohen 1985; Feeley and Simon 1992). The energy and resources of the new penology are introduced preemptively and premised on a sense of imminent danger from a criminal element beyond redemption and rehabilitation. Further, the state enlists the citizenry to participate actively in law enforcement (neighborhood watch) and in risk reduction (home security) and to accept without question intrusive interference (e.g., metal detectors) with everyday activities.

Retreat from criminal justice and the rule of law

Elements of this new penology are clearly at odds with the core values embodied in American justice. Gordon (1990, 16–35) notes the weakening of *Miranda* protections and the exclusionary rule, the expanding use of preventive detention, and the enormous increases in spending on criminal justice hastened by the punitive response to crack cocaine. For Gordon, these protections define our longstanding commitment to limited government, a commitment that is quietly eroding in the face of an expanding and interventionist "justice juggernaut." These trends ought to concern us, she says:

> [B]ecause the procedural protections of criminal law are emblematic of this society's commitment to limits in the state's authority over the citizen. . . . The rights of defendants are also the rights of students, employees, tenants, and everyone else who is ever in a position to be coerced by the exercise of government power over individuals. (p. 35)

It might be argued that Gordon and those who share her views of current developments are simply disappointed liberals complaining about the conservative shift in law enforcement—but there is more to the story than that.

Such developments seriously erode the common ground of criminal *justice* in the United States—common ground that, as Herbert Packer wrote many years ago, has united "due process" liberals and "crime control" conservatives. At the heart of this common ground are ex post facto restrictions requiring that law enforcement and the criminal process begin with a clear delineation of the conduct proscribed as criminal. In other words, "the criminal process ordinarily ought to be invoked by those charged with the responsibility for doing so, only when it appears that a crime has been committed and when there is a reasonable prospect of apprehending and convicting its perpetrator" (Packer 1968, 155).[9] All of this is put at risk by a new penology that anticipates criminal activity, acts on the probability that it is forthcoming, and targets *groups* of people. Although the state is implicated in, and influenced by, these repressive developments, these developments also play out at other sites of social control—the family, the workplace, and the community (Cohen 1985; Gilliom 1996; Garland 1996).

Weakening of inner-city families and communities

Christopher Stone of the Vera Institute noted that prisons are "factories for crime" (as cited in Schlosser 1998); increases in gang violence in our cities can be linked to the networking, recruiting, and leadership opportunities provided to gangs by incarceration. Blumstein, as we noted earlier, makes the same point in calling attention to the postrelease downside of incapacitation (1998, 133). But Stone's argument goes beyond the specifically criminogenic drawbacks of extensive incarceration. "[T]he culture of the prisons, he claims, is rapidly becoming the culture of the streets" (as cited in Schlosser 1998, 77). Michael Tonry (1995, 6–7) puts this broader point as follows:

> Particularly since 1980, the effects of crime control policies have been a major contributor to declining levels of lawful employment by young black males. The extraordinary levels of black male involvement with the justice system . . . are a serious impediment to the achievement of welfare policy goals. . . . No solution to the problems of the urban underclass . . . can succeed if young men are not part of it. The crime problem is no longer simply a criminal justice concern. Unless America can devise ways to make its crime control policies less destructive of poor black males and poor black communities, there can be no solution to the problems of the black underclass.

In addition to the social and fiscal burdens of a largely punitive and risk-aversive crime control regime, these policies and practices also have had a corrupting, albeit difficult to measure, impact on how we think about the nature of crime and crime control, and on political discourse more generally. The result is to impoverish public debate not only over crime and crime control but over the nature and condition of the social contract.

Meares and Kahan make a similar point about the impact of proactive policing that focuses on "the incarceration of geographically concentrated, low-level dealers inevitably lead[ing] to family disruption, unemployment, and low economic status—all of which create social *dis*organization" (1998, 813; italics in original). The underlying point is that there is a mutually reinforcing relationship between the incarceration of so large a proportion of African-American

113

males, the declining formal and informal control in communities, and the rise
of "no-go" areas that has been noted in the inner city (Dahrendorf 1985).

Contemporary prison construction and sentencing reform reveal a parallel problem of the *opportunity* costs of punitive policies. "Today the United States has
approximately 1.8 million people behind bars . . . more people than any other
country in the world" at a cost of approximately $35 billion a year (Schlosser
1998, 53–54). This reflects a choice to invest in a redistribution of resources
not only from other segments of the criminal justice system but also from
inner-city schools to rural prisons (Schlosser 1998). Beckett (1997, 106) stated:

> Between 1976 and 1989, the percentage of state budgets allocated to edu-
> cation and welfare programs declined dramatically—the former by 12%
> and the latter by 41%. Across the states, the average monthly welfare bene-
> fit shrank from $714 to $394 (in 1995 dollars) between 1979 and 1993. . . .
> Meanwhile, state and federal "correctional" expenditures grew by 95%
> and 114% (respectively) between 1976 and 1989 and continue to increase
> dramatically.

The budgetary impacts of these investment decisions were also apparent at the
Federal level as a result of the Reagan administration's war on drugs. From 1981
to 1991, Federal Bureau of Investigation antidrug funding increased from $8
million to $181 million, Drug Enforcement Administration funding increased
from $86 million to $1,026 million, and Department of Defense antidrug funding grew from $33 million to $1,042 million (Beckett 1997, 123, note 36). At
the same time, funding for the National Institute on Drug Abuse was cut from
$274 million to $57 million (1981–84) and Department of Education antidrug
funding dropped from only $14 million to a mere $3 million (Beckett 1997, 53).

Deterioration of political discourse

In addition to the social and fiscal burdens of a largely punitive and risk-aversive
crime control regime, these policies and practices also have had a corrupting,
albeit difficult to measure, impact on how we think about the nature of crime
and crime control, and on political discourse more generally. The result is to
impoverish public debate not only over crime and crime control but over the
nature and condition of the social contract.

Thus, current patterns for investing public dollars seem to reflect what Tonry
(1995) tellingly refers to as "malign neglect": political indifference and/or obliv-
iousness to the decimation of a generation and to the centrifugal forces that are
dividing the Nation against itself. Similarly, Sampson and Bartusch (1998) argue
that our current law enforcement practices are part of a broader range of social
policies that add to the disproportionate burdens borne by those who live in

neighborhoods of concentrated disadvantage. As they see it, escalating imprisonment rates, more intensive surveillance, less available health care, deteriorating
inner-city schools, and more aggressive police practices all add to the ordeal of
families and communities already most victimized by crime.

Currie (1998, 6) calls attention to the failure of political leaders to address
these broader issues and, in so doing, to settle for, and contribute to, an impoverished political discourse:

> Neither presidential candidate in 1996 spoke to the issues raised by the
> mushrooming of America's prisons or offered an articulate response to the
> crisis of violence among American youth. Instead, the candidates reached
> for the most symbolic and least consequential issues: both Clinton and Dole,
> for example, supported the extension of the death penalty, along with a vague
> call for "victims' rights," boot camps, and school uniforms. . . . The political
> debate, such as it is, has become increasingly primitive and detached from
> what we know about the roots of crime and the uses and limits of punishment.

In other words, candidates tend to ignore crime prevention and job creation
while their fixation with punishment leaves people confused and "continually
bombarded with the myths, misconceptions, and half-truths that dominate
public discussion, while the real story is often buried in a specialized technical
literature" (Currie 1998, 6–7) or obscured by circumlocutions central to law
enforcement (Klockars 1988).

The history of crack is one example of how disinformation impoverishes public
debate and has a destructive impact on those communities most victimized by
crime. According to a *New York Times* article, crack struck fear in American
society, but crack use fell long before harsh penalties were imposed, leaving a
legacy of continued drug use, harsh penalties, crowded prisons, aggressive
policing of minor disorders, and diminished respect for fairness in the criminal
justice system. "Crack prompted the nation to rewrite its drug laws, lock up a
record number of people and shift money from schools to prisons. It transformed police work, hospitals, parental rights, and courts. Crack also changed
the racial makeup of American prisons. . . . But the harsh laws responding to
crack have not reduced overall drug use" (Egan 1999).

Taken together, the costs of our punitive and preemptive campaign against
crime are socially and politically disabling. Even if the crime control case for
these policies was stronger than we believe it to be, this would be dubious
public policy at best. How then is the dogged adherence to a punitive policy
agenda to be explained? For us, as the title of this article clearly suggests, the
explanation is political.

The Political Construction of Crime and Punishment

A substantial, and in our view convincing, body of data indicates that the politics of crime and punishment are a classic instance of what Murray Edelman (1977) refers to as "words that succeed and policies that fail." Winning and holding public office, not crime control, are driving the policymaking process. And in politics, as Katherine Beckett (1997) has put it, "crime pays"—at least insofar as it becomes the occasion for a punitive political discourse and for punitive policy initiatives (Scheingold 1984, 71).

But why, how, and for whom do punitively inflected politics of crime and punishment pay? Just what are the political calculations that lead toward punitive policies? Our answer to these questions diverges sharply from the views of both the liberal and conservative mainstream. According to the mainstream commentators, the politics of crime and punishment are, for better (the conservative position: Wilson 1985) or worse (the liberal position: Windlesham 1998), driven *from below* by aroused citizens. In contrast, nonmainstream critics are inclined to attribute the politics of crime and punishment to the more or less conscious efforts of powerful elites to preserve the prevailing hegemony (Quinney 1980 and Hall et al. 1978).

To our way of thinking, these narratives at best tell only part of the story and at worst lead us astray in significant ways. Our reading of the data indicates that punitive policies are driven from above as well as from below. The *top-down* explanations are much closer to the mark and, at the very least, provide insightful correctives to the *bottom-up* mainstream narratives. Political leaders are not, however, free agents in this process. And although there is a punitive impulse from below, it is neither as insistent nor as decisive as the conventional wisdom suggests. Finally, the available data fail to establish a reliable association between crime, fear of crime, or criminal victimization and either punitive initiatives from above or punitive impulses from below. Instead, the politics of punishment draw sustenance from other more fundamental problems—many of which might reasonably be seen as root causes of crime.

All of this will be explored in more detail. For the time being, suffice it to say that our analysis leads to a more complex, multilayered, and interactive vision of the politics of crime and punishment than emerges from either the top-down or the bottom-up accounts. We also want to underscore the centrality of empirical evidence in our account and, thus, the sharp contrast between it and the impressionistic narratives dominating so much of public and criminological discourse on these political issues. As one of us has written elsewhere, "criminologists tend to think of the political side of things, when they think of it at

116

all, as both too simple and too elusive to warrant their attention" (Scheingold 1998, 860). Take, for example, the undocumented assertion of the otherwise scrupulously precise criminologist Alfred Blumstein:

> *It is clear* that in the current era, where the political expediency of indulging the public's intense concern about crime is sufficiently attractive and the political risk of failing to do so and being labeled "soft on crime" is sufficiently frightening—the role of research findings in the public policy arena does seem largely to have been put aside, though only temporarily one would hope. (1997, 359; italics added)

We are, of course, in complete agreement with Blumstein concerning the wide gap between criminological knowledge and crime control policy. But we take issue with Blumstein attributing punitive policies to "the public's intense concern about crime." We are not alone in calling attention to the constitutive contribution of politics to crime control policy, and the work of these political criminologists figures prominently in the analysis that follows.

Decoupling the politics of punishment from crime

Over the years, the substantial body of data generated in the United States has failed to establish the associations that might reasonably be expected between crime rates, on one hand, and fear of crime, punitive public attitudes, and incarceration rates on the other (Scheingold 1984, 38–49). Similarly, Tonry reprinted a U.S. Department of Justice table that indicates a lack of association between crime and incarceration rates (see exhibit 2).

Christie has found the same disassociation between incarceration and crime rates in a variety of countries in Eastern and Western Europe as well as in the United States—including, for example, Norway, Finland, and the Netherlands (1994, 22–33).

Beckett (1997, 28–44) and Savelsberg (forthcoming) interpret this disconnection between crime rates and a variety of political variables as an indication that public concern about crime follows rather than precedes punitive political initiatives like the war on drugs (see exhibits 3 and 4). According to this way of looking at things, crime control policy cannot properly be thought of as democracy at work. Political leaders simply do not seem to be responding to a frightened, victimized, and punitive public (Scheingold 1984, 49–54).

It seems much closer to the mark to think of punitive policies as starting at the top, so to speak, and being driven by the electoral needs of political leaders—rather than by either the crime rate or by public clamor. This is not to say that

Exhibit 2. Crime and incarceration rates, State and Federal prisons, 1960–90 (per 100,000 population)

	All crimes	Violent crimes	Incarceration
1960	1,887	161	117
1965	2,449	200	108
% change 1960–65	+30	+24	–8
1970	3,985	364	96
% change 1965–70	+63	+82	–11
1975	5,282	482	111
% change 1970–75	+33	+32	+16
1980	5,950	597	138
% change 1975–80	+13	+24	+24
1985	5,206	556	200
% change 1980–85	–13	–7	+45
1990	5,820	732	292
% change 1985–90	+12	+32	+46

Note: From William P. Barr, 1992, *The Case for More Incarceration*, Washington, D.C.: U.S. Department of Justice, Office of Policy Development, table 2; U.S. Department of Justice, Federal Bureau of Investigation, Uniform Crime Reports, various years; U.S. Department of Justice, Bureau of Justice Statistics, *Prisoners in America*, various years. Data presented in boldface not provided in *The Case for More Incarceration*.

Source: Tonry 1995, 23.

punitive policies are simply imposed on an acquiescent and disinterested public. Instead, the politics of crime and punishment emerge out of complex and reciprocal interactions mediated by a variety of values and institutions—most prominently via the media (Scheingold 1991, 172–192).

Consider, for example, the Savelsberg finding of, and explanation for, much higher incarceration rates in the United States than in Germany. He notes that "[n]either the German nor the American patterns are directly associated with changing crime rates" (Savelsberg 1994, 916). Whatever the linkage between crime rates and incarceration, Savelsberg argues that it must be seen as "mediated in complex ways by many factors" (p. 920), including the institutions and practices a nation-state selects for its criminal justice systems and the cultural resonance of punitive crime control messages. We will return to these intricate interactions shortly, but first we want to present further evidence of the disjunction between crime rates and the politics of punishment.

Consider the *negative* correlation between crime rates and imprisonment discovered by Davey (1998) in his bivariate correlations for all 50 States for the period

THE NATURE OF CRIME: CONTINUITY AND CHANGE

Exhibit 3. Correlation of the crime rate, media coverage, and political initiative with public concern about crime, 1964–74

Explanatory variables	Column 1 lag=0 3–5 months	Column 2 lag=1 6–10 months	Column 3 lag=2 9–15 months
Crime rate	–.0077 (.011)	–.0067 (.013)	–.005 (.022)
Media initiative	1.2504* (.5547)	1.3103** (.497)	1.2107* (.5372)
Political initiative	1.3711** (.3509)	1.3511** (.3364)	1.2721** (.3409)
Adjusted R^2	.5649	.5866	.5712

* $p<.05$
** $p<.01$
Source: Beckett 1997, 21.

1972–1992. He also ran a multiple regression analysis including socioeconomic, racial, and demographic variables and found that neither crime rates nor these other variables accounted for all of the variance in imprisonment rates. Finally, Davey selected six matched pairs of adjacent States, where one State had among the eight highest increases and the other among the eight lowest increases in imprisonment. Neither crime rates nor socioeconomic factors entirely accounted for the dramatic differences in imprisonment across these otherwise similar States.

The differences arose, Davey suggested, from gubernatorial values. States led by law-and-order governors experienced sharp increases in imprisonment rates. Adjacent States with more moderate governors avoided an incarceration explosion. For example:

■ From 1989 to 1993, Judd Gregg served as Governor of New Hampshire. In that period, the State's prison population increased from 103 to 157 per 100,000, while the crime rate fell 12 percent. Governor Gregg used deep cuts in State support for education to finance the increases in the imprisonment costs. He revised sentencing laws to keep young offenders in prison longer for more minor offenses and encouraged judges to get tough on crime. In addition, he expanded funding for drug enforcement while "New

119

Exhibit 4. Political initiatives and public concern about crime and drugs

	Political initiatives (above date line) and public concern (below date line)				
Case 1	.25	.52	1.03	.31	
Crime (January 1968–	1/68 →	4/68 →	7/68 →	10/68 →	1/69
January 1969)	8%	10%	13%	15%	12%
Case 2	.37	.50	.77	.50	
Crime (May 1969–	5/69 →	1/70 →	5/70 →	10/70 →	2/71
January 1971)	8%	12%	12%	22%	9%
Case 3	.38	.53	1.4	.83	
Drugs (September	9/88 →	1/89 →	5/89 →	9/89 →	1/90
1988–December 1989)	15%	11%	27%	64%	33%
Case 4	.24	.42	1.01	.19	
Drugs (January 1986–	1/86 →	4/86 →	7/86 →	10/86 →	1/87
January 1987)	1%	3%	8%	11%	5%

Source: Beckett 1997, 14.

Hampshire prisons lacked the funds to provide any kind of drug and alcohol treatment" (Davey 1998, 52–53).

■ For the same period in Maine—a State with another Republican Governor, John McKernan, a similar socioeconomic profile, and crime rates that also fell 11 percent—the prison population did not change.

Davey explains that what distinguished the two States was that Gregg was a law-and-order governor while McKernan took the "direct opposite" position—supporting gun control, for example, even though it was "not popular in rural Maine" (p. 54–55). Davey concludes that crime and punishment become public obsessions through "the political exploitation of public confusion and the fear of crime" (p. 48).

Of course, Davey's conclusion begs the question of how and why States with similar cultures and demographics elect such differently situated governors.[10] Although we do not directly address this puzzle, our analysis moves in that direction. We combine *macroanalytic* and *microanalytic* accounts of the politics of crime and punishment. The macroanalytic accounts attribute punitively inflected policies to structural failings of the liberal state. The microanalytic

Exhibit 5. Trends in incarceration rates in the United States and the Federal Republic of Germany, 1961–92

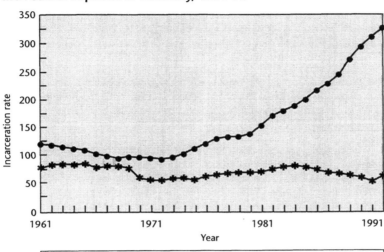

Note: For the United States, the incarceration rate is for prisoners sentenced to more than 1 year under the jurisdiction of State or Federal correctional authorities between 1961 and 1992 (see Cahalan 1986; U.S. Department of Justice 1990b, 1992a; figs. for 1992 are estimated). The incarceration rate (Gefangenenziffer) in Germany is based on Statistisches Bundesamt (1977, 1991; figs. for 1992 are estimated).

Source: Savelsberg 1994, 917.

accounts look directly at the policymaking processes at different levels of government. These accounts are not mutually exclusive; each makes meaningful contributions to our understanding of the politics of crime and punishment.

Punishment, governance, and the decline of the liberal state

Most broadly conceived, the punitive binge of recent years has been attributed to the inability of the liberal state to live up to its own ideals.[11] This broader vision is articulated in related but distinctive and not necessarily compatible ways in the works of Simon (1997, 1995), Garland (1996), Melossi (1993), and Christie (1994). For them, a postliberal state unable to maintain the economic and social conditions minimizing crime and maximizing the well-being of the society as a whole turns to punitive responses to crime. Incapable of building a

121

truly inclusive society and thus vulnerable to various kinds of disorder, the state turns to punishment, exclusion, and the "new penology" to maintain power and reinforce the prevailing hegemony. In the words of Jonathan Simon (1997), this amounts to "governance through crime." Although there is general agreement that the politics of crime and punishment are a direct reflection of the problems of the liberal state, the diagnoses diverge sharply.

Both Christie and Garland see the imposition of punitive crime control strategies as a more or less direct response to unacceptable levels of crime leading to, and resulting from, a transformation of consciousness. According to Christie (1994, 23–24):

> [We] are in a situation where the old defenses against committing unwanted acts are gone, while new technical forms of control have been created. God and neighbors have been replaced by the mechanical efficiency of modern forms of surveillance. We live in a concrete situation with crime as a mass-phenomenon. Here anger and anxieties [associated with crime] . . . become the driving force in the fight against *all* sorts of deplorable acts.

Garland (1996, 446) states:

> Despite the fact that crime has an uneven social distribution, and that high risk victimization is very much a pocketed, concentrated phenomenon, crime is widely experienced as a prominent fact of modern life. For most people, crime is no longer an aberration or an unexpected, abnormal event. Instead, the threat of crime has become a routine part of modern consciousness, an everyday risk. . . . My claim is that the normality of high crime rates in late modern society has prompted a series of transformations in official perceptions of crime, in criminological discourse, in modes of governmental action, and in the structure of criminal justice organizations.

In this scenario, elites deploy and play on the fear of crime to encourage acquiescence to the concentration of violence in the state. State violence can then be separated from the moral constraints constitutive of community life by encouraging the perception of "even minor transgressions of laws as crimes and their actors as criminals" (Christie 1994, 23–24).

Crime figures much less prominently in Melossi's analysis tracing punitive policies to the economic downturn of the 1970s:

> Abruptly, after 1973 the rate of growth in *real* weekly earnings dropped. From a 1973 peak of $327.45 in constant (1982–84) dollars, *real* weekly earnings slipped to $276.95 during the 1982 recession. In spite of the recovery and the long expansion of the 1980s they continued to fall to $264.76

THE NATURE OF CRIME: CONTINUITY AND CHANGE

in 1990. Thus seventeen years after . . . and in spite of the vaunted prosperity of the Reagan years, the real weekly income of the worker in 1990 was 19.1 percent *below* the level reached in 1973! (Peterson 1991, 30)

As working conditions became more onerous, Melossi argues, elites used the threat of punishment as a "social whip" to maintain discipline within an increasingly alienated workforce. At the same time, views about economic adversity shifted. Rather than acknowledging its structural sources, criminologists, politicians, and other opinionmakers directed attention to crime and criminals, and, in so doing, nurtured a "climate of social disciplining" (Melossi 1993, 266).[12] For Melossi, this reframing is better understood as a reassertion of hegemonic discipline than as effective crime control—as a way of directing attention away from a redistribution of income leading to more class inequality and poverty.

> But whatever the nature and sources of these threats to the liberal state, there is general agreement that they result in punitive policies diverting resources from social and economic policy to the agencies of the criminal justice system.

Clearly, Melossi points to a broader crisis in the authority of the liberal state— one that transcends crime. The breadth of Melossi's analysis lends weight to Simon's "governing through crime" thesis. Melossi moves beyond crime to challenges to political authority posed not only by the excluded underclass but also by the discontents among the working poor and other portions of the working and middle classes. Melossi's analysis also seems more compatible with data, already presented, that decouples crime rates from the politics of crime and punishment. Finally, the broader vision is more compatible with data showing how punitive preferences are more closely linked to a loss of status and sense of material deprivation than to fear of crime or victimization.

But whatever the nature and sources of these threats to the liberal state, there is general agreement that they result in punitive policies diverting resources from social and economic policy to the agencies of the criminal justice system. In addition, there is evidence that once under way, these policies generate their own momentum, driven by increasingly entrenched vested interests. Crime control is, after all, a big business (Christie 1994) and a huge job creation program (Schlosser 1998).

Schlosser (1998, 54) argues that decisions to invest in punishment and the prison construction frenzy that followed are evidence of:

[a] prison-industrial complex—a set of bureaucratic, political, and economic interests that encourage spending on imprisonment, regardless of the actual need. The prison-industrial complex is not a conspiracy. . . . It is a confluence of special interests. . . . [C]omposed of politicians, both liberal and conservative, who have used the fear of crime to gain votes; impoverished rural areas where prisons have become a cornerstone of economic development; private companies that regard the roughly $35 billion spent each year on corrections not as a burden on American taxpayers but as a lucrative market; and government officials whose fiefdoms have expanded along with the inmate populations.

In other words, not only is crime control inescapably sculpted within ongoing political struggles, but, in addition, the outcomes impact jobs, community, and citizenship.

From the macroanalytic perspective, then, there is a great deal at stake. To acknowledge that punitive crime control policy has failed, "would call into question not just the crime policies themselves but the success—and the humanity—of the vision as a whole" (Currie 1998, 8). It also would challenge the distribution of full employment, private-sector profits, and a widely accepted and comforting understanding of how to make sense of our social problems. This understanding is anchored in a dramatic and compelling "myth of crime and punishment" that conveys the dual message of acute criminality and of the crime control capabilities of professional law enforcement practices (Scheingold 1984, 60–75).

> *Broadly speaking, crime control policies in urban jurisdictions with the most crime tend to be distinctly less punitive than those developed by the Federal and State governments.*

At the same time, the macroanalytic, high-stakes politics of crime control, as identified by Garland, Christie, Melossi, and Simon coexist with, and are qualified by, a lower stakes political game. That political game is more fluid and adaptable. We now turn to this perspective with its potential for reform.

Punishment, politics, and contingency *within* the liberal state

From the macroanalytic perspective, the politics of crime and punishment may well be about the form and future of the liberal state. Another story needs to be told, however, about the interior politics of the liberal state. This story reveals a multilayered, fluid, less deterministic side of the politics of crime and punishment. Although these two perspectives are in tension with one another, they are not mutually exclusive. We seek to understand how they interact and, in so doing, to illuminate both the opportunities for, and the constraints on, reform of the emergent punitive state. By exploring and explaining the imposing variation that divides the general public and political elites on punitive approaches to crime control, we lay the foundation for examining reform.

National and State politics: Campaigning on punishment

It might be expected that reactions to crime by both the public and policymakers would vary directly with their proximity to crime, but this is not the case. Instead, insofar as there is a relationship, it is not direct but inverse. Consider, to begin with, the *fear of crime*:

> Research on fear of crime—the emotional response to possible violent crime and physical harm—began some 20 years ago with the idea that fear reflects the possibility of victimization. This notion foundered on two repeated findings: (1) fear levels do not closely reflect local crime rates when social class is removed from the relationship . . . and (2) fear levels of age-sex groupings are inversely related to their victimization rates. (Covington and Taylor 1991, 231)

For example, young males tend to be more victimized but less fearful while the elderly and women are less likely to be victimized but more fearful. The incongruities compound when we turn to *punitive attitudes* that do not seem to be associated with *either* victimization or fear. Thus, women are more fearful but less punitive (Scheingold 1984, 47–48). Most telling perhaps is the so-called "rural hunting culture" of white males in nonurban settings who are less victimized and less frightened but more punitive (Stinchcombe et al. 1980).

What is true of public attitudes is also reflected in policy. Broadly speaking, crime control policies in urban jurisdictions with the most crime tend to be distinctly less punitive than those developed by the Federal and State governments. These outcomes are generally consistent with the distribution of public attitudes. Since urbanites are the most ambivalent about punishment, it stands to reason that urban political elites would court controversy by politicizing crime and would simultaneously be more receptive to nonpunitive policies. Conversely, as the skeptical urban constituency is diluted at the State and Federal levels, the influence of the more distant and punitive publics probably increases. But how do we explain the underlying discrepancy between distance from and attitudes toward crime and punishment? Punitive attitudes are driven by expressive rather than instrumental motivations. Ellsworth and Gross (1994) report that respondents who support the death penalty do not necessarily believe in it as a crime control technique; nor, for that matter, does support

125

decrease as crime stabilizes or falls. These findings led Ellsworth and Gross to conclude that support for the death penalty is largely moral and absolute—expressive rather than instrumental: "Research suggests that fear is not the driving emotion. Future research should focus on other emotions, particularly frustration and anger. Anger is the most positive of the negative emotions, because it is the only one that confers a sense of power" (p. 45).

Note that Ellsworth and Gross mention frustration and anger but not specifically frustration and anger about crime.

The link between punitive attitudes and crime is further attenuated by data generated in Tyler and Boeckmann's (1997) study of "three strikes" legislation. They found both strong public support for a California "three strikes and you're out" initiative and reasons why that support cannot be taken at face value. Enthusiasm for the punitive three-strikes approach to crime control, it turned out, could not be traced directly to public reactions against crime but rather to public reactions against a rather amorphous sense that "social conditions" and "underlying social values" have become too precarious (p. 255). In short, those citizens who feel that the moral and social cohesion that holds society together is declining are more supportive of punitive public policies (p. 258).

Although crime may well be one indicator of social malaise, there are of course many others. Consider the unsettling *social* upheavals that this society has experienced in recent decades, the so-called "culture wars" (Hunter 1991) arising from challenges to established hierarchies along race and gender lines, and the struggle between secular and religious values. Consider also the neoliberal reconfiguration of the American economy with reduced job security, increased material inequality, and a weakened social safety net. Many Americans have, in short, been working harder but earning less in jobs that may be temporary and/or insecure.

Given this context, crime can serve as a condensation symbol—a vehicle for channeling other deeply felt concerns about society into amplified fears of crime (Melossi 1993; King 1989; Hall et al. 1978; Beckett 1997). For a host of reasons, those in distress might displace their anxieties onto crime—even if they themselves were not threatened by it. Kathlyn Gaubatz's research on "crime in the public mind" leads her to conclude that criminals are among the last socially acceptable targets for venting our anger and resentments in an increasingly tolerant society and thus our "insufficiently actualized negative feelings" are eagerly and resolutely directed at them.

> Many Americans have decided to tolerate behavior which they nevertheless find bothersome. Thus they go about their lives, still carrying the burden of feeling that their fellow citizens are engaging in activities which

THE NATURE OF CRIME: CONTINUITY AND CHANGE

are somehow distasteful, unnatural, sinful, dangerous, immoral, or uppity. But they choose not to release that psychological burden into advocacy of prohibitions on these activities. . . . [As a result, they have been] developing a pool of insufficiently actualized negative feelings, and . . . they [have] needed some place to put them. What better place than in strenuous opposition to the acts of criminal offenders? (1995, 162)[13]

Moreover, in contrast to the readily acknowledged complexity of economic, social, and cultural problems, taking a bite out of crime seems like a rather straightforward proposition. These simple truths about crime and punishment are readily accessible as common sense (Scheingold 1991, 4–7), although the available data lead in unequivocally counterintuitive directions.

There are also reasons why an expressive reaction to crime, generated at a distance from it to displace a broader malaise, would privilege punishment— regardless of beliefs about punishment's effectiveness. If, for example, the public turns to matters of crime and punishment in reaction to hard-to-grasp economic problems or to objectionable social and cultural changes, punishment tends to become an end in itself. As Ellsworth and Gross put it in connection with their research on support for the death penalty:

It is not hard to understand why many people support capital punishment even though they believe it does not deter crime and is not fair. The death penalty is concrete, it is forceful, and it is final (which nothing else seems to be); it is *something*, and being for it means that you insist that *something* be done. (1994, 42; italics in the original)

In short, the anxieties associated with unwelcome social, economic, and cultural transformations generate anger, and punishment becomes a vehicle for expressing that anger. Conversely, more permissive responses to crime are less likely to discharge anger and anxiety than to compound them.

It stands to reason that if we turn to the world of crime and punishment for solace, we are unlikely to be receptive to the messages of enlightened liberalism. We do not want to hear that we are all responsible or that there is no definitive solution to the problems of crime, nor that we should turn the other cheek. (Scheingold 1984, 71)

The problem with this vague message is that it imports into the world of crime and punishment the same sense of futility we are fleeing and also forecloses the opportunity to express anger.

Politicians are attracted to punishment in part because their constituents are attracted to it. Politicians are, of course, always in search of campaign issues. Valence (largely symbolic and expressive) issues, like anticommunism, for example, are particularly attractive in that they unite sizable majorities. The only challenge with respect to valence issues is to present them in ways that work for you and against your opponent. Certainly in presidential politics, street crime has frequently served as an effective valence issue, especially for conservative Republicans. Not only is there overwhelming agreement that street crime should be reduced, it has the added attraction of arousing strong emotions—something capable of gaining a firm grip on the public imagination (Scheingold 1984, 68). Much the same seems to be true at the State level—going back to the 1960s. Indeed, Ronald Reagan's 1966 law-and-order campaign for Governor set the tone for much of what was to follow in presidential politics (Berk, Brackman, and Lesser 1977, 59). More broadly, the California legislature seemed inclined to invoke criminal law indiscriminately. "[T]he almost universal response to a wide spectrum of perceived social problems was increased criminalization" (p. 300).

> *Proximity does not make people less concerned about crime. On the contrary, those closest to crime tend to be less punitive, in large part, precisely because they have a real, rather than a symbolic, stake in effective crime control strategies.*

This does not mean, however, that politicians are simply responding to the demands of their constituents, as many argue. On the contrary, politicians have their own reasons for stoking the punitive fires. Street criminals, who are objectionable in their own right, are also serviceable surrogates for displacing other discontents. Accordingly, campaigning on crime provides politicians with an opportunity to divert the public's attention to crime and away from underlying social, economic, and cultural problems. Dealing with these latter issues (e.g., reducing inequality, enhancing job security, and confronting cultural cleavage) is likely to be both costly and divisive. Although punishing criminals has been a fiscal burden, it has not been divisive and, indeed, has been the foundation on which enduring and successful political coalitions have been constructed at the national and State levels. Moreover, for presidential candidates and members of Congress to divert attention from the economy to crime is to refocus the public's attention from problems for which the Federal Government is responsible to a problem for which local and county officials have primary responsibility.

Urban politics: Punishment as contested value

Although a punitive consensus emerges readily among those who are distanced from crime, proximity seems to reduce, or at least to destabilize, both instrumental and expressive forms of support for punishment. Those living closest to crime are not as likely to embrace get-tough policies, and local political leaders are less inclined to campaign on crime. In short, a reverse synergy exists between politics and punishment in high-crime urban settings. The result is that, at the local level, both political leaders and the public tend to be more ambivalent about punitive responses to crime.

Proximity does not make people less concerned about crime. On the contrary, those closest to crime tend to be less punitive, in large part, precisely because they have a real, rather than a symbolic, stake in effective crime control strategies. For those in close proximity to crime, it is neither an expressive abstraction nor a political opportunity. The data also indicate that for both officials and the public generally, crime is not readily separable from a host of concrete structural problems, such as unemployment or inferior educational opportunities, that are associated with crime and, arguably, contribute to it. At the same time, those familiar with the forces driving marginalized Americans toward crime are less likely to be receptive to the moral case for punishment—especially punishment unaccompanied by measures to reduce crime and strengthen communities. In short, proximity to crime generates an intense engagement that casts doubt on both the easy moralizing and the superficial policy calculations associated with exclusively punitive crime control strategies.

Another reason that punitive wars against crime are of limited appeal in urban areas is because they tend to be racially divisive (Beckett 1997; Hall et al. 1978). Attitudinal research reveals that African-Americans respond to punishment with more skepticism than do whites. Although, at first glance, there appears to be "a fair degree of consensus between blacks and whites," with blacks only slightly less punitive than whites (Cohn, Barkan, and Halteman 1991, 291), this agreement is more apparent than real.

In the first place, blacks and whites invest their punitive preferences with distinctly different meanings. Cohn, Barkan, and Halteman found that punitive attitudes among blacks are instrumentally driven by a fear of crime, whereas among whites punitiveness is rooted in "prejudice" (1991, 293). Insofar as punitive preferences are driven by prejudice, they are visceral and expressive and are thus unlikely to be influenced by even the most successful crime control strategies. Recall the research mentioned earlier that found peak punitiveness within the rural white hunting culture—among those, that is, who are neither threatened by, nor fearful of, crimes. Conversely, insofar as blacks are responding to a fear of victimization, they are more likely to evaluate punishment in instrumental terms.

Moreover, although African-American attitudes toward punishment are not exclusively instrumental, the expressive element tends to mobilize blacks *against* punishment. Consider, in this regard, Sasson's focus group research conducted among African-Americans. His Boston area neighborhood crime watch groups were strongly attracted to conspiratorial explanations of the high crime rates among blacks. These African-American respondents were willing to attribute "the drug trade and 'black-on-black' violence to the clandestine actions of powerful whites" (Sasson 1995, 266). Starkly put, there was an inclination to credit what most Americans find incredible: high crime in African-American neighborhoods as the *intended* consequence of genocidal policies pursued by white elites. According to Sasson, blacks are receptive to conspiracy theories because of "the absence of a public discourse on crime corresponding to African-American popular wisdom" (p. 281).[14] Specifically, conspiracy theories flourish, he says, largely because there is no space in mainstream explanations of crime for one of the central "facts" of the African-American experience: the brutal reality of white racism.

If there are African-Americans who see crime itself as part of a deliberate plan fomented by whites to destroy black communities, it stands to reason that punitive responses to crime would be perceived as inextricably linked to the same plot. Blacks are, after all, being incarcerated in astonishing numbers while also being disproportionately subjected to police violence. Zero-tolerance policing, a centerpiece of urban anticrime strategies, is certainly intrusive and seems to be leading to increased police violence. Even police officers who believe in the effectiveness of zero-tolerance law enforcement are sensitive to its problematic repercussions. According to James Savage, president of the Patrolmen's Benevolent Association in New York City:

> When zero-tolerance tactics were first introduced by the department, crime was at an all time high. . . . Now that crime is way down, an adjustment of the strategy is required. If we don't strike a balance between aggressive enforcement and common sense, it becomes a blueprint for a police state and tyranny. (Cooper 1999)[15]

Presumably whites continue to be less afflicted by this increasingly punitive police presence—thus, further exacerbating the racial schism. According to Scheingold (1995, 3):

> [W]hites are likely to see the best police officers on their best behavior while African-Americans and other marginalized groups are likely to see the worst police officers at their worst. But it may also be because whites expect the police to treat "the dangerous classes" in just the ways that antagonize minorities. If so, then Andrew Hacker's ominous admonition that we are *Two Nations: Black and White, Separate, Hostile and Unequal* may apply at least as much to the fight against crime as to other areas of American life.[16]

130

THE NATURE OF CRIME: CONTINUITY AND CHANGE

In short, crime in general and punitive policy initiatives in particular tend to pit whites against blacks.

Sampson and Bartusch recently conducted a multilevel statistical analysis of survey data compiled from 8,783 residents of 343 neighborhoods in Chicago and found that proximity to crime and police misconduct contributed to more complex attitudes about the nature of crime and punishment.

> [N]eighborhoods of concentrated disadvantage display elevated levels of legal cynicism, dissatisfaction with police, and tolerance of deviance unaccounted for by sociodemographic composition and crime-rate differences. Concentrated disadvantage also helps explain why African-Americans are more cynical about law and dissatisfied with the police. Neighborhood context is thus important for resolving the seeming paradox that estrangement from legal norms and agencies of criminal justice, especially by blacks, is compatible with the personal condemnation of deviance. (1998, 777)

This does not mean that African-Americans are more accepting of crime, but their desire to reduce crime coexists with deep cynicism about, and distrust of, the criminal justice system (Podolefsky 1983; Hagan and Albonetti 1982). The increasing influence of minorities in urban electoral politics tends, then, to inject a moderating influence into policy choices.

With crime such a racially divisive issue, political and civic elites in urban areas have reasons not to campaign on crime—reasons for avoiding the issue rather than deploying it. Just this finding emerged from the most comprehensive available research, the Governmental Responses to Crime Project (Jacob and Lineberry 1982). Ten cities were examined over the 30-year period 1948 to 1978. To be sure, there were instances of successful campaigning on crime. The overall message of that research was, however, that most of the time, in most of the 10 cities, crime was not a salient issue. Similar findings emerged from a case study by one of the authors. That research, conducted in the 1980s, found that central city blacks were much less willing to support get-tough policies than were similarly situated whites (Scheingold 1991, 50–55). With civic elites arrayed against them, neither the law-and-order campaigns nor the campaigners were able to establish an influential, much less an enduring, political presence. Once again, occasionally successful law-and-order electoral campaigns were the exception that proved the rule (p. 66–69).

Electoral and commercial forces also contribute to policy moderation in urban areas. Civic elites are likely to see the politicization of street crime as bad for business—likely, that is, to drive people from the inner city to suburban shopping malls, housing developments, and business parks. Unlike their more distant counterparts in Washington, D.C., and even in State capitals, urban

131

political leaders and criminal process professionals are in the front line of "wars" waged against crime. They are directly answerable to an electorate that, on one hand, tends to see crime as one of a number of afflictions and, on the other, witnesses the collateral damage inflicted by overly zealous law enforcement (Scheingold 1995).

In racially heterogeneous urban settings, therefore, punishment and crime both become contested values rather than valence issues. Rather than symbolic expressions of putative support for punitive and exclusionary forms of social control, local crime control debates focus more on what will express moral approbation in a way that reduces crime and strengthens communities. For all of these reasons, we believe that urban policymaking processes are more inclined to take seriously the criminological knowledge that casts doubt on an exclusively punitive crime control strategy. It is no accident that more balanced and criminologically informed programs such as community policing and Weed and Seed programs are being embraced in urban areas. Consider also the findings emerging from a current study of the Weed and Seed program in Seattle. Local officials, responding to African-American constituents, have negotiated a partial reversal of the priorities of the Federal program—reducing its emphasis on punitive weeding provisions and giving more attention and resources to the preventive seeding provisions (Miller 1999).

This does not mean that the urban setting is devoid of punitive impulses or that the political ethos is not predominantly punitive from time to time and place to place.[17] Rather, our point is that there is substantial receptivity to nonpunitive responses to crime among local elites, the lay public, and criminal process professionals—or to punitive responses that are also reintegrative (Braithwaite 1989). Accordingly, there are definitely insistent political incentives to develop a more balanced and less obtrusively punitive policy agenda.

Beyond Punishment: Policy and Political Alternatives

In concluding this paper, our agenda is twofold. On one hand, we sketch in the broad outlines of a crime control strategy that we believe would make much better sense than either punishment, per se, or the pervasively intrusive practices of the new penology. On the other hand, we look more closely at what is politically feasible. To do so, we balance the opportunities for reform suggested by our analysis of the political process against the constraints that stem from the ongoing problems of the liberal state. To invoke the mantra of this paper once again, our claim is that crime control policies must be understood as political choices made in contexts where options are constrained by larger cultural and economic forces. Thus, although our analysis separates policy from politics, they are inextricably interdependent.

Beyond punishment: Strengthening communities and families

To discuss alternatives to punishment is in no way to argue against the need for punishment. In analyzing crime control debates, Currie is critical of the political right for dismissing prevention in favor of unlimited punishment. But he is also critical of the left for a failure to focus on crime prevention programs that work—and, instead, voicing uncritical support for social programs as being superior in all cases to punishment.

> Given what we've learned about crime prevention in recent years, four priorities seem especially critical: preventing child abuse and neglect, enhancing children's intellectual and social development, providing support and guidance to vulnerable adolescents, and working intensively with juvenile offenders. . . . The first priority is to invest serious resources in the prevention of child abuse and neglect. The evidence is compelling that this is where much of the violent crime that plagues us begins, especially the kinds of violence we fear the most. (Currie 1998, 81–82)

We see community policing as a step in the right direction but only insofar as it is rooted in a genuine partnership among police officers, police departments, city governments, and community residents. Community policing programs should manifestly demonstrate how they would strengthen the communities most victimized by crime.

Relying heavily on Currie's analysis and his proposals, we advocate an even-handed approach that takes more cognizance of the structural sources of crime and puts less emphasis on crime as a volitional act—a matter, that is, of strictly personal choice (Scheingold 1991, 7–15).[18] Fundamentally, this means, in effect, investing in noncriminal justice system programs that, according to the available criminological knowledge, have crime prevention value. In this way, it will be possible to reduce the need to resort to the punitive crime control strategies that provide short-term drama and serve political needs, but tend at the same time to weaken the communities that are most victimized by crime. But there are also worthwhile steps that can be taken within the context of crime control policy per se, and we will begin with them.

133

Nonpunitive crime prevention

Crime control policymakers would be well advised to heed medicine's first principle: Do no harm. Tonry's research indicates that this principle has certainly been violated in the so-called war on drugs. Its focus on street dealers and punitive sentencing policies has, he argues, had foreseeable and destructive impacts on African-American families and communities. Accordingly, he proposes reducing statutory maximums or establishing strong presumptive upper limits on punishment severity, abolishing all mandatory penalties, empowering judges to mitigate sentences based on individual circumstances, and "greatly limit[ing] the use of imprisonment" while using the money saved to invest in communities (1995, 41–46).

In addition to eliminating the *negative*, there are a variety of *positive* steps that can be taken within the criminal justice system itself. We believe these will promote both crime reduction and stronger families and communities. Programs for repeat offenders can be structured in ways that circumvent the exclusionary consequences of deterrent, incapacitative, and preemptive strategies. Hope (1995) and Tremblay and Craig (1995) argue for the crime prevention value of investing in vulnerable adolescents in ways that build concrete skills and support systems. According to Currie, this is the strength of programs like Job Corps, where intensive skill training "significantly reduced violent crime among its graduates" (1998, 102). The key remains a comprehensive and consistent approach that offers tangible supports (valued skills, activities, stipends, relational networks). Punitive programs (boot camps) that are currently popular but are of dubious value (Simon 1995) and treating offenders in isolation are a "prescription for failure" (Currie 1998, 105). When offenders are treated as "participants in a range of institutions, from the family to the school and beyond," success has been shown to be more likely (Currie 1998, 107).

Community policing has, of course, become a central feature of crime control strategies throughout the United States. We see community policing as a step in the right direction but only insofar as it is rooted in a genuine partnership among police officers, police departments, city governments, and community residents. Community policing programs should manifestly demonstrate how they would strengthen the communities most victimized by crime. Similarly, it is essential that aggressive crime suppression activity not be undertaken without a demonstrated consensus in the communities concerned over the definition of the problem and the proposed solution. Finally, self-consciously and in consultation with citizen partners, police must avoid practices that, even if effective in the short term, undermine the relational networks, resources, and informal social control mechanisms communities depend on to subject unaccountable power in their neighborhoods to critical public scrutiny (Lyons 1999).

134

Meares and Kahan (1998, 816–828) argue along these same lines that a focus on policing that strengthens communities of concentrated disadvantage would emphasize different police practices than those currently in place. Reverse stings, for instance, would spread the disorganizing impact of formal sanctions across many communities and are likely to be just as effective as buy-busts that concentrate that impact on those communities already least advantaged (see also Miller 1999). Curfew laws rather than aggressive gang units, order maintenance that does not rely on arrests and focuses on the concerns of all communities, and alliances with African-American churches can each contribute to both crime prevention and strengthening those communities most victimized by crime.

Structural responses to crime

But to focus on what criminal justice agencies can do on behalf of families and communities only scratches the surface of the problem. In the United States, "unlike other advanced societies, we cannot link our early-intervention programs to national-level health care" and "we have traditionally over-estimated the capacity of purely educational strategies to over-come the effects of endemic poverty, community disorganization, and economic insecurity" (Currie 1998, 98–100). In short, we agree with Currie that it is necessary to combine social service interventions with investments in structural reform.

Consider in this connection Tremblay and Craig's (1995) detailed review of the literature evaluating programs designed to prevent crime by reducing developmental risk factors. They conclude that "money invested in early prevention is money saved later on remedial services in school, social, physical, and mental health services for families and correctional services for juveniles and adults" (p. 224). Programs that target children engaging in unusually disruptive behavior, experiencing cognitive difficulties, or being subjected to poor parenting had "generally positive results" (p. 151).

> *Because areas of concentrated disadvantage lack precisely those resources needed to mobilize the informal social controls associated with strong communities, a failure to make the necessary structural investment inevitably leads to punishment as the only meaningful alternative.*

Tremblay and Craig's review covered many programs, but one common characteristic of success emerged consistently. The successful programs invested in teachers, parents, and children by distributing resources in the form of concrete *skills* (such as moral and legal reasoning skills, conflict management skills, study skills), consistent and

135

targeted *support* systems, caring relational *networks* (social bonding), and self-confidence stemming from concrete *achievements*. These investments paid off in terms of improved attitudes toward school, better academic performance, fewer school suspensions or expulsions, an increased capacity to hold a job after graduation, less drug abuse, and often significantly less criminal behavior (Tremblay and Craig 1995).

Child abuse itself is a crime linked to 5,000 deaths, 18,000 permanent disabilities, and 150,000 serious injuries per year. Children who survive this threat "are far more likely to turn to violence themselves as teenagers or adults" (Currie 1998, 82). Abused kids are more likely to engage in serious delinquency (Tonry and Harrington 1995). One key ingredient of crime prevention strategies is, therefore, early and consistent assistance for at-risk families (Currie 1998, 85–86). In reviewing a prenatal–early infancy program pioneered in Elmira, New York, Currie concluded that even for those families at greatest risk of producing delinquent children, timely and sustained investment that supported the parents and children led to crime rates that were lower than those of control groups.

> The families, in short, represented a tough population, and their children were heavily exposed to the multiple adversities of poverty and social marginality. . . . The control children were almost four times as likely to have a formal juvenile record (22 percent versus 6 percent of the program children). And even the relatively rare delinquencies of the program children were minor. (1998, 97)

Returning to Hope's review of the literature on community crime prevention, we note that he underscores the importance of investing in ways that counter the "nexus of youth poverty and crime emerging in areas where crime and poverty are concentrating" (1995, 77).[19]

In the final analysis, then, neither families nor communities are going to be strengthened without directly tackling the extreme deprivation that "inhibits children's intellectual development, breeds violence by encouraging child abuse and neglect, and undermines parents' ability to monitor and supervise their children" (Currie 1998, 135–140). In a context of predominantly punitive, politically appealing approaches to crime control, families are left without an alternative to poverty and dependence on state agency. Accordingly, Currie (1998, 150–157) proposes:

- Living wage campaigns to raise the minimum wage.

- Upgrading part-time work to include benefits and security against arbitrary layoffs.

- Providing universal health and child care nationally.

136

- Creating jobs in inner cities: jobs in child care, child protection, health care, and public safety.

In short, because chronic joblessness hurts families in ways that cause crime, Currie suggests that the most intelligent crime prevention approach would focus on reforming work rather than welfare. People who work should be able to earn enough to support their families. More broadly, the idea is to place the welfare of at-risk families and the well-being of communities most victimized by crime at the top of the criminal justice agenda. These are, after all, sites "where the strains and pressures of the larger society converge to influence individual development" (Currie 1998, 141).

Because areas of concentrated disadvantage lack precisely those resources needed to mobilize the informal social controls associated with strong communities, a failure to make the necessary structural investment inevitably leads to punishment as the only meaningful alternative. As Hope puts it: "Disintegrating urban communities may need significant social investment in their institutional infrastructure to offset the powerful tendencies of destabilization of poor communities within the urban free-market economy" (1995, 78). Unlike whites fleeing to the suburbs, privatization in fortress communities is not an option for these communities. For crime prevention to make sense, investment in the strength of these communities is an indispensable complement to punishment. As for punishment itself, there is reason to believe that forms of punishment that are reintegrative will strengthen communities more than those that are strictly exclusionary (Braithwaite 1989).

Beyond punishment: The politics of reform

The political struggle over crime control policy takes place inside and outside the communities most victimized by crime. Within the afflicted communities, the streets are the site of encounters over the status and funding of professional law enforcement, the tax burdens imposed on various business interests, and the electoral fortunes of political leaders and governing coalitions. We have already established that punitive tendencies are under considerable pressure in these urban settings. In our concluding pages, we will demonstrate that even outside the inner city, punishment is not uncontested, nor is a punitive agenda indispensable for electoral success.[20] It is, however, much less clear that a nonpunitive agenda will necessarily translate into the kind of structural reform that we claim is the key to strengthening communities and families in crisis.

A nonpunitive political ethos?

There are a number of indications that it is not only in the inner cities that support for punishment is equivocal. Most broadly, the political ethos has never

137

really been as punitive as is often thought to be the case (Gottfredson and Taylor 1987). Throughout the last decade, public opinion research has revealed a distinctly nonpunitive streak. In the same 1989 survey that found rehabilitation was preferred over punishment by 48 percent to 38 percent, it was discovered that, by a 61- to 32-percent margin, the public believed that attacking social problems was more likely to deter crime than improved law enforcement (Gallup Organization 1989, 31). Moreover, when asked about the factors that are responsible for crime, only 4 percent chose lenient courts and 4 percent chose lax punishment while 58 percent pointed to drugs, 14 percent to unemployment, and 13 percent to a breakdown in family values (p. 25). In other words, even if the public is inclined to treat known criminals harshly, they have a broad sense of the causes of crime and of ways to reduce it.

Consider also the moderation beneath surface enthusiasm for capital punishment. Between the mid-1960s and the mid-1990s, support for capital punishment grew from just above 40 percent to more than 75 percent (*American Enterprise* 1991, 80). It might seem at first glance that these numbers run counter to our proposition, but research by Bowers, Vandiver, and Dugan suggests why this is not the case. They report that these polls have been "misinterpreted" and that:

> [T]here is now solid evidence that the "prevailing wisdom" of "strong," "deep-seated" public support for the death penalty is mistaken. . . . When people are presented with an alternative to the death penalty that incorporates both lengthy imprisonment and restitution to murder victims' families, and are then asked whether they would prefer the death penalty to such an alternative, they consistently choose the non-death-penalty alternative. (1994, 79)

More specifically, in this research conducted in 1991 in New York and Nebraska, support for capital punishment was cut almost in half when respondents were presented with the alternative of life in prison without the possibility of release. Support dropped still further when restitution was added to the life in prison option (Bowers, Vandiver, and Dugan, 1994, tables 5 and 7). These findings do not, of course, reveal an aversion to punishment. Indeed, there was strong agreement in both States that we should be tough on criminals—even tougher than we already are (table 9). What is revealed, however, is that there is political space for enterprising political leaders who refuse to raise the punitive ante and instead choose the instrumental over the expressive.

Bowers and his associates further demonstrate the existence of this nonpunitive political space by the responses of legislators to capital punishment. On balance, the legislators were, if anything, slightly less punitive than their constituents (table 13). On capital punishment, however, they took a tougher line. Why? Bowers and colleagues state:

138

> Seven out of ten [New York] legislators believed that their constituents would prefer the death penalty over any of the other alternatives—when . . . only one in three voters statewide preferred it to [life without parole], and only one in five preferred it to [life without parole plus restitution]. (p. 139)

In other words, what drove capital punishment policy in New York was not so much a punitive public or a punitive legislature as legislative misperception of public preferences.[21]

Toward a structural crime control strategy?

The empirical record thus suggests that punitive policies are politically constructed on surprisingly uncertain foundations. Research suggests that the general public and State agencies are more ambivalent and more conflicted about punitive policies than a cursory reading of public opinion and State policy might suggest. Given these crosscurrents, punitively inflected politics of crime and punishment are hardly inevitable. On the other hand, there is no quarreling with the electoral success that has been achieved by hardline campaigning on crime in State and presidential politics.

So even if we are correct and it is *possible* to steer a nonpunitive course, is there any reason to believe that it is *likely*? And, moreover, is there any reason to believe that nonpunitive policies will progress to genuine structural reform? Certainly fiscal prudence would militate against further prison construction. But States continue to build prisons at an alarming rate. Perhaps fiscal discipline will kick in—but perhaps not. After all, as indicated previously, prison construction as well as many other policies and practices associated with the emergent punitive state have a built-in economic payoff.

We do, however, see a glimmer of hope elsewhere. Punitively inflected politics of crime and punishment resonate with anger and anxiety generated by the interaction of social, cultural, and economic instability. It is therefore hardly surprising that, given the high level of prosperity that this Nation has enjoyed during most of the 1990s, neither crime nor punishment has been the veritable political pot of gold that it once was. Although the rising economic tide has definitely not raised all boats, it is entirely plausible to believe the influential, so-called middle class has been sufficiently mollified that it offers less fertile soil in which to plant the seeds of law-and-order populism. Of course, insofar as we are correct, this respite from a punitive political ethos will last only as long as our current prosperity. Still, for the time being, it is reasonable to hope and expect that the nonpunitive approaches being developed in inner cities are less likely to be undermined by enterprising outsiders in Washington, D.C., and in the State capitals.

139

On the other hand, the prospects for genuine structural reform seem less promising. We do believe that with less free-floating public anger and anxiety for politicians to exploit, it will become increasingly difficult to deploy crime as a political fig leaf concealing the structural failings of our liberal-democratic state. But it also seems that the current prosperity has itself provided something of a fig leaf and, if so, we may be further from facing up to our structural problems.[22] In addition, the burden of these problems increasingly falls on those largely without political voice—the so-called dangerous classes that figure so prominently in the governing-through-crime literature.

Even if criminal justice agencies pursue more enlightened crime control policies and practices, there is no reason to believe that macroeconomic policy-makers will shoulder the redistributive burdens implied by genuine structural reform. Indeed, it may even be that the better the nonpunitive palliatives work, the less incentive there will be to undertake structural remedies. Further complicating policy choices is the distinct possibility that redistributive policies could generate a backlash by fueling the kinds of resentments on which law-and-order politicians have been preying for many years. Thus, one need not think of the crisis of the liberal-democratic state as a terminal condition to be pessimistic about the prospects for the kind of genuine structural reform that we see as a necessary component of an effective and inclusive crime control strategy.

Notes

1. Put another way, while criminologically speaking, the case for punishment is contested terrain, politically speaking, punishment tends to be largely uncontested. A heated debate among criminologists is thus politically transformed into widespread acclaim for punishment as both a necessary and a sufficient response to crime.

2. Strictly speaking, Wilson has always given priority to certainty, rather than to severity, of punishment—as the quoted statement clearly indicates. But this distinction is regularly lost in the public discourse on crime and punishment, and, even in its qualified form, there is a clear implication that punishment is exclusively about the relationship between the law-abiding citizens represented by the State and the criminal element.

3. According to Currie (1998, 29): "The incarceration rate has risen much more than anyone imagined. But there has been *no* overall decrease in serious criminal violence, and there have been sharp *increases* in many places—including many of the places that incarcerated the most or increased their rates of imprisonment the fastest. The national incarceration rate doubled between 1985 and 1995 alone, and every major reported violent crime increased."

4. Tonry goes on to note that this research was "commissioned and paid for by the Reagan administration's Department of Justice" but had no discernable effect on policy-makers who, Tonry concludes, could not have used the best available data in deciding to adopt punitive policies that depend on deterrence (1995, 17–18). The disconnect between criminology and policymaking is, of course, central to our underlying argument and will be revisited at length in the next section of this paper.

5. Further, Fagan (1994, 207) suggests that an approach that accounts for contextual factors like the job market will avoid the "counter-deterrent effects" of strictly punitive approaches.

6. Blumstein (1998, 132) makes the same point as part of a multifaceted, carefully bal-anced (but largely skeptical) account of the incapacitative contribution of punitive sen-tencing to crime reduction. "The incapacitative effects could have been diminished because the marginal prisoners brought into prison during the expansion [of incarcera-tion] had lower values of offending frequency . . . than might have been anticipated."

7. Blumstein (1998) agrees that recruiting replacement drug dealers is likely to reduce the incapacitative effects of stiff sentences (p. 131), and he takes advocates of incapaci-tation to task for ignoring its "postrelease" consequences. Unlike Currie, however, Blumstein believes that these consequences may be both positive and negative (p. 133).

8. In the past 5 years, there has been considerable discussion about the dramatic reduc-tion in urban crime—first noted in New York City and attributed to that city's zero-tolerance policing, and thus arguably, to punishment. As we see it, the returns are not yet in and other explanations should probably be taken into account—for example, the maturation of the drug markets and unemployment rates that are at an all-time low. It should also be noted that, while our focus is on the prevailing punitive trends in crime control policy, current policy also includes less punitive approaches, such as community policing, drug courts, and family violence courts. Clearly, nonincarcerative sanctions and a concern for rehabilitation remain part of the overall crime control picture. We see these less punitive approaches as both promising and, in the current punitive context, unlikely to realize that promise. As currently practiced, initiatives like community polic-ing, for instance, are often constructed as part of larger punitive efforts emphasizing public relations, aggressive law enforcement, and empowering the police department, often at the expense of strengthening those communities most victimized by crime (Lyons 1999).

9. In his classic study, *The Morality of Law*, Lon Fuller argues that these are among the defining elements of law—in his words, "the morality that makes law possible" (1964, ch. 2).

10. Davey also contrasts the incarceration rates of two other States with similar demo-graphics and Republican Governors. While South Carolina's incarceration rate jumped from 294 to 415 per 100,000 (1985–89), North Carolina's rate fell from 254 to 250. According to Davey, the elevated rates in South Carolina were because Governor Carrol

Campbell "knew well the value of exploiting the voter's fear of crime" (1998, 60). Meanwhile, in North Carolina, Governor James Martin did build some new prisons but only to ease overcrowding. Despite the danger that building prisons would inevitably lead to filling them, Davey argues that "in the absence of a 'law and order' governor, that apparently did not happen in North Carolina" (p. 62).

11. Blumstein (1998) provides a criminologically based explanation of the stunning acceleration of incarceration rates beginning fairly early in the 1970s (see exhibit 5). Blumstein traces the upturn to criminologist Robert Martinson's widely read 1974 *Public Interest* article "What Works? Questions and Answers About Prison Reform." Martinson's answer, drawn from more than a decade of empirical research, was that nothing worked. Blumstein claims that it was this criminological research that spearheaded a retreat from rehabilitation and an increasingly insistent demand to get tough with criminals. We see things differently. The years in which incarceration took off were also years of double-digit inflation, heated conflict over busing, and white flight—and just after the height of social turmoil over the war in Vietnam (Scheingold 1991, 66–71). In other words, for reasons detailed in the pages ahead, we look to the major dislocations of the 1970s to explain the upsurge in incarceration.

12. U.S. Census Bureau data lend credence to Melossi's analysis. From 1974 to 1994, the income of the poorest (lowest quintile) Americans fell from 4.3 percent to 3.6 percent of total income earned. Middle-class (the middle three quintiles) income fell from 52.2 percent to 47.3 percent. At the same time, the income of the wealthiest (highest quintile) Americans increased from 43.5 percent to 49.1 percent (U.S. Bureau of the Census 1996).

13. For a complementary psychoanalytic explanation that links the lure of punishment to perceptions of declining status and/or material well-being, see Chancer and Donovan (1994).

14. A newspaper report implicating the CIA in inner-city drug dealing both fueled the conspiracy fires and revealed how rapidly they tend to spread among African-Americans (Golden 1996).

15. Retiring San Diego Police Chief Jerry Sanders urges that this statement be taken at face value and not attributed to a hidden agenda or to political posturing. He argues, as we have, that "no one is more aware than officers on the beat that arrests and citations don't solve many long-term problems" (Sanders 1999).

16. Reactions to the O.J. Simpson trial revealed this same black and white division on matters of criminal justice, as did the earlier reactions to the Bernhard Goetz incident (Rubin 1986).

17. It is instructive that both of these studies found substantial urban politicization of crime only in the mid- to late 1970s—very close to the period when incarceration took off and society seemed to be coming apart at the seams. This is also, arguably, the period when conservative whites were making a kind of last-ditch stand against unwelcome changes in the racial composition and balance of political power in U.S. cities.

18. We realize that some of these proposals are controversial and that there are prominent figures, perhaps most notably Charles Murray, who doubt that they will work. Again, we are treading on contested terrain—rooted, in this instance, in competing and ultimately irreconcilable views of human nature. Thus, Murray rejects the investment of resources in improving inner-city schools, concluding that there is "little hope" for success because the contribution of formal education "has already been realized" (1984, 389). Further, he rules out several preschool programs he found to be effective, because they were too costly. He does not, however, contrast these costs with the $100 billion spent on crime control in 1993 (Beckett 1997, 3)—not to mention the many other costs that we analyzed earlier. We are under no illusions that we can resolve this longstanding and deep-seated conflict. Accordingly, our objective is to present the data on which our own judgment rests. In so doing, we offer what are, at the very least, plausible and promising additions to the crime control policy repertoire.

19. Hope also acknowledges the importance of incorporating the concerns of victims into such programs. Because these are areas with concentrations of victims, not just offenders, he argues on behalf of programs "to protect the fearful, vulnerable, and victimized if the destabilization of communities is to be arrested" (1995, 77). To ignore victims is likely to encourage destabilizing forms of flight, blight, and, perhaps, gentrification.

20. With that said, it is important to keep in mind that policies that are not overtly punitive do, nonetheless, contribute to the punitive tide. We have already called attention to the "new penology"—various forms of surveillance and separation. Although less overtly punitive, the intrusive practices of the new penology fall heavily on the powerless. For example, the *New York Times* recently editorialized about New Jersey's "racial profiling and drug interdiction" programs: "In the name of crime-fighting, the [New Jersey State Police] agency has created a vast surveillance network that engulfs large numbers of innocent hotel guests" (*New York Times* 1999, A30). Similarly, private-sector security devices that protect the social space of the privileged constrict the social space available to the marginalized. Thus, even if politics *within* the liberal State are more permeable and more protean than the politics *of* the liberal State, it does not necessarily follow that repression and exclusion will be avoided or mitigated.

21. Similar findings have been uncovered in Indiana by Edmund F. McGarrell and Marla Sandys (1993).

22. How all this plays out in the long run will depend on the extent to which neoliberal conceptions of freedom are internalized. As Nikolas Rose (1999, 156–166) persuasively argues, the insecurities of corporate downsizing, mid-career retraining, and the like are currently being touted as opportunities to display resilience and resourcefulness. Insofar as the vicissitudes of the neoliberal market are, thus, successfully transmuted into a hallmark of freedom, it could be argued that the there will be less anxiety and anger available to sustain the politics of law and order. On the other hand, to thus repress anxiety and insecurity might well trigger resentments that, although more deeply buried, could provide soil that is at least as fertile for the kinds of political mischief that we have documented in this paper.

References

American Enterprise. 1991. Crimes, cops, and courts. *American Enterprise* 2 (July–August): 74–82.

Banfield, Edward. 1970. *The unheavenly city: The nature and future of our urban crisis.* Boston: Little, Brown and Company.

Beckett, Katherine. 1997. *Making crime pay: Law and order in contemporary American politics.* New York: Oxford University Press.

Bennett, W. Lance. 1996. *News: The politics of illusion.* New York: Longman.

Berk, Richard A., Harold Brackman, and Selma Lesser. 1977. *A measure of justice: An empirical study of changes in the California penal code, 1955–1971.* New York: Academic Press.

Blumstein, Alfred. 1998. U.S. criminal justice conundrum: Rising prison populations and stable crime rates. *Crime & Delinquency* 44 (January): 127–135.

———. 1997. Interaction of criminological research and public policy. *Journal of Quantitative Criminology* 12 (4): 349–361.

Bowers, William, Margaret Vandiver, and Patricia Dugan. 1994. A new look at public opinion on capital punishment: What citizens and legislators prefer. *American Journal of Criminology* 22:77–150.

Braithwaite, John. 1989. *Crime, shame, and reintegration.* New York: Cambridge University Press.

Cain, Maureen. 1990. Towards transgression: New directions in feminist criminology. *International Journal of Sociology of the Law* 22:261–277.

Chancer, Lynn, and Pamela Donovan. 1994. A mass psychology of punishment: Crime and the futility of rationally based approaches. *Social Justice* 21:50–72.

Chicago Community Policing Evaluation Consortium. 1996. *Community policing in Chicago, year three.* Illinois Criminal Justice Information Authority.

Christie, Nils. 1994. *Crime control as industry: Toward gulags, Western style.* New York: Routledge.

Cohen, Stanley. 1985. *Visions of social control.* Cambridge, England: Polity Press.

Cohn, Steven, Steven Barkan, and William Halteman. 1991. Punitive attitudes toward criminals: Racial consensus or racial conflict? *Social Problems* 38:287–296.

Cooper, Michael. 1999. Police delegates rebuke the commissioner. *New York Times*, 14 April.

THE NATURE OF CRIME: CONTINUITY AND CHANGE

Covington, Jeannette, and Ralph Taylor. 1991. Fear of crime in residential neighbor-hoods: Implications of between- and within-neighborhood sources for current models. *Sociological Quarterly* 43 (Summer): 231–249.

Currie, Elliott. 1998. *Crime and punishment in America*. New York: Metropolitan Press.

———. 1991. The politics of crime: The American experience (A debate between Elliott Currie and James Q. Wilson). In *The politics of crime control*, edited by Kevin Stenson and David Cowell. London: Sage Publications.

Dahrendorf, Ralf. 1985. *Law and order*. London: Stevens.

Davey, Joseph Dillon. 1998. *The politics of prison expansion: Winning elections by waging war on crime*. Westport, Connecticut: Praeger.

Davis, Mike. 1990. *City of quartz: Excavating the future of Los Angeles*. New York: Vintage Books.

Edelman, Murray. 1977. *Political language: Words that succeed and policies that fail*. New York: Academic Press.

Egan, Timothy. 1999. The war on crack retreats, still taking prisoners. *New York Times*, 28 February.

Elias, Robert. 1986. *The politics of victimization: Victims, victimology, and human rights*. New York: Oxford University Press.

Ellsworth, Phoebe C., and Samuel R. Gross. 1994. Hardening of attitudes: Americans' views on the death penalty. *Journal of Social Issues* 50 (2): 19–52.

Erikson, Kai. 1966. *Wayward puritans: A study in the sociology of deviance*. New York: John Wiley & Sons.

Fagan, Jeffrey. 1994. Do criminal sanctions deter crimes? In *Drugs and crime: Evaluating public policy initiatives*, edited by Doris Layton MacKenzie and Craig Uchida. Thousand Oaks, California: Sage Publications.

Feeley, Malcolm, and Jonathan Simon. 1992. The new penology: Notes on the emerging strategy of corrections and its implications. *Criminology* 30 (4): 449–474.

Fuller, Lon L. 1964. *The morality of law*. New Haven: Yale University Press.

The Gallup Organization. 1989. *Gallup Report* 285 (June).

Garland, David. 1996. The limits of the sovereign state: Strategies of crime control in contemporary society. *British Journal of Criminology* 36:445–471.

Gaubatz, Kathlyn. 1995. *Crime in the public mind*. Ann Arbor: University of Michigan Press.

Gilliom, John. 1996. *Surveillance, privacy, and the law: Employee drug testing and the politics of social control.* Ann Arbor: University of Michigan Press.

Golden, Tim. 1996. Tale of CIA and drugs has a life of its own. *New York Times*, 21 October.

Gordon, Diana. 1994. *The return of the dangerous classes: Drug prohibition and policy politics.* New York: W.W. Norton.

———. 1990. *The justice juggernaut: Fighting street crime, controlling citizens.* New Brunswick, New Jersey: Rutgers University Press.

Gottfredson, S., and R. Taylor. 1987. Attitudes of correctional policymakers and the public. In *America's correctional crisis: Prison populations and public policy*, edited by S. Gottfredson and S. McConville. New York: Greenwood Press.

Greene, Jack, and Stephen Mastrofski, eds. 1988. *Community policing: Rhetoric or reality.* New York: Praeger.

Hagan, J., and C. Albonetti. 1982. Race, class, and perceptions of criminal justice in America. *American Journal of Sociology* 88:329–355.

Hall, Stuart, Chas Critcher, Tony Jefferson, John Clarke, and Brian Roberts. 1978. *Policing the crisis: Mugging, the state, and law and order.* London: Macmillan.

Hope, Tim. 1995. Community crime prevention. In *Building a safer society: Strategic approaches to crime prevention*, edited by Michael Tonry and David S. Harrington. Vol. 19 of *Crime and justice: A review of research.* Chicago: University of Chicago Press.

Hunter, James Davison. 1991. *Culture wars: The struggle to define America.* New York: Basic Books.

Jacob, Herbert, and Robert Lineberry. 1982. *Governmental responses to crime: Executive summary.* NCJ 81621. Washington, D.C.: U.S. Department of Justice, National Institute of Justice.

King, Michael. 1989. Social crime prevention a la Thatcher. *Howard Journal* 28:291–312.

Klockars, Carl. 1988. The rhetoric of community policing. In *Community policing: Rhetoric or reality*, edited by J. Greene and S. Mastrofski. New York: Praeger.

LaFree, Gary. 1998. *Losing legitimacy: Street crime and the decline of social institutions in America.* Boulder, Colorado: Westview Press.

Lyons, William. 1999. *The politics of community policing: Rearranging the power to punish.* Ann Arbor: University of Michigan Press.

Martinson, Robert. 1974. What works? Questions and answers about prison reform. *Public Interest* 35:22–54.

McGarrell, Edmund F., and Marla Sandys. 1993. Indiana citizens and lawmakers on the death penalty: Results of the 1992–1993 public and legislative surveys. Unpublished manuscript, July.

Meares, Tracey, and Dan Kahan. 1998. Law and (norms of) order in the inner city. *Law & Society Review* 32 (4): 804–838.

Melossi, Dario. 1993. Gazette of morality and social whip: Punishment hegemony and the case of the USA, 1970–1992. *Social and Legal Studies* 2:259–279.

Miller, Lisa. 1999. Taking control: Race, community, and the politics of crime prevention. Ph.D. diss., University of Washington.

Murray, Charles. 1984. *Losing ground: American social policy, 1950–1980*. New York: Basic Books.

New York Times. 1999. New Jersey's trooper scandal. Editorial, 30 April.

Packer, Herbert. 1968. *The limits of the criminal sanction*. Stanford, California: Stanford University Press.

Peterson, Wallace C. 1991. The silent depression. Challenge 34 (4): 29–34. Quoted in Dario Melossi, Gazette of morality and social whip: Punishment hegemony and the case of the USA, 1970–1992, *Social and Legal Studies* 2 (1993): 267–268.

Podolefsky, A. 1983. *Case studies in community crime prevention*. Springfield, Illinois: Charles C. Thomas.

Quinney, Richard. 1980. *State, class, and crime*. New York: Longman.

Rose, Nikolas. 1999. *Powers of freedom: Reframing political thought*. Cambridge: Cambridge University Press.

Rubin, Lillian. 1986. *Quiet rage: Bernie Goetz in a time of madness*. Berkeley: University of California Press.

Sampson, Robert, and Dawn Jeglum Bartusch. 1998. Legal cynicism and (subcultural?) tolerance of deviance: The neighborhood context of racial differences. *Law & Society Review* 32 (4): 777–804.

Sanders, Jerry. 1999. Refreshing copspeak. *New York Times*, 16 April.

Sasson, Theodore. 1995. African-American conspiracy theories and the social construction of crime. *Sociological Inquiry* 65:265–285.

147

Savelsberg, Joachim. Forthcoming. Kulturen staatlichen strafens: USA–Germany. (Cultures of state punishment: USA–Germany.) In *Die vermessung kultureller unterschiede: USA und Deutschland im vergleich*, edited by J. Gerhards. Opladen, Germany: Wesdeutscher Verlag.

————. 1994. Knowledge, domination, and criminal punishment. *American Journal of Sociology* 99:911–943.

Scheingold, Stuart A. 1998. Constructing the new political criminology: Power, authority, and the post-liberal state. *Law and Social Inquiry* 23 (Fall): 857–895.

————. 1995. The politics of street crime and criminal justice. In *Crime, communities, and public policy*, edited by Lawrence B. Joseph. Chicago: University of Chicago Press.

————. 1991. *The politics of street crime: Criminal process and cultural obsession.* Philadelphia: Temple University Press.

————. 1984. *The politics of law and order: Street crime and public policy.* New York: Longman.

Schlosser, Eric. 1998. The prison-industrial complex. *Atlantic Monthly* 282 (December): 51–77.

Schwendinger, Herman, and Julia Schwendinger. 1993. Giving crime prevention top priority. *Crime & Delinquency* 39 (October): 425–446.

Simon, Jonathan. 1997. Governing through crime. In *The crime conundrum: Essays on criminal justice*, edited by Lawrence Friedman and George Fisher. Boulder, Colorado: Westview Press.

————. 1995. They died with their boots on: The boot camp and the limits of modern penality. *Social Justice* 22:25–48.

Stinchcombe, Arthur, Rebecca Adams, Carol A. Heimer, Kim Lane Schepple, Tom Smith, and Garth Taylor. 1980. *Crime and punishment: Changing attitudes in America.* San Francisco: Jossey-Bass.

Tonry, Michael. 1995. *Malign neglect: Race, crime, and punishment in America.* New York: Oxford University Press.

Tonry, Michael, and David Harrington. 1995. Strategic approaches to crime prevention. In *Building a safer society: Strategic approaches to crime prevention*, edited by Michael Tonry and David S. Harrington. Vol. 19 of *Crime and justice: A review of research.* Chicago: University of Chicago Press.

————, eds. 1995. *Building a safer society: Strategic approaches to crime prevention.* Vol. 19 of *Crime and justice: A review of research.* Chicago: University of Chicago Press.

Tremblay, Richard, and Wendy Craig. 1995. Developmental crime prevention. In *Building a safer society: Strategic approaches to crime prevention*, edited by Michael Tonry and David S. Harrington. Vol. 19 of *Crime and justice: A review of research*. Chicago: University of Chicago Press.

Tyler, Tom, and Robert Boeckmann. 1997. Three strikes and you are out, but why? The psychology of public support for punishing rule breakers. *Law & Society Review* 31 (2): 200–214.

U.S. Bureau of the Census. 1996. Income, poverty, and valuation of non-cash benefits: 1994. In *Current Population Reports*, series P60–189. Washington, D.C.

Wilson, James Q. 1991. The politics of crime: The American experience (A debate between Elliott Currie and James Q. Wilson). In *The politics of crime control*, edited by Kevin Stenson and David Cowell. London: Sage Publications.

———. 1985. *Thinking about crime*. Rev. ed. New York: Vintage Books.

———. 1977. *Thinking about crime*. New York: Vintage Books.

Windlesham, Lord. 1998. *Politics, punishment, and populism*. New York: Oxford University Press.

Zimring, Franklin, and Gordon Hawkins. 1995. *Incapacitation: Penal confinement and the restraint of crime*. New York: Oxford University Press.

Name Index